ACTA
ARCHAEOLOGICA

Editor

KLAVS RANDSBORG

VOL. 79

OXFORD

WILEY - BLACKWELL

2008

Published by ACTA ARCHAEOLOGICA & Centre of World Archaeology (CWA), Director Klavs Randsborg
Archaeological division, SAXO Institute, University of Copenhagen, Njalsgade 80, DK-2300 Copenhagen, Denmark
Phone +45 35329478 Fax +45 35329495 randsb@hum.ku.dk
www.worldarchaeology.net

Editor Professor Klavs Randsborg

Type setting etc. by Rimas Steponaitis, rimas@rimas.info
Printing & reproduction house P. J.Schmidt Grafisk, Vojens
Publishing house Wiley - Blackwell
Orders: Wiley - Blackwell Publishing, 9600 Garsington Road, Oxford OX4 2DQ, UK
customerservices@oxon.blackwellpublishing.com

© 2008 by Wiley - Blackwell, Oxford

ISBN 9781405185707
ISSN 0065-101X
ISSN 1600-390 (online)

ACTA ARCHAEOLOGICA

ACTA ARCHAEOLOGICA SUPPLEMENTA

ACTA ARCHAEOLOGICA

SUPPLEMENTA

Editor

KLAVS RANDSBORG

VOL. X

OXFORD

WILEY · BLACKWELL

2008

ACTA ARCHAEOLOGICA Vol. 79, 2008
ACTA ARCHAEOLOGICA SUPPLEMENTA X
CENTRE OF WORLD ARCHAEOLOGY (CWA) - PUBLICATIONS 6

NORDIC WORLD

PREHISTORY TO MEDIEVAL TIMES

Edited by

KLAVS RANDSBORG

OXFORD

WILEY - BLACKWELL

2008

CONTENTS

Acta Archaeologica vol. 79, 2008, pp 1-23
Printed in Denmark • All rights reserved

KINGS' JELLING

GORM & THYRA'S PALACE
HARALD'S MONUMENT & GRAVE - SVEND'S CATHEDRAL

KLAVS RANDSBORG

In memory of C.J. Becker (1915-2001)

1. JELLING & DENMARK

... auk tani [karði] kristna

... and made the Danes Christian

(King Harald, the large Jelling rune-stone; 960s AD)

The Jelling monuments of the late-10th century AD and their importance for the Danish kingdom and empire of the late Viking Age are well known (cf. Jensen 2004).[1] Jelling is centrally placed very near the north-south going main road through Jutland (Jylland) (Randsborg 1980; 1991) (Fig. 1). Like a spider, it also holds the same land-

wards distance to a number of centres, which all were to become important cities in the 11th century: Ribe, Viborg, Århus, and Odense on Funen (Fyn). Even the great Hedeby/Slesvig, faraway to the south in Jutland, is not too far away, and thus the land routes in direction of Hamburg and Central Europe as well as towards Slavonian East Germany and on to Bohemia and Poland. Indeed, south of Jelling is the two-lane half a mile long wooden Ravning Enge Bridge across the watery Vejle River (Jensen 2004, 396f.). The bridge is easing access to the centre when approaching from the south, while at the same time demonstration the powers of the king.

Narrow valleys to the east of Jelling - easy to defend - are leading towards the inlet of Vejle Fjord, in turn opening into the Cattegat (Kattegat) Sea, connected with the Skagerac (Skagerak) and the North Sea, the roads to Norway and England. Frisia (and England) is reached from Ribe and - across a short stretch of land - from Hedeby/Slesvig. Through the Belts one enters the Western Baltic. In fact, all Danish Islands and even Scania (Skåne) and other eastern provinces were within easy reach by boat from the deep wooden lovely Vejle Fjord. Further into the Baltic are Sweden and other regions, including Russia and the routes to the Near East.

However, Jelling did not develop into a city. Rather, it was a gigantic estate centre or manor house, even a palace, in Western Denmark, which during the 10th century

1 The paper is dedicated to the memory of the late Professor C.J. Becker, an excavator with a vision, a very productive scholar, and editor of Acta Archaeologica. As a young man, he served as assistant to E. Dyggve during the excavation of the Southern Mound at Jelling. C.J. Becker devoted his life to the promotion of Danish archaeology and its empirical tradition. The author stands in debt to his inspiration, interest, and support.

Acknowledgements: The author stands in dept to the fine fieldwork of K.J. Krogh and the late E. Dyggve, their ideas, and perceptions. The author also appreciates the critical remarks to the above by the late H. Andersen, as well as information, ideas, and comments to the present work from N. Lund, N. Lynnerup, C. Adamsen (who in particular has provided useful comments and information), K. Christensen, M. Gelting, K. Ottosen, H. Skov, M. Warmind, and others. However, the author is sole responsible for the interpretations. Most observations, including those of the author, were presented at the First Jelling Conference, May 2008 organized by the National Museum of Denmark with support from the Bikuben Foundation, the new benefactor of investigations in a Jelling context.

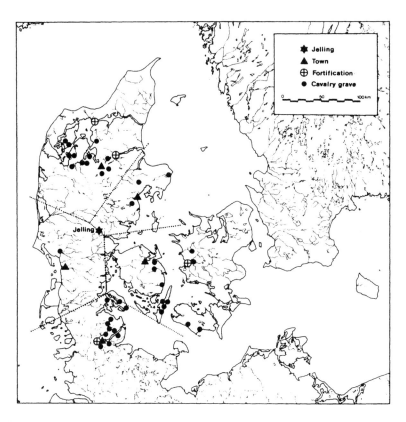

Fig. 1. Jelling and other important localities of the 10th century (after Randsborg 1991). The likely Trelleborg type fortress at Nonnebakken in Odense, Funen should be added to the map, as possibly the southwest Scanian ring fortresses at Trelleborg town & Borgeby village, near Lund - however somewhat differing.

The cited cavalry weapon graves all hold weapons, horse gear (including heavy bits and stirrups), and other items in an age with very modest grave goods (Randsborg 1980, 121f.). Obviously, the items have not been passed on to heirs, but serve to mark a particular occupation of the death men, perhaps as professional officers of the hirð, as well as owners of estates.

was adequately positioned for the king (cf. Jensen 2004, 371f.). This picture is highlighted by recent finds of a gigantic palisade fence around (1) two huge mounds, (2) a huge ship-setting with the Northern Mound as its centre, (3) two rune-stones erected by King Gorm and by King Harald: "Bluetooth" to later sources[2], who accepted Christianity, and (4) a large wooden church - in fact, three subsequent ones, the last one resting on boulders, the earlier ones with roof-supporting posts dug into the ground (cf. Krogh 1966 - then operating with only two wooden churches) (Section 4 below; and Appendix II). Mound burials and ship-settings are traditional symbols of high status and should therefore be considered non-Christian.

2   Short range wireless connectivity has, for unknown reasons, adopted the term "Bluetooth" from King Harald's later nickname, which actually means "Black Tooth". The logo is HB in runic letters.

The ship-setting is the largest ever found: 354 m, or exactly 1,200 Roman feet; this foot is the unit of measurement also used at the famous Trelleborg fortresses (*contra* Nielsen 1974).

The name of the church was perhaps St. Johannes (St. John the Baptist), since the frescos of the stone church from the beginning or the 12th century are devoted to Johannes "Døberen" (Haastrup & Egevang 1986, 64f.). The heavy palisade fence was seemingly erected to fit the ship-setting, and is thus defining the representative and ritual area. It is also so tall that one would only catch a glimpse of the top of the monuments from the outside. Studying King Harald's large and important rune-stone would only have been for the few.

The fenced area, of at least ten hectares, is nearly rectangular but only preliminarily investigated (Mohr Christensen & Wulff Andersen 2008) (Figs. 2a-b). Apart

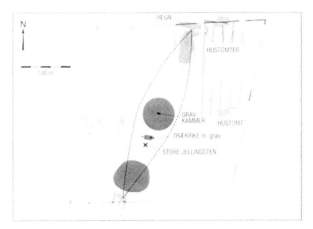 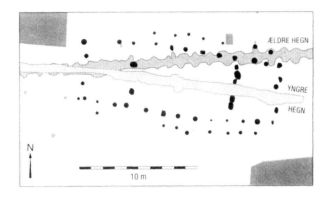

Figs. 2a-b. The Jelling monuments and finds as of early 2008 (after Christensen & Wulff Andersen 2008). Note the two huge mounds and the remains of the huge ship-setting. Also marked are the fields of excavation, in addition to modern roads. [Danish] Hegn = fence; Hustomt(er) = house structure(s); Gravkammer = Grave chamber; Trækirke m. grav = Wooden church w. grave; Store Jellingsten = Large Jelling [rune] stone. - Ældre hegn = older fence; Yngre hegn = later fence.

A riddle is the angle of the main axis of the whole monument, 24 degrees towards the east, hardly an astronomical cardinal point (Midsummer's sunrise is at 44 degrees towards the east in Denmark). The angle is partly reflected in the strange polygonal shape of the main fence.

Stop press note: The western fence was found in Oct. 2008, c 100 m to the west of the big rune stone.

from the monuments, it contains several halls of common type. One of these halls - from around 1000 AD - was built after the first palisade fence was removed (Mohr Christensen & Wulff Andersen 2008, 8). A later palisade fence, likely an adjustment to the first one, is seen in the same micro area, but the relative age of the hall and the late fence is unknown. The hall and the late fence have the same orientation as the wooden church, a couple of hundred metres away though and may be more or less contemporary. Likely, this whole area is the predecessor of the later "Bailiff Farm" at Jelling. Another major farm from recent times - "The Vicarage" - was placed to the south of the fenced area; also this may have a Viking Age predecessor.

The Northern Mound held a very large wooden chamber grave, heavily disturbed and now likely destroyed by digging and excavations since the early 19th century. The chamber has also been violently opened in times of old, as appears from descriptions and illustrations from the 19th century (cf. below). Another wooden grave chamber was found beneath the earliest wooden church, holding a re-buried male person. In both chambers were rich grave-goods, however fragmentary. Interestingly, from the chamber in the Northern Mound (or near it) come a few items that appear to be "Christian", including a small cross for hanging from the neck, two mountings (for a book?) with cross motives, and a wooden figure depict-

ing a dragon or snake slayer, perhaps even Christ himself (Krogh & Leth-Larsen 2007, 220f., 239f., and 173f.). The Southern Mound contained no central grave and appears empty, apart from parts of the large ship-setting and a few other structures of various kinds.

An idea of the economic might behind the provincial towns of the 11th century is yielded by the large contemporary farmsteads at Vorbasse and Østergård (Hvass 1986; Ethelberg et al. 2003, 448f.). In fact, Vorbasse gives the whole development of one and the same village from the birth of Christ till about 1100, with the farms being progressively larger in the 3rd and again in the late 7th and, particularly, in the late 10th centuries. Vorbasse is representing the new social energy of the Late Viking Age heralded by the Jelling monuments. This energy found an outlet in the creation of the High Medieval Danish landscape of estates based on permanently located large and small farms and cottages. In this landscape, villages had stopped moving around on their territories when new demands arose. But expansion continued, in the form of new villages of -torp ("secondary village") and -rød ("clearance") types, even founded in the 13th century.

In the late 7th century a series of production and trading sites were founded all over north-western Europe, like Ribe in Denmark (Ulriksen 1994). At Tissø on Zealand (Sjælland) such a site is attached to a magnate farmstead or manor house (Jørgensen 2003). What we are observing

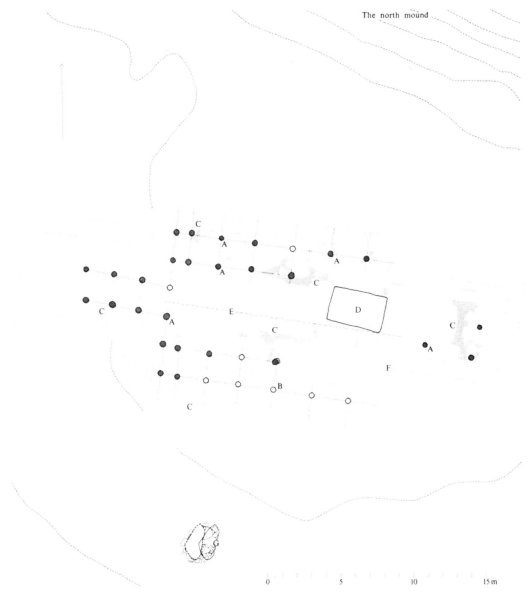

Figs. 3a-b. The first wooden church at Jelling with its chamber grave (after Krogh 1982) (Fig. 3a). A = post-holes; B = inferred post-holes; C = remains of floor-layer; D = chamber grave; E = longitudinal axis of church; F = outline of present stone-church; G = King Harald's rune-stone (broken line represents the previous tilted position). - Analysis and reconstruction by the present author; broken line = limit of upper floor/royal tribune (cf. Appendix II).

here is no doubt a novel stage in estate formation. Estates were becoming more than a series of dependant farms when they began to convert the surpluses of production into manufacture of objects which could be traded: Thus, the interlinked production and trading sites in an emerging international economical system.

Likely the early rune-stones were a part of this game: Conspicuous markers with inscriptions in "high language"

signalling new social (and economic) conditions of power in the Early Viking Age (cf. Wamers 1994, for a rare royal grave at Hedeby). In the 10th century, the region around Jelling saw many rune-stones, including those at Jelling related to Danish royalty: King Gorm and Queen Thyra, and their son King Harald, who became so mighty that he "won" "Denmark all" - "and Norway" - and "made the Danes Christian", as is stated on the largest of the Jelling

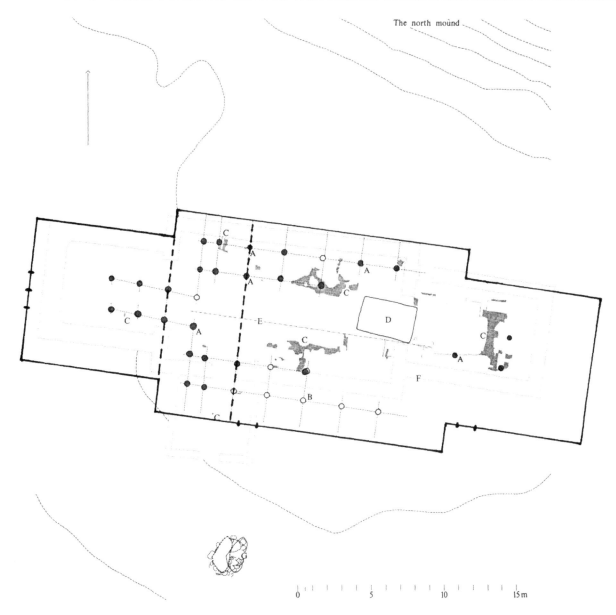

Fig. 3b. Attempt at reconstructing the plan of the first wooden church at Jelling.

rune-stones from the 960s, which also carries a representation of Christ (Jacobsen & Moltke 1942, Nos. 41-42; Randsborg 1980; Jensen 2004). Interestingly, Widukind (925-973+) claims that the Danes were Christian as of old (Widukind III.64f.). The Christian artefacts from the Northern Mound point in the same direction. The explanation might be that Harald was accepting Christ as the strongest deity in the 960s.

As M. Gelting and others have convincingly demonstrated, Archbishop Bruno of Köln (Cologne) (925-65;

Archbishop 953-65) was the likely force behind Harald's acceptance of Christianity. Bruno was Emperor Otto I's brother and acting "foreign minister" of Germany. The link to the court at Jelling was Bruno's secretary Poppo (Folkmar), who followed as archbishop of Köln (965-69) (Lund 2004 for various references).

In the early to mid 10th century the North, and not least Denmark, were economically very strong, as the stream of Islamic silver and other imports demonstrate. In the late 10th century Danish kings secured their realm by fortresses such as Fyrkat and Aggersborg in the north, possibly the Ravning Enge Bridge across Vejle River Valley, and certainly the Danevirke long-walls on the German frontier in the south, as well as the fortresses of Nonnebakken and Trelleborg - and the Scanian "Trelleborge" - towards the east (Jensen 2004). All these projects have Jelling as their geographical centre. A little later in time, new rune-stones were erected - several of them Christian - in Scania and North Jutland. Scania was now an integrated part of the empire, and the point of gravity moved from west to east - as the many coins minted in Roskilde and Lund (the future seat of archbishop) by King Knud "the Great" (Canute), King Harald's grandson, are demonstrating (Randsborg 1980). In this New Denmark, Jelling played only a modest role.

2. JELLING'S ARCHAEOLOGICAL FUTURE

The new Jelling initiative and archaeological programme, supported by the Bikuben Foundation, should as its minimum sphere of interest encompass the zone within ten-fifteen kilometres from Jelling to establish the development of the Viking Age settlement, including a reconstruction of the natural environment on the basis of geomorphology and pollen analyses. Hopefully, even an even larger area will be considered. A particularly interesting maritime locality is "Skibet" (The Ship) on the lower Vejle River, sitting back in a large watery and heavily forested area, which includes several valleys, including the dramatic one of Grejs River, emanating from Fårup Lake at Jelling. The area is ideal for building and harbouring of ships; it is also protected from direct attacks from the sea. No doubt it served the royal fleet attached to Jelling.

To the west of Skibet is the majestic Ravning Enge Bridge of the 980s and a nearby ring wall, Troldborg or Trældborg Ring (cf. the two "Trelleborg" ring fortress, the one on West Zealand, the other in south-western Scania). However, the small irregular Troldborg is likely a fortified farmstead of the Roman Iron Age (cf. H. Andersen 1992). Another ring wall with the same sort of name is Trælborg, 25 km to the south of Jelling; a hall at this site is of the Migration period, the overlying ring wall later (Voss 1957). An interesting natural fortification, very highly situated in the landscape, is Kollen on the Gudenå River, 35 km north of Jelling (Horsbøl Nielsen 2004). A defensive ditch was dug in the 10th century, and trees felled in c984. Nearby is

Sønder Vissing with a rune-stone raised by King Harald's wife Tove, daughter of Slavonian Prince Mistivoj, for her mother (Jacobsen & Moltke 1942, No. 55).

Sites in the Central Jutland region with 10th century rune-stones should also receive attention by the Jelling programme, like Bække (26 km to the south-west of Jelling), with a ship-setting (Jacobsen & Moltke 1942, No. 30). as should localities with particularly rich finds of noble metals or even prominent stone churches of the 12the century. They all probably indicate important manor houses. In fact, the localities of two late 10th century princely graves on nearby Funen - Søllested & Møllemosegård at Hillerslev - are also worth considering (Pedersen 1996), as are Funen localities with important rune-stones, like that of Glavendrup, even with an attached ship-setting (Jacobsen & Moltke 1942, No. 209). The manor house at Ladby, Funen, with the well-known royal ship-grave of the early 10th century, should also be located (Sørensen 2001).

The same is the case of Mammen in North Jutland, with a contemporary princely grave (Iversen 1991). Tamdrup at Horsens, 25 kilometres to the northeast of Jelling, has a fine stone Basilica church from 1100 with superb frescos paralleled in style and date to those of the stone church at Jelling. Tamdrup housed a golden altar of around 1200 with depictions of King Harald being lectured at, demonstrated the powers of Christ (through ordeal by fire), and finally baptized (Schiørring 1991; Haastrup & Egevang 1986, 72f.). In fact, contemporary sources do not indicate that King Harald was baptized when he accepted Christianity (cf. Widukind III.64f.). At Tamdrup remains of an 11th century manor house has been found.

A particular stress should be put on Jelling itself, the monuments, palaces, manor houses, villages and farmsteads. In spite of many previous investigations certain limited operations should be directed towards the two huge mounds, if only to check their state of preservation (cf. below). The rune-stones should be brought indoor for the same reason and copies erected in their place. Other copies should be placed in Copenhagen.

The royal compounds at Jelling may well turn out to have been much larger than even the huge newly found croft, and the number of royal burials higher than that of the huge Northern Mound and the grave under the first wooden church (cf. Figs. 2a-b). Also, we should expect ordinary Viking Age burials at Jelling; hundreds of people must have been engaged in running the estates and erecting the monuments.

In ancient West African kingdoms, for instance, each new king often built a palace of his own. Furthermore, the resting place of a dead king was not necessarily the official tomb (in the framed particular area for royal graves). The question is therefore if the detected Jelling compound is but the ritual area of King Gorm's palace, on which the monumental graves, the ship-setting, the rune-stones, and the church were erected, while King Harald of the large rune-stone resided elsewhere, perhaps on an even larger croft.

Questions are many, as always at Jelling, of which many are to be solved by help of archaeology. Apart from a huge settlement complex and the mounds, new excavations should be carried elsewhere in the area: older archaeologists re-educating the recent generation of fast diggers from the administrative excavations. Jelling is the family silver of Denmark, constantly renewed by each visit to the treasury. Unfortunately, the final reports on the excavations in the late 1970s are not yet fully published, including important information on the wooden churches, and thereby on the acceptance of Christianity (Krogh 1993; Krogh & Leth-Larsen 2007; cf. H. Andersen 1995). Studying the two important publications at hand gives rise to many thoughts, not least since there are obvious errors, some of which are due to recent finds.

The ship-setting, for instance, is now proved to be twice as long as hitherto suggested. It is, in fact, strange that the large stones in the modern cemetery did not give rise to the hypothesis that the ship-setting might have continued well to the north of the Northern Mound. O. Voss is the one exception, when he in newspapers of 1960s commented on the find of a row of large pits - possibly for stones - to the west of the Northern Mound. After all, Dyggve suggested that his pagan "vi", based on the fragmentary stone "V" found under the Southern Mound, continued all the way up to the flanks of the Northern Mound (Dyggve 1942; cf. 1954; 1964). Another overlooked issue is the possible role of King Svend, the son of Harald, and a military genius as conqueror of England. This short presentation and discussion should therefore end by raising new issues.

3. KING SVEND & THE JELLING MONUMENTS

It is chocking that the bones of the unknown re-buried person from the chamber grave under the first wooden church at Jelling have recently been re-buried once again,

and *in toto*, under the fine and almost untouchable modern stone art floor of the Romanesque church (Figs. 3a-b). The claim that the person in question is King Gorm is unfortunately not wholly convincing, in spite of the popularity that the hypothesis has won among high and low and how widespread in the literature as well as on the internet (www) it is (e.g., Jensen 2004; but see 582, note 148).

The standard theory is that Gorm is re-buried in the chamber under the first wooden church from the chamber in the Northern Mound upon King Harald's acceptance of Christianity in the 960s (Krogh 1993; but see H. Andersen 1995). King Harald's large rune-stone, the first wooden church, and even the Southern Mound are thus regarded as contemporary.

A series of wooden objects are claimed to relate to the violent opening of the wooden chamber in the Northern Mound. A Carbon-14 date of a spade to 1080+/-100 BP merely gives "Viking Age(+)"[3]; more important is the dendro-date on a secondarily placed twin branch of 964/65 AD (Krogh & Leth-Larsen 2007, 245 & 260, respectively)[4]. If the linkage is correct, the opening of the chamber is as accurately dated as its construction, which is given as a few years earlier, or 958/59+ (cf. Christensen & Krogh 1987; Krogh 1993).

The interpretation is less straightforward, however (if we rule out simple plundering for gain), since we do not know whether something was removed from the grave or entered into it. Since Queen Thyra died before King Gorm (according to the latter's rune-ston), the opening may have taken place to bury Gorm in the large chamber of Thyra. A third hypothesis is destruction of the grave by someone in opposition to the dead person. This is what probably took place at both the famous Oseberg ship-grave of the early 9th century in Norway and the Ladby grave in Denmark of the beginning of the 10th century (Sørensen 2001). Such practice is also known from the Bronze and Iron Ages and from other parts of the world, for instance the kingdoms of West Africa (Randsborg 1998). Finally, in a critique of the translocation of "Gorm", K. Ottosen

---

3 AD 810-1034 at 66.6%, 782-1034 at 68.2%, 694-1161 at 95.4%, and 657-1226 at 99.7% probability. A dendro-chronological study of the spade merely gave "(rather long) after 924 AD".

4 This important dendro-date is otherwise unpublished; like the others from the Jelling Mounds, it was carried out by K. Christensen (cf. Christensen & Krogh 1987; Krogh 1993). A full publication and renewed discussion of the basis for the dendro-dates is a high priority.

has stressed the fact that according to 10th century theology and liturgy the body of a heathen person could not become Christian by being moved to a church, or, in the present case, to a location on which a church is going to be built. In fact, for a fourth hypothesis, King Harald might even have wished for the bodies - and spirits - of Gorm and Thyra to be removed from their graves at his now Christian palace.

The person in the chamber grave of the church is likely a man, rather powerfully built. Tooth wear etc. indicate an age at death of around 35-40 years (new study of the CT-scans by N. Lynnerup, Panum Institute, University of Copenhagen). Some incisors are missing, as well as many other bones. If we exclude Queen Thyra, in spite of the rather feminine pelvis, Basse (or Bise) - named on a third but fragmentary rune-stone found in secondary position at Jelling (Moltke 1976, 177) - or, for that matter, any other historically known or unknown high-ranking person may be candidates. Saxo (close of the 12th century) relates that King Harald had an older brother Knud who died in Ireland on expedition shortly before King Gorm passed away, seemingly on hearing the news (Saxo IX.11.4f.). Doubts linger though, in particular since the tale is interwoven with a claim that Thyra died after Gorm, which is clearly wrong, as demonstrated by King Gorm's rune-stone for Thyra.

One would actually suggest King Harald "Bluetooth" himself (cf. H. Andersen 1995), a simple solution, even one only based on circumstantial evidence. Harald died in Slavonia after being mortally wounded in an uprising which gave the kingdom to his son King Svend (died 1014). The artefacts from the chamber grave under Jelling Church do not speak against a year of death around 970-75; incidentally the approximate date of the erection of the first phase of the empty Southern Mound cenotaph at Jelling (dendro-date). A princely grave from Mammen in North Jutland is dendro-dated to 970/71 (Iversen 1991, 43f./H. Andersen). The artefacts from this grave bear resemblance in style to King Harald's rune-stone (in "Mammen Style"), as well as to the items found in the chamber grave in Jelling Church.[5] Harald - if in fact the man in the chamber grave under the church - would thus have been born around 935, be 25-30

years at the death of King Gorm, and about 30 at the acceptance of Christianity in the 960s.

That King Harald is buried in Roskilde is a construction from the late 11th century by Adam of Bremen (c1-040-c1081), as N. Lund has demonstrated (Lund 1998). Even the pillar in the later cathedral supposedly holding Harald's bones is empty. Also Harald's long life is Adam's construction, placing Harald as a parallel to Archbishop Adeldag of Hamburg (937-988).

Harald disappears from the reliable written sources after the 960s (cf. Widukind; Thietmar). On the other hand, the son Svend only appears in the 990s but may well have been king earlier; perhaps the German attack on Denmark in 974 is a reaction to Harald's violent death (Appendix I). This would make Svend the builder of the Trelleborg fortresses plus, of course, the conqueror of England: An indeed interesting return to former ideas about a connection between the fortresses and the campaigns in England, resulting in the Danish conquest (Appendix III).

The huge Southern Mound cenotaph is very interesting. Geophysical anomalies at the northern edge, but still in the axis (defined by the two mounds and King Harald's rune-stone right in between), should evidently be investigated (H. Andersen 1994). The anomalies seemingly represent an about 25 m[2] large roundish heap of stones of unknown function. A suggestion, perhaps, is a heathen sacrificial site ("hørg") as has been found at Lejre on Zealand, though much larger (cf. Capelle & Fischer 2005, 131ff./L. Jørgensen, for Tissø).

The big wooden chamber of the Northern Mound is sunk into an older mound (likely of the Bronze Age). Importantly, the attached ship-setting must - to judge by its considerable width - have been erected after the Northern Mound was fully built to a height of 8½ metre and a diameter of 65 metre. As suggested, the chamber grave of the Northern Mound should likely be linked with King Gorm one way or the other. However, the find of an end board for a wagon body in the chamber might suggest that at first Queen Thyra (after 958/59), then King Gorm (before 964/65), were buried in the chamber, since prominent women were commonly given wagon bodies for coffin in the 10th century (Krogh 1993, 97f.; cf. Müller-Wille 1987, 26f., 140f.; for a newly discovered male grave, Lindblom 2008).

The Northern Mound would thus have been completed by King Harald and the ship-setting erected after 958 (according to the dendro-date of the pertaining chamber

---

5 Artefacts from the chamber grave in the Northern Mound in part define the typologically older "Jelling Style" (cf. Pedersen 1996). In fact, the two groups may represent the court styles of Kings Gorm and Harald, respectively. King Svend, or perhaps rather King Knud, may have been behind the Ringerike style. A contemporary English style of Knud (and others) is the Winchester Style.

tomb). Harald's large rune-stone from the 960s is placed in the main axis of the ship-setting to the south of the Northern Mound, and harmoniously balanced against the lines of the stone monument. The original position of King Gorm's stone is not known.[6]

The Southern Mound is erected as a parallel to the Northern Mound in the 970s (first phase), and in such a way that King Harald's large rune-stone is standing at the mid-point between the centres of the two mounds. The cenotaph is covering part of the ship-setting. On the one hand, this is a demonstration of continuity - one doubles the Northern Mound; on the other, it is the matter of a negatively loaded disturbance of the ship-setting. Both mound and ship-setting are traditional, non-Christian symbols. Incidentally, this interpretation recalls Dygve's suggestion that the heathen "vi" was destroyed by the Southern Mound erected in connection with the acceptance of Christianity.

It is therefore suggested that the cenotaph Southern Mound was erected by rebellious King Svend - perhaps as a traditional monument for Harald, but rather to honour the grandparents; this may also explain the traditional, although rather late, names for the mounds: Thyra's Mound (north) and Gorm's Mound (south) (cf. Saxo X.6). The erection of the Southern Mound is taking place in opposition to the ship-setting and thus to Harald as agent in the history of the monuments. Nevertheless, Harald's rune-stone still holds a central place in the overall monument. In this way, Harald's family and domestic, as well as national, position is acknowledged by King Svend, as is his role in the acceptance of Christianity.

4. THE FIRST WOODEN CHURCH

That the wooden church is a later addition to the Jelling monument seems clear from its "squeezed" and somewhat askew position between Harald's large stone and the mighty Northern Mound. The church, which is very large - in fact, a cathedral in size - has parallels among several 11th century wooden churches in Denmark with rows of internal roof-supporting posts near the long walls in a Basilica fashion (Liebgott 1989, 179 Fig. 141; Hauglid 1976, 144f., cf. Fig. 139; Wieczorek & Hinz 2000 for ear-

ly churches from Central Europe; cf. the general corpus in Ahrens 2001) (Figs. 3-5; Appendix II; Table I). Unfortunately, there is no 10th century material in Denmark for comparison. At Jelling there are even two rows of internal posts in the nave - like the double Basilica of Old St. Peter, Rome (e.g., Clapham 1930, 8 Fig. 3) - if we suppose that the outer rows are freestanding and not parts of the long walls. Such interpretation is confirmed by fragments of the floor layer beyond the outer posts.

The slightly askew posts to the west may look like supports for beams to carry church bells, but since they are very powerful and so to say "built into the structure" they rather represent a staircase - in fact a whole staircase tower, as a fragment of the said floor layer in this area would indicate; the entrance would have been to the west, perhaps the direction of the entrance to the croft or even of the royal palace itself. The staircase was giving access to a second level, revealed by the fortified western end of the nave where the posts are closer to one another. Certainly, the church at Jelling - likely of about 450 m² at ground level, and 39 metres long (width 13½ m) - must have set a standard for all large churches in Denmark before the coming of stone, and even beyond (Fig. 4). The first wooden church at Jelling is also of the largest wooden churches in Europe, at least in pre-modern times (cf. Ahrens 2001). Its height, although difficult to estimate, was certainly bigger than the two huge mounds.

Actually, the reconstructed plan of the first wooden church at Jelling is equivalent in proportions to one of the earliest (but much smaller) stone churches from Denmark, located at St. Jørgensbjerg near Roskilde and likely built by English stone masons in the late 1030s (Olsen 1960) (Fig. 6). Like Jelling, St. Jørgensbjerg has the characteristic wide choir found on Anglo-Saxon churches. Late Anglo-Saxon English churches may also have a western *piano nobile*, like St. Mary at Deerhurst near Gloucester (Taylor 1975). In fact, even the first Salvator/Trinitatis ("Drotten") Church in stone at Lund has a structure similar to the first wooden church at Jelling (Cinthio 1997; 2002; 2004). Depending on its date, this church might have been erected by King Knud (Canute), meant for the secondary burial of the body of his father King Svend. This church also seems to have had an upper level to the west, and eventually a west tower. It was perhaps built around 1020/30, but there is no confirmed date.

The large Carolingian Corvey Abbey basilica at Höxter on the Weser in Northwest Germany, with its famous

---

6 The above-mentioned stone-setting in the Southern Mound is a rather unlikely but not wholly impossible candidate. Incidentally, it seems to hold the same distance to King Harald's rune-stone as the latter to the edge of the Northern Mound.

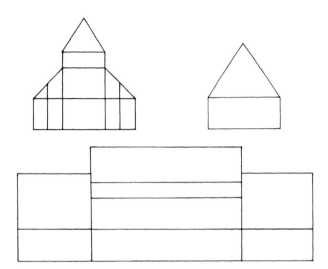

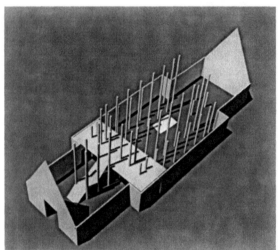

Fig. 4. Attempt at reconstructing the first wooden church at Jelling. The structural cross-sections of the church are reconstructed on the basis of the plan in Fig. 3b, in spite of great uncertainty concerning its heights. The concomitant uprights of the long walls of the church are also presented, as well as an equally simplified 3D edition of the church.

so-called westwork and upstairs imperial tribune (873 AD), may also be called upon as a model (Taylor 1975; Toman 2000, 36f.). A related structure is St. Pantaleon in Köln (964+ AD) built by Archbishop Bruno, who was likely behind King Harald's acceptance of Christianity (Braunsfeld 1981, 51; Toman 2000, 43). Quedlinburg Abbey (west of Magdeburg) from the close of the 11th century, a very beautiful basilica with an exquisite upper level in the west, is taking such architecture into the high Romanesque age, and in fact on to Danish churches of this period (Braunsfeld 1981, 411f.). Certainly, the first church at Jelling is a stone cathedral in wood.

It is difficult to escape the impression that the first church at Jelling cannot be from the age of King Harald but must later. Perhaps it is contemporary with the common hall structure from around 1000 AD on the former site of the big palisade fence connected with the ship-setting (cf. Mohr Christensen & Wulff Andersen 2008, 8) (Figs. 2a-b). Incidentally, the church, the said hall, and the second palisade fence all have the same orientation. The relative age of the second fence and the hall is not known, however.

If English impact is involved, this ought to be of the close of the 10th century, or even later. Harald may well have erected a court altar or chapel but hardly the basilica under discussion. Rather the situation resembles Lisbjerg near Århus, Jutland, where the church is erected on the croft of a Late Viking Age manor house (Jeppesen & Madsen 1995-96; Jeppesen 2004). The excavator of the wooden church cautiously supposed that he found the same sort of levelling fill at Harald's rune-stone as under the church (Krogh 1982, 211f.). This may be as it is and does not necessarily make the two elements contemporary. Perhaps it informs of a general levelling of the area in connection with the erection of King Harald's stone.

At any rate, with the erection of the church, King Harald's stone attained a second function, namely as a marker of the likely southern common entrance to the nave. In fact, the rune-stone explains the peculiar location of the church. Finally, as indicated, King Harald himself may rest in the chamber grave under the church, re-buried by the son Svend, who died in 1014; or even by the grandson Knud (Canute), who died in 1035 (cf. H. Andersen 1995). Svend died in England and was at first buried in York Minster, then in Denmark (Roskilde, or perhaps rather Lund), thus marking the new eastern area of gravity of Denmark, which was to remain so. Knud's bones are still in Winchester Cathedral.

This essentially novel overall model seems to cover all know facts. Whether it stands the test of time and new investigations is rather more doubtful. Notably, by accepting this model we do not have to explain how the re-buried body of the supposed "King Gorm" found in the chamber grave in Jelling Church had nearly completely decomposed in the few years between "after 958" and the (early) mid-960s. Rather, the huge wooden church and its prominent re-burial might be from the 980s or around 990: after the building of the Trelleborg fortresses but before Svend's campaigns in England: King Svend securing his empire and honouring his dynastic obligations before going abroad for conquest. A few years later the attention was on Roskilde and in particular Lund (cf. Andrén 1985).

A later date of the first wooden church of Jelling, to the reign of King Knud (Canute), or even to King Svend Estridsøn (reign 1047-74/76), is less likely. Svend Estridsøn was the organizer of the Church of Denmark, from its eight bishoprics - Slesvig, Ribe, Århus, Vendsyssel region, Odense, Roskilde, Lund and Dalby - and down. At Lund, dendro-dated wooden Basilica churches are of around 1050 (cf. Table I). Remains of a wooden Basilica with a

post-quem coin date to the reign of Svend Estridsøn have been found in Odense. This church was erected on the site of an earlier burned down wooden church, supposedly the one where King Knud "the Holy" (reign 1080-86) was killed in 1086 (Eliasen et al. 2001, 1736f.).

The cathedral size Basilica at Jelling would certainly befit a bishop (and a king). However, the 10th century German written sources do not know of a bishop of Jelling, only of Slesvig, Ribe, and Århus (948); and of Slesvig, Ribe, Århus, and Odense (988). However, these bishops may never have visited or even resided in Denmark. A bishop of Ribe of the early 11th century is mentioned by Adam of Bremen. The former had a Danish name, Odinkar (which is even heathen); Jelling District would likely have belonged to the see of Odinkar, or Ribe, as it certainly did later on.

The implication of this notion is also that the first wooden church at Jelling is of the end of the 10th century. However, the clerical ambitions were seemingly not met by nomination of bishops for Northern Jutland seated at Jelling (dioceses of Ribe and Århus and perhaps Odense as well); in fact, even Hedeby/Slesvig may have been due for inclusion, perhaps in a dream of an archbishopric. At any rate, the large first wooden church of Jelling towered over the traditional monuments at the site.

Finally, the highly prestigious very long wooden two-lane Ravning Enge Bridge is perhaps also a piece in this game. The bridge is dendro-dated to "after 980" (the statistical average being 986+/-) (Christensen 2003, cf. 220 Fig. 3). From Swedish rune-stones of the 11th century we know that building of bridges was considered a Christian act, securing access to the holy structure at all times of the year; several rune-stones even stood at bridges (Wilson 1994, 44). The Ravning Enge Bridge may thus have been constructed to serve the ambitious cathedral at Jelling. Certainly it was not built at the narrowest crossing. Archaeologically, one might claim that the bridge is dating the erection of the church.

It is quite possible that the cross type half bracteates coins, or at least one or more series of these from the final quarter of the 10th century, are contemporary with the first wooden church at Jelling (Malmer 1966, 229f.). These coins may well have been produced at Jelling around 980-85 in celebration of the cathedral rather than the much earlier acceptance of Christianity by King Harald. Certainly they are earlier then the first English impact on Danish in the 990s.

5. WIDER PERSPECTIVES

In conclusion, the Jelling monuments should be interpreted jointly and in their full context (Table II). They are symbolic expressions of a complex game of political "checks-and-balances", across three or more generations, where the stakes were the Danish empire. By implication, the ramifications are felt to this very day. Denmark is still - however heavily reduced in area by Swedish and German conquests - an independent nation: Even one of the best organized and wealthiest in Europe and the World, and certainly one with the least social problems.

Even more important than the long-term perspective are two other issues, which should also be tacked by the Jelling programme. The first one is the relationship in the 10th century between east and west in Denmark. As demonstrated already many years ago, Jutland and Funen and perhaps westernmost Zealand (indeed, the Greater Belt area) seemed to form a unity in a number of respects, in particular as studied from archaeology (Randsborg 1980). This implies that Zealand and Scania, regions of gravity from the 11th century onwards (as well as earlier), should also be considered when studying the Late Viking Age. Jelling is the core of a particular formation of kingdom or empire. But how were the other parts of Medieval Denmark integrated into the realm by Kings Harald, Svend, and Knud? Culturally, the regions were already integrated, and had long been so, but politically certain measures must have been put to work, in addition to ongoing estate formation, even colonization by the elites: archaeologically accompanied by a new type of hall, the prestigious Trelleborg hall.

The measures were doubtless those of dominance, instrumented by the same kings. Trelleborgs, in structure resembling the ones in the west but less strict in composition and manufacture were built in Scania. The runestone "custom" was extended to Scania around 1000 (likely with a novel group of royal magnates). Cities were established across Denmark around 1000 and in the 11th century, including Roskilde and in particular Lund, where most of King Knud's minting was taking place. Obviously, the conquest of England and the new flow of wealth helped integrate the country and fortify its imperial character. The church was another useful instrument of dominance. Great Basilica cathedrals and other churches were constructed by kings and magnates, not only at Jelling but in particular at Lund. An organization of parishes followed in the late 11th century. At that time, stone churches had already begun to replace the wooden ones. On could

continue, delving into military affairs, for instance, or the marvellous ships. What is summing it all up is a vision of empire engulfing earlier forms of kingdom.

The second important issue is the relationship between Denmark and the other kingdoms and empires surrounding the country. Obviously, Germany was the one great power always to consider. Slavonia as a whole remained on the principality and alliance level for a long time to come, even though kingdoms were evolving and consolidating themselves, in Bohemia under German impact, and in Poland. The most successful new entity was probably Russia; Hungary is a special case, even introducing a new language into Central Europe.

Sweden was then relatively far away from Denmark, while Southern Norway in many respects should be considered another region integrated into the Jelling Empire. England (and the British Isles) was important to Denmark, but most of France less so, except for Normandy - the Normans eventually building a new empire in England as well as expanding into the Mediterranean. At any rate, Denmark could not extend its measures of dominance to these regions, nor did the country try to expand its influence in the North Atlantic, leaving that to the remoter parts of Norway - the "Northern Way" - and eventually to a stronger Norwegian kingdom.

Far away, but with Christianity also a part of the Danish orbit, Rome (with Pope), and Constantinople, the centre of the Byzantine Empire, remained important. In Constantinople, military experience was valued; Scandinavian warriors served the emperor and no doubt brought back home Byzantine dresses and values, but not the "Greek" religion. By 1000 direct contacts with the Islamic World, so important in the decades around 800 and in the early 10th century, had almost ceased, to judge by the coins. Russia rose as a new middle man (as did the Spanish kingdoms and Italian cities). Russia supplied Europe with the produce of the great forests: fine furs and wax (for candles). Europe was becoming an entity onto itself, and Denmark was finding its place in the patch-work of empires, kingdoms and principalities - all of them competing dominance systems using various types of symbols of status and power.

In spite of a heavy Scandinavian involvement through the ages, never again did Denmark experience an expansion such as that of Kings Harald, Svend, and Knud - of Jelling: Thus, the ongoing debate about the centre and its character.

APPENDICES

APPENDIX I. THE GERMAN ATTACK OF 974

In the spring of 973, Danish ambassadors participated in the Imperial Easter meeting at Quedlinburg west of Magdeburg shortly before the death of Emperor Otto I (Thietmar, etc.; Ranft 2006) (Table II). Participants came from Denmark, Poland, Bohemia, Hungary, Bulgaria, The Pope/The Papal States, Benevento (in Southern Italy), Byzants, and the Spanish Caliphate: a truly remarkable gathering of almost EU proportions. Nevertheless, Christian Western Europe was not represented. The omission underlines Denmark's political position of balance (and strength) between The West, in particular England, Germany, and the Slavonian principalities. Denmark's position was also central regarding the rest of The North. Southern Norway should in many ways be seen as an extension of Denmark (cf. King Harald's claim on the large rune-stone). Sweden was farther away, behind large stretches of thinly populated lands.

ATTACKS & DEFENCES

The following year, likely rather early, Denmark was attacked by Emperor Otto II, according to an only slightly later and well-informed German written source, Thietmar (975-1018). Thietmar reports that "the Emperor hurried to Slesvig to attack the rebellious Danes" [obviously something had happened on the Danish side] (Thietmar III.6). He found the Danes in weapons, "manning the ditch [*fovea*] made for defence of the country and the gateway called Wieglesdor"[7]. "Upon advice" from his senior followers - Duke Bernhard of Saxony and Count Heinrich of Stade, Lower Saxony, the grandfather of Thietmar - the Emperor conquered "all these fortifications". This may be correct, or an exaggeration.

At any rate, this much sounds like an attack on Danevirke or a part of Danevirke, perhaps the front Kovirke long wall, which in German is actually called "Kograben", "Graben" meaning ditch (cf. H.H. An-

dersen 1998). The Kovirke Wall is only Carbon-14 dated, seemingly to the (late?) 10th century. However, it is often considered to be older. The reason is a description in the Frankish Imperial Annals of King Godfred's defensive wall of the year 808 AD; this wall had only one gateway, it was said (Rau 1974, 87f.; cf. "Wieglesdor" above). A wall phase with certainty dated to around 800 has not as of yet been located in the Danevirke system.

The ruler-straight and highly regular Kovirke Wall displays only one phase of construction and therefore much looks like an ad-hoc installation in preparation against a particular threat and line of attack (H.H. Andersen 1998, Pl. 23). The builders were likely an army under command. A narrow gateway has been located. At any rate, 10th century Kovirke was built in connection with a Danish military operation to safeguard Hedeby and doubly protect Danevirke against German (or Slavonian) assaults.

The Danevirke wall system was strengthened in 965/968 (dendro-dates), by linking the large so-called Main Wall to the heavy wall around Hedeby town. Interestingly, this is the exact time of King Harald's acceptance of Christianity. Obviously, the king is safeguarding his country in spite of - or even because of - the recent understanding with Germany in terms of the status of Christianity.

Kovirke may have been constructed at the same time (the Kovirke gateway may even be the "Wieglesdor" of Thietmar). More likely, however, it should be considered in connection with the Trelleborg fortresses of the late 970s, since Kovirke has the particular deep V-shaped ditch found at these installations. In fact, Kovirke may be the result of events leading to the German attack of 974. The wall may also, but this seems less likely, be connected with the military operations leading to the Danish attack to the south of Danevirke in 983 (cf. below). At any rate, Kovirke is creating defence in depth at Danevirke and Hedeby.

The only other piece of information by Thietmar in connection with the attack on Denmark in 974 is that "the Emperor founded a fortress (*urbs*) at the border and secured it by help of a garrison". No such fortress is known from South Jutland. It may have been situated in Holstein,

---

7 It has previously been claimed that the "ditch" is the Ejder River (Latin "Egidora") to the south of Danevirke and Slesvig/Hedeby, with the argument that "Wieglesdor" is a so-called kenning (circumlocution). This is not likely. Interestingly, The Frankish Annals for 808 are speaking of King Godfred's wall in terms of a defence rampart on the entire northern bank of the Ejder River, in spite of the fact that the Ejder is some 25 kilometres to the south of Danevirke (Rau 1974, 87f.).

for instance at Itzehoe in the south-west (from where fortresses are known), or even at Rendsborg on the Ejder, strategically a fine position (but no fortress is known from there). To suppose that the German "fortress" was Hedeby itself seems quite unlikely for a number of archaeological as well as other reasons. Rather than a symbol of Danish subjugation, the erection of the German fortress - likely in Holstein - may have covered a *de facto* retreat from the Danish frontier (cf. below).

The German attack of 974 much looks like a demonstration of power, possibly after the death of Otto I 973, but more likely in response to a shift of power in Denmark, where King Harald - a friend of Germany and the church, one supposes - was deposited by a rebellion. If so, King Harald must have died in 973, or in 974, at the latest.

WIEGLESDOR

Likely, the above "Wieglesdor" in Thietmar is German for Vigleksdør. Viglek is a Danish Saga King; his Latin name is Wiglecus (Saxo IV.2.1). "Ie" has the same sound in German as "i" in Danish (cf. "ee" in English). Dor (modern German "Tor") = Danish "dør", i.e., gateway (cf. English "door").

According to Saxo, Wiglecus was upset that Amlethus ("Amlet", cf. Shakespeare's Hamlet) had conquered Jutland. With support from Zealand and Scania, Viglek killed Amlet in battle. The son of Viglek was Vermund, whose grandson Uffe fought the Germans on the River Ejder, the very Slesvig frontier to the south of Danevirke (Saxo IV.4). Possibly a gate in the Danevirke walls, or rather in the front Kovirke wall, was so named to carry a highly relevant reference to these tales, certainly known in the 10th century, as well as to crucial contemporary affairs.

RUNESTONES

A couple of rune-stones at Hedeby may refer to fighting between German and Danish forces. The first stone is raised by Thorulv, member [most likely as an officer] of the personal guard of King Svend, for his fellow Erik, who was killed, when "drenge" [literally "boys", here warriors] were sitting around [likely, laid siege to] Hedeby; and he [likely, Erik] was a sea commander, a very high-born "dreng" (Jacobsen & Moltke 1942, No. 1). The other stone is raised by King Svend for the member of his personal guard [likely an officer] Skarde, who had gone

West, but now found death at Hedeby (Jacobsen & Moltke 1942, No. 3).

The monuments belong to a type of rune-stone postdating the Jelling rune-stones of Kings Gorm and Harald. The King Svend mentioned on the Hedeby stones can hardly be any other than the son of King Harald. The event is unknown, and several hypotheses have been put forward.

The hypothesis proposed here is that it is the matter of a Danish attack, likely a counterattack connected with the German assault of 974. The attack may have been spearheaded by a navy squadron under the command of King Svend going into the Sli Inlet (cf. the "sea commander" on Thorulf's rune-stone above). It is also possible that the Germans did penetrate Danevirke, or, for a minimum, Kovirke, in 974 but Danish fighters held out behind the heavy walls of Hedeby. The two rune-stones were raised in the open field to the south of the eastern part of the Connection Wall and Hedeby (but north of the Kovirke Wall), perhaps where the two commanders were killed; certainly, this is not where their estates were situated (as with other rune-stones). Supposing that the German conquest of "all these fortifications" in 974 was a boast and only involved Kovirke, this would explain a battle exactly in the area of the rune-stones.

The hypothesis that the battle at Hedeby mentioned on these rune-stones was linked with the Danish capture of the above-mentioned German "fortress" in the year 983 is less likely. Of course, several other scenarios are also possible, as well as yet other dates for the fighting.

ATTACK OF 934

The lack of a double defence line must have been sorely experienced in 934, when German King Heinrich I subdued Danish King Gnupa, after the Danes had attacked the Frisians, and forced the king to accept baptism (Widukind I.40). Gnupa is connected with two rune-stones at Hedeby, also mentioning King Sigtryg, a son of Gnupa (Jacobsen & Moltke 1942, Nos. 2 & 4) (cf. Table III for Adam's relations). The stones are raised by Queen Asfrid, daughter of Odinkar, mother of Sigtryg. One of the stones relates that Gorm wrote the inscription.

Names of the "writers" of rune-stone inscriptions are rarely mentioned. But the writers seem to have had a high status and should not be confused with the artisans actually cutting the letters. On the famous Early Viking Age rune-stone from Rök, Östergötland in Sweden, the writer appears to be the father of the dead person (Jansson 1976, 36f.).[8] On Glavendrup, Funen (likely of the early 10th century, and with a ship-setting) the dead person is the lord of the writer (Jacobsen & Moltke 1942 No. 209). On the late rune-stone from Tillitse, Lolland the writer is a step son (Jacobsen & Moltke 1942, No. 212).

Gorm of the Hedeby stone is no doubt a person close to Queen Asfrid and King Sigtryg, likely a member of the royal house, even of the royal family, and - a wild guess indeed - the future king of the Jelling rune-stones. The unusual promotion of Thyra on the two Jelling rune-stones and likely on other stones as well (Jacobsen & Moltke 1942 Nos. 29 & 33) might indicate that she is of the royal family, and that Gorm was acquiring his particular status through marriage to her. Perhaps the much discussed praise on King Gorm's rune-store for Thyra should again be read "Denmark's Remedy", rather than "Denmark's Adornment" (Moltke 1976, 162f.).

It has been suggested that the first defences at Århus date to "the early 930s" (advanced Carbon-14 date) (Damm 2005, 16); a second phase is dendro-dated to "sometime after 957" and "before or at 980". At Ribe, the first defences are possibly from the early 10th century (Feveile 2006, 48f.). The earliest fortification around Hedeby is considered to be of the middle or rather the first half of the 10th century (Elsner 1992, 38; H.H. Andersen 1998, 133f.).

In other words, it is just possible that the first fortifications of the three main towns in Jutland are of the same period and may relate to the German intimidation of 934.

---

8   Rök carries an indeed very long inscription, which even mentions Zealand and Theoderic the Great (454-526), king of the Ostrogoths and ruler of Italy.

The military logics behind such fortifications are on the one hand protection, on the other starvation of enemy operations. King Alfred's fortified "burhs", constructed against roaming Viking armies, served exactly this purpose, whether the Danes wished to trade in the towns, or to plunder them (cf. Randsborg 1998A). Seemingly, Danevirke was not strengthened in the early 10th century (H.H. Andersen 1998; cf. 2004).

ATTACK OF 983

Regarding the year 983, Thietmar reports that Duke Bernhard - *en route* to an Imperial meeting in Verona - turned around, "because one of his fortresses (*urbs*) ..., which the Emperor had secured against the Danes by wall and garrison, was once more sneakily conquered by those and burned down after the defenders were killed" (Thietmar III.24). Likely, it is the matter of the same fortress as the above-mentioned one from 974+ in the border lands between Denmark and Germany.

Interestingly, 983 is also the year of the great Slavonian rebellion against the German emperor and Christian institutions in the (northern) March. The revolt threw the Germans back across the Elbe until the early 12th century: estates, towns, and churches. Obviously, the Danes were linked with the revolt or used it to expand their own influence to the south of Danevirke and the Ejder River. The Danish attacks on England from the 990s onwards were thus taking place without a massive threat from Germany.

In fact, with a strong Danevirke, and the Trelleborgs, Denmark might have been likened to a veritable fortress, even patrolled by navy squadrons (cf. Appendix III).

APPENDIX II. THE FIRST WOODEN CHURCH AT JELLING

The reconstruction of the first wooden church at Jelling takes as its point of departure the plan published by the excavator (Krogh 1982, 195 Fig. 12) (Figs. 3a-b; Table I)[9]. It is acknowledged that the characteristic floor layer established by the excavator as lying under the original wooden floor of the church was also found beyond the outer lines of posts dug into the ground. This indicates that the outer walls of the whole structure were positioned beyond the lines of roof-supporting posts. Perhaps, the planks of these walls were nested in a horizontal beam lying directly on the ground (cf. the late construction in Christie 1981, 153; 169f.), or simply dug into the ground, as the churches in Lund and elsewhere (cf. Fig. 5). Likely, these wall lines were disturbed by the stone church and later digging, but there is still a chance to find elements of the first wooden church outside the stone church.

UPPER FLOOR & OTHER ELEMENTS

In the western end of the nave, several pairs of posts with only a narrow space in between indicate a demand for support of an upper level likely covering one fourth of the nave. The upper level was seemingly reached by a monumental staircase represented by the posts to the west of the nave, probably housed in a square tower (again to judge by the floor layer). The open part of the nave is reconstructed as a (near) square (a perfect square if the edge of the upper floor is extended a little towards the east). This allows for the single known post in the longitudinal axis of the church (marked with an "A") to the east of the chamber grave to stand at the border line between nave and choir. It is also seen that there is space left in the south-eastern part of the nave for one more chamber grave next to the excavated one (for King Svend?).

The choir is reconstructed as a square narrower than the nave. It is defined by the outer lines of posts in the nave, in accordance with other large wooden churches where the line of wall is preserved (cf. Fig. 5). The remaining two posts in the choir likely belong to an internal division, or are roof-supports, likely four posts arranged in a square, or a similar arrangement (eight posts in a rectangle?).

Finally, going back to the west tower, the choir may

have set the size of the former, making it large enough to serve as a hall (*narthex*), even though there is no firm evidence. This would yield symmetry to this magnificent structure. Actually, such plan is near identical in proportions to the one of one of the oldest stone churches in Denmark, the much smaller St. Jørgensbjerg at Roskilde, which was likely built by English architects in the late 1030s (Olsen 1960, 9 Fig. 5) (Fig. 6).

Three doorways are suggested: staircase tower (royalty, on special occasions) - likely towards the west and the main palace at the time (but it may also have been in the southern wall); nave (main entrance) - in the southern long wall at the westernmost part of the open nave and opposite King Harald's rune-stone; and, choir (clergy) - western part of the southern long wall. The oblique staircase allows for easy access to both levels from a western entrance.

Due to the second level, the nave must have been quite tall and in this resembled the well known superbly preserved Norwegian stave churches (of the late 12th century), even though the roof at Jelling was likely comparatively lower (Christie 1981; cf. Ahrens 2001). The earliest of the Norwegian churches is Urnes, from about 1130, incidentally giving name to the last of the traditional animal ornamental styles on the base of elegantly carved, but likely re-used timbers. One or more predecessors of Urnes Church, dated to the 11th century, had old-fashioned roof-supporting posts dug into the ground like the first wooden churches at Jelling (Krogh 1971).

A BASILICA

The roof is a particular problem. A large saddle roof is the simple solution, but the roofs of the Norwegian churches are more intricate. The basilica reference would, if taken at face value, indicate a main roof with at least one half-roof on either side. Adaptation to the requirements of the second level must also be taken into consideration.

The double rows of posts in the nave may even give rise to the hypothesis (however less likely) that narrow upper floors were also found on the long-sides, on either side of a rather limited open nave. One might even reconstruct the plan of the nave symmetrically with pairs of posts with only a narrow space in between also towards the east. But in this case the single post to the east of the chamber graves does not find ready explanation, and the

---

9 Ahrens' reconstruction is simplistic and does not take into consideration the actual area of the floor level (cf. Ahrens 2001, 202f. (Katalog)).

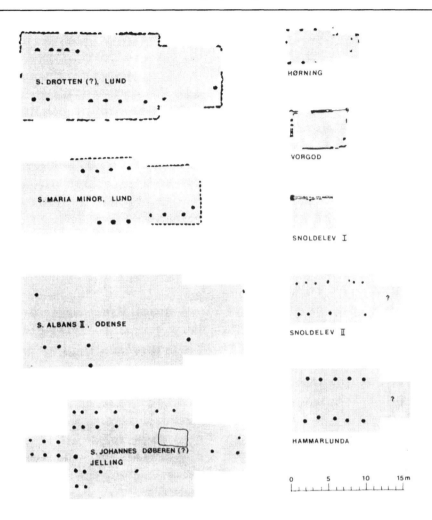

Fig. 5. Plans of Danish wooden churches of the 11th century AD (after Liebgott 1989): The Basilicas on the left are also presented in the Table I. The smaller churches on the right are likely with common saddle roofs.

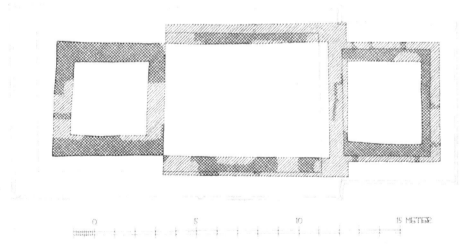

Fig. 6. Foundation ditches of St. Jørgensbjerg Church (stone) of the late 1030s (after Olsen 1960).

whole space is less harmoniously conceived. Excavation outside the stone church may provide further clues, although this is less likely. Incidentally, as the reconstruction stands, it is structurally not dissimilar to the symmetrical so-called Trelleborg halls.

At any rate, the first wooden church at Jelling is a highly advanced piece of wooden architecture finding parallels in high class dwellings of the mid-11th century, like Østergård in South Jutland (Ethelberg et al. 2003, 440 Fig. 5:3; 442 Fig. 5). In the present reconstruction, the church is about 450m[2] at floor level and 39 metres long (width 13½ m): one of the largest wooden churches in Europe in pre-modern times (Fig. 4). Its height, although difficult to

estimate, was certainly bigger than the two huge mounds. The quality of work is very high indeed and is reflecting knowledge of both wooden and stone architecture. The decoration has no doubt been lavish, as demonstrated by the evocative painted wood-carvings from the Northern Mound, and by the Norwegian churches (Krogh & Leth-Larsen 2007).

In Table I, the measurements of the first wooden church at Jelling are compared with those of other wooden Basilica churches as well as smaller wooden churches from the city of Lund (all of the 11th century) and other localities in Denmark (cf. Ahrens 2001; etc.).

APPENDIX III. *ENCOMIUM EMMAE REGINAE* ON KING SVEND

Encomium Emmae Reginae or *Gesta Cnutonis Regis* (writer unknown, but likely from the monastery of St. Bertin at St. Omer, near Calais) of 1041/42 is an illustrated book produced in honour of Queen Emma of Normandy, wife of King Knud (Canute), the son of King Svend of Denmark. It reports the following on the nature of Svend (cf. Campbell 1998, 9f.):

... The army, grieved by this, deserted the father [King Harald], adhered to the son [Svend], and afforded him active protection. As a result they met in battle, in which the father was wounded, and fled to the Slavs, where he died shortly afterwards. Sveinn [Svend] held his throne undisturbed. ... When Sveinn was at peace, and in no fear of any attack by his foes, acting always as if in danger, and

indeed of pressing danger, he attended to the strengthening of any positions in his fortress[10], which might not have resisted hostile forces, should they have appeared, and, preparing everything necessary for war, he permitted no remissness in his men, lest their manly spirit should, as often happens, be softened by inactivity. ... (Book I.1).

And so when in the continuity of a settled peace all matters were turning out favourably, the soldiers of the above-mentioned king, confident that they would profit by the firm steadfastness of their lord, decided to persuade him, who was already meditating the same plan, to invade England, and add it to the bounds of his empire by the decision of war. ... (Book I.2).

10　Denmark, with the Danevirke walls at the foot of Jutland, the Trelleborg fortresses, armed units across the country, and naval squadrons would indeed have seemed like one big fortress by the year 900 AD; however, also equipped for attack (cf. Appendix I).

BIBLIOGRAPHY

Adam of Bremen = Trillmich 1973; Lund 2000.

Ahrens, C. 2001. Die frühen Holzkirchen Europas. Schriften des Archäologischen Landesmuseums 7 [Schloss Gottorp, Schleswig]. Stuttgart (Theiss).

Andersen, H. 1992. De glemte borge. Skalk 1992:1. 19ff.

- . 1994. Den tomme Jellingehøj. Skalk 1994:2. 3ff.

- . 1995. The Graves of the Jelling Dynasty. Acta Archaeologica 66. 281ff.

Andersen, H.H. 1998. Danevirke og Kovirke. Arkæologiske undersøgelser 1861-1993. Moesgård Museums skrifter. Højbjerg (Jysk Arkæologisk Selskab/Aarhus Universitetsforlag).

- . 2004. Til hele rigets værn. Danevirkes arkæologi og historie. Højbjerg (Moesgård & Wormianum).

Andrén, A. 1985. Den urbana scenen. Städer och samhälle i det medeltida Danmark. Acta Archaeologica Lundensia. Series in 8° 13. Bonn/Malmö (Habelt/Gleerup).

Berg, K. (et al.) (ed.). 1981. Norges kunsthistorie 1. Fra Oseberg til Borgund. Oslo (Gyldendal Norsk).

Braunsfels, W. (etc.). 1981. Die Kunst im Heiligen Römischen Reich Deutscher Nation III. Reichsstädte, Grafschaften, Reichsklöster. München (Beck).

Capelle, T. & C. Fischer (eds.). 2005. Ragnarok. Odins verden. Silkeborg (Silkeborg Museum).

Campbell, A. (ed.) (et al.). 1998 (1949). Encomium Emmae Reginae. Camden Classic Reprints 4. Cambridge (Royal Historical Society/Cambridge University Press).

Christensen, K. 2003. Ravning-broens alder. En af Danmarks sikreste dendrokronologiske dateringer? Kuml 2003. 213ff.

Christensen, K. & K.J. Krogh. 1987. Jelling-højene dateret. Nationalmuseets Arbejdsmark 1987. 223ff.

Christensen, P. Mohr & S. Wulff Andersen. 2008. Kongeligt? Skalk 2008:1. 3ff.

Christensen, T. & N. Lynnerup (et al.). 2004. Kirkegården i Kongemarken. N. Lund 2004. 142ff.

Christie, H. 1981. Stavkirkene - Arkitektur. Berg 1981. 139ff.

Cinthio, M. 1997. Trinitatiskyrkan i Lund - med engelsk prägel. Hikuin 24. 113ff.

- . 2002. De första stadsborna. Medeltida gravar och människor i Lund. Stockholm (Symposion)

- . 2004. Trinitatiskyrkan, gravarna och de första lundaborna. N. Lund 2004. 159ff.

Clapham, A.W. 1930. English Romanesque Architecture. Before the Conquest. Oxford (Clarendon).

Damm, A. (ed.). 2005. Vikingernes Aros. Højbjerg (Moesgaard Museum).

Dyggve, E. 1942. La fouille par le Musée National danois du tertre royal sud à Jelling en 1941. Acta Archaeologica XII. 65ff.

- . 1954. Gorm's Temple and Harald's Stave-Church at Jelling. Acta Archaeologica XXV. 221ff.

- . 1964. Mindemærkerne i Jelling. Form og tydning. København (Nationalmuseet).

Eliasen, K., B. Bøgild Johannsen, H. Johannsen & M. Vedsø. 2001. Forsvundne middelalderkirker i Odense. Danmarks Kirker IX (Odense Amt) Vol. 3:18-19. København (Nationalmuseet).

Elsner, H. 1992. Wikinger Museum Haithabu: Et portræt af en tidlig by. Neumünster (Archäologisches Landesmuseum der Christian-Albrechts-Universität/Wachholtz).

Ethelberg, P., N. Hardt, B. Poulsen & A.B. Sørensen. 2003. Det sønderjyske Landbrugs Historie. Jernalder, Vikingetid og Middelalder. Skrifter udgivet af Historisk Samfund for Sønderjylalnd 82. Haderslev (Haderslev Museum & Historisk Samfund for Sønderjylland).

Encomium Emmae Reginae = Campbell 1998.

Feveile, C. (ed.). 2006. Ribe Studier. Det ældste Ribe. Udgravninger på nordsiden af Ribe Å 1984-2000. Vol. 1.1-1.2. Højbjerg (Jysk Arkæologisk Selskab/Den antikvariske Samling/Aarhus Universitetsforlag).

Frankish Imperial Annals = Rau 1974.

Haastrup, U. & R. Egevang (eds.). 1986. Danske kalkmalerier. Romansk tid 1080-1175. København (Nationalmuseet).

Hauglid, R. 1976. Norske stavkirker. Bygningshistorisk bakgrunn og utvikling. Norske minnesmerker. Oslo (Riksantikvaren/Dreyer).

Hirsch, P. (et al.) (ed.). 1935. Die Sachsengeschichte des Widukind von Korvei. Hannover (Hahnsche Buchhandlung). 5th ed.; Reprint 1977; only the Latin text.

Hvass, S. 1986. Vorbasse. Eine Dorfsiedlung während des 1. Jahrtausends n.Chr. in Mitteljütland, Dänemark. Berichte der römisch-germanische Kommission 67. 529ff.

Iversen, M. (ed.). 1991. Mammen. Grav, kunst og samfund i vikingetid. Jysk Arkæologisk Selskabs Skrifter XXVIII. Viborg Stiftsmuseums række 1. Højbjerg/Århus (Jysk Arkæologisk Selskab/Aarhus Universitetsforlag).

Jacobsen, L. & E. Moltke (et al.). 1942. Danmarks Runeindskrifter. Text & Atlas. København (Munksgaard).

Jansson, S.B.F. 1976. Runinskrifter i Sverige. Uppsala (Almqvist & Wiksell/AWE/Gebers).

Jensen, J. 2004. Danmarks Oldtid. Yngre Jernalder og Vikingetid. 400-1050 e.Kr. København (Gyldendal).

Jeppesen, J. 2004. Stormandsgården ved Lisbjerg Kirke. Nye undersøgelser. Kuml 2004. 161ff.

Jeppesen, J. & H.J. Madsen. 1995-96. Trækirke og stormandshal i Lisbjerg. Kuml 1995-96. 149ff.

Jørgensen, L. 2003. Manor and market at Lake Tissø in the sixth to eleventh centuries: the Danish 'productive' sites. Pestell & Ulmschneider 2003. 175ff.

Krogh, K.J. 1966. Kirken mellem højene. Skalk 1966:2. 5ff.

- . 1971. Kirkerne på Urnes. Aarbøger for nordisk Oldkyndighed og Historie 1971. 146ff.

- . 1982. The Royal Viking-Age Monuments at Jelling in the Light of Recent Archaeological Excavations. A Preliminary Report. Acta Archaeologica 53. 183ff.

- . 1993. Gåden om Kong Gorms Grav. Historien om Nordhøjen i Jelling. Vikingekongernes Monumenter i Jelling I. København (Carlsbergfondet og Nationalmuseet/Poul Kristensen).

Krogh, K.J. & B. Leth-Larsen. 2007. Hedensk og Kristent. Fundene fra den kongelige gravhøj i Jelling. Vikingekongernes Monumenter i Jelling II. København (Carlsbergfondet & Nationalmuseet).

Krogh, K.J. & O. Voss. 1961. Fra hedenskab til kristendom i Hørning. En vikingetids kammergrav og en trækirke fra 1000-tallet under Hørning kirke. Nationalmuseets Arbejdsmark 1961. 5ff.

Liebgott, N.-K. 1989. Dansk middelalderarkæologi. København (Gad).

Lindblom, C. 2008. Overraskelsen i Oens. Skalk 2008:3. 4ff.

Lund, A. (ed.). 2000. Adam af Bremens krønike. Oversat og kommenteret. Højbjerg (Wormianum).

Lund, N. 1998. Harald Blåtands død og hans begravelse i Roskilde? Roskilde (Roskilde Museum).

Lund, N. (ed.). 2004. Kristendommen i Danmark før 1050. Et symposium i Roskilde den 5.-7. februar 2003. Roskilde (Roskilde Museum).

Malmer, B. 1966. Nordiska mynt före år 1000. Acta Archaeologica Lundensia. Series in 8°:4. Bonn & Lund (Habelt & Gleerup).

Moltke, E. 1976. Runerne i Danmark og deres oprindelse. København (Forum).

Møller, E. & O. Olsen 1961. Danske trækirker. Nationalmuseets Arbejdsmark 1961. 35ff.

Møller, K. 1997. Vikingeætten. Brudstykker til et mønster. [Vemb/Holstebro] (own publisher).

Müller-Wille, M. (etc.). 1987. Das wikingerzeitliche Gräberfeld von Thumby-Bienebek (Kr. Rendsburg-Eckernförde) II. Offa-Bücher N.F. 62. Neumünster (Wachholtz).

Nielsen, A. Horsbøl. 2004. Sukkertoppen. Skalk 2004:4. 5ff.

Nielsen, H. 1974. Foden på Trelleborg. Skalk 1974:1. 19ff.

Nielsen, J.N. 2004. Sebbersund - tidlige kirker ved Limfjorden. N. Lund 2004. 103ff.

Olsen, O. 1960. St. Jørgensbjerg kirke. Arkæologiske undersøgelser i muværk og gulv. Aarbøger for nordisk Oldkyndighed og Historie. 1ff.

Østergaard, B. 1994. Sven Estridsens danmarkshistorie. Danmarks politiske historie ca. 890-965. Historie Jyske Samlinger 1994. 3ff.

Parsons, D. (ed.). 1975. Tenth-Century Studies. Essays in Commemoration of the Millennium of the Council of Winchester and the *Regularis Concordia*. London & Chichester (Phillimore).

Pedersen, A. 1996. Søllested - nye oplysninger om et velkendt fund. Aarbøger for Nordisk Oldkyndighed og Historie 1996. 37ff.

Pestell, T. & K. Ulmschneider (eds.). 2003. Markets in early medieval Europe: trading and 'productive' sites. 650-850. Macclesfield (Windgather).

Randsborg, K. 1980. The Viking Age in Denmark. The Formation of a State. London/New York (Duckworth/St. Martin's).

- . 1991. The First Millennium AD in Europe and the Mediterranean. An Archaeological Essay. Cambridge (Cambridge University Press).

- . 1998. Plundered Bronze Age Graves. Archaeological & Social Implications. Acta Archaeologica 69. 113ff.

- . 1998A. Offensive Armies and Navies. Acta Archaeologica 69. 163ff.

Ranft, A. (ed.). 2006. Der Hoftag in Quedlinburg 973. Von den historischen Wurzeln zum Neuen Europa. Tagungsband. Im Auftrag der Landesregierung von Sachsen-Anhalt sowie der Historischen Kommission von Sachsen-Anhalt. Berlin (Akademie-Verlag).

Rau, R. (ed.). 1974. Quellen zur karolingischen Reichsgeschichte I. Die Reichsannalen, Einhard Leben Karls der Grossen, etc. Ausgewählte Quellen zur deutschen Geschichte des Mittelalters V (ed. R. Buchner). Darmstadt (Wissenschaftliche Buchgesellschaft).

Saxo = Zeeberg 2000.

Schiørring, O. (ed.). 1991. Tamdrup. Kirke og Gård. Horsens (Horsens Museum & Foreningen til gamle bygningers bevaring/Skippershoved).

Sørensen, A.C. 2001. Ladby. A Danish Ship-Grave from the Viking Age. Ships and Boats of the North 3. Roskilde (The Viking Ship Museum in Roskilde, The National Museum of Denmark & Kertemindeegnens Museer).

Taylor, H.M. 1975. Tenth-Century Church Building in England and on the Continent. Parsons 1975. 141ff.

Thaastrup-Leth, A.K. 2004. Trækirker i det middelalderlige Danmark indtil ca. 1100. Hvornår blev de bygget? N. Lund 2004. 207ff.

Thietmar von Merseburg = Trillmich 1970.

Toman, R. 2000 (ed.). Romansk kunst. Köln (Könemann). (German edition 1995.)

Trillmich, W. (ed.). 1961. Quellen des 9. und 11. Jahrhunderts zur Geschichte des Hamburgischen Kirche und des Reiches. Rimbert Leben Ansgars, Adam von Bremen, etc. Ausgewählte Quellen zur deutschen Geschichte des Mittelalters (ed. R. Buchner) XI. Berlin (Rütten & Loening).

- . 1970. Thietmar von Merseburg Chronik. Neu übertragen und erläutert. Ausgewählte Quellen zur deutschen Geschichte des Mittelalters (ed. R. Buchner) IX. Darmstadt (Wissenschaftliche Buchgesellschaft).

Ulriksen, J. 1994. Danish sites and settlements with a maritime context: AD 200-1200. Antiquity 68 (No. 261), 797ff.

Voss, O. 1957. Trælborg. Skalk 1957:4. 14ff.

Wamers, E. (et al.). 1994. König im Grenzland. Neue Analyse des Bootkammergrabes vom Haiðaby. Acta Archaeologica 65. 1ff.

Wieczorek, A. & H.-M. Hinz (eds.). 2000. Europas Mitte um 1000. Beiträge zur Geschichte, Kunst und Archäologie 1-2 (& Katalog). Stuttgart (Theiss).

Widukind = Hirsch 1935.

Wilson, L. 1994. Runstenar och kyrkor. En studie med utgångspunkt från runstenar som påträffats i kyrkomiljö i Uppland och Södermanland. Occasional Papers in Archaeology 8. Uppsala (Societas Archaeologica Upsaliensis).

Zeeberg, P. (ed.). 2000. Saxos Danmarks Historie. København (Det Danske Sprog- og Litteraturselskab/Gad).

Author's address
SAXO Institute, University of Copenhagen, Njalsgade 80, DK-2300 Copenhagen, DENMARK
randsb@hum.ku.dk   www.worldarchaeology.net

TABLES

Table 1. Early Basilicas and smaller/simpler wooden churches from Jelling, Hørning, Vorgod, Sebbersund, Odense, Svorgerslev, Hammarlunda, and Lund, Denmark: Measurements in metres; approximate dates in brackets (cf. Ahrens 2001; Christensen & Lynnerup 2004; Cinthio 1997; 2004; Jeppesen & Madsen 1995-96; Krogh & Voss 1961; Møller & Olsen 1961; Nielsen 2004; Thaastrup-Leth 2004; etc.) (Cf. Fig. 5).

Jellling's measurements are reconstructed; Svogerslev (II) and Hammarlunda are uncertain as Basilicas; they may rank with Kongemarken (and Sebbersund?) as churches with internal posts that are not Basilicas.

	Total length	Length nave	Width nave	Length choir	Width choir
BASILICAS					
JELLING St. Johannes? First wooden church (980s?)	39.2	20.0	13.5	9.6	9.6
LUND St. Maria Minor (c1050)	>18 (24?)	>10.0	c10.0	8.0	c7.6
LUND Trinitatis?/Kattesund (c1050+) (ex-"Drotten", ex-St. Stefan)	25.7	17.9	10.6/10.8	8.1	7.5
? HAMMARLUNDA (I) St. Anna? (c1050+)	?	≥9.7	≥c5	?	?
? SNOLDELEV(II) (c1070)	?	≥9½	≥4½	?	?
ODENSE St. Albani (post 1086?)	?	≥18	≥12	≥7?	≥7
SMALLER CHURCHES					
LUND Trinitatis/"Drotten" (c990) (King Svend's church?)	?	?	c7.0	5.5	7.0
SEBBERSUND (c1000?)	c13	c13	4-6	-	-
KONGEMARKEN (c1000) (uncertain)	≥8	≥8	≥2	-	-
LUND St. Stefan (1049/50)	18.5	18.5	6.8	-	-
LUND ?/south of Kattesund (1057+)	19	15	6½	4	4
HØRNING (c1060+)	9.3	6.0	4.5	3.3	3.3
SNOLDELEV (I) (before 1070)	≥5½	≥5½	?	-	-
LISBJERG (close of 11th century)	8?	8?	6	?	?
VORGOD (-12th century)	7	7	5	-	-

Table II. Summary model of the chain of events: Jelling & Denmark, etc. in the late 10th century.

	FACTS	FACTS & FICTION
934	German attack, King Gnupa subdued	Fortification of Hedeby, Ribe, Århus (↓)
	King Sigtryg, son of Gnupa; "Gorm"	
		King Gorm's rune-stone for Thyra (↓)
958/59+	Chamber in the old Northern Mound	Queen Thyra/King Gorm buried in the chamber, at Jelling
		Northern Mound extension, huge ship-setting, large palisade fence, etc.
•960s, early	King Harald accepts Christianity	King Harald's rune-stone for Gorm & Thyra
964/65(?)	Chamber in Northern Mound opened	Queen Thyra/King Gorm exhumed, buried elsewhere*
965/68	Danevirke defences strengthened	
970/71	Mammen grave	King Harald dies, buried in Slavonia (↓)
•970s	Southern Mound (cenotaph)	
973	Danes at Quedlinburg imperial meeting	
974	German attack on Danevirke	Kovirke wall (?)
•970s, late	Trelleborg fortresses	Cross type half bracteate coins (Jelling?) ↓
983	Danish attack on German fortress	
c986	Ravning Enge Bridge	Wooden cathedral at Jelling,
		King Harald re-buried under the church
c990	1st wooden church in Lund	
•990s	King Svend attacking England	
1014	England conquered, King Svend dies	

*Alternatively, King Gorm was buried in the chamber at this date; in which case, the construction of the Northern Mound extension and the huge ship-setting, as certainly the acceptance of Christianity (cf. the large rune-stone), are later.

Table III. 10th century kings of Denmark before King Harald according to Adam of Bremen (Adam). The issue has been pondered endlessly in the literature, often without the archaeological and other knowledge we have today (e.g., Østergaard 1994; Møller 1997). Adam is a late source, his information incomplete, contradictory and appearing in several versions; in addition, Adam had his own "agendas" as a writer.

I.48 - source King Svend Estridsøn (died 1074): After the defeat of the Norsemen [Battle of Louvain 891] Heiligo [Helge] reigned, according to my knowledge, loved by his people for his justice and holiness [cf. German Heilig], followed by Olaph who came from Sweden and occupied the Danish kingdom by force of arms. He had many sons, of whom Chnob and Gurd took over the kingdom after the death of the father.

I.52 - source Svend Estridsøn, etc.: After Olaph, the First of the Swedes, who ruled in Denmark together with his sons, Sigerich took his seat. But already shortly after, Hardegon, a son of King Suein's [Svend], who came from Nortmannia [Norway or Normandy?], stole the throne from him. It is uncertain whether all these Danish kings, or rather tyrants, ruled the same time or lived shortly after each other.

I.55 - source likely local library: At that time, Hardecnudth Vurm reigned among the Danes; he was a very dangerous worm. [A *lacuna* has been suggested between Hardecnudth and Vurm, implying that Vurm is the son of Hardecnudt.]

I.57 - source unnamed Danish bishop: King Heinric invaded the land of the Danes with his army, scaring King Vurm, who promised to obey Heinrich.

I.59 - source likely local library: King Worm & son Harold [listed as contemporary with Archbishop Unni of Hamburg-Bremen (918-36)].

Interpretation: Chnob (Cnuba) must have reigned in 934; his son is Sigerich (Sigtryg). King Heinric (Heinrich) suppresses Cnuba, not Vurm. According to Adam, Sigerich is followed by Hardegon, who is likely identical with Hardeknuth [and perhaps = Knud I]. There is also a link between Hardeknuth and Vurm; Adam actually regards "Vurm" as a nickname. King Gorm (son Harold/Harald) is identical with Vurm/Worm. It is possible that the character behind Hardegon, Hardecnudth and Vurm/Worm is one and the same: King Gorm, who must have died around 960.

Acta Archaeologica vol. 79, 2008, pp 24-61
Printed in Denmark • All rights reserved

DIE WOHNSTALLHÄUSER
DER FEDDERSEN WIERDE
MASSE UND GEOMETRIE DER GRUNDRISSE
EXKURS: MEGARA IN PRIENE, TROJA

WOLF MEYER-CHRISTIAN

Den Ausgräbern Dank,
den Alten Meistern Bewunderung

DIE WOHNSTALLHÄUSER DER FEDDERSEN WIERDE
MASSE UND GEOMETRIE DER GRUNDRISSE, I

Anders als die Archaio-*Logie*, deren Funde, in Doppelbedeutung, direkte sprachliche Äußerungen aus der Alten Geschichte einschließen, kann die jüngere, unabhängig entstandene Vorgeschichtsforschung nur indirekt Schlüsse auf Tätigkeiten, Leistungen, und die dahinterliegende geistige Welt ihres Untersuchungsfeldes ziehen. Damit ist eine wesentliche Trennung der Methoden, der Ausbildung, des Forschungshorizonts gegeben.

Bauwerke, das umfangreichste Erbe aus allen Epochen der Vergangenheit, sind erst spät, nachträglich Forschungsgegenstand geworden; auch fehlte, mit Architekten als außenstehender dritter Partei, für ein eigenständiges Fach zunächst die Mitte. Der Abstand beider Geschichtsdisziplinen voneinander in Vorverständnis und Arbeitszielen hat von Anfang an zu einer Teilung in Kulturen und Regionen geführt und dann, unvermeidlich und folgenreich, auch die Bauarten getrennt, das handwerkliche, also 'kunstlose' frühe Bauen auf der einen Seite, die wesentlich ästhetisch definierte (definiert?) Architektur auf der anderen – ebenso schlicht in Holzbau und Werksteinbau zu teilen. Einer aufwendigen Befunderhebung und nahezu fehlenden Deutung auf der einen Seite steht die Suche nach dem Logos der fertigen Gestalt antiker Bauwerke gegenüber. Zusammen mit Schriftfunden hat sich so das feste Vorverständnis eines geistig-kulturellen Gefälles von Süd nach Nord gebildet. Gemein aber ist

beiden Linien, die Technik des Erbauens, ihre, seine Ratio nicht zu kennen, und in der geschichtlichen Entwicklung beider kein eigenes Feld für das Wirken menschlicher Intellektualität zu sehen.

Diese Lücke in der Bauforschung ist das Muster einer universitären Mißbildung. Obwohl unbestreitbar, daß alle Architektur nur aus dem Handwerk enstanden sein kann, ist bis jetzt nicht erkennbar, wo denn und welcher Art die Grenze sein soll, oberhalb derer aus einem Handwerk 'Architektur' wird, und natürlich, was überhaupt Architektur sein soll. Die deutende Bauforschung, die sog. Architekturtheorie – inzwischen sind Architekten beteiligt – hat dabei nicht nur in der Sache, sondern auch über sich selbst keine Theorie, noch nicht einmal eine Frage.

Eine der Schwierigkeiten ist, zu definieren, worin ein Typus besteht, in welche Entwicklungsreihe er gehört, und welche Verschiedenheiten ein Bauwerk zu einem Individuum machen, bis auf weiteres die Voraussetzung für die Zuweisung in den Bereich der Kunst. Typus allerdings bezieht sich auf Begriffe auf sehr verschiedenen Ebenen, die am fertigen Bauwerk zusammen in unterschiedlicher Ausprägung auftreten. Die variierenden Längen der Wohnstallhäuser auf der Feddersen Wierde und anderen Siedlungen werden als nutzungsbezogen gesehen, sie gehören damit in die entwerferisch niedere Realwelt. Aber sollten die auch bei gleichlangen Häusern dezidiert unterschiedlichen Längen der Boxen im Stallteil ebenso nutzungsbezogen sein? Versuche, nach bloßem Augenschein, hier aus Hauslängen und Jochabständen, Typen zu bilden, sind ohne Aussage. Dorische Tempel, auf der anderen Seite, typologisch ebenfalls stark gebunden, jedoch abgehoben, Kultbauwerke, werden in ihrer Gestalt auf die Geheimnisse eines jeweiligen Entwurfs, seiner Idee hin beforscht. Wie unabhängig von der Sinnlichkeit einer Kunstschöpfung aber, von ihrer Bildlichkeit im Ursprung dürfte solche Idee, eine τεχνη sein?

Bauwerke, mit ihrer durch die Zeit bleibenden Grundaufgabe, ein Innenklima in einer klimatisch wechselhaften Außenwelt zu erhalten, dabei gefahrlos, beständig, und für seine Benutzer am Ort herstellbar zu sein, besitzen schon im Ursprung einen Vernunftanspruch. Naturgesetzliche Notwendigkeiten, Verfahren als Antwort haben nicht einfach nur zu Techniken geführt; Erkenntnisse als Folge haben vielmehr auch eine Ebene rationalen Verhaltens, operativer Verselbstständigung entstehen lassen. Den wohl wichtigsten Teil dabei stellen Notwendigkeiten und Zwänge im *Ent-werfen*, dem Aufstellen eines Bauplanes dar, aus dem allein die Maße der anzufertigenden Teile abzuleiten sind. Die hier vorgelegten Planrekonstrukionen bieten einen völlig neuen Einblick in eine bisher ungeahnte Geisteswelt.

Hier nun hätte der Beitrag der Architekten liegen können, wären sie nicht erst nach dem Übergang zum Metersystem in die Bauforschung eingetreten – denn sie waren, bis dahin, noch im Besitz ihrer geschichtlichen Planungstechnik; Schinkel, Semper und alle anderen praktizierten sie, und sie hätten ohne Mühe nachvollzogen, was jetzt hier, traurig zu sagen, geringes Verstehen finden wird. Sie hätten auch einer heutigen ´Ästhetik´ widersprochen, die gefühlig die Wirkung geschichtlicher Bauwerke beschreibt, und, ohne die Inkongruenz zu bemerken, als ´Theorie´ nach formalen Rezepten für Säulenordnungen sucht. Sempers Darlegungen zeigen aber, daß er, wie alle, damals noch ein Berufsgeheimnis zu bewahren hatte.

Die Umstellung auf das amorphe Metersystem nach der Gründung des Kaiserreiches hat jedes *konstruktive* Denken der Architekten in einem Maß-, d.h. Zahlengefüge aufgehoben, und die entwurfliche Bindung an die Geschichte beendet. Die weitere Aushöhlung des Berufs durch den Übergang zu industriellen Bauverfahren, der Ingenieurswelt, Orientierungslosigkeit innerhalb wechselnder gesellschaftlicher Systeme, Reformen der Ausbildung ohne inhaltliche Ziele, sowie frühe Entscheidung Einzelner für

die Bauforschung, häufig ohne jede Baupraxis, schränken heute weiter die Wirkung ihrer Mitarbeit ein.

Zu prägenden Deutungen geschichtlicher Bauwerke kaum berufen haben Architekten Rekonstruktionsversuche deshalb anderen überlassen. Dabei verhält sich die naturwissenschaftlich arbeitende Seite unspezifisch; die kulturwissenschaftlich arbeitende aber sieht nur Sekundärmerkmale. Rekonstruktionen vorgeschichtlicher Holzbauten zeigen das Fehlen jeder Vorstellung zu dem wichtigsten Fortschritt in der Konstruktion seit den Bandkeramikerhäusern mit ihren stabil eingegrabenen Pfosten – die Dreischiffigkeit mit ihrer obenliegenden Längs- und Queraussteifung. Rekonstruktionen des ägäischen Lehmziegelmegarons auf der anderen Seite werden mit flachen Deckenplatten versehen, ohne Vorstellung, wie die Wassermengen dieser Winterregengebiete abgeleitet werden sollen, wie diese Dächer in der Nässe überhaupt bestehen könnten. Der Rauch des offenen Herdes zwischen den vier Pfosten wird, unbegreiflich, durch einen offenbar frei in der Dachplatte darüber hängenden Schornstein abgeführt. Es ist nicht zu erwarten, daß von hier aus das große Thema, die technische Evolution des Bauens, die zunehmenden Erkenntnisse aus den beiden Formen des Versagens, Querschnittsbruch im tektonischen Bereich, Kollabieren im konstruktiven, einmal gesehen und nachgezeichnet würde.

Die wesentlich von Wortwissenschaften geführte Bauforschung hat nur den fertigen Bau im Blick. Sie sieht dabei dessen Gestalt, ein *Bild*, und nimmt ohne zu fragen an, Bauwerke seien, wohl auf wundersame Weise, auch direkt aus der Vorstellung ´geplant´ worden. Bilder sind maßlos, Bauwerke aber, technisch gesehen, nichts als eine bloße Zusammenstellung von *Bauteilen*, die, um scharfkantig zusammenzupassen, *zuvor* über Maße, das sind *diskrete Zahlen*, definiert sein müssen.

Ein Plan stellt eine andere Ebene dar als ein Bild und kann nicht einfach aus diesem gewonnen werden. Das (königliche) ´Bild´ eines bis dahin nicht gekannten Bauwerks, der ersten Pyramide, Sakkara, kann sogar nur ein *Begriff* gewesen sein, der eines baulichen Machtzeichens (wem sonst gegenüber als der eigenen Priesterschaft?). Entstanden ist das Bauwerk dann als Form: Eine spezielle Geometrie für dieses Vorhaben, ein Stufenbau, zu errichten durch Trägerkolonnen, ist nach zu jener Zeit bereits bekannten Gesetzen, ´Pythagoras´, ´Thales´-Kreis entwickelt und der Bau begonnen worden. Die Erfindung einer bestimmten Krantechnik hat dann zu einer Überbauung nach einem zweiten, anderen Konzept geführt, mit einer neuen Geometrie. In dieser hat Imhotep dann von Grund auf die Pyramide des Nachfolgers noch beginnen können. Mit einer weiteren technischen Erfindung für den Steintransport, dem Hochrollen, ist schließlich die glatte 'klassische' Pyramidenform entstanden. Allerdings werden Bilder aus bestehenden Traditionen, anders als bei diesen kolossalen Erstschöpfungen, in der Planung der langen Reihen architektonischer Typen eine Anfangsbedeutung gehabt haben.

Pläne, wir sind in der Steinzeit, sind formale Konstrukte; sie stellen durch die gesamte Geschichte eine eigene geistige, eine *intellektuelle* Ebene und Realität der Bauwerke her, bereits vor ihrer Ausführung. Dies macht Bauwerke aller Epochen miteinander verwandt, und ihre Planung rekonstruierbar. Bauwerke sprechen, durch ihre Maße. Diese Geisteszeugnisse sind älter als die Schriftzeugnisse der Geschichte.

PLANUNG

Bauen, sowohl in Holz wie in Stein, besteht aus zwei Abschnitten, dem Herstellen der Teile, und ihrem anschließenden Zusammenbau. Ein Techniker wird das Bauwerk nicht als Ganzes, sondern als Summe dieser Bauteile sehen. Ziel, schon bald nach Aufnahme des Bauens, muß es gewesen sein, Bauteile der jeweiligen Gruppe gleichmäßig auszubilden, sie damit zu anonymisieren und in Bezug auf den jeweiligen Verlegeort austauschbar zu machen. Voraussetzung dafür ist, daß die jeweiligen Auflagerkanten parallel laufen. Dies bedeutet, daß das Bauwerk als Rechteckkörper aufgefaßt wird. Dieser Körper läßt sich dann planerisch in drei rechtwinklige Ebenen fassen. Diese Flächen, Grundriß, Längsschnitt, Querschnitt, können über berechenbare x- und y-Werte in Koordinaten *geteilt* werden, die die Kanten zusammenzubauender Teile darstellen und auf diese Weise deren Form definieren. Ein Bauen ohne Plan dagegen zwänge dazu, jedes einzelne Bauteil, erst während des Bauvorgangs, seinem bestimmten Verlegeort anzumessen, um es danach als Einzelstück herzustellen, undenkbar.

Eine fortgeschrittene Planungstechnik wird dann darin bestanden haben, Bauwerke in ihrer Größe, also die Gesamtrechtecke der drei Ebenen, nicht in Bauteile zu zerlegen, sondern umgekehrt, sie aus bewährten Konfigurationen von geometrischen Einzelfiguren, fertigen Sätzen, erstehen zu lassen, zusammenzusetzen.

Es gibt eine primäre Qualität aller Bauwerke der Vergangenheit, ihre Rechtwinkligkeit. Deren Herstellung auf dem Baugrundstück ist keine Banalität, sondern eine technische Leistung; sie ist, wie hier zu zeigen, überhaupt der Schlüssel zum Entwurf. Daß sie in der Forschung bisher ganz übersehen wird ist eine Aussage für sich.

Rechtwinkligkeit ergibt sich nicht einfach, sondern muß über eine bestimmte Geometrie hergestellt werden. Rechtwinkligkeit entsteht, wenn die zwei Schenkel eines Winkels über eine dritte Seite im richtigen Maße gespreizt werden. Die Länge dieser dritten Seite kann über zwei Rechenfiguren bestimmt werden, das Quadrat, und das sog. pythagoräische Dreieck; seine Kenntnis ist Jahrtausende älter als der zum Namensgeber gemachte Philosoph.

Pyth. Dreiecke (pDs), das kleinste ist das bekannte 3:4:5, liefern exakte rechte Winkel. Es gibt eine unbegrenzte Anzahl dieser Dreiecke, hier numeriert als -1, -2, -3 nach aufsteigender Länge der Hypotenuse. Dies ist die einzige eindeutige Reihenfolge und damit Bezeichnung. Da sie auch vergrößert auftreten, wird hier der Vervielfältigungsfaktor vorangestellt:

1-1 ist	3:4:5	2-1 ist	6:8:10
1-2	5:12:13	2-2	10:24:26
1-3	8:15:17	2-3	16:30:34usw.

Alle pDs besitzen ganzzahlige Seitenlängen. Es gibt Katheten, die mit mehreren Gegenkatheten pDs gleicher Länge, aber unterschiedlicher Breite bilden. Diese Eigenheit ist im Bauen wesentlich genutzt worden. Ein Beispiel für lange Katheten ist 24:7; 24:10; 24:18. Ein Beispiel für kurze Katheten ist 24:32; 24:45; 24:70. Dies bedeutet, daß mittels Überlagerung auf der gemeinsamen Länge 24 sechs verschiedene Höhen gewonnen werden können.

Quadrate besitzen im Gegensatz zu pDs nur ganzzahlige Seitenlängen oder eine ganzzahlige Diagonale, als Hypotenuse. Es gibt aber einige 'spezielle' Quadrate mit guter Annäherung an die Ganzzahligkeit aller drei Seiten, die kleinste ist 12:17 (16,9705...), eine bessere 99:140 (140,0071...). Mit 120:170 äg. ellen ist das vermutlich erste Projekt der erwähnten Stufenpyramide von Sakkara rechtwinklig ausgelegt worden. Ein bessere Bemessung weist das Grundquadrat des Aachener Münsters auf, 70:99 ellen (cubiti zu 1½ fuß), genau 98,9949..., eine Abweichung von 1,1 mm. Über demselben Quadrat, der Zahl nach als 99:140 (140,0071...) fuß verdoppelt, ist die Kuppel der Hagia Sophia errichtet worden.

Gemessen worden ist allgemein in fuß, ein Maß, das seinen Ursprung im Abstecken auf dem Boden nennt. Im Gegensatz dazu ist mit der Elle, ebenso sprechend, auf dem Tisch gemessen worden /1/. Für die Bemessung der Bauteile waren weiter Kleinmaße nötig, hand und finger (zoll). Das Problem der rechnerischen Einordnung dieser Kleinmaße bestand darin, daß der menschliche Fuß 3½ Handbreiten (ohne Daumen) lang ist. Um ganzzahlig im Körpermaß teilbar zu werden mußte dieser Wert entweder auf 4 aufgerundet, griechisch, oder auf 3 abgerundet werden, römisch und abendländisch. Es ist nun zu zeigen, daß vorgeschichtliche germanische Wohnstallhäuser, Ezinge, Feddersen Wierde, den fuß 'griechisch' teilen, also in 4h x 4 f = 16 zoll. Hier scheint ein Werkzeug für Zuweisungen im Alten Orient gegeben. Zu schließen ist, daß wir, wohl mit der Christianisierung, auf die römische Teilung in 3h x 4 f = 12" umgestellt worden sind /2/.

Aus der griechischen und der römischen Antike ist bekannt, daß die elle, der phcuV bzw. cubitus auf 1½ fuß normiert war. Nicht bekannt bisher ist, daß diese Praxis auch sowohl für den Alten Orient wie für das vorgeschichtliche Abendland galt, wo diese Bauelle, noch ohne Namen, später sehr wohl von den Handelsellen der Messung auf dem Tisch zu unterscheiden ist, die nicht nach der Fußteilung in hand und zoll unterteilt wurden.

Die Aufnahme des Bauens bedeutet nicht nur den Epochenschritt der Seßhaftwerdung. Hatten Jagd, Kampf und Krieg bereits eine lange Geschichte der Logistik hervorgebracht, so fand mit dem *Hausbau*, und dem *Bootsbau*, eine Berührung mit einer Logik neuer Art statt, mit der Technik des Planens und Messens. Eine neue geistige Ebene, Zahlen und gerade Linien, war erstanden, völlig fremd in der Naturumgebung bis dahin, aber wohl im Zeltbau bereits angelegt. Deren rechnerischer Zusammenbau über Maße muß als der Beginn der Geometrie gelten. Die stille Vorstellung, Mathematik sei aus sich selbst entstanden, kann für ihren Anfang keinesfalls zutreffen.

Da alle Kulturen, seit Aufnahme des Bauens, vor derselben Aufgabe standen, und es nur diese beiden Rechenfiguren gibt, sind alle Bauwerke der Vergangenheit aus diesen beiden zusammengesetzt. Damit gibt es zwischen Handwerksbauten und Kunstbauten, die nur aus dem Handwerk entstanden sein können, geometrisch, d.h. im wesentlichen, keinen Unterschied.

Der Zusammenbau der Rechenfiguren zu ganzen Feldern ist nur mit bestimmten Zahlen möglich, hierher

gehören zu allererst die 3, die 4, und die 12, dazu ihre Vielfachen. Sie sind als 'Heilige Zahlen' bekannt, weil sie Aufnahme in die Heilige Schrift, und damit einen neuen Ursprung gefunden haben – eine Umkehrung. Die kabbalistische Suche hat in ihnen entsprechend eine höhere Sinngebung erkannt, gedeutet und kanonisiert /3/; dagegen hat sich die erst aufkommende Philosophie an die bloße Verfahrenslogik gehalten. Es sind dies zwei unterschiedliche Kausalitätsableitungen, in ihrer Statik bzw. Dynamik geschichtsbildend, dabei bis in die Gegenwart Antinomien geblieben und nicht zu überbrücken.

Damit entsteht die Frage, ob eine Planungsgeometrie, oberhalb der ihr eigenen Gesetze, soweit wie möglich von geglaubten *Deutungen* formaler Beziehungen dieser Zahlen aus eingesetzt worden ist, nichtänderbare 'Erfüllung' /4/, oder ob sie das geblieben, als das benutzt worden ist, was sie am Anfang war, eine τεχνη /5/. Dies ist die Frage, die hinter der hier vorgetragenen Rekonstruktion der Planungsmaße liegt. Als sicher darf gelten, daß nur das technische Konzept frei genug war, mit dem Fortschreiten realer Erkenntnisse den Weg in die heutige Wissenschaft zu finden.

Formale Beziehungen der pDs untereinander könnten in ihren Maßzahlen und ihren Bezeichnungen liegen. Schließt man wegen ihrer Vielzahl aus, daß sie wirkliche Namen trugen, so bleibt blos eine Nummerierung in ihrer Reihenfolge, die dann nur die hier verwandte sein kann, eingeschlossen den Vergrößerungsfaktor. Es finden sich als denkbare Beziehungswahlen Auffälligkeiten wie Umkehrungen (1-5 und 5-1 in Abb.1h; 2-1 und 1-2 in Abb.12b) oder 'Berechnungen' (4-1 und 2-2 in Abb.9a). Ihre Anzahl ist jedoch gering, ihr Ansatz nicht spezifisch, und ihre Wählbarkeit durch die bauliche Typik wesentlich eingeschränkt.

Eine Rekonstruktion der Planungsmaße führt zum Auftreten geometrischer Mehrfachbestimmungen, einer Vielzahl sich nicht widersprechender Lösungen. Ungewiß bleibt dabei zunächst, welche von ihnen die einstige Planung darstellen. Zwar liegt es nahe, große Maße, Bauelle und Fuß, eher für geplante zu halten als die leichter einzupassenden Kleinmaße in Zoll. Aber erst ein Vergleich mehrerer Bauwerke kann formale Verwandtschaften als kanonisch und geplant wahrscheinlich machen, und der Unterscheidung zwischen einem deutenden und einem 'nur' technischen Grundkonzept näherbringen.

Es gibt weitere Fragen, vor allem, was der Beginn der Planung war, von wo aus, dem Schachspiel vergleichbar, die numerischen Zwänge aus den Überlagerungen jeweils geschlossener Gesamtkonfigurationen, Ebenen, die Zahl möglicher Entscheidungen immer kleiner gemacht haben, bis zu wenigen aufgehenden Typenlösungen.

War der *Querschnitt*, die geometrische Bestimmung der Längen der Hölzer und der Lage der Verbindungen, Höhe von First und Traufe konstruktiv, also als erstes festzulegen, so kann der *Grundriß* als ´Reihung von Querschnitten´ verstanden werden, die über Pfetten und Kopfbänder in Längsrichtung verbunden waren. Für die Hausgröße, d.h. die Länge des Grundrisses war, bei feststehender innerer Organisation, wohl der Bauherr zuständig: Zahl der Viehboxen sowie ggf. die Anlage eines Werkraumes. Daß hier auch ein Gemeinschaftsbeschluß zu suchen war ist nach dem Bild geordneter Siedlung zu erwarten.

Die Geometrie des Grundrisses in seiner wählbaren Länge hatte die Aufgabe, den Bau rechtwinklig aufzustellen. Diese Längengeometrie ist schematisch aus den Breitenmaßen des typisierten Querschnitts abgeleitet, und auch hier standen fertige Sätze, Typen zur Verfügung. Erst die innere Teilung, die Jochabstände, ist nicht mehr schematisch, eine grundlegende Unterscheidung. Es soll abschließend dann das Beispiel einer erstaunlichen Gesamtplanung unter Einschluß des Grundstücks gezeigt werden, die als solche wohl einen verwalteten Regelakt, technisch aber ein überraschendes, eigenständiges Konzept darstellt.

Eine Planrekonstruktion steht vor der Aufgabe, über eine unbekannte Entwurfsgeometrie die Größe des Fußmaßes zu ermitteln, die zu Maßen führt, mit denen wiederum die Entwurfsgeometrie rekonstruiert werden kann. Dics ist möglich, wcil die Entwurfsgeometrie der Vergangenheit in ihren Grundzügen inzwischen bekannt ist, und die Rechenfiguren des Schemateils nicht einzeln eingesetzt worden sind, was auf einen freien Entwurf hinausliefe, sondern als größere Sätze, Konfigurationen. Es sind sind diese, die den Typencharakter herstellen.

Ziel der vorliegenden Arbeit ist die Rekonstruktion der Plangeometrie als Prinzip. Dabei stellt sich die Frage, wieviele Beispiele nötig sind, um zwischen Typen- und Einzelfallplanung zu unterscheiden. Eine kaum zu beantwortende weitere Frage ist, wo ein mittlerer Wert zwischen steigender Gewißheit und abnehmender Übersichtlichkeit liegen soll.

FEDDERSEN WIERDE

Die Wohnstallhäuser auf der Feddersen Wierde /6/ sind in ihren acht Horizonten über etwa vier Jahrhunderte im Typus und in der Konstruktion unverändert geblieben. Da Konstruktion, Aufbau des Querschnitts, und die lichte Breite von 18´ mit dem der etwa ein halbes Jahrtausend älteren westgermanischen Häuser von Ezinge /7/ identisch sind, wird die typologische Verschiedenheit der Grundrisse beider Siedlungen nicht auf den ersten Blick erkennbar. In Ezinge ist eine Abtrennung des Wohnteils, mit Herd, vom Stallteil wenig deutlich; Fragen bleiben auch in Bezug auf die Eingänge. Am Grundrißtypus der Feddersen Wierde dagegen läßt sich mit seiner klaren Dreiteiligkeit, Wohnteil, Flett mit Seiteneingängen, und Stallteil mit Deele und Giebeleingang eine Andersartigkeit erkennen, die auf eine andere Herkunft deutet.

Die ´Trennung´ in Wohnteil und Stall, jeweils unterschiedliche Funktionsteile mit eigenem Bewegungskonzept, verbunden durch das Flett mit seiner Quererschließung, ist richtiger wohl als Zusammenschaltung zweier Nutzungstypen zu sehen; Feddersen Wierde ist, als Komposittypus, deshalb unverwandt mit Ezinge. Dies führt zu weiteren Fragen.

Das querliegende Flett (engl. flat) erlaubt die Erschließung nach beiden Seiten, und wird auch als Hauswirtschaftsraum gedient haben. Mit seinen beiden Eingängen bietet es einen indirekten, aber kurzen Zugang zum nach außen öffnungslosen Wohnraum /8/; eine Schwelle in diesen, ausmittig, ist in FW 2/10 erhalten. Dieses Haus besitzt am Stallgiebel neben der Schwelle des üblichen schmalen Eingangs, nicht leicht zu erklären, eine weitere, für einen breiten Eingang (?). Die Hauseingänge im Flett scheinen in mehreren Fällen in der Art eines Schotts auf Schiffen mit höhergelegter Schwelle ausgebildet worden zu sein.

Der Wohnraum zeigt sich im folgenden als ein alter Typus, Anlaß für einen Exkurs. Die Frage nach der Entstehung des Stallteils, Ezinge vergleichbar, bleibt hier unbehandelt; es wäre da zu fragen, ab wann nach dem Übergang zur Dreischiffigkeit in welcher Gegend Vieh eingestallt worden ist. Daß links und rechts des Mittelganges „Jaucherinnen" (P.Schmid) gelegen haben sollen bedarf, bei ihrer Ausführung in luftgetrocknetem Lehmausstrich, der Erläuterung.

Der Wohnteil der großen Häuser ist in der Regel als Einraum mit 2 Pfostenjochen, 4 Pfosten ausgeführt, doch gibt es Ausnahmen. Im Haus 2/14 scheint es keine Wand zum Flett gegeben zu haben, auch stünde sie, wenn, in der zweiten Pfostenachse. Haus 3/10 wiederum scheint 3 Pfostenachsen im Wohnteil zu besitzen.

Bemerkenswert ferner, daß im Wohnteil der offene Herd teils mittig im Feld liegt, teils aber auch fast im Joch, so in Haus 1d/7, 2/4, 5/10. Das Windauge (engl. window) im Dach darf auf der Wohnraumseite angenommen werden. Ein Dachboden, nur sinnvoll mit eingelagertem Heu, wäre durch Funkenflug gefährdet, ein Abzug des trägen Rauchs offener Herde unterhalb eines Dachbodens, in Kopfhöhe, ebensowenig vorstellbar. Bei der halbkreisförmigen Aufstellung der Häuser in den jüngeren Schichten, die Wohnteile zum Platz hin gelegt, entstehen um fast 180° unterschiedliche Windanblasrichtungen; die Entrauchung der Dächer scheint trotzdem keine Schwierigkeit bereitet zu haben.

In mehreren Häusern zeichnen sich Schlafplätze an den Seiten des Wohnraums ab. Für eine solche Anordnung sind Beispiele, Schlafschränke, noch aus dem Mittelalter und später bekannt. Die Weiterentwicklung bestand darin, im Giebel eine Reihe von Schlafkammern abzutrennen, und mit einer Decke nach oben zugfrei abzuschließen. Erweitert wird daraus die Stube /9/, mit durchgehender Decke, womit der offene Herd in das Flett zu verlegen war. Mit diesem für die Gesundheit wichtigen Schritt ist ein rauchfreier Wohn-/Schlafbereich entstanden, über eine Takenplatte oder einen feuerlosen Ofen (Bilegger) vom Flett aus beheizt, einer Lufterwärmung an Stelle der Strahlungsheizung des Herdes.

In gewisser Weise offen ist die Bestimmung des Hauses 5/12. Es finden sich an der Innenseite der gut erhaltenen Außenwände keine Ansätze für Boxenwände, es finden sich keine 'Rinnen', und es scheint der Giebeleingang zu fehlen. Andererseits entspricht der innere Aufbau des Hauses völlig dem der anderen Wohnstallhäuser.

Die Größe der Stallteile der Häuser weist auf einen Viehbestand, der den erwartbaren Eigenbedarf an Milch und Fleisch in vielen Fällen überschreitet /10/. Bei gewerblicher Milchwirtschaft wären Räumlichkeiten für die Käseherstellung zu erwarten. Von den hier behandelten Häusern scheint nur das Haus 5/10 /11/ zwischen Flett und Stall einen Lager- oder Arbeitsbereich zu besitzen. Voraussetzung für gewerbliche Viehhaltung wären weiter erreichbare Böttcher-, Töpfer-, und auch Stellmacherwerkstätten; Weberei wäre hauseigen. Die interessanteste Frage aber wäre die nach Handel und Abnehmerkreis.

Eine weitere Auffälligkeit ist, daß drei der hier behandelten Häuser Wohnteile gleicher Größe aufweisen, das zweitgrößte Haus, 5/10, jedoch einen kürzeren. Ein Nutzungsbezug erscheint als fraglich, da die Zahl der zu erwartenden Kinder wohl kaum vorher bestimmbar war.

Sind die großen Häuser wegen ihrer gleichbleibenden Breite als Standardbauten anzusprechen, so

zeigen sich doch im Inneren Verschiedenheiten, die einem Standard deutlich widersprechen und die Bauten wieder zu Einzelwerken machen. Die auffälligste Nicht-Regelmäßigkeit ist der wechselnde Abstand der tragenden Joche im Stallteil, besonders aber in den gleichgroßen Wohnteilen; außerdem liegen Giebeleingänge in die Deele nicht in der Mittelachse.

Dem aufgehende Reihungen unterschiedlicher Gleichmaße gewöhnten Betrachter von Architektur müßte, nähme er denn solche Bauwerke in Augenschein, derartige Abweichungen als der Widerspruch erscheinen, der dazu zwingt, und der es erlaubt, zwischen Kunst und Handwerk eine entschiedene Grenze zu ziehen, letzteres wie bisher aus der Betrachtung auszuschließen. Die Frage ist aber nun, ob es neben der zu zeigenden durchaus starren Formalität der Grundrisse, einer Rationalität der Sache, auch Willkürentscheidungen, auf den ersten Blick irrationale, gegeben hat, überhaupt geben kann.

Es gibt, d.h. gab in den Handwerken gewiß manche Traditionsentscheidung, deren ursprünglicher Sinn nicht mehr bekannt war. Gerade diese aber erlauben, insbesondere im baulich-konstruktiven Bereich, keine Einzelbehandlung. So sind es denn erst diese durchaus unterschiedlichen Jochabstände, Nichtstandardentscheidungen, in denen die Tiefe der planerischen Durchdringung, die ganze unerwartete Kunst der Alten Meister sichtbar wird.

Diese wie zu zeigen überragende Qualität der Planung kann nur das Werk ausgebildeter Baumeister gewesen sein. Entwurf und Einmessung erfordern Kenntnisse, die das Handwerk nicht nach außen trägt, auch ist für die Herstellung der Holzverbindungen berufsspezifisches, eisernes Werkzeug erforderlich. Für einen Baumeister und wohl auch seine kleine Schar von Zimmerleuten wird es in schon bestehenden Dörfern nicht ausreichend zu tun gegeben haben. Sie werden deshalb, auftragsbedingt, als Wanderhandwerker tätig gewesen sein, eine Tradition im Zimmerhandwerk bis in die Gegenwart.

PLANGEOMETRIE

Die hier zu behandelnden vier großen Wohnstallhäuser haben eine Innenbreite von 18′ (12ᶜ; 288″), und eine Außenbreite von 13ᶜ (312″). Sie sind hierin identisch mit den Häusern A und B von Ezinge. Die Lichtweiten des Mittelschiffs betragen in den FW-Häusern 9 bzw. 10′; hier findet sich, mit 9′, eine Entsprechung in Ezinge nur in Haus A. Die bauliche Gleichheit ist aber nichts anderes als die Gleichheit der Geometrie, in der ihr Querschnitt aufgebaut ist.

Gegenüber dieser Typenbreite sind die Längen der Häuser unterschiedlich. Ihre Grundrisse aber definieren sich nicht einfach durch eine frei wählbare Anzahl gereih-

ter (Querschnitts-)Joche – deren Abstände wären dann auch nicht derart ungleich – sondern ebenfalls geometrisch. Da die Grundrisse vor Beginn des Zusammenbaus rechtwinklig auszulegen sind, muß ihre Geometrie auf der des Querschnittes aufbauen, sie geht in den Grundriß ein. Damit sind für die Hauslänge ebenfalls Typen entstanden, allerdings zahlreicher, und damit gebunden wählbar.

Querschnitte sind in große Quadrate eingebunden, oder in ihnen entwickelt worden /12/. Bemerkenswert dabei, daß die Quadrate der Typenbreiten der folgenden vier Häuser, 288, 312, 336, 360″, nicht zu den erwähnten ′speziellen′ Quadraten gehören.

Aus Quadraten und pDs Nr. -1 (3:4:5) entstehen als

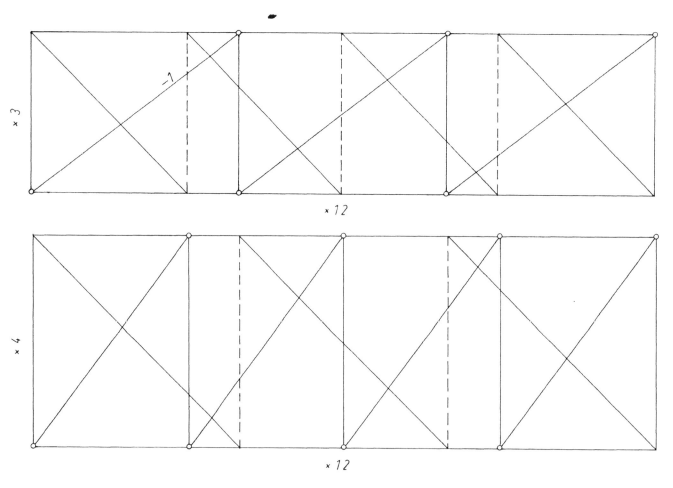

Abb. 1A, 1B

Rahmen (Grundkonfigurationen) aus 4 Quadraten und 3 pDs -1 bzw. 3 Quadraten und 4 pDs -1

3 pDs	n-1:	n(3:4:5)	= 3:4	3*4	12
4 Q		n*3		4*3	12
4 pDs	n-1:	n(3:4:5)	= 4:3	4*3	12
3 Q		n*4		3*4	12

Reihungen zwei traditionelle, urtümliche Konfigurationen, ein Rechteck n*3 auf n*12 (Abb.1A) bzw. n*4 auf n*12 (Abb.1B):

Eine vielleicht fortgeschrittenere Konfiguration ohne Quadrate entsteht aus einer Reihung von 7 pDs Nr. -2 (5:12:13), d.i. 12:35 unter durchbindendem pD Nr. -6 (12:35:37). Diese Reihungen sind, umgekehrt, als Teilungen zu verstehen, die Teilstücke wären dann Vitruvs moduli, bisher nicht verstehbar.

Es gibt nun Detaillierungen dieser 5 langen Teilstücke, der in Abb.1C stehenden pDs -2 (ᶜ), die quer dazu

die Lichtbreite 12ᶜ (288") derart teilen, daß ein 10' (160") breites Mittelschiff und zwei 4' (64") breite Seitenschiffe definiert werden (Abb.1d). Dieselbe Querteilung ergibt sich auch bei einer Teilstücklänge von 168" (7ᶜ, Abb.1e):

Was bei den Griechen ʹSym-Metriaʹ genannt wurde, ein Zusammen-Maß-Geben, zeigt sich auch in anderen Verbindungen, den Teilstücklängen 8ᶜ (192"), 252" und 20' (320") (Abb.1f, 1g, 1h). Die Dreischiffteilungen unterscheiden sich hier in den Quermaßen; die Mittelschiffsbreite ist jetzt 9' (144"), und die Überdeckungen

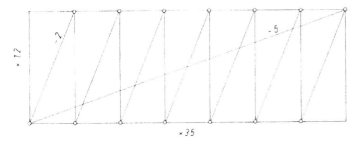 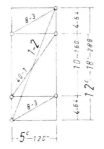 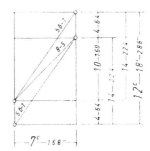

Abb. 1C, 1d,1e

Eine weitere Grundkonfiguration aus 7 pDs -2 und 1 pD -6.

Teilstücke der Längen 5ᶜ (120") und 7ᶜ (168") auf die Lichtbreite 12ᶜ (288"), darin Konstruktion eines 160" (10') breiten Mittelschiffs.

7 pDs	1-2	1(5:12:13)	=	5:12	7*5	=	35ᶜ
	1-6	1(12:35:37)	=	12:35	1*35	=	35ᶜ
	8-3	8(8:15:17)	=	64:120	1*120	=	120"
	40-1	40(3:4:5)	=	120:160	1*120	=	120"
	56-1	56(3:4:5)	=	168:224	1*168	=	168"
	8-5	8(20:21:29)	=	160:168	1*168	=	168"

 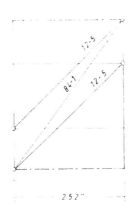 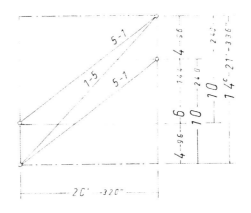

Abb. 1f, 1g, 1h

Drei Teilstücke unterschiedlicher Länge, Breite 15ᶜ (360"), Traufkantenbreite, bzw. 14ᶜ (336"), Breite über die Fußpfetten. Mittelschiffsbreite 6ᶜ (9', 144").

pD	1-3	1(8:15:17)	=	8:15	1*8	=	8ᶜ
	2-1	2(3:4:5)	=	6:8	1*8	=	8ᶜ
	84-1	84(3:4:5)	=	252:336	1*252	=	252"
	12-5	12(20:21:29)	=	240:252	1*252	=	252"
	1-5	1(20:21:29)	=	20:21	1*20	=	20'
	5-1	5(3:4:5)	=	15:20	1*20	=	20'

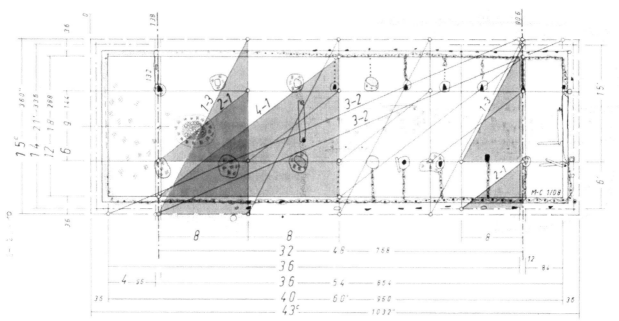

Abb. 2 Das Gerüst, Schema, Haus 2/10

Die in moduli zu teilende Grundstrecke beträgt 32^c, (48′; 768″) als Achsabstand der Endjoche. Teilung 4 nach 1f. Über je 2 Teilstücken liegt pD 4-1 (^{c}) mit 12:16.

Eine weitere Teilung (rechts) in 6*8′ = 48′ greift mit den pDs 1-3 und 2-1 mit 15+6 = 21′ die Achsweite 14^c (336″) der Fußpfetten auf; sie erscheint möglicherweise nur rechnerisch.

Das Außenwandrechteck mit der auf andere Weise festgelegten Innenlänge 40^c (960″) wird über 2 gespreizte pDs 3-2 mit 15:36 (^{c}) in der Länge derart (Außenseite 132 bzw. Innenseite 900) auf das Gerüst bezogen, daß 2 ungleiche Endfelder von 96″ und 84″ entstehen.

Weil dieser Planungsteil vollständig in den ersten drei pDs und im großen Maß (^{c}) darstellbar ist könnte dieses Haus soweit ein Standardhaus sein.

erreichen eine Breite von 15^c (360″), Traufkantenbreite, bzw. 14^c (336″), Breite über die Fußpfetten:

Mit diesen fünf verschiedenen Teilstücklängen können, additiv, unterschiedliche Gesamtlängen mit daran gebundenen unterschiedlichen Mittelschiffsbreiten 9 bzw. 10′ gebildet werden. Da bei formalem Planen ihre Auswahl, Zusammenstellung, und Anzahl aber unbestimmt wäre, können sie nur ein auf andere Weise definiertes Grundrißrechteck ausgefüllt haben. Dies sind die Grundkonfigurationen 1A, 1B und 1C; es gibt, hier nicht aufgeführt, weitere rahmende Konfigurationen. Die Teilkonfigurationen 1d und 1e bilden mit ihrer Höhe 288″ nur die Lichtbreite, die 1f die Traufkantenbreite 360″, 1g, 1h die Fußpfettenpfostenbreite 336″ (14^c); diese ist hier im Befund, anders als in Ezinge, kaum nachzuweisen.

Im folgenden werden gezeigt:

　　Querteilung und Länge des Gerüsts, als Schema

　　das Außenwandrechteck der Standardbreite, als Schema

　　die Trennwand

　　die Lage von Giebeleingang und Herd

　　der Wohnteil als das *Alte Haus*,

ein Exkurs über das ägäische *Megaron* als das Alte Haus,

Bemessung der ungleichen Jochabstände, als Systema

eine Grundstücksplanung

Es werden vier Häuser gleicher Breite vorgestellt, die ersten beiden mit gleicher Länge, aber unterschiedlicher Mittelschiffsbreite, danach ein langes Normalhaus, und schließlich ein Sonderfall. Der ′Zähler′ bezeichnet den Siedlungshorizont, der ′Nenner′ die Nummer des Hauses.

Es ist noch zu sagen, daß die Plangeometrie dem Entwurf, d.h. der Dimensionierung der Bauteile und ihrer Abstände dient, und nicht gleichzusetzen ist mit der praktischen Einmessung beim Zusammenbau.

DAS GERÜST, SCHEMA (ABB. 2, 3, 4, 5)

Das nordalpine Normalhaus besitzt bis in die Gegenwart ein Sattel-Steildach, dessen begrenzte Höhe aus Mindestneigung zugleich die Breite des Hauses bestimmt. Dächer im städtischen Wohnbau sind auf einen steifen

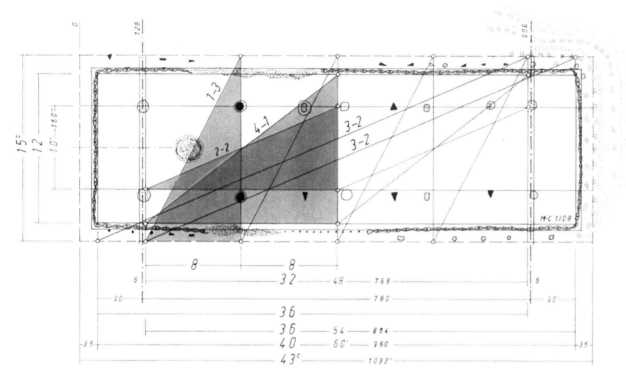

Abb. 3 Das Gerüst, Schema, Haus 5/12

Teilung des Endjochabstands 32ᶜ w.v., jedoch der Lichtweite. Rechnerische Dicke der Joche 12" wie die der Außenwände. Mittelschiffsbreite 10′ gebildet mit pD 2-2 (′), d.i. 2(5:12:13) = 10:24 auf 24′(16ᶜ). Standardhaus w.v.;

Anbindung des Außenwandrechtecks an das Gerüst wechselseitig mit 2 pDs 3-2 (ᶜ) w.v.; durch den Lichtweitenansatz werden die Endfelder mit 90"
gleichgroß. Ob die Wahl eines breiteren Mittelschiffs den Zweck hatte, die Endfelder gleichgroß machen zu können, bleibt offen.

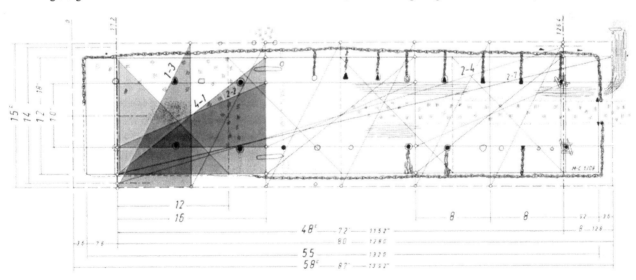

Abb. 4 Das Gerüst, Schema, Haus 1d/7

Teilung des Endjoch-Achsabstands 48 (ᶜ) (72′; 1152") nach Grundkonfiguration 1A auf die Lichtbreite 12ᶜ, darin Mittelschiffsbreite 10′ mit 3 pDs 2-2
(′) w.v. Über die Teilung in 6*8ᶜ Traufkantenbreite 15ᶜ mit pD 1-3. Fußpfettenachsbreite 14c über pD 2-4 (ᶜ) auf Grundlänge 48ᶜ.

Anbindung des Außenwandrechtecks an das Gerüst nur einseitig von der Achse 112 auf gegenüberliegendes Dachende mit pD 2-7 (′), d.i. 2(9:40:41)
= 18:80.

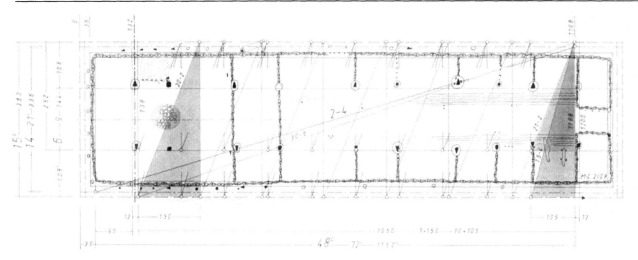

Abb. 5 Das Gerüst, Schema, Haus 5/10

Teilung des Endjoch-Lichtabstands 1050" zwischen den Koten 138 und 1188 in 7*150; mit 7 pDs 30-2 auf 1 pD 30-6 stellt sich die Grundkonfiguration 1C auf Traufkantenbreite 360" (15ᶜ) dar. Eine weitere Teilung (rechts) in 10*105 ergibt mit pD 15-4 ("), d.i. 15(7:24:25) = 105:360 ebenfalls die Traufbreite, sowie pD 21-2 (105:252) auf Kante Mittelschiff (hier wie auch sonst nur einseitig dargest.)

Wie die nichteingebundenen Stiele des Endjochs rechts zeigen, liegt dessen Achse nicht mittig in der Wand 1188-1200. Die Anbindung des Außenwandrechtecks erfolgt mit pD 2-4 (14:48c) einseitig von der Kante 1188" auf Innenkante 36".

Kleinteiligkeit und Nichtaufgehen der Gerüstgeometrie verrät einen Einzelentwurf mit besonderen Zielen.

Rechteckkasten aus Fachwerk oder Mauern aufgesetzt, die Trennung bildet eine begehbare Decke. Das Dach ist in diesem Falle selbsttragend und ebenfalls in sich steif gegen seitlichen Wind, es gibt dessen aufgenommene Horizontalkraft an den Hauskasten ab, auf dem es konstruktiv befestigt aufliegt. Die Beheizung dieser Häuser ist nur durch Öfen, mindestens Kamine, gemauerte, halbgeschlossene Feuerplätze mit durch den Dachraum geführtem gemauerten Schornstein möglich /13/.

Die eingeschossigen, landwirtschaftlich genutzten Wohnstallhäuser des F-W Typus und ihre Nachfahren besitzen eine gänzlich andere Struktur; es gibt keinen steifen Hauskasten, sondern nur ein aufgeständertes Dach, und ein 'freies' Außenwandrechteck. Der entscheidende Fortschritt der dreischiffigen Bauweise gegenüber der primitiven und robusten Vier- und zweischiffigen mit in den Boden eingespannten Pfosten ist nicht einfach der freie Mittelgang, sondern die entfallende direkte Unterstützung des Firstes. Die Pfosten beiderseits des Mittelganges in ihrer nach wie vor begrenzten Länge müssen nicht die Firsthöhe erreichen, sondern nehmen ihren Anteil der Dachlast in halber Dachhöhe auf. Das ganze Dach, First und Traufe, kann damit erheblich höher liegen, auch an den Außenwänden wird jetzt eine bequeme Kopfhöhe erreicht.

Eine weitere wichtige Verbesserung ist der sparsame Holzverbau durch Aufkeilen der Stämme. Die so entstandenen zarten, tortenstückähnlichen Querschnitte erlauben keine Einspannung im Boden mehr, wären also ohne obenliegende Verbände nicht einsetzbar, schon garnicht im weichen Grund der Marsch. Hier wären übrigens auch die stärkeren Querschnitte der Bandkeramikerpfosten nicht stabil einzuspannen.

Diese Bauten *mit in den Dachraum* ragendem Gerüst besaßen damit als *Halle* einen offenem Dachraum; in diesem lagen die Verbände zur Quer- und Längsaussteifung. Eine Nutzung des Dachraums, würde ein begehbarer Dachboden eingelegt, wäre damit kaum möglich.

Es ist leicht zu sehen, daß die Aufstellung dieses Gerüsts aus steifen Jochen den ersten Abschnitt des Bauvorgangs bildet; die Herstellung der Außenwände, die die Baustelle dann nur noch durch die Türöffnungen betretbar machen, den nachfolgenden. Die 'grundlegende' Einmessung erfolgt deshalb mit der Auslegung dieses Gerüsts. Es zeigt sich dann aber, daß die Planung wohl nicht entsprechend in zwei Abschnitte geteilt werden kann, Gerüst mit Dach, Rechteck der Außenwände – sie ist, wie zu zeigen, vielmehr eine Gesamtplanung.

Das Gerüst besteht aus einer Anzahl von Stielpaaren, deren Abstand die Breite des Mittelschiffs darstellt.

Schema bedeutet hier, daß die Grundstrecke, die Länge zwischen den beiden Endjochen, jenseits derer die abgewalmten Giebel liegen, ganzzahlig geteilt wird in der Art, daß auf diesen Teilstücklängen, Vitruvs *moduli*, die vorgegebenen Breiten des Standardquerschnitts geometrisch aufgenommen werden. Die innere Ausbildung in ungleiche Jochabstände bleibt vom Schema unberührt. Diese werden, nach einer Definition hier, über das *Systema* bestimmt.

Außerdem ist es noch nötig, die Lage des Außenwandrechtecks in *Längsrichtung* gegenüber dem Gerüst festzulegen. Die beiden Endfelder zwischen Gerüst und Giebel-Außenwand sind in Haus 2/10 ungleich lang, im ebensolangen Haus 5/12 aber gleichlang, gewiß nicht grundlos.

Diese Lage des Gerüsts im Außenwandrechteck wird durch 2 gespreizte, von einem Endjoch bis zum gegenseitige Giebel durchgehende Groß-pDs bestimmt. Die unterschiedlichen Endfeldbreiten der Häuser 2/10 und 5/12 begründen sich daraus, daß die in beiden Häusern gleichgroße Grundstrecke 48′ (768″) in Haus 2/10 in der Endjoch-Achse ansetzt, im Haus 5/12 aber den Lichtabstand bildet, eine Differenz von 2*6 = 12″. Diese Verschiedenheit beruht auf einer unterschiedlichen Systemateilung, bedingt durch die unterschiedliche Mittelschiffsbreiten von 9′ bzw. 10′.

FW 5/10, ein Haus mit mehreren Besonderheiten, zeigt im Endjoch rechts ein Nichtaufgehen der Überlagerung von Schema mit Systema – Zwänge mit besonderer Aussage.

DAS WANDRECHTECK, SCHEMA
(Abb. 6a, 6b, 7a, 7b, 8a, 8b, 9a, 9b, 9c)
Die hier vorgestellten 4 Häuser der Horizonte 1, 2, und 5 besitzen einen geometrischen Aufbau des Außenwandrechtecks entsprechend dem schematischen des Gerüsts. Dabei zeigt sich, daß sie auf die bereits festgelegten Standardbreiten je 2 Schemata in der Länge besitzen, auf die lichte Innenlänge, und auf die Länge Giebel-Fußpfettenachse (+ 2*24″), bei Haus 1d/7 nur auf die Giebelwand-Außenkante.

Drei der Häuser definieren ihre Länge außerdem auch durch 2 lange pDs auf eine halbe Breite und über die Giebel-Fußpfettenachsen, das Haus 5/10 aber durch 1 langes pD auf die Lichtbreite; es erscheinen hier formal auch zwei Innenlängen. An den beiden gleichlangen Häusern

2/10 und 5/12 wird sich zeigen, daß diese Halbierungen in einen anderen Zusammenhang gehören (Abb. 16,17)

Aus den Längen der Häuser ist die Größe des verwendeten Fußmaßes zu errechnen. Es hat mit 0,332 m eine erhebliche Größe, und kann verglichen werden mit einem in Troja nachzuweisenden (Exkurs)

| Haus | Längen | | 0,332 F-W | 0,3313 (Troja) |
	Ist [m]	Plan [′]	Soll [m]	
1d/7	27,80	84	27,89	27,83
2/10	21,00	63	20,92	20,87
4/27	18,90	57	18,92	18,88
5/10	25,80	78,5	26,06	26,01
5/12	20,95	61,5	20,42	20,38

Das letzte Beispiel weist eine größere Abweichung auf. Bei wie zu zeigen konventioneller Geometrie und in gleichem Horizont wie 5/10, also unverändertem Fußmaß, wird eine Erklärung dafür in einer Bodenverformung zu suchen sein.

DIE TRENNWAND
(Abb. 10, 11)
Mit der Abtrennung des Wohnraums in den Wohnstallhäusern, anders gesehen, mit dem Anfügen von Flett und Stall hat es wie im folgenden zu zeigen eine besondere Bewandnis – beide Teile enthalten eigene, unabhängige Planungsteile. Diese werden zunächst nur für die hier als standardnah angenommenen Häuser 2/10 und 5/12 gezeigt, Flett und Stall der beiden anderen in Abb. 17,18.

Den beiden Häusern 2/10 und 5/12 gemein ist, daß ihr Wohnteil in den letzten beiden Feldern des Gerüsts als Quadrat auf die Außenwandbreite 13c (312″) aufgebaut ist, zum einen außenseitig (Abb.10), zum anderen im Lichten (Abb.11). Dabei unterscheidet sich der weitere innere Aufbau entsprechend der unterschiedlichen Mittelschiffsbreite von 9′ (144″) bzw. 10′(160″). Das Haus 1d/7 scheint ohne Quadrat geplant zu sein, Haus 5/10 zeigt eine Sonderlösung (Abb.18).

DER GIEBELEINGANG
(Abb. 12a, 12b, 12c, 13a, 13b, 14a, 14b)
Mit der geometrisierten Planung von Eingangsbreite und Lage des Eingangs im Außenwandrechteck verlassen wir das Feld bautechnisch begründeter Planung und betreten

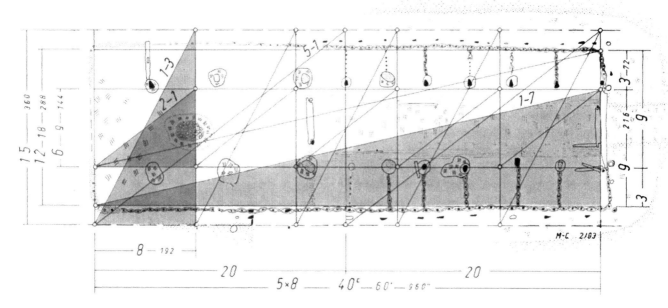

Abb. 6a Das Außenwandrechteck, Schema, Haus 2/10

Die lichte *Innenlänge* beträgt 40ᶜ (960"), geteilt in 5 Teilstücke 1f. Es erscheint weiter eine Reihung von 2 pDs 5-1 (ᶜ), Traufenbreite, die aber, weil ohne Bezug, hier als nur rechnerisch gelten könnte.

Die lichte Innenbreite von 12ᶜ wird durch 2 lange pDs 1-7 aufgenommen, die gespreizt wechselseitig die Mittelschiffsbreite überdecken.

1 pD   1-7:   1(9:40:41)   = 9:40   = 40ᶜ

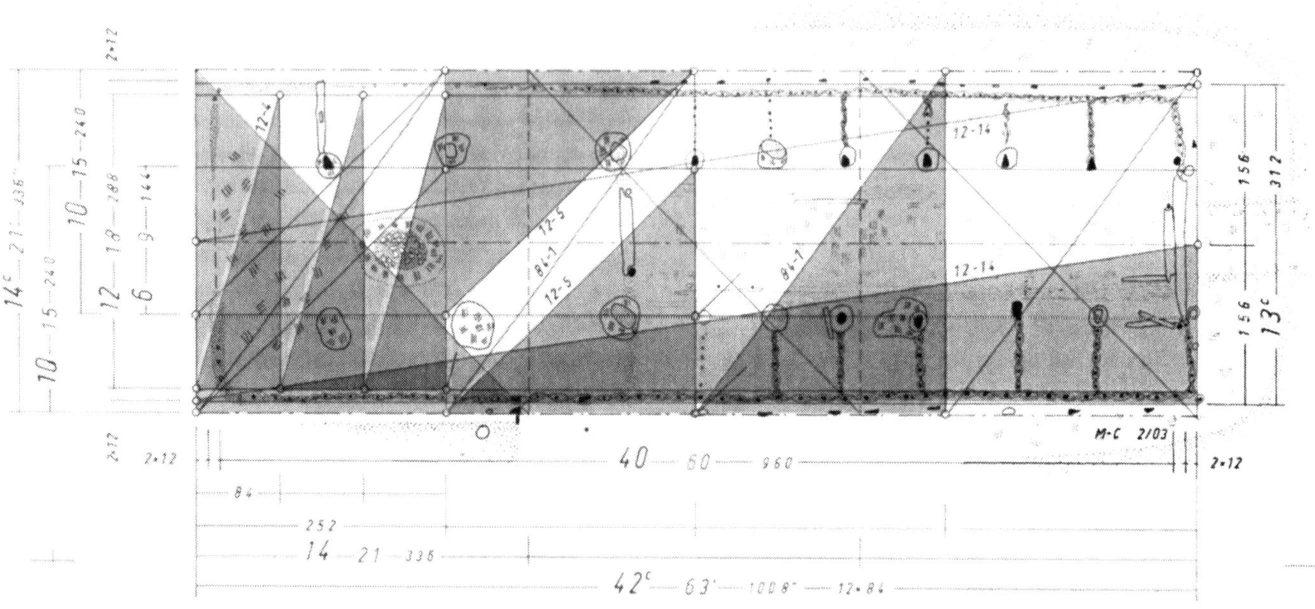

Abb. 6b Das Außenwandrechteck, Schema, Haus 2/10

Die *Außenlänge* über die Fußpfettenachsen der Giebel beträgt Innenlänge zzgl. beidseitig Wanddicke und Pfostenabstand, d.i. 960+2*24 = 1008" (42ᶜ). Dieser Rahmen wird gebildet von der Grundkonfiguration 1B mit 3 Q 14ᶜ sowie 4 pDs 84-1 (", 3. Fach). Auf dieser Vierteilung liegt auch die Teilstückkonfiguration 1g, es erscheinen darin auch je 3 pDs 12-4 auf das Innenlichten 288". Die Länge 1008" wird außerdem mit 2 langen pDs 12-14 auf die halbe Außenbreite 312" (13ᶜ) gebildet.

1pD   12-14:   12(13:84:85)   =   156:1008   1*1008   =   008"

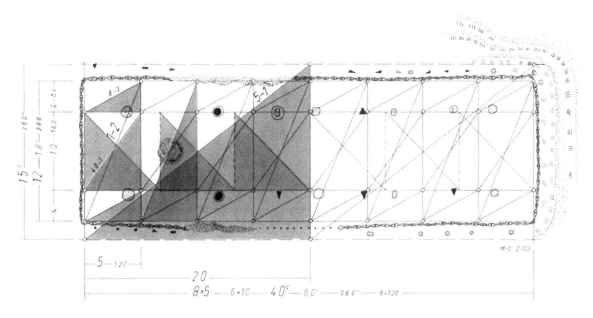

Abb. 7a Das Außenwandrechteck, Schema, Haus 5/12

Die lichte Innenlänge beträgt w.v. 40ᶜ (60′, 960″), geteilt in 8 Teilstücke 1d. Mit dieser Innenfigur wird die Mittelschiffsbreite 10′ (160″). Die beiden Hälften werden mit je 1 pD 5-1 auf die Traufkantenbreite bezogen, im Mittelschiff erscheinen je 3 Quadrate. 2 lange pDs, gespreizt um die Mittelschiffsbreite (vgl. Abb. 6a), gibt es hier nicht.

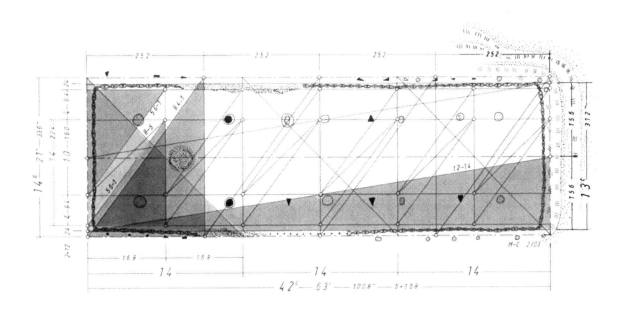

Abb. 7b Das Außenwandrechteck, Schema, Haus 5/12

Die *Außenlänge* über die Fußpfettenachsen der Giebel beträgt 1008″ (42ᶜ), gebildet mit Grundfiguration 1B w.o. Die Länge wird durch 6 Teilstücke 1e gebildet, mit der Mittelschiffsbreite 10′. Die Länge 1008″ wird w.o. (Abb. 6b) mit 2 langen pDs 12-14 auf die halbe Außenbreite 312″ (13ᶜ) aufgenommen.

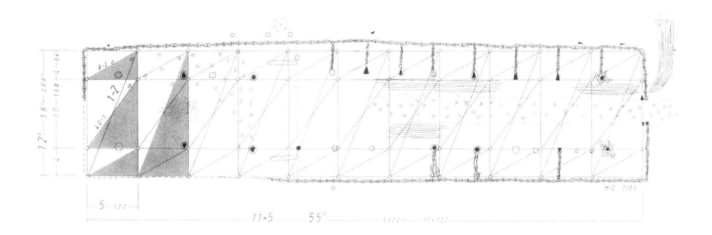

Abb. 8a Das Außenwandrechteck, Schema, Haus 1d/7

Die lichte *Innenlänge* beträgt 55ᶜ (1320"), geteilt in 11 Teilstücke 1d. Mittelschiffsbreite w.v. 10′ (160"). Weitere Teilungen erscheinen als nur rechnerische.

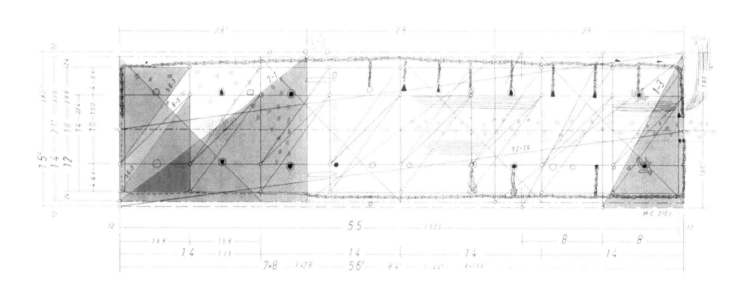

Abb. 8b Das Außenwandrechteck, Schema, Haus 1d/7

Die Außenlänge ist geometrisch nur zwischen den Giebelwand-Außenkanten zu rekonstruieren. Sie baut sich aus der Grundfiguration 1A mit 4 Q 14ᶜ und 3 liegenden pDs 7-1 (′) auf, darin Teilstücke 1e.

Die Länge 56c (1344") ist außerdem in 7*8ᶜ teilbar, womit sich 7 pDs 1-3 auf die Traufkantenbreite 15ᶜ ergeben (rechts).

Die Länge 1344" wird w.v. durch 2 lange pDs 12-19 gebildet/aufgenommen, welche die Traufkantenbreite 360" (15c) halbieren.

1pD 12-19: 1(15:112:113) = 180:1344   1*1344 = 1344"

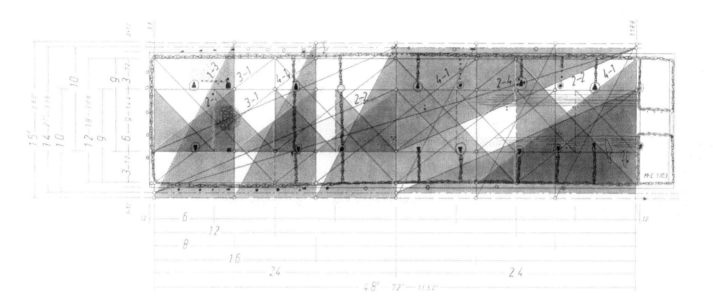

Abb. 9a Das Außenwandrechteck, Schema, Haus 5/10

Dieses durch Lager (?) und Futterkammern (?) erweiterte Haus besitzt eine *Innenlänge* netto von 48^c (72′, 1152″) zwischen den Koten 36 und 1188 (vgl. Abb. 5), gedeckt durch die Grundkonfiguration 1A auf die Lichtbreite 12^c (rechts), mit 4 Quadraten 12^c und 3 pDs 4-1 (^{c}).

Die Länge 48^c ist weiter teilbar in 6 Teilstücke 1f auf die Traufkantenbreite, sowie 8 Q 6 (^{c}) auf die Mittelschiffsbreite. Das Mittelschiff ist weiter bezogen mit 2 Paaren gespreizter pDs 2-2 (rechts) sowie 4 Paaren gespreizter pDs 3-1 (^{c}) (links).

Auf ganze Länge 48^c greift auf die Breite der Fußpfettenachsen (14^c) das pD 2-4.

$$1 \ pD \quad 2\text{-}4: \ 2(7\text{:}24\text{:}25) \ = \ 14\text{:}48 \quad 1*48 \ = \ 48^c$$

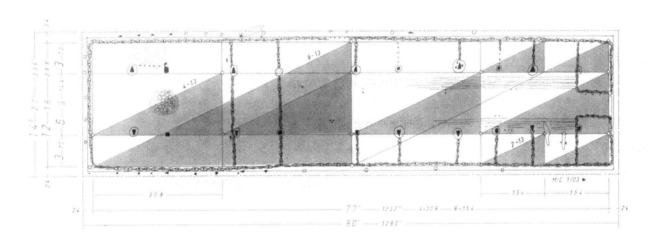

Abb. 9b Das Außenwandrechteck, Schema, Haus 5/10

Auf die Innenlänge brutto, 77′ (1232″), enthält dieses besondere Haus eine Überraschung, die zu der Frage führt, ob die geometrische Konstruktion hier eine absichtsvolle Besonderheit als Einzelleistung darstellt. Mittelschiff, Seitenschiffe, und Gesamtlichten sind auf einem einzigen, dem höherzahligen pD -13 auf die Brutto-Innenlänge aufgebaut.

$$8 \ pDs \quad 2\text{-}13: \ 2(36\text{:}77\text{:}85) \ = \ 72\text{:}154 \quad 8*154 \ = 1232″ \ \text{usw.}$$

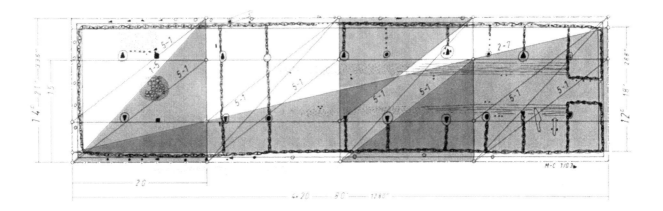

Abb. 9c Das Außenwandrechteck, Schema, Haus 5/10

Äußere Planungslänge über die Fußpfettenachsen der Giebel wie die Häuser 2/10 und 5/12. Die Länge 80′ wird dabei von den Teilstücken 1h gebildet, und von dem durchgehenden pD 2-7 (′) auf die Lichtbreite 18′ (12ᶜ).

1 pD   2-7:   2(9:40:41)   =   18:80   1*80   =   80′

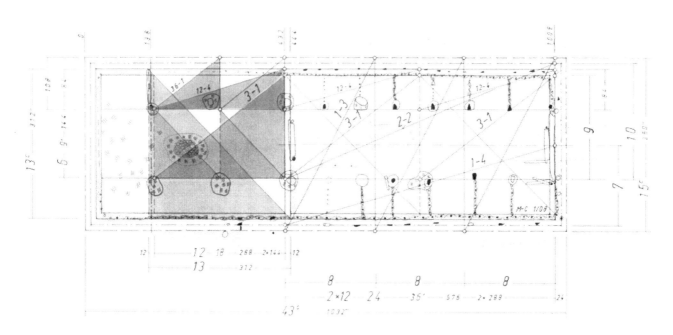

Abb. 10 Die Lage der Trennwand, Haus 2/10

Die beiden Joche des Wohnteils haben einen Lichtabstand von 12ᶜ (288″), und einen Außenseitenabstand von 13ᶜ (312″); dieser entspricht der Wand-Außenbreite, womit über beiden ein Quadrat entsteht.

Auf die Innenlänge 12ᶜ (288″) liegen über Mittel- und Seitenschiffsbreite 2 gespreizte pDs 3-1 (ᶜ) (wie auch sonst nur 1 dargest.), auf Breite 84″ das pD 12-4. Auf halbe Länge im Mittelschiff 2 Q 6, bis zur Traufkante je 1 pD 36-1.

Der Stallteil besitzt, bei Überdeckung der 12″ Trennwand, eine Länge von 24ᶜ, teilbar in 2*12ᶜ und Aufbau wie Wohnteil, sowie 3*8ᶜ, Aufbau nach 1f.
Auf der halben Traufpfettenbreite liegen das pD 1-4 mit 7:24 (ᶜ), auf der Breite 10ᶜ bis zur Traufpfette die gespreizten pDs 2-2 mit 10:24ᶜ.

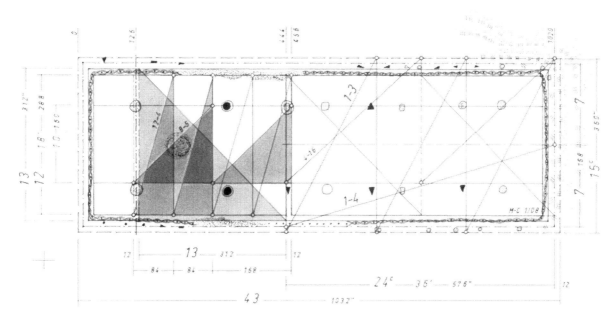

Abb. 11 Die Lage der Trennwand, Haus 5/12

Endjoch und Trennwand sind gegenüber Haus 2/10 (Abb. 10) um je 12" nach außen gerückt, womit das Q 13 über die Außenwandbreite jetzt das Lichten bildet. Der außenseitige Jochabstand beträgt 14ᶜ (336" = 312 + 2*12); auf dieser Länge decken 2 pDs 8-5 das Mittelschiff, und 4 pDs 12-4 die Lichtbreite 288".

Der Stallteil ist aufgebaut w.v., doch ist wegen des breiteren Mittelschiffs das pD-Paar 2-2 ersetzt durch 2 pDs 4-16, d.i. 4(65:72:97) = 260:288" auf die Traufkante.

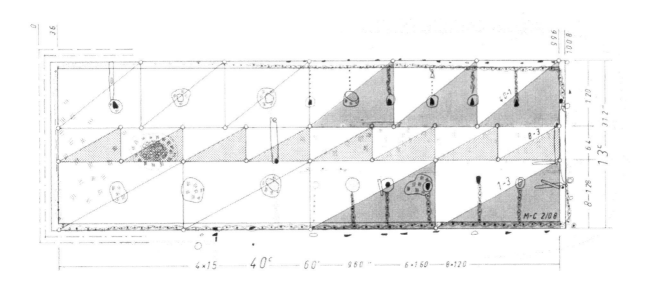

Abb. 12a Der Giebeleingang, Haus 2/10

Der Giebeleingang besitzt eine Breite von 64" (4′), auf dem Lichtmaß 960" (60′) angelegt mit 8 pDs 8-3, d.i. 8(8:15:17) = 64:120 ("). Dieser Streifen ist ausmittig mit 8′(128") und 120" auf die Außenbreite 312" bezogen. Auf diese Kanten entsteht eine 2er- bzw. 3er-Taktung mit pD 1-3 (′) bzw. 40-1.

In der Giebelwand liegt eine zweite, breitere Schwelle, die sich in anderen Häusern, vgl. insbesondere 5/10, nicht findet. Ob hier eine (komplizierte) Doppeltür zu rekonstruieren ist bleibt offen.

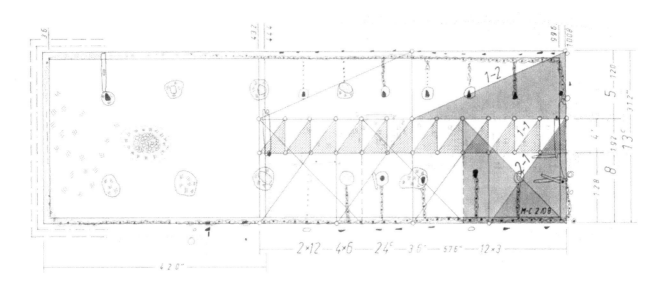

Abb. 12b Der Giebeleingang, Haus 2/10, Stallteil

Auf der Grundlänge 36′ (576″) der Stalllänge außen wird die Eingangsbreite 4′ wieder in die Außenbreite eingebaut, mit der Grundfiguration 1B auf 8c, übergreifend, und einer Taktung nach beiden Seiten.

Erkennbar ist, daß der Eingang zum Wohnteil nicht in der Flucht liegt.

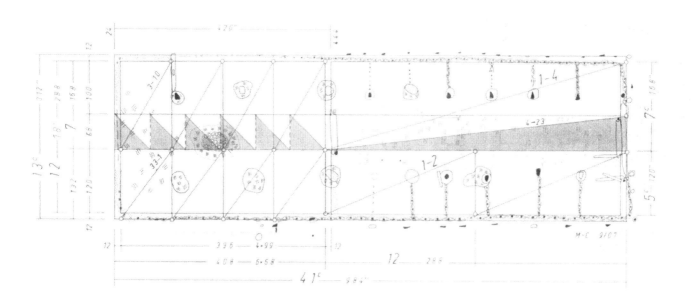

Abb. 12c Der Wohnteileingang, Haus 2/10

Dieser Eingang ist mit 68″, offensichtlich aus geometrischem Zwang, breiter als der 64″-Giebeleingang. Auch dieser Durchgang ist zwiefach bestimmt, im Wohnteil ohne Taktung und mit 12″ Differenz in der Giebelwand, im Stallteil nur mit dem hochzahligen pD 4-23, d.i. 4(17:144:145) = 68:576 (″).

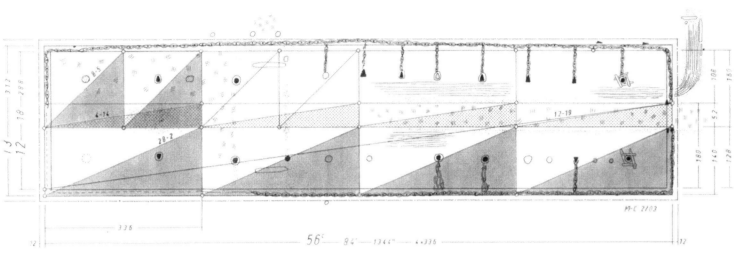

Abb. 13a Der Giebeleingang, Haus 1d/7

War die Grundstrecke der geometrischen Teilung für den Giebeleingang in Haus 2/10 das lichte Längsmaß, so ist es hier die Außenlänge 1344" des Wandrechtecks. Die Taktung bedarf keiner Erklärung. Ob das durchgehende pD 12-19 zur Planung gehört bleibt offen, es erscheint aber konstitutiv in Abb. 15a.

$$4 \text{ pD} \quad 4\text{-}14: \quad 4(13:84:85) \quad = \quad 52:336 \quad 4*336 = 1344"$$
$$12\text{-}19: \quad 12(15:112:113) \quad = \quad 180:1344 = 1344"$$

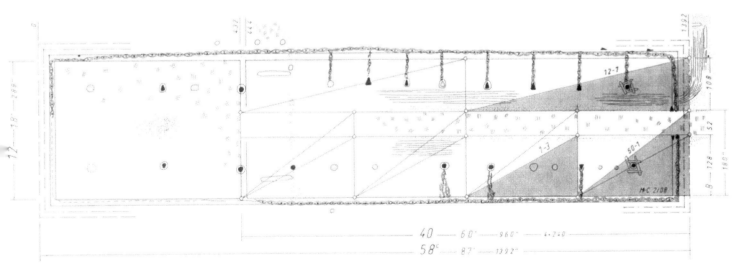

Abb. 13b   Der Giebeleingang, Haus 1d/7, Stallteil

Auf der viele Möglichkeiten bietenden Grundlänge 60′ (576"), 432 bis zur Walmgiebeltraufkante 1392, ist mit den Festlegungen nach Abb. 13a eine einfache Taktung auf die Innenbreite 288" zu rekonstruieren.

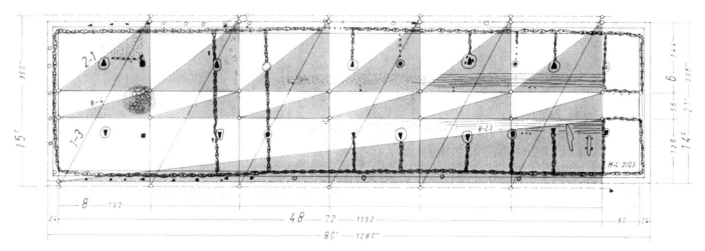

Abb. 14a Der Giebeleingang, Haus 5/10

Das etwas besondere Haus 5/10 bietet eine nahezu vollkommene Taktung auf die Traufkantenbreite 15c und zugleich auf die Achsbreite der Fußpfetten, 336" (14c), und die lichte Nettolänge 48c (1152").

1 pD 8-23:   8(17:144:145) = 136:1152 = 1152"

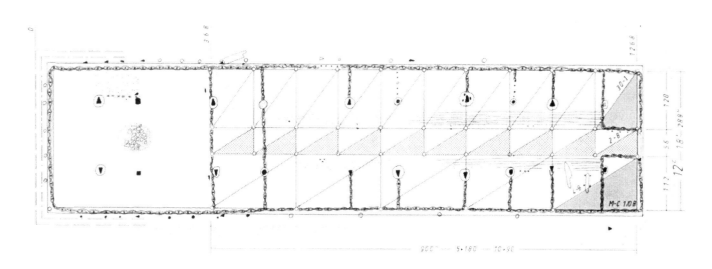

Abb. 14b Der Giebeleingang, Haus 5/10, Stallteil

Auf andere Weise einfach ist die Taktung des Giebeleingangs über Stallteil und Flett, auf die Lichtbreite 288". Auch hier zeigen die wenig oder nichteingebundenen Stiele (vgl. Abb. 5), daß die Jochachse 368" die Mittelachse der Wand zum Wohnteil verfehlt; diese liegt bei 366" (vgl. Abb. n)

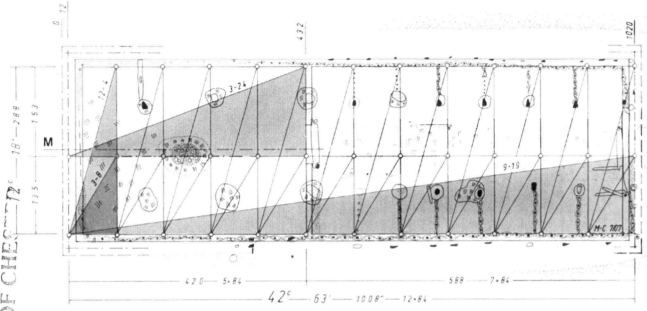

Abb. 15a Der Herd, Haus 2/10, Längsachse

Die beiden pDs 3-8, d.i. 3(28:45:53) = 84:135 und 12-4, d.i. 12(7:24:25) = 84:288 takten zwiefach, wie die Giebeleingänge, hier zwischen den Koten 12 und 432 ebenso wie zwischen 432 und 1020".

5 pDs	12-4:	12(7:24:25)	= 84:288	= 420"
5	3-8:	3(28:45:53)	= 84:135	= 420"
1	3-24:	3(51:140:149)	= 153:420	= 420"
1	9-19:	9(15:112:113)	= 135:1008	= 1008"

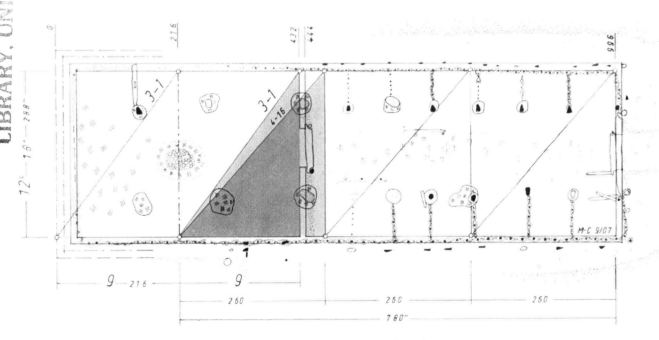

Abb. 15b Der Herd, Haus 2/10, Querachse

Der gleiche Anspruch ist in der Länge verwirklicht worden, der Herdmittelpunkt liegt in der Mitte zwischen den beiden pDs 3-1 (c). Das zweite pD 3-1 bezieht die Herdmitte auf die Trennwand 432/444", 3 pDs 4-16, d.i. 4(65:72:97) = 260:288 mit 780" auf die Wandkante 996".

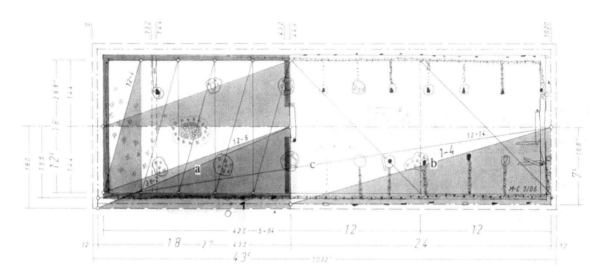

Abb. 16 Das Alte Haus, 2/10

Die Außenlänge 420" und die Innenbreite 288" werden gebildet durch 5 pDs 12-4 längs, d.i. 12(7:24:25) = 420:288, und 2 pDs 12-6 quer, d.i. 12(12:35:37) = 288:420. Weitere Bezüge

übliche für Mittelschiff, Außenbreite, Fußpfettenachsbreite, und Traufbreite (nicht dargest.).

Bemerkenswert hier aber das Halbierungskonzept. Das lange pD 12-14 (c) auf die Fußpfettenachsen der Giebel (vgl. Abb. 6b, 7b) ist durch die Trennwand des Wohnraums geteilt in 2 pDs für Wohnraum und ´Anbau´, pD 36-2 (a), mit 180:432 und und pD 1-4 (b), mit 7:24 (c).

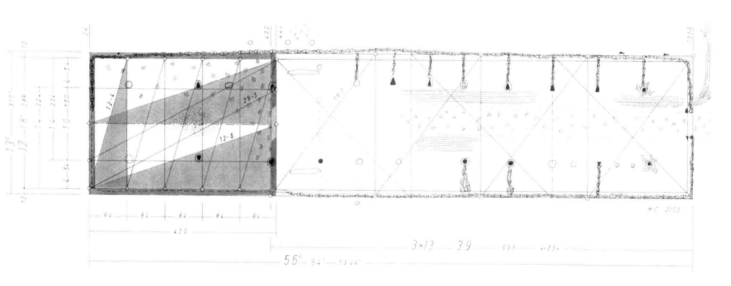

Abb. 17 Das Alte Haus 1d/7

Länge 420" wie Abb. 16, Mittelschiff wie Abb. 17. Anbau von Flett und Stall nach Grundkonfiguration 1B.

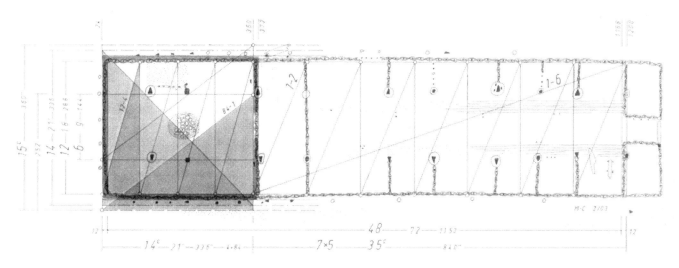

Abb. 18 Das Alte Haus 5/10

Länge bis zur Innenkante der Trennwand 336 (14c), darüber Quadrat auf die Fußpfettenachsbreite, sowie 4 pDs 12-4. Das Mittelschiff ist mit 2 gespreizten pDs 84-1 gebildet. Anbau von Flett und Stall nach Grundkonfiguration 1C.

das einer rein formalen. Deutlich wird die erhebliche Variationsbreite des Verfahrens, aber auch die Meisterschaft in seinem Gebrauch. Es müßte dann auch hier unterschieden werden zwischen bloßem technischen Aufgehen, der allgemeinen rechnerischen Abstraktion, und dem Herstellen symbolischer Bezüge. Für diese aber gibt es keinen Anhalt.

Es ist bereits festgestellt worden, daß die Giebeleingänge in keinem der drei Fälle mittig liegen, eine häufige Erscheinung aus gleichem Grund auch in der weiteren Baugeschichte.

Die Eingänge in den Häusern 1d/7 und 5/10 sind eng. Daß die Eingangsbreite 52" (1,08 m) die kleinste ist, für das größte Haus, zeigt die rigorose Formalität des Planungserfahrens. Dieses besteht darin, daß die Eingangsbreite auf die Innenlänge (Haus 2/10 und 5/10) oder die Außenlänge (Haus 1d/7) geometrisch aufgehen muß, zugleich taktend mit den beiderseitigen gleichlangen Reststreifen, mit denen die Lage des Eingangs bestimmt ist (Abb.12a,13a,14a).

Eine überraschende zusätzliche Bedingung ist, daß diese drei Streifen geometrisch auch auf die Länge nur bis zur Trennwand des Wohnteils, also die Länge von Stallteil und Flett aufgehen müssen. Die Bedeutung dieser Forderung wird sich im zweiten Teil zeigen (Abb.12b,13b,14b).

In dem Haus 2/10 hat sich auf der Flettseite vor der Wohnraumtrennwand eine Schwelle erhalten. Sie liegt nicht in der Achse des Giebeleingangs, und ist, gegen heutige Erwartung, 4" breiter als der Hauseingang im Giebel. Damit wird ein weiterer Nachweis für die Planung möglich (Abb.12c).

DER HERD
(Abb.15a, 15b)

Daß der Herd als Platz des Opfermahls seit Urzeiten den Mittelpunkt häuslicher Bezüge darstellt bedarf keiner Ausführung. Sein geometrischer Einbau in den Hausplan ist deshalb kaum überraschend. Interessiert am Prinzip, mag es in diesem Falle genügen, die Lage des Herdes nur an dem Beispiel des Hauses 2/10 zu rekonstruieren; das Besondere hier ist seine Lage außerhalb der Längsachse.

Die Verschiebung in der Breite, 135 und 153", erlaubt eine vollkommene Taktung mit den pDs 12-4 und 3-8 gleichartig auf die beiden Längen, Wohnteil (420") und Gesamtlänge Fußpfettenachsen (1008"), auf die Lichtbreite 288". In den Breiten wird 153" nur auf 402" gedeckt, 135" nur auf 1008"; es legt sich der Gedanke nahe, diese Konfiguration könnte der erste Zug der (Standard-) Planung gewesen sein.

DIE WOHNSTALLHÄUSER DER FEDDERSEN WIERDE
MASSE UND GEOMETRIE DER GRUNDRISSE, II
EXKURS: MEGARA IN PRIENE, TROJA

DAS ALTE HAUS

(Abb. 16, 17, 18)

Es scheint noch nicht bemerkt worden zu sein, daß mit dem Zusammenfügen zweier Funktionsteile, dem Ein-raum-Wohnhaus und dem dreischiffigen Stall, mit dem 'Leerraum' des Fletts dazwischen, der Urahn des (Nie-der-)Sachsenhauses entstanden ist. Zusammenfügung bedeutet, daß die beiden Funktionsteile selbst nicht erst zu diesem Zeitpunkt entstanden sein können. Der Stallteil findet sich bereits in Ezinge. Der Wohnteil mit seinen vier Pfosten und dem Herd (meist) in der Mitte aber ist – das ägäische Megaron.

Die Gleichheit des Grundrißaufbaus beider Einraum-häuser, Herd zwischen vier Pfosten, ist mehr als deut-lich. Sind sie als Typus gleichzusetzen, so bedeutet ihre bauliche Verschiedenheit, Staken-Flechtwerkswand und Lehmziegelmauer, daß beide Ausführungen nicht gleich-zeitig entstanden sind. Damit stellt sich die Frage, welche die ursprüngliche, oder, welche aus der anderen entstan-den ist /14/.

Nun liegt der Ursprung der Pfostenpaare, damit der Dreischiffigkeit, in der Einführung der obenliegenden Queraussteifung; sie gehören also zum Holzbau, dieser ist der ursprüngliche. Das Lehmziegelmegaron bedarf keiner Aussteifung. Die Umformung in die Ziegelausfüh-rung muß bei der Einwanderung in mediterrane Länder erfolgt sein – nicht unbedingt, weil diese schon unter Holzarmut gelitten hätten, sondern wegen eines notwen-digerweise anderen Wärmeschutzkonzeptes. Die thermi-sche Trägheit der Ziegelmauern und der dazugehörigen Lehm-Dachplatte, die ihrerseits gegen Regen geschützt werden muß, stellt im Hausinneren einen Mittelwert zwi-schen Tages- und Nachttemperatur her.

Die Abdeckung, das auf dieser Lehmdecke auflie-gende Dach, konstruktiv getrennt von den (ehemaligen) Jochpfosten, ist damit eine Neubildung. Es ist, mit bes-serem Regenschutz durch gebrannte Dachziegel spä-ter, das Tempeldach. Dessen jetzt flache Neigung, d.h. geringe Höhe, hat einen freien Abzug des Herdrauchs (unter dem Dach, durch eine Aussparung in der Leh-mdecke) nicht mehr erlaubt, weshalb der Herd für das Opfermahl ins Freie vor den Tempeleingang verlegt werden mußte.

Ein anderer, hier vorzulegender Nachweis der Iden-tität beider Hausarten liegt in der Geometrie. Die Wohn-teile der ersten drei FW-Häuser weisen ein identisches Planungsfeld mit identischen Maßen auf, 420" zu 288" (Abb.16,17,18). Die beiden gleichlangen Häuser, hier als 'standardnah' gesehen, enthalten außerdem ein Quadrat auf die Wandaußenseiten (Abb.10,11). Beide Elemente, das Planungsfeld 420/288, und das die Außenbreite de-ckende Quadrat, zeigen sich in zwei älteren Bauten in der Ägäis (Exkurs).

Der geometrische Aufbau der Alten Häuser ist ein ein-faches Längs- und Querschema. Die davon unabhängige Planung des Anbaus, Flett und Stall, ist für die beiden Häuser 2/10 und 5/12 bereits gezeigt worden (Abb.10,11); sie besteht bei Haus 1d/7 in der Grundkonfiguration 1B (Abb.17), bei Haus 5/10 in 1C (Abb.18).

Die beiden 'standardnahen' Häuser 2/10 und 5/12, nicht die beiden langen Häuser, enthalten ein weite-res überlagerndes Planungsmerkmal. Die Länge des Halbierungs-pD 12-14 (Abb. 6b, 7b) wird durch die Trennwand geteilt derart, daß für beide Hausteile eigene Halbierungs-pDs entstehen (Abb. 16; in Haus 5/12 iden-tisch, nicht dargest.). Dieses Konzept wird sich dann im Systema der Jochteilung erneut zeigen; hier wichtig, daß eine vergleichbar eingesetzte Halbierung sich aber auch im folgenden findet (Abb.19 und 25).

EXKURS: MEGARA IN PRIENE, TROJA

Das in den Alten Häusern aufgefundene Quadrat ist ein konstituierendes Planungselement auch der ägäischen Megara. Deren Herkunft ist ungeklärt, das älteste bisher bekannte Beispiel gehört nach Südrußland /14/. Gezeigt wird der Zeustempel an der Agora in Priene, 4. Jahrh. v. Chr. /15/ und das Megaron VIa in Troja, 'mykenisch', nach 1900 v.Chr. /16/. Eine vollständige Bearbeitung bei-der Bauwerke soll a.a.O. vorgelegt werden.

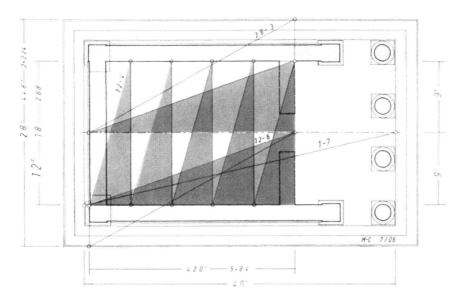

Abb. 19 Priene, Zeustempel I

Planungsfeld 420:288" und entsprechend Geometrie w.v. (Abb. 16). Eingesetzt auch hier das Konzept der Halbierung: Mit pD 1-7 (´), d.i. 9:40:41 ist die Länge der obersten, mit pD 28-3 ("), d.i. 420:224, die Breite der untersten Krepisstufe bestimmt.

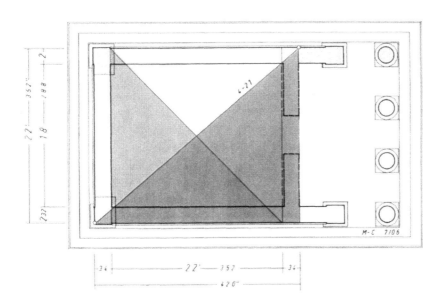

Abb. 20 Priene, Zeustempel II

Das Innenlichten 22´ längs entspricht der Außenbreite (vgl. Abb. 10, 11), womit über ein Quadrat und das pD 4-21, d.i. 4(88:105:137) = 352:420 die Mauerdicken 32 bzw. 34" bestimmt sind.

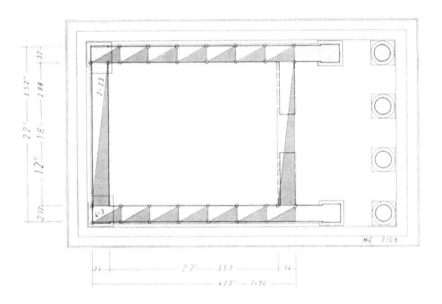

Abb. 21 Priene, Zeustempel III

In aller Architektur sind die Mauerstärken eigendefiniert innerhalb des Gesamtnetzes; sie sind Einbettungen. Mit pD 2-23, d.i. 2(17:144:145) = 34:288 werden die Maße nach Abb. 20 aufgenommen.

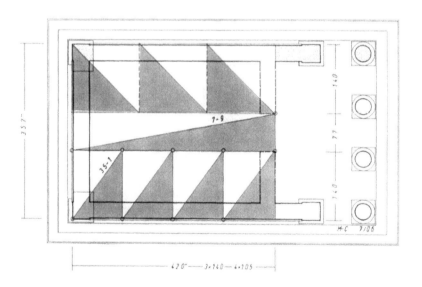

Abb. 22 Priene, Zeustempel IV

Wie in den Wohnstallhäusern ist auch hier die Eingangsbreite bestimmt, die Breite 357", mit Eckvorlagen, wird geteilt in pD 7-9, d.i. 7(11:60:61) = 77:420, sowie beidseitig Grundkonfiguration 1B.

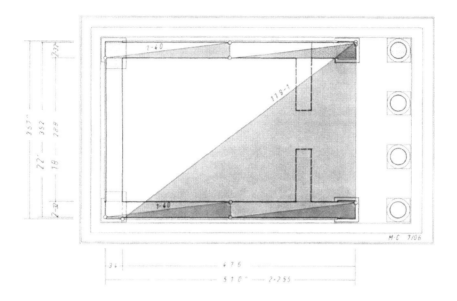

Abb. 23 Priene, Zeustempel V

Diese Bruttobreite 357" ist Breite des pD 119-1, mit dem, auf die Länge 476" die Tiefe des Vorplatzes bestimmt wird. Mit 2 pDs 1-40, d.i. 1(32:255:257) = 32:510 war zugleich die Dicke der Seitenmauern auf die neue Länge zu bestätigen.

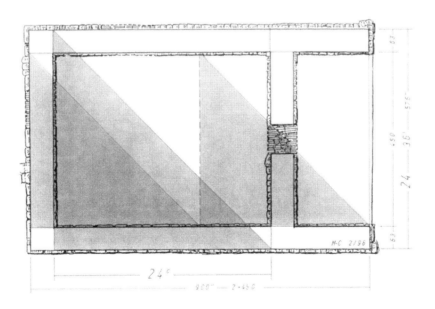

Abb. 24 Troja, Megaron VIa, I

Das Grundquadrat 24ᶜ deckt wie in Priene die lichte Länge und die Außenbreite. Die Lichtbreite 450" erscheint über 2 Q 450 als Gesamtlänge 900".
Die Seitenmauern sind damit 63" dick.

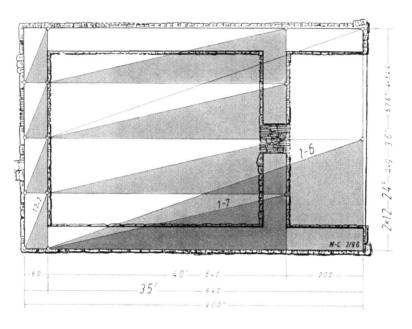

Abb. 25 Troja, Megaron VIa, II

Das Halbierungskonzept ist mit dem pD 1-6 (^c), d.i. 12:35:37, auf 12^c, der halben Breite, eingeführt. Die Außenbreite 36′ wird querlaufend mit 4 pDs 1-7, d.i. 9:40:41 auf die Länge 40′ gedeckt. Sym-metrisch dazu die Giebelmauer, Dicke 60", mit 4 pDs 12-2.

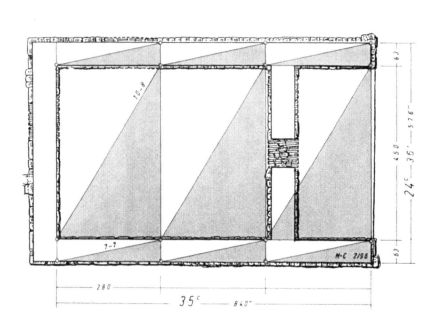

Abb. 26 Troja, Megaron VIa, III

Die Länge 840" ist teilbar in 3*280; Lichtbreite 450" und Mauerdicke 63" werden mit den pDs 10-8 bzw. 7-7 symmetrisch gedeckt.

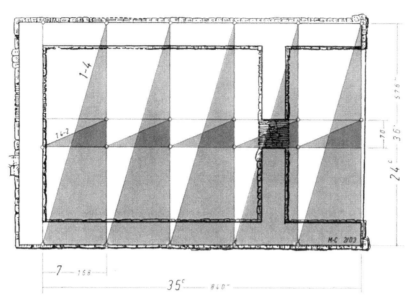

Abb. 27 Troja, Megaron VIa, IV   c

Die Eingangsbreite, von Dörpfeld markiert, beträgt 70". Sie bindet mit pDs 14-2 sym-metrisch in die Schemareihung von 5 pDs 1-4 ( ) der Gesamtbreite ein.

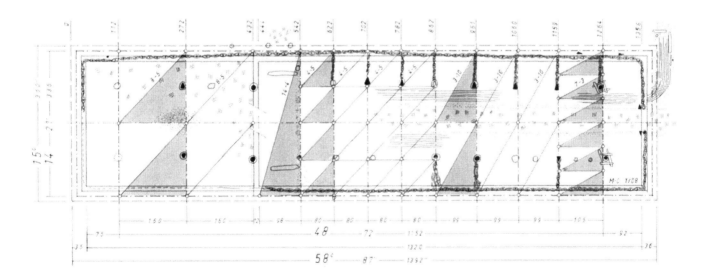

Abb. 28 Systema der Jochabstände II, Breiten, Haus 1d/7

Der Wohnteil enthält 2 Joche zu 160" Breite, es folgt das Flett mit 98", dann der Stallteil mit 4 Jochen zu 80", 2 Jochen zu 99", und 1 Joch zu 105". Die Länge dieser Querstreifen ist wie in den anderen Häusern durchgehend die Achsweite der Fußpfettenpfosten, 336" (14ᶜ). Summe 1152" als Achsweite der Endjoche (Abb.4).

Diese Anordnung ist noch keine Ordnung in sich; die Verteilung der Jochbreiten unterliegt vielmehr einem überlagernden Konzept I

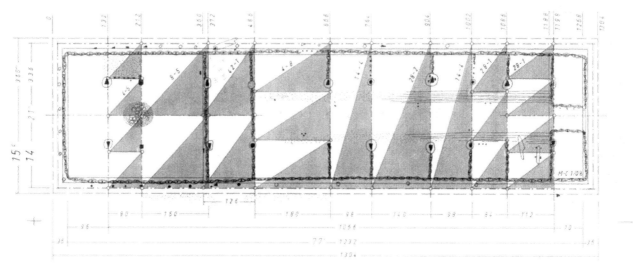

Abb. 29 Systema der Jochabstände II, Breiten, Haus 5/10

Dieses Haus weist nicht w.v. 5 verschiedene Jochbreiten auf, sondern deren 8, auch wird die Trennwand des Wohnteils nicht übersprungen, sondern doppelt belegt. Die Summe 1066" liegt um 4" außerhalb der Mitte Wandachse (1194") Endjoch rechts (Abb.5) bei Kote 1198".

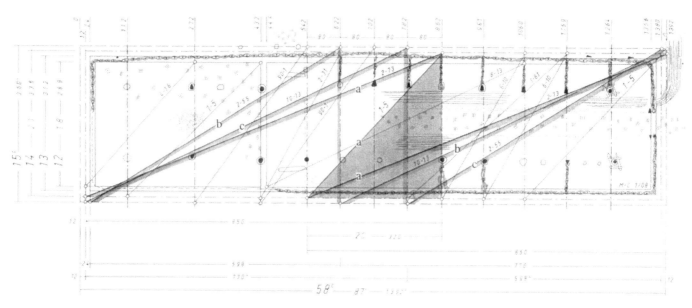

Abb. 30 Systema der Jochabstände I, Verteilung, Haus 1d/7

Das wegen seiner geringen Zahl von Wahlmöglichkeiten primäre Konzept der Verteilung stellt sich in diesem Haus in einer überraschenden, überragenden Lösung dar:

(a) Mit dem pD 2-73, d.i. 2(168:425:457) = 336:850 werden Kote 12 bis 862 gedeckt;

pD 1-5 (´) deckt mit 20:21 rückwärts Kote 542 bis 862 – das sind jene 4 Joche zu 80";

ein zweites pD 2-73 deckt den Bereich Kote 542 bis 1392.

Dieses offenbar bewußte Spiel wird fortgesetzt mit den Ansätzen (b) und (c):

(b) Das pD 2-55, d.i. 2(180:299:349) = 360:598 deckt den Bereich der Koten 24 bis 622;

das anschließende pD 10-13, d.i. 10(36:77:85) = 360:770 deckt den Bereich Kote 622 bis 1392;

1. (c) die Umkehrung von (b), mit pD 10-13, pD 2-55 anschließend.
2. Die weitere Verteilung ist selbsterklärend.

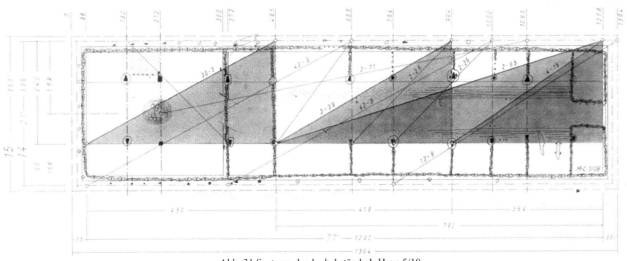

Abb. 31 Systema der Jochabstände I, Haus 5/10

Die Lösung für das primäre Konzept der Verteilung der Jochabstände in diesem Hause ist anders, aber ebenso eindeutig. Eingesetzt sind 4 pDs identischer Breite, 240". Das erste deckt Wohnteil und Flett, das zweite und dritte den Stallteil, zusammengefaßt durch das vierte.

					Koten
30-3:	30(8:15:17)	=	240:450	36	486
2-39:	2(120:209:241)	=	240:418	486	904
4-18:	4(60:91:109)	=	240:364	904	1268
2-65:	2(120:391:409)	=	240:782	468	1268

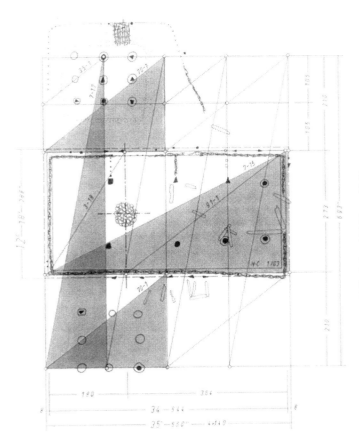

Abb. 32 Haus 5/30, I

Das Haus besitzt Auwandmaße 34′ (544") auf 273", über die der Herd in Längsrichtung angelegt worden ist mit pD 3-18, d.i. 3(60:91:109) = 180:273, und pD 91-1 mit 364:273. 180+364 = 544.

Mit einem Überstand von beidseitig 8" entsteht eine Länge des Planungsfeldes von 35′ (560"); in diesem liegt das pD 7-15, d.i. 7(39:80:89) = 273:560, sowie je 2 pDs 70-1 mit 210:280" auf die Außenachsen der beiden Speicherbauten. Mit 210+273+210 entsteht die Breite 693" des Planungsfeldes. Die Länge 560 ist schematisch geteilt auf die Breite mit 4 pDs 7-17, d.i. 7(20:99:101) = 140:693". In dieser 4-Teilung erscheint die Breite des oberen Speichers mit 105", ebensogroß der Abstand vom Haus.

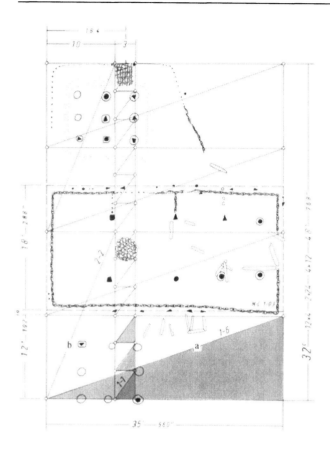

Abb. 33 Haus 5/30, II

eine 5-Teilung der Länge nimmt mit pD 14-3, d.i. 112:210" die Außenbreite der Speicher auf (a, a). Mit dem auf die Breite 105" gespreizt angesetzten pD 4-8, d.i. 4(28:45:53) = 112:180 (c) wird die Grenze des Grundstücks erreicht; das Planungsfeld erhält damit die vielseitig beplanbare Breite 48′ (768") (vgl. Abb. 2, 3).

Der untere Speicher, in der Länge gegenüber dem oberen versetzt, ist in der Breite durch pD 14-7, d.i. 14(9:40:41) = 126:560" definiert (d), in seinem Abstand durch pD28-1 mit 112:84 (b).

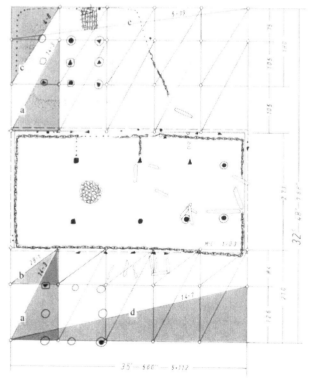

Abb. 34 Haus 5/30, III

Die Breite 48′ wird auf die Länge 35′ mit 4 ′gestapelten′ pDs 1-6 gedeckt (a). Daß diese einen Bezug zum Hausdach haben ist nicht anzunehmen, weil der Überstand der Traufkante gegenüber der Fußpfettenachse dann mit 18" anderthalbmal größer wäre als bei den 4 größeren Häusern.

In diese 4 pDs 1-6 fügt sich je 3 mal die Breite der Eingangspforte, 3′, mit pD 1-1 (′), und auch ihr Abstand von dem Rand des Planungsfeldes, 10′, mit 2 pDs 2-2 (b). Der Herd, auf den ersten Blick eingeschlossen, liegt mit 188" (Abb. 32) nicht in der Mitte des Eingangs, Achse 184".

PRIENE, ZEUSTEMPEL
(ABB.19, 20, 21, 22, 23)

Der Tempel besitzt mit der Lichtbreite 18′ (288″) und dem Außenmaß 420″ dieselben Abmessungen wie die drei ′Regelhäuser′ der Feddersen Wierde (Haus 5/12 zzgl. Wanddicke). Damit ist auch die Geometrie für das Feld 288/420 identisch.

Auffällig sind zwei weitere Entsprechungen. Das Quadrat der FW-Häuser bestimmt auch hier die Außenbreite, 22′, mit Seitenmauern der Dicke 2′ (32″); Front- und rückwärtige Mauer 34″ (Abb. 20). Weiter ist auch das Halbierungskonzept nachzuweisen, es bestimmt die Länge der obersten, und die Breite der untersten Krepisstufe (Abb. 19)

Ein kanonisches Erfordernis der Architekturplanung ist, Mauerdicken ebenfalls in pDs bzw. Quadraten zu definieren; hier bestätigen sich die genannten Mauerdicken (Abb. 21). Es ist offenbar, daß die aufgehende Fügung allein dieser 3 Ebenen, die armonia, real gemeint ist, nicht etwa ästhetisch.

Mit je 2½ ″ dicken Eckvorlagen wird die Bruttobreite 357″, in der in üblicher Weise die Eingangsbreite festlegt worden ist, mittig (Abb. 22).

Der gedeckte Vorplatz, pronaoV , ist geometrisch eingebunden (Abb. 23). Er darf als das Flett der Wohnstallhäuser angesehen werden, dessen Zugang von der Seite geschaffen werden mußte, als der Stall angesetzt wurde. Es müßte sich dann wohl eine Geometrie auch für das um das Flett erweiterte Alte Haus nachweisen lassen.

TROJA, MEGARON VIA
(ABB. 24, 25, 26, 27)

Das von Dörpfeld in Troja ausgegrabene Megaron bestand nur noch aus der Feldstein-Grundmauer. Der Lehm-Trockenziegelaufbau war abgespült, läßt sich aber in Anwendung bisheriger Planungsrundsätze rekonstruieren. Der fuß ist griechisch geteilt, er enthält 4 hand zu 4 finger.

Erkennbar ist das Grundquadrat 24 ^{c}, wie in Priene lichte Länge und Außenbreite deckend. Die Lichtbreite 450″ erscheint über 2 Q 450 als Gesamtlänge 900″. Die Seitenmauern sind damit 63″ dick (Abb. 24).

Die Querteilungen, als Halbierungskonzept, bilden bereits das, was hier als Systema bezeichnet werden soll. Auf 12 ^{c}, der halben Breite, liegt das pD 1-6 (^{c}), die Länge abzgl. rückwärtige Giebelmauer deckend; Cellalänge,

ebenso, mit 4 pDs 1-7 (′). Die Giebelmauer, Dicke 60″, ist mit 4 pDs 12-2 sym-metrisch gedeckt (Abb.25). Entsprechendes gilt für die Seitenmauern (Abb.26). Für die Eingangöffnung, 70″, ergibt sich keine Formulierung der Restbreiten.

Das Gerüst, Systema der Jochabstände II
(Abb. 28, 29)

Mit der Planungtechnik des Schemas sind aus den Breiten des Typenquerschnitts Standardlängen des Grundrisses bestimmt worden. Die innere Partitionierung, zunächst die Dreiteilung in Wohnteil, Flett, Stallteil, dann darübergelegt die auffällig ungleichen Jochabstände, wird von der Schemaplanung nicht definiert. Hier setzt eine andere Technik an, die als Systema bezeichnet werden soll und die auch an anderen Bauplanungen nachzuweisen ist /17/. Sie besteht in der schematischen Einzeldefinition der Querstreifen, die bei einer inneren Partitionierung auf die Länge des Grundrisses entstehen.

Diese Definition bestimmt die Breiten der Querstreifen (Längsrichtung des Grundrisses) auf eine gegebene feste Länge, d.i. hier, entsprechend der praktischen Einmessung des Grundrisses, die Achsweite der Fußpfetten, 336″ (14c). Die Breiten sind, an den Jochabständen abzulesen, recht ungleich, müssen sich aber als Summe in den Abstand der Endjoche einordnen. Man wird sich aus heutiger Sicht wundern, daß diese Länge nicht, technisch sinnvoller, einfach in gleiche Abstände geteilt worden ist. Es kann aber, nach allem, kein Zweifel daran bestehen, daß die Wahl der Breiten sowie die Verteilung dieser ungleich breiten Querstreifen auf die Länge einem rationalen Konzept unterliegt.

Planerisch besitzt diese Definition der Querstreifen, Jochabstände, eine größere Anzahl an Lösungen, ist anpaßbarer, weshalb sie als zweiter Schritt, (II), nachgeordnet erscheint.

Die permutative Verteilung der Streifen unterschiedlicher Breiten dagegen ist dann nach einem zusammenfassenden, übergreifenden Konzept mit entsprechend geringeren Wahlmöglichkeiten vorgenommen worden, das deshalb als primär gelten muß, (I). Dieses Konzept läßt sich in den beiden langen Häusern klarer zeigen als in den beiden kurzen, die noch weniger Wahlmöglichkeiten bieten. Dem leichteren Verständnis zuliebe erfolgt die Darstellung (II) zuerst.

Das Gerüst, Systema der Jochabstände I
(Abb. 30, 31)

Die scheinbare Willkür in der Verteilung der ungleich breiten Jochabstände verwandelt sich in eine außerordentliche planerisch-rechnerische Leistung bei Rekonstruktion der überlagernden zusammenfassenden pDs; eine Vorabfestlegung stellen dabei die Wohnteil-Trennwände dar. Es gibt zwei Arten dieser zusammenfassenden pDs, die durchgehenden eines Entwurfs, hier blau gekennzeichnet, und die Einzelfallüberlagerungen.

Die pDs des Entwurfs folgen in beiden Häusern unterschiedlichen Konzepten. In Haus 1d/7 erscheinen 3 Folgen, die erste aus 3 pDs (a), die beiden anderen aus 2 pDs, aneinander anschließend, und gespiegelt. In Haus 5/10 erscheint 1 Folge aus 3 pDs, aneinander anschließend, von denen die beiden des Stallteils von einem vierten überlagert werden; alle vier besitzen die selbe Breite.

EIN GRUNDSTÜCK, HAUS FW 5/30

Der neue Einblick in geistige Leistungen der sog. Vorgeschichte soll abgeschlossen werden mit der Darstellung einer planerischen Grundstücksordnung. War die geometrische Konzipierung in den vorgestellten Beispielen direkt auf das Haus und seine Bauteile bezogen, hatte sie, auch in ihrer Formalisierung, einen technisch-praktischen Zweck, so soll das letzte Beispiel zeigen, in welch ausgreifender, geradezu erschreckender Weise die Geometrisierung sich auch auf das nächste Umfeld erstreckte.

Das Haus 5/30, kleiner als die anderen hier behandelten, unterscheidet sich von diesen auch durch die sehr unterschiedliche Breite der Giebel-Endfelder. Auf der Wohnteilseite muß das Dach deshalb als abgewalmt, auf der gegenüberliegende als einfacher senkrechter Satteldachgiebel vor auskragenden Pfetten angenommen werden. Die geometrischen Kanten der Länge 35′ (560"), Überstand 8", müßten damit auf der einen Seite als Fußpfettenachse, auf der anderen als Dachkante, Ortgang angesehen werden. An den Traufseiten erscheint, mit einem Abstand von 7½ ", der Achsabstand der Fußpfetten, 18′ (288").

Zwei Speicher gleicher Länge, aber unterschiedlicher Breite, mit hochgelegter Lagerfläche, sind in ungleichen Abständen parallel zum Haus angelegt. Ein kurzes Stück einer Grundstücksgrenze zeichnet sich ab, eine Pforte, mit befestigtem Boden. Jenseits wäre damit ein öffentlicher Weg anzunehmen.

Die Rekonstruktion der Planung erlaubt erstmals, geistige Arbeit in vorliterater Zeit direkt nachzuweisen. Dabei ist die Frage ′wie?′ weitgehend, aber nicht vollständig gelöst. Vor allem bleibt eine wichtige Frage vorerst offen, die nach der Reihenfolge der Planungsschritte. Hier begänne die Frage ′warum?′. Sie ist auf zwei Ebenen zu stellen, der technischen, und der einer möglichen Bedeutung.

Ist die Wiederkehr der Maße 420/288" eine kanonische Bindung, oder bloße Praktikabilität? Für eine Bindung spricht das Quadrat, das in verschiedenen Größen, aber in gleichem Bezug auf die Außenwandbreite auftritt. Es fällt nicht schwer, darin ein früheres quadratisches Zelt zu sehen.

Ist weiter auch die gewiß festliegende Reihenfolge der Planungsschritte im Einzelnen als Kanonik verstanden worden, oder als bloße Handwerksregel? Ersteres würde mit den langen Zeiträumen der Konstanz harmonieren; es stellte sich dann aber auch die Frage, ob Konzepte wie in Abb. 30 und 31 Standardlösungen waren, oder immer wieder mögliche Einzelberechnungen innerhalb der Kanonik. Hat es, nach der geometrischen Bewahrung des Alten Hauses, kanonische Bindungen auch zwischen einzelnen Bauteilen, Bezüge des Halbierungsverfahrens etwa gegeben?

Gern wüßte man auch, ob Erfindungen Diskussionen, Konflikte hervorgerufen haben, und ob diese in der Öffentlichkeit, oder nur unter den Meistern ausgetragen wurden. Wieviel haben die Bewohner des Grundstücks 5/30 von der Planung ihres Anwesens gewußt, wieviel hätten sie verstanden? Hat es ein Verhalten der Gesellschaft gegenüber dem planerischen Niveau und einer derart durchdringenden Regulierung ihrer Alltagswelt gegeben?

Holzbauwerke des Handwerks erreichen nur bescheidene Größen, und das Feld möglicher Erfindungen ist ebenfalls begrenzt. Nach dem grundlegenden Fortschritt, dem Wechsel zum Dreischiffhaus, war als Fortschritt nur die ′Verselbstständigung′ des Daches möglich, der Einbau von Kehl- und Hahnenbalken in Steildächern, das Hochrähm- und das Niederrähmhaus der Neuzeit. Häuser in Süddeutschland und im Alpenraum mit ihren flachen, schneehaltenden Dächern sind von Anfang an bei der bandkeramischen Firstunterstützung geblieben /18/.

Der Grund für die geringen Möglichkeiten der Konstruktionsentwicklung ist, daß Hölzer eine begrenzte Länge haben, und daß ihr Zusammenbau statische Systeme mit

Druck und Zugkräften entstehen läßt. Die dem Handwerk möglichen Holzverbindungen aber können nur geringe Zugkräfte übertragen. Außerdem sind hölzerne Strukturen leicht, und die Hauptgefahr ist und war der Wind. So blieb der Zusammenbruch im Bereich bloßer Tektonik, und die Erfahrung der Realität beschränkte sich auf den erklärbaren einfachen Faserbruch. Erst die Einführung eiserner Verbindungsmittel, Bolzen, ggf. mit Laschen oder Dübeln hat Zugkräfte in voller Größe übertragbar gemacht, und den Handwerksbau in einen Ingenieursbau verwandelt. Sprungartig wurden große Spannweiten möglich, Großraumkirchen, Theater, Reithallen. Eiserne Verbindungsmittel waren bereits den Römern bekannt, sind aber erst in der Neuzeit wieder eingesetzt worden. An den damit entstehenden neuen Konstruktionen aus linearen Gliedern hat sich die Theorie der Statik/Mechanik entwickelt.

Daß Zahlen, die sich als Maße fügten, ursprünglich als Ordnung, von einer überweltlichen Macht eingesetzt, erlebt worden sind darf allgemein wohl angenommen werden. Weil aber nun die Hölzer nach Länge und Dicke naturbeschränkt waren, Leistung und Versagen der Strukturen direkt den Holzverbindungen zuzuschreiben, könnte die Geometrie der Planung als abhängig, als bloßes Werkzeug zur Bemaßung gesehen worden sein. Es stellt sich die Frage, ob sie – es gibt nur eine – von den ersten Siedlern entwickelt und ihre Praxis später auf ganz andere übertragen worden ist, oder ob dieselben Notwendigkeiten zu verschiedenen Zeiten überall zu denselben Verfahren geführt haben.

Holzbauer mußten die Maße ihrer Hölzer von Anfang an geometrisch festlegen. Waren sie es dann auch, die als Benutzer bloßer Technik hier auch schon Ansätze zu einem Verstehen der Geometrie als solcher entwickelt haben? Immerhin ist jetzt die Frage offen, wie die Kenntnis hochzahliger pDs wie der in den Abb. 30, 31 erlangt worden ist.

Wie völlig neu den Holzbauern der Steinbau im römischen Besetzungsgebiet erschienen sein muß kann kaum eingeschätzt werden; denn sie werden bald erkannt haben, daß seine Planungsgeometrie die war, die sie in eigener Tradition selber einsetzten, alle Raffinessen eingeschlossen. Das Neue für sie aber war, daß es im Massivbau keinen Bezug auf naturgegebene Bauteillängen gab, weil die Mauern in allen drei Dimensionen aus beliebig vielen Bausteinen aufzubauen waren. Das war ursprünglich schlicht additiv möglich gewesen; trotzdem war, sollten hier Erfahrungen der Standfestigkeit tradiert werden, in

Querschnitt und Grundriß die Bestimmung der Dicken, also der Innen- und der Außenseite, mittels Geometrien nötig. Formalistisch dabei ist die zusätzliche, innenliegende geometrische Verbindung beider Seiten, die zu einer Verwandtschaft aller Kubaturen führt. Waren Bauteile und Geometrie derart aneinander gebunden, so waren Massivbauwerke, anders als Holzbauten, nicht mehr aus ihrem Baustoff, sondern direkt als Geometrie zu planen, und in diesen auch weiterzuentwickeln.

Die kritische Größe, Grunderfahrung der Massivbauer, war hier zunächst das Verhältnis von Mauerdicke zu -höhe, die Schlankheit, bei der, unter Mitbedenken von Baustoffschwere und innerem Verbund, sowie der konstruktiven Aussteifung, zwischen Feldstein-, Werkstein- und Backsteinbau sehr klar unterschieden werden mußte. Die eigentlichen Erfahrungen aber sind im Wölbbau gewonnen worden – er war das überragende bauliche Thema des auch hierin einzigartigen abendländischen Mittelalters. Mehr noch als die Technisierung des Bauvorgangs, neuen Bauformen damit, trieben hier die Zusammenbrüche die Entwicklung an, die immer wieder, immer genauer zu Fragen nach der Ursache, und damit nach dem Sinn der festen geometrischen, nicht als diesseitig verstandenen Gesamtordnung führen mußten. Denn die geometrische Bindung hatte die schwere Folge, daß die mindestens fünf Komponenten, Spannweite, Kämpferhöhe, Busung u.a. nur sprungweise, nicht in kleinen Schritten an die jeweiligen Grenzzustände herangeführt werden konnten. Diese Zusammenbrüche waren jetzt kein schlichter Materialbruch, Querschnittsversagen, sondern ein Kollabieren der Struktur, aus verschiedenen Gründen, ein weites Feld der Diskussion. Die in den Zusammenbrüchen allmählich erkennbar werdenden Schrägkräfte mußten die Wirklichkeit einer durch höhere Ordnung stabilisierten baulichen Struktur immer ungewisser machen. Neue Fragen nach Ursachen taten sich auch sonst auf, das Ende der Baukunst und einer ganzen Epoche war schließlich gekommen, der Übertritt in eine andere, immer weiter aus Realien ableitbaren Wissenschaft wurde der einzige Weg durch die Zeit.

ZUSAMMENFASSUNG

Bauforschung, entstanden als Stilgeschichte, ist bis heute wesentlich geprägt von der kunstgeschichtlichen Forschung. Sie beschränkt sich auf die Forschung an Architekturwerken, und sucht deren Ursprung im mittelmeerischen

Massivbau. Dabei ist der Begriff Architektur nach wie vor undefiniert. Handwerkliches Bauen, ihr Ursprung, bleibt außerhalb, damit auch der gesamte nordalpine Holzbau. Architekten haben Bautechnisches als Grundlage nicht einbringen können, sie haben Entwürfe auch da nicht rekonstruiert, wo die Fußmaßgrößen, seit dem 18. Jahrh., bekannt waren.

Die als Grundrisse z.T. gut erhaltenen Wohnstallhäuser der Feddersen Wierde nördlich Bremerhavens, 1955..61 ausgegraben /11/, erlauben eine weitgehende Rekonstruktion ihrer Planung. Diese folgt einer bereits Jahrtausende alten Technik, Rechtwinkligkeit der Bauwerke und ihrer inneren Verbindungen über Quadrate und 'pythagoräische' Dreiecke (pDs) als Rechenfiguren herzustellen. Das Verfahren besteht darin, eine Zusammenstellung von Teilstücken (Abb. 1d..h) in Grundkonfigurationen (Abb. 1A..C) einzusetzen.

Die hier rekonstruierten vier Grundrisse besitzen eine Typenbreite von 18´ im Lichten, dabei je 2 mit einer Mittelschiffsbreite von 9´ bzw. 10´. Die Größe der Häuser variiert nur in der Länge.

Die Struktur der Häuser besteht aus in Querrichtung windsteifen Rahmen, die in Längsrichtung gereiht ein dachtragendes Gerüst bilden. Anders als bei den bandkeramischen Häusern erlaubt der nichtunterstütze First dreischiffiger Häuser ein Hochlegen des Daches, damit auch der Traufe.

Gezeigt wird die Geometrie des Gerüsts (Abb.2..5) sowie des Außenwandrechtecks

(Abb.6..9) als Schemaplanung. Fest eingebaut ist die Trennwand, die den Wohnteil von Flett und Stall trennt (Abb.10, 11 und 16, 17). Schematisch eingebaut sind, wie in Ezinge /7/, der Giebeleingang (Abb.12..14) und der Herd (Abb.15).

Der Wohnteil erweist sich mit 4 Pfosten und Herd als Ursprung des ägäischen Megarons. Die Maße 420/288" erscheinen auch im Zeustempel von Priene (Abb.19,20); hier und im Megaron VIa in Troja (Abb.24) auch das auf der Außenseite ansetzende Quadrat. Auch das Halbierungskonzept ist kanonisch.

Die erheblich ungleichen Jochabstände entstammen einer hier als Systema bezeichneten Überlagerung zweier unabhängiger Konzepte, möglichweise Einzelfallberechnungen. Die Jochabstände als Querstreifen auf die Länge 21´, den Achsabstand der Fußpfettenpfosten aufgehend, decken als Summe die Gerüstlänge (Abb.28,29). Ihre Verteilung ist derart, daß sie mit Groß-pDs takten (Abb.30,31).

Eine planerische Grundstücksordnung zeigt abschließend einen erstaunlich abstrakten Zugriff auf den Nahbereich.

Das Zurichten der Hölzer vor dem Verbau muß bald nach Aufnahme des Bauens in eine geometrische Maßberechnung geführt haben. Die leichten Strukturen sind windgefährdet; der Zusammenbruch ist ein Faserversagen in zugbeanspruchten Verbindungen, seine Deutung technisch einfach.

Der durch römische Besatzung bekannt gewordene Massivbau war als Steinbearbeitung neu, neu auch das Denken in additiven Größen, und das veränderte Konzept der Aussteifung. Die geometrische Planungstechnik aber war bekannt, da identisch. Die eigentliche, und einzigartige Leistung abendländischen Bauens war dann die Entwicklung der Gewölbe als Gesamtstruktur.

QUELLEN UND ANMERKUNGEN

/1/ Ensprechend phcuV bzw. cubitus (verwandt mit (Arm-)Beuge bzw. cubare). Die Handelselle wurde im Abendland nicht in hand und zoll geteilt, sondern in einer Halbierungsreihe.

/2/ Der engl. Zoll, inch, sowie ounce, von uncia, der zwölfte Teil; das Dutzend (afrz. dozeine) aus duodecim.

/3/ Ein Beispiel, für gewöhnliches Verständnis unbegreiflich, ist die Zahl der genau 153 Fische, die Petrus bei der dritten Offenbarung Jesu aus dem See Genezareth im Netz fängt (Joh. 21,11). Schon Augustinus soll sich um eine Deutung bemüht haben; eine Aussage für sich, denn die Zahl ist die der kurzen Kathete der pDs

51-1	153: 204	12 x 17
3-24	153: 420	12 x 35
9-23	153: 1296	12 x 108

Darin ist 12 der Teilungfaktor semitischer und römischer Maße, im Gegensatz zur 16 der griechisch-germanischen Sphäre. Für 17, 35, 108 gibt es jeweils eine Reihe von Bezügen. Die hebräischen Zähleinheiten, auch die der Gewichte, sind dagegen, hand/finger bezogen, auf dem Teilungsfaktor 10 aufgebaut. An gewissen Stellen der Hlg. Schrift läßt sich eine Auseinandersetzung zwischen beiden Systemen ablesen.

/4/ Die 99 als Seitenlänge des Kuppelquadrats der Hagia Sophia (´) und als Diagonale des Grundrißquadrats des Aachener Münsters

(°) ist mit I.Mose 17.1,.20 in das 12er-Meßsystem eingebaut worden. Die Diagonale in Aachen wird durch das innere Oktogon in 3 Teile von 33c Länge geteilt, der Lebenszeit Christi auf Erden, in der Trinität aufgehoben.

/5/ Die Zahlennennungen der Hlg.Schrift sind teils Mengen, Anzahlen, teils Maße. Zwischen dem Zählen mit 10 Fingern und dem Messen mit dem Fuß, und seiner Kleinteilung in 3 hand zu 4 finger, d.i. 12 Zoll, entsteht damit der bis in die Gegenwart wirkende Basisgegensatz von 10 und 12. (vgl. Fußn. /7/, 159f.

In der Lieder-Edda (Codex regius) finden sich nur Anzahlen, keine Maße. Obwohl eine Fingerzählung naheliegt, auf diese auch mit ´elf´ und ´zwölf´ (got. ain-lif, twa-lif (left)) zu schließen ist, findet sich in den Götter-Liedern kein Bezug auf die 10. Statt dessen:

3 Asengötter, Nornen, Riesen, Töchter der Riesen, Hähne, weise Jungfrauen, 3 mal verbrannt, 3 mal geboren; wohl zugehörig, Troika;

Die 8 mag zwei Grundlagen haben: Odins, des Einäugigen Roß Sleipnir ist 8-füßig, für doppelte, überirdische Geschwindigkeit, während 8 Nächte, 8 Tage, 8 Winter kalendarisch sind.

´odín´ ist eins (russ.), eine Umkehrung von unus, wie temnein >< Messer, causa >< Sache, terra >< Erde, küssen >< saugen usw.

9 Welten, 9 Räume des Weltenbaums, mit 3 Wurzeln nach 3 Seiten kennt die Seherin;

11 Äpfel Iduns für ewige Jugend, 11 Paläste;

33 Zwerge;

„Fünfhundert Tore und vierzig dazu
sind in Walhalls weitem Bau".

Bezüge weder auf das Zählen noch auf das Messen sind hier zu erkennen. Als erstaunlich wird sich da die Rechentechnik erweisen.

/6/ Die Hausgrundrisse sind dankenswerterweise vom Niedersächsischen Institut für historische Küstenforschung, Wilhelmshaven, W.H.Zimmermann, zur Verfügung gestellt worden. Längenmaße nach Angabe von R.Stamm.

Es bleibt zu wünschen, daß zeichnerische Aufnahmen mit Maßen oder durchgehendem Maßstab versehen würden.

/7/ Acta Archaeologica 75:2, 2004, 172ff. Eine gewisse Verschiedenheit liegt in den Pfosten der Fußpfette. Diese sind in Ezinge Rundhölzer, vollständig und bemeßbar im Abstand 12" vor den Außenwänden erhalten, auf der Feddersen Wierde jedoch Keilhölzer, in weniger klarer Form. Anders wiederum Häuser von Flögeln (W.H.Zimmermann, Die Siedlungen des 1. bis 6. Jahrh. n.Chr. von Flögeln-Eeckhöltjen, Niedersachsen: Die Bauformen und ihre Funktionen, Probleme der Küstenforschung im südlichen Nordseegebiet Bd.19, 1992, 140).

/8/ Ausnahme etwa Haus 2/13, möglicherweise ohne Flett

/9/ vgl. engl. stove

/10/ Über die Kopfzahl der jeweiligen Siedlungsgemeinschaften, die Größe ihrer landwirtschaftlichen Erzeugung, über Selbstverbrauch und vermarktungsfähigen Überschuß gibt es noch keine näheren Erkenntnisse. Handwerkliche Tätigkeit ist für Schmiede nachgewiesen, verschiedene Werkzeuge sind gefunden worden. Das Fehlen von Rennfeueröfen führt zur Annahme, fertige Roheisenstücke seien zur Verarbeitung erhandelt worden, ebenso Holzkohle, und alles Bauholz, das sich auf der Marsch nicht findet (P.Schmid, Feddersen Wierde, in

Reallexikon der Germanischen Altertumskunde, Berlin, New York, Bd.8, 1994)

Nach Schmid sind dem Viehbestand entsprechend große, mittlere, und kleine Höfe zu unterscheiden, große mit 24..30, kleine mit 12..18 Rindern. Bei einer Familiengröße von 6..10 Personen und 142 kg Fleisch/a und Kopf seien damit die kleinen Höfe nicht mehr fähig zur Selbstversorgung gewesen, sondern haben von den großen Betrieben mitgetragen werden müssen. (Es stellt sich die Frage, worin der Sinn für den Bau eines normalen Hauses im unterwirtschaftlichen Bereich gelegen haben kann.). Dabei sei Ernährungslage insgesamt nur ausreichend gewesen. Zugleich wird aber ausgeführt, der Handel mit der Geest sei über Naturalien erfolgt, also Überschüsse.

Der Gesamtfleischverbrauch pro Kopf betrug 2003 in Deutschland 91,8 kg; EU-Mittel 97,6 kg, darin 19,5 kg Rind- und Kalbfleisch (ZMP, Holzmann Verlag).

Der Gesamtfleischverbrauch pro Kopf betrug 1913 im Deutschen Reich 51,7 kg, 1937 53,2 kg; darin Rind- und Kalbfleisch 14,6 kg (´Schlag nach´, Bibliograph. Institut AG, Leipzig, 2.Aufl. 1939,148)

/11/ in W.Haarnagel, Feddersen-Wierde, Wiesbaden 1979, Abb. 29, S.106 als 4/10 geführt.

/12/ Die Querschnittsrekonstruktionen für beide Mittelschiffsbreiten der F-W Häuser sind fertiggestellt. Sie sollen in anderem Zusammenhang veröffentlicht werden.

/13/ Fachwerk, stapelbar als geschoßhohe Kästen, ist auf einem Kranz von Feldsteinen hochgelegt und frei von Bodenfeuchte. Die Wandscheiben bestehen aus Stielen und Schwellen, tragende Decken sind zwischen Rähm und Saumschwelle eingelegt. Steifheit in der Ebene durch Streben. Fachwerk ist als räumliche Struktur in sich steif und gänzlich unverwandt mit der dachtragenden Gerüststruktur des ´Scheunentyps´. Da keine Vorform und keine Entwicklung des Fachwerks denkbar sind, handelt es sich um eine Erfindung. Nimmt man den Verbau kurzer Hölzer hinzu, entsteht das Bild transportfähiger vorgefertigter Häuser – also das einer Erfindung römischer Ingenieure im nordalpinen Raum. Hierher gehören, begrifflich und in der Sache, fenestra, cella, und caminus.

/14/ „Die Herkunft des Megarons in der Ägäis ist noch immer ungeklärt." (Der Kleine Pauly Bd.3, 1149)

/15/ W.Höpfner u. D.Schwandner, Haus und Stadt im klassischen Griechenland, 1986, Abb. 156

/16/ W.Dörpfeld, Troja und Ilion, Athen 1902, Fig. 56. Aus den angetragenen Maßen (nur) zweier Außenseiten der Grundmauer ergibt sich ein Fußmaß von 0,3313 m.

/17/ Verf., Babylon, die Stadtmauer Nebukadnezars II., Maße und Geometrie, Ausschnitt, Mitt. d. Dt.Orientges. zu Berlin, 138/2006, 199..209, Abb. 4

/18/ vgl. das lange Haus in Manching (W.Krämer, Germania 40, 1962, Beil. 4).

Author's address
Emmerichstrasse 13
D - 34119 Kassel
Deutschland
wmeyerchristian@unitybox.de

Acta Archaeologica vol. 79, 2008, pp 62-78
Printed in Denmark • All rights reserved

PROMINENT MIGRATION PERIOD BUILDING

LIPID AND ELEMENTAL ANALYSES FROM AN EXCAVATION AT ALBY, BOTKYRKA SÖDERMANLAND, SWEDEN

Björn Hjulström, Sven Isaksson & Christina Karlsson

Houses of a special character referred to as hall buildings in the literature, were constructed in Central Sweden from around the 4th century onwards (e.g. Herschend 1993, 1998). These are more prominent than other houses and served other functions as well as that of dwellings. In the saga literature the hall is closely related to various forms of feasting (gästabud or banquets), gift giving, cults and other phenomena connected with the customs of the aristocracy and their exercise of power (see Brink 1996; Enright 1996; Herschend 1997, 2001; Lönnroth 1997; Sundquist 2002). The special function of a hall building may have been restricted to a separate room in the house (sal) or in other cases it may have applied to the whole house. Although buildings labelled as halls share some common attributes, there are certain characteristics that distinguish between them with regard to their setting, architecture and find material. These differences may be difficult to grasp, however, because of the varying scale of the excavations and the particular methods employed (Söderberg 2005). Some of these differences may be explained by chronological changes or variations in the wealth of the farms they belonged to. Were all these 'special' buildings used for the same purpose, or did they fulfil different purposes? The Archaeological Research Laboratory (ARL) at Stockholm University (SU) excavated a prominent house foundation (Raa 131) in the parish of Botkyrka in 2006 and 2007 and performed lipid analyses and elemental analyses on the occupational layer in order to obtain more insights as to whether there were several smaller rooms or a large room and to see what activities might have taken place in this particular building.

Our notions regarding the cultural and social importance of food, drink and feasting in Iron Age society have been revised in recent years, and the importance of food, not only as a possible source of power but as a means of making and confirming differences and similarities between individuals and groupings in a society, has been stressed (see Herschend 1997; Isaksson 2000, Isaksson 2003; Söderberg 2005). Hence the pottery use in a building may be of great importance for the understanding of the building. Lipid analyses have been carried out on ceramics found in and around houses to get an indication of the practice and ideas of food preparation and how food culture was expressed. The results of lipid analyses performed on ceramics from Alby have been compared with analyses of ceramics from contemporary settlements that all belong to a wealthy category (Vendel, Valsgärde and Tuna in Alsike). The ceramic material from Vendel comes from a three-aisled building that has been interpreted as a multifunctional house with a possible central 'hall' or representational area (sal) (Isaksson 2000). Seven of the samples from Vendel were found in a storage area and the remaining ones come from the potential representation or dwelling area. The ceramics from Valsgärde were collected from post-holes in a settlement context, close to a hall building and in the vicinity of a boat-grave cemetery, and are dated to c. 7th century (Norr 1997). Based on lipid analysis of the ceramics, these samples may represent some sort of estate buildings specially connected with the handling of vegetable products (Isaksson 2003). The material from Valsgärde is rather limited and consists of only 6 shards. The third set of material, comprising 11 samples, comes from a cultural layer at Tuna in Alsike that has been dated to the 6th-7th century (Hjulström & Isaksson 2005). The whole deposit from which these samples were collected has been interpreted as residue largely from feasting activities and the preparation of food (Olsson & Isaksson 2007). The samples from Alby will also be compared here with pottery use in more explicitly ritualised contexts, i.e. as found in contemporary mortuary practice (Forsgren 2007).

THE MIGRATION PERIOD LANDSCAPE AT ALBY

Ancient Monuments, Finds and Landscapes
Botkyrka, situated by Lake Mälar, c. 15 km southwest of Stockholm, is close to several important Iron Age sites, such as Helgö, Birka, Adelsö and Gåseborg (see Figure 1). Its proximity to the waterways of Lake Mälar and to the historical main road to Götaland (götalandsväg), makes it centrally located with regard to both significant sites and communication routes. In earlier times, when roads followed natural features rather than arranged paths, the road to Götaland most probably followed the heights from the passage between Lake Alby and Lake Tullinge and passed the excavated house foundation Raa 131 (see Figure 2). Björn Ambrosiani drew attention to the area's importance in 1964 and discussed the history of the parish from the Bronze Age up to the Viking Age, while Åke Hyenstrand (1974) used Botkyrka as an area site for his evaluation of settlement organisation during the Iron Age.

The northern part of the parish Botkyrka, together with the excavation site (Raa 131), is shown in Figure 2. The richest Migration Period and Vendel Period burials in the parish are found at Hundhamra (Raa 8) and Skrävsta (Raa 36). The main burial in the large mound at Hundhamra, the largest in the parish (39-46 metres in diameter x 6 metres in height), contained a fragment of a gold hilt of a sword, a scabbard of silver and part of a gilded bronze fitting, all dated to c. 650-700 AD. (Nerman 1961), while a grave with quite ordinary superstructure at Skrävsta contained artefacts of the highest quality, such as a Frankish garnet sword pommel and fragments of a spear, shield and helmet (ATA dnr 1968/40). Several Migration Period burial grounds of more ordinary character were excavated during the construction of the residential township of Alby just north of our excavation site (e.g. Raa 115, 116 and 120) (see Bennett 1987). The richest stone setting from Raa 120 contained a fragmentary relief brooch and clasp button, together with a fragmentary animal head of bronze and more exclusively a fragmentary comb with a early runic inscription (Bennett 1972). Few settlements with satisfactory results regarding dating and size have been excavated in the parish. Among the recently excavated settlements are an imposing three-aisled house 50 metres long located on clay soil next to the burial ground at Skrävsta (Bratt & Wertwein 1999), and a terraced house dated to the Late Roman Iron Age - Migration Period situated in the Eriksberg industrial area, c. 500 metres west of Raa 131 (Schützler 1996).

The closest non-excavated Iron Age remains to the house foundation are the Early Iron Age stone settings at Raa 132 and 333. The two burial grounds Raa 124 and 130 both have similar grave forms, with mounds and stone settings, and can be dated to the Migration Period - Viking Age (see Figure 2). Two features recorded as heaps of fire-cracked stones are located only 20-30 metres south of the foundation, but their shape and location made us believe that they were graves. An unpublished geophysical and geochemical investigation showed that the conductivity in the middle of the construction differed from that at its edges and the phosphate content was low and evenly distributed, which should not be the case if it is a heap of fire-cracked stones. Hence it is more likely that these are indeed graves, and if so, they should be more or less contemporary with the house foundation. Raa 131 has been surrounded by known farm and hamlet sites (Älvesta, Alby, Segersby and Nibble) during historical times, although none closer then 0.5 km.

THE ALBY PLATEAU

The House Foundation
The location for the house was obviously chosen by the builders (or the person who engaged them) in order to be as prominent and scenically central as possible. In this respect the natural ridge of Raa 131, a spike protruding from a larger till and bedrock elevation, was a perfect setting (see Figure 3). It was evident prior to the excavation that the plateau had been strengthened with a stone terrace around the eastern gable and a row of stones (Ø 50-150 cm) along the north side, and it became clear from the trial excavation that there had been buildings standing on the plateau, for which a date between the 5th and 9th centuries was suggested (Hjulström 2006:7). As seen in Figure 3, there are considerable slopes on all sides except at the western gable. The less steep area on the long southern side is believed to be a ramp leading to the entrance to the house.

Acta Archaeologica

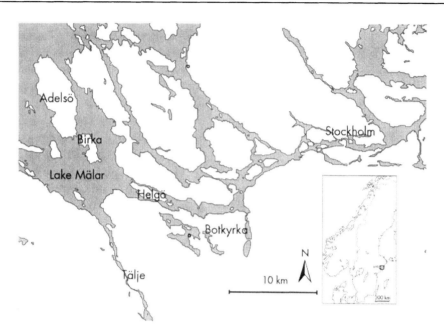

Figure 1. The parish of Botkyrka and its surroundings. Tälje and Stockholm are situated on inlets from the Baltic Sea to Lake Mälar. The location of the map is shown in the inset.

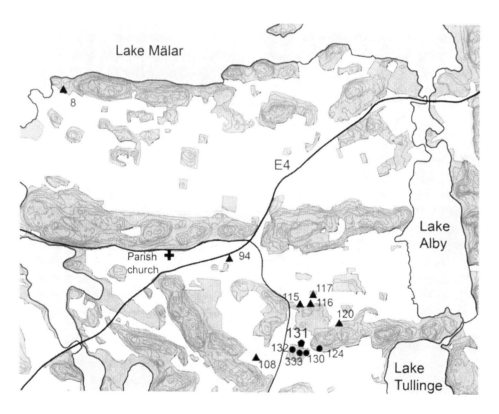

Figure 2. Map of northern Botkyrka showing the positions of the sites mentioned in the text. The topography is a typical Mälar Valley setting with a fissure-valley landscape. Till and bedrock are shown in grey and the clay-filled valleys in white. Important modern roads are shown as points of reference.

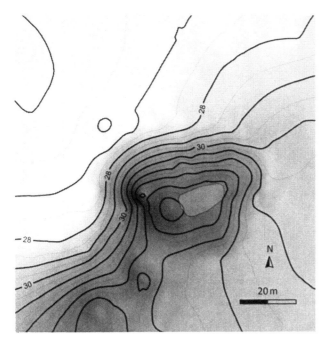

Figure 3. Contour map of the location of the house (grey) illustrating its enhanced position in the landscape.

The excavation showed that the stone terrace around the eastern gable consisted of several layers of stones (Ø 6-50 cm) up to 50 cm thick, while another smaller patch of stone packing with only one layer of stones is linked to the principal row of stones in the northwest. These stone terraces were not the only layers that had been brought in, however, as beneath them, covering the eastern half of the plateau and running along both long sides all the way to the western gable, was a layer of gravely sand that was thickest at the eastern gable and northeast of the long side (5-30 cm) and only a few centimetres deep in the southwestern and middle parts (see Figure 4). The function of the row of stones on the northern slope became more evident during the excavation; it was intended to keep the layer in place at the point where the slope was steepest.

The Buildings

Two three-aisled houses subsequently stood on the plateau. Both had a roof-bearing construction with a pair of posts forming three interlinked trestles, as shown in Figure 4. Since none of the features of the two houses overlap, it has not been possible to see in which order they were erected, but since house 1 had been dismantled once it was abandoned while the posts in house 2 had been left

in their holes, it is easy to favour the interpretation that house 1 is the earlier of the two.

The roof-bearing construction in house 1 evidently consisted of three evenly placed trestles located 6.2 and 6.1 metres apart. House 1 is both longer and wider than house 2. Five stake holes situated in a row along the southern side follow the same direction as house 1 and are interpreted as a part of the wall. As is often the case with similar buildings, it has not been possible to identify the gable construction, although various suggestions can be made.

House 2 is very similar in layout to house 1, although it is 2 metres shorter as measured between the outer pair of posts and there is a slight deviation in the direction (1.5 degrees). In contrast to house 1, house 2 was not dismantled, and the carbonised posts were still in situ in their stone-lined holes. As with house 1, it is not possible to conclude the construction of the eastern gable, but at the western end it is possible that one post belonged to the gable construction, since it bore a greater similarity to the roof-bearing posts. The post-hole was lined with stones, and even though the post was not carbonised there were mouldy traces of it to be seen. Three smaller posts are interpreted as remains of the northern wall. The reason for connecting these posts with house 2 rather than house 1 is that the distance would be slightly too short compared with the southern wall of house 1. In the southwest is a furrow, 3 metres long, running in the same direction as house 2 and interpreted as related to the wall.

Although no architectural evidence of an entrance was recovered, we hypothesize that the entrance was located on the south side of the building, since that area is somewhat flatter and gives easier access to the house. Also, there is some stone packing in line with the wall posts for house 1 and the traces of both the wall of house 1 and the furrow related to house 2 end just there. No architectural evidence of internal dividing walls was to be found. Such walls have previously been shown to coincide with roof support posts, as recognized by soil chemistry (Isaksson et al. 2000), and the house is divided into four hypothetical rooms based on the trestle positions.

One of the roof-bearing posts from house 2 was sent to the Laboratory for Wood Anatomy and Dendrochronology at Lund University, where it was concluded that the type of wood that had been used was pine and the age of the tree when it was cut down was estimated to have been 70-90 years, although only the first 60 rings from

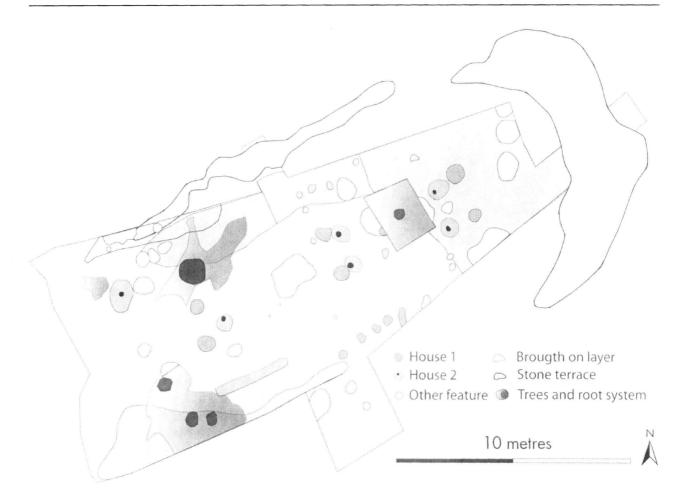

Figure 4. Plan of the excavation. Features interpreted as belonging to the same house are given the same colour, while other features are white. Note that the northern post-hole in the western trestle of house 2 is covered by a root system. The root system around the oak in the eastern part of the house partly covers a hearth.

the centre outwards were intact (Hans Linderson, pers. comm). It was not possible to date the post from the dendrochronological sequence, but three annual rings with known intervals were sent for 14C analysis (see Table 1). Matching of the results gives a probable year of felling in the interval 436 - 480 1σ (see Table 2). The interval is extended by the fact that the actual age of the tree is not certain, but even so the date is unusually precise.

Finds and Offerings
The fact that the total weight of all finds was just over 600 grams gives the impression that the houses had been carefully tidied. Most finds were made in the occupation layer, the fill in the eastern terrace and the layers outside the entrance. Among the finds in the occupational layer are two unidentified iron objects, burned bones, ceram-

ics, fragments of loom weights, burned clay (including some with the imprints of twigs that was presumably from the wattle and daub walls) and a glass shard. This latter, which measures only c. 1 x 2 centimetres, is green in colour with an on-laid glass thread in the same colour. The glass is of a fairly typical species which has been found repeatedly at wealthy settlements dating from the Migration Period (e.g. Helgö and Tuna in Alsike). The imported built-up layer mostly contained burned bones, but also some ceramic shards, while both burned bones, ceramics and resin caulking were found in the layer from the trench outside the entrance. Three of the shards had small decorative knobs on the rim.

The osteological assessment of the bones yielded a rather surprising result, with human bones identified in three contexts. One certain and two probable human bone fragments were identified in the stone construction around the eastern gable, fragments of human cranium were identified in layers outside the entrance and in the imported layer, and there were also fragments of dog jawbones in both of these layers. One explanation could be that the foundations are situated on an older burial ground with indistinct cremation graves, but there were no traces whatsoever of any activity on the site earlier than the construction of the houses. The closest graves (Raa 132 & 333), which have the appearance of being older than the house, are located c. 120 metres from the terrace, but they are easily visible and it is unlikely that the imported material could have been taken from the burial ground by accident. In addition, the sandy material that was used for the foundations of the houses can be found much closer to the house. Hence there are several indications that the human bones had been incorporated in the foundations intentionally.

Offerings of human origin are often said to be the most prestigious or powerful of all (see Carlie 2004), but the human material from the Alby house is not interpreted as an offering per se, which would imply that a human life had been taken, but as an action where the dead, possibly from an older grave context, were incorporated in the foundations. Since there is no known contemporary equivalent house offering in the area around Lake Mälar, the closest parallel is a Migration Period house at Brista, in the parish of Norrsunda, Upland, where a child was buried in a post-hole (Renck 2000). It is probable, however, that this burial had not taken place when the house was erected but directly after it had been destroyed by fire.

House offerings differ with regard to the building concerned and the milieu that it belongs to. What they have in common, however, is that they seem to represent an aspiration for prosperity, either for the household or for the kin or perhaps the region. This raises the question of the character of the Alby house. Through analogies with ethnographic material, the deposition of human bones can be seen as an expression of an ancestral cult and that the presence of the ancestors gave protection and blessing (Artelius 1999; Hardacre 1987).

METHODS

Sample Preparation

The soil samples were collected in a 2-metre grid system from a dark occupational layer c. 2-5 cm thick that cov-

ered more or less the full area of house 2. The layer had a homogeneous mineral composition and since the pattern of several nearby samples has a similarly deviant elemental composition, this is most probably explained by anthropogenic influences. Visible organic material such as roots and charcoal was removed. Samples were partially crushed with a pestle and mortar and subsequently sieved to obtain a particle size fraction of 0.07 mm - 0.5 mm. The potsherds were carefully collected during excavation and wrapped in aluminium foil. They were never handled with bare hands. All the samples were stored frozen until analysed.

Lipid Extraction and Derivatisation

A 1-3 g sample was ground off each potsherd after removing the outer millimetre in order to avoid contamination from the soil. 5 g of the same fraction as for the element analyses was analysed in the case of the soil samples. The lipids were extracted into a chloroform/methanol (2:1) solvent by sonification. with n-hexatriacontane (C36) added as an internal standard. Following centrifugation, the extracts were transferred to a vial and the solvent removed with a stream of nitrogen. The lipid residues were treated with bis(trimethylsilyl)triflouracetamide with 10% (v) chlorotrimethylsilane to produce trimethylsilyl derivatives and analysed by gas chromatography and mass spectrometry (GC-MS). The derivatisation and GC-MS parameters were the same for both soil lipids and lipids from the ceramics.

Gas Chromatography – Mass Spectrometry

The analysis was performed on a HP6890 Gas Chromatograph equipped with a SGE BPX5 capillary column (15 m x 220 µm x 0.25 µm). Injection took place by the pulsed splitless technique (pulse pressure 17.6 Psi) at 325°C through a Merlin Microseal™ High Pressure Septum. The oven was temperature-programmed with an initial isothermal of 2 min at 50°C per minute to 350°C, followed by a final isothermal of 15 min at this temperature. Helium was used as the carrier gas and kept at a constant flow of 2.0 ml per minute throughout the analysis.

The GC was connected to a HP5973 Mass Selective Detector via an interface with a constant temperature of 325°C. The compounds separated were fragmented by electronic ionisation (EI) at 70eV. The temperature at the ion source was 230°C, and the mass filter was set to scan between m/z 50 and 700, providing 2.29 scans per second.

The temperature of the mass filter was 150°C. The data were processed using the HP Chemstation™ software.

Atomic Absorption Spectrophotometry (AAS)

The elemental analyses were performed using a Z-5000 Polarized Zeeman AAS to determine the concentrations of calcium (Ca), copper (Cu), iron (Fe), potassium (K), magnesium (Mg), manganese (Mn) and zinc (Zn). For each sample 1 gram of soil was digested with 10 ml Aqua Regis (nitric acid : hydrochloric acid vv 1:3) in a MARSX microwave oven ramped for 20 minutes to 175°C and held there for 10 minutes. The samples were filtered and the filtrate diluted to 25 ml and then by a suitable factor depending on the element to be analysed. The concentrations in the solutions were measured and recalculated to concentrations in the soil, presented as parts per million (ppm).

Analysis of Lipids on the Ceramics

Unglazed pottery may adsorb lipids (fats, oils, waxes) from foods or other products stored or processed in them (see Evershed et al. 2001). The process by which lipid residues are formed is complex, and it may prove difficult to determine exactly what went into a pot (see Barnard et al. 2007). Lipids from pottery most probably represent the last or last few uses of a vessel (Craig et al. 2004). The composition of the lipid residues was employed to place the samples in a number of broad use classes based on the following assumptions. The presence of cholesterol is evidence of animal lipids and the detection of phytosterols, waxes or wax residues is indicative of plants (see Charters et al. 1997). A high ratio of C18:0 to C16:0 alkanoic acids (> c. 0.5) is a typical sign of a contribution from terrestrial animal lipids and a low ratio for plant or fish lipids. For the positive identification of milk and ruminant lipid residues the analysis of stable carbon isotopes of individual alkanoic acids ($\delta 13CC16:0 - \delta 13CC18:0$) by gas chromatography combustion isotope ratio mass spectrometry (GC-C-IRMS) should be used (Evershed et al. 2001), although the ratio of C17:0 branched-chained fatty acids to C18:0 straight-chained fatty acids may be used as an indication of the contribution of ruminant fat in general, including milk (cf. Dudd et al. 1999:1480). Analyses of stable carbon isotopes of individual alkanoic acids have been performed on a limited number of Iron Age potsherds from Sweden, and correlation of the C17:0branched /C18:0straight ratios with $\delta 13CC16:0 -$

$\delta 13CC18:0$ values shows that there are statistically significant close correlations between these measures (n = 6, r = 0.905, r2 = 0.820, t = 4.26, p = 0.013). There is a statistically significant difference (t=3.101, df=4, p=0.0362) in the C17:0branched /C18:0straight ratios between samples characterised as ruminant or milk (C17:0branched /C18:0straight ratio > 0.020) and samples characterised as non-ruminant (C17:0branched /C18:0straight ratio < 0.0077). Based on these observations the C17:0branched /C18:0straight ratio was used as a proxy variable for the isotopic data in this paper. Certain triunsaturated alkanoic acids (C16:3, C18:3, C20:3) are transformed to ω-(o-alkylphenyl)alkanoic acids when heated (Matikainen et al 2003:567f). C18 is an indication of plant oil, but together with C16 and C20 it denotes marine animal residues (Isaksson et al. 2005; Hansel et al. 2004; Olsson & Isaksson 2007). Heating can start reactions between free fatty acids that produce ketones, which thus serve as an indicator that the vessel has been used for cooking (Evershed et al. 1995).

All the shards from Alby showed traces of lipids of animal origin, either through the presence of cholesterol or a high C18:0/C16:0 ratio, often both of these indicators combined. The only exceptions were samples 9 and 15, where the ratio was not as evident, although cholesterol was identified on both shards. All the samples also had an input from plants, as indicated by phytosterols, wax residues and also phytanic acid in two samples. No traces of cooking or heating as indicated by ketones or ω-(o-alkylphenyl)alkanoic acids could be identified, but diterpenes and triterpenes in quantities that indicate smoke were found in 6 samples. The Alby material therefore shows a fairly homogeneous composition. All the samples contained lipids of both animal and vegetable origin, and in six cases there were indications that the animal fat was derived from ruminants. There were no traces of heating, suggesting that the vessels had been used as serving dishes rather than cooking vessels.

The pottery use classifications for Alby and the sites taken for the comparison are presented in Figure 5. There was a statistically significant difference in pottery use between Alby and each of the other sites when compared individually, as seen in Table 3. The main difference between Alby and Vendel is that no vessel from Alby had a purely vegetable content and that there was no indication of ruminant fat in the ceramics from Vendel. It is interesting, however, to see that when the samples from the

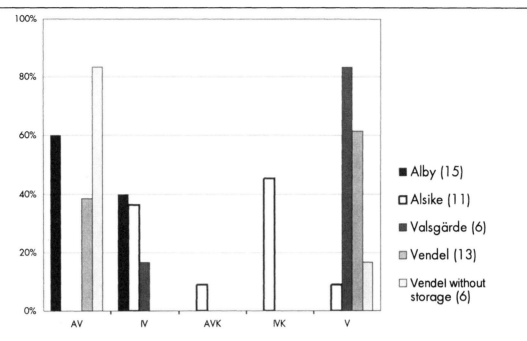

Figure 5. Bar-charts representing the percentage distribution of pottery use at four sites. The material is represented by 15 samples from Alby, 11 from Alsike, 6 from Valsgärde and 13 from Vendel. The samples from Vendel are shown both with and without the 7 samples from the storage area. A= Terrestrial animals; V=Vegetables; I=Ruminant animals; K=Cooking.

storage area in the house at Vendel are removed, there is no statistically significant difference between Alby and the central area of the Vendel house, which had been a dwelling area with the possible function of a hall or representational area. One major difference between Alby and Valsgärde is that Alby has many more vessels with traces of animal fat, although it has a lower percentage of vessels with ruminant fat than at Tuna. Also, the ceramics from Tuna often show traces of cooking. Hence Alby is distinguished by the presence of a relatively high amount of animal fat, but with no traces of cooking, and the fact that 9 of the 15 samples had indications of fat from non-ruminant animals.

Several statistically significant differences could be seen when Iron Age ceramics from burial contexts in the Mälar region (27 samples) were compared with ceramics from settlements (79 samples) (Forsgren 2007). The ceramics from the settlements had more often been used to cook or heat food ($\chi2=5.76$; df=1; p=0.016) and also included a higher proportion of vessels that contained lipids from agricultural products as their only contents and when meat was identified a larger number of the vessels contained lipids from ruminant animals (t-test on the C17:0branched/C18:0straigth ratio, t=2.895; df=69; p=0.005) (Forsgren 2007). Since the food in grave goods

more often contains animal fat than that recovered from settlements and has not been cooked in, the vessel use at Alby has more in common with ceramics from a ritualised context. The difference relative to the ceramics from the dwelling/representational area at Vendel is that those from Alby more often contain fat from non-ruminant animals.

GEOCHEMICAL ANALYSIS

Elemental Analysis

Elemental analysis of soil samples has been used for a long time to identify sites and to obtain space-use and activity interpretations for archaeological structures (e.g. Aston et al. 1998; Middleton & Price, 1996; Wells, 2000; Terry et al., 2004; Cook & Heizer, 1965; Konrad et al., 1983). Although the elemental signature of several activities can be foreseen, it is difficult to connect the result to a specific activity (Middleton 2004). These analyses are nevertheless often successful in identifying different areas of activity, which in itself is of great interest in a house such as the one at Alby, where no other traces of space-use could be seen. The possibilities for identifying the activities increase when this approach is combined with lipid analysis, for instance.

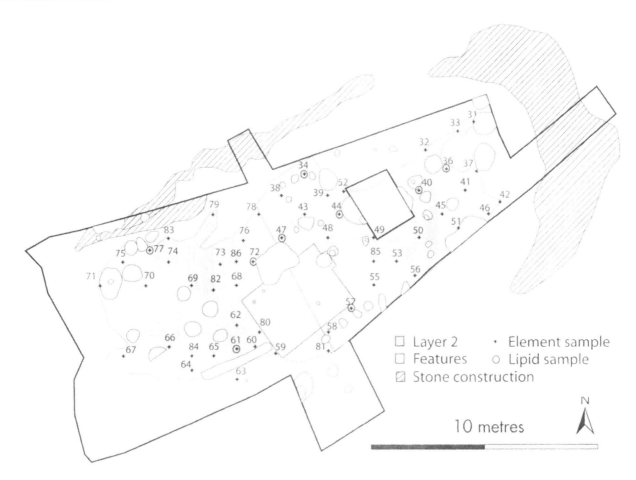

Figure 6. Sampling and extent of the occupational layer (layer 2).

The results are presented in the form of isopleth maps in Figure 7 , in addition to which a data set with standardized values for all samples and elements was used for a principal component analysis. The first two principal components (PCs) account for 63% of the total variance. The factor loadings are shown in Table 4. Factor 1 is mainly influenced by depleted K, Ca and Mn and enhanced Mg, while the two major features bringing about a high factor 2 are enhanced Zn and Cu. The first two PCs for each sample are plotted in Figure 8, on the basis of which the samples can be grouped into three larger clusters, mainly by reference to factor 1. An isopleth for the factor 1 loadings is shown in Figure 7, and the distribution of the cluster from the PCA in Figure 9. Some space-use areas with internally similar elemental compositions can be distinguished on the basis of the isopleths, as shown in Figure 10. The space-use area 2 traverses the hypothetical rooms 1 and 2, space-use area 3 traverses rooms 2 and 3, and space-use area 5 traverses rooms 2, 3 and 4. These are strong indications that at least rooms 2, 3 and 4 constituted one open space, although separated into a number of space-use categories which are not related to the room division. The box and whisker chart in Figure 11 shows the mean and standard deviation for each element in each space-use area. The elements with enhanced values in area 3 are Ca, Fe, K, Zn and Mn, while Mg is depleted (see Figures 10 and 11). Area 3 and area 4 are rather similar, the only difference being that area 4 has lower Zn and Mn values and somewhat higher Fe. In area 5, K is depleted while Mg is enhanced. Area 6 consists of only two samples, which detracts from the significance of the mean and standard deviation statistics. The samples in area 6 have enhanced Cu values but are otherwise rather similar to those in area 5.

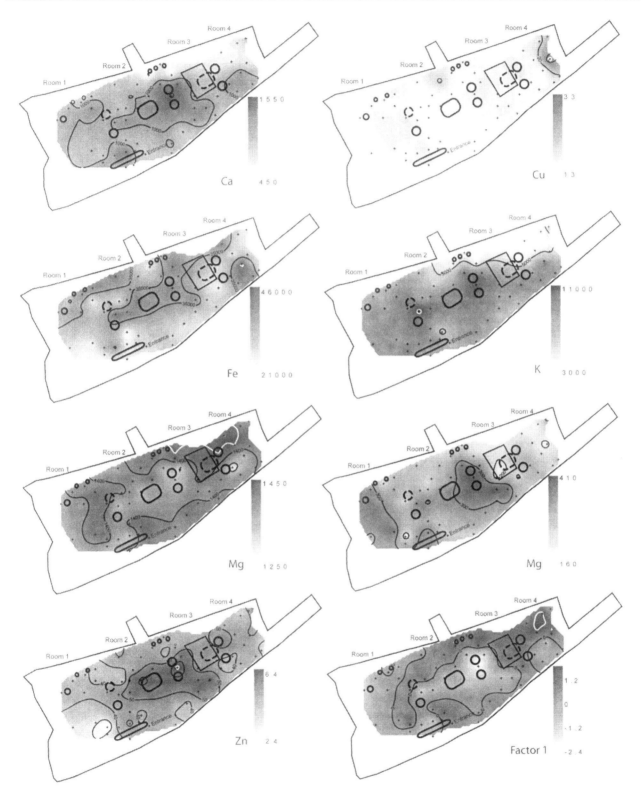

Figure 7. Variations in Ca, Cu, Fe, K, Mg, Mn and Zn content across the occupational layer. Factor 1 plan show the scores for the first principal component in PCA as an isopleth. (obs several figures, included separately for now).

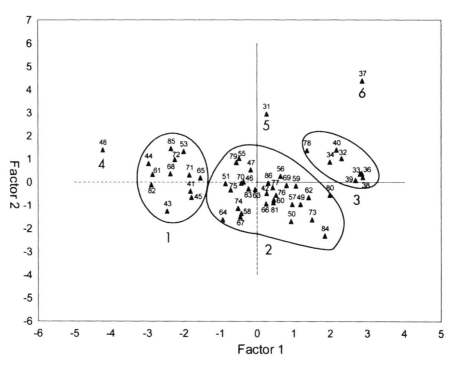

Figure 8. Scatter plot of the PCA results for all elements.

Although there are several pitfalls when elemental analyses are used to deduce activities and not only space use, as mentioned above, we should still consider what can be seen in the areas identified here. Apart from somewhat enhanced Mn, the elemental values in room 1 are not uniform and the room probably did not have any restricted function or activity. The doorways and entrances, which will have suffered more wear and tear, and repeatedly have low concentrations of chemical residues, due to erosion (Barba 2007, Middleton 2004). This can be observed to some extent for the proposed entrance to room 2 in the Alby house, except for Mg, which is clearly elevated at the entrance. Wood-ash is rich in K, as a function of the uptake of this element by plants, and the archaeological significance of Ca should be more or less the same, as plants also take up large amounts of Ca. K combined with Mg has been used to identify areas with hearths (Middleton & Price 1996), and iIn a recent study enhanced K proved to be indicative of a stable (Hjulström & Isaksson, manuscript). When Ca accompanies K, as in areas 3 and 4, wood ash is a more likely source, but Mg is depleted in these areas , suggesting either a different origin for the enhanced K and Ca rather than ash from a hearth, or an activity that deposited a high amount of Mg

in areas 2, 5 and 6 making the relative Mg value less in areas 3 and 4. Since K is depleted in area 5, a source other than ash accumulating along the walls must explain the enhanced Mg. Hence, the composition must depend on other parameters besides the hearth. The clearly divergent elemental values in area 5 cannot be given any clear-cut explanation.

The floor layer may have been affected as a result of benches or other constructions along the wall, or else some more restrictive use may have been made of the area furthest away from the entrance. Fe and Zn are abundant in meat and Mn is abundant in cereals, hence these elements can be seen as general indicators of food. All of them are elevated in area 3. The areas at the gables, area 1 and area 6, respectively, should probably be seen as refuse 'traps' where it has been difficult to tidy organic material away, resulting in divergent elemental values. As seen, even though some spatial differentiation can be seen, it is hard to identify specific activities from the elemental composition of the floor layer in the house.

Lipid analysis
The internal relations between the three predominant long-chained fatty acids (FA) in each sample are shown in

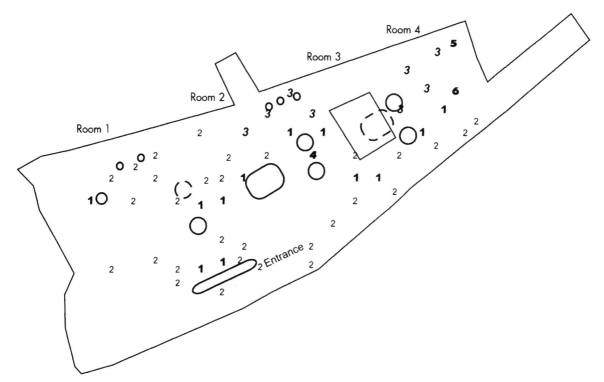

Figure 9. Plan of the distribution of samples falling into different clusters in the scatter plot (Figure 8).

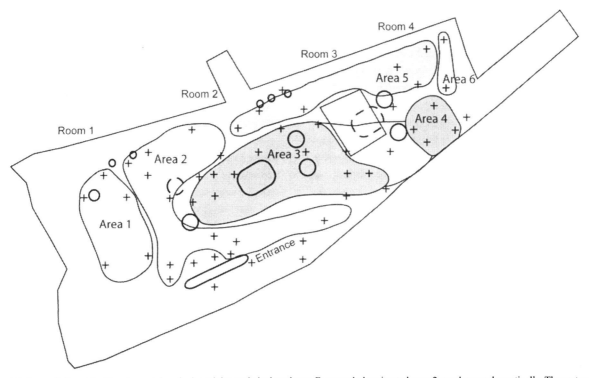

Figure 10. Areas distinguished by elemental analysis and the statistical analyses. Features belonging to house 2 are shown schematically. The rectangular feature shown with a broken line in room 3 is the partly excavated hearth.

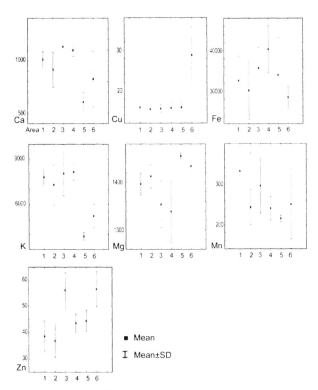

Figure 11. Box and whisker plots of mean values and standard deviations
for the element concentrations in the space-use areas.

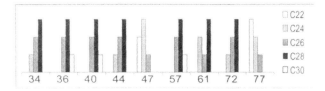

Figure 12. The three dominant long-chained fatty acids in each soil
sample.

Figure 12. In seven of the nine samples from Alby are the
C28 FA predominate, followed by C26. In an unpublished
study we analysed reference soils from different vegeta-
tional surroundings in the Tyresta National Park, south of
Stockholm, where land use during historical times is well
documented. The FA distribution in the samples from
Alby corresponds best to the references from a decidu-
ous forest with grass undergrowth. In two of the samples
(47, 77), C24 and C22 respectively, were dominant, and
these samples are more similar to the reference samples
taken in a coniferous forest, where C22 FA was dominant,
followed by C24, in six out of eight cases. Traces of dehy-
droabietic acid, which is widely used as a conifer biomar-
ker and is stable over geological time periods (Simoneit
1986), could be detected in all the samples from Alby.
Hence one of the conclusions from the lipid analysis is
that the long-chained FA distribution reflects the present
vegetation, which is dominated by sparsely growing de-
ciduous trees, such as oak and hazel, with some grass undergrowth and occasional pinaceae growing nearby.

Traces of manuring (Allard, 2006; Jandl et al. 2005;
van Bergen et al. 1997; Wiesenberg et al. 2004) and stab-

ling (Hjulström & Isaksson, manuscript) have repeatedly
been identified in soil analyses by studying coprostanol
and related compounds (see Eneroth et. al 1964; Leeming
et. al. 1996). Since we could not detect coprostanol or any
related compounds in the samples from Alby, it must be
said that there are no traces of stabling in the house.

Previous studies have identified specific activities
using certain markers and ratios with diagnostic relevance. Culinary areas, for instance, have been identified
through the analysis of sterols and their corresponding
5α-stanol (Isaksson 1998). In a study of a reconstructed Iron Age house (Hjulström & Isaksson, manuscript)
we were able to distinguish a dwelling and a dwelling/
cooking area based on the sterol ratio (cholesterol/[stig-
masterol + β-sitosterol + campesterol]), as this ratio was
not only enhanced around the hearth, where cooking had
taking place, but in the whole dwelling area, showing
that spilling had also contributed to the sterol composition. Hence the ratio is not a marker of a specific activity
such as food preparation, but a result of a more intensive
use resulting in general debris from everyday activities,
including food consumption. As individual compounds,
stearic (C18) and palmitic (C16) fatty acids are not sour-
ce-specific. Biohydrogenation of the more abundant C18
unsaturated fatty acids causes the ratio of C18/C16 fatty
acids to shift and this ratio can thus be used for geochemical source apportionment studies. In a study of surface
soil and fugitive dust from open lot dairies and cattle
feedlots, significant differences in the C18/C16 ratio were
recognized, ranging from 0.2 in the reference samples to
3 in the soils from the dairies and feedlots (Rogge et al.
2006). Our assertion with regard to the use of the C18/
C16 ratio is that it may also be affected by other forms of
organic input.

The sterol ratio and C18/C16 ratio results are shown
in Table 5. The samples with a higher proportion of cholesterol are fairly well concentrated in the house (see Fig.
12) and correlate with the cluster 1 samples in the PCA,
being centrally located in area 3. Three of the four samp-

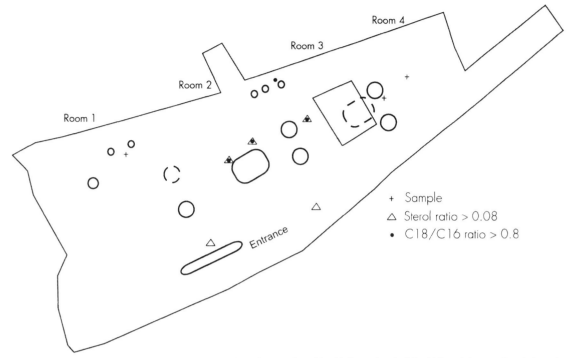

Figure 13. Plan of sterol ratios and C18/C16 ratios in the samples. The samples with a high sterol ratio fall within activity area 2 and along the southern wall, and those with a high C18/C16 ratio have a similar distribution, 3 out of 4 being in activity area 2.

les with the highest C18/C16 ratio are the same as those with a high sterol ratio, coinciding with high Fe and Zn values. Moreover, the samples with a high C18/C16 ratio are centrally located, showing a pattern that must be explained by the activities that have taken place in the house. The central area 3 was the most intensively used, and the activities that took place there have resulted in a sterol ratio and a C18/C16 ratio similar to reference samples from dwelling and food preparation areas. Since the ceramic analysis nevertheless shows that no evidence of food preparation can be seen in the house, the lipid ratios may be the result of spillage from the eating and serving of food in areas 3 and 4.

Feasting (with the Ancestors - for the Offspring)
The placing of human bones in the foundations of the house is an unusual form of offering for this time and region. We regard this desire to include the ancestors in the house as being intimately connected with its function and purpose. Houses located on a crest, creating a plateau-like position, are well-known from the Iron Age (Hedman 1991), even though few similar Migration Period buildings have been excavated. We do not, therefore, consider this building and it finds to be unique. In-

stead, it is possible that the results show that there was a division among the houses classified as hall buildings and that this type of house had been built for a particular purpose.

As mentioned above, Raa 131 is centrally located in the parish, and is surrounded by graves and burial grounds in all directions. Finds that probably belong to a late Bronze Age or Pre-Roman Iron Age settlement have been reported in the clayey field west of Raa 132, and it is possible that there was a farm located on the clay land that surrounds Raa 131 during the Roman Iron Age as well, although there are no visible remains of a settlement from any period in the nearby till soils. In terms of the location of a historically known farm or visible traces of earlier farms one cannot connect Raa 131 or its house with any specific farm.

Other known house terraces in the parish are of a more common type and probably represent dwelling houses, although prominent ones and possibly combined with a representational or ritual function, while Raa 131 is the only one of its kind in the parish. It may be that the building did not belonging to one single farm but was of importance for several of the farms and hamlets that surrounded it.

The space-use areas that could be discerned from the elemental analysis suggest that there was a large open space (sal) in the house that was not divided by internal walls. As indicated by the sterol ratio and elemental composition, some spillage from eating may have occurred on either side of the hearth in areas 3 and 4. It is not possible, of course, to discuss the form and context in which the eating took place based only on the sterol ratio, but when the results of the excavations and the conclusions regarding vessel use are considered together, it is very possible that activities that included the consumption of food of cultural significance took place in the house. The exclusivity of the vessel use, for the serving of food with a high proportion of meat (especially from non-ruminant animals), demonstrates a close affinity to the ritual sphere. According to the general conception of Iron Age gastronomy, the food culture recognized in this Alby house could be interpreted as related to rituals or feasting, or both, since no clear-cut distinction can be made between

the two. The glass beaker and the feasting in the hall allude to the famous description of how Queen Waltheow received Beowulf in the great hall of Heorot (612-630).

"Wealtheow came in, Hrothgar's queen, observing the courtesies. Adorned in her gold, she graciously saluted the men in hall, then handed the cup first to Hrothgar, their homeland's guardian, urging him to drink deep and enjoy it because he was dear to them. And he drank it down like the warlord he was, with festive cheer. So the Helming woman went on her rounds, queenly and dignified, decked out in rings, offering the goblet to all ranks, treating the household and the assembled troop until it was Beowulf's turn to take it from her hand. With measured words she welcomed the Geat and thanked God for granting her wish that a deliverer she could believe in would arrive to ease their afflictions. He accepted the cup, a daunting man, dangerous in action and eager for it always" (Transl. Heaney 1999).

LITERATURE

Allard, B., 2006. A comparative study on the chemical composition of humic acids from forest soil, agricultural soil and lignite deposit: Bound lipid, carbohydrate and amino acid distributions. Geoderma 130, pp 77-96.

Ambrosiani, B., 1964. Fornlämningar och bebyggelse. Studier i Attundalands och Södertörns förhistoria. (KVHAA). Stockholm.

Artelius, T., 1999. Den döde vid dörren. Reflektioner kring förfäderskult utifrån fynd av människoben i två halländska långhus från järnåldern. Kring västsvenska hus. Boendets organisation och symbolik i förhistorisk tid (eds. L. Ersgård, E. Englund and T. Artelius). Göteborg.

Aston, M. A., Martin, M. H. & Jackson, A. W., 1998. The use of heavy metal soil analysis for archaeological surveying. Chemosphere 37, pp 465-477.

Barba, L., 2007. Chemical residues in lime-plastered archaeological floors. Geoarchaeology 22(4): pp 439-452.

Barnard, H., Ambrose, S. H., Beehr, D. E., Forster, M. D., Lanehart, R. E., Malainey, M. E., Parr, R. E., Rider, M., Solazzo, C. & Yohe II, R. M., 2007. Mixed results of seven methods for organic residue analysis applied to one vessel with the residue of a known foodstuff. Journal of Archaeological Science 34, pp 28-37.

Bratt, P. & Werthwein, G., 1999. Hallen i Skrävsta. Arkeologisk för- och delundersökning av fornlämning 36, Botkyrka socken och kommun, Södermanland. Rapport Stockholms läns museum 1999:16. Stockholm.

Bennett, A., 1972. Gravfält och fynd från järnåldern: en kort översikt över 1970-1971 års utgrävningar i Botkyrka. Fornvännen 3-4, pp 239-254.

Bennett, A., 1987. Graven - religiös och social symbol: Strukturer i folkvandringstidens gravskick i Mälarområdet. Theses and papers in North-European archaeology 18. Stockholm.

Van Bergen, P. F., Bull, I. D., Poulton, P. R. & Evershed, R. P., 1997. Organic geochemical studies of soils from the Rothamsted Classical Experiments - I. Total lipid extracts, solvent insoluble residues and humic acids from Broadbalk Wilderness. Organic Geochemistry 117-135.

Brink, S., 1996. Political and Social Structures in Early Scandinavia. A Settlement - historical Pre-study of the Central Place. TOR 28, pp 235-281.

Bronk Ramsey, C., van der Plicht, J., & Weninger, B., 2001. 'Wiggle matching' radiocarbon dates. Radiocarbon 43 (2A), pp 381-389.

Carlie, A., 2004. Forntida byggnadskult: Tradition och regionalitet i södra Skandinavien. Arkeologiska undersökningar, skrifter, 57. Stockholm.

Charters, S., Evershed, R. P., Quye, A., Blinkhorn, P. & Reeves, V., 1997. Simulation experiments for determining the use of ancient pottery vessels: the behaviour of epicuticular leaf wax during boiling of leafy vegetable. Journal of Archaeological Science 24, pp 1-7.

Cook, S. F. & Heizer, R. R., 1965. Studies on chemical analysis of archaeological sites. University of California Publications in Anthropology No. 2, Berkeley.

Craig, O. E., Love, G. D., Isaksson, S., Taylor, G. & Snape, C. E., 2004. Stable carbon isotopic characterisation of free and bound lipid constituents of archaeological ceramic vessels released by solvent extraction, alkaline hydrolysis and catalytic hydropyrolysis. Journal of Analytical and Applied Pyrolysis 71, pp 613-634.

Dudd, S. N., Evershed, R. P. & Gibson, A., M., 1999. Evidence for Varying Patterns of Exploitation of Animal Products in Different Prehistoric Pottery Traditions Based on Lipids Preserved in Surface and Absorbed Residues. Journal of Archaeological Science 26, pp 1473-1482.

Eneroth, P. K., Hellstrom, K. & Rhyage, R., 1964. Identification and quantification of neutral fecal steroids by gas-liquid chromatography and mass-spectrometry: studies of human excretion during two dietary régimes. Journal of Lipid Research 5, pp 245-262.

Enright, M. J., 1996. Lady with a mead cup. Ritual, property and landship in the European warband from La tène to the Viking Age. Four Courts Press, Dublin.

Evershed, R. P., Stott, A. W., Raven, A., Dudd, S. N., Charters, S. & Leyden, A., 1995. Formation of Long-Chain Ketones in Ancient Pottery Vessels By Pyrolysis of Acyl Lipids. Tetrahedron Letters 36, pp 8875-8878.

Evershed, R.P., Dudd, S.N., Lockheart, M.J. & Jim, S., 2001. Lipids in archaeology. Handbook of Archaeological Science. (Eds. D.R. Brothwell & A.M. Pollard), Wiley, cop(??), Chichester.

Forsgren, A., 2007. Dödsgott med käk i kistan. Graduate thesis. Archaeological Research Laboratory, Stockholm University.

Hansel, F. A., Copley, M. S., Madureira, L. A. S. & Evershed, R. P., 2004. Thermally produced [omega]-(o-alkylphenyl)alkanoic acids provide evidence for the processing of marine products in archaeological pottery vessels. Tetrahedron Letters 45, pp 2999-3002.

Hardacre, H., 1987. Ancestors: ancestor worship. The Encyclopedia of Religion, Vol. 1, (ed. M. Eliade). Macmillan. New York.

Heaney, S. 1999. Beowulf. A new translation. Faber and Faber limited. London.

Herschend, F., 1997. Livet i hallen. Occasional Papers in Archaeology 14. Uppsala.

Herschend, F., 2001. Journey of civilisation. The late Iron Age view of the human world. Occasional Papers in Archaeology 24. Uppsala.

Hjulström, B., 2006. Arkeologisk förundersökning inom fastighet Botkyrka-Alby 15:32, RAÄ 131. Rapporter från Arkeologiska forskningslaboratoriet 5. Stockholm.

Hjulström, B. & Isaksson, S., 2005. Tidevarv i Tuna. Arkeologiska undersökningar i Tuna by, Alsike sn, Uppland. Rapporter från Arkeologiska forskningslaboratoriet 3. Stockholm.

Hyenstrand, Å., 1974. Central settlement - outlying districts: Principal structural, economic and administrative features in the late Iron Age in Middle Sweden. Studies in North-European archaeology 5. Malung.

Isaksson, S., 1998. A kitchen entrance to the aristocracy - analysis of lipid biomarkers in cultural layers. Laborativ Arkeologi 10-11, pp 43-53.

Isaksson, S., 2000. Food and rank in early medieval time. Theses and Papers in Scientific Archaeology 3. Stockholm.

Isaksson, S. 2000b. The culture of food in Early Medieval Middle Sweden. A pottery use perspective. Food and rank in early medieval time (Ed. Isaksson, S). Theses and Papers in Scientific Archaeology 3. Stockholm

Isaksson, S., 2003. Vild vikings vivre. Fornvännen 2003:4, pp 271-288.

Isaksson, S., Olsson, M. & Hjulström, B., 2005. De smorde sina krås. Spår av vegetabilisk olja i keramik från yngre järnålder. Fornvännen 2005:3, pp 179-191.

Jandl, G., Leinweber, P., Schulten, H.-R. & Ekschmitt, K., 2005. Contribution of primary organic matter to the fatty acid pool in agricultural soils. Soil Biology and Biochemistry 37, pp 1033-1041.

Konrad, V. A., Bonnichsen, R. & Clay, V., 1983. Soil chemical identification of ten thousand years of prehistoric human activity areas at the Munsungun lake thoroughfare, Maine. Journal of Archaeological Science 10, pp 13-28.

Leeming, R., Ball, A., Ashbolt, N. & Nichols, P., 1996. Using faecal sterols from humans and animals to distinguish faecal pollution in receiving waters. Water Research 30, pp. 2893-2900.

Lönnroth, L., (1997) Hövdingahallen i fornnordisk myt och saga. "...gick Grendel att söka det höga huset..." Arkeologiska källor till aristokratiska miljöer i Skandinavien under yngre järnålder. Rapport från ett seminarium i Falkenberg 16-17 november 1995. (eds. J. Callmer & E. Rosengren). Halmstad.

Matikainen, J., Kaltia, S., Ala-Peijari, M., Petit-Gras, N., Harju, K., Heikkilä, J., Yksjärvi, R. & Hase, T., 2003. A study of 1,5-hydrogen shift and cyclization reactions of an alkali isomerized methyl linolenoate. Tetrahedron 59, 567-573.

Middleton, W. D. & Price. D. T., 1996. Identification of activity areas by multi-element characterization of sediments from modern and archaeological house floors using inductively coupled plasma - atomic emission spectroscopy. Journal of Archaeological Science 23: pp 673-687.

Middleton, W. D., 2004. Identifying chemical activity residues on prehistoric house floors: A methodology and rationale for multi-elemental characterization of a mild acid extract of anthropogenic sediments. Archaeometry 46: pp 47-65.

Nerman, B., 1961. Till vilken ätt ha de stora gravhögarna vid Norsborg i Botkyrka socken hört? Fornvännen 2-3, pp. 97-109.

Norr, S., 1997. (Ed.) Rapport från utgrävningarna i Valsgärde. Svealand i Vendel och vikingatid. Uppsala.

Olsson, M. & Isaksson, S., 2007. Molecular and isotopic traces of cooking and consumption of fish at an Early Medieval manor site in eastern middle Sweden. Journal of Archaeological Science, doi:10.1016/j.jas.2007.06.009

Renck, A. M. 2000. Den helgade marken: ritualen som dokument. Människors platser (ed. L. Ersgård). Stockholm.

Rogge, W. F., Medeiros, P. M. & Simoneit, B. R. T., 2006. Organic marker compounds for surface soil and fugitive dust from open lot dairies and cattle feedlots. Atmospheric Environment 40, pp 27-49.

Schützler, L., 1996. Arkeologisk fosfatkartering, provundersökning och delundersökning: Ett boplatskomplex från yngre brons- och järnålder vid Eriksbergs industriområde, Södermanland, Botkyrka socken, Tumba 7:2, Eriksberg 2:1, RAÄ 108, 331. Rapport UV-Stockholm, Vol. 1996:87.

Simoneit, B. R. T., 1986. Cyclic terpenoids of the geosphere. Methods in Geochemistry and Geophysics 24.

Sundqvist, O., 2002. Freyr´s offspring. Rulers and religion in ancient Svea society. Acta Universitatis Uppsaliensis. Historia Religionum 21. Uppsala.

Söderberg, B., 2005. Aristokratiskt rum och gränsöverskridande. Riksantikvariämbetet, Arkeologiska undersökningar, Skrifter No 62.

Terry, R. E., Fernandez, F. G., Parnell, J. J. & Inomata, T., 2004. The story in the floors: chemical signatures of ancient and modern Maya activities at Aguateca, Guatemala. Journal of Archaeological Science 31, pp 1237-1250.

Wells, C. E., Terry, R. E., Parnell, J. J., Hardin, P. J., Jackson, M. W. & Houston, S. D., 2000. Chemical Analyses of Ancient Anthrosols in Residential Areas at Piedras Negras, Guatemala. Journal of Archaeological Science 27, pp 449-462.

Wiesenberg, G. L. B., Schwarzbauer, J., Schmidt, M. W. I. & Schwark, L., 2004. Source and turnover of organic matter in agricultural soils derived from n-alkane/n-carboxylic acid compositions and C-isotope signatures. Organic Geochemistry 35, pp 1371-1393.

Authors' adresses
The Archaeological Research Laboratory, Stockholm University, SE 10691 Stockholm, SWEDEN bjorn.hjulstrom@arklab.su.se

TABLES

C14 labnr	Annual ring	Result BP	Sigma 1	Sigma 2
Ua-34166	1-3	1675 - 30	340-415	250-430
Ua-34167	22-26	1685 - 30	260-280; 330-410	250-430
Ua-34168	57-60	1570 - 30	430-540	420-560
Trädets egenålder uppskattat till 70-90				

Table 1. Radiocarbon dates for three annual rings in one of the carbonised posts. Calibrated according to Stuiver et al. (1998).

Felling date Posterior if 70 year		Felling date Posterior if 90 year	
Sigma 1	Sigma 2	Sigma 1	Sigma 2
436 - 460 AD	423 - 472 AD	456 - 480 AD	443 - 492 AD

Table 2. Wiggle-matching of the tree-ring sequence (Bronk Ramsey et al. 2001).

	Degrs. of Freedom	Max. Lik. Chi-squ.	Probab. p	Pearson Chi-squ	Probab. p
Vendel vs Alby	2	15.67	0.0004	13.25	0.00133
Valsgärde vs Alby	2	14.68	0.00065	13.98	0.00092
Tuna vs Alby	4	15.89	0.00317	13.71	0.00827
Vendel without storage vs Alby	2	4.25	0.11971	3.88	0.14371

Table 3. Results of $\chi 2$ tests of pottery use distributions.

Factor loadings		
Variable	Factor 1	Factor 2
K	-0.797	-0.356
Ca	-0.911	-0.022
Mg	0.892	0.047
Mn	-0.705	0.148
Fe	0.36	0.221
Zn	-0.375	0.777
Cu	0.175	0.738
Variation	43.7%	19.3%

Table 4. Factor loadings for the two most influential factors in the PCA.

Sample	Sterol ratio	C18/C16
34	0.06	1.04
36	0.04	0.58
40	0.05	0.55
44	0.15	0.97
47	0.10	0.85
57	0.08	0.66
61	0.10	0.70
72	0.08	0.98
77	0.05	0.05

Table 5. Sterol ratios and C18/C16 ratios for the nine soil lipid samples.

Acta Archaeologica vol. 79, 2008, pp 79-109
Printed in Denmark • All rights reserved

Copyright 2008
ACTA ARCHAEOLOGICA
ISSN 0065-101X

TÆBRING, NW DENMARK, AD 600-1100
AN ARCHAEOLOGICAL AND ARCHAEOBOTANIC STUDY

POUL MIKKELSEN, ANNINE S.A. MOLTSEN & SØREN M. SINDBÆK[1]

He came to a hall,
a door was up, on the lintel,
In he stepped,
a fire was on the floor ...

In the poem Rigsþula, preserved in the poetic Edda, we learn of Rig's (Wodan's) visits to the house of a yeoman. Entering the dwelling, Rig found the owners, Afi and Amma, occupied with household tasks: The man carving wood for the weaving-beam, the woman spinning yarn. Unlike the thralls, whose hut Rig had just left, the couple was well clad. Still, they had no wide south-facing portal and strewn floor as in the earl's hall, for which Rig was eventually heading; and their guest was not entertained as there with fresh game, roasted fowl and wine in pitcher on a clothed table. He was seated in the midst of the room and was served a sturdy dish of boiled veal (Dronke 1997 165f).

This brief scene, written down in 13th-century Iceland but arguably composed in the 10th Century, has long remained as useful a picture of late Iron Age housing in Scandinavia, as any supplied by archaeology.

Between 1999 and 2003, parts of an unusual settlement dating to the 7th –11th centuries AD were uncovered at Tæbring on the island Mors in the Western Limfjord, North West Denmark. A number of unusual features were investigated, amongst them iron-smelting furnaces, and turf-walled buildings. But the most remarkable structures were uncovered beneath the collapsed walls of the turf buildings: hearths, ovens, a cellar, stone paving, wall-benches, and clay floors from several older houses. Associated with this were cultural layers containing artefacts as well as rich archaeobotanic evidence: seeds, husks, chaff, and sprigs. All this gives an exceptional opportunity to describe the interior of dwellings from the Late Iron Age – the Merovingian and Viking periods – to a level of contextual detail rarely reached before. The aim of this article is to present an inter-disciplinary analysis of the three best-preserved buildings of the site.

The analysis will demonstrate that the basic domestic unit at this site from the 7th century onwards was a two-room structure, sometimes combined with more rooms in the same building. The functional distinction between the two basic rooms seems to fit with the distinction between salhus and ildhus known in the earliest Danish law texts from the 13th Century. The observations imply that some kitchen activities were moved out of the central living room as early as by the 7th century – a transformation hitherto assumed not to have occurred in Scandinavia before the Late Viking Age.

HOUSING IN SOUTH SCANDINAVIA IN THE LATE IRON AGE

Over the past generation, Scandinavian Late Iron Age longhouses have become familiar structures. In Denmark alone, their remains have now been examined at more than 250 sites, nine tenth of which were investigated within the last 25 years. Yet, as regards the inner organization of the buildings, the increasing number of excavations has added little to our knowledge. In the bulk of sites investigated in later years (mostly as rescue excavations), buildings were preserved only in the shape of post-holes and sometimes wall-trenches.

1 *Acknowledgements.* The present investigation was made possible by a generous donation from Queen Margrethe the II's Archaeological Foundation. The excavations in Tæbring (MHM 1335) were financed by the Danish Council of Cultural Heritage and Morsland Historical Museum.

More information is supplied almost exclusively by a few early investigations, e.g. Aggersborg (Schultz 1949; Roesdahl 1986, 64ff), Sædding (Stoumann 1980, 106ff), and Omgård (Nielsen 1980, 184). In Norway and Sweden, as well as in Denmark, Late Iron Age housing is poorly illuminated as compared to the Early Iron Age (e.g. Schmidt 1994; Myhre 1980, 370; 2000, 37; Göthberg, Kyhlberg & Vinberg 1995). From the 12th century onwards, we begin to get better evidence, as in Tårnby or Kyrkheddinge (Kristiansen 1998; Sabo 2001). Between these examples, the Late Iron Age houses known so far stand out as mere shells, the spatial and social structure of which remains hidden. Therefore, the unusually well-preserved houses excavated in the North Atlantic islands, e.g. Stöng in Iceland, Toftanes in the Faroese Islands or Unst in Shetland, have often served as illustrations of the building customs of the Viking period (e.g. Águstsson 1982; Hansen 1991, 2000). However, excavations have long since shown the North Atlantic buildings to be anything but true copies of those in the Viking homelands.

Customs and conventions of housing are essential to the understanding of any culture or society. Domestic space is a medium through which people may constitute and negotiate principles of order and classification, general cosmological categories, relations of status and gender, or relations between individuals in a group (Parker Pearson & Richards 1994, 40). In a well-worn phrase, the spatial order of houses is medium and outcome of the daily practices they provide the setting for, and recursively structure (Giddens 1984, 25).

In keeping with the available evidence, the study of Late Iron Age houses long remained a field concerned with the useful basics of understanding constructional details (Schultz 1949; Olsen & Schmidt 1977; Schmidt 1994). As the material basis grew, researchers became occupied with the equally indispensable task of constructing typological and chronological schemes (Myhre 1982; Hansen, Hvasss & Mikkelsen 1991; Tesch 1993; Jørgensen & Eriksen 1995; Skov 1995; Göthberg et al. (eds.) 1995). A social perspective on Late Iron Age and medieval housing was introduced early (e.g. Stenberger 1943; Steensberg 1952), and has to some extend been sustained (Myhre et al. 1982). But as significant new evidence is almost absent, even recent contributions remain visibly restrained (Samson 1990; Price 1995; Artelius, Englund & Ersgård (eds.) 1999; Mikkelsen 2003). Our problems begin at the level of seemingly trivial features. Wall-benches along the walls have been identified in a number of buildings. But were they simply seats or bedsteads, or perhaps semi-independent rooms? Remains of central fireplaces are commonly interpreted as open hearths, but ovens are also testified. Was the long-fire indeed a staple feature of Late Iron Age living rooms? Not infrequently, several hearths occur in the same building. Were they separate arrangements for heating, cooking, and perhaps for crafts? How did individual rooms communicate?

Ethnologists pose questions as to the organization of domestic practices from different perspectives. It has been noted that words documented in 13th-century law-texts and assumed on etymological grounds to have first designated the integrated family room of the Iron Age farm, the ildhus ('fire house') or salhus ('hall') have lived on in Danish dialects as a name for the kitchen and the main farmhouse respectively. It is commonly assumed that this change of meaning happened when the stue ('sitting-room') was introduced as a separate room for residence and representation, expelling other domestic activities to separate rooms (Stoklund 2003, 20). Did this transformation occur in the early medieval period, or was it already introduced in the Viking Age?

Generally, in previous research Late Iron Age long-houses have been considered either a setting of domestic activities or a scene of social representation. The first perspective is prominent in archaeobotanic and geochemical studies (e.g. Viklund 1998; Isaksson 1998; Isaksson, Wojnar & Hjulström 2000; Hansson 2003). The second perspective has appeared almost exclusively in discussions of the great chieftains' halls (e.g. Christensen 1993; Lundqvist 1996; 1997; Herschend 1997; Jørgensen 2003; Herschend & Mikkelsen 2003; Söderberg 2005). Though the two aspects are essentially complimentary, they have tended to conduct ideas into very different orbits.

Approach and presentation must have been important on formal occasions even to the common yeoman. Yet, little attention has been paid to the representational aspect of more ordinary farms. All housing provide the setting of both 'economic' and 'symbolic' practices. Houses can be arranged to respond to this need, e.g. by dividing space into presentable 'front' and out-of-sight 'back' regions (cf. Parker Pearson & Richards 1994, 51f). How would an ordinary Late Iron Age residence in South Scandinavia present itself to someone approaching it the 'right way'? What rooms would be encountered as one was received – and what would remain hidden to the eye of the visitor?

The large crofts of Late Iron Age farms in South Scandinavia have normally left very faint cultural layers that has long since been destroyed by ploughing. However, in the coastlands and islands of the Western Limfjord, Late Iron Age settlements with dense cultural layers have been encountered on several occasions. In these areas, turf was employed from the 11th century as an insulating material for outer walls. After the abandonment of the houses, material from the heavy walls sealed and protected the floors. Moreover, turf was used in the medieval period for fertilizing fields, sometimes sealing the remains of earlier settlements under metres of accumulated topsoil. Tæbring belongs among these settlements.

THE TÆBRING INVESTIGATION

With its 362 square kilometres, Mors is the largest island in the Limfjord (Fig. 1). It is mentioned by Adam of Bremen in c. 1075. In sharp contrast to the almost riverlike eastern part of the Limfjord, the western part is characterised by much more open waters. Mors is surrounded by four narrow straits alternating with more open waters. The coastline of the island varies considerably. Some parts, for instance the major part of the northern coastline, is characterised by steep slopes, while the rest of the coastline has steep slopes varying with a much more open coast with forelands, capes, and bays.

The importance of the Limfjord in the Merovingian and Viking periods can hardly be overestimated. It connected the North Sea area with the inner Danish waters and played an important part in the local and interregional exchange of goods. The topography of the Western Limfjord made it suitable for the gathering of the fleets that set out for raids on the British Isles and later maintained the connections between Denmark and England. Some of these events are known from written sources, and the obvious royal interest in the area has been accentuated (Birkedahl & Johansen 2000, 25f). With its central location in the middle of the Western Limfjord area and the many villages by the coast, Mors must have played a role in the events that took place in the Viking Age.

LATE IRON AGE SETTLEMENT ON MORS

On Mors, 18 settlements from the Late Iron Age are known, but many other evidently existed, as stray finds

Fig. 1. Map of the Western Limfjord Region with places referred to in the text.

indicate. Half of the known sites are located on the coast. Fourteen of the settlements have been subject to archaeological investigations.

The best-known settlement is Karby. It was discovered in 1976 and in the following years, several minor excavations took place in the village, some of which resulted in the establishment of a local chronology for the ceramic material (Madsen & Vegger 1992, 133f). Karby is characterised by cultural layers sealed under a thick humus horizon. For some years, Karby played a role in the debate concerning the character of the settlements where trade was performed (Nielsen 1985, 270f).

In Dalgård on the east coast of Mors nine sunken feature buildings have been excavated near the old coastline below the steep slope. A rectangular iron brooch dates the sunken feature buildings to c. 725800 (Nielsen 1985, 266). Above the coastal slope, two longhouses were excavated along with six sunken feature buildings. Traces of more longhouses as well as pits and fences have been recorded (Nielsen 1976; Vegger 1987). In this area a similar iron brooch was found, and another example is known from Karby. At least ten brooches of the same type have been found at Bejsebakken near Aalborg (Nielsen 2002, 207), and the type is also known from Aggersborg – probably a type specific to Northern Jutland. In connection with surface reconnaissance in 2004 with a metal detector, a small ornamented rectangular brooch of bronze from the 7th century and an Islamic silver coin from the 9th century were found.

At Løngård on the southwest coast of Mors, a small excavation was carried out in 197677 (unpublished). Numerous pits and postholes were recorded and a single sunken feature building was excavated. A beakshaped brooch from the 7th century was collected from the surface.

The Kokkedal site at the northwest coast of Mors showed almost the same picture. A small excavation in the mid-1980's and a later trial excavation revealed extensive traces of a large coastal village (MHM j.nr.1609; both excavations unpublished). In some parts of it, the cultural layers were preserved, while other parts were heavily disturbed by modern farming. The finds indicate a rather rich locality. The number of finds was surprisingly high and varied and comprised several glass beads, shards of soapstone vessels, whetstones of slate, quernstone fragments of garnet-muscovite-chist, several iron objects including an arrowhead, a brooch fragment without a spring construction, and decorated pottery.

At present, the four localities mentioned above form the best local comparative material to the results from the excavations at Tæbring. Karby and Dalgård has been characterised by Jens Ulriksen as specialised landing places (Ulriksen 1998, 147; 159f). Adopting Ulriksen's terminology, it seems more reasonable to characterise all four sites as agrarian landing places, rather than as specialised landing places. The finds and structures recorded suggest that they were used for the general seawards activities of a farming community rather than for special engagements like long-distance trade or military activities. All the villages seem to have been founded in the 7th century, and to have covered an extensive area from the very beginning.

THE EXCAVATIONS

Tæbring lies on the west coast of Mors on the south side of Dragstrup Vig. The Late Iron Age village lies south of the Romanesque church, while the modern village is to the north. The small church is almost provocatively built at the steepest and most spectacular part of the coastal slope. From the area near the church, there is an impressive view over Dragstrup Vig. Test trenches have shown that the village covers an area of at least 60.000m². It lies on an oblong moraine formation divided into four smaller hills separated by minor bowl-shaped depressions. To the south and west, the area is bounded by Votborg Å and its moist meadow lands. Along the entire east side of the excavated part of the village, a sunken road leading to the coast is still visible. In earlier days, the road continued eastwards along the coast leading to the inner part of Dragstrup Vig. South of the village, the sunken road probably crossed Votborg Å at the same place as the modern road crosses the stream.

Back in 1938, a loom weight of burnt clay was dug up at the playground of the school in Tæbring. The settlement was first noticed in the mid-1980s by Knud Høirup through field reconnaissance. A number of shards, a loom weight, a spindle whorl, and pieces of soapstone vessels were found on that occasion, but no excavation was made to examine the character of the site.

In 1992, Morslands Historiske Museum made a small excavation some 75m south of the Romanesque church (MHM j.nr. 1958x). Three trenches covered a relatively small area, and only sparse settlement remains were found. Because of the presence of a circular trench, a characteristic feature known from other sites, the remains were dated to the Viking Age.

In 1999 new field reconnaissance of the area made it clear that it was under heavy destruction. Large areas with ploughed-up cultural layers were recorded – some of which contained a lot of charred grain – and on the surface, pottery, pieces of soapstone vessels, a whetstone of slate, a piece of a quern made of garnet-muscovite-chist, and small fragments of bronze were found. As a result of the new surface finds, a trial excavation was made. This demonstrated that numerous interesting features were still to be found almost undisturbed. Because of the promising results and the obvious threat to the remaining settlement traces, the southernmost part of the settlement (6.000m²) was fully investigated during the years 2000-2003.

The preservation conditions varied considerably. In some areas, only the 20-30 centimetres thick topsoil with modern plough marks in the subsoil could be observed, while in other areas, the topsoil combined with a thick

House I

House VII

House IV

N

0   25m

Fig. 2. Plan of the excavated area.

humus horizon, partly because turf had been introduced as building material in the latest phase of the village and had sealed the settlement traces.

UNCOVERED FEATURES

The almost triangular excavated area is well defined: to the east and west by sunken roads, to the north by a lowering in the terrain, and to the south by the meadows bordering Votborg Å. It therefore seems reasonable to assume that the excavated area represents only one farmstead, with the oldest farm dating to the 7th century and the latest to the 11th century. The trial trenches documented that the excavated farmstead lies in the outskirts of the village, while the village centre is situated on the flat terrain to the north. Here the preservation conditions were surprisingly good, with totally undisturbed turf-build buildings and ditches covered by a 1m thick humus horizon, a result of sod fertilization in the Middle Ages and later, when the area was in use as the infield of the younger Tæbing village. The markedly sloping terrain to the south might seem to have been less attractive for building purposes, but the area was build upon from the very beginning.

The excavated structures may be divided into two: structures in the subsoil and structures in the cultural layers. Cultural layers are also associated with these latter, but most of their features are recorded in the subsoil. Seven buildings were recorded at the subsoil level. The houses discussed below, number IV and VII, were partly covered by later buildings and cultural layers, and structures such as clay floors, fireplaces, and ovens were preserved. The buildings belong to well-known types that can be dated from the 7th to the 11th century. The houses IV and VII were longhouses with dwellings combined with stables or byres, while the other, smaller buildings served other purposes.

In addition to this, 14 sunken feature buildings were excavated. The floor-layers were preserved in two cases, both containing collections of loom weights made from burnt and non-burnt clay. In some cases, the fill in the rest of the sunken feature buildings indicates the period when the hut was in function.

The largest of the sunken feature buildings was filled with waste material such as ashes and a great deal of slag. In the ash layers, a complete pair of tongs was found, probably lost by accident. In this area, a complete slag-pit from an iron production process was excavated. Besides this, several traces of local iron production were recorded, including five other bottoms of ovens used for iron production. Local iron production played a minor role, and no doubt, the majority of the iron used in the settlements of Northern Jutland was imported from Norway (Birkedahl & Johansen 2000, 29; Nielsen 2001, 206). Analyses of a few nails and knives from Tæbring show that two knives were probably made of locally produced iron, while the rest of the objects were of iron produced elsewhere in Jutland or in Norway or Germany (Jouttijärvi 2003). Although the iron production in Tæbring was minimal, the presence of ovens for producing iron is remarkable.

A well with organic material preserved in the bottom-layers, among other things a wooden trough, has been radiocarbon dated to around AD 1000 (j.nr. AAR 8934 Mikkelsbakke). A lot of different pits were recorded. Remarkable are a series of large pits found in the western part of the area, all of which contain numerous fire-cracked stones, including very large ones. These pits may have had a function in connection with flax production (Hansen & Høier 2000, 68f). Some fences were also located, characterised by narrow ditches with a curved bottom. A number of broader and deeper ditches are interpreted as toft demarcations. They all belong stratigraphically to the final village phase.

Numerous features were excavated from the cultural layers. Most important are the two buildings I and III. Besides these buildings, two other structures were found, but the character of these is uncertain. In connection with the buildings, the remains of more dikes were recorded, which divided the farmstead area into different functional areas. The broad ditches running north-south mark the limit of the toft with openings to the west.

In the same strata, the bottom of an oven and an oven-like structure were excavated, and a couple of pits can be connected to this settlement phase by means of the ceramics. In the area around and south of house I, an older phase in the cultural layers was indicated. The oven and the clay floor belonging to the older house VII was located in this layer. From this layer comes a small Thor's hammer pendant of iron and a much worn square or cross shaped bronze brooch with animal ornament. Both objects date from the 10th century (Skibsted Klæsøe 1999, 96f).

The most remarkable object, however, was found with a metal detector in the topsoil after the excavation had finished. It was a strike-a-light (fig. 11c). The familiar

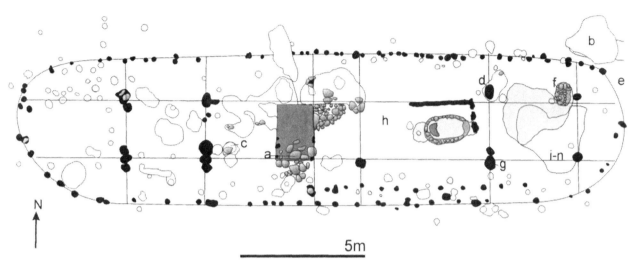

Fig. 3. Plan of house IV. Features that are interpreted as belonging to the building are marked by black (postholes or grooves) or grey shading (stones and clay floors); fills and other features are marked by open signatures; Individually marked finds: a) S-shaped brooch; b) rectangular brooch; c-e) spindle whorls; f-n) ceramic shards, including i) miniature ceramic vessel. Drawing: S. Sindbæk.

strike-a-lights from the Viking period known from settlements and graves are of a simple type made of iron/steel. The one from Tæbring is unique as it has a handle of gilded bronze and a piece of steel attached to it by two small rivets. The curved handle is decorated with two gripping beasts in the Borre style, which dates from the end of the 9th and the 10th centuries. The form and ornamentation of the handle has a striking similarity with a group of the so-called hogback gravestones in Northern England. The ornament much reminds of the gravestones from the church in Brompton in Yorkshire (Schmidt 1970,18; Lang 1984, 106-109, 120-121).

THE ORGANIZATION AND DEVELOPMENT OF THE SETTLEMENT

The development of the settlement can be divided into three main phases. The oldest farm in Tæbring consisted of a house (house IV) and two smaller buildings. Three sunken feature buildings are probably contemporary, according to the ceramics from the fill layers in these buildings. The house does not seem to have been repaired. The farmstead with a dwelling-cum-byre, smaller buildings, and some sunken feature buildings corresponds to the published farms from the 7th-8th centuries from Nr. Snede and Vorbasse (Hansen, Hvass & Mikkelsen 1991).

Like the older farm, the middle farm in Tæbring consisted of a house (House VII), two smaller buildings,

and a number of sunken feature buildings . Some of the recorded fences are perhaps connected with this farm. The house had a longer function period than the older one with several traces of repair and modifications. The house typology does not allow a more precise dating than the Viking Age. However, the few metal objects from the cultural layer support a dating to the late 9th and the 10th centuries.

The latest farm probably consisted of two turf-buildings (buildings I and III), in combination with turf-built dikes. Building I was the dwelling house, while building III probably served other functions. The find-material is almost exclusively attached to house I, and it is obvious that the main activities primarily took place in and around this house. Traces of ovens/fireplaces outside the buildings show that certain processes took place outside the buildings. The well was probably in function in this period. The radiocarbon dating and a large rim sherd from a soapstone vessel in the bottom layer of the well support this conclusion. The toft of the latest farm is obviously a bit smaller than those belonging to the older farms. The area was not continuously occupied during the 400 years. In some periods, it must have been without buildings and may have served other purposes, for instance the production of flax or as a forging area.

The village was abandoned around 1100. Later ceramics has not been recorded from the excavation or the topsoil, and this indicates that there are no younger, com-

Fig. 4. Photo of house IV during excavation, seen from west. The cellar, stone pavings, wall bench, and central hearth or oven are clearly visible. Photo: P. Mikkelsen.

pletely destroyed buildings. The farmsteads moved a few hundred metres to the west and grouped in the low area where Votborg Å flows into the Limfjord. The old village area now functioned as a well-manured infield supplied by sod-fertilization.

THREE HOUSES

House IV (7th century)

The earliest phase of the settlement is represented by a longhouse set across a slightly sloping hillside in the southern part of the excavated area. The middle section of the building was partly covered by the construction of a younger building (see plan Fig. 2). The length of the building is 24m and the width at the centre is 6m (Fig. 3). The clearly marked southern and northern walls are straight. The gables are less clear, but appear to be rounded. The closing set of roof posts in each end is set well behind the gable. The construction points to a date for this house to the 6th or 7th century. The building is fixed to the later part of this range by finds of an S-shaped and a

rectangular brooch, and by ceramic finds. A rim of a hemispherical vessel may suggest that the building remained in use into the 8th century (Fig. 7).

The constructional frame of the building is marked by two sets of symmetrically set posts at each end of the building, each pair with a distance of 3.5m between them. A third set of posts divides the space between the two pairs into two longer sections of 6.9m and 4.2m respectively.

The building can be separated into at least five rooms. In the western section of the building, few intelligible features can be made out. A door may be indicated in the gable by a pair of double-set wall posts at intervals of c. 90cm. A set of doors can also be surmised in the north and south walls just east of the second set of internal posts, but merely on strength of gaps in the line of wall-posts. Additional postholes on the centre-side of three roof posts may indicate doorways, byre constructions, or most likely repair. By analogy with other Late Iron Age houses, we would expect the part of a longhouse lacking hearths to have contained a stable or byre, or possibly a barn. The dampness of a stable or byre would agree well with the apparent need to repair the posts, a need which seemingly did not occur in the rest of the house.

In Danish Late Iron Age longhouses, byres are almost always found in the east end. An exception to this rule, however, is house D at Aggersborg (Roesdahl 1986, 65) and, in so far as the plans can be made out, also some buildings at Lindholm Høje (Pedersen 1994, 40). Perhaps we are dealing with a peculiarity of the Limfjord region.

Towards the middle of the building, a small cellar fills out the central aisle between the roof post (Fig. 4). On the south side, a partially destroyed stone paving indicates that the feature could be by-passed this way (the partial destruction of the paving is most likely connected with the construction of the younger building, which just reaches it). The cellar is 1.5m long, 2.3m wide and approximately 30cm deep below floor level. It was entered from the northeast corner where a stone paving gave way to a slightly sunken stepping-stone made from a large sandstone block. Four posts supported the walls of the southern section; no similar arrangement was observed in the northern part. The cellar was packed with a uniform dark fill that was completely void of artefacts except for some large stones broken up from the stone paving on the south side. Neither were any archaeobotanic remains noticed. Due to the lack of finds, the function of the cellar is difficult to determine. The most obvious reason for including a sunken feature in a residential space is to secure a cool, dark and damp environment for storage of foodstuff. Technically, it is more reasonable to place such a store outside the heated dwelling. The decision to locate it in the middle of the house (and opening towards the residential section) may express a wish for easy accessibility or control of access.

Unlike in the Early Iron Age, cellars were not a regular feature in Late Iron Age houses. Examples are known in Trelleborg (Nørlund 1948, 85f) Gl. Lejre (Christensen 1991; 1993), Gl. Hviding (Jensen 1987), and possibly in Jannerup, Thy (Bertelsen 1992) – all in marginal parts of houses, not as here in the centre of the dwelling. In the light of the depth of the feature, more examples would certainly have come to light, had they been common. Perhaps the cellar in Tæbring never functioned according to intention? From the west side an erosion channel left by running water leads to the cellar. While it may well relate to the abandonment of the house, it reminds us that it could have been difficult to protect this particular

Fig. 5. Photo of the central hearth or oven in house IV, seen from southwest. Photo: S. Sindbæk

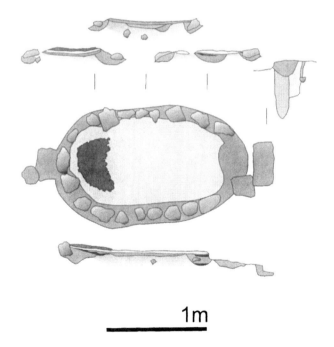

1m

Fig. 6. Drawing and section of hearth or oven in house IV. Drawing: S. Sindbæk.

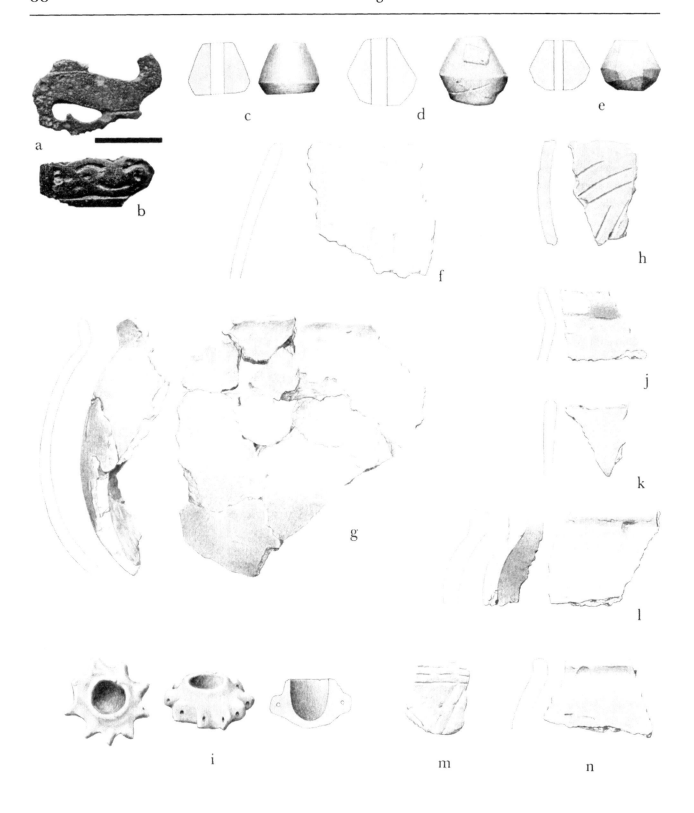

Fig. 7. Finds associated with house IV. a) S-shaped brooch; b) rectangular brooch; c-e) spindle whorls; f-n) ceramic shards, including i) miniature ceramic vessel. See plan Fig. 3 as to the position of the individual finds. Drawings: Helle Johansen.

longhouse, placed almost like a dam on a sloping hill-side, from intruding water during heavy rains or thaw. Is this why no finds were made in the feature? However this may be, the comparative material known at present would suggest that the cellar represents an experiment that was not taken up more generally.

In line with the eastern end of the cellar, two roof posts mark the passage to the next section of the house. The posts were placed in the side aisles, well off the line marked by the other wall-posts. A similar construction was noticed recently in Skåne (Ståstorp house 3, see Jacobsson 2002). In the latter case, it was interpreted as a support for a beam that would bind the roof laterally, but not acting as a roof-support proper. In Tæbring, a more obvious explanation is that the posts were set aside to make way for passage around the cellar. The foot of the northern post was packed with three large, flat stones. This was necessary as, unlike all other roof post, this one was not dug into the natural, but in a filling of dark earth (or rather a patch left of the old topsoil) along the north wall in the entire mid-section of the house. This fill lev-elled the north-south slope inside the building, creating a 1.7m wide bench along the wall. In the corner by the entrance to the cellar, two flat stones marks a step to the top of the bench. This enables us to fix the height of the bench to 20cm above the stone pawing (Fig.4). The pav-ing below the bench is set directly into the natural. This suggests that the levelling of the site was in fact achieved by partly digging away the topsoil.

Internal stone pawing is known from the pre-fortress houses in Aggersborg (Roesdahl 1986, 65), where they occur in stables/byres and entrance halls – i.e. where people enter a clay or earthen floor from an often soggy outside. The shattered paving on the south side of the cel-lar in Tæbring house IV, giving access to the stable, byre or barn, may have acted in this way. The paving in the northern part of the room, on the other hand, covered only a corner of the floor, and must be regarded as a remedy against erosion by the steps to the cellar and by the wall-bench.

The stone-settings suggest that this room served main-ly as a passage, giving access to the cellar, to the stable or byre along the south wall, to the top of the bench, and into the living room to the east. But there was probably no entrance directly from the exterior in the passage room of Tæbring house IV, as the line of outer wall posts appears to be uninterrupted at this stretch. This fact supports the idea that the cellar was intended as a particularly guarded space, reached only from the strictly residential section of the house.

East of the stone-paved corner, a setting of four large stones probably served as the sill of a roof post. The feature is on top of the wall bench, but aligned with the northern row of roof post and pairs well with a posthole to the south. Most probably, this pair of roof posts was part of a partition wall. No direct traces were observed of such a wall, but its presence may be assumed for practical reasons: The hearth or oven of the living room was placed close to the eastern end of the room and could hardly have provided efficient heating for a room that continued all the way to the cellar. Conversely, the supposed purpose of the cellar, to provide cool storage, would be counteracted if it communicated directly with the best-heated room of the house.

In the following room the hearth or oven covered the eastern half of the mid-aisle. This heating unit marks the room as the central living room of the house. The feature was outlined by a 2m long and 1.2m wide horseshoe-shaped setting of stones set in a groove filled with dark brown, sandy clay (Fig. 5-6). The pan delimited by this was patched with a concave layer of sandy clay strongly blazed by fire. In the western end the colouration of the clay showed an undisturbed sequence, topped by a crisp, dark grey sintering. In the eastern end, the traces of heat-ing were less intense, and the clay coating had been re-peatedly dug into. In this end the encircling line of stones was left open. Taken together, these observations may in-dicate that the structure was a vaulted oven rather than an open hearth. This certainly was the case in house VII (see below). The presence of ovens in Merovingian period houses in South Scandinavia was recently attested in Jär-restad, Skåne (Söderberg 2003, 288). In Tæbring house IV, no trace was found of the vault itself. Neither were there any traces of stakes to support it. Oven domes could be supported without stakes, as observed e.g. in Nødskov Hede (Steensberg 1952, 266). On the state of evidence, the question of oven or hearth can hardly be settled con-clusively. The construction is strongly reminiscent of the structure in PK-banken in Lund described as an oven (Nielsson 1976; cf. fig. 17h), but caution should be taken, as the latter structure is 400 years younger.

At the eastern end of the hearth or oven, a deep-set, sturdy post may have served as a gallows for cooking vessels. Oven or not, the position of the main activity-

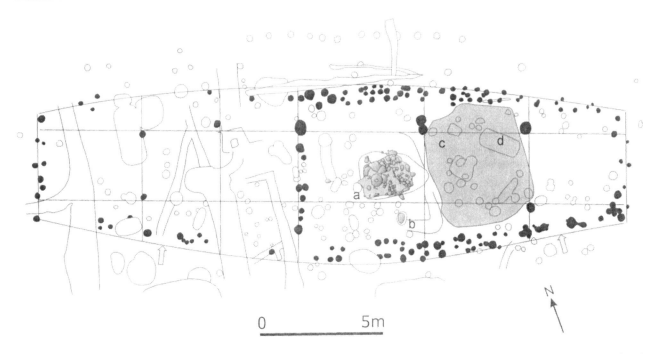

Fig. 8. Plan of house VII. Signatures as in Fig. 3. Individually marked finds: a) whetstone of grey slate; b-c) loom-weights; d) arrowhead. Drawing: S. Sindbæk.

Fig. 9. Photo of the central part of house VII during excavation, seen from north. Photo: P. Mikkelsen.

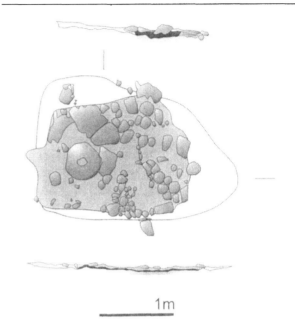

Fig. 10. Drawing and section of oven in house VII. Shaded dark grey: stones. Light grey: greyish soil. Mid-tone grey (surface): red-burned clay. Black: Charcoal-rich sand. Shaded light grey (bottom): Fire-blazed natural clay. Drawing: S. Sindbæk.

area near the eastern end of the structure would mean that fuel and ashes could have been transported through the next room to the east without entering the central living room. Ventilation for the fire was also available through the eastern room that had one or several doors to the exterior. With doors open, cooking on the central hearth might even be supervised from the eastern room. This could suggest that efforts were taken to keep "dirty" household activities away from the central living room.

North of the hearth or oven, a shallow groove was observed across a 2.5m distance in direct continuation of the wall bench noted in the passage room. This must imply that the bench continued through the living room, delimited by a plank following the inner line of the roof post. Intact wall-benches are often found in Viking Age and Medieval Norse settlements in the North Atlantic. Their traces were observed in the houses of the Fyrkat fortress (Olsen & Schmidt 1977), in Sædding (Stoumann 1980, 106ff), Hedeby (Schietzel 1984), and Elisenhof (Bantelman 1975). In these cases, the benches are seemingly placed symmetrically on either side of the central aisle. In the present case, however, there was no sign of a bench to the south. Several observations may indicate that there never was one. While the northern bench served to level the slope of the terrain, a southern bench would have

counteracted this. A line of posts running parallel to the south wall may indicate a narrow bench, a reinforced wall, shelves or whatever, but evidently a construction quite different from the one in the northern section. It is tempting to compare this arrangement with the high seat of aristocratic halls – i.e. the seat of the owners and honorary guests of the house during feasting. Some more modest reflection of this arrangement is likely to have existed in farmer's houses as well. Frants Hershend has pointed to indications that the high seat had its traditional place along one side of the main room before it was moved to the end of the building, supposedly at some point during the Viking Age (Herschend 1997).

Few finds appeared in the living room: Some shards, a spindle whorl, and a droplet of bronze. Their sparseness reflects the absence of an actual floor layer, and they do little to clarify the room function further.

A partition wall must have separated the main living room from the eastern part of the building. This is indicated by the fact that the northern wall bench evidently terminated just before the penultimate set of roof post, to give way for a clay floor that seems to have covered the entire floor of the last room in the same level as the central aisle of the living room. Because of the resulting difference in floor level in the northern aisle, the passage between the two rooms must have been through the central aisle (or just possibly the southern one). The clay floor of the eastern room was worn down to a concave pan later destroyed near the walls but still preserved in the middle. In the northeastern corner of the room, a paving of cobblestones covered an area of 100 x 70cm right next to the terminal roof post. The stones and the earth beneath them were marked by fire. The proximity to the roof post implies that the structure was an oven rather than an open hearth. It may be noted that the arrangement of the two heating units is almost identical to the situation in Sædding house III (see Fig 17c).

The eastern room had several possible entrances from the outside. One is marked by a double set of posts in the northern wall close to the small oven. There are several openings in the line of the southern wall, but on balance (and comparing with contemporary buildings) it appears most probable that a southern entrance faced the northern one symmetrically. The badly preserved gable makes it impossible to determine whether an opening existed here too. Two postholes behind the wall line in the northeast corner may just possibly mark a wide, oblique en-

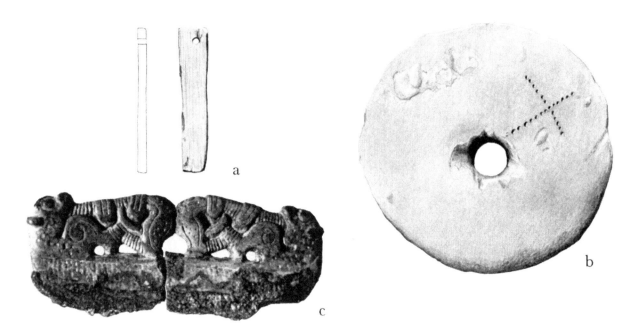

Fig. 11. Finds associated with house VII. a) whetstone of grey slate; b) loom-weight; c) the strike-a-light was not directly associated with the house, but was found close to it, and must belong to the period when it was in use. See plan Fig. 8 as to the position of the individual finds. Drawings: Helle Johansen.

trance, but on lack of analogous examples, this seems less likely.

The southern part of the clay floor was partly covered by an ashen layer. A layer of the same colour and consistence was found outside the north-eastern corner of the building, right by the northern entrance, and seems to mark a refuse heap. In both layers, a number of finds were unearthed. Those from inside consisted of ceramics, among them one unusual and complete miniature vessel with nine perforated bosses or ears (Fig. 7e). Miniature vessels with mostly three similar ears are known from a number of Late Iron Age sites, but no exact parallels to the present find are known to the authors. A rich archaeobotanic material was also secured from this layer (see below). The finds from outside included one square brooch (Fig. 7b), a spindle whorl and fragments of amber.

HOUSE VII (9TH OR 10TH CENTURY)

Some 25m to the north of house IV another building with preserved internal structures was uncovered. The outline of the building is quite different from the first one, with curving walls and straight gables. The length was 24m

and the in width the middle 7m. Five sets of roof posts were set at regular intervals through the building, while a final set stands in each gable. This type of building is known through the 9th and 10th century. The few artefacts directly associated with the building do nothing to narrow this frame, but from finds in the general area, a phase of activity around 900 is evident.

The southern face of the house curves more strongly than the northern. This is not infrequently seen in Late Iron Age houses, and may at least in the present case have a constructional explanation: the house was set on a gentle, southward slope. In order to obtain a symmetrical roof construction (which was indispensable for the stability of the building), the builders had to either give the southern face extra height, or let the roof descend a bit further on this side. The latter and probably more graceful solution would make the wall line protrude a bit further in the middle of the convex façade, exactly in the way recorded here.

The house was in an area marked by a great deal of later activity that somewhat confuses the plan. Part of the outer wall and several roof posts could not be traced. It seems, however, that the house was composed of six

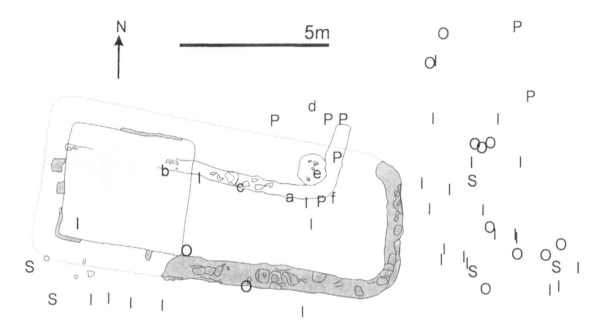

Fig. 12. Plan of house I. Signatures as in Fig. 3, except dark shading used for turf walls. Finds associated with the house are marked with P = ceramics; I = iron; S = soapstone, and O = other materials. Individually marked finds: a) Harthacnut coin, 1040-42; b) ingot of copper alloy; c-e) ceramic shards; f) Soapstone shard. Drawing: S. Sindbæk.

Fig. 13. Photo of house I during excavation, seen from southeast. Tæbring church and the Limfjord are visible in the background. Photo P. Mikkelsen.

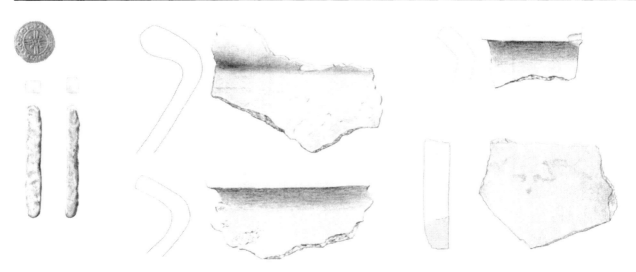

Fig. 14. Selected finds associated with house I. a) Harthacnut coin, 1040-42; b) ingot of copper alloy; c-e) ceramic shards; f) Soapstone shard. See plan Fig. 12 as to position of the individual finds. Drawings: Helle Johansen.

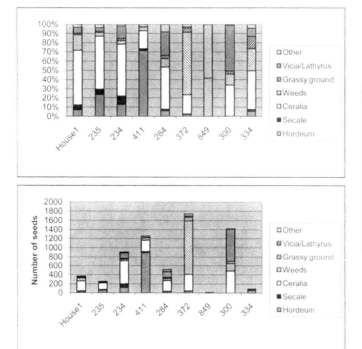

Fig. 15 The distribution of cereals, weeds, meadow species, and Vicia/Lathyrus. a) distribution expressed in percentages, b) number of seeds. By the calculation 4 fragments = 1 grain and 1 ear = 1 unit.

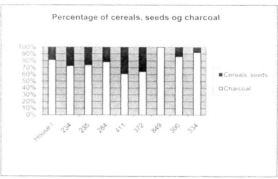

Fig. 16 Distribution of cereals and seeds vs. charcoal and other remains in the floated samples expressed in percentages.

sections, four of which were 3.5m long, while two sections serving for residential area were stretched to 4.9 and 4.15m respectively.

Three rooms can be discerned in the building. The western part of the house is badly disturbed by later ditches. It seems that the walls were of a less firm construction than in the domestic section. The reconstruction must be regarded as a rational conjecture. Few internal structures can be discerned here, but on the absence of any arrangement for heating, we expect this section to be a stable, byre, or barn. As in house IV, this would mean that the general orientation of the house was reverse to the situation commonly found. One or several doors probably existed in this section, but their location cannot be determined.

A partition wall with a door in the middle gave way to the central room of the house. The walls of this part are marked by closer and deeper set posts than the western section. The wall line is continuous to the north as well as to the south, so there was hardly an entrance directly to this room from the outside. The swarm of wall posts visible in this section in particular is quite different from the single line of posts commonly seen but has close parallels in the pre-fortress buildings in Aggersborg (Fig. 17d-e). Here they have been interpreted as a result of frequent repair (Olsen & Schmidt 1977, 112f), but this does not explain why similar features do not occur along the entire wall. In Aggersborg as well as in Tæbring, the 'post-swarm' wall are associated with the dwelling section of the house, a fact that must point to a particular and probably more insulating construction.

As in house IV, the central room is focused on its heating-unit. There is no doubt that this was an oven: Remains of the collapsed dome were found on top of the structure. The foundation consisted in a 2.1 by 1.4m large rectangular plate of clay covered with stones. In the eastern end, the material used was mainly small cobblestones, but in the west, where the mouth had been, large flat slabs of sandstone were preferred (the same material as was used for the step to the cellar in house IV). Among them were also the bedstone of a rotating quern of gneiss. Its position here had no relation to its primary function – as is often seen in Iron Age houses a worn-out quern became a useful slab. On either side of the oven, and in the eastern end, separate large stones were set, probably as a support to the dome.

The identification of the central heating unit in this house as an oven invites us to reconsider other cases.

If a few more centimetres had been dug away, no trace would have remained of the vault. In most cases the fireplaces in Late Iron Age houses have been traced only as a colouration of the subsoil. They are routinely assumed to be hearths – but how many others could have been ovens?

Except for the oven, no intelligible structures are noted in the central room. The location of the oven and its dimensions leaves room for the wall-benches, but there are no visible traces of such. No floor level was preserved. The finds are accordingly few. A loom weight was found in the southern part of the room (fig. 11b). Except for the reused quern, the only other find was a small whetstone of grey slate (fig. 11a). It was neatly polished on all sides and had a perforation for suspension. Evidently being a piece of personal equipment, it fits well in the living-quarter of the house.

The passage to the next room is marked by a clay floor that just reached the next set of roof posts and almost touched the oven. There seems to be little doubt that a partition wall separated these two sections of the building. No traces of a doorway between the rooms were found, but it can be surmised to have been in the middle aisle like the western door of the living room. There were no indications of a fireplace. No obvious place for an entrance from the outside can be pointed out in the wall line, although a pair of particularly strong posts in the southeastern corner may be an indication of its position. The clay floor produced a couple of interesting finds: a rather large bronze object, the poor condition of which unfortunately has not allowed an identification, and a barbed arrowhead of iron.

While the two central rooms exhibit a striking correspondence with the organization of the residential area of house IV, the presence of yet another room in the eastern gable presents a marked difference. The separate position of this room is brought out by the termination of the clay floor. No trace of a floor cover was found in the gable room. As the walls were equally well preserved as in the previous rooms, the difference must be genuine. There is little to indicate the function of the gable room. An opening in the south wall with sturdy posts on either side may indicate an entrance in the same position as we tend to find it in contemporary houses (see e.g. Fig. 17g), but a note of caution should be voiced as just here, the wall line was disturbed by a sunken feature.

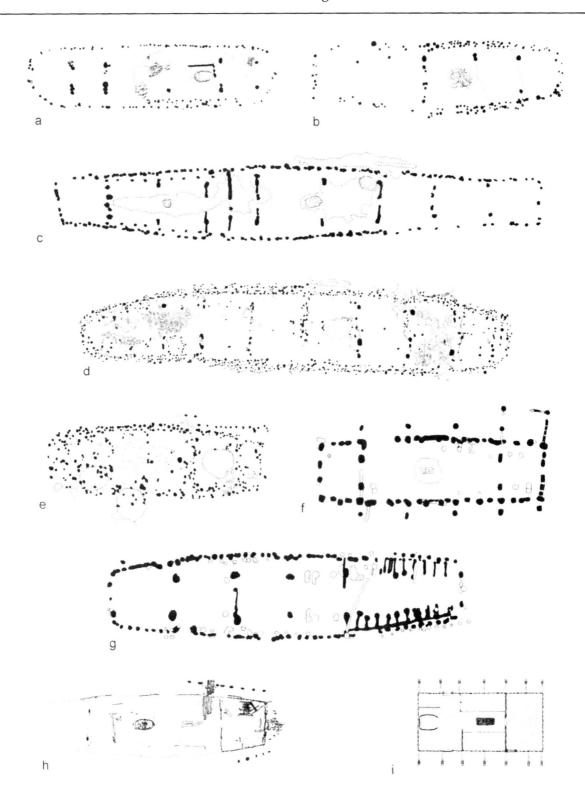

Fig. 17. Tæbring house IV and VII (a-b) drawn to scale with comparative house plans: c) Sædding III; d-e) Aggersborg D & A; f-g) Vorbasse CII and CCIII; h) PK-banken Lund; i) Hedeby. All plans except Tæbring from Schmidt 1999.

House I (11th century)

House I was the best-preserved building of the 11th century phase, characterised by outer walls made of turf. Turf buildings represent a local development radically different from the mainstream domestic architecture in late Viking Age and early medieval Denmark, which features large houses from which non-residential activities had been moved to separate buildings. Similarly, the turf-buildings were exclusively residential buildings, albeit smaller than traditional houses.

Anne-Louise Haack-Olsen has recently demonstrated that the custom of building in turf in Late Viking Age and early medieval Denmark was restricted to the north-western part of the country (Olsen 2005). She observes that the Danish buildings are constructed from rather small, rectangular turfs, unlike the turf buildings in the North Atlantic islands, which were constructed as double-faced turf or stone shells with a rubble core. In all likelihood the Danish technique was adopted from the Frisian area, where a similar technique is documented in the Viking Age.

On the outside the present house was 12.5m long and 5m wide. The thickness of its outer walls varied from 50 to 80cm – quite modest compared to North Atlantic turf buildings and also distinctly less than the nearest Danish parallels in Nødskov Hede and Sjørring. In the neatly preserved southern wall and in both gables, the individual sods could be clearly traced, whereas the northern wall was disturbed in part by a later phase of the house. South of the house, two turf dikes enclosed a yard measuring 8x20m. Within this yard, immediately to the east of the building, a refuse-layer was uncovered, which contained a rich artefact material. The dating of the house is determined by the occurrence of hard-fired globular pots with sharp rim profiles, which appear in Denmark in the late 10th century, and soapstone vessels that generally do not occur later than c. 1050. The dating to the first half of the 11th century is confirmed by the coins found inside and outside the building (see below).

The house consisted of two separate rooms. It was most probably entered through a door in the destroyed west end of the south wall. At least the eastern part of the south wall shows no disruption; whether an entrance had been situated in the north wall cannot be determined because of its partial destruction, but as comparable turf buildings had only one entrance and the general orientation of the house can be assumed to have been towards the yard on the south, this possibility appears unlikely.

Inside the building, a stamped clay floor covered the western third of the floor area. No remains of a floor were found in the east. This section may simply have had an earthen floor, but could also have been covered with planks. In any case, the change of floor cover must indicate that the house had two rooms. The clay floor in the western room was partly covered by a refuse layer, which provided a rich archaeobotanic material (see below). But only two artefacts were found: part of a horsebit in the southwest corner, and a small bronze ingot in the northwest section (fig. 14b). Towards the east, an area with fire-cracked stones by the middle of the northern wall marked the position of a fireplace or possibly oven. Around this, a number of ceramic shards were found, as well as a piece of a soapstone vessel. Other finds from this room include an iron nail and a loom-weight found in the south-east corner.

A coin issued by Harthacnut Oxford 1040-42 was found close to the fireplace (fig. 14a). The find conditions, however, did not make it clear whether the coin was indeed deposited inside the house, or perhaps just outside the walls of the later building that partly covered it. More coins were found in the refuse layer immediately to the east of the building. Wound together by silver thread, probably the remains of a purse, was a lump of six coins: three fragments of English coins issued by Cnut and Harold between 1017-1040, two German coins (one complete and one cut in half) from the first half of the 11th century, and one indeterminate fragment (Aarsleff 2003, 87). Finally, a German coin, issued by Konrad II in Duisburg between 1024-1039, was found outside the opening in the southeastern corner of the dike. Whether this last coin is associated with House I is unclear.

The finds from the refuse-layers around the house and on its western side in particular are of the same general types as those from the inside: Shards of mainly hard-burnt globular pots with sharply profiled rims, iron object and shards of soapstone vessels (distribution shown in fig. 12). It is an interesting fact that all soapstone-shards found in Tæbring occurred within the yard of house I and must be associated with this particular building.

ARCHAEOBOTANICAL INVESTIGATIONS

During the investigations in Tæbring, the excavators took a number of samples for plant macrofossil analysis. The samples were taken from houses or other features where cereals became visible during excavation. The time available for the excavation did not allow for more systematic sampling. The purpose of the macrofossil analysis is in part to give a functional determination of individual features or part of features, in part to investigate the agrarian activities on the site.

The samples, each of app. 25 litres, were floated in Skive Museum. The floated material was collected in a set of sieves with a mesh size of 2.0mm and 0.5mm respectively, and subsequently dried in coffee-filters. The volume of the individual samples was measured in a measuring cup with a 5-ml scale, while the volume of cereals and seeds separated out was measured in a measuring cup with a 0.25-ml scale. As some of the floatation residues were very large, they were divided through a grid separator.

Before floatation, a sub-sample of app. 1 litre was subtracted from several samples in order to investigate the contents of heavy components, which do not show in the floated samples, and a possible content of un-charred organic material. The non-floated sub-samples were described and then washed through a set of set of sieves with a mesh size of 0.5mm and 0.25mm respectively. The contents of the residues were then inspected through a stereo-magnifier by up to x40 magnification. The main samples were inspected through a stereo-magnifier by up to x80 magnification. The contents of the sample were recorded, and seeds and other identifiable material were separated out. The seeds are identified by reference to literature and by comparison to recent material.

The description of the non-floated samples, the volume of the samples, and their contents apart from seeds and cereals appears from table 1. The contents of seeds and cereals appear from table 2. In table 2 "ruderal and weeds" are the annual species found in disturbed soil, often in fields or close to settlements. "Meadow plants" are perennial species that are found in a more stable and closed vegetation, while "others" are seeds that could not be determined to the level of species, for which reason their ecological habitats cannot be stated.

Cereals
All samples contained hulled barley (Hordeum vulgare), as well as grains and ears of rye (Secale cereale).

Hulled barley (Hordeum vulgare) is known in Denmark since the Early Neolithic period, but appears in general to replace the more common naked barley only in the Late Bronze Age, and then to expel it entirely during the Roman Iron Age (Robinson 1994b). Recent investigations indicate, however, that naked barley remained the more common variety in the sandy soils of northern and western Jutland well into the Roman Iron Age (Henriksen in press).

Barley is the cereal most commonly found in charred samples from prehistoric settlements. The reason may be that the grains were more frequently brought into contact with fire in a complete state, either because they were used as such for cooking, or because they were roasted to improve the taste, or to remove the chaff. A further possibility is that the grains were dried over a fire in order to reduce the content of water before grinding, as a great content of water creates a putty-like substance on the grinding-stone. Before storage, the grains must also be dried in order to reduce the content of water, as they will otherwise go mouldy or germinate.

Barley may also have been roasted as malt for beer. But in that case, the grains should first have germinated, for which there is no indication in any of the samples. Brewing, then, does not appear likely in this context.

Rye (Secale cereale) is known in Denmark since the Late Bronze Age, but becomes common only in the Merovingian and Viking periods (Robinson 1994b). The proportion of rye grains was low in all samples. Unlike barley, a few ears of rye were found in several samples. Possibly rye was present as a remnant crop in a crop rotation system and hence occurred in the harvest of barley. Another possibility is that they were less frequently in contact with fire in a complete state.

A few grains of oats (Avena) were identified, but as the diagnostic scar in the lower floret was not present, it was not possible to determine whether we are dealing with cultivated oats (Avena sativa) or a wild species, e.g. wild oat (Avena fatua) that occurs as a weed in cultivated fields.

Wheat (Triticum) was not found in any of the analysed samples. From Viking Age Denmark, a few grains of wheat are known from Aggersborg and Gammel Lejre (Robinson 1994a), as well as from Hundborg in Thy, a mere 25km's from Tæbring. The samples from Hundborg were taken from a layer of charred material found outside a house excavated by Thisted Museum (sample THY3432x702A). The content of cereals in this sample appears from table 3. Except for cereals, the sample contained very few seeds of weeds, among which Fat-Hen (Chenopodium album), Redshank (Persicaria maculosa), Nipplewort (Lapsana communis), Sun Spurge (Euphorbia helioscopia), Vetches (Vicia sp.), and Sedge (Carex sp.) are present. The small proportion of weeds suggests that the cereal was cleaned.

Because of the find circumstances (see below) the proportion of the individual cereals in the samples from Tæbring cannot be used as a quantitative measure reflecting the proportion of cereals cultivated in the village. Their representation is rather influenced by the preparation and treatment of the individual cereals. The sample from Hundborg, on the other hand, seems to consist of stored, cleaned grain, for which reason the sample gives a more realistic impression of the cereals cultivated at this site. But in general, too few macrofossil analyses have been conducted from Late Iron Age settlements in Denmark to conclude on the relative occurrence of the individual cereals.

No other cultivated crops were identified in the samples. Among the grains that could not be determined to the level of species, the majority appears to belong to barley.

Weeds
All samples contained seeds of Fat-Hen (Chenopodium album) and Oraches (Atriplex sp.). Both species are found in fertilized soils, as is the case with Small Nettle (Urtica urens), found in a single sample. Pale Persica (Persicaria lapathifolia ssp. pallida) and Redshank (Persicaria maculosa), both associated with waterlogged disturbed soil, were encountered more sporadically in the samples. Peas or Vetches (Lathyrus /Vicia) were found in several samples, albeit not in the samples from house VII. There was a sporadic occurrence of Knottgrass (Polygonum aviculare), Corn Spurrey (Spergula arvensis), Sheep's Sorrel (Rumex acetosella), and Wild Radish (Raphanus raphanistrum), all to be found in slightly more poor and dry soils. All weeds mentioned occur commonly in samples from the Iron Age, including the Viking Age, in Denmark (e.g., Henriksen & Robinson 1994, Moltsen 2005, Robinson 1994a).

Only sample x372 from house IV seems to contain unrefined cereals (see below). The content of weeds hence has limited value for determining the ecological conditions in the fields, as the majority of weeds are lacking. It is not possible to determine in every case whether the material represents weeds that have grown along with the harvested crops, or a later mixture – or even more importantly, whether the material is deposited in a short episode or over a prolonged period of time. If the weeds come from the cultivated fields, the presence of seeds of species associated with both wet and dry soils probably reflects local variation in humidity in the fields. The same may be the case with the nutritional conditions.

The weeds may also be used to estimate whether the seed was sown in autumn or spring. If the soil is worked in the spring, the species that germinate and generate vegetative parts in autumn will be destroyed, and only the summer-annual species that germinate in spring will be present. Conversely, the winter-annual species will be present in case the crops are sown in autumn. The weeds found in the samples are summer-annual, for which reason we must be dealing with spring-sown cereals.

Crop-processing
Figure 15a shows the relative occurrence of barley (Hordeum vulgare), rye (Secale cereale), cereals (Ceralia), weeds, meadow plants, peas/vetches (Vicia/Lathyrus) and "others."

A large percentage of cereals and a low content of weeds in the samples is commonly an indication of cleaned cereals. If the cereal is cleaned by winnowing, as it is known from the Iron Age (Viklund 1998, Henriksen & Robinson 1994), the fraction with the largest grains will contain the largest and heaviest grains of weeds, but also round seeds that roll. Small and light seeds of weeds, on the other hand, will land closest to the point from which the crop is thrown. Correspondingly, a large content of seeds of weeds together with a large number of grains will usually be interpreted as unrefined cereals.

It will appear that the samples from house I (xHouse I, x234, x 235), and sample x411 from an oven-like feature, contained a large proportion of cereals (70-90 %) and very few seeds of weeds. This should indicate cleaned cereals. In the samples x284, x372, x300, and x334 the concentration of cereals is far lower (25-50%), lowest in sample x372. This will normally imply that the cereals are less well cleaned, or that the sample belongs to a different fraction of the cleaned cereals. Sample x372 seemingly contained unrefined cereals. The samples x284 and x300 contained a large proportion of vetches or peas (Vicia/ Lathyrus). Both genera have pods that burst by drying, so that the seeds roll out. It is not possible to determine if the relative content depends on accidental variation, the harvest-season, or something else.

As it appears from Fig. 15b, the total content of seeds in x849 is very low, for which reason no certain conclusions can be drawn.

By retrospective analysis it is often possible to calculate how cereals are cleaned, which stage in the process the sample corresponds to, or which fraction of the material is concerned. For this, however, it is necessary to know the find circumstances. As explained below it is not clear whether the material in the samples concerned is deposited in one episode, and thus corresponds to an isolated, distinct fraction, or a mixture from several episodes. If the material is deposited as waste over a period of time, it will not represent a distinct fraction. Because of this uncertainty, the present material is not considered suitable for this type of analysis.

Meadow plants

In all samples meadow plants comprise a very small proportion, albeit as much as 15% in x334. For the most part species of Sedge (Carex sp.) are found in the samples. It is not unusual to find seeds of Sedge in this type of samples, though no obvious explanation for their presence has been found. Species of Sedge are perennial herbs that generally cannot survive in well-worked soils. A certain determination to the level of species is difficult and often impossible on the basis of seeds alone, a fact that adds to the problems of finding a cause to their presence in the samples. It has been suggested that the seeds come from hay used as material for the roof. This is unlikely, though, as we should then expect a combination with other meadow plants. Only sample x334 contained other types of meadow plants. They were mainly species associated with wet or moist soil. In the same sample charred stems and leafs were found. Alltogether, this may indicate that the meadow plants in this sample were the remains of turf used as fuel.

Fuel

All samples contained charcoal and stems/roots from Heather (Calluna vulgaris). Lumps of turf were found in sample xHouse I, and charred straws were found in samples x372, x849 and x300. Together with the content of seeds from meadow plants that do not occur in cultivated fields, this suggests that turf, together with Heather (Calluna vulgaris) and wood has been employed as fuel in the features concerned.

FUNCTIONAL ARCHAEOBOTANIC DETERMINATION

The most convincing method for a functional determination of houses, or sections of houses, based on charred plant macrofossils has been designed by Karin Viklund (Viklund 1998). Viklund's investigations of mainly Roman Iron Age houses are based on the relative content of cereals, weeds, and meadow plants respectively in samples from holes of roof posts from longhouses. Viklund interprets a large content of cereals with little weeds as cleaned cereals. This distribution is most frequently encountered in postholes near the hearth where dry conditions have prevailed. A large content of meadow plants with little cereals indicates byres. Finally, Viklund interprets a large content of weeds together with cereals as evidence of threshing. The latter also presupposes, however, that the room has a solid floor, for instance of clay, that the room is large enough to swing a flail, and that there are doors or similar openings for ventilation. It should be added that Viklund's method for a functional determination yields its best results when applied to burnt-down houses.

Even if the organization of houses – and possibly also the methods for processing crops – changes substantially between the Roman Iron Age and the Viking Age, the model seems to provide a suitable basis for interpreting the samples from Tæbring.

House IV

Sample x372 is taken from a layer covering a clay floor in the eastern part of the house, immediately south of the oven (Fig. 3). The sample contained relatively little cereals and a large amount of weeds. Cereals and weeds together comprised 40% as compared to the content of charcoal. It was in this sample that the largest amount of meadow-plants was recorded. In addition, the sample contained a small volume of white-burned bone.

The sample contained some white slag, probably moulted clay, but also small flecks of burnt clay and bog iron ore. Both demand quite high temperatures, which would agree well with the material having been charred in the oven. As previously mentioned, the large content of seeds from meadow-species may derive from turf used for fuel. The bog iron ore may also derive from this turf. As there were no signs that the house had burned, the material on the floor most probably derives from the oven. The varying state of preservation of the seeds may either be due to differences in the charring-process, or perhaps some seeds have been left in areas without mechanical wear, whereas other have been more exposed.

At face value, the substantial content of seeds from weeds seems to indicate non-cleaned cereals. Taken together with the few fragments of bone, this may indicate that the feature has been used for preparing both animal and vegetable food. It cannot be determined whether the deposition happened during one or several episodes.

House VII
A single sample (x849) was taken from a posthole in the western part of this house. No cereals were found in the sample, and the content of weeds was very low. The material may have slipped into a depression at the foot of the post during the period when the house was in use. No inference can be made from the isolated sample.

House I and oven-like feature (x411)
The samples xHouse I, x234, and x235 were all taken from above the clay-floor, which covered the western third of this house (Fig. 12). The material was deposited as an approximately 5cm thick layer of reddish ashes. Sample x411 was taken from a small oven-like feature in the courtyard south-west of house I. The feature overlies house VII and is presumably contemporary with house I.

In all three samples from the house (xHouse I, x234 and x235), the volume of seeds and cereals made up 20-25% of the total volume of the sample (Fig. 16). The samples contained a rather low concentration of weeds. The proportional distribution of seeds from weeds and cereals seems to indicate cleaned cereals, for which reason it would seem natural to assume storage or food preparation. It would take some sort of accident, however, for a stored material to become charred, e.g. a restricted fire. According to the excavator, there were no signs of conflagration, but in the eastern part of the building, a feature with fire-cracked stones is interpreted as a heating unit.

The majority of the grains of cereals were quite worn and fragmented. This presumably indicates great mechanical wear. Except for charcoal, charred twigs and roots of heather, and lumps of turf, no other components were found in the samples.

In sample x411 from the oven-like feature, the proportional distribution of seeds of weeds and cereals did not deviate significantly from the samples taken inside the house. The cereals in sample x411 were far better pre-

served; almost 80% of the grains could be determined to the level of species. Cereals and weeds made up 40% of the total volume. As concerns the contents, the samples from house I and from the oven-like feature were very similar. However, x411 contained a certain amount of white slag, presumably moulten clay. This implies that rather high temperatures have been present – which is of course fully consistent with the interpretation as an oven. The better conditions of preservation in x411 must be due to the fact that the grains here were protected by the structure, while those on the clay floor had been exposed to mechanical wear. The better-preserved pieces from the house may derive from corners or structures that protected them from being trampled. No charred bones were found in any of the samples.

Quite likely, the oven in the courtyard was the primary location for drying or roasting cereals. The cause for the presence of cereals inside the house is less clear. Accidentally relocated material in these amounts is not possible. A deposition of ashes from the fireplace in the eastern end of the house could be an explanation – especially as no finds of molten clay or other kinds of slag that might indicate that the material derived from an oven were found. If this was the case, the fireplace must have been used for drying, roasting, or preparing the cereals. On the other hand, the idea of ashes being deposited inside the house appears odd. Could there have been a fireplace or the like in the western part of the house that could not be traced by the excavation?

It cannot be determined whether the material from the respective features was deposited in one episode or by recurrent activities. It seems less likely, though, that the material from the floor of the house was deposited during a single episode.

Sample x 334 is from the layer in the western part of the house. The sample contained a small amount of burnt bone, which together with the content of cereals indicate that the sample derives from a structure used for preparing animal as well as vegetable food. As it appears from Fig. 15b, the content for seeds was very low in this sample, even though largely the same species as in the material from the other samples from the house are present. As the sample is taken from material deposited later, it may have been mixed with that below. Charred bone was not found in any of the samples taken from immediately above the clay floor. It is uncertain if the sample should be referred to the primary function of the house or whether it derives from fill deposited when or after the house was abandoned. In any case, the content of bone seems to indicate the preparation of meat, for which no other traces were present in the house.

Other features

Sample x284 was taken from a feature identified during excavation as building II (not discussed in this article). The interpretation of the structure is uncertain – it may have been either a house or some kind of oven. The feature is probably contemporary with House I. The material was evenly spread in a strictly defined zone within the feature. Another sample from the same feature was previously analysed (Mikkelsen 1999).

The proportional distribution by volume shows that the sample contained as much as 20% cereals and seeds. The sample also contained some fire-cracked stone and a small amount of burnt bone. Together with the content of cereals, this may indicate that the feature was used for preparing both meat and vegetarian food.

The grains were very worn, and no slag of molten clay was found. This rather speaks against the interpretation of the feature as an oven. The sample also contained a few small, rounded pieces of amber. As the pieces were rounded, they can hardly be refuse from amber carving. More likely, the amber was dragged in accidentally together with other material, such as seaweed. In all probability, the structure was used for preparing food.

Sample x300 is taken from the floor layer in the sunken feature building, number XV – the largest of its kind on the site. It is dated to the period 700-1000. The sample contained a fair amount of cereals, albeit so badly preserved that none of the grains could be determined to the level of species. There was a proportionally large amount of Peas or Vetches, but it is not possible to determine whether this was due to random variation or to a specific function.

In comparison with the other samples analysed, the proportional content of cereals was quite low (10 %). Some refuse from forging was found in the building, a fact that agrees well with the large content of charcoal in the sample. The function of the sunken feature building is not clear from the samples analysed. A function as a smithy does not explain the presence of cereals and weeds. Perhaps the fireplace was also used for drying cereals.

The large content of cereals and weeds in all samples suggests that hearths and ovens were extensively em-

ployed for roasting or perhaps preparing the cultivated crops. Only the samples x284 taken from a posthole in house IV, the sample from "building II," and the cleaning-layer from of house I contained fragments of burnt bone, which could indicate that the ash layers contained the remains from the preparation of meat.

What remains puzzling is why or how the material was deposited on the clay floors. The ashen material seems to have been a rather dirty surface to move about on. One possibility is, of course, that the sediments reflect the last activities before the houses were abandoned. This would explain the limited fragmentation: under normal circumstances, charred material would soon be pulverized on a hard floor with frequent trampling. Another possibility is that ash had a value, for which reason it was stored. We know from medieval sources that the alkaline and corrosive potash can be produced from wooden ash by a very simple process. Potash has been used in connection with dying textiles, for tanning, soap, fertilizing, etc. (Wergeland 1829-1834).

Perspectives

The remarkable preservation conditions for cereals, and their ample occurrence, make the site particularly well suited for a functional determination of the houses. In future excavations it must be recommended that samples are collected in a finely meshed grid covering the entire house so that the samples may be compared internally. This method was recently employed in the functional determination of an 11th century workshop from Viborg Søndersø (Moltsen 2005). A denser sampling can offer a much more detailed impression of the use of houses. Moreover, the charred material, i.e. the material that was brought into contact with fire, only reflects certain kinds of activities. Other activities that took place outside, and which did not produce charred material, may be detected in samples from waterlogged soils. For these we must search in pits in wet areas, in wells, and in humid depressions.

Tæbring holds a great potential for illuminating day-to-day activities in the Late Iron Age, as well as for developing methods for functional determination. By future examinations, a very detailed picture may be obtained of the function of individual structures, as well as activities carried out in the open area, in particular if other relevant scientific disciplines are also employed.

Conclusions

In their formal appearance, the three houses discussed show an otherwise conventional sequence from the Late Iron Age and Middle Ages in South Scandinavia. From the 7th century, we find a longhouse with straight walls and rounded gables. In the 9th or 10th century, a slightly broader house with curving walls and straight gables appears. In the 11th century we meet – entirely in accordance with local custom, even if diverging from the mainstream of South Scandinavian architecture – a rather small turf-walled building. Given the long intervals between the constructions, this sequence hardly represents directly successive stages of one farm, but three arbitrary sections through the history of a village community.

Through all stages, and regardless of the outer construction of the buildings, we find a similar arrangement of the basic, domestic quarter of the house. A central room of 25-30m² centred on a heating unit – open hearth or oven – and next to it a slightly smaller room with a clay floor and at least in the earliest house with a second heating unit. The archaeobotanical investigations indicate that the second room was used for drying, preparing, and storing vegetable and to some extent meat. In the earlier two houses further rooms with other functions, e.g. byre or stable, supplemented this basic domestic section.

If we return to some of the few contemporary buildings where internal structures can be discerned, evidence of a similar arrangement will be readily found, even if this has not previously been recognized. In Sædding house III (Fig 17c), presumably from the 9th century, the arrangement of the two heating units and a clay floor in the middle section of the building is identical with Tæbring house IV. The house from Hedeby (Fig. 17i), built in a very different technique, has a similar division.

The analysis of the three houses from Tæbring suggests that the basic domestic unit in this site through the period AD 600-1100 was a two-room structure: One room was a relatively spacious, heated compartment, the other a smaller room where rough processing of cereals and doubtless other foodstuffs took place. The comparison with spatial arrangement in contemporary houses suggests that this was in fact a general feature of houses of the period.

The observations imply that at least some kitchen activities moved out of the central living room as early as by the 7th century – if not even earlier (cf. Lund 2003, 68). While it would be anachronistic to think of a "kitchen",

we can see that a separate unit existed for some kinds of food processing at least.

The description of these two rooms fits surprisingly well with the distinction between salhus (hall) and ildhus ("fire house") documented in the 13th Century law-texts. For lack of earlier textual evidence, we cannot know if a similar, conceptual distinction was made in the Late Iron Age. But if it was, it seems reasonable to assume that the Tæbring houses show the kind of arrangement it referred to.

If this identification is allowed, the early occurrence of this functional division is the great surprise. Such a transformation of the dwelling is commonly assumed not to have occurred in Scandinavia until the Late Viking Age. Moreover, this is a point on which the house diverges markedly from the North Atlantic examples often referred to as typical "Viking houses". While Icelandic houses had special facilities for processing and storing dairy products, the Tæbring houses were organized to sustain the core of a South Scandinavian economy: the cereal harvest.

From a social and symbolic perspective, it would appear that the buildings had a low hierarchy of accessibility. Taking the earliest, best-preserved house as example, there were several entrances, and all rooms except the cellar could be entered without passing more than one other room. The house was concentrically organized: The hearth was the centre of the living room, which was the centre of the house, which was probably again in the centre of the toft. But the concentric arrangement was not a symmetrical one: Assuming a stable or byre to the west, the living room would be set between the humid animal world to the west and the heated, dry room where cereals were taken in and prepared to the east. An equally clear opposition existed between the brightly lit southern façade of the house facing the valley and probably visible from afar, and the dark northern side hiding against the hill-slope, where the refuse-heap was found.

Returning to the theme of our introduction, we may thus visualize how this house would have faced a visitor: Coming from the road he would approach the building from the east and enter through the south-eastern doorway – like other things and beings coming from the fields. Once seated in the warm, clean living room, he would have passed through a dry room with a swept clay floor, where supposedly, he would have seen plenty of stored foodstuffs. Implements for textile production, undoubtedly including a loom, a sign of female virtue, would also have been in one of the rooms. In contrast, he would not have passed the heap of ashes and refuse from the food-preparation hiding behind the northern wall, nor would he have entered the stable or byre. And perhaps disappointingly, he would have known as little as we do what was kept in the cellar, the most inaccessible room of the building. Though the finds give no evidence of great prosperity, the owners of the house would certainly have shown their hospitality by feeding their guest – perhaps like Rig with meat from a cooking-vessel over the fire.

Great halls achieved their splendour by ousting everyday domestic activities to separate buildings. In the late 10th and 11th century, this became emulated by more average farms. Earlier farms like house IV and VII in Tæbring may have aspired to the same by dividing living space up into separate rooms, so that some kitchen activities, and perhaps even the maintenance of the fire was moved out from the central living room. There is little doubt that the yeoman and housewife of Tæbring would have wanted to present their residence well to kinsmen or strangers – no less so than the earl in his hall. The observations made here suggest some of the ways in which they may have sought to show that theirs was a house of good standing.

Considered from the viewpoint of the ideal site, the evidence of the Tæbring houses is meagre enough: The conditions that ensured the preservation of older structures also caused considerable disturbance. The simplicity and completeness of house plans sometimes achieved on sites without cultural layers is rarely attainable in a situation where thick sediments challenge the mere disentanglement of individual features. Although important archaeobotanic results were obtained, richer evidence could undoubtedly have been acquired if the extraordinary features had not appeared unexpectedly during an emergency excavation, but through a systematic sampling strategy.

In spite of this, the presentation has demonstrated how the complexities of a multi-level site permits insights that are missed in the mechanical excavation of large, open surfaces that has been the paradigm of later decades. The preservation state of the houses from Tæbring allows us to discuss a number of issues normally absent from the discourse of Iron Age housing: not only practical function, spatial organization or social presentation, but also individuality, innovation, and unintended consequences. These are aspects that have long been marginal to discussions on housing, due to failure of evidence. Scandinavian settlement archaeology was long focused on technical construction and typology. The detailed investigation of densely informative sites like Tæbring may offer a new departure towards individual biographies of houses as unique historical sequences of cultural configuration.

REFERENCES

Aarsleff, E. 2003: Vikingemønter fra Mors. Nordisk Numismatisk Unions Medlemsblad. 2003:5-6. 86-88.

Ágústsson, H. 1982: Den islandske bondegårds udvikling fra landnamstiden indtil det 20. århundrede. In: Myhre et al. (eds.). 255-268.

Anderberg, A.L. 1994: Atlas of seeds and small fruits of NorthwestEuropean plant species with morphological descriptions. Part 4. RecedaceaeUmbelliferae. Stockholm (Swedish Museum of Natural History).

Artelius, T., E. Englund & L. Ersgård (eds.): Kring västsvenska hus – boendets organisation och symbolik i förhistorisk och historisk tid. Gotarc Ser. C. Arkeologiska Skrifter 22. Göteborg (Göteborg Universitet, Inst. för Arkeologi).

Bantelmann, A. 1975: Die frühgeschichtliche Marschensiedlung beim Elisenhof in Eiderstedt. Landschaftsgeschichte und Baubefunde. Studien zur Küstenarchäologie Schleswig-Holsteins, Serie A, 1.

Berggren, G. 1981: Atlas of seeds and small fruits of Northwest European plant species with morphological descriptions. Part 3. SalicaceaeCruciferae. Stockholm (Swedish Museum of Natural History).

Bertelsen, J. Brinch 1992: Nederby på Fur – en landsby grundlagt i yngre jernalder. Et bidrag til belysning af vikingetidsbebyggelsen i den vestlige del af Limfjorden. Kuml 1990. 99-118.

Birkedahl, P. & Johansen, E. 2000: The Eastern Limfjord in the Germanic Iron Age and the Viking Period. Internal Structures and External Relations. Acta Archaeologica 71. 25-33.

Christensen, T. 1991: Lejre – syn og sagn. Roskilde (Roskilde Museum).

Christensen, T. 1993: Lejre beyond Legend – the Archaeological Evidence. Journal of Danish Archaeology 10 (1991). 163-185.

Dronke, U. 1997: The Poetic Edda, edited with translation, introduction and commentary. Vol. II : Mythological poems Oxford (Clarendon).

Giddens, A. 1984: The constitution of society. Cambridge (Polity Press).

Göthberg, H, O. Kyhlberg & A. Vinberg 1995: Hus och gård i det förurbana samhället. Riksantikvarieämbetet, Arkeologiska undersökningar. Skrifter nr. 13. Stockholm.

Hansen, K.M. & H. Høier 2000: Næs - en vikingetidsbebyggelse med hørproduktion. Kuml. 59-89.

Hansen, S. Stummann 1991: Toftanes: A Faroese Viking Age

farmstead from the 9-10th centuries A.D. Acta Archaeologica 61. 44-53.

Hansen, S. Stummann 2000: Viking Setlement in Shetland. Chronological and Regional Contexts. Acta Archaeologica 71. 87- 103.

Hansen, T. Egebjerg 1995: Vikingetidsgård ved Vesterbygård I Tarm. Fram 1995. 114-116.

Hansen, T. Egebjerg, S. Hvass & D. Kaldal Mikkelsen 1991: Landbebyggelsen i 7. århundrede. In: P. Mortensen & B.M. Rasmussen (ed.): Høvdingesamfund og Kongemagt. Fra Stamme til Stat i Danmark 2. Jysk arkæologisk Selskabs skrifter XXII:2. Århus (Aarhus Universitetsforlag).

Hansson, A.-M. 2003: Plant remains from Borg I:1. In: G.S. Munch, O.S. Johansen & E. Roesdahl (ed.). 87-107.

Henriksen, P.S. & D.E. Robinson 1994: Ældre jernalders agerbrug: arkæobotaniske analyser af kornfund fra Overbygård, Østerbølle, Fjand og Alrum. NNU-rapport nr. 12 (1994). København (Nationalmuseet).

Henriksen, P.S, D.E Robinson & K. Kelertas (in press): Bronze Age agriculture, land use and vegetation in Bjerre Enge based on archaebotanical investigations. In: J.-H. Bech (Ed.): Bronze Age Settlement Structure and Land Use in Thy, NW Denmark - primarily based on settlements from Bjerre Enge, Northern Thy.

Herschend, F. 1997: Livet i Hallen. Tre fallstudier i den yngre järnålderns aristokrati. Occasional Papers in Archaeology. Institutionen för arkeologi och antik historia. Uppsala Universitet. Uppsala.

Herschend, F. & D. Kaldal Mikkelsen 2003: The Main Building at Borg (I:1). In: G.S. Munch, O.S. Johansen & E. Roesdahl (ed.). 41-76.

Hvass, S. 1993: Bebyggelsen. In: S. Hvass & B. Storgaard (eds.): Da klinger i muld... 25 års arkæologi i Danmark. Århus (Aarhus Universitetsforlag). 187-194

Isaksson, S. & Hjulström, B., 2000. The spatial variation of alkanoic acid and n-alkane distributions in ancient anthropogenic soils. In: S. Isaksson (ed.): Food and Rank in Early Medieval Time. Archaeological Research Laboratory, Stockholm University, Stockholm.

Isaksson, S., M. Wojnar-Johanson & B. Hjulström 2000: The spatial organization of subsistence at an Early Medieval manor. An application of soil chemistry at a settlement in the Vendel parish, Uppland, Sweden. In: S. Isakssen (ed.) Food and Rank in Early Medieval Time. Archaeological Research Laboratory, Stockholm University, Stockholm.

Isaksson, S. 1998: A kitchen entrance to the aristocracy – analysis of lipid biomarkers in cultural layers. Laborativ Arkeologi 10-11. 43-53.

Jacobsson, B. 2002: Ståstorp – en gård från sen vendeltid och vikingatid. I: M. Mogren (red.): Märkvärt, medeltida. Arkeologi ur en lång skånsk historia. Riksantikvarieämbetet Arkeologiska undersökningar Skrifter 43. Stockholm. 99-126.

Jensen, S. 1987: Gårde fra vikingetiden ved Gl. Hviding og Vilslev. Mark og Montre 1986-87. 5-26.

Jouttijärvi, A. 2003: Slagger og jern fra Tæbring. MS. Heimdal-arkæometri.

Jørgensen, L. 2003: Manor and Market at Lake Tissø in the Sixth to Eleventh Centuries – A Survey of the Danish 'Productive' Sites. In: T. Pestell & K. Ulmschneider (eds.): Markets in Early Medieval Europe. Trading and 'Productive' sites, 650-850. Macclesfield (Windgather). 175-207

Jørgensen, L. Bender & P. Eriksen (eds.) 1995: Trabjerg. En vestjysk landsby fra Vikingetiden. Jysk Arkæologisk Selskabs Skrifter XXXI:1. Århus (Århus Universitetsforlag).

Kristiansen, M.S. 1998: Tårnby – a farm of the period 1100-1800. An analysis of the medieval farm. Journal of Danish Archaeology 12, 1994-95. 171-195.

Lang, J. 1984: The Hogback: A Viking Colonial Monument. Anglo-Saxon Studies in Archaeology and History 3. Oxford (Oxford University Committee for Archaeology).

Lund, J. 2003: Boligfunktioner I jernalderhuse omkring Kristi Fødsel. In: E. Roesdahl (ed.), 67-76.

Lundquist, L. 1996: Slöinge – en stormansgård från järnåldern. In: L. Lundquist, K. Lindeblad, A. Nielsen & L. Ersgård (eds.): Slöinge och Borg. Stormansgårdar i øst och väst. Riksantikvarämbetet. Arkeologiska undersökningar. Skrifter nr. 18. 9-52.

Lundquist, L. 1997: Central Places and Central Areas in the Late Iron Age. Some Examples from South-western Sweden. In: H. Andersson, P. Carelli & L. Ersgård (eds.): Visions of the Past. Trends and Traditions in Swedish Medieval Archaeology. Lund Studies in Medieval Archaeology 19. Riksantikvarämbetet. Arkeologiska undersökningar. Skrifter nr. 24. 179-193.

Madsen, H. J. & Bugge Vegger, P. 1992: Karby på Mors. En landsby fra vikingetiden. Kuml 1990. 133-150.

Mikkelsen, D. Kaldal 2003: Boligfunktioner i vikingetidens gårde. I: E. Roesdahl (red.): Bolig og familie i Danmarks middelalder. Århus (Jysk arkæologisk selskab). 77-87.

Mikkelsen, P.H. 1999: Arkæobotanisk undersøgelse af prøver fra Tæbring (MHM 1335). Unpublished report.

Moltsen, A.S.A. 2005: Lag- og makrofossiler. In: M. Iversen, D.E. Robinson, J. Hjermind & C. Christensen (eds): Viborg Søndersø II 1018-1030. Arkæologi og naturvidenskab i et værkstedsområde fra vikingetid. Jysk Arkæologisk Selskabs Skrifter nr. 52. Højbjerg (Aarhus Universitetsforlag).

Munch, G.S., O.S. Johansen & E. Roesdahl (ed.) 2003: Borg in Lofoten. A chieftain's farm in North Norway. Trondheim (Tapir).

Myhre, B. 1980: Gårdsanlegget på Ullandhaug I. Gårdshus i jernalder og middelalder i Sørvest-Norge. AmS-skrifter 4. Stavanger (Arkeologisk museum).

Myhre, B. 1982: Bolighusets utvikling fra jernalder til middelalder i Sørvest-Norge. In: Myhre et al. (eds.). 195-217.

Myhre, B. 2000: The early Viking Age in Norway. Acta Archaeologica 71. 35-47

Myhre, B., B. Stoklund & P. Gjæder (eds.) 1982: Vestnordisk byggeskikk gjennom to tusen år. Tradisjon og forandring fra romertid til det 19. århundre. AmS-skrifter 7. Stavanger (Arkeologisk museum).

Nielsen, J. N. 2002: Bejsebakken, a central site near Aalborg in Northern Jutland. In: B. Hårdh & L. Larsson (eds.): Central Places in the Migration and Merovingian Periods. Papers from the 52nd Sachsensymposium, Lund, August 2001. Uppåkrastudier 6. Acta Archaeologica Lundensia Ser. in 8° no. 39. Lund (Almqvist & Wiksell). 197-213.

Nielsen, L.C. 1980: Omgård. A Settlement from the Late Iron Age and the Viking Period in West Jutland. Acta Archaeologica 50. 173-208.

Nielsen, S. 1976: En vikingetidslandsby på Mors. MIV 6. 52-61.

Nielsen, S. 1985: Karby-udgravningen på Mors. Med nogle bemærkninger om den keramiske udvikling i yngre jernalder. Aarbøger for Nordisk oldkyndighed og Historie 1984. 260-281.

Nielssen, J.N. 2002: Flammernes bytte. Skalk 2002:6.

Nielsson, T. 1976: Hus og huskonstruktioner. In: A.W. Mårtensson (ed.): Uppgrävt förflutet för Pkbanken i Lund. En investering i arkeologi. Archaeologica Lundensia investigationes de antiqvitatibus urbis Lundae. Lund (Kulturhistoriska museet). 41-72.

Nilsson, Ö & H. Hjelmqvist 1967: Studies on the nutlet structure of south Scandinavian species of Carex. Botaniska Notiser 120, 46085.

Nørlund, P. 1948: Trelleborg. Nordiske Fortidsminder IV:1. København (Nordisk Forlag).

Olsen, O. & H. Schmidt 1977: Fyrkat. En jysk vikingeborg I.

Borgen og bebyggelsen. Nordiske Fortidsminder B 4. København.

Olsen, Anne-Louise H. 2005: Af tørvehusets saga. Skalk 2005:4. 20-27

Parker Pearson, M. & Richards, C. (eds.) 1994: Architecture & Order. Approaches to Social Space. London & New York.

Pedersen, A. 1994: Landsbyerne på Lindholm Høje. I: E. Johansen & A. Lerche Trolle (ed.): Lindholm Høje. Gravplads og Landby. Ålborg. 39-52.

Price, N. 1995: House and Home in Viking Age Iceland: Cultural Expression in Scandinavian Colonial Architecture. In: D. N. Benjamin (ed.): The Home: Words, Interpretations, Meanings, and Environments. Avebury.

Robinson, D.E. 1994a: Plants and Vikings: Everyday life in Viking Age Denmark. In: J.H. Dickson & J.H. Lennard (eds.): Plants and People. Botanical Journal of Scotland 46(4), 542-551.

Robinson, D.E 1994b: Dyrkede planter fra Danmarks forhistorie. Arkæologiske Udgravninger i Danmark 1993. København (Det Arkæologiske Nævn).

Roesdahl, E. 1977: Aggersborg. The Viking settlement and fortress. Chateau Gaillard VII:I. 269-278.

Roesdahl, E. 1986: Vikingernes Aggersborg. IN: F. Nørgaard et al. (eds.): Aggersborg gennem 1000 år. Herning (Poul Kristensens forlag). 53-93.

Roesdahl, E. (ed.) 2003: Bolig og familie i Danmarks middelalder. Århus (Jysk arkæologisk selskab).

Sabo, K. 2001: Vem behöver en by? Kyrkheddinge, struktur och strategi under tusen år. Riksantikvarieämbetet Arkeologiska Undersökningar Skrifter 38. Stockholm.

Samson, R. (ed.) 1990. The Social Archaeology of Houses. Edinburgh.

Schietzel, K. 1984: Die Baubefunde in Haithabu. In: H. Jahnkuhn et alii (red.): Archäologische und naturwissenschaftliche Untersuchungen an ländlichen und frühstädtliche Siedlungen im Deutschen Küstengebiet vom 5. Jahrhundert v. Chr. bis zum 11. Jahrhundert n. Chr. Bd. II: Handelsplätze des frühen und hohen Mittelalters. Weinheim (Acta Humaniora), 135-158

Schmidt, H. 1970: Vikingernes husformede gravsten. Nationalmuseets Arbejdsmark 1970. 13-28.

Schmidt, H. 1994: Building customs in Viking age Denmark. Herning.

Schultz, C.G. 1949: Aggersborg. Vikingelejren ved Limfjorden. Fra Nationalmuseets Arbejdsmark 1949. 91-108.

Skibsted Klæsøe, I. 1999: Vikingetidens kronologi – en nybearbejdning af det arkæologiske materiale. Aarbøger for Nordisk oldkyndighed og Historie 1997. 89-142.

Skov, H. 1995: Hustyper i vikingetid og middelalder. hikuin 21, 139-162.

Stace, C. 1991: New Flora of the British Isles. Cambridge (Cambridge University Press).

Steensberg, A. 1952: Bondehuse og vandmøller i Danmark gennem 2000 år. København.

Stenberger, M. (ed.) 1943: Forntida gårdar i Island. København.

Stoklund, B. 2003: Andre veje til middelalderhuset – en filologisk-etnologisk tilgang. I: E. Roesdahl (red.): Bolig og familie i Danmarks middelalder. Århus (Jysk arkæologisk selskab). 15-29.

Stoumann, I. 1980: Sædding. A Viking-age Village near Esbjerg. Acta Archaeologica 50. 95-118.

Söderberg, B. 2003: Integrating Power. Some aspects of a Magnate's Farm and Presumed Central Place in Järrestad, South-East Scania. In: L. Larsson & B. Hårdh (eds.): Centrality – regionality. The social structure of southern Sweden during the Iron Age. Uppåkrastudier 7. Acta Archaeologica Lundensia Ser. in 8° no. 40. Lund (Almqvist & Wiksell). 283-310.

Söderberg, B. 2005: Aristokratisk rum och gränsöverskridande. Järrestad och sydöstra Skåne mellan region och rike 600-1100. Riksantikvarieämbetet Arkeologiska undersökningar Skrifter No 62. Stockholm (Riksantikvarieämbetet).

Tesch, S. 1993: Houses, Farmsteads, and Long-term Change. A Regional Study of Prehistoric Settlements in the Köpinge Area, in Scania, Southern Sweden. Uppsala (Uppsala University, Dept. of Archaeology).

Ulriksen, J. 1998: Anløbspladser. Besejling og bebyggelse i Danmark mellem 200 og 1100 e.Kr. Roskilde (Vikingeskibshallen).

Vegger, P.B. 1987: Dalgård. In: Danmarks længste udgravning. Arkæologi på naturgassens vej. Nationalmuseet & De danske Naturgasselskaber. 252-253.

Viklund, K. 1998: Cereals, Weeds and Crop Processing in Iron Age Sweden. Methodological and interpretive aspects of archaeobotanical evidence. Archaeology and Environment 14. Umeå.

Wergeland, H. 1829-1834: Den Norske Bondes Nyttige Kundskab. In: H. Jæger, D. Arup Seip, H. Koth & E. Højgård (eds): Samlede skrifter. Afhandlinger, oplysningsskrifter IV, vol. 1. Kristiania/Olso (Steenske forlag) 1918-1940. 87-132.

Authors' addresses
Poul Mikkelsen, Morslands Historiske Museum, Dueholm Kloster, DK-7900 Nykøbing, Mors, Denmark dueholm@museum.dk
Annine S.A. Moltsen, NOK – Natur og Kultur, Valdemarsgade 19a 2.mf., DK-1665 Kbh.V., Denmark nok@nokam.dk
Søren M. Sindbæk, Institute of Anthropology, Archaeology & Linguistics, Aarhus University – Moesgaard, DK-8270 Højbjerg, Denmark farksms@hum.au.dk

TABLES

Table 1. Analysed samples – volume and contents except seeds.

Sample no.	Feature	Sample ml	Analyzed Volume ml	Cereals, weeds ml	Contents
xHouse I	House I	205	57	13	Grey sand. After floatation a small residue was left, consisting in ¾ fine sand and ¼ coarse sand. The sample contained a little charred turf, charcoal, charred twigs and roots from Calluna vulgaris, as well as many recent roots.
x234	House I	167	72	27	A few pieces of charcoal, some twigs and small braqnches.
x235	House I	106	32,25	11,25	Charcoal, charred twigs and roots from Calluna vulgaris, rather coarse material.
x334	House I	54	25	2,1	Fine grey-brown sand. Middle-sized residue of fine sand and a tiny amount of coarse sand. The sample contained charcoal, twigs and roots from Calluna vulgaris and a few fragments of burned bone.
x284	" House II"	253,1	79,5	21,5	Fine grey-brown sand. Middle-sized residue of fine sand and a tiny amount of coarse sand. The sample contained charcoal, twigs and roots from Calluna vulgaris, some fragments of burned bone, as well as a few, small rounded lumps of amber and fire-cracked stones.
x411	Oven-like feature	72	72	46	The sample contained a few pieces of charcoal and some white slag with air bubbles.
x372	House IV	176	41	22,75	Fine light-brown sand. After floatation a middle-sized residue was left, consisting in 2/3 fine sand and 1/3 coarse sand. The sample contained small and somewhat larger pieces of charcoal, some small fragments of burned clay or bog-iron, a few fragments of burned bone, some charred twigs from Calluna vulgaris, charred straw, a few pieces of burned flint and some amount of white slag with air bubbles.
x849	House VII	10	10	< 1	The sample contained charcoal, charred straw, and a few charred twigs.
x300	Sunken feature building XV	245	245	38,75	The sample consisted in red-brown sandy ashes. It contained large pieces of charcoal, fine stems and roots from Calluna vulgaris and straw.

Table 2. Content of cereals and seeds in the analysed samples.

			House I				Oven	"House II"	House IV	House VII	Sunken feature building
	Danish navn	English name	MHM 1335 hus I	MHM 1335 235	MHV 1335 234	MHV 1335 334	MHM 1335 411	MHV 1335 284	MHV 1335 372	MHM 1335 849	MHV 1335 300
Cultivated species											
Hordeum vulgare	Almindelig Byg	Hulled Barley	26	18+42cf	116	5	895	31	36		
Secale cereale	Almindelig Rug	Rye	18+2 ears	15	83+1 ears	2	24 +1 ears	2 ears 7	12+2 ears		5 ears
Ceralia	Korn		144+292f	133+45f	387+498f	27+45f	118+507f	123	265+379f		460+80f
Weeds											
Chenopodium album	Hvidmelet Gåsefod	Fat-Hen	28	6	27	15	31	30	561	4	107
Atriplex sp.	Mælde	Oraches	30	3	1	4	6	6	22		22
Brassica sp.	Kål/Turnips	Cabbages									2
Fallopia convolvulus	Snerle-Pileurt	Black-bindweed		1	5			1	5+1f		15
Polygonum aviculare s.l.	Vej-Pileurt	Knot-tgrass	1						28		2
Poa annua	Enårig Rapgræs	Annual Meadow-grass							20		
Raphanus raphanistrum	Kiddike	Wild Radish					2 joint	1/4 silique	3/2 joint		
Plantago lanceolata	Lancet-Vejbred	Ribwort						1	4	1	1
Rumex acetosella	Rødknæ	Sheep's Sorrel					4		419		
Persicaria maculosa	Fersken-Pileurt	Redshank	2		1		2	3	4		
Urtica urens	Liden Nælde	Small Nettle							1		
Persicaria lapathifolia ssp. pallida	Bleg Pileurt	Pale Persicaria	1		2	1	6	5½	95		17
Spergula arvensis	Almindelig Spergel	Corn Spurrey					1		23		
Stellaria media	Almindelig Fuglegræs	Common Chickweed							1		2
Bromus sp.	Hejre	Bromes							cf. 286		
Meadow species											
Bolboschoenus cf. maritimus	Strand-Kogleears	Sea Club-rush							7		
Calluna vulgaris	Hedelyng	Heather							2 flowers		2 flowers
Carex nigra	Almindelig Star	Common Sedge							5		
Carex sp.	Star	Sedge	6	4	19	12		17	58		45
Lycopus europaeus	Sværtevæld	Gypsy-wort							2		
Luzula sp.	Frytle	Wood-rushes				2					
Malva sp.	Katost	Mallows							1		

	Danish navn	English name	House I				Oven	"House II"	House IV	House VII	Sunken feature building
			MHM 1335 hus I	MHM 1335 235	MHV 1335 234	MHV 1335 334	MHM 1335 411	MHV 1335 284	MHV 1335 372	MHM 1335 849	MHV 1335 300
Rhinanthus sp.	Skjaller	Yellow-rattles							2		
Myrica gale	Mose-Pors	Bog-myrtles						1			
Eleocharis sp.	Sumpstrå	Spike-rushes							2		
Others											
Galeopsis sp.	Hanekro	Hemp-nettles	1	1					7		2
Galium sp.	Snerre	Bedstraws									1
Avena sp.	Havre	Oats	6	6	1	1	29		6		
cf. Avena	Havre lign	Oats							8½		
Carduus/ Cirsium	Tidsel	Thistles	1								
Viola sp.	Viol	Violets							3		
Lathyrus/Vicia	Latyrus/Vikke	Peas/Vetches	24	9	122	8	6	130	17+18/2		707
Poaceae	Græs	Grass	3	2	9	3	2	32		4	
Poa sp.	Rapgræs	Meadow-grass									2
Ranunculus sp.	Ranunkel	Butter-cups						1	10		
Trifolium sp.	Kløver	Clovers					2		2		
Silene sp.	Limurt	Campions			1				1		
Rumex sp.	Skræppe	Docks	1	1	6			8½	7	1	5
Potentilla sp.	Potentil	Cinque-foils						1	2	2	1

Table 3. Content of cereals in sample x1033 from Hundborg (THY 3432), cf. Moltsen 1999.

Latin name	Danish name	English name	Number	Weight
Secale cereale	Rug	Rye	365	2 g
Hordeum vulgare	Byg (flere avnklædte)	Barley	364	3,7 g
Avena sp.	Havre sp.	Oats	155	0,9 g
Triticum compactum	Dværg-Hvede	Club Wheat	165	1,1 g

Acta Archaeologica vol. 79, 2008, pp 110-144
Printed in Denmark • All rights reserved

MAGNATE ESTATES ALONG THE ROAD
VIKING AGE SETTLEMENTS, COMMUNICATION AND CONTACTS IN SOUTH-WEST SCANIA, SWEDEN

ANNE CARLIE

INTRODUCTION

Just a few decades ago, the research picture of the social dimensions of Iron Age settlement in southern Scandinavia was still rather hazy. As a result of the more systematic use of metal detectors on sites, the state of our knowledge today is completely different, and details are beginning to stand out. One of the phenomena that can be clearly discerned is the complexes of large estates with halls from the Late Iron Age and Viking Age. Based on similarities in building styles and organization, it has been suggested that these sites should be regarded as exponents of a collective aristocratic network of individuals and groups which gave certain families a special social position above others. A characteristic feature of these estates, which is believed to distinguish them from other more ordinary farms, is the occurrence of sequences of halls. In a study of the complex at Järrestad in south-east Scania, Bengt Söderberg uses the hall as a distinguishing element, which can be followed on the same site during several successive phases (Söderberg 2005, 107).

Excavated farms with sequences of halls are at present known from five places in southern Scandinavia. Apart from Järrestad there are three sites in Zealand, represented by Tissø on the west side of the island, towards the Great Belt (Jørgensen 2002), Lejre in Roskilde Fjord (Christensen 1997), and Strøby Toftegård at Stevns on the east side of the island, by the Sound (Tornbjerg 1998). The fifth site is at Slöinge in Halland, by the Kattegat (Lundqvist 2003). Uppåkra in south-west Scania should also be added to the group, with its sequence of halls, although the relationship to a contemporary estate complex has not yet been clarified (Larsson & Lenntorp 2004). In a comparative study Söderberg urges caution, saying that we should not ascribe too much importance to the

geographical distribution of the sites, since new finds can quickly change the picture. At the same time, he notes the lack of sites with sequences of halls in Jutland and Funen, despite the fact that several large estates with halls have been excavated in these areas (Söderberg 2005, 112f).

Smaller magnate estates[1] from the Late Iron Age and Viking Age, that is, estates not belonging to the uppermost stratum of society, but to individuals or collectives who were lower down the social ladder, have attracted much less attention in the archaeological discussion (but see e.g. Widgren 1998; Ethelberg 2003, 310ff; Carlie & Artursson 2005, 218ff). These are estate complexes which differ from the mass of farms through their appearance and size, but do not show any explicit traces of an aristocratic lifestyle or special functions such as specialized craft.

In this article I have chosen to focus on one such type of smaller magnate estate. The empirical point of departure is the Västervång site at Trelleborg in south-west Scania, where the Southern Excavations Department (UV Syd) of the National Heritage Board a few years ago investigated parts of a large settlement from the Late Vendel Period and Viking Age which also contained remains of a large estate complex (Ericson & Carlie 2006). The estate can be followed during two settlement phases on the site, but otherwise does not distinguish itself by its finds.

The aim is to understand what the estate at Västervång and other similar complexes represented in their own times. Should the size of these units in relation to other contemporary settlement be viewed solely as a reflection

---

[1] At the moment we lack adequate terminology to describe different types of Iron Age farms in terms of social and settlement hierarchy. I have chosen the term "smaller magnate estate" to distinguish these sites from larger estate complexes with a clear aristocratic character.

of greater prosperity? Or are there signs suggesting that these belonged to a local elite with social contacts that extended outside the local district? My thesis is that we should look at the estate complexes from the latter perspective, mainly because of the similarities in building styles that can be detected in the archaeological record from contemporary estates in different parts of southern Scandinavia. In Scania and Zealand one can see clear influences in the architecture of the buildings from western Denmark and houses of Sædding type. In Scania it is striking that the estate complexes with Sædding-like houses that we know of were all located along one of the major roads in the region, running between Uppåkra and Trelleborg on the south coast of Scania. I would not go

Fig. 1. Section of the Scanian Reconnaissance Map from 1812–20. This shows the location of the Västervång site in relation to known graves and settlement sites from the Vendel Period and Viking Age in the vicinity. The map also shows the location of three of the four Köpinge-places north-east of Trelleborg. Illustration: Henrik Pihl.

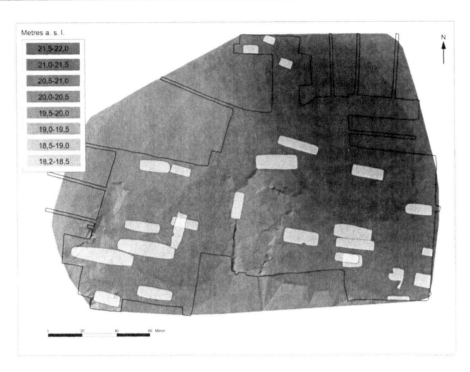

Fig. 2. GIS model of the microtopography of the site, with the houses marked. The model is based on a large number of altitude figures measured all over the site under today's topsoil cover and preserved layers, which means that this captures the variation in the early surface topography of the site, before the effects of modern agriculture. The altitude varied between 19 and 23 metres above sea level and is shown in the GIS model with 0.5 metre equidistant contours, with light areas marking higher terrain and darker areas lower sections. GIS model: Karin Lund. Illustration: Henrik Pihl.

so far as to ascribe political implications to the similarities in building style, that is, viewing these as expressions of regional or supra-regional alliances between different individuals or collectives. The adoption of a new building tradition should instead be regarded as an active choice, through which the owner/builder manifested his social affiliation.

The article consists of four parts. The first part presents the settlement site and magnate farm at Västervång, after which the site is related to the Late Iron Age settlement and graves in the surrounding district. The introduction to the site and the landscape around Trelleborg is followed by an analysis of the architecture of the estate. The focus is on the appearance and construction of the main building on each site, which is discussed from a comparative southern Scandinavian perspective. I argue that the influences on the house types should be sought in Jutland in houses of the type called after the example at Sædding. The third part of the article asks how we should interpret the similarities in the buildings on the estates. To answer that question I choose to look more closely at how the

Scanian farms were localized in the landscape, which provides a foundation for putting them into a contemporary social context. The article is followed by an appendix, where the Late Iron Age settlement at Västervång is presented in more detail. The emphasis is on an analysis and description of the spatial and social organization of the settlement.

VÄSTERVÅNG SETTLEMENT

Västervång is situated in south-west Scania, just north of the town of Trelleborg (Fig. 1).[2] The Iron Age settlement was located on a noticeable height, about 19 to 23 m above sea level, some two kilometres from the coast and with a view of the sea. The distance to the coast is approximately two kilometres. To the south, west, and east of the height the terrain slopes gently down towards slightly wetter land. Less than a kilometre north-west of

---

2 Historical maps show that the site is in the west field belonging to the town lands of Trelleborg, hence the place-name *Västre vång*.

the site there is a small watercourse lined by wetlands, which discharges into the sea just west of the town.

Besides a short phase in the Bronze Age, the settlement at Västervång can be followed on roughly the same site from the fifth century BC until the Late Viking Age, that is, for almost one and a half millennia.[3] Most of the long-houses were on small ledges and/or heights in terrain gently sloping towards the south and west. The location of the houses is evident from the GIS-based terrain model in Fig. 2, which shows a reconstruction of the early topography of the site. The soils are mainly till and boulder clay without much stone; experiments have shown that this clay is suitable for use as daub.[4] In the excavated area there were also a very large number of pits, probably dug to extraction of clay.

The Early Iron Age settlement consisted of single farms which moved at regular intervals – perhaps with each new generation – to a new location on the cultivated lands. It was not until the eighth century AD that settlement became more stationary and a village was established on the height. In the oldest phase (c. 770–900 AD) the village consisted of at least four or five farms.[5] These were built around a natural depression which had been filled in with soil during the Early Bronze Age, roughly two thousand years earlier. One of the farms, placed slightly on its own to the west of the depression, was much larger than the other units. With its 37-metre longhouse and extra buildings the farm had a building area of approximately 380 m², which can be compared with the smallest farm in the village with an area of less than 100 m². The big estate and two more farms were rebuilt in the Late Viking Age (900–1050 AD, while other units were abandoned or moved from the site.[6]

In both phases the main building of the estate was virtually identical in appearance and proportions, 37 and 34 metres long respectively, with convex long walls and a maximum width of 8.7 metres at the middle of the house. In their external construction both houses display influences from the building tradition of western Denmark and houses of Sædding type, while the internal plan seems to have a more local touch.

In both phases the estate had extra buildings. In the later phase, however, the estate took on a more complex composition, in that it probably had two extra post-built houses besides the main building. One of these - a 20-metre-long single-aisled building - was at right angles to the long-house and was joined to it. The estate also had a medium-sized house south of the main building. This meant the estate had buildings with a total area of about 510 m². The increased building area suggests that the economy of the estate had changed, perhaps towards a greater emphasis on grain production, which required extra space in the form of barns for threshing, storage, and so on.

The village probably also had a small workshop area, located at the south-east of the site.[7] The remains consisted of a small post-building with an open side and windbreak, which was possibly used as a forge. Among the finds there were occasional objects indicating that textile and antler crafts were pursued in the vicinity. There were no sunken-floor huts, however, and there is no evidence of specialized craft on the site. The finds are instead dominated by ordinary domestic pottery and animal bones.[8]

LATE IRON AGE AT TRELLEBORG
GRAVES
The area surrounding Trelleborg is very rich in antiquities. The Iron Age remains mostly consist of graves and cemeteries, whereas settlements from the period are not as well known. A large cemetery (Trelleborg RAÄ 2), which is contemporary with the village and the estate, is located roughly one kilometre south-west of Västervång (see Fig. 1). The cemetery has been excavated several times between 1916 and 2005. Approximately 40 graves have been investigated, but the cemetery has been damaged by gravel quarrying, and the total number of burials has been estimated to be twice as high. The burial ground is thus one of the biggest known in the area around Trelleborg. The cemetery was in use during a time extending over both the Vendel Period and the Viking Age. 14C dates obtained from the skeletal material show, however,

---

3 The dating of the settlement is based on a combination of different materials, consisting of ¹⁴C samples, the architecture of the houses and the objects found, chiefly pottery. For a presentation of all the settlement phases (1–6) readers are referred to the report (Ericson & Carlie 2005; Carlie 2008).

4 Personal communication, Ylva Kristina Ekelund, Trelleborgen.

5 See *Appendix*, phase 5.

6 See *Appendix*, phase 6.

7 See *Appendix*, phase 5.

8 The pottery has been analysed by Ole Stilborg of the Ceramic Research Laboratory, Lund University (Stilborg 2006), while the animal bones have been identified by Annica Cardell (2006).

that the majority of the graves date from the tenth century. The graves mostly consist of flat-earth inhumations, but there are also traces of kerb trenches, probably remains of removed burial mounds (Hellerström 2005; Arcini & Jacobsson 2008).

Yet another large cemetery, Järavallen (Maglarp RAÄ 5), is situated on the coast about four kilometres south-west of Västervång. The cemetery consists of 80 or so small barrows, but it was originally larger. Earlier excavations indicate that the barrows were built in the Late Iron Age, from the Migration Period up to the Viking Age, but that the site was also used for burials in the Pre-Roman Iron Age and the Roman Iron Age (Hansen 1945; Jacobsson 2003, 197f). Single graves or small groups of inhumation graves from the Late Iron Age have also been found at other places around Trelleborg (see Fig. 1, Trelleborg RAÄ 18, 19, and 21). For instance, a group of three inhumation graves was discovered just south of a Viking Age ring-fort in the town of Trelleborg at the end of the 1980s (see below) (Jeppsson 1995).

Fredrik Svanberg, in his study of Viking Age graves and funeral rituals in south-east Scandinavia, interprets south-west Scania as a separate tradition area (2003), characterized by inhumation graves with few grave goods. Cremation graves also occur, but to a much lesser extent. Most inhumation graves have been found under flat earth. Svanberg considers it likely, however, that many graves were originally covered by flat mounds which have been destroyed by later ploughing; he refers to the barrow cemetery at Järavallen. Svanberg simultaneously stressed that the burial tradition in south-west Scania should be regarded as part of a more widespread ritual tradition that also existed in much of present-day Denmark (ibid., 85ff).

SETTLEMENT SITES

The large number of graves in the Trelleborg area suggests that it was heavily populated in the Late Iron Age. Current excavations occasioned by the extension of the E6 in the plains north-west of Trelleborg confirm this picture, having uncovered remains of Late Iron Age settlement at a number of sites along the road (Jacobsson & Riddersporre 2007). There are in total ten or so sites located near the historical villages of Maglarp, Skregrie, Hermanstorp, Södra and Norra Håslöv, and Vellinge. The excavations hitherto show that settlement consists of both long-houses and sunken-floor huts. From several sites there are also metal finds, including different types

of costume brooches from the Vendel Period and Viking Age (beak fibulae, equal-armed brooch, circular flat fibula, Urnes brooch) and a couple of Arabic silver coins.[9] All in all, the excavations indicate very dense settlement in the area in the Late Iron Age. The frequent occurrence of sunken-floor huts is especially interesting, contrasting it with the settlement at Västervång.

If we look instead at the area immediately surrounding Trelleborg, there are only two excavated sites in the inland with Late Iron Age settlement apart from the Västervång site (see Fig. 1). The nearest settlement is about one and a half kilometres east-south-east of Västervång (Trelleborg RAÄ 21). The excavation uncovered traces of settlement in the form of long-houses and sunken-floor huts, and pottery from the Vendel Period or Viking Age. Otherwise the extent and size of the settlement site is unknown (Jacobsson 1996). The other settlement is at Ståstorp, about two and a half kilometres west-south-west of Västervång (Västra Tommarp RAÄ 38). Here a well-preserved farm in two settlement phases was excavated. In both phases the farm consisted of a roughly 25-metre long-house, a large outbuilding, and one or more small outhouses, including a sunken-floor hut (Jacobsson 2002).

Apart from the settlement sites in the inland, parts of a large coastal settlement from the Vendel Period and Early Viking Age were excavated in the present-day town of Trelleborg, in connection with various building projects and inspections there (Trelleborg RAÄ 19) (Jacobsson 2000). Besides remains of settlement, chiefly in the form of sunken-floor huts (about 25 in number) but also post-built houses, evidence of a large occupation layer was also found. The layer is up to about 30 centimetres thick and can be followed within an area some 800 metres long and 100–200 metres wide along the former shoreline (Fig. 3). The finds mainly consist of pottery and animal bones, but there are also quite a few everyday objects, including loom weighs, spindle whorls, and bone needles, testifying to the pursuit of textile craft on the site. There is no sure evidence that specialized craft was pursued on the beach ridge. On the other hand, there is quite a lot of pottery of foreign provenance, suggesting that there was some trade or exchange on the site. It is above all early Slavic pottery (AII) of the Feldberg and Fresendorf types. There are also sherds from pots of Tatinger type (AI) from Frisia, and oc-

---

9 Personal communication, Bengt Jacobsson and Bengt Söderberg, National Heritage Board UV Syd, Lund.

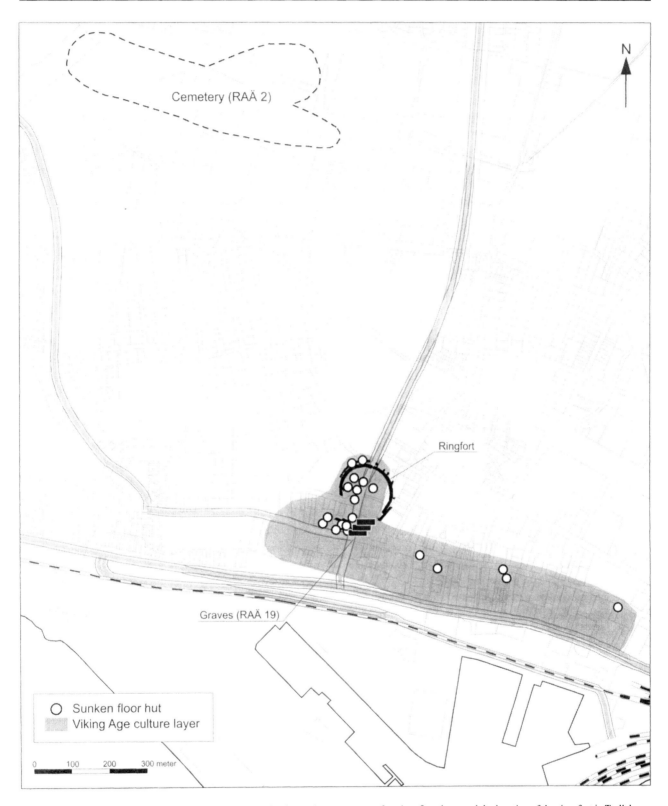

Fig. 3. The map shows the extent of the Viking Age occupation layer, the occurrence of sunken-floor huts, and the location of the ring-fort in Trelleborg.
Illustration: Henrik Pihl.

casional sherds of glass beakers, probably of Western European provenance (Jacobsson 2000, 51ff; cf. Brorsson 2003). Like other coastal sites in southern Scandinavia, the settlement at Trelleborg has its chronological centre of gravity in the eighth and ninth centuries and some time into the tenth century. This is confirmed both by pottery and by 14C dates, which show that the settlement ceased to exist some time in the first half of the tenth century, after which parts of the area were cultivated (Jacobsson 2000, 142).

Apart from the large coastal site, a small Iron Age farm has been excavated near the shore east of Trelleborg (Dalköpinge RAÄ 35). The farm is interesting through its location, just 300 metres from today's coastline. Despite this, the farm seems to have been geared to agrarian production, and there are no traces of sunken-floor huts on the site (Aspeborg 2008).

THE RING-FORT

Some time after the coastal settlement had been abandoned, probably in the mid-tenth century, a ring-fort of Trelleborg type was built on the site. Even before the fort was discovered at the end of the 1980s, archaeologists and historians suspected that there must have been a Trelleborg fort that gave its name to the town. The fort, which was partially excavated between 1988 and 1991, was found in the north-west part of the site. It was on a natural rise in the landscape with a view of the sea and surrounded by protective wetlands (see Fig. 3). The excavations have shown that the fort was built in two phases. The older ring-fort with an external diameter of 135 metres was probably constructed in the mid-tenth century, while the younger building phase, when the surrounding circular rampart was reinforced and supplemented with an outer ditch, can be assigned to the last decades of the tenth century. The younger phase of the fort thus coincides in time with the building of the west Danish Trelleborg forts which are dated to the 980s (Jacobsson 2000, 77f and 148). It may be added that the placing of the fort gates to the north and south coincides with the course of one of the oldest streets in the town, Bryggaregatan, which in turn in linked to the main road that can be followed in the oldest maps, from Trelleborg on the plains of Söderslätt up towards Uppåkra and later Lund (Erikson 2001). This means that the main road probably also passed the Iron Age village at Västervång (see the section Along the Road).

In its basic fortification design, that is, the outer timber cover of the front wall and gates, and the berm and moat, the ring-fort in Trelleborg is very similar to the forts in western Denmark, while also showing significant differences. Perhaps the most important differences are that the site lacks traces of contemporary settlement, and it does not have the same basic symmetrical shape as the Trelleborg forts in Zealand, Nonnebakken in Funen, and the forts of Fyrkat and Aggersborg in north Jutland. This has led to intensive debate among Danish and Scanian archaeologists as to whether the Scanian ring-forts in Trelleborg and Borgeby should be regarded as "genuine" Trelleborg forts (Svanberg & Söderberg 1999, 57; Jensen 2004, 384; Petersson 2008). The ring-fort was used for only a short time, and was probably abandoned, like the forts in western Denmark, at the end of the tenth century.

THE HISTORICAL VILLAGES AND THE TOWN OF TRELLEBORG

The predominant soil in the Trelleborg area is what is known as south-west till, a coarse boulder clay characterized by a high content of clay and a low proportion of stone. This, in combination with the fact that the clay rests on a bed of limestone, makes the area one of the most fertile in Scania. The good conditions for agriculture, both animal husbandry and tillage, generated a surplus in agrarian production, which is reflected in the Middle Ages in the greater population density than in, say, the interior and northern parts of Scania. The high population density is illustrated not just by the number and size (i.e. the number of farms) of the historical villages, but also the size and number of the parishes in the area (Skansjö 1983, 171f with reference to A. E. Christensen 1938).

Around Trelleborg, counting from west to east, are the historical villages of Ståstorp, Västra Tommarp, Tågarp, Västra Vemmerlöv, Gylle, and Kyrkoköpinge (see Fig. 1). All the settlement names have second elements testifying to a high age, going back to the Viking Age or Early Middle Ages (names in torp and köpinge), or before the Viking Age (names in lev/löv and hög). Early written sources testify to yet another village, Västra Köpinge, which was just under a kilometre south-west of the Västervång site. The village were probably abandoned in the latter part of the fifteenth century, in connection with an economic upswing for urban trades in Trelleborg, when the village lands were incorporated with those of the town, under the name Östre vång ("The East Field", Skansjö 1983, 94ff, 218f). An archaeological investigation in the mid-1990s confirmed the occurrence of a medieval settlement in the area. The excavation also revealed remains of a settlement from the Late Iron Age (Trelleborg RAÄ 21, cf. above). Västra Köpinge is the westernmost of four köpinge-villages situated at a distance of a few kilometres in from the coast east of Trelleborg, consisting of Dalköpinge, Mellanköpinge, Kyrkoköpinge, and Västra Köpinge. The köpinge-names suggest that there was a trading centre in the Viking Age or Early Middle Ages near one of these villages. The exact location of the place is not known. The village of Dalköpinge, however, has been suggested as the most likely candidate, since there are some signs of urbanization in the village and parish, indicating economic resources over and above what agriculture alone could offer, such as a brick church from the 1270s and a chapel by the shore (Skansjö 1983, 177ff, note 6).

The town of Trelleborg was probably founded in the first half of the thirteenth century, and written sources show that the place received its borough charter in 1257. There is a great deal to suggest that the rich herring fishery, which began during the twelfth century, played an important part in the growth of the place. The development of the town thereby came under Hanseatic influence, which steered and dominated the herring fishery in the region at an early stage. In the mid-fifteenth century there is also information that the town was one of the places in Scania where herring was salted and herring markets were held (Jacobsson 1982, 8 and works cited there).

VÄSTERVÅNG - A LINK BETWEEN THE COASTAL SETTLEMENT & UPPÅKRA?

All in all, it may be observed that the area on the south coast of Scania that developed into the town of Trelleborg in the mid-thirteenth century was already strategically interesting in the eighth century as a meeting place for the pursuit of craft and trade. The problem is that we have long lacked knowledge of what Late Iron Age settlement looked like in the area around the coastal settlement. What was here before this was founded, and what relations did the inhabitants of the coastal site have with the people at other settlement sites in the district? Nor do we know who was behind the establishment of the place. Was there a local elite in the area, with special interests in trade and craft? Or should we instead envisage a scenario

in which the coastal site was a pawn in a larger economic and political game staged by the ruling elite in south-west Scania, with Uppåkra as the regional centre? Evidence for this could be that the course of one of the main roads in this part of Scania ran from Trelleborg to Uppåkra. The question is the role played by the big estate at Västervång in this context.

Søren Sindbæk, in his dissertation *Ruter og rutinisering* (2005), mentions the coastal site at Trelleborg as one example of a large number of Scanian and Danish find spots which, because of their coastal location, and traces of sunken-floor huts linked to textile production, have been held up in the literature as "local trading sites". He believes instead that these places are rather representatives of other activities than trade and exchange, or else that they were used for a shorter period than the large contemporary maritime trading places with their copious finds, such as Hedeby, Birka, and Ribe. I agree with Sindbæk's critique, but as regards Trelleborg he evidently did not know of the excavations of recent years, as a result of which he underestimates the character of the place (2005, 74f).

Investigations show that the coastal settlement, judging by extant occupation layers, was of significant size, with an estimated area of between 80,000 and 120,000 m². In this respect it resembles several of the other contemporary places in Scania, such as Löddeköpinge by the River Kävlingeån (Olsson 1976), the Tankbåten block west of Ystad (Strömberg 1978), and the sites on the River Helgeå south of Åhus (Callmer 1991). As at those places, the finds from Trelleborg show a not insignificant element of early Slavic pottery, chiefly of the Feldberg and Fresendorf types, which is dated to the period c. 775 to 825 (Brorsson 2003, 232). Petrographic analyses of the pottery show that this is both imported and locally produced. Torbjörn Brorsson has suggested, against this background, that the pottery should not just be seen as trading commodities, but was probably brought along by Slavic traders/craftsmen or manufactured locally by them while they were staying here (ibid., 232f). Unlike other large coastal sites in Scania from the Vendel Period and the Early Viking Age, there is as yet no sure evidence of specialized craft in Trelleborg. Bengt Jacobsson therefore believes that the place should be interpreted as a trading site combined with agrarian operations and fishing (Jacobsson 2000, 144). The find of bronze scales from Trelleborg strengthens the assumption that the site was used for trade and craft (Strömberg 1961, 64).

The village and estate at Västervång were founded at roughly the same time as the settlement on the beach ridge. The distance between the places is just a couple of kilometres. This suggests that there must have been close contacts between the two places. The type of relations is, however, uncertain. Was the coastal site founded on the initiative of the big local farmers, or at the command of the elite in Uppåkra? The small quantity of finds from Västervång, mostly consisting of local domestic pottery, unfortunately offers no foundation for further comparisons between the places. It should be mentioned, however, that finds of early Slavic and other pottery of foreign provenance, which are relatively well represented at the coastal site, are not documented from the village.

Another contemporary site which can help to shed light on the relationship between the village and the coastal site is the big cemetery in the Verkstaden block (Trelleborg, RAÄ 2), located in between the two places (Arcini & Jacobsson 2008). A recent osteological analysis shows that the burial ground, like several contemporary cemeteries, was spatially divided into areas for children and adults. According to Arcini and Jacobsson, this, in combination with the fact that the graves show an equal gender distribution, suggests that the burial ground was not linked to a settlement with special functions, but probably to a large village or several farms.

The majority of the buried individuals have grave goods of very ordinary character, or none at all. They can consist of various personal objects such as iron knives, whetstones, spindle whorls, and bone combs. But there are also a number of graves with objects indicating greater prosperity, in the form of beads, brooches, and mountings of various kinds.[10] Both the inner and the outer mortuary practice, along with the character and composition of the grave goods, thus suggest a varied social structure among the deceased, which agrees well with conditions in the village at Västervång and other contemporary settlements.

An interesting element in the cemetery is the occurrence of buried individuals (men), whose upper front teeth had filed grooves (Arcini & Jacobsson 2008). The phenomenon has been particularly discussed by Caroline Arcini, who has drawn attention to the fact most of the known examples of individuals with filed teeth have been found in Gotland. There are 65 of them, all men, of whom 42 are from Kopparsvik and 12 from Slite Torg. Against this background, she believes that the two men from the cemetery in the Verkstaden block probably come from Gotland. The social meaning of the custom of filed front teeth is not known to us today. Arcini speculates about the possibility that it could be a social marker of people connected to the hird or possibly to trade (ibid.). Regardless of the meaning that should be ascribed to the phenomenon, its occurrence shows that the cemetery was not just used for the local population but also for people from outside. The cemetery in the Verkstaden block can thus be viewed not just as a uniting link between the village and the coastal site, but also as testimony to contemporary inter-regional contacts and exchange.

MAGNATE ESTATES, BUILDING TRADITIONS, AND CONTACTS

After this introduction to the settlement at Västervång and its hinterland, the spatial perspective will now be widened in order to elucidate the social and political composition of the settlement. The overall aim is to understand what the magnate estate at Västervång and other similar complexes represented in their own times. To approach this question I have chosen to look more closely at similarities and differences in the building style of the estates. Before I embark on the comparative analysis, however, I must comment on Viking Age building traditions in southern Scandinavia.

VIKING AGE BUILDING TRADITIONS

The building traditions of the Late Iron Age and Viking Age have previously been examined by several scholars (see e.g. Egebjerg Hansen et al. 1991; Schmidt 1994; Skov 1994; Bender Jørgensen & Eriksen 1995; Ethelberg 2003; Artursson 2005). The tradition has its origin in the buildings of previous periods, characterized by three-aisled post-built houses of varying size and number of trestles. As in the Late Roman Iron Age and the Migration Period, the long-houses could have a straight or a convex

---

10 As examples of graves from the Verkstaden block displaying a certain degree of prosperity we may mention graves 12 and 9 (excavated 1953–54). Grave 12 contained remains of a large hexagonal coffin measuring 1.85 × 1 metre. Among the grave goods were a brooch and a Carolingian strap-end mount of bronze with plant ornamentation). Grave 9 contained a small set of beads, including a gold-foil bead. In the same grave there were also a spindle whorl, an iron knife with remains of a wooden handle, and a bone needle (Svanberg 2003, 293, Cat. No. 232). Another grave (A958, excavated 2005) contained a ring pin of bronze together with an iron knife and a bone comb (Hellerström 2005).

form. The general trend, however, is that the outer walls were given an increasingly convex form and that the construction of the gables was reinforced. Several scholars have emphasized the occurrence of roof-bearing posts in the gable structure as a characteristic feature of Viking Age architecture (Egebjerg Hansen et al. 1991, 19f; Skov 1994). According to Hans Skov, this phenomenon became increasingly common in the eighth century (ibid., 139f). In the Viking Age it is above all long-houses of Sædding type that show this structural detail (Bender Jørgensen & Eriksen 1995, 20), but it is found in smaller post-built houses as well. The placing of roof-bearing posts in the gables has been associated with the introduction of a new type of gable structure, in which the rounded gables and hipped roofs of the Early Iron Age were replaced by a straight plank wall with a saddle roof or a half-hipped roof (see e.g. Ethelberg 2003, 343ff, figures 206–207).

The internal roof-bearing structure also underwent several modifications during the Early Iron Age. In the Late Roman Iron Age and the Migration Period the width of the roof-bearing trestles had gradually narrowed. This development reached its peak in the Early Vendel Period, when the trestle width could be as little as 1.2–1.5 metres, and then in the later part of the period and at the start of the Viking Age the width increased once again to three and sometimes four metres. These changes in the internal construction meant that the weight of the roof was shifted, so that instead of resting on the posts in the outer walls it was carried by the inner trestles.

In the course of the Viking Age there were also other changes in the mode of building. Besides the three-aisled roof-bearing construction, people started to experiment with new technical solutions, probably to gain greater space in the houses without obstruction from posts. At this time they also built houses of one- and two-aisled design, and in the big three-aisled long-houses there were sometimes combinations of trestles and separate central posts, to increase the length of the span and the space between the trestles. The classical Trelleborg houses may be viewed as the final stage in this development, in that the number of trestles was reduced to two, placed relatively close to each gable in order to give a large, hall-like room in the middle of the house. In the Trelleborg houses the weight of the roof rests in large measure on the outer walls as well, and to ensure the durability of the structure the wall was buttressed with extra diagonal posts (Olsen & Schmidt 1977; Schmidt 1994, 108ff).

Houses of Sædding type, which precede the Trelleborg houses typologically and chronologically, are characterized by a traditional three-aisled design and a convex shape. Houses of this type, which are dated from the eighth to the tenth centuries, have above all been documented on sites in southern and western Jutland. Apart from the eponymous Sædding near Esbjerg (Stoumann 1980), the type is represented at places such as Vorbasse, Omgård, and Trabjerg (Hvass 1980; Nielsen 1980; Bender Jørgensen & Eriksen 1995). The Sædding houses vary in size, from 7–12 metres long with three roof-bearing trestles, two of which are placed in the gables (group 1), up to 32–56 metres long and 5–8 metres wide, with five to ten trestles including gable posts (group 5). The roof-bearing trestles were often placed at relatively equal intervals, usually 4–6 metres. Examples of shorter or longer spans do occur, however, above all in the bigger and more complex long-houses. Another characteristic feature of the Sædding houses is that the width of the inner trestles is often relatively large, between three and four metres. This means that little of the weight of the roof rested on the outer walls, the posts in which could be easily repaired and replaced (Stoumann 1980, 100) (see Fig. 5).

COMPARISONS

Building traditions in Scania and southern Scandinavia in the Iron Age and Viking Age have recently been examined by Magnus Artursson as part of the West Coast Line Project (2005). In his compilation, however, there are no examples of big three-aisled convex long-houses of the type found at Västervång. This is because houses of this type have only recently been found in Scania, and the new material was not published when Artursson did his study. Houses of similar type, but smaller in size, have however been excavated at several places, chiefly in southern and western Scania and in southern Halland.[11]

Parallels to the Västervång houses have been discovered in recent years at three places in the Malmö area: Lockarp 7A, the site of the village of Lockarp, and Sun-

---

11 Houses of Sædding type have been found in Scania at places such as Löddeköpinge 90:1 in Löddeköpinge Parish (Svanberg & Söderberg 2000), Ståstorp in Västra Tommarp Parish (Jacobsson 2002), Bjärred 9:5 in Flädie Parish (Pettersson & Brorsson 2002), Svågertorp 8A in Malmö (Rosberg & Lindhé 2001, 76ff), and Vantinge in Barkåkra Parish (Schmidt Sabo 2000, 16f). In south Halland the house type has been found at Ösarp, Laholm Rural Parish (Viking & Fors 1995, 21ff) and Stenstorp, Slöinge Parish (Johansson 2000).

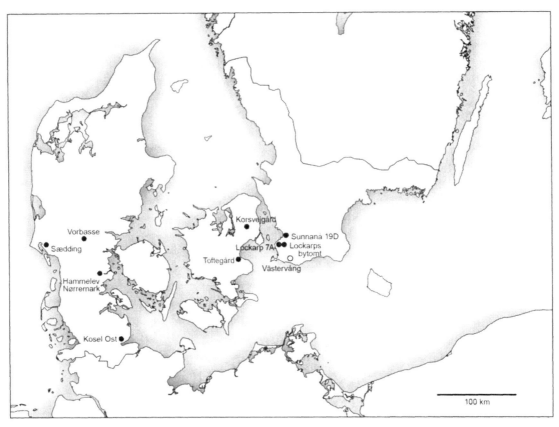

Fig. 4. Places with houses of Sædding type discussed in the article. Map: Thomas Hansson.

nanå 19D. In the report on the Sunnanå site Morten Stei-necke, in connection with the analysis of a Viking Age farm complex at Holmängen by the River Segeå, dis-cusses the possibility that the main building of the farm (house XXI) may have been influenced by the Jutlandic building tradition and houses of Sædding type (Steinecke et al. 2005, 195f). House XXI, according to Steinecke, above all displays similarities in the construction to the later Sædding houses, characterized by a convex inner and outer construction and roof-bearing posts in the ga-bles, although individual details in the roof-bearing con-struction differ (ibid., 196).

The big long-houses from Västervång are built with a similar technique to the house from Sunnanå and thus also to houses of Sædding type. This is an important starting point for the comparative analysis. To broaden the material in the study I have therefore chosen to look at contemporary houses from Jutland and Zealand as well. In selecting material I have applied the following criteria:

(1) The houses should resemble the Västervång houses, that is, have a convex outer form, they should be large or very large (25 metres or more) and have a width of at least 6 metres or more.
(2) The houses should preferably have been interpreted as the main building on a large farm.
(3) The houses should be contemporary with the Västervång houses; that is dated to the Late Vendel Period and Early Viking Age, the time period from the end of the eighth century to the start of the tenth century.
(4) The houses should be well-preserved, to increase the potential for comparisons of construction and spatial division.

The assembled material comprises 14 long-houses from Scania, Zealand, and Jutland (Fig. 4, Table 1).[12] The study is arranged in three steps. First I discuss a selection of representative Jutlandic houses of Sædding type. I then present the houses from Scania and Zealand, and finally extend the discussion to a comparison of the eastern and western Danish tradition.

12 Despite searches of the literature I have not found any examples of large houses of Sædding type from anywhere north of Scania.

Table 1. Sites with buildings of Sædding type discussed in the article.

Site	House	Size	No. of pair of posts	With between posts in pair	Distance between each pair of posts	Reference	Dating
Västervång	House 6	37 x 8.7 m	11*	2.2–3.0 m (approx. 30%)	1.85–6.95 m	Ericson & Carlie 2006	Late Vendel Period– Early Viking Age
Västervång	House 7	34 x 8.7m	7–8*	2.15–3.2 m (31–36.5%)	2.25–11.90 m	Ericson & Carlie 2006	1095±40 BP 890–990 AD 1 s
Sunnanå 19D	House XXI	31.5 x 7.35 m	8*	1.8–3.87 m (45–52.5%)	2.7–7.8 m	Steinecke et al. 2005	1155±70 BP 790–980 AD 1 s
Lockarps bytomt	House 1	29 x 7.7 m	7	2.0–3.3 m (36.5–37.5%)	3.6–4.6 m	Heimer et al. 2006	1055±35 BP 900–1030 AD 1 s
Lockarp 7A	House 6	>38 x 6.0–6.4 m	10*	2.0–2.9 m (50%)	3.0–4.6 m	Rudin & Brink 2002	1150±60 BP 820–980 AD 1 s
Korsvejgård	House 24	44.5 x 5.5–8.0 m	10	1.95–2.2 m (27%)	1.6–8.8 m	AUD 1994 Boye pers. com.	Early Viking Age
Korsvejgård	House 2	26 x 5.5–8.0 m	8*	2.0–3.4 m (36.25–42.5%)	3.1–5.5 m	AUD 1996 Boye pers. com.	Early Viking Age
Toftegård	House 5	40 x 10.5 m	6	2.5–3.6 (34%)	2.6–12.5 m	Tornbjerg 1998	Early Viking Age 9th–10th C
Toftegård	House 4	38 x 10.5 m	6	2.8–4.0 m (38%)	2.5–12.0 m	Tornbjerg 1998	Early Viking Age 9th–10th C
Hammelev Nørremark	House I	30 x 5.5–6.4 m	6*	2.0–2.9 m (approx. 42%)	5.10–6.10 m	Ethelberg 2003	Late Vendel Period 8th C
Sædding	House XL	44 x 4.5–7.0 m	10*	3.2–4.8 (61%)	4.2–7.0 m	Stoumann 1980	Early Viking Age 9th–10th C
Sædding	House LXXXVII	26 x 6.7 m	6*	2.6–3.8 m (52–56.5%)	4.7–6.0 m	Stoumann 1980	Early Viking Age 9th–10th C
Sædding	House LXV	28 x 6.6–6.8 m	6*	2.4–3.8 m (53–55.8%)	4.7–6.0 m	Stoumann 1980	Early Viking Age 9th–10th C
Vorbasse	House CCIII	33 x 5.5–8 m	7*	2.7–4.2 m (50–52.5%)	3.6–6.5 m	Hvass 1980	Early Viking Age 9th C
Vorbasse	House CCXXIII	33 x 5.5–8 m	11*	2.7–4.0 m (approx. 50%)	2.7–6.0 m	Hvass 1980	Early Viking Age 9th–10th C
Kosel Ost	–	36.5 x 5.5–7.0 m	9–10	2.7–3.2 m (approx. 46%)	–	Ethelberg 2003	Early Viking Age 9th–10th C

* One pair of posts in each gable.

JUTLANDIC HOUSES

From the very large material from western Denmark I have selected seven long-houses which satisfy the majority of the stated criteria. These are three houses from Sædding (houses XL, LXXXVII, and LXV) (Stoumann 1980), two houses from Vorbasse (houses CCIII and CCXXIII) (Hvass 1980), and one house from Hammelev Nørremark (house 1) (Ethelberg 2003) in southern and western Jutland. In addition, a large long-house from the Kosel Ost site east of Hedeby in Schleswig (ibid.) has been included in the sample (Fig. 5). The houses can be divided into three groups based on size:

A. Long-houses which are 26–30 metres long and 6.4–6.8 metres wide with six trestles in the roof-bearing structure, one of which is incorporated in each gable. This group is represented by houses XXXXVII and LXV from Sædding and by house 1 from Hammelev Nørremark.

B. Houses that are 33–36 metres long and 7.0–8.0 metres wide with 8–11 trestles in the roof-bearing structure, with one trestle in each gable. This group consists of houses CCIII and CCXXIII from Vorbasse and a house from Kosel Ost in Schleswig.

C. Houses more than 40 metres long and 7.0 metres wide, with nine roof-bearing trestles, with one in each gable. This category is represented by the 44-metre long house XL from Sædding.

A characteristic of all the houses is that the form is clearly convex, as regards both the inner and the outer construction. Another shared feature is that the houses had a balanced or over-balanced design, so that the weight of the roof rested both on the inner trestles and the outer walls. The over-balanced houses (52–61%) are all from Sædding, while the balanced houses (42–50%) come from Vorbasse, Hammelev, and Kosel Ost. In most of the houses the roof-bearing trestles are at relatively even intervals, the distance varying from 4–5 metres up to 6–7 metres. Exceptions to this are the two houses from Vorbasse, with a roof-bearing structure showing a more irregular placing. These are also the only houses in the material with distinct traces of a division into stalls in the eastern part. Yet another characteristic feature is that the houses often have several entrances, both in the long walls and in one or both gables. The entrances can either be counterposed, as in the big house XL from Sædding, or asymmetrically placed, as in house 1 from Hammelev Nørremark and house CCIII from Vorbasse. Judging by the placing of the entrances and the occurrence of inner partition walls, the houses had between three and five rooms, depending on differences in size. A more exact assessment of the function of the rooms has not been possible in this context.

SCANIAN HOUSES

Apart from the Västervång houses I have found three comparable houses from the Malmö area in south-west Scania in the published material. These are house 6 from Lockarp 7A (Rudin & Brink 2002), house 1 from the Lockarp village site (Heimer et al. 2006), and house XXI from Sunnanå 19D (Steinecke et al. 2005) (Fig. 6). These houses were all discovered by the excavations conducted

for two major infrastructure projects, the Öresund Fixed Link and the City Tunnel. The distance between these places and Västervång, as the crow flies, is 20–25 kilometres.

The magnate estate at Västervång can be followed in two building phases on the same site. In the first phase the farm consisted of a main building (house 6) and a smaller post-built house (house 9), the latter placed south of and parallel to the long-house.[13] House 6 was about 37 metres long with a distinctly convex shape. The maximum width at the middle of the house was 8.7 metres, narrowing to approximately 5.5 metres at the gables. The roof-bearing structure is under-balanced (approx. 30%) and consists of 10 or 11 trestles, many of which are not complete. The first trestle coincides with the straight west gable of the house, while the east gable was probably open. The house had at least four rooms and three entrances, two on the north side and one on the south. In the western part there were two rooms, seven and eight metres long. These were followed in the middle section by a ten-metre room, which in turn was followed by an eleven-metre room at the eastern end, where the open gable suggests a function as a cart shed. It is uncertain which part of the house was used as a dwelling. It may have been the middle section, although this is made less likely by the closely spaced posts in this part of the house, which would rather indicate a function as a byre or stable. An alternative interpretation is that the dwelling was in the western part of the east room, where the occurrence of stone lining in several post-holes indicates a reinforcement of the construction.

During the second phase the estate consisted of two large buildings placed in the form of an L, with the main building (house 7) oriented east–west.[14] This long-house is a direct successor of the very similar house 6 in the first phase. The post-built house running north-south (house 8) has no inner roof-bearing posts and its south gable is joined to the north long wall of the main building. The estate probably also had a smaller long-house, house 10.

House 7 is almost identical in style to house 6. The building was 34 metres long with convex walls. The maximum width of the house was 8.7 metres, with the walls narrowing towards the gables, which were about 6 metres wide. The house, like the older main building, had at least three entrances, two on the north side and one

---

13 See *Appendix*, Fig. 11.
14 See *Appendix*, Fig. 11.

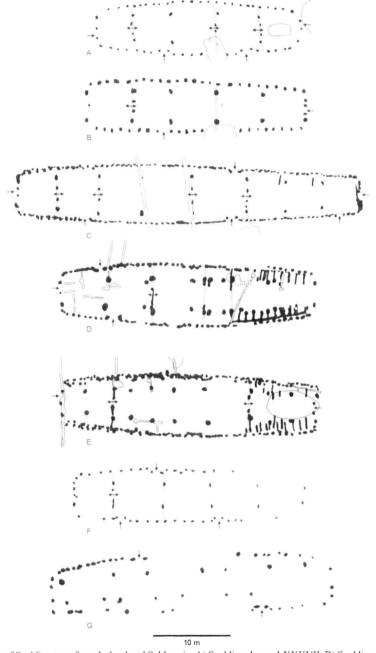

10 m

Figure. 5. Examples of houses of Sædding type from Jutland and Schleswig. A) Sædding, house LXXXVII, B) Sædding, house LVI, C) Sædding, house XL, D) Vorbasse, house CCIII, E) Vorbasse, house CCXXIII, F) Hammelev Nørremark, houses I and G) Kosel Ost, Schleswig. For the dimensions of the individual houses see table 1. Illustrations: Anne Carlie and Thomas Hansson.

on the south, and an open gable in the east. The biggest difference is in the roof-bearing structure, although it is still under-balanced (approx. 31–36%). Whereas the older house 6 had ten or eleven trestles, six of them placed more closely together in the middle section of the house, the younger house had only seven or eight trestles. The room with the longest span, which has the proportions of a hall, was in the middle section. Otherwise the plan of the building was virtually identical; besides the hall it had two large rooms in the western part and a room in the eastern part, where the open gable indicates a function as a cart shed.

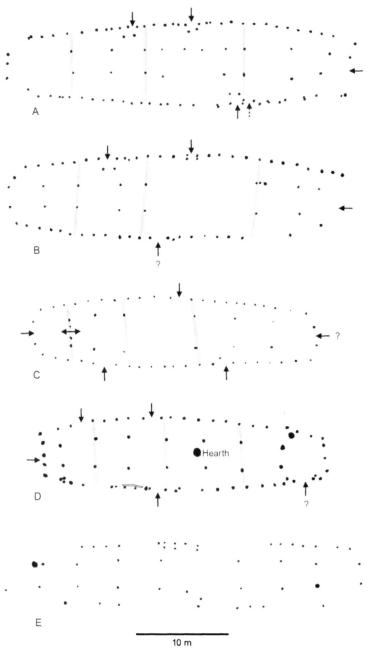

Fig. 6. Houses of Sædding type from Scania. A) Västervång, house 6, B) Västervång, house 7, C) Sunnanå 19D, house XXI, D) the Lockarp village site, house 1, E) Lockarp 7A, house 6. For the dimensions of the individual houses see Table 1. Illustrations: Anne Carlie and Thomas Hansson.

The buildings on the Lockarp village site are interpreted as a farm unit, with site continuity from the seventh century to the second half of the tenth century. House 1 is the main building on a U-shaped farm with the opening towards the east belonging to the second building phase, dated from the late ninth century to the mid-tenth century. In this phase of the complex there was probably also a fourth building, located north of and parallel to the main building (Heimer et al. 2006, 151ff). House 1 has a ground plan that is very similar in form and appearance to houses 6 and 7 from Västervång. The most important differences are that house 1 from Lockarp is slightly

Fig. 7. Houses of Sædding type from Zealand. A) Toftegård, house 4, B) Toftegård, house 5, C) Korsvejgård, house 2, D) Korsvejgård, house 24. For the dimensions of the individual houses see table 1. Illustrations: Anne Carlie and Thomas Hansson.

shorter and narrower (approx. 29 × 7.7 m) and that the roof-bearing trestles are spaced more regularly (ibid., 38f). Like the Västervång houses, the house from Lockarp has several partly asymmetrically placed entrances in each of the long sides. On the other hand, the house seems not to have had an open gable in the east. In the second half of the tenth century the farm was rebuilt and a new main building was erected (house 7). The house was at least 22 metres long, showing great similarities in

construction to house 1. The remains of the house were not in such a good state of preservation, however, so it has not been included in this study. In the latter half of the tenth century the farm was moved to a new location in the vicinity. On the new site the farm developed in the mid-eleventh century into something close to a splendid magnate estate complex, with no less than five different buildings of Trelleborg type, including a small post-built house interpreted as a chapel (ibid., 153ff).

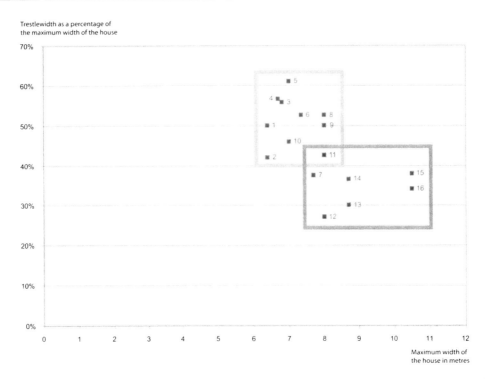

Trestlewidth as a percentage of
the maximum width of the house

Maximum width of
the house in metres

Fig. 8. Differences in building style between long-houses from magnate estates in Scania (Sk.), Zealand (Sj.), Jutland (Jy.), and Schleswig. Black rectangles indicate houses with balanced and over-balanced inner structure and grey rectangles mark houses with an under-balanced structure. 1) Sk. Lockarp 7A, house 6; 2) Jy. Hammelev Nørremark, house I; 3) Jy. Sædding, house LXXXVII; 4) Jy. Sædding, house LVI; 5) Jy. Sædding, house XL; 6) Sk. Sunnanå 19D, house XXI; 7) Sk. Lockarp village site, house 1; 8) Schleswig. Kosel Ost, house; 9) Jy. Vorbasse, house CCIII; 10) Jy. Vorbasse, house CCXXIII; 11) Sj. Korsvejgård, house 2; 12) Sj. Korsvejgård, house 24; 13) Sk. Västervång, house 6; 14) Sk. Västervång, house 7; 15) Sj. Toftegård, house 4; 16) Sj. Toftegård, house 5. For the dimensions of the individual houses see table 1. Illustration: Anne Carlie and Thomas Hansson.

House XXI from Sunnanå 19D (Holmängen) was the main building in a complex from the Late Vendel Period/ Viking Age, which also had two smaller post-buildings (Steinecke et al. 2005). The farm was found just south of the River Segeå, close to one of the major passages over the river on the main road running from Lund/Up-påkra south to Trelleborg on the coast. Also connected to the settlement was a crescent-shaped post structure about 200 metres long, beside the course of the river, interpreted as a possible jetty. This, in combination with the lack of traditional settlement site remains, led the excavators to interpret the settlement at Holmängen as a reloading place for goods, from water to further transport on land (ibid., 210ff). House XXI is, if possible, even more like the Västervång houses than is house 1 from the Lockarp village site. The building is almost identical in form and was only slightly shorter and narrower than houses 6 and 7 (approx. 31.5 × 7.35 m). As in house 7, the roof-bearing trestles in the Sunnanå house are irregularly placed,

with sometimes short, sometimes long spans. An interesting feature of the construction is the almost eight-metre long span in the middle of the building, giving a hall-like room. The same technical solution is also found in the younger of the houses from Västervång (house 7). House XXI, like houses 6 and 7, has several asymmetrically placed entrances in the long walls, and probably one entrance in each gable. The only major difference from the Västervång houses is that the roof-bearing structure has a more convex shape and that the trestle width is greater than at Västervång, meaning that the building was almost perfectly balanced (approx. 45–50%). In this respect the house is more like the west Danish houses of Sædding type, to which I shall return later. House XXI has been 14C-dated to 790–980 AD (1155±35 BP), which makes it contemporary with either house 6 or house 7 from Västervång.

The third example from south-west Scania is house 6 from Lockarp 7A. This almost forty-metre building was probably part of a farm together with a small four-post house (house 26) (Rudin & Brink 2002). House 6 is less well preserved than the other houses in the Scanian material, chiefly as regards the construction of the outer walls and the number and placing of the entrances. This, in combination with the fact that the roof-bearing trestles are spaced at relatively even distances, means that the evidence is too scanty to enable an interpretation of the spatial division of the house. Analyses of macrofossils from post-holes, however, indicate that the dwelling was in the eastern part and that the western part was used to stable horses (ibid., 251, fig. 215). The total length of the house is also uncertain, since the gable posts are not preserved. Judging by the inner structure, the building was at least 38 metres long with ten roof-bearing trestles. The outer walls had a slightly convex form, with a maximum width of 6.4 metres. Unlike the Västervång houses, this one had a balanced construction (50%), with the weight of the roof resting in equal measure on the inner trestles and on the outer walls. In this respect the Lockarp house follows the west Danish building tradition, although it is a little narrower. House 6 has been 14C-dated to 820–980 AD (1150±60 BP), and may thus be contemporary with both houses 6 and 7 from Västervång.

ZEALANDIC HOUSES

From eastern Denmark I have found just a few examples of large long-houses of Sædding type in the published material, which satisfy the criteria above. These are four houses from eastern Zealand, two of them from Strøby Toftegård (houses 4 and 5) at north Stevns east of Køge (Tornbjerg 1998) and two houses from Korsvejgård (houses 2 and 24) on the western edge of Greater Copenhagen (Fig. 7).[15] As in Scania, this type of house is documented at several other places, e.g. at Bøgelund, Varpelev Parish outside Køge (Tornbjerg 1992, 73ff) and at Vallensbæk in the Copenhagen area (Kaul 1985).

Houses 4 and 5 from Strøby Toftegård have been published by Sven-Åge Tornbjerg (1998). The houses, together with a further three big long-houses, are located in the central part of the settlement site and are interpreted as the two youngest phases of a manor with a hall function. A large number of outhouses both large and small

can also be linked to the estate. From the Toftegård site there is a rich and varied assemblage of finds testifying to prosperity and long-distance contacts, and craft activities are chiefly represented by bronze casting. Among the finds there are parts of glass beakers of Frankish origin, gold-foil figures, weighs, parts of weapons and warrior's equipment, and pieces of precious metal. Houses 4 and 5 are dated, among other things, by finds of Baltic ware to the ninth and tenth centuries.

Houses 4 and 5 at Strøby Toftegård are 38 and 40 metres long respectively and have a virtually identical ground plan. The houses have clearly convex long walls with a maximum width of about 10.5 metres. The inner roof-bearing construction is also slightly convex. Like the Västervång houses, these ones are under-balanced (34% and 38% respectively in proportion to the total width). As with the Scanian houses, the Toftegård houses had several entrances in the long walls and an opening in the east gable. The greatest difference is that the houses are larger than the Scanian examples, and that the roof-bearing trestles are irregularly spaced, giving a partly different plan. Houses 4 and 5 both had at least four rooms, one of them a small room at the west gable, two rooms in the east and a large hall measuring 12–13 metres in the middle section (Tornbjerg 1998, 221ff). It is worth noting here that house 7 from Västervång and house XXI from Sunnanå also had a hall-like room in the middle.

Houses 2 and 24 from Korsvejgård at Måløv in western Copenhagen were the main buildings on two farm complexes from the Early Viking Age, of which the smaller unit was fenced. The farms were just a few hundred metres from each other and are possibly contemporary.[16] The bigger long-house, no. 24, is almost 45 metres long and 8.0 metres wide, with ten roof-bearing trestles, while the smaller one, no. 2, is 26 × 8 metres with eight trestles in the roof-bearing structure. Despite the differences in size, the houses display interesting similarities above all to the Västervång houses. Besides the convex shape, they had several asymmetrically placed entrances in the long walls. The bigger house, moreover, is likely to have had an open east gable. The distances between the roof-bearing trestles varies, and in both houses there

---

15 The comparative material has mainly been collected from published studies. Special thanks to Linda Boye, Kroppedal Museum, for material from the Copenhagen area.

16 The houses at Korsvejgård were excavated in 1994 and 1996 by the Copenhagen County Museum Council, now Kroppedal Museum. The material has not been published; I have only had access to descriptions of houses in the technical report. Cf. AUD 1994, no. 40, pp. 113, SØL 463, and AUD 1996, no. 45, pp. 129, SØL 905.

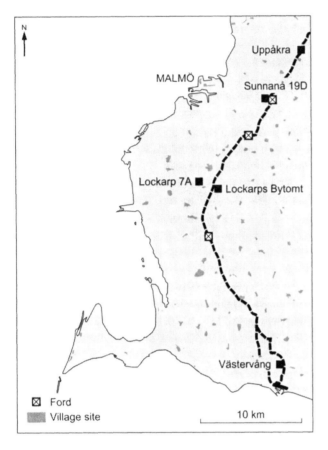

Figure. 9. The course of the main road between Uppåkra and Trelleborg in relation to the historical villages. As the map shows, the four magnate estates with houses of Sædding type are located along the road. After Erikson 2001. Map: Thomas Hansson.

are short and long spans. The longest span is almost nine metres and is in the eastern part of house 24. The placing of the trestles and entrances indicates that the houses were divided into at least three and five rooms respectively. The data are insufficient to allow us to determine the function of the rooms. Finally, the houses from Korsvejgård, like the houses from Västervång and Toftegård, are under-balanced. This feature is particularly clear in the bigger house, where the width of the roof-bearing trestles is only about 27% of the total width.

RESULTS

The comparative study of the main buildings from the Early Viking Age is based on a small sample, and the conclusions drawn should therefore be regarded as preliminary. Some tendencies can nevertheless be discerned

in the material. The appearance and construction of the long-houses reveal several interesting similarities between the long-houses from Scania and Zealand and houses of Sædding type in Jutland. Among the distinctive features in the west Danish building tradition that also occur in the east Danish houses we may mention the convex shape, the occurrence of roof-bearing posts in the gables, numerous and often asymmetrically placed entrances in the long walls, and the occurrence of entrances or openings in the gables.

At the same time, the study shows that the west Danish building tradition was not directly copied; it was incorporated into the indigenous tradition. It thus seems as if people sought primarily to copy the convex shape and outward appearance of the west Danish houses, but for the inner construction they preferred to stick to the older custom of building with an under-balanced roof structure. In the majority of the houses from Scania and Zealand the width of the roof-bearing trestles is less than a third of the total width of the house. Approximately the same proportions are found in other contemporary houses from these areas. In western Denmark, in contrast, houses were often built balanced or over-balanced, which meant that a larger share of the weight of the roof rested on the outer walls. This method not only gave the house increased stability but also allowed greater flexibility for repair, rebuilding, and extension without any negative effect on the roof-bearing structure. In the Scanian material studied here, only two of the examples, house 6 from Lockarp 7A and house XXI from Sunnanå, follow the west Danish tradition with an almost perfectly balanced construction.

Another thing that distinguishes Scanian and Zealandic houses from the west Danish tradition is that the roof-bearing trestles are often unevenly spaced, with short and long spans, while houses of Sædding type generally have equal spans (but the Vorbasse houses have unequal spans). The distance between the roof-bearing trestles is closely connected to the spatial and functional division of the house. Against this background the constructional differences between the west and east Danish houses probably reflect cultural differences in the outlook on the functional divisions of the long-house. For example, several of the Scanian and Zealandic houses seem to have had an open gable construction in the east, which indicates that this part of the house was used as a cart shed. Several of the west Danish long-houses, on the other hand, show clear traces of stall partitions in the eastern part,

revealing a function for housing animals. Another difference is that, in some of the east Danish houses there was
a large, hall-like room of the same kind as found in the
Trelleborg houses. These are houses 4 and 5 from Strøby
Toftegård, house 7 from Västervång, and possibly house
XXI from Sunnanå. The occurrence of a hall suggests that
these long-house were used for special purposes, for example, major religious festivals or feasts (cf. Herschend
1993). None of these long-houses has been dated exactly;
they are dated on the basis of pottery and 14C in general
terms to the ninth and tenth centuries. The inspiration for
the technical construction of a large hall probably comes
from large contemporary aristocratic estates, such as
those excavated at Lejre (Christensen 1997) and Järrestad
(Söderberg 2003).

What, then, is the meaning of the interregional similarities in building style? Was the west Danish tradition
spread as an effect of increased travel, whereby people
brought home new trends to their farm or village? Or
should the new mode of building long-houses be regarded
as a conscious choice among the local landowning elite,
who used this as a way to show that they were a part of
the "big" world? To shed light on these questions we must
look more closely at how the Scanian estates were located
in the landscape, in relation to important communications
and contemporary power centres.

ALONG THE ROAD

It is reasonable to assume that the ruling elite in the Late
Iron Age, with increased travel and transports of goods,
felt a greater need to control important communication
routes. We know that one of the main roads in south-
west Scania ran from Lund/Uppåkra, over the Söderslätt
plain, down to Trelleborg on the south coast, a distance
of roughly thirty kilometres (Fig. 9). The historical geographer Marja Erikson, in a cartographic analysis, has
shown that the main road passed through the lands of no
less than 23 villages in 17 different parishes.[17] An interesting observation is that the road only exceptionally ran

through the actual village sites. In Erikson's opinion, this
strengthens previous assumptions about the great age of
the road, and that it reflects an older route that preceded
the establishment of the villages. The age of the main
road is not known, but the close spatial connection to areas with prehistoric graves and monuments - particularly
Bronze Age barrows - has led to speculation that it could
go back to prehistoric times, perhaps the Bronze Age
(Erikson 2001, 172; Samuelsson 2001).

A few kilometres south of Uppåkra the road crosses
the Segeå, at Görslöv Bridge, which in historical times
was known as one of the most important passages across
the river in the inland. It is also here, about one and a
half kilometres west of the bridge, that we find one of
the farms in the comparative analysis (Sunnanå 19D), to
which we shall have reason to return. Another few kilometres south of the river the road passed the village site
of Östra Skrävlinge, where parts of a settlement from the
Late Viking Age and Early Middle Ages, with long-
houses and sunken-floor huts, has been excavated by
Malmö Heritage.[18] At Östra Skrävlinge a large road joins
the main road from the south-east; in Erikson's analysis
this is called the East Road. It is identified with the early
Ystad road, which continues to the north-west towards
Malmö, founded in the thirteenth century (Erikson 2001,
172). The reason the crossroads is located in Östra Skrävlinge, according to Erikson, is that it crosses the Rise-
bergabäcken, a small watercourse with adjacent wetlands
that limited accessibility in the landscape (ibid., 172f).

Further south, the road runs through the lands of Fosie
village, where extensive remains of settlement, above all
from the Early Iron Age, but also the Late Iron Age, have
been excavated by Malmö Heritage (Björhem & Säfves-
tad 1994; Björhem & Magnusson Staaf 2007). Further
south again, the road passes through the lands of the villages of Lockarp and Fjärdingslöv, where it also crosses
an east–west road called "The Vintrie Road", which links
the main road with the coast to the west (Björhem &
Magnusson Staaf 2007, 230f; Eliasson & Kishonti 2007,
330, fig. 61). Here too, Malmö Heritage, in connection
with the Öresund Fixed Link Project, excavated large areas with extensive remains of settlement from the Early
Iron Age. In the area there was also settlement from the
Vendel and Viking periods (Björhem & Magnusson 2007,
219ff). Two of the estate complexes that are included in

17 The road was noticed at the start of the 1960s, when the historian
Per Edvin Sköld, after studies of Gerhard Buhrmann's map of Scania
from 1684 and the Scanian Reconnaissance Map from 1812–20,
presented a reconstruction of the early course of the road (1963). Sköld's
proposal was on a small scale and of a general character. As part of the
Uppåkra Project a more detailed study was conducted by the historical
geographer Marja Erikson, based on large-scale land survey maps from
the eighteenth century (Erikson 2001).

18 Personal communication, Ulrika Sjöstrand, Malmö Heritage.

the comparative analysis come from the area at Lockarp (cf. Lockarp 7A and the Lockarp village site). The eastern farm can be followed on the same site during several phases (Heimer et al. 2006, 151). In the latter half of the tenth century the farm was moved to a new and topographically more prominent location nearby. In this higher new place it developed into a magnificent complex which may be assumed to have functioned as the seat of the local landowning elite. The most complex settlement belongs to the youngest phase of the estate, dated to 1050–1150. At this time the estate consisted of no less than seven buildings, including several of Trelleborg type and a wooden church or chapel at the centre of the farmstead. Production is assumed to have been based on agriculture, but various forms of specialized craft, such as glass bead manufacture, smithwork, textile production, woodwork, and leather craft, were also pursued here. A varied range of finds testify to long-distance contacts, for instance with southern Germany and south-east England (Heimer et al. 2006, 152ff).

A few kilometres further south the road passes through the site of Hököpinge village, where it follows the damp terrain along the course of the Pilebäcken. Like the köpinge-places around Trelleborg and other places in Scania, Hököpinge has been suggested in earlier research to have served as a centre for a big farmer's trade in the Late Viking Age and Early Middle Ages (Cinthio 1975; Ersgård 1986). No archaeological excavations have been undertaken to confirm this kind of activity on the site, but a Viking Age silver hoard has been found within the area of the medieval village site (Rosborn 1984). The hoard comprises 422 coins and a piece of hack silver. The coins are mainly German and English with a small admixture of Byzantine and occasional Swedish-minted coins.[19] Although the find in itself does not testify to non-agrarian activity on the site, it is indirect evidence of a large Viking Age settlement in the vicinity.

South of Hököpinge the road veered towards the southeast, passing the lands of the villages of Södra Åkarp and Västra Skrävlinge. Erikson's cartographic analyses show that the road then continued south through the sites of Fuglie, Östra Värlinge, and Tågarp and on down to the coast just east of where the Albäcken flows into the sea,

west of the medieval town of Trelleborg (Erikson 2001, 169ff). Bengt Jacobsson's studies of the Viking Age ringfort in Trelleborg, however, suggest that the main road north of the town also had an easterly course. Under one of the main streets running north–south in the medieval town, Bryggaregatan, remains were found of an earlier predecessor following the same course and running straight through the north gate of the ring-fort and out through the south gate (Jacobsson 2000, 149). Where exactly the road split into a westerly and easterly route north of Trelleborg is unknown. If one looks at the local topography in the area, it seems reasonable to assume that it was up in the hummocky landscape, perhaps just south of the village of Östra Värlinge, in order to use the high parts of the terrain. The east route then probably ran through the lands of the village of Hammarlöv and then curved in a gentle arc down to the town of Trelleborg. In the Viking Age this would mean that the eastern road passed the village and the magnate estate at Västervång and then continued south to the coastal settlement/ring-fort.

If we look at the four places with smaller magnate estates with main buildings in Sædding-like style, we see that they are all located on the main road between Uppåkra and Trelleborg. The spatial connection between the farms and the road may of course be coincidental. On the other hand, if there is a historical basis for it, we must then ask why the estates are situated where they are. Did they have functions other than purely agrarian? What type of functions could this be?

SCANIAN MAGNATE ESTATES IN THEIR OWN TIME

In Viking Age society, various social resources, besides kinship, were used to confirm and regulate mutual obligations, such as friendships, marriage alliances, and ties of loyalty. In the social elite or the aristocracy this resulted in complex social networks between different individuals and collectives, where personal bonds functioned as guarantees of support and protection in critical situations (Skre 1998, 18ff). According to Lars Hermansson, who has studied elite political culture in twelfth-century Denmark, this led to the creation of broad horizontal and constructed "kin groups", the composition of which varied depending on different political circumstances (Hermansson 2000, 9).

Kinship-like social relations existed not just in the upper social strata but also at other levels in society (Skre

---

19 One of the German coins in the Hököpinge find gives a *terminus post quem* of 1002, which suggests that the hoard ended up in the ground some time at the start of the eleventh century (Hårdh 1976, 54, cat. no. 76).

1998, 18f). The most common relationship, however, was probably that between the peasant and his lord, where the need for personal security was a central theme. By submitting to a landowning lord, the peasant had access not just to food but was also guaranteed protection in the event of attack, and help to assert his right in conflicts (ibid., 20f).

The written sources (chiefly runic stones and Norwegian kings' sagas) testify to a wide range of social functions or titles in Viking Age society that were not based on kinship but on different types of reciprocal social relations. The most common titles on Scanian runic stones are dreng and thegn. There is a general opinion that these refer to royal vassals who served in the lord's hird in return for landed property (Randsborg 1980, 31ff; Anglert 1995, 36ff). Examples of other titles in the sources connected to the upper class and royal power are bryde (steward), landman (royal vassal), and godi (pagan priest). Other titles occur, however, such as bonde (big farmer) and boman (probably a small landowner). The epithet godi here is thought to indicate a close relationship or loyalty to the king, as his subject or rather vassal (Randsborg 1980, 34ff, 40).

Smaller magnate estates with big long-houses of Sædding type probably did not belong to people in the elite or the aristocracy, but to individuals slightly lower on the social scale. Perhaps we should regard these persons as belonging to the local landowning elite, best designated as big farmers or, to use the contemporary social title, bonde. These persons too, of course, were a part of the social network of the time. The question is at what level and how we should understand the estates and their inhabitants in contemporary terms.

The estates at Sunnanå, Lockarp, and Västervång in south-west Scania were founded at a time when the old order with Uppåkra as the power centre prevailed and represented normality.[20] High-class finds of important prestige objects in the form of exclusive fibulae and sherds from glass beakers show that the social elite in Uppåkra, from the fifth century onwards, maintained long-distance contacts with areas above all in Western Europe (the Rhineland, southern England, France), but also in Southern Europe (southern Germany and northern Italy) (Helgesson 2002, 48; Hårdh 2003, 43). In the Vendel Period the material undergoes a change in character; the proportion of exclusive objects decreases while fibulae and craft-related finds take on a more local or provincial touch (Helgesson 2002, 51, 63f). At the same time, interregional contacts seem to have flourished, with finds of gold-foil figures and patrices for gold-foil figures linking Uppåkra with other contemporary central places, such as Sorte Muld in Bornholm and Strøby Toftegård in eastern Zealand (Watt 1999). Another category of find testifying to the maintenance of long-distance contacts is the unusually large proportion of Arabic coins found on the site (Silvegren 1999; von Heijne 2004, 253).[21] The pure silver content of the coins makes it likely that they were used to a large extent as raw material for craft work, for example, for making jewellery. In view of the considerable metalwork and jewellery production at Uppåkra, there must have been a large flow of coins to the site.

Based on studies of the historical villages and place-names, Johan Callmer and Mats Anglert have argued that Uppåkra in the Late Iron Age constituted some form of magnate's domain extending from the Höjeå in the north to the Segeå in south (Callmer 2001; Anglert 2003). Opinions are divided as to how large a geographical area Uppåkra was the political centre of (cf. Larsson 2006, 181). The international network of contacts to which the place belonged at the time, however, suggests that the elite established points of support in the landscape in order to control important routes and thus secure communications. My thesis is that the smaller magnate estates in Scania represent these places. It is thus probable that the estates, from the end of the eighth century to the mid-tenth century, were linked to the organization of the Uppåkra elite, functioning as territorial points of support for controlling

---

20 Recent decades' extensive research around Uppåkra as part of the project *The Social Structure in Southern Sweden in the Late Iron Age* has shown that for a very long time, probably from the third century AD until the end of the Viking Age, the place served not just as a political and economic centre but also as a religious centre for people in south-western and western Scania. Although the main central functions of the place probably changed character over the centuries, it is above all the long continuity of the site, and the size and composition of the finds, that testify to a complex organization. The Uppåkra Project is run by Prof. Lars Larsson and Prof. Birgitta Hårdh at the Department of Archaeology and Ancient History, Lund University, in collaboration with various scholars. The results of the project are continuously presented in the series Uppåkrastudier.

21 The Arabic coins from Uppåkra consist above all of Abbasid coins from present-day Iraq, minted 749–902. But there is also a relatively large share of Samanid coins from the eastern parts of the Caliphate, minted between 893 and *c.* 950. Because of the predominance of Abbasid coins, the chronological centre of gravity in the Viking Age coins from the site is thus in the eighth and ninth centuries. This can be compared with, e.g., the Carolingian coins, of which there are just seven examples from the site (von Heijne 2004, 253; cat. find 1.155).

important transports and other movements. Evidence for this comes above all from the fact that the estates were strategically placed for communications beside the old road network and the main route between Uppåkra and the coastal settlement at Trelleborg on the south coast. They were close to important river crossings, major crossroads, or large coastal settlements. I have previously mentioned the estate at Sunnanå as a probable reloading place beside one of the most important passages over the Segeå. The two estates at Lockarp likewise have a strategic location along the main road at an important crossroads. Finally, the big estate at Västervång, on a prominent height, offering a good view of the lowlands and the sea, was strategically placed to control travellers and transports of goods between the coast and the inland. It is possible that the construction of the ring-fort in Trelleborg, the earliest phase of which is in the mid-tenth century, should be viewed in this context, that is, as one of the Uppåkra elite's territorial points of support in the landscape.

It is thus likely that the owners of the four estates in the Early Viking Age were in some form of dependence on the leading elite in south-west Scania. We cannot say anything about the precise nature of the relationship, but it cannot be ruled out that they served as some kind of vassals to the ruler in Uppåkra. It should be mentioned here that the smaller estates lack traces of sunken-floor huts, specialized craft, or ritual feasting in halls. This distinguishes the sites from contemporary aristocratic estate complexes such as Järrestad, which are distinguished by precisely this type of activities.[22]

It is probable that the adoption of a new style of building with influences from western Denmark was a way for the owners to manifest their social affiliation. By building their houses in accordance with the latest trends in the "big" world, they showed that they belonged to the "right" social networks.[23] The big long-houses of Sæd-

ding-like type can be viewed here as a kind of parallel phenomenon to the Trelleborg houses in the Late Viking Age. Like the big long-houses of Sædding type, those of Trelleborg type or similar chiefly occur on slightly larger and more prosperous estates (see e.g. Ethelberg 2003, 354ff). Regional analyses of building practices, however, in southern Halland, suggest that each house was constructed individually by different builders with knowledge of the new technique (Wranning 1999, 47f). This indirectly supports the thesis that the local landowning elite, even in the Late Iron Age, used this building style as a way to display their social affiliation.

At the end of the tenth century the political and religious scene in Scania changed, when the area was integrated into the kingdom of Denmark and Christianity acquired a stronger foothold among the population. At the same time as the town of Lund was established, we see changes in the finds from Uppåkra suggesting that the central functions of the place had dwindled in significance. The exclusive imports were now much rarer than before, but the occurrence of weighs testifies to continued trade. On the other hand, the proportion of coins from the later part of the tenth century and into the eleventh century is very limited, represented only by a few English and Danish coins (von Heijne 2004, 253, cat. no. 1:155). There is also a small number of finds testifying to an early Christian mission, in the form of an encolpion and an early Christian burial (Anglert 2003, 134).

The town of Lund was established, probably at the command of the Danish king Harald (Bluetooth), as a new political and religious centre in the region.[24] The foundation of the town has been dated by new archaeological evidence (dendrochronological dating) to around 990. There have been different explanations for the origin of the town and why it was founded. Whereas earlier research chiefly sought economic explanations, the most recent contributions to the debate have highlighted the significance of the place as a political, administrative, and religious centre (Andrén 1980; see also Larsson 2006, 175ff and works cited there). Many people have pointed out that early medieval Lund in several respects shows clear English influences. The early minting, under the rule of Sweyn Forkbeard, is an example of this, and has been interpreted by Anders Andrén and Peter Carelli

---

22 At Sunnanå, Lockarp, and the Lockarp village site, the excavated area was so large that the absence of sunken-floor huts must reflect the reality. For Västervång the situation is harder to assess. Although there are indications that crafts were pursued in the village (textiles, antler craft, possibly smithwork), there are no traces of sunken-floor huts. Sunken-floor huts could possibly have stood on the edge of the village, e.g., beside the wetlands to the south, which was not covered by the excavation. Another explanation for the lack of sunken-floor huts could be that they were located outside the village and should instead be sought down at the coastal settlement, a couple of kilometres from there (Ericson 2007).

23 Houses of Sædding type are not yet known from Uppåkra. Only a small part of the large settlement has been excavated, however, and the picture could change quickly.

---

24 Editorial note: King Harald may have died already in the (early) 970s, cf. Randsborg this vol.; this does not alter the argument.

as a desire to manifest himself as a Christian king in keeping with the ideals of the time (Andrén & Carelli 1998, 28). In Lund, as in Löddeköpinge, a large central cemetery was created, probably to function as a burial place for a large area in Scania, that is, for the people in the aristocracy who chose to manifest their new religion and were loyal to the Danish king (Anglert 2003, 134; cf. Lihammar 2007, 175).

In the discussion about the foundation of Lund, several researchers have drawn attention to the placing of the town in relation to the old road network and the main road running northwards from Uppåkra. The prevailing opinion is that the reason for this placing should be sought in the ambition of the Danish king to control important communication routes and thus movements in the landscape (Larsson 2006, 179ff). Anna Lihammar thinks that the foundation of Lund should be regarded as one of the most important symbolic royal acts in western Scania around the year 1000 (Lihammar 2007, 180). It was a way for the king and the Christian church to display its power and ambition vis-à-vis the old political and religious order. Instead of viewing Lund as succeeding the old central place at Uppåkra, Lihammar argues that the foundation of Lund was a deliberate provocation against the old power.

The Danish king's ambitions to acquire control over important communication routes in the landscape around Lund/Uppåkra probably also included strategies to create territorial points of support. We may assume here that the king was primarily trying to integrate existing places, either by winning over the local elite to its side, or if this failed, by appointing loyal new subjects in these places. Several scholars think that the Trelleborg houses could be viewed as an expression of loyalty to the Danish crown (Anglert 2006, 46). It is interesting in this connection that two of the smaller magnate estates discussed here also have remains of Trelleborg houses. On the Lockarp village site, when the big estate was moved to a new site at the start of the eleventh century, several of the new buildings were constructed in Trelleborg style. This can be interpreted to show that the local elite in Lockarp actively supported the Danish king and the ideals of the new age, thus turning their backs on the old order and the Uppåkra elite (Heimer et al. 2006, 156f; Anglert 2006, 46).

The youngest buildings at Västervång are contemporary with the youngest ones in the ring-fort in Trelleborg, which are dated to the last two decades of the tenth century. The rebuilding of the fort coincides in time with the other Trelleborgs in western Denmark, which are assumed to have functioned as a kind of bridgehead in the expansion of Danish royal power (Randsborg 1980, 99ff; Anglert 1995, 46ff, 53f). This suggests that the Danish king took over and integrated the Scanian fort as a point of support in his own organization. The role played by Västervång in this is uncertain. Here too, however, the fact that the main building on the youngest estate, at least its interior, was built in Trelleborg style may indicate a change of loyalties in favour of the Danish king.

FINAL REMARKS

In this article I have sought to highlight a group of non-aristocratic estates from the Viking Age which have not previously received much attention in the archaeological discussion. By studying the building style of the estates and their placing in the landscape, I found several interesting tendencies in the material which do not seem to be random, instead calling for some form of historical explanation. In the article I suggest that the estates in Scania in the Early Viking Age were linked to the Uppåkra elite and that they probably served as territorial points of support to control important routes and movements. At the end of the tenth century, when Scania was integrated in the Danish power sphere, there are signs that some of the farms were taken over and integrated in the new administration.

The thesis at present still rests on a shaky foundation, and naturally needs to be substantiated in different ways to gain in plausibility. What is needed is more "good" examples, with Iron Age settlement being analysed from a social perspective and in terms of settlement hierarchy, while the places are simultaneously put into a larger landscape context. I hope that this article will inspire other similar works that put Iron Age settlement and farms at the centre.

APPENDIX
VÄSTERVÅNG: DEVELOPMENT & ORGANIZATION 770–1000 AD

PHASE 5: LATE VENDEL PERIOD AND EARLY VIKING AGE (770–900 AD)

The settlement at Västervång was probably established in the latter half of the eighth century, when three farms (I:a, II:a, and III:a) were set up on the site. The farms were built around a natural depression which had been filled in with earth during the Early Bronze Age (Fig. 10). In the latter part of the period yet another farm was built (IV) at the far east of the site, and at the same time two small buildings (houses 18 and 26) were erected south-east of farm III:a. The latter may have had something to do with craft activities, in the form of bone and antler craft and possibly smithwork. A fifth farm was located west of farm II:a (cf. house 11). The dating of the house is uncertain, however, and it may also belong to phase 6.

The size and composition of the farms vary. The biggest farm, I:a, was on a small but noticeable height south-west of the depression. The farm consisted of a big long-house (house 6) and a smaller post-built house (house 9), the latter placed about 15 metres south of and parallel to the main building. Farm II north of the depression, besides its long-house, probably had an extra post-building, placed at an angle south-west of the main building. Other units consisted of just a small or medium-sized long-house (Fig. 11).

The main building of the magnate estate (farm I:a) is a 37-metre long-house with convex walls. The maximum width of the house at the middle is 8.7 metres, which then narrows towards the gables to about 5.5 metres. The roof-bearing structure consists of 10 or 11 trestles, most of which are not complete. The first trestle coincides with the straight west gable of the house, while the east gable was probably open. The trestle width in the house is relatively narrow (2.2–3.0 m), which gives the building an under-balanced construction (31–36,5%). The distance between the spans varies from 1.90–6.85 metres, with the shortest spans in the centre of the house. It had at least three entrances, two of them on the north side and one on the south. The latter had been moved to the side some time during the life of the house.

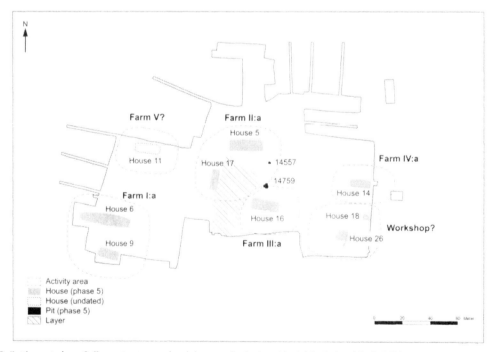

Fig. 10. Settlement phase 5. Farm structure and activity areas in the Late Vendel Period and Early Viking Age (c. 770 BC–900 AD).
Illustration: Henrik Pihl.

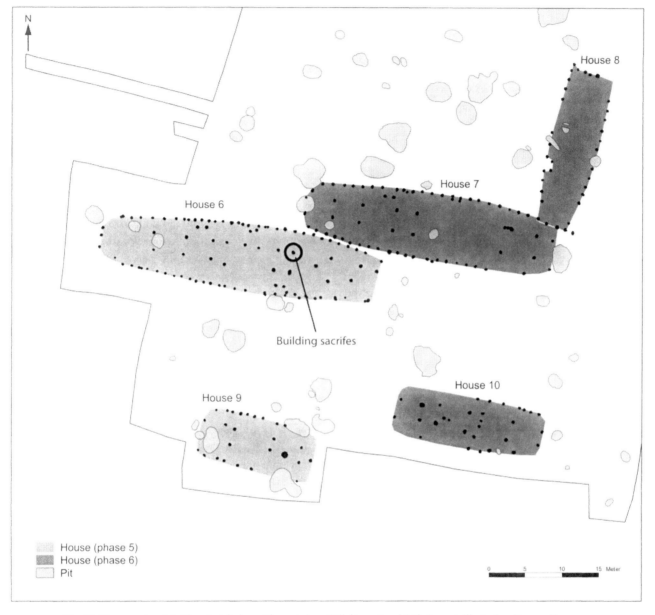

Fig. 11. The magnate estate (farm I:a) during settlement phase 5 (light grey) and 6 (dark grey). Illustration: Thomas Hansson.

House 6 probably had at least four rooms, two of them in the western part, 7 and 8 metres long respectively, a 10-metre room in the middle section, and an 11-metre room at the eastern end, where the open gable indicates a function as a cart shed. It is uncertain which part of the house the people lived in. One possibility is that the dwelling was in the middle room, although this is contradicted by the close placing of the posts in this part of the house, which would suggest a function as a byre or stable.

An alternative interpretation is that the dwelling was in the western part of the eastern room, where the occurrence of stone lining in several post-holes indicates that the structure was reinforced. In one of these post-holes, for the north-west corner post (A11606) in the eastern room, there was a ritual deposit consisting of a spindle whorl, a smoothing stone, and part of a rib. The objects were found at the bottom of the post-hole, which suggests an inauguration sacrifice when the house was built (Fig.

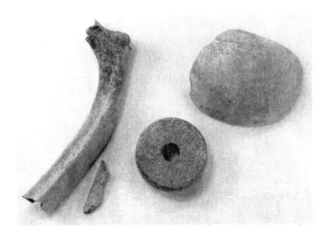

Fig. 12. Inauguration sacrifice from the main building of the magnate estate (house 6). Photo: Staffan Hyll.

12). The composition of the finds is interesting, since the objects have a female touch through their connection to textile crafts (Carlie 2004, 171).

House 6 shows great similarities in building technique to house XXI from Sunnanå, house 1 from the Lockarp village site, and house 6 from Lockarp 7A, located in the Malmö district and dated to the Viking Age.[25]

The other building on the estate (house 9) is a post-built house measuring about 15.5 × 6.9 metres with three roof-bearing trestles and slightly convex outer walls. The house probably had two rooms, one of them in the western part of the house with an entrance on the south side and a smaller room in the eastern part, where a centrally placed hearth between trestles 2 and 3 suggests a dwelling function. House 9 shows similarities in width and post positions to several of the Early Viking Age houses from Bjärred, although these are somewhat longer (Pettersson & Brorsson 2002, 41).

A waste pit (A6936) north-east of house 9 should probably be linked to the location of the farm. In the pit there were small quantities of cattle bones and an iron object of indeterminate type. No other features or activities can be linked to the farm.

The north farm, II:a, likewise consisted of two buildings. These were at an angle to each other, with the long-house (house 5) placed on a rather steep slope towards the west and an outbuilding (house 17) set in a north–south direction just west of the depression. The long-house was about 20.5 metres long and 8.5 metres wide with almost

straight long sides and with an internal construction of four or possibly five trestles. The placing of the trestles gives no hint as to the inner spatial arrangement of the house. A waste pit (A14557) containing remains of four large vessels of domestic type is contemporary with the farm and was dug south-east of the long-house (Stilborg 2006). The pit also contained small quantities of animal bones (150 g) from cattle and sheep/goats (Cardell 2006).

The other two farms (III:a and IV) belonging to settlement phase 5 consisted of a solitary long-house each. Of these, the long-house on farm III:a (house 16), east of the depression, was roughly the same size as the long-house on farm II:a. The house has six roof-bearing trestles, of which the outermost one was part of the gable. The placing of the trestles and an entrance on the south side suggest that the house had at least three rooms, with the biggest span of about six metres in the middle of the house, probably marking the dwelling section. House 16 shows clear parallels to house 2, on the contemporary settlement site of Ståstorp, located about two and a half kilometres west of Västervång (Jacobsson 2002).

A waste pit (A14759) with remains of five pots of domestic type was found north of the long-house. The pottery is typologically dated to the Vendel Period and can thus be linked to the farm (Stilborg 2006). A relatively large amount of animal bones was also retrieved from the pit (816 g), consisting of bones of cattle and sheep/goat (Cardell 2006).

Farm IV was approximately 50 metres east-north-east of farm III:a and is represented by house no. 14. This long-house measures about 15 × 5.8–6.3 metres, which means that the building is somewhat smaller and narrower than other long-houses in this phase. The interior is also of different design, consisting of a combined two- and three-aisled construction. Just a few post-holes were excavated, which leaves the spatial division of the house uncertain.

To phase 5 we should probably also assign a workshop area in the south-east corner of the excavation site (see Fig. 10) . Two buildings, houses 18 and 26, were found in this area. House 26 is a small three-aisled post-built house of roughly 35 m². The building had an open gable and windbreak towards the south, where there were also discreet traces of a fireplace. No craft-related finds were discovered in the house; it is instead the construction that indicates a workshop, possibly a forge. House

---

25 See the section on *The Scanian houses* in article.

18 is likewise a three-aisled post-built house, although the size is unknown, since the house is only partly within the excavated area. In the house was a pit (A8363) with finds including a bone needle, a comb (see below), a possible iron knife, and fragments of red deer antler showing traces of working. Unburned bones (327 g) from cattle, sheep/goat, pig, and a herring jawbone were also found in the pit, suggesting a secondary use of the pit for waste. The element of craft finds indicates that textile and antler crafts were pursued nearby. However, no sunken-floor huts were found, despite a thorough search of the excavation area.

DATING AND ORGANIZATION.

In phase 5 the dating of the settlement is likewise based on 14C, finds and house typology. Six 14C dates, all obtained from houses, can be assigned to the Late Vendel Period and Early Viking Age (Table 2).[26] A combined calibration of all the samples gives a dating to c. 770–900 AD (1160±16 BP). There are no datings from the main building of the magnate estate, house 6; instead the dating is based on the appearance of the house and the building method, and on the spatial placing in relation to the later and virtually identical long-house, no. 7 (see Phase

6: Late Viking Age). The distance between the long walls in houses 6 and 7 is only about half a metre. This suggests that the younger house was built shortly after the older main building had been demolished.

The finds that indicate a dating consist mainly of pottery and the remains of a comb (Fig. 13). The comb plate has iron rivets and is decorated with crosses and straight lines. It probably belongs to Ambrosiani's type B1:1, with an approximate dating to the first half of the tenth century (Ambrosiani 1981, 25, 62–64). The pottery comes from two pits (A14557 and A14759) close to the long-houses on farms II and III. The pottery from pit 14557 comprises the remains of at least four vessels. In every case they are large barrel-shaped vessels of domestic type, made of coarse ware. In the other pit (A14759) remains were found of at least five vessels, two of which were fully represented while the other three pots were represented by a single rim sherd. These posts too are of domestic type but they seem to be slightly smaller (Stilborg 2006).

The number and dating of the houses is evidence that there was more settlement on the site in phase 5 than in previous periods. Both the 14C dates and the appearance of the houses suggest that occupation was relatively brief, from c. 770–900 AD, that is, a period of about 150 years. It is likely that the magnate estate (farm I:a) and farms

---

26 Calibration of ^{14}C values was done with the program Oxcal v. 3.10, Bronk Ramsey 2005.

Table 2. Late Iron Age. Radiocarbon datings from Västervång, Trelleborg, Scania.

Lab. No	Context	[14]C BP	+/-	1 sigma	2 sigma	Material
Ua-27713	Post-hole, house 20	1620	45	390AD-540AD (68,2%)	330AD-550AD (95,4%)	Charcoal (Quercus sp)
Ua-27707	Post-hole, house 27	1550	35	430AD-560AD (68,2%)	420AD-590AD (95,4%)	Charcoal (Prunus sp?)
Ua-27705	Post-hole, house 7	1395	35	620AD-665AD (68,2%)	585AD-680AD (95,4%)	Charcoal (Quercus sp)
Ua-27703	Post-hole, house 2	1360	40	630AD-690AD (66,8%)	600AD-720AD (86,4%)	Charcoal (Alnus)
Ua-27677	Post-hole, house 9*	1180	40	770AD-900AD (68,2%)	760AD-980AD (91,4%)	Macrofossil (Hordeum)
Ua-27681	Post-hole, house 17*	1180	40	770AD-900AD (68,2%)	760AD-980AD (91,4%)	Macrofossil (Seeds)
Ua-27674	Post-hole, house 16*	1175	40	770AD-900AD (68,2%)	770AD-980AD (92,9%)	Animal bone
Ua-27712	Post-hole, house 5*	1165	40	780AD-900AD (58,5%)	770AD-990AD (95,4%)	Charcoal (Pomoideae)
Ua-27680	Post-hole, house 14*	1140	40	860AD-980AD (65,7%)	770AD-990AD (95,4%)	Macrofossil (Ceralia)
Ua-27682	Post-hole, house 26*	1130	35	885AD-975AD (68,2%)	800AD-990AD (93,6%)	Macrofossil (Triticum)
Ua-27676	Post-hole, house 7**	1095	40	890AD-990AD (68,2%)	860AD-1030AD (95,4%)	Macrofossil (Triticum)
Ua-27678	Post-hole, house 10**	1065	40	890AD-1020AD (68,2%)	890AD-1030AD (95,4%)	Macrofossil (Triticum/Hordeum)
Ua-27679	Post-hole, house 13**	1045	40	960AD-1030AD (62,5%)	890Ad-1040AD (95,4%)	Macrofossil (Hordeum)
*Comb. Cal.		1160	16	860AD-900AD (41,2%)	770AD-900AD (74,8%)	
**Comb. Cal.		1068	23	970AD-1020AD (61,4%)	940AD-1020AD (77,3%)	

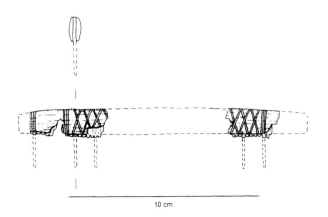

Fig. 13. Reconstruction of a comb from pit A8363. Drawing: Annica Jeppsson.

II:a and III:a, located respectively to the west, north, and east of the depression, were built at roughly the same time at the end of the eighth century or the start of the ninth. The dates from farm IV and the workshop area indicate that these are slightly later, perhaps built in the latter half of the ninth century. Farm V, located north of the magnate estate, is possibly be linked to the village as well, although the dating of the house is uncertain. The number of farms in the village could perhaps have been even greater, since the outer limits of the site were not determined to the south, where the topography would allow room for another couple of farmsteads.

The suggested interpretation means that the settlement for the first time displays a denser structure and greater stability. This picture contrasts with the earlier phases, which are instead characterized by an open and scattered settlement structure with great mobility. Another interesting feature in the settlement is that it now shows an internal hierarchy among the farms. This is evident, for instance, in the area of the buildings, which varies from small units of 90–160 m², via a medium-sized farm of about 290 m² (II:a) to the magnate estate (I:a), with an area of about 380 m². The estate also distinguishes itself in another way form the other farms in the village, in that the main building was erected on a slight ridge running east–west, in a somewhat secluded location west of the depression. The long-house on the estate also differs in building style from the other farms, being more like long-houses of Sædding type which have been found in other magnate settings from the same time in southern Scandinavia (see the article).

PHASE 6:
LATE VIKING AGE (900–1000 AD)

In the Late Viking Age we see a clear continuity in the organization of settlement on the site, although the number of farms decreased somewhat from that in the preceding phase. In phase 6 settlement consisted of three or possibly four farms (Fig. 14), of which the two largest units (farms I:b and III:b) were respectively east and west of the filled-in depression. The dubious farm is represented by house 11, the dating of which is uncertain; the farm could also belong to phase 5.

The magnate estate to the west, farm I:b, consisted of two large buildings placed in the form of an L, with the main building, house 7, oriented east–west (see Fig. 14). This long-house is a direct successor of the very similar house 6 in the preceding phase. The north–south post-built house (house 8) lacks inner roof-bearing posts and its south gable is joined to the north long wall of the main building. Probably also belonging to the estate is a small long-house, house 10, located about 15 metres south of house 7.

The main building on the magnate estate (house 7) is almost identical in style with house 6. The building is 34 metres long with convex outer walls and a maximum width at the middle of about 8.7 metres, narrowing towards the gables which were roughly 6 metres wide. The house, like house 6, had at least three entrances, two of them on the north side and one on the south and an open gable in the east. The trestle width is also approximately the same (2.15–3.2 m), i.e., under-balanced (31–36.5%). The greatest difference is in the roof-bearing structure. Whereas the older house 6 had 10 or 11 trestles, six of them placed more closely together in the central section of the house, the younger house 7 had only seven or eight trestles. The room with the longest span, which had hall-like proportions, was in the central section of the house. Otherwise the house has a virtually identical plan; besides the hall it comprised two large rooms in the western part and a room in the eastern end, where the open gable indicates a function as a cart shed.

The estate had two more buildings. One of these, a single-aisled post-house about 20 metres long and 4.1–6.45 metres wide with convex long walls and straight gables, was at an angle to the main building, with its south gable joined to the north-east long side and corner of the long-house. The house shows similarities to Jutlandic houses of Margrethehåb type with their characteristic slightly

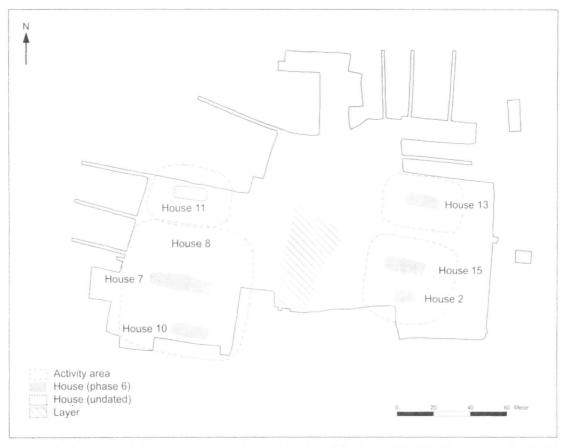

Figure. 14. Settlement phase 6. Farm structure and activity areas in the Late Viking Age (c. 900–1000 AD). Illustration: Henrik Pihl.

convex outer walls and no inner roof-bearing structure (Bender Jørgensen & Eriksen 1995, 19ff). House 8 had at least one entrance placed slightly south of the middle on the west side. The function of the house is uncertain, but it may have been an outbuilding of some kind.

The other house (house 10) was about 15 metres south of the main building and parallel to it. The main reason why the house is not interpreted as a separate farm unit, but as part of the magnate estate, is the short distance to the main building, and the fact that a similar building can be linked to the estate during the earlier phase. It is a traditional three-aisled long-house, roughly 20 metres long and 6.8 metres wide. The house had five trestles, of which no. 5 at the far east was probably part of the gable. The house probably had several rooms, but because of the poor state of preservation the division cannot be ascertained. Several of the excavated post-holes contained small quantities of unburned animal bones (7–28 g), and the identified fragments are mandibles of pig. A fragment

of a comb was also found in the hole for one of the roof-bearing posts in the western part of the house. The element of animal bones in the house is interesting in view of the fact that bones otherwise were very scarce in the filling of the post-holes. This suggests that the house had a dwelling function and that some form of food preparation and/or consumption of meat took place in the building.

The eastern farm, farm III:b, consisted of a long-house (house 15) and a smaller post-built house (house 2) placed about seven to eight metres south of and parallel to the long-house (Fig. 15). The long-house is 22 metres long and 6.1–8.0 metres wide, with four trestles, placed in two pairs towards the gables. Between these there is larger span of about 10.5 metres. Inside and parallel to the line of the south wall there is a row of post-holes 7–10 metres long, which probably had some kind of function supporting a wall-mounted bench. The house displays several features similar to houses of Trelleborg type, with convex outer walls and widely spaced trestles with a hall-

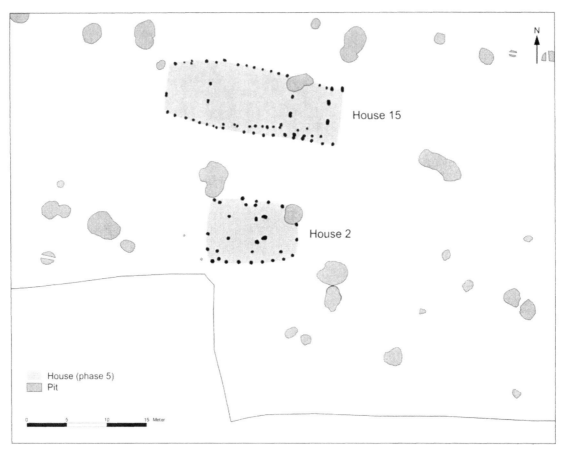

Fig. 15. The eastern farm (farm III:b) during settlement phase 6. Illustration: Thomas Hansson.

like room in the middle. The house, however, can hardly be described as a classical Trelleborg type since it lacks the outer row of oblique supporting posts (Nørlund 1948; cf. Artursson 2005, 131ff, with references).

There are traces suggesting that the house underwent rebuilding or repair. All the roof-bearing posts in the southern row are doubled, probably because posts were replaced. In the south line of the wall in the eastern part of the house there are also traces of double post-holes, most likely as a result of a rebuilding of the wall. In two of the post-holes in the south long wall there were parts of two extremity bones from cattle. There is a tibia from an animal aged 2–2.5 years in a post-hole belonging to the original wall and a whole metacarpus from a post-hole belonging to the rebuilt outer wall. Only occasional animal bones were found in other parts of the house, which corroborates the unusual character of the find. Against this background it is probable that the bones were ritually deposited, no doubt in connection with the rebuilding of the house, when

the old wall was closed and the new one was inaugurated. The deposited bones should thus be viewed as votive offerings after ceremonial meals to protect the house against misfortune and evil forces (Carlie 2004, 190).

The eastern farm also had a small post-built house (house 2), located about eight metres south of and parallel to the long-house. The building is 11.5 metres long and 6–8 metres wide, and like the long-house it had convex long walls. The entrance to the house is in the middle of the north side, thus facing the long-house. House 2 has not been 14C-dated; the interpretation that it is contemporaneous is based on the appearance of the house and its spatial placing in relation to the main building. It is difficult to say what the function of the smaller house was, but traces of several retracted wall posts suggest that it either had a double wall or some kind of wall-mounted benches. This indicates that it was not used as an outhouse but had other functions – perhaps as a workshop or a dwelling for the servile labourers on the estate.

The third farmstead, farm II/IV:b, is in the north-east part of the area, almost thirty metres north of farm III:b. This unit consisted of a single medium-sized long-house (house 13) with five roof-bearing trestles. An interesting technical detail in this house is the oblong shape of the post-holes, indicating the use of hewn timber. The positions of the inner posts and the span length suggest a traditional tripartite division of the house, with the dwelling to the west, an outhouse to the east, and a centrally placed entrance hall.

DATING AND ORGANIZATION

As in phase 5, the dating of the settlement is based on 14C and house typology. Three 14C dates belong in the Late Viking Age (Table 2), all taken from houses (houses 7, 10, and 13). A combined calibration of the samples gives a dating of 940–1020 AD (1068±23 BP). Neither pottery nor other date-indicating finds can be linked to the settlement. This may be due to a change in the handling of butchering and household waste, which was no longer deposited in pits on the site but spread on the fields when they were manured (Stilborg 2006).

The settlement in phase 6 is a direct continuation of the settlement in the preceding phase. A slight decline can be seen, however, in that the number of farms decreased from four/five to three/four, and the activities in the workshop area in the south-east probably ceased. Based on 14C dates and the building method of the houses, the settlement can be dated to c. 900–1050 AD, a period of about 150 years, after which it was moved away from the site. Three farms display continuity from the preceding phase, the magnate estate (farm I:b) and farms III:b and II/IV:b, located respectively east and north-east of the depression. Both the magnate estate and farm III:b were built on almost the same plots, with only a minor shift towards the east, while the long-house on the third farm may be a successor of either farm II or IV.

In the Late Viking Age the magnate estate took on a more complex composition. Apart from the big main building, it comprised two post-built houses, one of them a roughly 20-metre single-aisled building at right angles to the long-house and joined to it. Also belonging to the estate was a medium-sized long-house south of the main building. This gave the estate a total building area of approximately 510 m², an increase by 130 m² or some 25% compared to the preceding phase. It is chiefly the north–south-oriented house 8 that accounts for this increase in

area, while the main building (house 7) is actually slightly smaller than house 6. This increase in the area of the buildings must mean that the economy of the farm changed, perhaps towards a greater emphasis on grain production, which would no doubt have required more room in the form of a threshing barn or stores for the estate's products and equipment. Perhaps the extra long-house south of the main building was also used to house the workforce.

In the last phase farm III also became slightly larger, with an increase in the area of buildings from 160 to 250 m². In this case too, it is an extra post-built house (house 2) south of the long-house that accounts for the increase. As mentioned above, the interpretation of the function of this house is uncertain. Its structure, however, does not suggest that it was used for livestock or storage, but more likely for craft activities or as a dwelling.

An interesting detail in this phase is the different building traditions of the farms. The buildings on the magnate estate display both older and younger elements, with the main building, at least externally, being a virtual copy of the older long-house (house 6). At the same time, in the later phase we see a change of the inner organization, as the central section now has hall-like proportions. Innovation is also seen in house 8, which was built without inner roof-bearing posts and with bearing walls, a practice that became increasingly common in the second half of the Viking Age (Bender Jørgensen 1995, 19ff). It we look instead at farm III:b, we see no older features in the construction; the long-house was built in a style showing distinct influences of houses of Trelleborg type, with noticeably convex long walls and widely spaced trestles giving a large hall-like room in the middle section of the house (Olsen & Schmidt 1977; Schmidt 1994). House 15, however, lacks the outer buttressing posts of the classical Trelleborg house, with a simple wall construction in its stead.

The differences in building styles are probably due to the farms being built with a few decades' interval, so that new architectural preferences gained a foothold among the inhabitants of Västervång. Since the buildings on the magnate estate also show novelties in the technical construction, the difference in time between the farms ought not to have been greater than that they stood simultaneously on the site for at least part of the period. As the long-house on farm III displays several traces of rebuilding or repairs, this could hypothetically represent the last farm standing on the site, after the settlement had been abandoned to be moved to another place, probably in the vicinity.

REFERENCES

Ambrosiani, K. 1981. Viking Age combs, comb making and comb makers: in the light of finds from Birka and Ribe. Stockholm Studies in Archaeology 2. Stockholm.

Andrén, A. 1980. Lund. Riksantikvarieämbetet & Statens historiska museer. Rapport Medeltidsstaden 26. Stockholm

Anglert, M. 1995. Kyrkor och herravälde. Från kristnande till sockenbildning i Skåne. Lund Studies in Medieval Archaeology 16. Almqvist & Wiksell International, Stockholm.

Anglert, M. 2003. Uppåkra. Bland högar, ortnamn och kyrkor. In Anglert, A. & Thomasson, J., eds., Landskapsarkeologi och tidig medeltid – några exempel från södra Sverige. Uppåkrastudier 8. Acta Archaeologica Lundensia Series in 8° No. 48, pp. 115–144. Stockholm: Almqvist & Wiksell International.

Anglert, M. 2006. Landskapets Malmö. In Larsson, S., ed., Liljan. Om arkeologi i en del av Malmö, pp. 31–47. Stockholm/Malmö: Riksantikvarieämbetet & Malmö kulturmiljö.

Arcini, C. & Jacobsson, B. in press. Vikingarna från Vannhög. Ale Historisk tidskrift för Skåne, Halland och Blekinge nr 1 2008, pp. 1–14.

Artursson, M. 2005. Böndernas hus. In Carlie, A., ed., Järnålder vid Öresund. Band 1. Specialstudier och syntes. Skånska spår – arkeologi längs Västkustbanan, pp. 76–161. Stockholm: Riksantikvarieämbetets förlag.

Bender Jørgensen, L. & Eriksen, P. 1995. Trabjerg. En vestjysk landsby fra vikingetiden. Holstebro Museums række. Jysk arkæologisk Selskabs skrifter XXXI:1.

Björhem, N, & Magnusson Staaf, B. 2006. Långhuslandskapet. En studie av bebyggelse och samhälle från stenålder till järnålder. Öresundsförbindelsen och arkeologin. Malmöfynd nr 8. Malmö: Malmö kulturmiljö.

Brorsson, T. 2003. The Slavonic Felberg and Fresendorf Pottery in Scania, Sweden. In Larsson, L. & Hårdh, B. eds. Centrality – Regionality. The Social Structure of Southern Sweden during the Iron Age. Uppåkrastudier 7. Acta Archaeologica Lundensia Series in 8° No. 40, pp. 223–224. Stockholm: Almqvist & Wiksell International.

Callmer, J. 1991. Platser med anknytning till handel och hantverk i yngre järnålder. Exempel från södra Sverige. In Mortensen, P. & Rasmussen, B.M., eds., Høvdingesamfund och Kongemagt. Fra Stamme til Stat i Danmark 2. Jysk Arkæeologisk Selskabs Skrifter XXII:2, pp. 29–47, Højbjerg: Jysk Arkæeologisk Selskab.

Callmer, J. 2001. Extinguished solar systems and black holes. Traces of estates in the Scandinavian Late Iron Age. In Hårdh, B., ed., Uppåkra. Centrum och sammanhang, Uppåkrastudier 3. Acta Archaeologica Lundensia Series in 8° No. 34, pp. 109–137. Stockholm: Almqvist & Wiksell International.

Cardell, A. 2006. Slaktavfall och matrester. Unpublished report. Riksantikvarieämbetet.

Carlie, A. 2004. Forntida byggnadskult. Tradition och regionalitet i södra Skandinavien. Riksantikvarieämbetet Arkeologiska undersökningar Skrifter No. 57, Stockholm: Riksantikvarieämbetets förlag.

Carlie, A. 2008. Västervångsboplatsen under 1500 år – bebyggelseutveckling och social organisation. Bilaga till rapport för Västervång 3:14 m.fl., Trelleborgs stad/socken, Trelleborgs kommun, Skåne. Arkeologisk slutundersökning 2005. RAÄ UV Syd Dokumentation av fältarbetsfasen 2006:1.

Carlie, A. & Artursson, M. 2005. Böndernas gårdar. In Carlie, A., ed., Järnålder vid Öresund. Band 1. Specialstudier och syntes, Skånska spår – arkeologi längs Västkustbanan, pp. 162–245. Stockholm: Riksantikvarieämbetets förlag.

Christensen, T. 1997. "Hallen i Lejre". In Callmer, J. & Rosengren, E., eds., "Gick Grendel att söka det höga huset…" Arkeologiska källor till aristokratiska miljöer i Skandinavien under yngre järnålder. Rapport från ett seminarium i Falkenberg 16–17 november 2005, pp. 47–54. Halmstad: Hallands länsmuseer.

Cinthio, E. 1975. Köping och stad i det tidigmedeltida Skåne. Ale 1975:1, pp. 1–10.

Danmarks Arkæologiske Udgravningar, 1994 & 1996.

Egebjerg Hansen, T., Kaldal Mikkelsen, D. & Hvass, S. 1991. Landbebyggelserne i 7. århundrede. In Mortensen, P. & Rasmussen, B. M., eds., Fra stamme til Stat 2. Høvdingesamfund og Kongemagt, Jysk Arkæologisk Selskabs Skrifter XXII:2. pp. 17–27. Højbjerg.

Eliasson, L. & Kishonti, I. 2007. Det funktionella landskapet. Naturvetenskapliga analyser ur ett arkeologisk perspektiv. Öresundsförbindelsen och arkeologin. Malmöfynd nr 10. Malmö: Malmö kulturmiljö.

Erikson, M. 2001. En väg till Uppåkra. In Larsson, L., ed., Uppåkra. Centrum i analys och rapport. Uppåkrastudier 4. Acta Archaeologica Lundensia Series in 8° No. 36, pp. 167–176. Stockholm: Almqvist & Wiksell International.

Ericson, T. & Carlie, A. 2006. Västervång. En boplats från äldre och yngre järnålder. Skåne, Trelleborgs kommun, Trelleborgs stad/socken. Västervång 3:14 m.fl. Arkeologisk slutundersökning 2005. RAÄ UV Syd Dokumentation av fältarbetsfasen 2006:1.

Ersgård, L. 1986. Kämpinge och köpingarna – om tidigmedeltida handelsplatser i Sydvästskåne. In Andrén, A. et al., eds., Medeltiden och arkeologin. Festskrift till Erik Cinthio. Lund Studies in Medieval Archaeology 1, pp. 313–323. Lund.

Ethelberg, P. 2003. Gården og landsbyen i jernalder og vikingtid (500 f.Kr. – 1000 e. Kr.). In Det Sønderjyske Landbrugs Historie. Jernalder, vikingetid og middelalder, pp. 123–373. Haderslev: Haderslev Museum og Historisk Samfund for Sønderjylland.

Fenger, O. 1971. Fejde og mandebod. Studier over slægtsansvaret i germansk og gammeldansk ret. København: Juristforbundets Forlag.

Hansen, F. 1945. Järnåldersgravar vid Albäcksåns mynning nära Trelleborg, Meddelanden från Lunds universitets historiska museum 1945, pp. 44–67.

Heimer, O., Ifverson, P. & Persson, J. 2006. Lockarps bytomt – delområde 8. Citytunnelprojektet Rapport över arkeologisk undersökning. Malmö kulturmiljö. Rapport nr 45.

von Heijne, C. 2004. Särpräglat. Vikingatida och tidigmedeltida myntfynd från Danmark, Skåne, Blekinge och Halland (ca 800–1130). Stockholm Studies in Archaeology 31. Stockholm: Stockholms universitet.

Helgesson, B. 2002. Järnålderns Skåne. Samhälle, centra och regioner. Uppåkrastudier 5. Acta Archaeologica Lundensia Series in 8° No. 38. Stockholm: Almqvist & Wiksell International.

Hellerström, S. 2005. Gravar från yngre järnålder. Skåne, Trelleborgs kommun, Kvarteret Verkstaden 3, RAÄ 2. Arkeologisk slutundersökning. RAÄ UV Syd Dokumentation av fältarbetsfasen 2005:5.

Hermansson, L. 2000. Släkt, vänner och makt. En studie av elitens politiska kultur i 1100-talets Danmark. Avhandlingar från Historiska Institutionen, Göteborgs universitet, 24. Göteborg.

Herschend, F. 1993. The Origin of the Hall in Southern Scandinavia. Tor, vol. 25, pp. 175–199.

Hvass, S. 1980 Vorbasse. The Viking-age Settlement at Vorbasse, Central Jutland. Acta Archaeologica, Vol. 50 1979, pp. 137–172.

Hårdh, B. 1976. Wikingerzeitliche Depotfunde aus Südschweden. Katalog und Tafeln. Acta Archaeologica Lundensia Series in 4° No. 9. Bonn A.R./ Deutschland: Rudolf Habelt Verlag, Lund/ Sweden: CWK Gleerup.

Hårdh, B. 1984. Inventering av järnåldersmaterial i Skytts och Oxie härader. In Pugna Forensis –? Arkeologiska undersökningar kring Foteviken, Skåne 1981–83, pp. 86–112. Malmö: Länsstyrelsen i Malmöhus län.

Hårdh, B. 2003. The Contacts of the Central Place. In Larsson, L, & Hårdh, B., eds., Centrality – Regionality. The Social Structure of Southern Sweden during the Iron Age. Uppåkrastudier 7. Acta Archaeologica Lundensia Series in 8° No. 40, pp. 27–66. Stockholm: Almqvist & Wiksell International.

Jacobsson, B. 1982. Trelleborg. Riksantikvarieämbetet & Statens historiska museer. Rapport Medeltidsstaden 38. Stockholm.

Jacobsson, B. 1996. Arkeologisk utredning steg 2. Trelleborg, Västervång-Vipeängen, område 1, 6, 7 och 9. RAÄ 2, 20 och 31. 1995. Riksantikvarieämbetet Rapport UV Syd 1996:52.

Jacobsson, B. 2000. Trelleborgen i Trelleborg. Förhistoriska boplatslämningar och gravar, vikingatida ringborg och medeltida bebyggelselämningar. Skåne, Trelleborg, kv Gröningen, kv Kråkvinkeln, Bryggaregatan och Svenstorpsgatan. Arkeologiska undersökningar. Riksantikvarieämbetetet UV Syd rapport 1999:93.

Jacobsson, B. 2002. Ståstorp – en gård från sen vendeltid och vikingatid. In Mogren, M., ed., Märkvärt medeltida. Arkeologi ur en lång skånsk historia. Arkeologiska undersökningar Skrifter no. 43, pp. 99–126, Stockholm: Riksantikvarieämbetets förlag.

Jacobsson, B. 2003. Trelleborg and the Southern Plain during the Iron Age. A Study of a Coastal Area in South-West Scania, Sweden. In Larsson, L. & Hårdh, B. Centrality – Regionality. The Social Structure of Southern Sweden during the Iron Age. Uppåkrastudier 7. Acta Archaeologica Lundensia Series in 8° No. 40, pp. 191–221. Stockholm: Almqvist & Wiksell International.

Jacobsson, B. & Riddersporre, M. 2007. Väg E6 Trelleborg–Vellinge. Ett motorvägsbygge. Skåne, Maglarp, Skregire, Håslöv och Vellinge socknar, Trelleborgs och Vellinge kommuner. Arkeologisk utredning steg 2 2006. Riksantikvarieämbetet UV Syd Rapport 2007:9.

Jensen, J. 2004. Danmarks Oldtid. Yngre Jernalder og Vikingetid 400–1050 e. Kr. København: Gyldendal. Nordisk Forlag A/S.

Jeppsson, A. 1995. Skåne, Trelleborg. Kvarteret Katten 12, 27 och 29. RAÄ 19. Arkeologisk slutundersökning 1987 och 1988. Riksantikvarieämbetet RAÄ Rapport 1995:9.

Johansson, N. 2000. Boplatser och fossilt odlingslandskap vid Stenstorp i Slöinge socken. In Strömberg, B., ed., Boplatser och fossilt odlingslandskap. Arkeologi längs väg E&/E20 i södra halland. Del III 1993–1996. Sträckan Kvibille–Slöinge. Riksantikvarieämbetet. UV Väst rapport 1998:21, pp. 97–130.

Jørgensen, L. 2002. Kongsgård – kultsted – marked. Overvejelser omkring Tissøkompleksets struktur og funktion. In Jennbert, K., Andreén, A. & Raudvere, C., ed., Plats och praxis – studier av nordisk förkristen ritual. Vägar till Midgård 2, pp. 215–247. Lund: Nordic Academic Press.

Kaul, F. 1985. A Settlement Site of the Later Iron Age at Vallensbæk near Copenhagen. Journal of Danish Archaeology vol. 4, pp. 31–54.

Larsson, L. & Lenntorp, K.-M. 2004. The Enigmatic House. In Larsson, L., ed., Continuity for Centuries. A ceremonial building and its context at Uppåkra, southern Sweden, Uppåkrastudier 10. Acta Archaeologica Lundensia Series in 8° No. 48, pp. 3–48. Stockholm: Almqvist & Wiksell International.

Larsson, S. 2006. Gestaltningen av några skånska städer. In Larsson, S. Centraliteter. Människor, strategier och landskap, pp. 167–292. Stockholm: Riksantikvarieämbetets förlag.

Lihammar, A. 2007. Bortom Riksbildningen. Människor, landskap och makt i sydöstra Skandinavien. Lund Studies in Historical Archaeology 7. Lund.

Lundqvist, L. 2003. Slöinge 1992–96. Undersökningar av en boplats från yngre järnålder. Slöingeprojektet 2. Gotarc Serie C. Arkeologiska Skrifter No. 42. Göteborg.

Nielsen, L.C. 1980. Omgård. A Settlement from the Late Iron Age and the Viking Period in West Jutland. Acta Archaeologica, Vol. 50 1979, pp. 173–208.

Nørlund, P. 1948. Trelleborg. Nordiske Fortidsminder IV, 1. København.

Ohlsson, T. 1976. The Löddeköpinge Investigation I. The Settlement at Vikhögsvägen. Meddelanden från Lunds Universitets Historiska Museum 1975–75, pp. 59–161.

Olsen, O. & Schmidt, H. 1977. Fyrkat. En jysk vikingeborg. I. Borgen og bebyggelsen. Nordiske Fortidsminder. Serie B, bind 3. Det Konglige Nordiske Oldskriftselskab. København.

Olson, T., Regnell, M., Nilsson, L., Erikson, M. & Brorsson, T. 1996. Arkeologisk slutundersökning. Boplatslämningar från neolitikum, bronsålder och äldre järnålder. Skåne, Väg 108, N Nöbbelövs, Stångby, Vallkärra och Lackalänga socknar, Lunds och Kävlinge kommuner. RAÄ UV Syd Rapport 1996:60.

Petersson, B. 2008. Skåne mellan nationerna. Arkeologi och regional identitet. In Carlie, A., ed., Öresund – barriär eller bro? Kulturella kontakter och samhällsutveckling i Skåne och på Själland under järnåldern. Centrum för Danmarksstudier 18. pp. 309–320. Göteborg/ Stockholm: Makadam förlag.

Pettersson, C. & Brorsson, T. 2002. "Bott vid en landsväg…" In Mogren, M., ed., Märkvärt medeltida. Arkeologi ur en lång skånsk historia. Arkeologiska undersökningar Skrifter no. 43, pp. 9–98. Stockholm: Riksantikvarieämbetets förlag.

Randsborg, K. 1980. The Viking Age in Denmark. The Formation of a State. London: Duckworth.

Rosberg, A. & Lindhé, E. 2001. Öresundsförbindelsen Svågertorp 8A. Rapport över Arkeologisk slutundersökning. Malmö kulturmiljö Rapport nr 13.

Rosborn, S. 1984. Hököpinge – Pile. Medeltida centralbygd i Sydvästskåne. In Pugna Forensis –? Arkeologiska undersökningar kring Foteviken, Skåne 1981–83, pp. 69–85. Malmö: Länsstyrelsen i Malmöhus län.

Rudin, G.-B. & Brink, K. 2002. Öresundsförbindelsen. Lockarp 7A. Rapport över arkeologisk slutundersökning. Malmö kulturmiljö. Rapport nr 16.

Samuelsson, B.-Å. 2001. Kan gravar spegla vägars ålder och betydelse? Ett exempel från Söderslätt i Skåne. In Larsson, L., ed., Uppåkra. Centrum i analys och rapport. Uppåkrastudier 4. Acta Archaeologica Lundensia Series in 8° No. 36, pp. 177–184. Stockholm: Almqvist & Wiksell International.

Schmidt, H. 1994. Building customs in Viking Age Denmark. Published by Poul Kristensen.

Schmidt Sabo, K. 2000. Vikingatid långhus och en bysmedja. Skåne, Barkåkra socken, Ängelholms kommun, Vantinge bytomt, Vantinge

1:29. Arkeologisk för- och slutundersökning. Riksantikvarieämbetet UV Syd Rapport 2000:101.

Silvegren, U. W. 1999. Mynten från Uppåkra. In Hårdh, B., ed., Fynden i centrum. Keramik, glas och metall från Uppåkra. Uppåkrastudier 2. Acta Archaeologica Lundensia Series in 8° No. 30, pp. 95–112. Stockholm: Almqvist & Wiksell International.

Sindbæk, S. 2005. Ruter og rutinisering vikingetidens fjernhandel i Nordeuropa. København: Forlaget Multivers.

Skansjö, S. 1983. Söderslätt genom 600 år. Bebyggelse och odling under äldre historisk tid. Skånsk senmedeltid och renässans. Skriftserie utgiven av Vetenskaps-societeten i Lund 11. Lund: CWK Gleerup.

Skov, H. 1994. Hustyper i vikingetid og tidlig middelalder. Udviklingen af hustyper i det gammeldanske område fra ca. 800–1200 e. Kr. Hikuin 21, pp. 139–162.

Skre, D. 1998. Herredømmet. Bosetning og besittelse på Romerike 200–1350 e. Kr. Scandinavian Oslo: University Press Universitetsforlaget.

Söderberg, B. 2003. Järrestad. Huvudgård i centralbygd. Arkeologiska undersökningar Skrifter No. 51. Stockholm: Riksantikvarieämbetets förlag.

Söderberg, B. 2005. Aristokratiskt rum och gränsöverskridande. Järrestad och sydöstra Skåne mellan region och rike 600–1100. Arkeologiska undersökningar Skrifter No. 62. Stockholm: Riksantikvarieämbetets förlag.

Steinecke, M. Ekenberg, A., Hansson K. & Ifverson, P. 2005. Öresundsförbindelsen. Sunnanå 9A–F. Rapport över arkeologisk slutundersökning. Malmö kulturmiljö. Rapport nr 34.

Stilborg, O. 2006. Västervång. 1000 års brukskeramik. Keramiska Forskningslaboratoriet, Kvartärgeologiska avdelningen, Lunds Universitet. KFLrapport 06/08/14.

Stoumann, I. 1980. Sædding. A Viking-age Village near Esbjerg. Acta Archaeologica, Vol. 50 1979, pp. 95–118.

Strömberg, M. 1961. Strömberg, M. 1961. Untersuchungen zur jüngeren Eisenzeit in Schonen. Völkerwanderungszeit-Wikingerzeit. Bd II. Acta Archaeologica Lundensia Series in 4o No. 4. Lund.

Strömberg, M. 1978. En kustby i Ystad – före stadens tillkomst. Ystadiana XXIII, 1978, pp. 7–101.

Svanberg, F. 2003. Death Rituals in South-East Scandinavia AD 800–1000. Decolonizing the Viking Age 2. Acta Archaeologica Lundensia Series in 4° No. 24. Stockholm: Almqvist & Wiksell International.

Svanberg, F. & Söderberg, B. 1999. Den vikingatida borgen i Borgeby. Arkeologiska studier kring Borgeby och Löddeköpinge 1. Lund.

Svanberg, F. & Söderberg, B. 2000. Porten till Skåne. Löddeköpinge under järnålder och medeltid. Riksantikvarieämbetet. Avdelningen för arkeologiska undersökningar. Skrifter No. 32.

Tornbjerg, S.Å. 1992. Jernalderbebyggelser ved Køge. In Sjællands jernalder. Beretning fra et symposium 24. IV 1990 i København. Arkæologiske skrifter 6. Arkæologisk Institut, Københavns universitet, pp. 51–80.

Tornbjerg, S.Å. 1998. Toftegård – en fundrig gård fra sen jernalder och vikingetid. In Hård, B. & Larsson, L., eds., Centrala platser – centrala frågor. Samhällsstrukturen under järnåldern. Acta Archaeologica Lundensia Series in 8° No. 28, pp. 217–232. Stockholm: Almqvist & Wiksell International.

Viking, U. & Fors, T. 1995. Ösarp. Vikingtid och tidigmedeltida agrarbebyggelse i södra Halland. Arkeologisk undersökning. RAÄ 197 Ösarp 1:21, 2:15, Laholms lfs, Halland. Stiftelsen Hallands länsmuseer, Uppdragsverksamheten. Halmstad.

Watt, M. 1999. Guldgubber og patricier til guldgubber fra Uppåkra. In Hårdh, B., ed., Fynden i centrum. Keramik, glas och metall från Uppåkra. Uppåkrastudier 2, Acta Archaeologica Lundensia Series in 8° No. 30, pp. 177–200. Stockholm: Almqvist & Wiksell International.

Widgren, M. 1998. Kulturgeografernas bönder och arkeologernas guld – finns det någon väg till en syntes? In Larsson, L. & Hårdh, B., eds., Centrala platser, centrala frågor. Samhällsstrukturen under järnåldern. En vänbok till Berta Stjernquist. Uppåkrastudier 1. Acta Archaeologica Lundensia. Series in 8° No. 28, pp. 281–296. Stockholm: Almqvist & Wiksell International.

Wranning, P. 1999. Sydhalländska Trelleborgshus – lokala variationer av ett senvikingatida byggnadsskick. In Artelius, T., Englund, E. & Ersgård, L., eds., Kring västsvenska hus – boendets organisation och symbolik i förhistorisk och historisk tid. Gotarc Serie C. Arkeologiska Skrifter No. 22, pp. 37–50. Göteborg.

Author's address
National Heritage Board, Archaeological Excavations Dept. UV Syd, Odlarevägen 5, 226 60 Lund, Sweden
anne.carlie@raa.se

Acta Archaeologica vol. 79, 2008, pp 145-184
Printed in Denmark • All rights reserved

Copyright 2008
ACTA ARCHAEOLOGICA
ISSN 0065-101X

BLÓT HOUSES IN VIKING AGE FARMSTEAD CULT PRACTICES

NEW FINDINGS FROM SOUTH-EASTERN ICELAND

Bjarni F. Einarsson

INTRODUCTION

Many researchers have argued that there are no traces of Viking Age *blót*[1] houses to be found in Iceland and that these types of buildings have never even existed (Foot & Wilson 1970:398; Eldjárn 1974(b): 111f; Steinsland 1993:148) but in this article, based on new findings discovered close to Hornafjörður (Höfn) in southeast Iceland, it is my intention to argue otherwise.

The archaeological investigations relevant to this matter began in 1996 with the Viking Age burial situated on a hill, or a mound, at Hólmur. Initially the excavations were instigated in order to search for a farmstead which might be connected to the burial, the presence of which had been known for quite some time prior to the excavations. In 1997 the remains of a house were examined, at what was presumed to be the farmyard of the previously unknown farmstead, c. 250 metres away from the Viking Age burial and while sections of the farmyard were being excavated the site of the known burial was re-examined, approximately 100 years after being excavated the first time. It was at this time that traces of activity were discovered close to the burial and it was presumed that these were in some way connected to the burial. Furthermore the remains of a ritual cult site were also evident but it was not until the summer of 1999 that traces of the first Icelandic *blót* house were discovered at the cult site.

In the summer of 1999 a pit house was documented on the mound in close proximity to the grave and it included the traces of a number of different ritual activities. In my opinion the pit house should, without doubt, be interpreted as the remains of a *blót* house; a house that would have been used for private cult celebrations at the Hólmur farmstead. Furthermore the evidence also suggests that ritual activities continued after the pit house was no longer in use. It is this *blót* house and its significance for our understanding of Viking Age cult practices that this article will deliberate.[2]

---

1 Due to the complexities embedded in translation it has been decided that the Icelandic terms *hof*, *hörgur* and *blót* will not be translated to English. The meaning of these words is explained in the main body of the text in an attempt to preserve the multidimensionality of the words.

---

2 I would like to take this opportunity to thank all the friends and colleagues that have worked with me at Hólmur during the period 1996-2002, including; Eiríkur Páll Jörundsson former museum director in Höfn, Björn G. Arnarsson antiquarian in Höfn, Daniel Lindblad archaeologist, Andreas Åhman archaeologist, Kristján Mímisson archaeologist, Gísli Sverrir Árnason former museum director, Leif Jonsson osteologist and archaeologist, my family and all others participants of the excavations for shorter or longer periods of time, both those employed and the volunteers. At times things were difficult but when the spirits were good so too the results. I would also like to thank those that financed the excavations: The parliament of Iceland, Hornafjörður-Council, The Ministry of Education and Culture, the County Museum in A-Skaftafellssýsla, Hornafjörðurs Savings Bank, the Jökulsárlón Travel Agent, Skinney - Þinganes and Hafnar Chemist. Finally I would also like to thank my friends in Sweden; Dr. Curry Heimann that read the manuscript during its various stages and who contributed to my conviction that this is better than what I could have done myself, and Lars Lundqvist, who provided reading suggestions. Thanks also to the translator Dr. Fiona Campell. The excavations were carried out by Fornleifafræðistofan (The Archaeology Office - *Arkeologiska kontoret*), a company under the direction of the author which, since 1997, has worked with contract archaeological projects within the Icelandic Heritage Board, focusing on archaeological excavation, environmental assessments and ancient remain surveying.

I. VIKING AGE EVERYDAY CULT PRACTICES - THEORIES AND WRITTEN SOURCES

1 THEORETICAL POINTS OF DEPARTURE

One of the greatest problems when dealing with matters concerning Viking Age religious life is the lack of authentic, contemporary sources and explicit archaeological remains that can testify to different religious activities and their related constructions. One part of the problem is our own lack of knowledge and our inability to identify such remains, in other words, knowing what to look for. As Andrén writes:

> Pagan rites could be carried out at particular sacred sites, in and around special cult houses and with the guidance of religious leaders but undoubtedly different kinds of people could also have carried out rites in a variety of different places in the landscape. (Translated from Swedish - Andrén 2004:227).

Needless to say I agree, but this still does not tell us what these types of houses looked like. Furthermore the early literary sources are primarily descriptions written by Christians several hundred years after these religious events took place (Hultgård 1996:25) and as such these descriptions are products of a society with completely different religious and political beliefs. Subsequently these were often written for the purpose of being used to deal with their own time's contemporary social conflicts.

There are, however, a number of contemporary sources which provide a fragmented glimpse into Iron Age religious life. Such sources include rune stones, law texts and the ancient poetry (e.g. the Eddaic poems) as well as the tales of travellers, for example Ibn Fadlan's account, which inform us to some extent but at the same time it is important to remember that these are full of the storytellers' prejudices and moral beliefs about right and wrong (Vikingerne ved Volga 1981). Unfortunately none of these sources tell us what the buildings or constructions, which we expect to find as archaeological remains, looked like. Therefore one of the fundamental questions in research projects related to Iron Age religious life becomes: How can archaeology discern the differences between sites and buildings of potential religious significance and more profane remains? As Finnestad has suggested:

> The religious ideas and values will necessarily be reflected, in some way or other, in every sector of the culture, also the utilitarian ones – even the struggle for existence: the concrete ways of making a living, the economic system, and the relationship with the natural surroundings. (Bjerre Finnestad 1986:23).

Theoretically, all material is religiously relevant, and thus a source for the study of religion. The task is to specify more precisely the relevancy in the given instance. (Ibid. 1986:24).

It can also be argued that all material remains in a religious context are informative about society in general and in this matter it is possible to maintain that graves

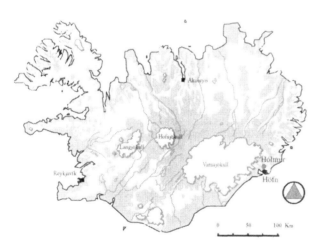

Figure 1. Hólmur and Hornafjörður (Höfn) in SE-Iceland. See figure 3 for more detailed map.

Figure 2. The mighty ridge and cult site from the west. In the background the mountain Bergárdalsheiði can be seen (Digital photo nr. 38. Photo BFE).

and grave-goods are some of the most important sources for understanding a society and its economical, technological, demographical and even ecological spheres. According to Artelius:

> Without a doubt it can be argued that these people [prehistoric] had a religious way of defining reality in the sense that profane everyday life was part of some spiritual reality. (Translated from Swedish - Artelius 2000:20).

So what can we expect to find at a Viking Age cult site and how do the archaeological remains reflect religious beliefs?

2 THE MATTERS BEING DEALT WITH

In this article I will attempt to demonstrate that a pit house discovered in 1997 at Laxárdalur, in southeast Iceland, five metres away from a known Viking Age burial located on a mound, on the slope of an impressive beach ridge, is in fact a *blót* house and that the site is a cult site - a site for offering, worship and sacrifice (Einarsson 1996, 1998(a & b), 2000(b), 2001, 2002 & 2003).

The term *blót* house refers to a house where religious activities have taken place, a place for discussion and communication between people and the gods in a systematic and regulated manner. No attempt will be made here to decide if the house has been a *hof* or a *hörgur* because such a definition is at best difficult and not especially meaningful. The various definitions could just as easily be more recent time explanations created from Christian influences in an attempt to understand a multidimensional and complex religion that there was no longer any daily contact with. The terms could even be synonymous. *Hof* appears in the literature as both a farmstead *hof* and as a district *hof*, for example Þorólfs heljarskinn's farmstead

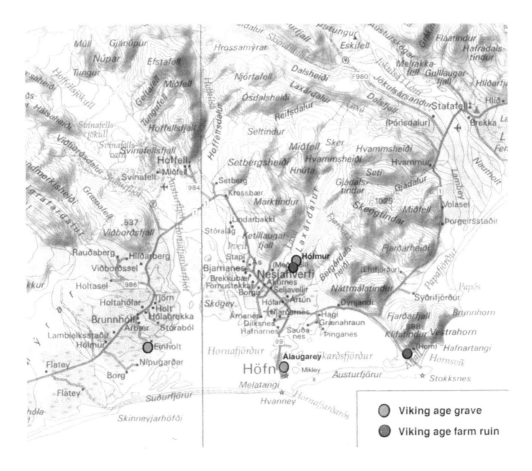

Figure 3. Map of parts of A-Skaftafellsýsla, around Höfn. A burial might exist at the farmstead ruins to the left (blue circle) but these have not been excavated and at present have no name. The dating of these is therefore very uncertain but could be Viking Age. In the text there are several place names mentioned and those not marked on this map can be found on maps further down the text (Kortabók, map 37 & 38).

hof in Forsæludal mentioned in the Vatnsdæla saga (Íslensk fornrit VIII:82), or the district *hof* in Gaul in Norway found in *Egil's saga* (Íslensk Fornrit II:124).

Both Ólsen and Bruun argue, in some detail, that the *hörgur* can be both a house and a special place (Ólsen & Bruun 1903:9-16) and accordingly the *hörgur* ought then to have been a private cult site, and the *hof* a more public cult site (Ibid. 1903:13). Based on this definition the *blót* house at Hólmur is a *hörgur* but this definition was probably of little relevance in Icelandic Iron Age society, where no centralisation of power existed and where the differences were more likely to have been found between the religious activities on the individual farmsteads and the activities of several farmsteads at shared sites (Olsen 1966:103). Moreover the terms *hof - hörgur* could have been completely independent of whether or not cult sites were public arenas or private ones and the same site could even have been used as a *hof, hörgur* and *blót* house. Originally the word *hörgur* meant rock, boulder or pronounced rock face and according to ancient provincial law *hörgur* could have been built as houses (Hultgård 1996:33). Hultgård maintains that:

> Originally these were cult sites out in the open, on raised surfaces in agreement with the natural meaning of the word *hörgur* [Sw: *harg*]. At times, however, *hörgur* have been added onto, using different kinds of stone or timber constructions. (Translated from Swedish – Hultgård 1996:31).

It is, however, not my intention to present all sources where the terms *blót* or *blót* house appear but a selection of these sources will be discussed later on in this text. For further reading a more in-depth presentation can be found in the work of Aðalsteinsson (1978 & 1997).

3 RITUAL TRACES

In "The Penguin Dictionary of Archaeology" from 1970 ritual is defined as:

> Connected with some magic or religious practice. With the near-impossibility of understanding beliefs from archaeological evidence alone, the term is sometimes used simply to mean that no functional explanation can be found for the site or object so described. The usage is to be deprecated: honesty is the best policy (Bray & Trump 1970:198).

This definition is, to say the least, a very reserved definition but it also reflects its own time where everything that could not be understood was given some diffuse, cult/ritual meaning. Zuesse (1987) suggested a somewhat more functional definition in 'The Encyclopedia of Religion'. He defines the term ritual as:

> ... those conscious and voluntary, repetitious and stylized, symbolic bodily actions that are centered on cosmic structures and/or sacred purposes. (Verbal behaviour such as chant, song, and prayer are of course included in the category of bodily actions).

DuBois adds further that:

> Ritual is an enacted communication that may be intercepted or shared by other humans but that is directed primarily toward an efficacious god or intermediary. It can record, reenact, even reactivate an earlier act of communication in the here and now, drawing on a symbolic idiom established during a seminal communication in the past. It can persuade its supernatural audience to act favorably toward the human community. (1999:122).

Ritual is therefore systematic, regulated and stylised physical or metaphysical communication directed towards cosmic or sacred entities or beings and its communication can be vocalised or silent. Needless to say how the ritual activities reveal themselves in different cultures varies and these can be expressed in many ways; through song and dance, the consumption of food and drink, in silent or verbalised prayer, sexual actions and in the sacrifice of material objects, food or artefacts. In this manner sacrificial actions become a way of establishing and confirming a desired relationship between society and the supernatural or between the living and the dead and some kinds of sacrifices might even fulfil the demand or need for material/food by the deceased on his or her journey to some final destination.

Renfrew and Bahn have provided a number of archaeological criteria to be used whilst searching for remains of ritual activities:

Focusing of attention:
1. Ritual may take place in a spot with special, natural associations (e.g. a grave, a grove of trees, a spring, or mountain top).
2. Alternatively, ritual may take place in a special building set apart for sacred functions (e.g. a temple or church).
3. The structure and equipment used for the ritual may employ attention-focusing devises, reflected in the architecture, special fixtures (e.g. altars, benches, hearths), and in the movable equipment (e.g. lamps, gongs and bells, ritual vessels, censers, altar clothes, and all the paraphernalia of ritual).
4. The sacred area is likely to be rich in repeated symbols (this is known as "redundancy").

Boundary zone between this world and the next:
5. Ritual may involve both conspicuous public display (and expenditure), and hidden exclusive mysteries, whose practice will be reflected in the architecture.
6. Concepts of cleanliness and pollution may be reflected in the facilities (e.g. pools or basins of water) and maintenance of the sacred area.
7. The association with a deity or deities may be reflected in the use of a cult image, or a representation of the deity in abstract form (e.g. the Christian Chi-Rho symbol).

Presence of the deity:

8. The ritualistic symbols will often relate iconographically to the deities worshipped and to their associated myth. Animal symbolism (of real or mythical animals) may often be used, with particular animals relating to specific deities or powers.
9. The ritualistic symbols may relate to those seen also in funerary ritual and in other rites of passage.
10. Worship will involve prayer and special movements - gestures of adoration - and these may be reflected in the art or iconography of decorations or images.

Participation and offering:

11. The ritual may employ various devices for inducing religious experience (e.g. dance, music, drugs, and the infliction of pain).
12. The sacrifice of animals or humans may be practiced.
13. Food and drink may be brought and possibly consumed as offering or burned/poured away.
14. Other material objects may be brought and offered (votives). The act of offering may entail breakage and hiding or discard.
15. Great investment of wealth may be reflected both in the equipment used and in the offerings made.
16. Great investment of wealth and resources may be reflected in the structure itself and its facilities.

> In practice, only a few of these criteria will be fulfilled in any single archaeological context. (1991:359f).

These criteria ought to be kept in mind when discussing discovered cult houses and the majority of these criteria match surprisingly well with the cult site at Hólmur.

The grave from Hólmur, which will be described in detail later on, is in itself a trace of conscious ritual activity that is based on a set of specific ideas shared by those affected by the burial and even at this stage a dialogue between the living and higher supernatural powers has taken place. This dialogue or communication continued at the site and was expressed both inside and outside the house via the remains left behind from food preparation and mealtimes, in the scattering of fire-cracked stones, in the offerings of amongst other things food, bloomery iron, and the placing (offering) of loom weights, in the fires lit and in some of the activities around a pair of poles at the cult site.

The grave at Hólmur could have been of such importance for the collective cult of the farmstead that it might even have been a central site for religious and legislative actions and/or a centre for ancestral worship (cf. Birkeli 1938:56, 87ff. Magnus & Myhre 1986:267. Baudou 1991:73. Kristoffersen 1993:201. Kaliff 1997:20. Østmo 2004:188. Carlie 2004:32).

4 WRITTEN SOURCES AND *BLÓT*

> Þórólfr lagðisk á fé manna ok gerðisk hinn mesti þjófur; hann átti ok *blót*grafar, því at menn hugðu at hann *blót*aði bæði mönnum og fé.
> (Ísl. Fornrit VIII:82).

Thorolf stole men's livestock and became the worst of thieves. He also had trenches for sacrifice and the belief was that he offered up both men and animals. (The complete Sagas of Icelanders IV. 1997:41).

The *Vatnsdæla saga* describes Þórólfr Heljarskinn of Forsæludal in this way and following this presentation of him it tells of how he is visited in his home and murdered.

> Jökull gat þá at líta hvar Þórólfr kom upp ór *blót*gröf sinni og hljóp ór virkinu, en Jökull eptir honum.
> (Íslensk Fornrit VIII:83).

> Jokul then managed to catch sight of Thorolf as he emerged from his sacrificial trench; he leapt down from the fortification, with Jokul in hot pursuit
> (The complete Sagas of Icelanders IV. 1997:41).

With regards to this description Aðalsteinsson says, amongst other things:

> With regards to the *blót*-grave it is difficult to provide an exhaustive explanation of the term. It does not, however, need to be anything other than a kind of pit house where deity worship occurred. (Translation from Icelandic to Swedish by author, from Swedish to English by Fiona Campbell - Aðalsteinsson 1997:99).

In the *Landnámabók* (the book of settlement) the term *blót* is mentioned several times and it mentions, for example, how Þorsteinn rauðnefur (red nose) worshiped the waterfall (Ísl. Fornrit I:1968:358), how Þórir snepill (Lapp) worshiped a tree grove (Ibid. 1968:270), how Þórólfr smjör (butter) worshiped his dead father (Ibid. 1968:59), how the relatives of Auður djúpúðga (the philosopher) worshiped hills (Ibid. 1968:139-40) and how Eyvindur Loðinsson, Þórir snepill's neighbour, worshiped stones (Ibid. 1968:273; Ólafur Briem 1945:130). With regards to Auður djúpúðga and her family's religious activities the Landnámabok states the following:

> Hon hafði bænahald sitt á Krosshólum; þar lét hon reisa krossa, því at hon var skírð ok vel trúuð. Þar höfðu frændr hennar síðan átrúnað mikinn á hóla. Var <þar> þá gör hörg, er *blót* tóku til; trúðu þeir því, at þeir dæi í hólana, ok þar var Þórðr gellir leiddr í, áðr hann tók mannvirðing, sem segir í sögu hans. (Ísl. Fornrit I:1968:139-40).

> She had her prayer station at Cross-Knolls; there she caused them to raise crosses because she was baptized and was a true believer. Her kinsfolk had great faith in those knolls. There they made a temple and there they sacrificed, and it was the firm belief of them that they should die into the mound, and Thord the Yeller was led thither before he took over his lordship of a Godi, as is related in his saga. [3] (The Book of the Settlement of Icelanders, 1898:65).

This is an interesting source because it suggests that the same site could have been of significance for both

---

3   This Saga does not exist.

Christians and non-Christians, or at least it appears to have been possible for the Christian writers of the saga. The idea that pagan sites became Christian ones is not completely unheard of in Scandinavia but at present in Iceland this has not been proven beyond doubt. There are, however, some slight indications that this might be the case. Furthermore the chance of a Christian site becoming pagan is most probably not as common.

In the poems of the Edda a number of fragmentary descriptions of *hof* and other cult houses appear alongside other phenomena connected to these. Some examples include, for example, the Beowulf poem, where a *hörgur*-tent (et heargtrafum. verse 175. Osborn 1983:7) is mentioned. Olsen writes:

> Here it is obviously a matter of some kind of super-structure over a shrine, but at the same time the choice of words appears to suggest that this super-structure does not have the same character as a proper building. (Translated from Danish -1966:76).

In *Völuspá* (Eddukvæði 1949:3, verse 7) there is a very well known and frequently quoted verse:

Hittusk æsir
á Iðavelli,
þeir er hörg ok hofhátimbruðu;
alfla lögðu,
auð smíðuðu,
tangir skópu
og tól gerðu.
At Ithavoll met
the mighty gods,
Shrines and temples
they timbered high;
Forges they set,
and they smithied ore,
Tongs they wrought,
and tools they fashioned.
(The Poetic Edda 2004:5).

In *Grímnismál* (Eddukvæði I. 1949:86ff) the different dwelling places of the gods are described and, for example, in verses 10 and 22 we can read:

Mjök er auðkennt,
þeir er til Óðins koma
salkynni at séa:
vargr hangir
fyr vestan dyrr,
ok drúpir örn yfir

Easy is it to know
for him who to Othin
Comes and beholds the hall;
There hangs a wolf
by the western door,
And o'er it an eagle hovers.
(The Poetic Edda 2004:89).

Valgrind heitir,
er stendr velli á
heilög fyr helgum durum;
forn er sú grind,
en þat fáir vitu,
hvé hon er lás of lokin.

There Valgrind stands,
the sacred gate,
And behind are the holy doors;
Old is the gate,
but few there are
Who can tell how it tightly is locket. (Ibid. 2004:93)

In the Scandinavian provincial laws (Swedish; landskapslagarna) certain kinds of cult sites or cult houses were noted as being forbidden. In the law code known as the *Gulatingslagen*, from 1000 AD, cult practices at a *hörgur* [Sw. *harg*] or mound were forbidden (chapter 29) and it was also stated that if a house is built and called a *hörgur* fines of three marks would have to be paid to the bishop. The same fines would be demanded, according to the Gutalagen (1220 AD) if one were caught eating and drinking in a non-Christian manner (Hultgård 1996:33f). In the law book *Upplandslagen* (1296 AD) it is written that: *"Ingen skall blota år avgudar, och ingen skall tro på lundar eller stenar". [No-one shall worship or idolize, and no-one shall believe in groves or stones.* (Translated from Swedish - Andrén 2004:213)].

In the Icelandic law *Grágás* from the latter part of the 12th century it is written that if a person sacrifices or makes offerings to pagan gods/beings, or is practicing magic or eating horse meat then this person will be sentenced to *fjörbaugsgarð* (*Grágás* 1992:19 & 32), which means that anyone committing such offences would have three years in which to leave the country and then once they had left they would have to stay away for a further three years.

When Icelanders converted to Christianity in 999/1000 AD several exceptions were made to the Christian rules. According to the Íslendingabók one was allowed to abandon a baby to die in the open air, to eat horsemeat and one was allowed to make offerings in secret but these exceptions were revoked several years later (Íslensk fornrit I 1968:17).

Parallel to an increasing interest in prehistory during the 19th century *hof* and *hörgur* sites were found in several different places in Iceland and the numbers increased to over 100 when they reached their peak at the beginning of the 20th century (Olsen 1966:172). In the *Landnámabók* 13 *hof* are mentioned and the place names *hof* or *Hofstaðir* are known at 37 farmsteads or derelict farms

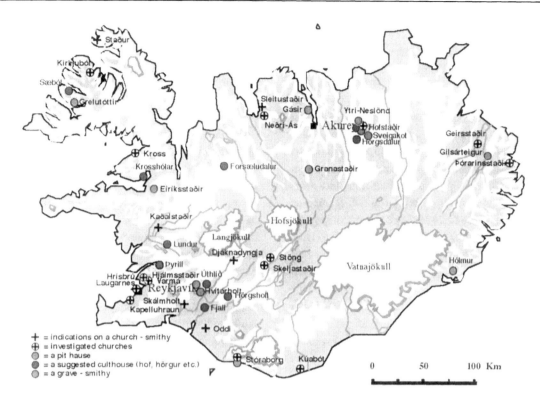

Figure 4. Map of known pit house sites and excavated churches in Iceland as well as sites with indications of churches – forges. A little more than half of the marked pit house sites have two or more pit houses. The positioning of the majority of other place names mentioned in the text can be found on other maps at the beginning of this article.

and there are many place names that contain the word *hof* or can be derived from it (Briem 1945:137). Significantly fewer sites have connections to the word *hörgur* (Ibid. 1945:134). Amongst the innumerable *hof* ruins that are known in the literature the following can be mentioned: Þyrill in Hvalfjörður, western Iceland (Vigfússon 1881:74ff & 1882:3ff), Sæból at Dýrafjörður, northwest Iceland (Vigfússon 1883:19f), Lundur at Lundarreykjadalur, western Iceland (Vigfússon 1885:97ff), Úthlíð and Fjall, southern Iceland (Jónsson 1894:6-9), and more than any other is *Hofstaðir* at Mývatn, in northern Iceland (Bruun & Jónsson 1910:265ff)[4]. None of these, apart from Hofstaðir, are believed today to be *hof* ruins and it has even been suggested that *Hofstaðir* ought to be removed from the list of religious buildings (Friðriksson & Vésteinsson 1997:110).

With regards to the place names connected to *hörgur* at least two ruins have been recognised. One of these ru

ins is in Hörgsdalur at Mývatn (Ólsen & Bruun 1903:1-16) and the other is in Hörgsholt at Hrunamannahreppur, southern Iceland (Jónsson 1900:28). Ólsen and Bruun write that the *hörgur* at Hörgsholt because of its slightness in size, it was only 1.48 m wide, has barely been a house (Bruun & Jónsson 1903:16) and even if Olsen was not certain he believed the ruin could be of Viking Age (Olsen 1966:208).

At the turn of the century several of the *hof* ruins ceased to be acknowledged as genuine and instead it was argued that these were more likely to have been sheep pens, horse stables or other types of farmstead buildings (Brunn & Jónsson 1910:308ff. Roussell 1943:216). This tendency, to reject the hof, continued throughout the entire 20th century and in the 1960's Olaf Olsen came to the conclusion that all hof/*hörgur* ruins were not these kinds of ruins at all. Only *Hofstaðir* at Mývatn, one of Iceland's largest hall-buildings from the Viking Age, was allowed to remain classified, in Olsen's opinion, as a *hof* or rather as a banqueting hall (Olsen 1966:198, 201).

---

4   During the years 1880 – 1908 the annual publication *Árbók Hins íslenska fornleifafélags* (the Icelandic archaeological society's yearbook) was filled with speculations regarding the *hof* and *hof* ruins.

Bruun and Jónsson excavated the hall at *Hofstaðir* along with a pit directly south of it in 1908 and they came to the conclusion that there had been a *hof* at *Hofstaðir* and that there had also been a rubbish pit to the south of it (Bruun & Jónsson 1910). Sixty years later Olsen excavated the pit once more and decided that it had been a large cooking pit instead and that the hall had been a large hall used for festivities (Icelandic – veisluskáli) which would have functioned as a dwelling house on an everyday basis. During certain periods of time, however, the hall would have been used for cult practices such as offerings and other religious activities and in connection with these feasting occurred (Olsen 1966:191-92). During these times the cooking pit would have played a vital role because it could cater for the vast amount of food required for such an offering (for an entire district?). This pit was 4.60 – 5.40 m in diameter and 1.8 m in depth (Ibid. 1966:189) making it one of the largest cooking pits to have ever been discovered! Needless to say, this interpretation seems quite irrational and in my opinion, this pit was not a rubbish pit or a cooking pit. In my opinion, in accordance with Margret Hermanns-Auðardóttir, this pit was a pit house (Einarsson 1989:52 & 1992:102, Hermanns-Auðardóttir 1989:107) and new excavations seem to confirm this. Furthermore the hall at *Hofstaðir* has been dated to a time somewhat later than expected (900-1000 AD) and the pit house is earlier (late 800 AD). In other words these two are not contemporary at all (Friðriksson & Vésteinsson 1998:68).

Olsen came to the conclusion that houses specifically designed for religious activities during the Viking Age have not been found, either in Iceland or in other parts of the North (Olsen 1966:198). He maintains that these houses, which he calls 'theatre buildings' were not constructed for cult activities either and that instead cult activities were practiced outdoors, or in festivity halls at the manors of small communities (Ibid. 1966:66, 83). Since then this idea that has dominated and become an accepted theory in Iceland (Foot & Wilson 1970:398. Eldjárn 1974(b): 111f; Steinsland 1993:148) and as a consequence it has even been suggested in recent years, as mentioned above, that the remains at *Hofstaðir* are not to be understood as having any kind of religious significance.

The picture portrayed by Olsen, however, hardly agrees with the circumstances on the smaller farms of Iceland because during the first period of settlement no centralised religion existed in Iceland and both large and small farmsteads were relatively independent of each other. As such these ought to be regarded as independent units from both economic and religious perspectives. Furthermore the fact that specific cult buildings have not yet been discovered is not in itself evidence that these have never existed and it is probably more a reflection of the implemented excavation strategies as well as being due to the fact that so few archaeological excavations of Icelandic Viking Age farmsteads have taken place at all. With all this in mind Olsen's theory ought to be questioned. Of those that have argued that houses specific to cult activities do not exist the majority are not particularly categorical in their standpoint and furthermore most do point to the fact that no definite houses have been found yet or that the uncertainty of their existence is great.

Aðalsteinsson and others believe that people in Iceland practiced their religion in both specific houses and outdoors and that this could be due to the climate (Aðalsteinsson 1988:45). In his dissertation he maintains that Olsen and other likeminded have not provided any evidence to confirm the lack of buildings particular to religious activities, but rather the opposite (Ibid. 1978:37) and even Olsen does not entirely reject the possibility of special *blót* houses. Olsen writes:

> That there could have been special *blót* houses or offering huts, on Icelandic farmsteads towards the end of pagan times, is a possibility that cannot be discarded. It is, however, important to underline that the existence of such buildings is based completely on hypothetical foundations. In the contemporary historical sources this theory is not supported. (Translated from Danish - 1966:112)

Furthermore Olsen maintains that the *Landnámabók* and the Icelandic sagas are limited in terms of their value as sources with regards to Viking Age religion. The stories are more or less fictional sagas that have been re-shaped in an oral tradition and coloured by a Christian view of life. In other words locating any core facts that might be hidden in them is a difficult task (Olsen 1966:54, 175f).

Written sources of all kinds (the Eddaic poetry, the travellers' tales, the rune stones, the Icelandic sagas, Adam av Bremen etc.) have been used in order to prove or reject the idea that special religious houses existed during the Viking Age in the North and not much progress has been made archaeologically either for the simple reason that remains of religious buildings from the Viking Age cannot be proven unequivocally to exist, even if things are beginning to change. Additionally the remains that do exist have often been interpreted differently in the literature of the discipline and as such they are absent in discussions related to these matters.

Näström has pointed out the importance of carefully examining simple small buildings in close proximity to larger farmsteads because there could be, for example, deity images hidden there (Nästsröm 2004:53).

Andrén has suggested the same:

> A relatively new category of finds is the small 'annexes' that have been discovered in recent decades. These are relatively small rectangular houses, at times enclosed, which are consistently found southwest of larger hall buildings at some settlements in Denmark and Sweden: Tissø and Leijre on Själland, Järrestad in Skåne, Borg in Östergötland and possibly Sanda in Uppland... The function of these 'annexes' and the areas surrounding them seems to have clearly been ritual in character. (Translated from Swedish - 2004:214)

Many archaeologists have used this negative picture to support the theory that these houses have never existed whilst others have been more cautious, including Olsen himself, and Johansen believes that there are obvious disparities between the written sources and the archaeological material with regards to the religious sphere and he speculates as to whether one of these sources might be misleading or if they both perhaps merely reflect different aspects of society (Johansen 1986:68). Explanation might partly be found in the fact that the written sources, generally speaking, do not describe contemporary phenomena because these were written in a completely different religious reality than the one being described, in other words the written sources are indirect.

There is, however, hardly any doubt that fragments of pagan religious understanding can be discerned in all these legends and stories about pre-Christian religion. The religious representations were of great significance for people understanding of their own reality and some of the pre-Christian ideas survived in the old Nordic provincial laws and to some extent continue to survive in Iceland today, like for example the relatively strong belief in elves, fairies and such beings that live in stones, hills and mountains (Icelandic- álfar – huldufólk)[5]. The present day meal-wakes in Russia, Belarus and Serbia that occur at the graveside have probably also survived from pre-Christian times and the same applies to the customs of preparing food at the graveside, for example in Bosnia and Herzegovina (Birkeli 1938:67f).

In this context there is an interesting story in the Svarfdæla saga about the settler Þorsteinn svörfuður, from the north of Iceland, but this saga seems to have been written during the 14th century and has been saved for prosperity in the manuscripts of more recent times but fragments of earlier stories or sagas could have been incorporated (pers. communication Professor Jónas Kristjánsson; The complete Sagas of Icelanders IV, 1997:149). There is also another action related to pagan religion that can be found in the sagas and this is connected to the destruction of objects.

> Þorsteinn garpur fór nú millum fjals og fjöru og lagði undir sig allan dalinn öðrumegin ár. Hann fer til fjalls og gerir þar kennimark sem hann kom framast og braut þar í sundur kamb sinn og kastaði niður kambsbrotunum og lætur eftir silfur í þremur stöðum, hálfa mörk í hverjum stað og er sá rimi kallaður að Kambi." (Íslendinga sögur 1986:1795)

> Thorstein the Tumultuous now took control of the valley between mountain and fjord on the other side of the river. He went to the mountains and erected a boundary stake at the uppermost edge and broke a comb and threw the pieces on the ground. Afterwards he had silver buried in three places, a half mark in each place, and that strip of mark is called Kamb. (The complete Sagas of the Icelanders IV, 1997:161)

To destroy private possessions in ritual context, in this instance a comb, is well known in the archaeological literature and one example of this is the c. 40 broken comb cases found in the warrior house at Birka (Carlie 2004:174).

From this perspective it is evident that archaeology has potential to shed light on the complexities of these fragments and place them in their rightful context. Furthermore the data collections continue to increase over the years compared to the philological sources!

It has been pointed out that many alternative ideas about life after death could have existed in late Iron Age Scandinavian society and that the religion, which to some extent is reflected in the written sources, has been the religion of the aristocracy and that this was not necessarily shared by the majority of the people. Other groups might have had different understandings but at the same time certain elements could still have been based on the same religious belief (Kaliff 1997:21f). It is perhaps at this level we ought to discuss public and private religion, or regulated and unregulated religion. This difference ought to have been expressed at several levels in society for example in the decoration of grave-goods, in dwelling houses etc. One such Christian environment could be the churches which on the one hand offered official, publicly displayed decoration and on the other contained unofficial, unassuming

---

5 Elf/Fairy dwellings are treated as ancient remains in accordance with Icelandic ancient remain legislation and these are protected in the same manner as other ancient remains (Þjóðminjalög 2001).

graffiti on the walls and benches in the less obvious nooks and crannies (Einarsson 2006).

5 CULT HOUSES – *BLÓT* HOUSES

It has been suggested that religious buildings do not have to differ so radically from other types of buildings (Briem 1945:133). On this subject Olsen expressed his thoughts as follows:

> With regards to the insufficiency of historical sources one must, on the whole, keep an open mind with regards to all forms of unusual occurrences in connection with homesteads –quite regardless of whether or not these occurrences fit in with our historical knowledge of pagan cult phenomena. (Translated from Danish -1966:178f)

The problem, however, with regards to, for example, *blót* houses – cult houses and other religious constructions is that we do not really know what these look like in the archaeological material. *"We know practically nothing about pagan temples except for the fact that they existed."* (Translated from Swedish - Sawyer 1985:167)

Needless to say cult houses were built using traditional materials (stone, peat, wood, bone, clay, leather and textiles) just like other houses and there is probably very little in the actual construction or architectural de-

sign that points to specific religious functions. In other words it is not certain that architectural elements differentiate the function of the house. Many believe that sacred remains ought to differ from profane ones, as Olsen has suggested above, without defining how this might be expressed (Roussell 1943:220). Others believe that we should expect to find fire-places, animal and human bone, post-holes, ritual pits and in rare instances even alters. (Davidson 1993:12 & Olauson 1995:55).

Nevertheless this does not imply that the finds, material or constructions necessarily differ from profane material. Instead it is the context, the find assemblages and the distribution of finds that decide the difference as well as the relation of the finds to the settlement sites, the topographical environment, the burial monuments and other remains. Everyday artefacts, objects that originally had some kind of practical function, could have completely new functions in connection with rituals, mortuary practices, or if used as offerings. Grindstones, that are frequently found in fire-cracked stone mounds and in graves from the Bronze Age, are one example of artefacts that alter their identity (see e.g. Lundqvist 1991; Kaliff 1997:88; Carlie 2004:84ff). The stones can be seen as symbols for

Figure 5. Aerial photograph from SSE. The immmense beach ridge is seen crossing the valley (Phtoto BFE).

a transition from the profane to the religious or for rebirth in a farming society. In a non-agricultural farming society, like for example in Iceland where animal husbandry was the primary source of subsistence, it is possible that other types of artefacts were of significance for a similar kind of transition. In this context the finds of deposited loom weights at Hólmur are of interest. Loom weights can be seen as a symbol for the transition from wool to textile and these implements could have been used, for example, to weave the cloth used in the clothes worn by the deceased at the time of burial. In other words these loom weights have had structural similarities to the burial as phenomenon; both are phases of a transformation process, situated between two stages of existence. Weaving is also connected to mythology via *Urðr, Verðandi* and *Skuld*, the three norns that weaved the fate of human beings (Aðalsteinsson 1978:47; Bæksted 1988:49 & 215f.).

The abundance of bloomery iron fragments found at Hólmur can also be seen in this light. These have come into existence through the effects of fire and there was a very concentrated distribution on the mound and these have probably had some connection to the post-holes at the site because bloomery iron fragments had been thrown through the paired posts (the passage/gate to the cult site?).

All objects being offered can be seen in this vein; as everyday objects that receive new meaning to become part of eternity, just like the one receiving the offerings, whether it is the recently departed in need of their tools on the other side or a revered deity.

Cult sites or sacred sites are not presumed to be randomly chosen but rather the opposite, consciously selected and unique (Olausson 1995:55; Artelius 2000:33). The site might have been chosen due to some natural, physical phenomenon in the landscape, for example a mound or hill, a water source, a large stone etc. but its sacredness could also have been indicated by the presence of a building or some other kind of construction (Carlie 2004:24). In other words, in this context it does not matter whether or not special buildings existed at the site or not.

At Borg, in the province of Östergötland, in Sweden, the remains of a Viking Age house were discovered and interpreted as the remains of a cult house (Nielsen 1996)

even though nothing in the construction of the house or in its architecture revealed its function. It was a timber house, 6 x 7.5 metres in size, and the direction of the house was north-south, with its entrance in the west. The floor was paved with round stones and the house had two rooms and this house was regarded as unique (Ibid. 1996:89).

No artefacts were found inside the house but outside 75 kg of unburnt bone and a hoard of 98 strike-a-light shaped amulet rings, several finished and others semi-finished, were discovered. Two ovens for the production of iron were found west of the house and this suggests that the rings were manufactured at the site. Similar artefacts are at times connected to offering, both in houses and graves.

The bone material consisted of an unusual amount of skull and jaw sections and there was an abundance of bone from horse and dog. Furthermore there was bone found from cat, red deer, goose, snake, fox, beaver, badger, salmon, sheep, cattle and pig. One interesting point here is that there was a very restrictive distribution of pig bones and these were boar and sow separated. The cult house was used during 900 AD and abandoned sometime during 1000 AD and it has been suggested that the abandonment occurred in the form of the ritual burial of the house. Only 100 metres east of the cult house a medieval church had been built (Ibid. 1996:102). Yet another example of bone material indicating signs of burial in ritual circumstances can be found at Järrestad, in the province of Skåne, in Sweden (Nilsson 2003).

The *blót* house discovered at Hólmur was in several ways different from the house at Borg. Firstly it was smaller and had a NW-SE orientation and its entrance was most likely facing northwest. The orientation could very likely have been affected by the direction of the valley, which is NE-SW, that is, at a right angle to the *blót* house, and this seems to have been a recurring theme with the Viking Age halls in Iceland. Generally speaking the house at Hólmur does seem to be even more complex than the one at Borg and in addition to this it was dug down. In other words this was a typical pit house (a more in-depth discussion to follow).

II. HÓLMUR – A VIKING AGE FARMSTEAD WITH *BLÓT* HOUSE

6 HÓLMUR, SOME BACKGROUND INFORMATION

The history of Hólmur begins at the turn of the 20th century when erosion in the area exposed several human bones. The site is located on a mound in southeast Iceland, beneath an immense beach ridge at the opening of the Laxárdalur Valley known as Selhryggur or Hryggurinn, an eye catching and unique mound on an otherwise flat and even beach ridge. Alongside the human bones there were also horse bones and artefacts and when the Dane Daniel Bruun excavated the site several years later, in 1902, he found a number of different artefacts and an amount of charcoal. In his report he writes:

> Several years ago (1899 or 1900) a man, who has since immigrated to America, dug the mound presumably because he came across a burial which was brought to light by the eroding soils. Here he found human bones that lay in the same direction as the mound; head pointing south and feet towards the north. He also found some horse teeth scattered about, two whetstones, three large multicoloured (black, red and blue) and unicoloured glass beads, a rusty piece of iron, six inches long, which could not have been an axe but possibly a knife; placed west of the skeleton…
>
> In the southern section of the mound, which seemed to have been disturbed, he found a complete whetstone and the residues of a thin charcoal layer that appeared to have been scattered around the deceased where he lay. Horse teeth were also found scattered along the northern section of the mound, just north of the place where it is presumed that the dead man had been laid to rest. (Translated from Swedish -1903:24)

According to information found in the autobiography of Þorleifur Jónsson, a farmer and parliamentarian from the area, the burial was found in 1894. He writes that the bone found south of Selhryggur was discovered by a farmer from the farm at Dilksnes, situated c. 10 km southeast of Hólmur, and that they subsequently visited the site together and rummaged about a little on the mound. Þorleifur writes:

> It was not necessary to dig deep and very soon badly preserved bone was found. The skeleton lay in a north-southerly direction. We also found two fragments of whetstone, three large glass beads, two red and one blue if I remember rightly, a very rusty piece of iron, c. 6 inches long. This could have been the remains of an axe or a sword, but most likely a carving knife. Beneath and around the bones there was charcoal and we even found some horse teeth. (Translated from Swedish -[Jónsson] 1954:386).

Þorleifur attempted to explain the remains in the following way:

> But it is quite strange that a man, who died at home, had been buried at this peripheral site quite some way from the settlement. Perhaps there had been a serious argument between two people, which resulted in conflict, and the plains south of Hryggur were chosen as the site to settle the quarrel. One has been killed and buried with his horse at the site, which was named after him [Icelandic: Skora á hólm. Swedish: Utmana till holmgång = Hólmur. English: challenge to a fight/duel]. The place name Hólmur [which means islet] is otherwise incomprehensible because there is no islet restricted by water or anything like that in this area. (Translated from Swedish -1954:388).

This account is interesting because it shows how the locals tried to explain the ancient remains in their own way and these kinds of explanations are common in Iceland. In this particular case it is the absence of a known farmstead along with an old and apparently illogical place name that has been the foundation for their interpretation of the remains.

In a presentation of place names from the latter half of the 1920's it is stated that a man, named Eymundur from the farmstead Dilksnes, did some digging at the site and found the remains of weapons (Örnefnaskrá) but this must be a misunderstanding.

In his dissertation, Kuml og haugfé, Kristján Eldjárn mentions the grave and he finds it remarkable that the grave was situated so far from the settlement (Eldjárn 1956:187).

Based on all this information attempts were made in 1996 to locate the farm site which, according to the author, ought to have been connected to the grave and some indications of ruins were found approximately 250 m southwest of the grave, somewhat further away from the beach ridge, by a small stream that ran into the larger River Laxá. On the basis of these finds trial excavations were carried out the same year and showed that culture layers and walls did exist, c. 1 metre beneath the surface. The following year a house at the farmstead was excavated (Einarsson 1996, '98(a) and '98(b)) and in the summer to follow excavations of the farmstead continued, on a smaller scale, but the hall could not be found. Finally, in the summer of 2002, the hall was located and partially excavated and as a result Hólmur is now the first definite Viking Age farmstead site in the county of Austur-Skaftafellssýsla.

In addition to the site at Hólmur only two definite Viking Age burials in the county are known to exist (see fig.

Figure 6. The cult site from SE prior to excavation. The mountain in the background is Ketillaugarfjall (Slide 2:10. Photo BFE).

Figure 7. This picture is taken from the beach ridge towards SSW. The cult site is primarily what is seen and at the foot of the ridge the farmstead is just slightly visible in the middle of the picture, to the left. The mountain to the right is Meðalfell (Digital photo nr. 89. Photo BFE.).

2). One of these is a grave located on the island Álaugarey at Höfn discovered in 1934 (Þórðarsson 1936). The other burial was found in 1974 at the farmstead Einholt, only a few metres away from remains known as the "Völvuleiði" (The grave of the seeress, Kristjánsdóttir 1994:74).

Álaugarey was a small island that nowadays is connected to the mainland and the village of Höfn. It is believed that the island would have been too small to have contained a farm and subsequently it is thought that the farm might have been located on the adjacent island of Mikley (=the large island) (Einarsson 1998(b):49f)[6].

Another area of interest is the foot of the mountain Horn, immediately east of Höfn. Here several different artefacts have been found along with the remains of badly eroded buildings suggesting that these might have been the remains of a Viking Age farmstead. The site has not, however, been closely examined and the artefacts have long since disappeared (Einarsson 1998(b): 14). Finally a recently discovered farm ruin in the western section of the county ought to be mentioned. This ruin is located in Steinadalur Valley, c. 5 km east of Jökulsárlón, and the test excavations carried out here indicated the presence of buildings. It is quite possible that the earliest of the two, investigated in the test trench, could be a hall but both

remains are situated quite some way beneath the tephra layers created during volcanic eruptions in 1362 and 1340 and the earlier ruin could be from either the Viking Age or from early medieval times (Einarsson 2002).

Attempting to connect known ruins in the landscape with stories from the world of the sagas is quite common practice in Iceland and Hólmur is no exception.

In the *Landnámabók* it is written that:

> Ketill hét maðr, er Hrollaugr seldi Hornafjarðarströnd útan frá Horni ok in til Hamra; hann bjó at Meðalfelli; frá honum eru Hornfirðingar komnir. (Íslensk fornrit I. 1968:319).

> There was a man named Ketil, to whom Hrollag sold Hornfirthstrand, east of Horn, west to Hamrar; he dwelt at Middlefell; from him are the Hornfirthers descended. (The Book of the Settlement of Iceland 1898:180-81).

According to the *Landnámabók* Hólmur is situated on the land that belonged to Ketill and the farmstead Meðalfell is located west of River Laxá, south of the mountain Meðalfell, which is situated at the opening of the Laxárdalur Valley, a few kilometres southwest of Hólmur.

In *Hrafnkell's saga Freysgoða* the following is written about the marriage of Hrafnkell: *"Hrafnkell fekk Oddbjargar Skjöldólfsdóttur ór Laxárdal."*[7] Hrafnkel married Oddbjorg Skjoldolfsdottir from Laxardal (The complete Sagas of Icelanders V, 1997:262). A footnote to

---

6 During a survey of the island no remains were located that suggested a farm had existed here. On the other hand, however, a number of sheep houses from more recent times were discovered in the northern part of the island, in the vicinity of where the farm might have been located. Sheep houses (Icelandic: beitarhús) are often built on top of earlier remains for the simple reason that the material necessary for construction is readily available in these locations and there is also plenty of grass.

---

7 Þórður Tómasson, museum director in Skógar in southern Iceland, showed me this note in the saga.

the saga indicates that there were some problems with the name Laxárdalur and to where it referred, and if it was referring to a valley which one it might be or if it referred to a farmstead instead. Besides Laxárdalur in Nesjum, where Hólmur is located, there are two other valleys with this name in eastern Iceland. One of these has also been connected to the Laxárdalur in the saga. It is situated in central eastern Iceland, close to the Jökuldalur Valley opening but no farmstead ruins have been found there (Ibid. 1950:98). The other valley with this name is situated in Lón, immediately north – northeast of Hornafjörður, and even this has no known farmstead remains.[8] In other words no Viking Age farmstead ruins are known in any of these valleys with the exception of Hólmur discovered in Laxárdalur in Nesjum, but whether this is Oddbjörg's home place or not is a very different matter indeed.

7 THE CULT SITE

The test pits excavated during the summer of 1997 showed traces of human activity over the entire mound, which is 15x 25 m in size and c. 2 m high and in addition to this the burial site was excavated once again. During the next season, which was the summer of 1999, the pit house was discovered and excavated in its entirety and this has now been interpreted as a *blót* house. During the summer of the year 2000 an area of 49 m2 was excavated on the southern side of the mound, immediately east and south of the *blót* house. A culture layer, 0.1 – 0.3 m in depth, was found which more or less covered the entire mound and it contained cremated bone, charcoal, fire-cracked stones and other artefacts. In total there was c. 200 litres of fire-cracked stone recovered from this area and this means approximately 4.1 litres per square metre, an amount that is to be understood as the absolute minimum.

In the summer of 2001 a further 107.5 m2 were excavated on the north section of the mound. The volume of fire-cracked stones in this section reached a total of approximately 148 litres or c. 1.4 litres per m2. It is worth noting that the differences in the amounts of fire-cracked stones per square metre are partially due to the fact that the fire-cracked stones collected during the summer of 1997 are not included in the calculation. If, however, this area of approximately 25 m2 is taken into consideration

Figure 8. View from the hall towards the cult site and Laxárdalur. The cult site is to the left, below the beach ridge. A secundary entrance is to be seen on the south gavel of the longhouse. All the wals are of turf alone, with jellow and blach vulcanic ash. The small river in between is Hólmslækur which has its origin in the spring Hólmslækjaruppspretta. Today this spring is the main water resource for Höfn village (Digital photo nr. 246. Photo BFE).

then the amount of fire-cracked stones would be approximately 1.8 litres per square metre and again this amount is to be regarded as the absolute minimum.

Needless to say areas containing such vast amounts of fire-cracked stones are hardly there for people to walk on and at normal settlement sites these kinds of stones usually end up in waste piles or pits, where people do not come into contact with them. These fire-cracked stones ought therefore to be interpreted as being consciously discarded, probably in connection with some religious intention. These could be seen as a cleansing fire symbol or as stones that might have transformed a piece of meat into food for people, a kind of 'rit de passage' phenomenon. Perhaps one can connect fire-walking with this? Other similar examples of concentrations of fire-cracked stones have been found at a cult house in Ringeby, in the prov-

---

8 The author of this article surveyed this valley with farmstead remains in mind but no results were forthcoming.

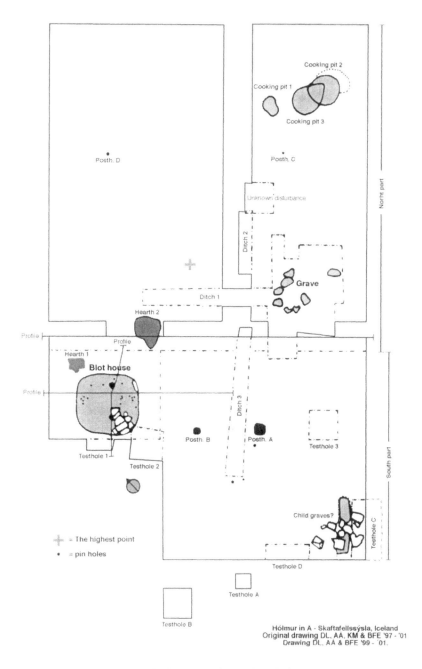

Figure 9. The constructions at the cult site.

ince of Östergötland, in Sweden (Kalliff 1997:55) but this house, from 500–700 BC, was much earlier than the one at Hólmur. Similar layers of fire-cracked stones have been found in other parts of Sweden too, e.g. at Husaby in Glanshammar parish, at Järrestad in the province of Skåne as well as at Lejre in Denmark.[9] A similar context

has also been discovered at Lunda just outside Strängnäs, in Sweden and there are also examples of burials being found in the fire-cracked stone layers. No unified interpretation with regards to these fire-cracked stones exists but interpretations similar to the ones related to the cult site at Hólmur have been proposed.

9 www.raa.se/ur/jarrestad/j03-07.htm (05.03.21). See also Söderberg 2003:135.

8 PLACE NAMES AND TOPOGRAPHY

The site name 'Hólmur' (English = islet) was created by the author, which he borrowed from the small valley Hól- mur (Örnefnaskrá) where the farmstead is located. The valley is restricted in the north by the immense beach ridge Selhryggur or Hryggurinn, sometimes Selmýrarhry- ggur, (Engl. = the Shealing Ridge or The Ridge or some- times the Shealing-marsh Ridge), that crosses the main Laxárdalur Valley. In the south the valley is restricted by a gravel and mountain ridge named Skógarenni (Engl. = Forest brow). In the west the River Laxá is its bound- ary and in the east the large, 448 m high, mountain ridge Bergárdalsheiði east of Hólmur frames the valley in. West of the River Laxá the mountain Ketillaugarfjall rises 668 m above sea level.

The Viking Age farmstead is situated on a small, dry shelf surrounded by wet marshlands in the middle of the valley and has now been given the name Hólmur. Imme- diately north of the farmstead (c. 10 - 20 m.), in-between the farmstead and the cult site there is a stream known as Hólmslækur (Engl. = Islet Stream) which has its source in the spring Hólmslækjaruppspretta (Engl. = Islet Stream Spring).

In the southern section of the valley, south of the stream, there is a grassy wet marshland which contains a small number of solitary, dry, raised surfaces. Loose soil formations (c. 1 metre for the last thousand years) have caused the ground water level to rise considerably and have most likely altered a previously dry grassy area into a wet marshland. North of the stream the valley depres- sion is seriously eroded and further north into the valley, c. 250 metres northeast of the farmstead the grave and the cult site are located on a small mound where the unique *blót* house is situated at the foot of the immense beach ridge.

The beach ridge, which is c. 30 metres high, domi- nates the landscape surrounding it. The top and sides are almost flat and only interrupted by the river (Laxá) in the west. On the lower section of the ridge, on its southern side, there is one irregularity, a very visible mound, and it is on this mound that the grave, the cult site and *blót* house were found.

9 THE *BLÓT* HOUSE

The *blót* house was situated at a cult site c. five metres west of where the grave is presumed to have been located.

Figure 10. Laxárdalur, the southernmost part. Photo: Landmælingar Íslands. With permission).

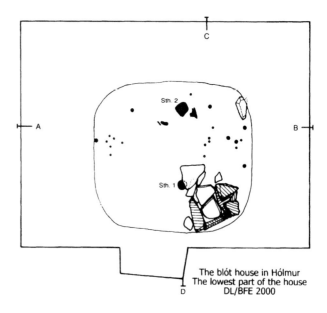

Figure 11. A plan-drawing of the *blót* house at Hólmur (Phase 6).

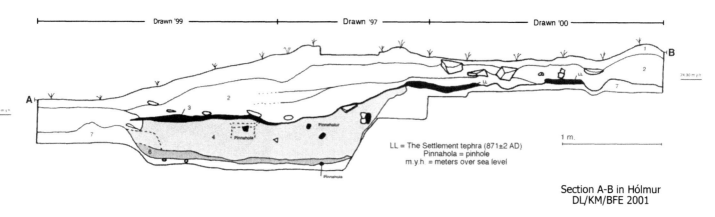

Section A-B in Hólmur
DL/KM/BFE 2001

Figure 12. A section cut through the *blót* house and part of the cult mound. Over the pit house there is a culture layer (layer 3) which indicates activity on the hill after the house was abandoned. These activities included the burning of fires and parts of animals.

The house was found just beneath the highest point of the mound's western slope and not on the crown. The grave was not on the crown either but slightly east of the highest point of the mound, and this positioning of graves on smaller mounds or hills and raised surfaces seems to be a recurring element.

The house was excavated in two stages; first a test pit during the summer of 1997 and then the house in its entirety during the summer of 1999.

The floor of the house was approximately 0.75m below the LL-tephra layer (volcanic ash), which is believed to have fallen in the year 871±2 AD (Grönvold et.al 1995:150-153). It is the usual kind of pit house with

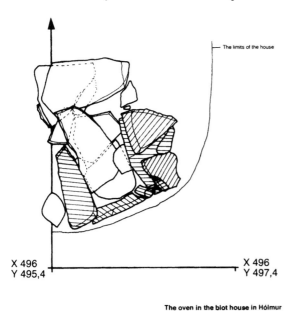

Figure 13. The oven in the cult house.

two opposed post-holes on each side (type B according to Einarsson 1992:110). The house was 2 x 2.16 m in size (measured just above floor level) or barely 4.32 m2, and almost quadratic in shape with rounded corners. The direction of the house was NA – SW (the same direction as the Laxárdalur Valley). It has had two roof supporting posts and there was an oven in the southeast corner. The entrance has not definitely been found but it was presumably in the northwest wall (close to the western corner farthest down the slope) and opposite the oven. The walls have most likely consisted of the mound itself, possibly with the highest or upper sections in wattle and daub. No traces of peat walls (or walls what so ever) were discovered. Furthermore the Hólmur house is one of the smallest pit houses known in Iceland.

The filling of the house contained a number of twig, or pin holes which were found in both vertical and level positions and those that were level were as a rule north-south or east-west oriented. A small number of very rotten boards were found with the same orientation and twig holes were also found in the floor. The twigs in the filling have been interpreted as the remains of the roof construction, perhaps made out of a gate or wattled branches. The species of one of the burnt timber boards was identified and determined to be birch (betula, sample nr. 18). Traces of hair were also found in the sample and this could indicate that skins had been placed on top of the wattled branches. In the section profile close to the floor there was a thin reddish layer interpreted as the possible remains of skins. The soil analysis (sample nr. 8) from the layer did, however, not show any signs of hair. In all seven wood species analyses were taken inside or close to the

Figure 14. The oven in the cult house (Digital photo nr. 36, part of. Photo BFE).

Figure 15. The oven in the cult house after the removal of the slabs of stone on top (Digital photo nr. 42. Photo BFE).

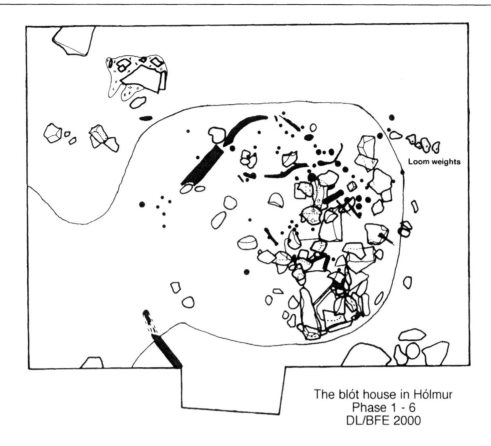

The blót house in Hólmur
Phase 1 - 6
DL/BFE 2000

Loom weights

Figure 16. Phases 1 – 6 of the *blót* house.

pit house and all resulted in birch (betula). Four of them were also C-14 dated (see section 12).

Amongst the objects found inside the house there were two pieces of whale bone vertebrae with cutting abrasions (chopping blocks) on the floor in front of the oven, strike-a-light-stones, iron nails, a spindle whorl in three pieces, a loom weight, a soapstone fragment from a pot, two beads of glass and amber, a polishing stone and a worked disc-shaped piece of soft rock (round disc) were found. In addition to these objects charcoal, cremated bones and fire-cracked stones were frequently found and the two unburnt jawbones from cattle, discovered on the floor in front of the oven, were exceptionally prominent. Many of the artefacts had been affected by fire. It should be mentioned that all these find categories have been found in earlier farmstead excavations and all the various types have previously been found in Icelandic graves, with the exception of the loom weights, the round disc and the chopping blocks. These find categories are in fact quite common except for the round stone disc, the func-

tion of which is unknown. A similar disc made out of very hard rock was also found in the courtyard at Hólmur and other similar discs have been found in Reykjavík (two), (Nordahl 1988:69, fig. 91), at Ísleifsstaðir in western Iceland (Stenberger 1943:166, fig. 111) and in Herjólfs-dalur on the Vestmanna Islands (Hermannsl-Auðardóttir 1989:25-26).

The disc from Ísleifsstaðir was decorated on both sides with relatively poor carvings. Stenberger only mentions the decoration on one side, i.e. the possible walrus head but further examinations revealed that the other side was decorated too with the shape of indiscernible scrib-bles, possibly the mark of ownership? (Einarsson 2006). The disc from Herjólfsdalur had grooves on both sides and because of these the disc has been interpreted as a whetstone. The discs from Hólmur and Reykjavík had no grooves and are otherwise undecorated. The larger disc from Reykjavík resembles the one from the Hólmur cult site most.

Immediately next to the eastern corner of the house

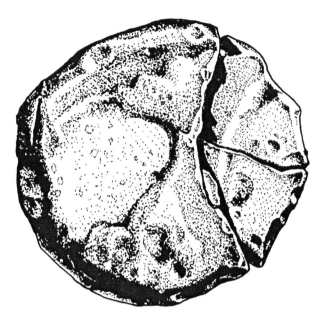

Figure 17. Drawing of the disc from Hólmur. The edges were retouched (artefact nr. 45, drawing Andreas Åhman).

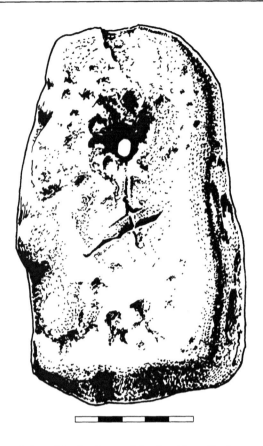

Figure 18. One of the four loom weights found immediately next to the *blót* house at Hólmur (artefact nr. 54, drawing Andreas Åhman).

four loom weights were found that had probably been hanging on some kind of string (all holes in a straight line – like when stringed). The loom weights had been consciously placed there, perhaps a votive find? In 2001 loom weights were found in a similar context in Lunda, the county of Sörmland, in Sweden.

On top of the filling of the house, which consisted of humus and loose soil containing cremated and unburnt bone, charcoal, fire-cracked stones as well as a whale bone vertebrae, there was a 7 cm thick charcoal layer (layer 3) which suggested that activities continued after the *blót* house had been abandoned.

10 OTHER FEATURES

10.1 The grave

The grave was either discovered in 1894, 1899 or in 1900 and was first excavated in 1902. Even then the grave was badly eroded and bones were exposed to the elements. The direction of the burial was N – S, in other words the same direction as the mound and the head of the buried faced south (towards the farmstead!), according to those who found the grave. The actual direction ought to have been NNW-SSE but the exact position of the grave cannot be determined today because only a small number of flat slabs, that were transported to the eastern section of

the mound, are all that remain as a probable indication of the place. In addition to these similar slabs of rock were found surrounding what are believed to be child burials. These slabs were not found in any other location on the mound and they are not natural features of the area and it is likely that they have been taken from the mountains close by. Even the farmers in this area have pointed to this site as the site of the grave and the general description given by Bruun in 1903 (finds south and north of the grave) fits in well with this site. The location, just below the highest point of the mound, appears to have been commonplace in Iceland (Einarsson 1998(a): 18).

The size of the grave cannot be given accurately and no construction details have been possible to discern, other than as a simple stone-setting, which most likely had some kind of low super-structure of slabs and soil. Surrounding the skeleton (beneath and on top) there was charcoal, which possibly came from one of the hearths on the mound or from the oven in the *blót* house.

When the grave was found there was two whetstones, three glass beads, a piece of iron, horse teeth and charcoal amongst the finds. In 1902 at the same site a further whetstone, horse teeth and charcoal were discovered.

It has been possible to determine that the grave was situated on top of the LL-tephra layer from 871±2 AD or it might have been dug through.

10.2 Child graves

The excavations revealed more than one grave and a pit house located on the mound. In the lower section of the mound (towards SE) two rectangular pits were discovered. The most southerly pit was 0.4 x 0.76 m in size and 0.3 m in depth (after removing the top soil). The most northerly pit was 0.36 x 0.86 m in size and just as deep as the first. Around and partly covering these there were stone slabs similar to the ones at the grave. The filling was humus without any elements of culture layer and these pits have been interpreted as possible child graves.

Slabs similar to the ones found over the pits were only present at one other construction on the mound, the grave, and it is worth mentioning that these presumed child graves were located below one of the post-holes (see next section 10.3). These child graves are reminiscent of the ones found in the vicinity of church cemeteries, i.e. graves not situated in consecrated ground but immediately outside or in the churchyard walls.

10.3 The post-holes

Several metres southeast of the pit house two post-holes were found. The one furthest away from the pit house (post-hole A) was 0.64 x 0.73 m in size and 0.76 m in depth. The second post-hole was situated 1.8 m NW of the first one and the size of this (post-hole B) was 0.46 x 0.46 m and 0.38 m in depth.

The post-holes could be said to form some kind of passage/entrance or gate to the mound! Such an entrance is reminiscent of the gate mentioned in Grímnismál, verse 22, quoted in section 3.

Two other post-holes (post-hole C and D) were found in the northern section of the mound but these were a lot smaller. Post-hole C was 0.14 m in diameter and 0.21 m in depth, and post-hole D was 0.24 m in diameter and 0.15 m in depth. Both post-holes leaned towards each other or towards the highest point of the mound.

It is also possible that twig holes were found below the poles (A and B) but this is not conclusive.

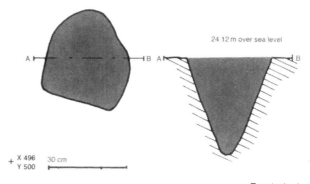

Figure 19. Posthole A at the cult site (drawing BFE).

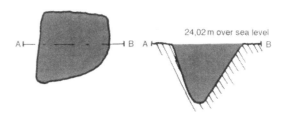

Figure 20. Posthole B at the cult site (drawing BFE).

10.4 Hearths

Immediately north of the pit house remains of a hearth (hearth 1), c. 0.5 x 0.5 m in size, were found. It was constructed using thin (1 – 1.5 cm) stone slabs, both for the base and the sides and the hearth could have been quadratic.

Slightly east of the pit house another hearth was discovered (hearth 2). It too was fragmented but built in the same way and had the same shape and was probably just as large as hearth 1 but it was more dispersed. In this hearth two loom weights were found and in its peripheral areas two gaming pieces of red sandstone, one more loom weight and a probable iron fishing hook were found. There was also cremated bone present in the hearth but this could not be identified.

10.5 Cooking pits

Three cooking pits were found on the north-eastern section of the mound. There were two different types.

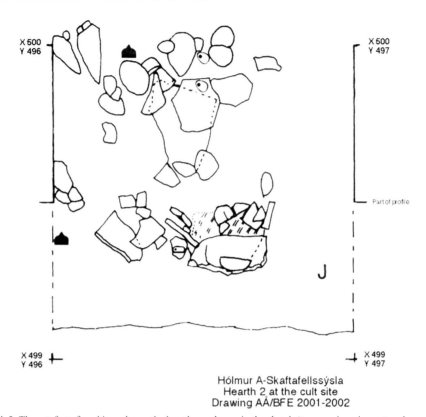

Hólmur A-Skaftafellssýsla
Hearth 2 at the cult site
Drawing AÅ/BFE 2001-2002

Figure 21. Plan of hearth 2. The artefacts found in and near the hearth are shown in the sketch (two gaming pieces, two loom weights -one was further away from the hearth, a stone with a hole and a fishing hook).

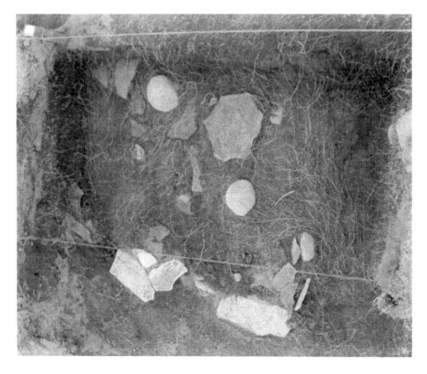

Figure 22. Hearth 2 (Digital photo nr. 138, part of. Photo BFE).

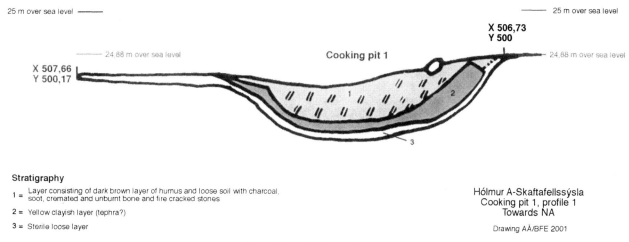

Stratigraphy

1 = Layer consisting of dark brown layer of humus and loose soil with charcoal, soot, cremated and unburnt bone and fire cracked stones

2 = Yellow clayish layer (tephra?)

3 = Sterile loose layer

Hólmur A-Skaftafellssýsla
Cooking pit 1, profile 1
Towards NA

Drawing AÅ/BFE 2001

Figure 23. Profile in cooking pit 1.

Cooking pit 1 was situated furthest west and was very difficult to discern after the surface had been cleared but at the top there was an abundance of rotten, unburnt bones (extremities). The pit was c. 0.7 x 1.6 m in size and 0.3 m in depth and it was lined with a yellow layer, 0.06 – 0.12 m thick, which probably consisted of fine grained, almost fatty, tephra (type H3 or H4[10]). The actual filling consisted of a dark brown layer of humus and loose soil containing charcoal, soot, cremated and unburnt bone and fire-cracked stones (1 – 1.5 litres of fire-cracked stones). In the lower section of the filling the forefoot bone from a calf was found.

Cooking pit 2 was situated furthest east. It was 0.9 - 1 m in diameter and 0.35 – 0.4 m in depth and a stone slab had been placed at the base, 0.25 x 0.4 m in size. The pit was lined internally with the same layer found in pit 1, 0.03 – 0.07 m thick. On top of this was a very thin layer of charcoal, unburnt fish bone and some animal teeth (layer 5). On top of this a light layer like the one at the base was present. The next layer again was a thin layer of charcoal and cremated bone. Yet again the yellow layer appeared with a layer of charcoal, soot and cremated bone on top. And finally there was a filling of loose, brown soil with a few pieces of charcoal and fire-cracked stones. This layer sequence suggested that the pit had been re-used on a number of occasions.

Digging had occurred to produce a further cooking pit through cooking pit 2. This pit, cooking pit 3, appeared to

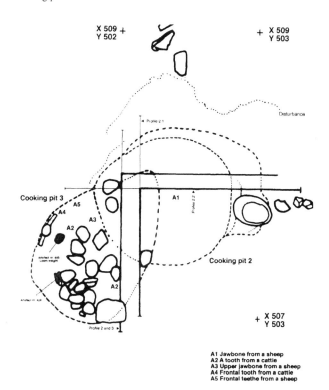

A1 Jawbone from a sheep
A2 A tooth from a cattle
A3 Upper jawbone from a sheep
A4 Frontal tooth from a cattle
A5 Frontal teethe from a sheep

Figure 24. Cooking pits 2 and 3.

be later than cooking pit 2 even if this is not conclusive because another section profile contradicts this. It would seem, however, likely that pit 2 is earlier. In cooking pit 2 an unburnt jaw tooth, a left and right jawbone with teeth and a toe bone from sheep/goat were found. In addition to these a foot bone and a left jaw bone with teeth from a

10   H3 and H4 are prehistoric ash layers (tephra) after the eruption of the volcano Hekla, H3 = 2900 BP. H4 = 4500 BP.

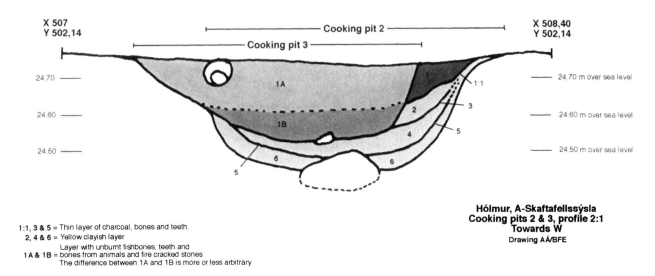

X 507
Y 502,14

Cooking pit 2

Cooking pit 3

X 508,40
Y 502,14

24.70 ——
24.60 ——
24.50 ——

1A
1B
1:1
3
2
5
4
6
6
5

—— 24.70 m over sea level
—— 24.60 m over sea level
—— 24.50 m over sea level

1:1, 3 & 5 = Thin layer of charcoal, bones and teeth.
2, 4 & 6 = Yellow clayish layer
1 A & 1B = Layer with unburnt fishbones, teeth and bones from animals and fire cracked stones
The difference between 1A and 1B is more or less arbitrary

**Hólmur, A-Skaftafellssýsla
Cooking pits 2 & 3, profile 2:1
Towards W**
Drawing AA/BFE

Figure 25. Profile 2:1 in cooking pits 2 and 3.

medium sized animal, an anklebone from cattle and an un-burnt backbone from cod were also discovered. There were also other bones present but these could not be identified.

Cooking pit 3 was situated in-between the other two cooking pits. It was 0.8 x 1.2 m in diameter and 0.25 – 0.3 m in depth. At the base of the pit there was a thin layer of unburnt fish bones (skull bone, most likely cod and backbone from cod) and teeth from both cattle and sheep. In the northern section of the pit two rows of up-per jawbones were found with teeth from an adult sheep, both from the right and left sections. The jaws were place on top of each other and these possibly represented two skulls that had been split. In the eastern section of the pit teeth from an upper jawbone from a calf were found.

In the upper section of the pit (layer 1A) grains were found (Einarsson 2003[11]). These were of hulled barley (Hordeum vulgare sp.), barley (*Hordeum sp.*), non-iden-tifiable grain (*Cerelia*), grass seeds (*Carex sp.*) and seeds from sedges (*Cyperaaceae*).

At the bottom of the pit a U-shaped artefact of wood and iron (Fnr. 424) had been deposited and this is possi-bly the remains of a wooden handle with an iron loop.

In the eastern and western sides of the pit there were burnt, sooty flat stones, including liparit (sour rock from the mountains nearby) and approximately 30 – 32 fist-

sized fire-cracked stones (cooking stones) were found in the lower section of the pit (layer 1B), one of which later revealed itself to be a loom weight (Fnr. 445). Other finds from the pit included pieces of slag, iron and a rivet.

The bone material, which could be identified, discov-ered in the three pits came from cattle, sheep/goat and cod. There were no traces of bone from horse or pig!

Three types of fire constructions were found at the cult site; two ordinary hearths, one classic cooking pit with fire-cracked stones (cooking stones) and two lined cooking pits containing no more than a few fire-cracked stones. The fire-cracked stones in cooking pits 1 and 2 were much more fragile than in cooking pit 3. All these constructions were located outdoors and in addition to these an oven was present inside the pit house, making this the fourth type of fire construction present at the site.

Based on these findings it is feasible to suggest four possible different types of food preparation on the mound: frying, baking, grilling and boiling. The pits might, if they were used for food preparation at all, represent differ-ent types of food preparation, i.e. baking using cooking stones directly in the pit and boiling using cooking stones in water in pits 1 and 2. The two lined pits might have been filled with both water and food and cooking stones could have been placed inside. In the oven inside the pit house it would have been possible to fry, grill, cook or bake. The outdoor hearths have most likely been prima-rily used as a source of heating to heat the cooking stones.

11   The soil samples from Hólmur were analysed in Sweden by Annika Söderlind and the results can be found in her report: "Interesting plant macro-fossils have been found at Hólmur", which is published as an appendix in Einarsson 2003.

Figure 26. The large stone at the bottom of the cooking pit 2. To the right some of the cooking stones from cooking pit 3, which is in the background, can be seen (Digital photo nr. 164. Photo BFE).

The oven in the pit house could occasionally have been used for this purpose too.

The hearths could of course even have been used in rituals both in connection with the preparation of food or in other ways and finally it cannot be excluded that one or some of the pits, primarily pit 1 and 2, might have been used in connection with the production (tempering or sharpening) of iron tools (see e.g. Gansum & Hansen 2004). In this instance it is possible to argue that knives/axes were sharpened at the pits and then later used to cut the meat on the chopping board inside the pit house.

Bearing in mind the bad preservation conditions it is surprising that the skeleton in the grave, excavated in 1902, could be observed at all because the other bone material, that was not cremated, was both rare and extremely badly preserved. The only exception was the whalebone found in the pit house. The badly preserved bone material has therefore brought to the fore the matter of whether the bones could have been cooked in the open fire or in the oven and as such been found in a much worse state than the human (and the whale) bones.

The type of cooking pits that the cooking pits 1 and 2 represent (lined with tephra or clay) have only been found at a number of locations: Áslákstunga Innri (Erlingsson 1899:33-34), Isleifsstaðir (Stenberger 1943:164f), Bólstaður (Þórðarson 1932:5-6 & 13-

16) and at Bergþórshvoll (Eldjárn & Gísli Gestsson 1952:31f). In the first three mentioned cases it was a matter of indoor pits in hall buildings and the first mentioned is understood to have belonged to a forge. One of the pits at Bergþórshvoll, most likely all of them indoors too, is also thought to have been a forge.[12] There is also a possible fourth site at Írskubúðir on the peak of Snæfellsnes, south of Hellissandur (Einarsson 2000(a)) and a further two ought to be mentioned; the two pits inside the great hall at *Hofstaðir* in Mývatnssveit. The first of these was layered like the cooking pits 1 and 2 at Hólmur and these too have been re-used. The filling consisted of a mixture of slag, charcoal and soil and this is considered to have been part of a forge (Friðriksson &Vésteinsson 1998:85).

The pit at Isleifsstaðir is thought to have been used for cooking but the three pits at Bólstaður (in two houses) and some at Bergþórshvoll are believed to have been used for fluids, probably water (food or washing). These too were layered like the pits at Hólmur and the pits from Isleifsstaðir and Hofstaðir. It would seem that all the pits

12 Several pits of this kind could have been discovered at the site (i.e. in floor nr. 32 and northwest of the trench nr. 2), but due to a very coarse excavation technique and insufficient documentation it is not possible to draw any definite conclusions on this matter. The excavation took place in the years 1927 – 28.

found have been indoor pits, with the exception of the pits at Hólmur.

11 BONE MATERIAL

The bone material confirms that the majority of animals usually connected with the settlement of Iceland are represented in the bone material.[13] There was bone from cattle, horse, pig, hen, sheep and probably also goat. Besides these bones, from fish (cod) and whale have also been found but bone from cat or dog were not identified in the material and in addition to these bones there was also the wing bone of a ptarmigan, a peregrine falcon foot bone and a toe bone probably from a wild duck or wader. It is interesting to note the abundance of teeth and skull bones in the bone material, which was scattered over the entire mound, as well as larger limb bones e.g. foot bone. There are similarities here to the bone material from Järrestad in the province of Skåne in Sweden (Nilsson 2003) but in this context it is also worth remembering Daniels Brunn's description of the grave at Hólmur, where he points to the horse teeth found scattered on the northern section of the mound, immediately north of the grave itself (Bruun 1903:24).

At *Hofstaðir* a total of eleven craniums were found next to the walls in the great hall building. These have probably been hanging on the outside of the walls and ended up underneath when the walls of the hall collapsed (Friðriksson et. al. 2004:196). The craniums with the horns still attached to most of them were from cattle with the exception of one, which was sheep and bearing in mind that the hanging of birds and craniums above entrances in order to keep evil spirits out has been a custom that continued well into the 20th century in Scandinavia it is quite feasible that these craniums had some religious – magic purpose. (Carlie 2004:104). On Björkö (Birka), in Sweden, pieces of cattle craniums with the horns still attached were found along with several other artefacts in a foundation trench to two parallel houses. Other bones in the trench included two wing bones from eider and a human shoulder blade (Ibid. 2004:119).

> It was also custom in forefather cult practices to deposit human bones in the foundations of the house, under the walls and at the entrances, as protection against illness and evil spirits. This custom is only represented in very few examples in the survey in question,

including Eketorp on Öland and Orred in Halland. The bones in question are of discrete character and most often the material consisted of small, individual fragments. There is therefore reason to presume that there is a large unseen presence in the archaeological material with regards to this kind of deposition. (Translation from Swedish - Carlie 2004:144)

Many of the cattle teeth recovered, during the excavations at Hólmur during the period 1997 – 2001, were unburnt and this could indicate that they represent uncooked offerings, whilst the cremated bones on the other hand might be indicative of the cooking of food for the people participating in acts of offering. The unburnt bones could also have been cooked as mentioned above.

The bird bone found on the surface was in the area where the bloomery iron was scattered. What significance this might have had cannot be determined but it is possible that its distribution is related to the pair of poles or the gate.

Closer analysis of the bone material (e.g. distribution of individual species, inside and outside, in the cooking pits, body parts, chopping abrasions, decomposition etc.) could provide a more detailed picture of the cult site.

12 C-14 DATING AND THE TEPHRA LAYERS

There are four C-14 datings from the cult site, all of which were acquired from charcoal from local tree species, or birch (betula). Two of the samples (H99: 19 & 20) were taken from the oven in the pit house, one from its floor (H97: 10) and one from a culture layer that covered the pit house (H97: 09). The samples indicate that the site was used during the entire Viking Age (800-1000 AD) and from an Icelandic point of view the datings are, to some extent, very early. One sample, however, with a deviating and extremely early dating (H99: 20), cannot be perceived as reliable.

The tephra layer, which more or less covers the entire mound, is known as the *landnamstephra* layer (LL - tephra). This layer comes from a volcanic eruption that occurred in the year 871±2 AD (Grönvold et. al. 1995). The layer did not cover the mound completely, partly because of the depositions from the Viking Age and partly due to erosion processes from more recent times. It is therefore not possible to establish conclusively whether or not there was human activity prior to the arrival of the tephra layer. What is certain is that activities did take place during the period shortly after. The grave and the *blót* house are both later than the landnamstephra layer. It must therefore be

---

13 Osteologist Leif Jonsson, from the 'Arkeologiskt Naturvetenskapligt Laboratorium', at the Department of Archaeology, Göteborg University, Sweden analysed these bones.

Table 1. Radiocarbon analysis samples from the cult site at Hólmur. All the samples were yielded from birch (betula). (Bronk-Ramsey 1995, 2001 using atmospheric data from Reimer et al. (2004)).

Test nr.	Lab nr.	C-14 year	C13/C12 ratio	1 zigma 68,2%	2 zigma 95,4%
H97:09	T 13781	1245±40	-28.2‰	680 (65,6%) – 810/ 840 (2,6%)- 860AD	670 - 880AD
H97:10	Beta 109905	1070±40	-30.4‰	890 (16,0%) – 920/ 960 (52,2%) – 1020AD	890 – 1030AD
H99:19	Beta 143634	1200±60	-27.6‰	710 (9,4%) – 750/ 760 (58,8%) – 900AD	680 – 980AD
H99:20	Beta 143635	1450±70	-27.4‰	540 – 660AD	430 – 680AD

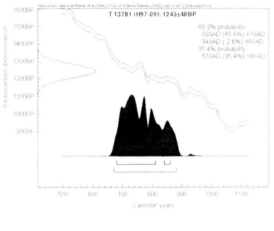

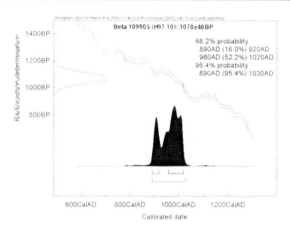

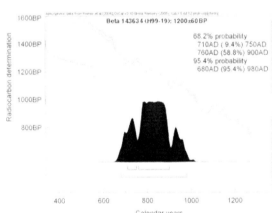

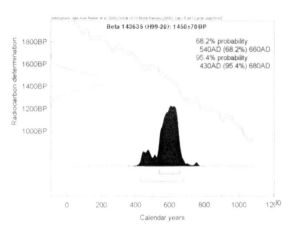

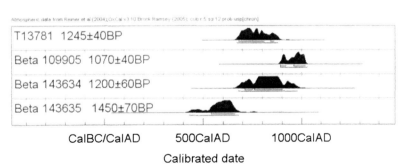

Figure 27 - 31. Calibrated C-14 dates from Hólmur.

concluded that activities on the mound occurred at the end of 800 AD, i.e. a short time after the period 869 – 873 AD.

At the farmstead site several tephra layers have been observed and the most significant of these are the 1362 layer (Öræfajökull 1362) and the "a"- layer (Vatnajökull 1477). Both layers are far above all the culture layers at the farmstead and therefore 'much' older than it (Einarsson 1998(b)).

13 FINDS

When compared to other Viking Age remains in Iceland the cult site at Hólmur is unusually rich and varied in its find collection. None of the artefacts were, however, unique even if some objects are rarely found and one particular category, i.e. the round discs of stone, is hardly ever found in Viking Age contexts in Iceland. As far as I know these have only been found at three locations; one at Ísleifsstaðir in western Iceland (Stenberger 1943), two in Reykjavík (Nordahl 1988) and one in Herjólfsdalur on the Vestmanna Islands (Hermanns-Auðardóttir 1989).

Several of the find categories, not including the bone material, are particularly interesting; the bloomery iron, the fire-cracked stones and the loom weights. These finds represent iron, fire and textiles, and all of these had some fundamental cultural significance. Furthermore no other site in Iceland has provided so much crude iron in such a restricted area as the cult site at Hólmur and no other site has contained fire-cracked stones so evenly scattered over such a large area than the cult site at Hólmur.

The crude iron was located in a very restricted area south of the pair of post-holes, interpreted as traces of a gate (passage) and a total of c. 650 g of crude iron was found, including three pieces that weighed 104.2 g, 110 g and 210 g respectively. The distribution pattern suggests that the iron had been thrown through the gate and not one piece of crude iron was found outside this area. The iron at the cult site was not manufactured on the site but it is possible that manufacturing occurred at a site close to the bogs north of the immense beach ridge, east of River Laxá.

It is possible to argue that the prospect of domestic iron manufacturing created the conditions necessary for the successful colonisation of Iceland. No other production demanded as much energy as iron but the knowledge required to transformed bog ore into iron was a decisive factor in terms of having access to usable iron which in turn was a decisive factor in human survival. Fortunately there is an abundance of bog ore in Iceland (Friðriksson & Hermanns-Auðardóttir 1992) and furthermore bog ore is present at Hólmur, both in the valley north of Selhryggur and in smaller amounts in-between the farm and cult site. It is therefore not surprising that the significance of iron is reflected in the materiality of cult practices (Burström 1990; Gansum & Hansen 2004).

A total of 14 loom weights were found at the cult site, one which being a stray find discovered just outside the location. Only one spindle whorl (in three pieces) was found. As previously mentioned four loom weights lay in a row immediately next to the pit house and these were most likely deposited attached to a string. Three loom weights lay in or close to hearth nr. 2 and two were found in the pit house whilst the remaining others were scattered on the mound. It is hard to imagine a weaving loom in the pit house or on the mound, outdoors so perhaps the presence of the loom weights ought to be explained in another way. Loom weights provide a direct link to sheep, wool production and the weaving of cloth and as such are an explicit element in the religion and cult as expressed through Urður, *Verðandi* and *Skuld*.

From the image proffered by the finds it is feasible that the crude iron and loom weights were used as offerings.

More than 214 artefacts were found at the cult site and include the following (figure 32 shows the distributions of the finds):[14]

> 60 iron objects (rivets, nails, fishing hooks, iron ribbons, hooks etc.)
> 40 slag fragments
> 23 pieces of bloomery iron.
> 19 strike-a-light stones of flint, obsidian or jasper
> 19 soapstone fragments (of which at least 9 are from pots)
> 14 flakes of flint or jasper
> 12 beads of amber, glass and stone
> 9 smaller stones with holes
> 8 whetstones (of which 4 were whetstone pendants)
> 8 décor-stones (Icelandic. "skrautsteinar")
> 2 gaming pieces [15]

The flakes of flint or jasper can be seen as parts of tools used for cutting meat in the same manner as found at the Viking Age farm Granastaðir. The flakes can also be seen as parts of strike-a-light stones (Einarsson 1995).

14 The list of finds includes a mixture of both definite and uncertain classifications as well as stray finds. Bone material was not included in the list of finds and finds recovered from around the turn of the 20th century have not been included either. The stray finds and the finds from around 1900 are not represented in the distribution map in figure 25.

15 An additional 15 beads and 11 whetstones would have been on this list if the findings from the excavations in1894/1899/1900 and 1902 had been included.

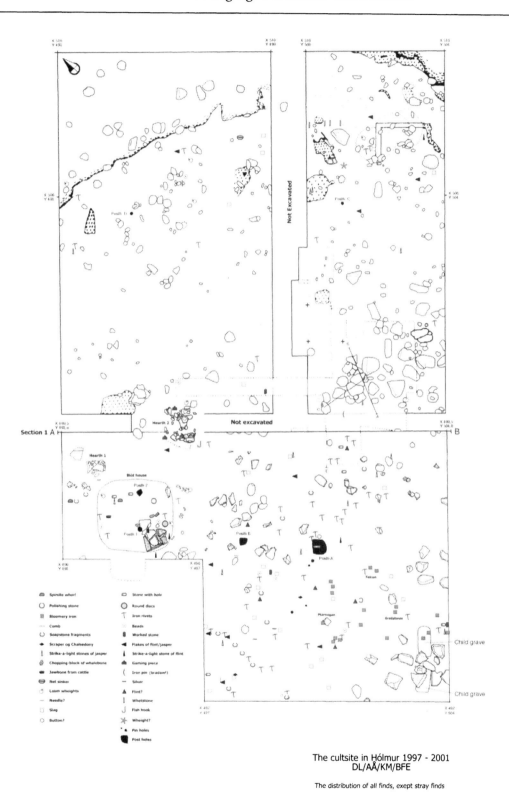

The cultsite in Hólmur 1997 - 2001
DL/AÁ/KM/BFE

The distribution of all finds, exept stray finds

Figure 32. Distribution of finds at the cult site in Hólmur. Neither the stray finds or the bone material is marked. The broken line in the eastern section of the surface close to the grave marks some of the test pits and test trenches from 1997.

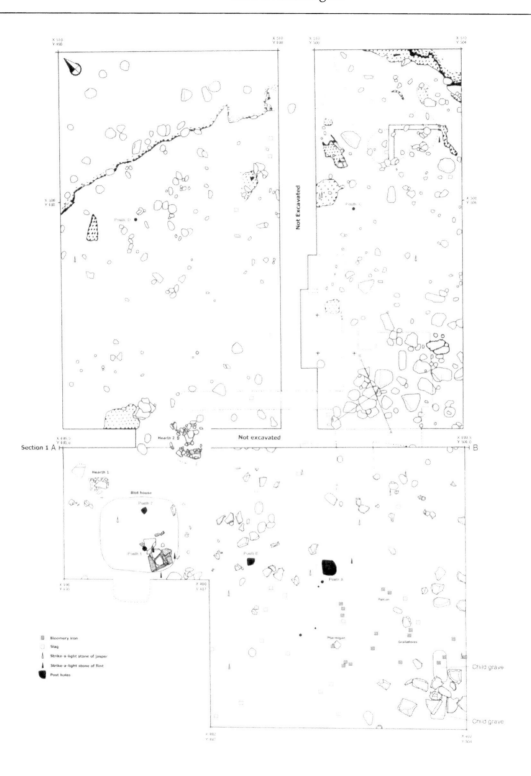

Figure 33. Distribution of the bloomery iron fragments, slag and some selected artefacts.

III. PIT HOUSES – *BLÓT* HOUSES – CHURCHES
A DISCUSSION

14 ICELANDIC PIT HOUSES

Pit houses were excavated for the first time in Iceland during the time period 1963 – 1967 at Hvítárholt in southern Iceland (see figure 4). In all five pit houses were found at the site and all were excavated (Magnússon 1972). Ten years later two pit houses were excavated at Grelutóttir, in northwest Iceland (Ólafsson 1980). In northern Iceland two pit houses were discovered at Granastaðir and one of these has also been excavated (Einarsson 1989 & 1992). In addition to these one, of the two pit houses found at Hofstaðir, has also been excavated (Friðriksson & Vésteinsson 1998 & *Hofstaðir* 2002 & 2003) as well as the medieval trading site at Gásir, where an unknown number of pit houses were discovered (Margrét Hermanns-Auðardóttir 1999). These and a number of recently discovered pit houses at Sveigakot[16] have all been found in the north or northeast of Iceland (Vésteinsson 2005:56-59).

In southern Iceland one pit house at Stóraborg (Snæsdóttir 1991) and one at Hjálmsstaðir were excavated (Ólafsson 1992) making Hólmur the ninth site where definite traces of a pit house have been found in Iceland.[17]

Interpretations as to the function of pit houses have varied. At Hvítárholt these houses were interpreted as bathhouses, whilst the ones at Grelutóttir were interpreted, like the house at Hjálmsstaðir, as both work sites for women (Icelandic "dyngjur") and as bathhouses.

The pit house at Granastaðir has been interpreted as the first settlement at the site, first as a dwelling house and then as a workplace and during the last phase of use it was used as a rubbish pit.

At Stóraborg the function of the house has not been determined, the house is the worst preserved of all known Icelandic pit houses and its dating is uncertain. The houses at Gásir have been interpreted as trading huts and they are the only ones that are not definitely Viking Age, besides of course the uncertain house at Stóraborg. It is not known which function the pit house at *Hofstaðir* has had, other than that it is a pit house and not primarily a rubbish pit or cooking pit (Friðriksson et. al. 2004:193-95). The house could well have ended up as a rubbish pit like the Granastaðir-house, several of the Sveigakot-houses and many of the other Scandinavian pit houses (Ohlsson 1976). The recently excavated houses from Sveigakot are believed to be first and foremost dwelling houses (Vésteinsson 2005:58).

Finally a possible and partially excavated pit house at Eiríksstaði in western Iceland ought to be mentioned (Erlingsson 1899:57).

A point of interest is that many pit houses seem to occur in pairs on farmstead sites. It is also worth noting that the pit house at Hólmur, Iceland's smallest pit house is the only one in Iceland that is not located on a farmstead or a trading site. Yet another interesting detail is the fact that sites, which have had continuous settlement from the Viking Age up until more recent times (Stóraborg, Hjálmsstaðir and Hofstaðir), are all situated at sites where churches have stood for longer or shorter periods of time. In 1942 early medieval graves were found at Hjálmsstaðir and this indicates that a church has existed at the site, possibly built before 1200 AD. At *Hofstaðir* the place name suggests the presence of a church or a chapel (Friðriksson & Vésteinsson 1998:68) and quite recently the church was found and excavated in 2001-2002 (Gestsdóttir 2003). At the trading site Gásir there was a church too (Hermanns-Auðardóttir 1989). The other farms (Hvítárholt, Grelutóttir, Granastaðir, Sveigakot and Hólmur) were all abandoned, at the latest c. 1000 AD or earlier, before the Christianisation of Iceland and it is possible that Grelutóttir had been moved to a new site and renamed Eyri or Hrafnseyri where there is a church.

---

16   Five pit houses were presumed to be found at this site. It is, however, debatable as to whether or not three of these houses are common type pit houses.

17   A dug out house in Breiðuvík NE of Húsavík in NE - Iceland has not here been counted as a pit house (Ólafsson 2001). Another dug house in Kópavogur just outside of Reykjavík cannot either be counted as a pit house (Sveinbjarnardóttir 1986). The known pit houses are:
- Hvítárholt in southern Iceland, 5 pit houses (Magnússon 1972)
- Grelutóttir, north-western Iceland, 2 pit houses (Ólafsson 1980)
- Granastaðir, nothern Iceland, 2 pit houses (Einarsson 1989 & 1992)
- Hofstaðir, north-eastern Iceland, 2 pit houses (Friðriksson et. al. 1998 & *Hofstaðir* 2002 & 2003)
- Gásir, northern Iceland, unknown number of pit houses (Margrét Hermanns-Auðardóttir 1999)
- Stóraborg, southern Iceland, 1 pit house (Snæsdóttir 1991)
- Hjálmsstaðir, southern Iceland, 1pit house (Ólafsson 1992)
- Sveigakot, north-eastern Iceland, at least five presumed pit houses (Vésteinsson 2005)
- Hólmur is the ninth site where a pit house has definitely been found in Iceland

Pit houses have been interpreted as multifunctional houses suitable for different purposes (Ohlsson, 1976:95. Einarsson 1989:61). They have been used as temporary dwelling houses, as work sites for a variety of productions, as animal houses, storage rooms, trading huts, court houses etc. etc. It has even been suggested that they functioned as saunas, as "dyngjur" for example in the form of weaving cottages or other work places for women or even as bakeries. Now it would appear that they have even functioned as *blót* houses. All pit houses in the Nordic countries have been found on farmsteads, in villages or at trading sites. The question is if more of the many pit houses in the North have functioned as *blót* houses. (See for instance Carlie's list of houses in Scandinavia 2004:264ff).

In a new country, as was the case with Iceland, with no infrastructure or any centralised power, both at a worldly and religious level there was no need to erect large houses in order to practice religious acts. It was relatively unnecessary to spend enormous amounts of effort on monumentality when no given opponent existed. A general prototype as to what religious houses should look like hardly existed and the social and religious pressure for a particular shape or size was not that great. A relatively liberal choice of solutions could have existed and as such the rules regulating the shape and design of *blót* houses, or other types of religious buildings could have varied in the different regions and therefore ought to have been flexible. With the new cult, Christianity, this drastically changed, even if it might have taken a while, and even if in accordance with prevailing attitudes but perhaps the differences were not that great, perhaps it is possible to discern characteristics common for both the Viking Age and the early Middle Ages. Hopefully current excavations of church sites will shed more light on this matter.

15 EXCAVATED CHURCH SITES

Several early medieval churches have been excavated around the country in recent years, some of which were not known prior to excavation and this implies that more churches from this period have existed than was previously thought. It is also quite possible that there was one church for each farmstead of rank (Icelandic, lögbýli) and maybe also for the larger tenant farms.

In 1947 a church ruin was excavated at the farmstead Kross in western Iceland. Its interior measured 2.5 x 5 m and although the dating is uncertain written sources suggest that a church was present at Kross in 1327 (Eldjárn 1974(a):143-44).

Some years later, in 1950, a chapel was excavated in Hafnarfjörður, west of Reykjavík. The chapel interior measured 2.2 x 2.4 m and even though the dating could not be determined exactly it is known to be earlier than 1550 (Eldjárn 1957).

At Varmá in western Iceland a church was excavated during the years 1968-1969. Its interior measured 3 x 5 m but again the exact age of the church could not be established. It is, however, mentioned as early as 1397 and has probably been used by several generations prior to this time. Furthermore a forge had been built on top of the church (Rafnsson 1971:37-40).

At Stóraborg in southern Iceland post-holes were discovered in a churchyard at the end of the 1970's and interpreted as the remains of a church. The size of the church could have been 3 x 3.75 m, not including the choir. No definite dating of these remains exists but their approximate age is hardly later than the 16th century (Ágústsson 1988:43).

At Stöng in Þjórsárdalur in southern Iceland a previously unknown church was discovered at the beginning of the 1990's with an interior that measured 2,8 x 3,3 m, not including the choir. This church, which is dated to early 11th century, was abandoned before 1200 AD and a forge was located beneath the church (Vilhjálmsson 1996:131).

The interior of a recently excavated church at Geirsstaðir in eastern Iceland measured 3 x 5 m, not including the choir, which was 1 x 1 m in size. The church was dated to the 11th century and built on top of a forge. The floor was dug down c. 1 m below the surface (Kristjánsdóttir 1998:10) and around the church there were traces of charcoal which were quite obviously the remains of a fire that had burnt when the church was in use (Ibid. 1998:11-12). Beneath the southern wall a pit was found containing amongst other things fragmented human bones (incl. two finger bones). One interpretation, in my opinion, is that these bones were deposited for the purpose of magic in a way similar to the ones from Eketorp in Öland, Vallhagar in Gotland, Orred in Fjärås and Birka in Uppland, all in Sweden. The first three are pre-Viking Age (Carlie 2004:141f) but whether these houses were pagan cult houses or not is another matter, but it is not improbable. No graves were found at Geirsstaðir but under the floor four pits were situated, two filled with slag, charcoal and soot and two filled with charcoal and soot (Kristjánsdóttir 1998:26ff). The house was located c. 100 m north of the farmhouse or hall. This is a long distance for a church!

At Neðri-Ás in northern Iceland a church was excavated at the end of the 1990's. The earliest church build-

ing appears to be from the very beginnings of Christian times (i.e. 11th century) but the section that was excavated provided a dating from the beginning of the 13th century. Furthermore one or more forges were built on top of the church ruin shortly after the church was abandoned (Bergsteinsson 1997:18, Vésteinsson 1998).

Table 2. List of excavated medieval churches and chapels in Iceland (excluding the churches at the bishopric Skálholt in southern Iceland and Hólar in northern Iceland as well as the churches at Gásir (market place) in northern Iceland and Skriðuklaustur (monastery) in eastern Iceland, where excavations are still in progress).

Site	Location	Excavated	Size m	Choir m	Dating	Graves	Forge
Skeljastaðir[1]	Árnessýsla	1939	c. 4 x c. 8	?	1100 AD+	Yes	No
Kross	Dalasýsla	1947	2.5 x 5 (int)	No	-1327	Yes	No
Kapelluhraun	Gullbringus.	1950	2.2 x 2.4 (int)	No	-1550	No	No
Varmá[2]	Kjósasýsla	1968-69	3 x 5 (int)	c. 1.5 x 1.5	-1397	Yes	On top
Kúabót[3]	V-Skaft.	1974	3.2 x 5.3 (int)	No	1400 AD+	No	Below
Stóraborg	Rangárv..s.	1975	3 x 3.75	Yes?	-	Yes	No
Kirkjuból[4]	Ísafjarðars.	1984	3.5 x 5.7	Yes	1400?	Yes	No
Stöng	Árnessýsla	1991-2	2.8 x 3.3 (int)	c. 1 x 1.5 (int)	1000 AD+	Yes	Below
Laugarnes[5]	Reykjavík	1993	8 x 11	?	1794	Yes	No
Geirsstaðir	N-Múlasýsla	1997	3 x 5 (int)	1 x 1.5 (int)	c. 1000 AD	No	Below
Neðri-Ás[6]	Skagafj.s.	1997-8	3.5 x 5.65	No	1200 AD+	Yes	On top
Þórarinsstaðir	N-Múlasýsla	1998-99	2.7 x 4.8 (int)	1.5 x 1.5 (int)	c. 1000 AD	Yes	No
Hofstaðir[7]	S-Þingeyjars.	-2002	3.4 x 3.6 (ext)	No	12 – 1300+	Yes	No
Hrísbrú[8]	Gullbringusýs.	2001-	3.2 x 4.3	2.5 x 2.5	c 1000 AD	Yes	No
Brattahlíð	Greenland	≈1960	2 x 3.5 (int)	No	c. 1000 AD	Yes	No
Sandur[9]	Faeroe islands	1969-70	4 x 5 (ext)	2 x 2.5	1100 AD+	Yes	No

1 Þórðarson 1943:134. No traces of the actual church were found. These figures are the absolute maximum sizes.

2 Sveinbjörnsson 1971:36. The length of the church is some what overestimated according to a plan drawing. The size of the choir is estimated by the author.

3 Árnadóttir 1987:57-62.

4 Þorkelsson 1985:4.

5 Einarsson 1993:7 & 13. Only archeometric investigation (georadar) occurred.

6 Earlier churches did exist during this time.

7 Gestsdóttir 2003:26.

8 Byock, J et.al. 2003 and www.gagarin.is/moso

9 Krogh, K.J. 1975:33.

At Þórarinsstaðir in eastern Iceland a church, that was dated to approximately 1000 AD, was discovered and excavated at the end of the 1990's. The size of the church during its earliest phases was 2.7 x 4.8 m, and the choir was 1.5 x 1.5 m in size. This church is not mentioned in any of the written sources and was in all probability aban-

doned before the year 1200 AD (Kristjánsdóttir 2004).

In Brattahlíð (Thjodhilds-church) on Greenland one of the smallest churches of the Northern countries appears to have been found. It was only 2 x 3.5 m in size (Krogh & Jørgensen 1964:4) but it is still larger than the chapel (Kapelluhraun) at Hafnarfjörður!

On the island Skellig Michael, west of Ireland, there are two small churches at a cloister complex. The interior of the larger of the two was 2.3 x 3.5 m in size whilst the interior of the smaller one measured only 1.85 x 2.45 m (Eldjárn 1989:81).

Besides these excavated churches, built on top of or beneath a forge there are several other churches that should be mentioned. These have not been excavated but are still evidence of a connection to forges (see table 3). Needless to say, it is enticing to put forward the hypothesis that the size of many of the early churches in Iceland could indicate a continuity of a farmstead cult in the small *blót* houses. Both types of buildings served a small group of people on the farmsteads, perhaps only for certain parts of a family or a select number of individuals. Icelandic Iron Age society, with no king and no centralised power did not need all-encompassing religious buildings or large monumental burials. It was the family or extended family of the farmstead that was of central importance.

It is also interesting to note that the church at Geirsstaðir was dug down into a slope and this seems to indicate that the digging of such cavities was accepted practice, even for such an 'important' house. Another point of interest is the fact that forges frequently occurred on top of or beneath the churches. This strengthens the interpretation that iron during the early Middle Ages had a continued significance both practically and ritually.

Christianity did not imply any great differences as such but should rather be seen to continue the acknowledgement of the ritual significance of iron.

In Iceland there are two Viking Age burials which can be linked with iron production or the remains of such an activity. In 1956-57 two Viking Age graves were discovered on a hill or mound called "Smiðjuhóll" (Engl. = Smithy Hill) on land belonging to the farmstead Gilsárteigur in eastern Iceland (Jón Steffensen 1959:121ff). One account states that pieces of charcoal and slag were found amongst the grave-goods but this description does not in any way suggest that this was a slag heap.

The forge has been linked to religious representations for a long period of time from prehistoric times up to the present day. In various places around the world it has been believed to be a great and almost supernatural art (Burström 1990:265; Gansum & Hansen 2004:359ff). Mythology tells of the master smithy Völund and the dwarves, of Thor's hammer, and folk tales tell of the

smithy's connection to the supernatural, Odin, the devil and other non-human beings. Fire cleansed from evil and objects of iron could have been used for a variety of purposes, for example to protect, heal or destroy (Schön 1988:61; Íslenskar þjóðsögur 1978:293f & 296f; Íslenskar þjóðsögur og ævintýri 1954:178, 258 & 323). There is a story of a man that only ceased his haunting after three iron nails were hammered into his grave (Íslenskar þjóðsögur 1978:292). Another tale tells us that if an iron rod or bar was placed upon the tongue it was possible to learn what one wanted to know and if it was held in the hand instead it was possible to learn a desired craft (Íslenskar þjóðsögur og ævintýri 1964:23).

In another story there is a farmer who took a rune stone from a grave, broke it into three pieces and used it in his forge. The following night he dreamed that a proud, large and heavy man in dark clothes came to him and said:

> It was bad to take my stone yesterday and break it into pieces. The stone was the only thing that kept my name alive, but this you could not allow me the pleasure of keeping. I will take revenge in a terrible way. Put the pieces back on my grave immediately, the same way they were before but because you broke my stone you will never walk again as a healthy man." (Translated from Icelandic to Swedish by author and from Swedish to English by Fiona Campbell - Ísl. þjóðsögur 1927:235).

The owner of the stone was the renowned hero Kjartan Ólafsson who died in 1002 (Laxdæla saga) and the farmer was never the same again. The stone in question is, however, much later - 14th - 15th century (Kålund 1985:32f).

To build a church on top of a forge was some kind of insurance that the site was purified and to construct a forge on top of a church was to invest in the success of the production of iron objects.

16 HÓLMUR'S SIGNIFICANCE IN UNDERSTANDING VIKING AGE PRIVATE CULT PRACTICES

Fire has played a very important role at the Hólmur *blót* site. It was burnt both inside and out. The artefacts, the fire-cracked stones and bone material, which are the result of the fire, are scattered over the entire mound and the effects of its presence depicts events that have previously not been recognised in Iceland, a country where cremation burials are not known to exist. There are, however, a number of cases (10 definite graves at 10 different sites) where it has been possible to confirm the presence of charcoal in Ice-

Table 3. Indications of the connections between churches and forges in Iceland during the Middle Ages.

Site	Location	Type	Churchyard	Forge
Skálmholt[1]	Árnessýsla	Chapel	Yes	On top
Djáknadyngja[2]	Árnessýsla	Ruin	?	?
Kaðalstaðir[3]	Mýrasýsla	Chapel	-	On top
Sleitustaðir[4]	Skagafjarðarsýsla	Chapel	Yes?	On top
Oddi[5]	Rangárvallasýslu	Church	Yes	On top
Staður[6]	Strandasýsla	Church?	-	Below

1 Jarðabók II. 1918-1921:178f.

2 Jarðabók II. 1918-1921:276. There is no definite information about a church here even if oral stories suggest this to be the case. The site has even been known as "Djáknadys" (Engl. = The Deacon's grave). At the site there is a ruin where slag and similar kinds of finds have been found. According to oral tradition a scholar lived there and was buried close to where his grave was thought to be visible. According to another oral tradition he was a smithy. In *c.* 1700 AD some farmers dug the ruins but no human remains were found. Instead they found animal bones, different kinds of ore fragments and stones (Frásögur um fornaldarleifar 1983:213).

3 Jarðabók IV. 1925 & 1927:321.

4 Jarðabók IX. 1930:226f.

5 Frásögur um fornaldarleifar 1983:141. This site is interesting because of a story from 1818 about how a church was moved from a farm named Jólgeirsstaðir. The church was placed late in the day to the east of the farmstead in Oddi, where a forge now (1818) stands but when the people woke the next day the church stood west of the farm. The church was located west of the farm at Jólgeirsstaðir, which was unusual.

6 Frásögur um fornaldarleifar 1983:439. In a story from 1817 a priest tells of a ruin, which he believed was a church ruin. He dug in the ruin and found large fragments of slag and charcoal.

landic graves but this is the closest we can come to the idea of cremation burials, for the time being at least.[18] One early explanation for the presence of charcoal in the graves is that it is to postpone decomposition (Stefánsson 1898:39). Eldjárn argues, with reference to Norwegian research, that the use of charcoal could have been a symbolic custom originating from cremation practices and he believes that the charcoal originated from ritual fires at burial sites (1956:245f). Remains of such ritual fires have, however, never been found in Iceland prior to the excavations at Hólmur and in Iceland the custom of spreading charcoal over the dead continued even after the introduction of Christianity (Kristjánsdóttir 2004:101).

With regards to the significance of iron it is worth mentioning the similarities between a site like Borg in Sweden and Hólmur. In Borg amulet-rings of iron were offered, at Hólmur bloomery iron was offered and it would seem that iron and the art of forging held magical powers and played an important role in pre-Christian religion (Burström 1990:265-66; DuBois 1999:95; Gansum

& Hansen 2004; see also verse 7 in Völuspá quoted in section 3 of this article).

The probable child burials are possibly located outside the sacred arena at Hólmur for reasons akin to the Christian practices for children that were not baptised or those classified as unwanted (e.g. criminals and the mentally ill) buried close to churchyard cemeteries. Close proximity to the sacred site would still somehow ensure the dead a piece of eternity or at the very least, perhaps provide them with a better chance of getting into heaven.

Magnus and Myhre believe that the occurrence of solitary mounds at farmsteads could also indicate some kind of forefather worship. Only a select few were honoured with such a memorial and they provided the farmstead with strength and prosperity. Such sites were worshipped and offerings were made to them (Birkeli 1938:47; Magnus and Myhre 1986:267 et.al. at the beginning of the article). The mound where the offering site is located could very well have functioned as a mound in this instance. An important person is buried at this site and with time the site became more than just a burial site.

18   At the excavation in progress at Hrísbrú, several burnt human skulls have been found in a presumed grave mound some meters away from the cemetery. The results of these investigations have not yet been published and as such can hardly be treated as a cremation burial, yet.

Acta Archaeologica

Figure 34. The cult house after excavation. The weather was terrible during the entire season of 1999 (Slide 9:25. Photo BFE).

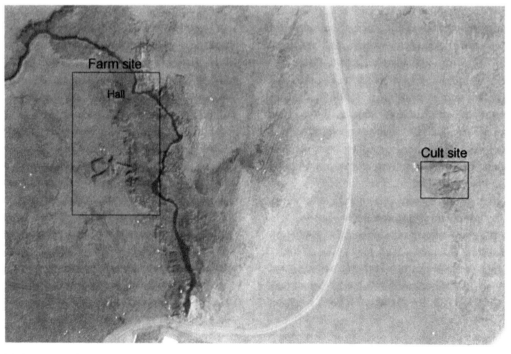

Figure 35. Aerial photograph of Hólmur from SE. The house in the lower part of the picture is situated at the top of the spring Hólmslækjaruppspretta
(Slide 2004:29. Photo BFE).

IV CONCLUDING REMARKS

The mound beneath the immense beach ridge that crosses the valley of Laxárdalur is physically quite protruding on the otherwise even slope of the beach ridge. It is almost alien-like and unnatural from a geological and ocular perspective and I can find no rational justification to explain its coming into being. It is practically a geological impossibility and the beach ridge seems to function as some kind of theatrical backdrop (amphitheatre) to the mound and the activities that took place there, as seen from the farmstead. Besides this the mound protects against the cold and the bitter north wind from the high mountains and could symbolically act as a safeguard against intrusion from the realm of the dead, "Hel".

Generally speaking Icelandic graves have not been examined in any great detail and in most cases it has been a matter of close inspection of the grave in question and subsequently emptying it of its contents. In contrast to this the stratigraphical contexts and the area in close proximity to the graves have not been subject to a closer inspection. Only a few exceptions exist in the literature where several graves have been excavated at the same site, but their surroundings have not. The total number of Viking Age graves is a little more than 300 and approximately one third of these occur as solitary burials giving an average of less than two graves per site (Einarsson 1995:46). An overwhelming amount of these graves were excavated at the turn of the 20th century and during the 1930's and 1950's (Ibid. 199:54).

The excavations of and at the grave in Hólmur were in part an attempt to break this tradition and as such an attempt to see if human activities could be traced in the environment in close proximity to the grave. Another aim with this project was to confirm the idea that there was a farmstead not too far away from each grave and to test the theory that an unbroken visual line existed between the two sites (Einarsson 1998(b)).

The excavations at the cult site at Hólmur have now ended but the farmstead is only partially excavated and all future work is dependent upon the acquisition of financial and other support. Finally it can be worth summarising some of the salient factors that I believe support the idea that the mound and the pit house at Hólmur were connected to cult practices.

- the mound is restricted and striking, c. 250 m from a farmstead, both dated to the Viking Age. In-between these a stream ran from a water source.
- on the mound there is a grave and a pit house from the Viking Age.
- on the mound, besides the grave and the pit house, there are also hearths and cooking pits, all located outdoors.
- on the mound there is a pair of post-holes which indicate the presence of a gate or an entrance and all the constructions are situated on one side of this entrance with the exception of the two presumed child graves. Beneath or immediately next to the entrance the only bird bones on the mound were found.
- two presumed child burials are located outside the entrance and outside the presumed sacred site.
- there was a relatively even distribution of fire-cracked stones which were not suitable for walking on – on an everyday basis. These stones more or less covered the entire area.
- on the mound there was one very concentrated distribution of bloomery iron which had obviously been thrown through the entrance.
- the size of the pit house is consistent with the size of the earliest churches.
- the pit house is the only pit house in Iceland that is not situated at a farm site,
trading place or assembly site. This probably also applies for the entire Scandinavian region.

Hólmur ought to be understood as a private cult site in a settler environment where a public cult had not been necessary. The site perhaps ought to be understood as an addition to the collection of similar sites, e.g. Borg, Lofoten, Slöinge, Järrestad and several other high ranking farmsteads where public cult practices took place.

The excavations at Hólmur have been exceedingly taxing and difficult for me personally but I never considered abandoning the project, not even because others wanted to interpret things differently or because many colleagues and historians in Iceland do not consider my interpretation of the site acceptable. To be of a different opinion is not unusual in other Nordic countries, but unfortunately in Iceland the tolerance levels are much, much lower.

REFERENCES

Aðalsteinsson, Jón H. 1978 Under the Cloak. The Acceptance of Christianity in Iceland with Particular Reference to the Religious Attitudes Prevailing at the Time. Acta universitatis Upsaliensis. Uppsala.

Ibid. 1988 „Norræn trú." Íslensk þjóðmenning V. Trúarhættir. Ed. F. F. Jóhannesson. Reykjavík.

Ibid. 1997 Blót í norrænum sið. Rýnt í forn trúarbrögð með þjóðfræðilegri aðferð. Reykjavík.

Ágústsson, Hörður. 1988 „Minnisgrein um kirkjugrunnsleifar á Stóruborg." Árb. Hins ísl. fornleifafélags 1987. Reykjavík.

Andrén Anders. 2004 „Platsernas betydelse. Norrön ritual och kultplatskontinuitet." Mellom himmel og jord. Foredrag fra et seminar om religionsarkeologi. Isegren 31. januar – 2. februar 2002. Red. Iene Melheim, Lotte Hedeager & Kristin Oma. Oslo. Archaeological Series Nr. 2. Oslo.

Árnadóttir, Lilja. 1987 „Kúabót í Álftaveri VI." Árbók Hins ísl. fornleifafélags 1986. Reykjavík.

Artelius, Tore. 2000 Bortglömda föreställningar. Begravningsritual och begravningsplats i halländsk yngre järnålder. Göteborg.

Baudou, Evert. 1991 „Helgedom, hus och hög." Gravundersökningar och gravarkeologi. Red. Agneta Lagerlöf. Forskning för kulturmiljövård 3. Riksantikvarieämbetet. Stockholm.

Bergsveinsson, Sigurður. 1997 „Neðri Ás í Hjaltadal, fornleifarannsókn." Greinargerð um stöðu og verkefni Fornleifadeildar Þjóðminjasafns Íslands árið 1998. Reykjavík.

Birkeli, E. 1938 Fedrekult i Norge. Et forsøk på en systematisk-deskriptiv fremstilling. Skrifter utg. av det Norske Videnskaps-Akademi i Oslo. II. Hist. – Filos. Klasse 1938. No 5. Oslo.

Bjerre Finnestad, R. 1986 „The Part and the Whole: Reflection on Theory and Methods Applied to the Interpretation of Scandinavian Rock Carving." Words and Objects. Towards a Dialogue between Archaeology and Religion. Ed. Gro Steinsland. Oslo.

Bray, Warwick & Trump, David. 1970 The Penguin Dictionary of Archaeology.

Briem, Ólafur. 1945 Heiðinn siður á Íslandi. Reykjavík.

Bruun, Daniel. 1903 „Nokkrar dysjar frá heiðni, II. Hólmsfundurinn." Árbók Hins íslenska fornleifafélags 1903. Reykjavík.

Bruun, D & Jónsson, F. 1910 „Om Hove og Hoveudgravninger på Island." Aarb. for nord. Oldk. og Hist. 1909. København.

Burström, Mats. 1990 „Järnframställning och gravritual. En strukturalistisk tolkning av järnslagg i vikingatida gravar i Gästrikland. Fornvännen 85. Stockholm.

Byock, Jesse, Walker, P., Erlandsson, J., Holck, P., Eng, J., Tveskov, M. Sigurgeirsson, M., Lambert, P., Moss, M., Prizer, K., Reid, M., Zori, D., Byock, A., & Fyllingen, H. "A Viking Age farm, church, and cemetery at Hrísbrú, Mosfell Valley, Iceland" Antiquity Vol 77. No 297. September 2003.

Bæksted, Anders. 1988 Nordiska gudar och hjältar. Gjövik.

Carlie, Anne. 2004 Forntida byggnadskult. Tradition och regionalitet i södra Skandinavien. Riksantikvarieämbetet. Arkeologiska undersökingar, Skrifter No 57. Malmö.

Davidson, H.E. 1993 The Lost Beliefs of Northern Europe. London.

DuBois, T. A. 1999 Nordic religions in the viking age. Philadelphia.

Edda Snorra Sturlusonar. 1949 Nafnaþulur og skáldatal. Guðni Jónsson bjó til prentunar. Íslendingasagnaútgáfan. Reykjavík.

Eddukvæði (Sæmundar Edda). 1949 I – II. Guðni Jónsson bjó til prentunar. Íslendingasagnaútgáfan. Reykjavík.

Einarsson, Bjarni. F. 1989 „Jaðarbyggð á Eyjafjarðardal. Víkingaaldarbærinn Granastaðir. Fornleifarannsókn á skála, jarðhýsi og öðrum tilheyrandi fornleifum sumrin 1987 og 1988." Súlur. Norðlenskt tímarit. XVI árg. 29. hefti 1989. Akureyri.

Ibid. 1992 „Granastaðir-grophuset och andra isländska grophus i ett nordiskt sammanhang. Deras funtion och betydelse i kolonisationsförloppet i Island." Viking. Tidskrift for norrøn arkeologi. Norsk Arkeologisk Selskap. Bind LV. Oslo.

Ibid. 1993 Laugarnes. Greinargerð um fornleifar á Laugarnesi í Reykkjavík. Skýrslur Árbæjarsafns XIX. Reykjavík.

Ibid. 1995 The Settlement of Iceland. A Critical Approach. Granastaðir and the Ecological Heritage. Reykjavík.

Ibid. 1996 -Hólmur í mynni Laxárdals - Skýrsla yfir prufurannsóknir á fornbýlinu Hólmur
í mynni Laxárdals, Austur-Skaftafellssýslu, 13.-16. ágúst 1996. Manuskript. Reykjavík.

Ibid. 1998(a) -Hólmur í mynni Laxárdals II. Skýrsla yfir fornleifarannsókn á fornbýlinu Hólmi og kumli í mynni Laxárdals, Austur-Skaftafellssýslu, 26. júní t.o.m. 18. júlí 1997. Manuskript. Fornleifafræðistofan. Reykjavík.

Ibid. 1998 (b) „Hólmur. Kuml og landnámsbær í mynni Laxárdals í Nesjum." Skaftfellingur. Þættir úr Austur-Skaftafellsýslu. 12. árg. Höfn.

Ibid 2000(a). Írskubúðir. Landnámsbýli á utanveru Snæfellsnesi. Skýrsla um fornleifarannsóknir haustið 1999. II. skýrsla. Manuskript. Fornleifafræðistofan. Reykjavík.

Ibid. 2000(b) -Hólmur í mynni Laxárdals- Blóthús undir [Selhrygg]. Skýrsla III. Manuskript. Fornleifafræðistofan. Reykjavík.

Ibid. 2001 -Hólmur í mynni Laxárdals- Blóthús undir Selhrygg. Skýrsla IV. Manuskript. Fornleifafræðistofan. Reykjavík.

Ibid. 2002 -Hólmur í mynni Laxárdals- Blóthús og bæjarstæði undir Selhrygg. Viðauki: Vindás/Hof. Forn rúst á Steinadal í Suðursveit. Skýrsla V. Manuskript. Fornleifafræðistofan. Reykjavík.

Ibid. 2003 -Hólmur í mynni Laxárdals- Blóthús og bæjarstæði undir Selhrygg. Skýrsla VI. Manuskript. Fornleifafræðistofan. Reykjavík.

Ibid. 2006 „Ekki er allt sem sýnist. Þáráð, krotað og rist til forna." Árbók Hins ísl. fornleifafélags 2004. Reykjavík 2006.

Eldjárn, Kristján. 1956 Kuml og haugfé. Úr heiðnum sið á Íslandi. Akureyri.

Ibid. 1957 „Kapelluhraun og Kapellulág." Árbók Hins ísl. fornleifafélags 1955-56. Reykjavík.

Ibid. 1974(a) „Kirkjurúst á Krossi á Skarðsströnd." Árbók Hins ísl. fornleifafélags 1973. Reykjavík.

Ibid. 1974(b) „Fornþjóð og minjar " Saga Íslands I. Reykjavík.

Ibid. 2000. Kuml og haugfé. Úr heiðnum sið á Íslandi. 2. útgáfa. Ed. Adolf Friðriksson. Reykjavík.

Ibid. 1989 „Papey. Fornleifarannsóknir 1967 – 1981. Guðrún Sveinbjarnardóttir bjó til prentunar og samdi viðauka." Árbók Hins ísl. fornleifafélags 1988.

Eldjárn, Kristján & Gísli Gestsson. 1952 „Rannsóknir á Bergþórshvoli." Árbók Hins ísl. fornleifafélags 1951-52. Reykjavík.

Erlingsson, Þorsteinn. 1899. Ruins of the Saga Time: Being an account of travels and excavations in Iceland in the summer of 1895. London.

Foot, P.G. & Wilson, D.M. 1970 The Viking Achievement. The society and culture of early medieval Scandinavia. London.

Frásögur um fornaldarleifar 1817–1823. 1983 Sveinbjörn Rafnsson bjó til prentunar. Reykjavík.

Friðriksson, A. & Vésteinsson, O. 1997 „Hofstaðir Revisited." Norwegian Archaeological Review. Vol. 30, No 2.

Ibid. 1998 „Hofstaðir í Mývatnssveit – yfirlit 1991 - 1997." Archaeologica Islandica1. Tímarit Fornleifastofnunar Íslands. Reykjavík.

Friðriksson, A. Vésteinsson, O. & McGovern, T. 2004 „Recent Investigations at Hofstaðir, northern Iceland." Atlantic Connections and Adaptations. Economies, environments and subsistence in lands bordering the North Atlantic. Ed. R.A. Housley and G. Coles. Oxford.

Friðriksson, Thorbjörn Á & Hermanns-Auðardóttir, Margrét. 1992 „Ironmaking in Iceland. " Bloomery ironmaking during 2000 years. Seminar in Budalen 1991. Ed.

Esplund. Trondheim.

Gansum, Terje og Hansen, Hans-Johnny. 2004 „Fra jern til stål." Mellom himmel og jord. Foredrag fra et seminar om religionsarkeologi. Isegren 31. januar – 2. februar 2002. Red. Iene Melheim, Lotte Hedeager & Kristin Oma. Oslo Archaeological Series Nr. 2. Oslo.

Gestsdóttir, Hildur. 2003 „The Chapel." Hofstaðir 2002. Framvinduskýrslur/Interim Report. Ed. Gavin Lucas. Reykjavík.

Grágás. 1992. Lagasafn íslenska þjóðveldisins. Gunnar Karlsson, Kristján Sveinsson og Mörður Ágústsson sáu um útgáfuna. Reykjavík.

Grönvold, K., Óskarsson, N., Johnsen, S., Clausen, C., Hammer, U., Bond, G. & Bard, E. 1995 „Express letter. Ash layers from Iceland in the Greenland GRIP ice core correlated with oceanic and land sediments." Earth and Plenetary Science Letters 135.

Hermanns-Auðardóttir, Margrét. 1989 Islands tidiga bosättning. Studier med utgångspunkt i merovingertida – vikingatida gårdslämningar i Herjólfsdalur, Vestmannaeyjar, Island. Studia Archaeologica Universitatis Umensis 1. Reykjavík.

Ibid. 1999 „Arkeologiska undersökningar av handels-platsen vid Gásir." Gásir – en international handelsplass i Nord-Atlanten. Senter for middelalderstudier. Skrifter nr. 9. Red. Axel Christophersen & Audun Dybdahl. Trondheim.

Hofstaðir 2002. 2003 Framvinduskýrslur/Interim Report. Ed. Gavin Lucas. Reykjavík.

Hultgård, Anders. 1996 „Fornskandinavisk kult - finns det skriftliga källor?" Religion från stenålder till medeltid. Red. K. Engdahl och Aders Kaliff. Riksantikvarieämbetet. Arkeologiska undersökningar. Skrifter nr 19. Linköping.

Íslendinga sögur og þættir. 1986. Síðara bindi. Ed. Bragi Halldórsson, Jón Torfason, Sverrir Tómasson & Örnólfur Thorsson. Reykjavík 1986.

Íslensk Fornrit I. 1968 Íslendingabók-Landnámabók. Jakob Benediktsson gaf út. Reykjavík.

Íslensk fornrit II. 1933 Egils saga Skalla-Grímssonar. Sigurður Nordal gaf út. Reykjavík.

Íslensk fornrit VIII. 1939 Vatnsdæla saga m.m. Einar Ólafur Sveinsson gaf út. Reykjavík.

Íslensk Fornrit XI. 1950 Austfirðingasögur. Hrafnkels saga Freysgoða. Jón Jóhannesson gaf út. Hið isl. fornritafélag. Reykjavík.

Íslenskar þjóðsögur. 1978 Ólafur Davíðsson. Þorsteinn M. Jónsson bjó til prentunar. Bjarni Vilhjálmsson sá um útgáfuna. I Bindi. 3. útg. Reykjavík.

Íslenskar þjóðsögur og ævintýri. 1927 Safnað hefur saman Jón Árnason. I.3. Nákvæm eftirmynd af frumútgáfunni. Bindi. Reykjavík.

Íslenskar þjóðsögur og ævintýri. 1954 Safnað hefur saman Jón Árnason. Ný útgáfa. I Bindi. Reykjavík.

Ibid. 1964 Safnað hefur saman Jón Árnason. Ný útgáfa. II Bindi. Reykjavík.

Jarðabók Árna Magnússonar og Páls Vídalíns. 1918-1921 II. bindi. Kaupmannahöfn.

Jarðabók Árna Magnússonar og Páls Vídalíns. 1925 og 1927 IV. bindi. Kaupmannahöfn.

Jarðabók Árna Magnússonar og Páls Vídalíns. 1930 IX. bindi. Kaupmannahöfn.

Johansen, Øyvind. 1986 „Religion and Archaeology: Revelation or Empirical Research."Words and Objects. Towards a Dialogue between Archaeology and Religion. Ed. Gro Steinsland. Oslo.

Jónsson, B. 1894 „Rannsóknir í ofanverðu Árnesþingi sumarið 1893." Árbók Hins íslenska fornleifafélags 1894. Reykjavík.

Jónsson, G. 1900 „Fornleifar í Hörgsholti." Árbók Hins íslenska fornleifafélags 1900. Reykjavík.

[Jónsson], Þorleifur. 1954 Þorleifur í Hólum. Ævisaga. Reykjavík.

Järrestad. Huvudgård i centralbyggd. 2003. Red. Bengt Söderberg. Riksantikvarieämbetet. Arkeologiska undersökningar, Skrifter No 51. Malmö.

Kaliff, Anders. 1997 Grav och kultplats. Eskatologiska föreställningar under yngre bronsålder och äldre järnålder i Östergötland. Aun 24. Uppsala.

Kortabók 2000 Road atlas 1:300 000. Mál og menning. Reykjavík.

Kristjánsdóttir, Steinunn. 1998 Geirsstaðir í Hróarstungu – stórbýli á landnáms- og söguöld. Niðurstöður fornleifarannsóknar Minjasafns Austurlands sumarið 1997. Skýrslur Minjasafns Austurlands.

Ibid. 2004 The Awakening of Christianity on Iceland. Discovery of a Timber Church and Graveyard at Þórarinsstaðir in Seyðisfjörður. Gotarc. Gothenburg Archaeological Theses. Series B, No. 31. Reykjavík.

Kristjánsdóttir, Unnur. 1994 „Völvuleiðið í Einholti." Skaftfellingur. 10. árg. 1994.

Kristoffersen, S. 1993 „Gård og gjenstandsmateriale - social sammenheng og økonomisk struktur." Arkeologiske skrifter fra Historisk Museum. Universitetet I Bergen. No. 7. Bergen.

Krogh, Knud J. 1975 „Seks kirkjur heima á Sandi." Mondul nr. 2. I. árg. Føroya Fornminnissavn. Torshavn.

Krogh, Knud & Jørgensen, J. Balslev. 1964 „Dette hus blev kaldt Tjodhilde kirke." Skalk 4. Århus.

Kålund, P.E. Kristian. 1985. Íslenskir sögustaðir II. Vestfirðingafjórðungur. Íslensk þýðing Haraldur Matthíasson. Reykjavík.

Lundqvist, Lars. 1991 „Undersökta skärvstenshögar i Västsverige." Arkeologi i Sverige. Ny följd 1. Stockholm.

Magnus, Bente & Myhre, Björn. 1986. Norges historie. Bind I. Forhistorien. Fra jegergrupper til høvdingsamfunn. Red. Knut Mykland. Østerås.

Magnússon, Þór. 1973 „Sögualdarbyggð í Hvítárholti." Árbók Hins íslenska fornleifafélags 1972. Reykjavík.

Nielsen, Ann-Lili. 1996 „Hedniska kult - och offerhandlingar i Borg." Religion från stenålder till medeltid. Red. K. Engdahl och Aders Kaliff. Riksantikvarieämbetet. Arkeologiska undersökningar. Skrifter nr 19. Linköping.

Nilsson, Lena. 2003. „Blóta, Sóa, Senda. Analys av djurben." Järrestad. Huvudgård í centralbyggd. Red. Bengt Söderberg. Riksantikvarieämbetet. Arkeologiska undersökningar, Skrifter No 51. Malmö.

Nordahl, Else. 1988 Reykjavík from the archaeological point of view. Aun 12. Uppsala.

Nordal, Sigurður. 1940 Hrafnkatla. Studia islandica 7. Reykjavík.

Näström, Britt-Mari. 2004. „Vid gudarnas bord – heliga platser och offerplatser i fornskandinavisk religion." Mellom himmel og jord. Foredrag fra et seminar om religionsarkeologi. Isegren 31. januar – 2. februar 2002. Red. lene Melheim, Lotte Hedeager & Kristin Oma. Oslo Archaeological Series Nr. 2. Oslo.

Ohlsson, Tom. 1976 The Löddeköpinge Investigation. The Settlement at Vikhögsvägen. Meddelanden från Lunds universitets historiska museum 1975-1976. Lund.

Ólafsson, Guðmundur. 1980 „Grelutóttir. Landnámsbær á Eyri við Arnarfjörð." Árbók Hins íslenska fornleifafélags 1979. Reykjavík.

Ibid. 1992 „Jarðhús að Hjálmstöðum í Laugardal. Rannsókn 1983-1985." Árnesingur II. Selfossi.

Ibid. 2001 Fornt jarðhús í Breiðuvík og fleiri minjar á Tjörnesi. Rannsókn vegna vegagerðar. Rannsóknarskýrslur 2000. 7. Þjóðminjasafn Íslands. Reykjavík.

Olausson, Michael. 1995 Det inneslutna rummet – om kultiska hägnader, fornborgar och befästa gårdar i Uppland från 1300 f Kr till Kristi födelse. Riksantikvarieämbetet. Arkeologiska undersökningar. Skrifter 9. Stockholm.

Olsen, Olov. 1966 Hørg, hov og kirke. Historiske og arkeologiske vikingetidsstudier. København.

Ólsen, B.M. & Bruun, D. 1903 „Hörgdalsfundurinn." Árbók Hins íslenska fornleifafélags 1903. Reykjavík.

Osborn, M. 1983 Beowulf. A Verse Translation with Treasures of the Ancient North. London.

Rafnsson, Sveinbjörn. 1971 „Kirkja frá síðmiðöldum að Varmá." Árbók Hins ísl. fornleifafélags 1970. Reykjavík.

Renfrew, C & Bahn, P. 1991 Archaeology. Theories, Methods and Practice. London.

Roussell, Aage. 1943 „Islands gudehove." Forntida gårdar i Island. Meddelanden från den nordiska arkeologiska undersökningen i Island sommaren 1939. Red. M. Stenberger. København.

Sawyer, Peter H. 1985 Kungar och vikingar. Norden och Europa 700l-1100. Malmö.

Schön, Ebbe. 1988 „Smeden i folktron." Mest om järn. Svenska turistföreningens årsbok 1989. Uppsala.

Snæsdóttir, Mjöll 1992 „Jarðhýsið á Stóruborg undir Eyjafjöllum." Árbók Hins íslenska fornleifafélags 1991. Reykjavík.

Stefánsson, Jón. 1898 „Leiði Guðrúnar Ósvífursdóttur." Árbók Hins ísl. fornleifafélags 1898. Reykjavík.

Steffensen, Jón. „Kumlafundur að Gilsárteigi í Eiðaþinghá." Árbók Hins ísl. fornleifafélags 1959. Reykjavík.

Steinsland, Gro. 1993 „Nordisk hedendom" Viking og Hvidekrist. Norden og Europa 800 - 1200. Nordisk ministerråd i samarbejde med Europarådet. Sverige.

Stenberger, M. 1943 „Ísleifsstaðir, Borgarfjarðarsýsla." Forntida gårdar i Island. Meddelanden från den nordiska arkeologiska undersökningen i Island sommaren 1939. Red. Mårten Stenberger. København.

Sveinbjarnardóttir, Guðrún. 1986 Rannsók á Kópavogsþingstað. Kópavogur.

Sveinsson, Einar. Ó. 1948 Landnám í Skaftafellsþingi. Skaftfellingarit. II. bindi. Skaftfellingafélagið gaf út. Reykjavík.

Söderberg, Bengt. 2003. „Järnålderns Järrestad. Bebyggelse, kronologi, tolkningsperspektiv." Järrestad. Huvudgård i centralbygd. Red. Bengt Söderberg. Riksantikvarieämbetet. Arkeologiska undersökningar, Skrifter No 51. Malmö.

The Book of the Settlement of Iceland. Translated from the original Icelandic of Ari the Learned. Rev. T. Ellwood. Kendal 1898.

The poetic Edda: the mythological poems. Trandlated from the Icelandic with an Introduction and Notes by Henry Adams Bellows. New York, 2004.

The complete Sagas of the Icelanders; including 49 tales. IV. General ed. Viðar Hreinsson. Reykjavík 1997.

The complete Sagas of the Icelanders; including 49 tales. V. General ed. Viðar Hreinsson. Reykjavík 1997.

Vésteinsson, Orri. 1998 Fornleifarannsókn á Neðra Ási í Hjaltadal 1998. Fornleifastofnun Íslands. Reykjavík 1998.

Ibid. 2005. „Samantekt." Archaeological investigation at Sveigakot 2004. Ed. Orri Vésteinsson. Fornleifastofnun Íslands [ses]. FS265-00215. Reykjavík.

Vigfússon, Sigurður. 1881 „Rannsókn á *blót*húsinu að Þyrli og fleira í Hvalfirði og um Kjalarnes." Árbók Hins íslenska fornleifafélags 1880-81. Reykjavík.

Ibid. 1882 „Um *hof* og *blót*siðu í fornöld." Árbók Hins íslenska fornleifafélags 1882. Reykjavík.

Ibid. 1883 „Rannsókn um Vestfirði 1882 einkanlega í sambandi við Gísla Súrssonar sögu." Árbók Hins íslenska fornleifafélags 1883. Reykjavik.

Ibid. 1885 „Rannsókn í Borgarfirði 1884." Árbók Hins íslenska fornleifafélags 1884-85. Reykjavík.

Vikingerne ved Volga. 1981 Ibn Fadlans rejsebeskrivelse rsumeret, deloversat og kommenteret af Jørgen Bæk Simonsen. Århus.

Vilhjálmsson, Vilhjálmur Ö. 1996 „Gårde og kirke på Stöng i Þjórsárdalur. Reflektioner på den tidligeste kirkeordning og kirkeret på Island." Nordsjøen. Handel, religion og politikk. Kamøyseminaret 1994 og 1995. Red. Jens Flemming Krøger og Helge-Rolf Naley. Stavanger.

Zuesse, E.M. 1987 The Encyclopedia of Religion. Ed. Mircea Eliade. S.v. "Ritual," vol. 12: 405-422. New York.

Þjóðminjalög nr. 107, 20. maí 2001. Þingskjal 1490, 126.

Þorkelsson, Magnús. [1985] Nokkrar hugleiðingar um fornleifarannsóknir að Kirkjubóli við Skutulsfjörð og á Búðasandi í Hvalfirði sumrin 1984 og 1985. Manuskript.

Þórðarson, Matthías. 1936 „Rannsókn nokkurra forndysja, o.fl. Dys í Álaugarey í Hornafirði."Árbók Hins íslenska fornleifafélags 1933-36. Reykjavík.

Ibid. 1943 „Skeljastaðir, Þjórsárdalur." Forntida gårdar i Island. Meddelanden från den nordiska arkeologiska undersökningen i Island sommaren 1939. Red. Mårten Stenberger. København.

Ibid. 1932 „Bólstaður við Álftarfjörð. Skýrsla um rannsókn 1931." Árbók Hins ísl. fornleifafélags 1932. Reykjavík 1932.

Örnefnaskrá. Árnanes. Skrásetjari: Stefán Einarsson, prófessor. Manuskript. Örnefnastofnun slands.

Østmo, Mari. 2004. „Symbolikk I landskapet – grenser, kosmologi og ritualer." Mellom himmel og jord. Foredrag fra et seminar om religionsarkeologi. Isegren 31. januar – 2. februar 2002. Red. Lene Melheim, Lotte Hedeager & Kristin Oma. Oslo. Archaeological Series Nr. 2. Oslo.

Author's address
Archaeological Office
Ægisgötu 10, IS -101
Reykjavík, Iceland
bjarni@fornstofan.is

Acta Archaeologica vol. 79, 2008, pp 185-207
Printed in Denmark • All rights reserved

Copyright 2008
ACTA ARCHAEOLOGICA
ISSN 0065-101X

THE MEANING OF WOMENS' ORNAMENTS & ORNAMENTATION
EASTERN MIDDLE SWEDEN IN THE 8ᵀᴴ AND EARLY 9ᵀᴴ CENTURY

JOHAN CALLMER.

1. INTRODUCTION

A common point of departure for many studies of the spiritual culture of the later prehistory of Scandinavia is its alleged similarity in various parts of this ethno-geographical unit and its alleged conservatism at least from the 5th and 6th centuries to the end of paganism. Notwithstanding excellent work on source-criticism this is probably still the effect of the total domination of West Nordic (read Icelandic) written sources. This is a most unlikely position, which is not supported by data from other relevant disciplines. For some reasons scholars treating the question of the pre-Christian religion (or religions) in Scandinavia cannot rid themselves of this prejudice. Most strikingly place-name studies have revealed how i.a. gods, hardly known from the West were very important in the East. Also from a general cultural historical point of view it is improbable that there were no regional variations and little historical change. Certainly there were differences in emphasis, patterns and symbols over time and in different cultural provinces. Furthermore we have good reason to count with differences between social strata. Especially the highest social stratum, the aristocrats, and the lowest, the serfs, are unlikely to have shared identical beliefs. Equally important are the differences between the spiritual culture of masculine and feminine gender. The masculine social and cultural role was certainly predominantly linked to a certain proportion of the system of beliefs and the feminine role had another spiritual emphasis. This does not mean that there were not parts of the same religion, which had a central meaning for both gender roles.

2. THE FEMININE SOCIAL AND CULTURAL ROLE AND OLD NORSE RELIGION

In this contribution I will try to concentrate on the feminine social and cultural role. As we shall see, this is a most natural choice because there is a very real dearth of relevant archaeological sources for the masculine side during the period of interest in Eastern Middle Sweden. Consequently it is necessary to make some remarks considering the character of the feminine gender role in the Late Iron age of Scandinavia. The feminine role was certainly a complex one as many scholars have pointed out starting with pioneering studies by Hjörungdal and Lillehammer (Hjörungdahl 1991, Lillehammer (1985)1996, cf. also Arwill-Nordhbladh 1994, Dommasnes 1994 and Gräslund 1997). The feminine gender, i.e. the chosen sex role, was elementary in a society, in which the maintenance of the family line and kin was of outmost importance. It is most improbable that there was anything more essential in this archaic society than the reproduction of the lineage. Producing heirs and as second choice heiresses was the central point in this sexual role. There was however more to this complex role. Although Old Norse society in many ways can be looked upon as a patriarchal society, it is probably well motivated to look for patterns and strategies to ensure a relative equilibrium in the relationship between the two roles. An important basis for this was the social territory exclusively reserved for the feminine gender and a vast number of different activities connected to it. The sexual division of labour and of various cultural practices from simple practical household tasks to ritual was fundamental. This division was not directly motivated by the reproductive role of the feminine gender but created to establish a balanced relationship and a dimension of integrity. Under special circumstances, like the absence or the incapability of the masculine part, the scope of the feminine role could be considerably expanded and could encroach on the masculine domain (Steinsland & Meulengracht Sörensen 1994 p. 117). Certainly there was a socially recognized limit to this but where exactly it was fixed was probably the result of the individual relationship between the two gender roles. With the feminine role also went a special gift to transcend the limits of human experience (Strömbäck 1935, Solli 2002). This was perhaps not something just anybody of the feminine gender could perform. It was limited to certain individuals but it seems likely that the potential to develop this competence was always there. These individuals could see into the future and they could also see and communicate with the dead: So much for the role of the individual. All these aspects of social life were modified in married status by the influence and the activity of the lineage on both sides. It was partly regulated by practice connected with marriage itself.

The different character of masculine and feminine life means, according to the West Nordic (Icelandic) written sources, that religion had another emphasis and that the pantheon of the feminine gender was differently structured. It does seem likely that the vanir gods were more central to the feminine aspect of religion than the masculine. The association with the aesir is weaker. Although the authenticity of this accentuated dichotomy between vanir and aesir can be questioned the difference in thematic spheres connected with the gods is there Turville-Petre 1964 pp. 156-179, Schjödt 1991). The general importance of the vanir gods is well demonstrated by their frequent occurrence in pre-Christian place-names. A consequence of this special feminine emphasis on the vanir domain is also the more differentiated and closer association with the alfs, the diser and the giants. In the feminine aspect of the pre-Christian religion the giants appear in a more positive context: they are attractive (beautiful?), intelligent, skilled and they possess very valuable and desirable things. The importance of the cult of giants and giantesses has been stressed by Steinsland (1986). She argues that the West Nordic written sources throughout underrate the religious significance of giants. She also touches on the great significance of other supernatural potent beings like diser and alfs.

3. CHRONOLOGICAL AND SPATIAL LIMITS OF THE STUDY

When we turn to the region of our study, Eastern Middle Sweden, we have virtually no written sources at all. The Vita Ansgarii has, as you could expect, little to say about pagan religion. Runic inscriptions are few and of little importance for the period. Traces of grave ritual are documented in great numbers but relatively little analytical work has been done in this field. Settlements could also provide interesting contexts but the number of excavations is still very limited. Religious sites with special deposition practices do exist but they have only recently been recognized (Andersson 2006). What remains is a relatively rich find material of artefacts not seldom with figural ornamentation, from the graves. The relevant source material is above all iconographic. I have chosen to concentrate on a relatively short period: the second half of the 8th century and around A.D. 800. This choice is partly motivated by a concern to recognize change. Of course relatively short spells of time mean that we come closer to an understanding of processes in the past in relationship to the experience of the individual. Since it is an ambition to look for contrast also the first half of the 8th century and the beginning of the 9th century will be shortly considered. The main phase is of considerable interest because we are at the threshold of the Viking Period. It is also the time when the earlier types of animal ornamentation and iconography are more or less completely discontinued. It is a time with radical changes in the material culture. Later material culture has much less regional variation. With regard to material culture we are consequently located between two rather different worlds.

I have chosen to consider the region of Eastern Middle Sweden including the historical provinces (landskap) of Gästrikland, Uppland, Västmanland, Närke, Södermanland and the Åland Islands (Fig. 1). In the 8th century this region developed a special variant of the Scandinavian material culture. This distinctive character comprises both special forms and a special ornamental art. Closely related artefacts are also found in the province of Östergötland and along the coast of the Baltic down to northeastern Scania including the island of Öland but not Gotland (with a few exceptions). This is a most attractive region since we have at our disposal an unusually large source material thanks to many industrious excavators-archaeologists. Most finds are as already stated grave

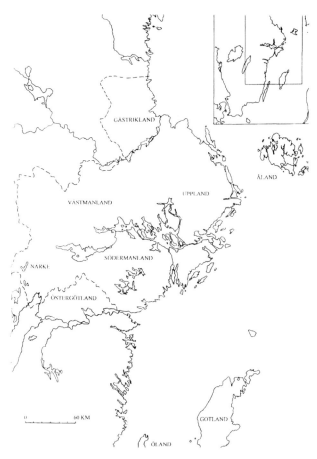

Fig. 1. Eastern Middle Sweden: the boundaries of the region studied.

finds but there are also a few stray finds.

My ambition, and this is also a methodologically important stand, is to put together all ornamentation whatsoever from this chronological phase and from this region in the database. This means that I have not just arbitrarily chosen some striking specimens. It is more important to consider the, until now, known part of the lost totality. For practical reasons I will however not describe the material in the database in any detail in this communication.

As already stated we will discuss a material almost exclusively related to the feminine sphere of society. How come? In order to be able to understand this we must look back in time a little. After the vitality of Salin's style I animal ornamentation with style II becomes increasingly monotonous and stereotype. In the 7th century begins a gradual shift away from a more or less equal representation between feminine and masculine artefacts and even sometimes-masculine dominance of ornamenta-

tion. This process continues throughout the 8th century and already by the middle of the 8th century animal ornamentation on men's equipment was more or less completely abandoned. A rich man's grave outfit with plenty of ornamental artefacts like Valsgärde 6 was still possible to bring together in the early 8th century (though we may maintain that a substantial part of the outfit in this grave was produced up to a generation earlier) (Arwidsson 1942B). Animal ornamentation in the masculine sphere was almost totally gone on weapons, armour (helmets), belts, girdles and bandoliers but lingered on almost exclusively on some bridles, of which we have fine examples from the famous graves Valsgärde 13 (unpublished) and Vendel II and VII (Stolpe&Arne 1912). Why men on the Scandinavian mainland chose to appear without the magnificent animal decoration in the 8th century is little known. On Gotland ornamentation on male attributes stayed on for a little longer. International trends should not be overlooked however. On the continent the development within the Late Merovingian and Carolingian state and among Saxons and Frisians as well as on the British Isles is very similar. Only in the late 8th century the Tassilo-chalice style and somewhat later the Carolingian plant ornamentation reappear on men's equipment.

4. FEMALE DRESS JEWELLERY IN THE FIRST HALF OF THE 8TH CENTURY

In the 8th century the feminine display dress is the context of the bronze (rarely silver) jewellery on which animal ornament is found (Fig. 2). However first considering the situation in the first half of the century we may conclude that the use of animal ornament is restricted. The standard jewellery set is composed of a button-on-bow fibula, two oval fibulae, two armlets and beads. The button-on-bow fibula was signalling high social rank in local society. Functionally it held together a cape of fine wool cloth over the shoulders, an integral part of a standardized ideal dress depicted on figure foils and cast figurines of the 7th and 8th centuries. Surprisingly the button-on-bow fibulae of the first half of the 8th century largely lack animal ornamentation and the fields with garnets on the head plate and the foot are rectangular and small. The single element of animal ornament is the two bird-of-prey heads set symmetrically on the footplate. This is a stereotype ornamental element brought on from the relief brooches

Acta Archaeologica

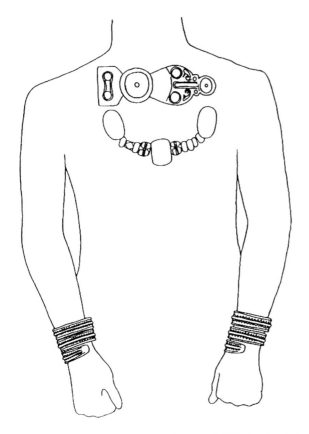

Fig. 2.The standard feminine dress set in Eastern Middle Sweden during the first half of the 8th century.

of the Migration period. There are also a small number of button-on-bow fibulae in Eastern middle Sweden with animal ornaments (Arwidsson's style D) but they are in my opinion rather imports from the south. The second component in the jewellery set is the oval fibulae carried in pairs. They are small and it is unlikely that they had the carrying function typical of the classical Viking Period oval fibulae. The oval fibulae in this region either completely lack ornamentation or have a simple non-figurative decoration: edge line, simple dividing line and bull's eyes. The shape is often not symmetrical but slightly egg like. On the breast, where the oval fibulae were set, also a collier of glass and occasionally rock crystal and bronze beads was carried.

The third component in the jewellery set is band-shaped armlets of bronze or occasionally silver (Ørsnes 1966 p. 166). The armlets never have decoration of animal character but only central and lateral ridges and geometrical stamp impressions. Around A.D. 700 we still

find some armlets with animal ornamentation but they are then soon gone. With the notable exception of Gotland later Scandinavian armlets of the 8th century and of the Viking Period never display animal ornament. In addition to these button-on-bow fibulae, oval fibulae, armlets and beads there are a few round pendants and bead spacers featuring dragon heads plus interlace or a simple linear pattern. Functionally these bead spacers should rather be interpreted as decorative dress applications. It should also be pointed out that combs, which obviously play an important role in the visual display of the social role, with only one exception lack animal ornament completely with only one exception (from a high status male grave). It could have posed no problem to let animal ornament free on the broad connection plates of the combs or on the open fields and the terminals of the arm rings but it was not done. This must have a special meaning. Without going into details of ideological and religious interpretation yet, we may conclude that animal ornament does not play an important role as decoration on visible dress items in Eastern Middle Sweden in the first half of the 8th century.

5. FEMALE DRESS JEWELLERY IN THE SECOND HALF OF THE 8TH CENTURY

In the second half of the 8th century this pattern of display changes, perhaps not radically, but all the same significantly (Fig. 3). As already stated for the first half of the century, the masculine sphere is almost completely devoid of artefacts with animal ornaments. Weapons and equipment lack ornaments completely. Equipment like mounts and buckles and even masculine fibulae not even feature animal heads. The feminine dress jewellery is now much richer than in the first half of the century. More than triple the amount of bronze is invested in a full dress set. Among the dress items there is both continuity and discontinuity in forms and ornament. The button-on-bow fibula is much bigger than before reaching almost double the size of the earlier representatives of this type. The variant typical of the region is almost completely lacking animal ornament and is decorated with a monotonous chequer pattern. A small number of fibulae feature animal ornament in local variants of Arwidsson's style E. Also the two bird's heads on the footplate are no longer distinct. Only relics of the eyes remain as decorative but-

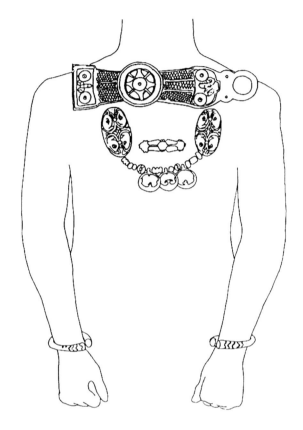

Fig. 3. The standard feminine dress set in Eastern Middle Sweden during the second half of the 8th century and the time ca. A.D. 800.

tons. The oval fibulae worn in pairs have also grown considerably in size they are no longer plain but have a rich animal decoration. The oval space free for decoration is either divided lengthwise, crosswise or symmetrically in oval medallion fields. The most common division is into four medallions. Each field or medallion features an animal figure, either a quadruped or a bird. Sometimes the jewellery set also comprises an equal armed fibula (Nerman 1952). These fibulae often display animal elements like limbs and torsos but never a complete animal. Animal heads and masks are extremely rare. In the second half of the 8th century ornamental pendants are among the most common types of jewellery. The vast majority of these pendants have a pelta or strike-a-light shape (Almgren 1955). Often there is additional animal ornamentation. Beside the pelta shaped pendants we also encounter different circular and lunula shaped pendants. The "bead spacers" are still there and very often feature rich animal ornamentation (Ørsnes 1966 pp.175-176). The jewellery

set is completed with armlets of massive bronze. The band shaped armlets are gone and we meet open armlets with thick ends and very often with half-moon shaped stamps set with alternating orientation in transversal lines giving the ornament a distinct, wavy look (Ibidem p.167). As already stated these armlets never feature animal ornament. Beads are of course carried and combs always have non-figurative ornaments.

6. FEMALE DRESS JEWELLERY IN THE EARLY 9TH CENTURY

In the 9th century there is considerable change. The button-on-bow fibulae become obsolete and the local oval and equal armed fibulae are replaced by Scandinavian standard jewellery distributed all over Northern Europe from Jutland to the Åland Islands and from Schleswig to Lofoten (cf. Petersen 1928). Pendants are seldom carried, whereas the armlets slightly changed are still used. With this dominance of cosmopolitan forms we have no possibility to discuss regional patterns with reference to the ornamentation of artefacts any more.

7. FIGURATIVE ORNAMENTATION AND MEANING

I will now turn to the ideological and religious message of the artefacts of the female sphere. This of course means that we are convinced that ornaments are intentional and significant. It is consequently meaningful to try to decode the ornaments. We shall proceed along the path of classical iconographic method sensu Panoffsky. Consequently we shall first have a close look at the ornaments themselves. In the second phase we shall try to find plausible interpretations of themes and attributes. In the third phase we shall try to generalize the information in the ornaments. We shall here concentrate on the animal ornaments. Beside the figurative ornamentation (complete or fragmentary bodies) we shall also look for signs and symbols. Had our literary sources been geographically relevant, complete and contemporary we could have hoped for a, if not total, then very far reaching reconstruction. Our sources also seem to be socially and sexually biased. I stress this since comparison with literary sources is the only possibility to link up with the Old Norse religion specifically. General analogies e.g. from other religions could also be sought, but they must be considered more

Fig. 4. Lunula-shaped and cirkular pendants of the 8th century featuring Migration Period design patterns.

Fig. 5. Dress mount from Berga and Folkesta, Tumbo parish, province of Södermanland with close links to bracteate design of the Migration Period.

unreliable. We are not prepared to use our methods as a quasi explanation like Leroi-Gourhan (1965), when he falsely denied having used analogies in the deciphering of the ornamentation of Lascaux. It is consequently a folly to think that all this ornamentation with its background in pre-Christian religion and ideology will be fully explained and understood. However, since so little has been achieved until now in the study of the pre-Christian iconography we find it likely that some positive results can be reached.

When we now cautiously turn to the interpretation of the figurative ornamentation of the display dress metalwork we should start with a division into different motive spheres: 1. traditional elements and stereotypes of the pre-Christian religion and mythology, 2. the quasi-Christian/ pagan sphere of the compact animals, non-aggressive birds and related symbols, 3. the beheaded animal, 4. the Christian motives and symbols. This division is of a general heuristic character and cannot be given its full background and motivation here for lack of space. Below the arguments for each group will however be clarified.

7.1. Traditional Elements and Stereotypes of the Pre-Christian Religion and Mythology

The first group of motives is strongly bound to traditional elements of the pre-Christian religion of considerable antiquity. It is in this connection of great interest that we can point at a number of signs of a keen interest by the 8th century population in the material culture and especially the iconography of the Migration Period. There are a number of fragments of Migration Period ornamental metalwork converted and exposed in jewellery sets. Some other artefacts are presumably strongly influenced by Migration Period design like the singular fibula from Öja (Magnus 1999) and the sword pommel from the rich male grave at

Löta (Arwidsson 1942A p.108), both in the province of Södermanland. There are also circular pendants with St. John's crosses and lunula-shaped pendants clearly closely linking up with Migration Period bracteates and pendants (Fig. 4). Another striking example of this intimate knowledge of standard design patterns of the Migration period is an ornamental dress mount from Södermanland (Fig. 5). The mount features the well-known standard design of the migration Period C-bracteates with the masculine head (here frontal) and the beast/horse. Both the head and the animal have been rendered according to the conventions of the late eighth century. Anthropomorphic heads are always depicted en-face and the body of the beast is slit open in oval fields according to the local style E (sensu Arwidsson) variant. Special interest is connected with the massive armlets with thickening ends and stamp decoration forming wavy transversal lines. They very closely correspond to a well-known Migration Period neck ring type often produced in gold. Since we know that many Migration Period inhumation graves in Eastern Middle Sweden have been plundered at an early date like Danmark village, cemetery No. 100 in Danmark parish (unpublished; information from the excavator A. Wexell, M.A.), and Hemmet, Lovö parish (Lamm1973), both in Uppland, we may form the hypothesis that the fine metalwork in precious metals was important for the 8th century inhabitants of Eastern Middle Sweden and that it was actively sought for. These antiquities considerably contributed to the formation of the notion that there had been a past more glorious and richer than the present. In comparison the material culture of the early 8th century could appear rather poor and bleak. Through this intimate knowledge of a distant magnificent past the idea of the

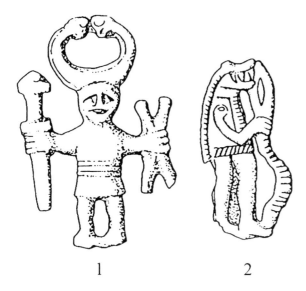

Fig. 6. Figurines with Migration Period connections from Ekhammar, Kungsängen parish, province of Uppland.

succession of ages and the dramatic decline and fall of the society of old was forcefully enhanced and given a central role in religion and myth. It is one of the main elements in the Ragnarok myth. The motive itself is a stereotype well known from other religions but possibly based on similar observations.

The links backward not only suggest this idea of the past but also an unchanged continuity from the past. Some other motives provide strong evidence that at least from ca. A.D. 600 very specific mythological traditions had continuously been of great cultural and religious importance. A very interesting example is the so-called guldgubber, obviously still vital around A.D. 800. We shall not look into this example of an almost unchanged stereotype. Instead we shall turn to the remarkable Ekhammar (Kungsängen parish, Uppland) find (Ringquist 1969). The two Ekhammar figurines (Fig. 6) stem from a rich cremation grave of the latest part of the 8th century. The two figurines are examples of a small number of virtually unchanged stereotypes created on the continent or in Southern Scandinavia in the late 5th or 6th centuries. One of the figurines holds a sword in one hand in a ceremonial pose and in the other hand two crosswise held spears. The headgear is crowned by corniform attachments with bird's head terminals. This motif has often been interpreted as a stereotype representation of Woden (cf. Hauck 1981). This interpretation has been repeated so many times that it has been considered a fact.

The mytho-religious character of the motif is obvious but the identification with Woden seems to be very uncertain. The pose of the figures is often very special, the unusual, curved lines rendering it an illusion of movement, perhaps dance. The weapons are always carried in a non-offensive way, clearly ceremonial. The figures are with two exceptions never one eyed. When this occurs (Björnhovda-very uncertain- and Uppåkra) the eye is only secondarily removed. This makes it likely that the one-eyedness was attributed to these artefacts only late when the original idea behind the motif was blurred. Another argument against the Woden-interpretation is that the headgear carried terminals with birds of prey heads. This circumstance makes it unlikely that they are representations of Hugin and Munin, the two ravens of Woden. It is most likely that the craftsmen behind the designs would be able to tell the characteristic difference between the picking bill of the Corvidae and the ripping beak of the Falconidae. Falconry with hawks and eagles was evidently widely practised among the local upper strata of society in Scandinavia. Difficulties to find a close and direct connection with Woden make it worthwhile to reconsider the interpretation suggested by B. Almgren (1948 p. 97). According to this scholar the motif was developed under strong influence of the emblemology of the Late Roman army where a special corps of cornuti existed. Consequently a mythological rather than a downright religious interpretation is to be preferred. A mythical warrior hero and helper of old, sometimes with a twin brother or a companion, whom we shall meet next, is a most likely interpretation. But for the iconographic material this myth is completely lost.

The other figurine in the grave context at Ekhammar is another stereotype very often appearing together with the horned figure. A bear mask and an animal torso, but human hands and limbs are standard characteristics. The Ekhammar figurine grips and bites a large snake. This combination with the snake is unique. In my opinion it is most unlikely that this is a rendering of the fatal combat between Thor and The Midgard worm at Ragnarok. In other renderings of the motif the bear man carries a lance and a sword. More convincing is an interpretation along the same lines as the preceding example. The figure has all the characteristics of a signifer, a standard bearer, of the Roman army. The non-divine character of the motif is also corroborated by its close connection with the other figure forming a special theme i.a. on stamped sheet decorations on scabbards and helmets. The most convincing interpretation is that of mythological warrior heroes of a more glorious past called upon to support men and ultimately women of later days. Were the two some sort of Mandrake and Robin figures of old days? Tales of the military power of the Empire must have been widely known several centuries later. It is very important to note that these motives like some other are appearing in a feminine milieu only when they have been abandoned in the masculine sphere.

Another but different example of motif continuity is presented by the birds of prey heads on the footplates of button-on–bow fibulae. Lateral animal heads are well known from the relief fibulae of the Migration Period, initially featuring both quadruped heads and bird's heads. Later the bird of prey head becomes the customary form. The bird connection of these prominent fibulae certainly has a long history, which should not be overlooked. The bird of prey is an important but ambiguous symbol of potency, power and strength. The bird of prey is connected to some Germanic gods as an alter ego or disguise, but they are also connected with giants and thurs. The feminine connection of these symbolic renderings of the bird of prey is problematic and cannot be easily solved but should be viewed from the perspective of its long tradition and its non-ethnic and cosmopolite connection.

The lateral bird's heads on the button-on-bow fibulae become much reduced in size in the Late Migration Period and in the early Vendel Period. They are not intimately connected with other design patterns on the fibulae and in the 7th century parallel to a dramatic shrinking of their size the bird's heads become indistinct and you can only guess their earlier place in the design. By the end of the 7th century and in the early 8th century there is a revitalisation of the bird's head element (Fig. 7). However, again in the late 8th century the bird's heads become indistinct. If this revitalisation of the design ca. A.D. 700 is a result of actual observations of Migration Period "antiques" is not possible to decide, but it is not unlikely.

One of the aims of this study is to ascertain if there is a special feminine ornamentation in the eighth century and around A.D. 800. The fact that masculine ornamentation is mainly lacking in our material makes this difficult and we have to use a retrospective method. The Ekhammar figurines definitely establish a link with a motif sphere, which in the preceding period was predominantly masculine.

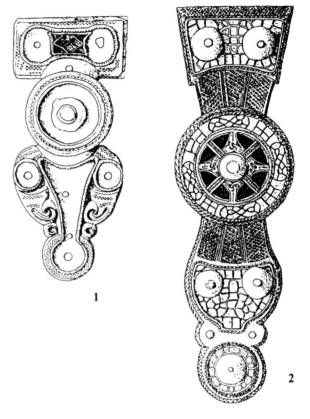

1

2

Fig. 7. Button-on-bow fibulae from the beginning (1) respectively the end of the 8th century (2) in Eastern Middle Sweden.

The female dress during our period of interest may include an ornamental dress mount. With very few exceptions these dress mounts are designed according to another stereotype from the masculine sphere (Fig. 8). The motif is an animal with a profile head with mighty jaws brandishing forceful teeth. A standard detail is the attack of smaller, lentiform animals, very often undisputable snakes, on the big animal. The shape of the body of the animal is elongated and spool-shaped (symmetrical). The stature of the body is remarkably stiff. The marked tail is always symmetrically designed with elements suggesting a bird's or fish-tail and symmetrically folded feet. The body of the animal may show off a uniform pattern suggesting a perfect and strong body (with interlace or garnet inlay) or enclosed minor lentiform animals attacking the intestines (?) of the big animal. Only two mounts from Eastern Middle Sweden have a deviating design featuring a bird of prey head and in one case an enclosed bird figure.

This motif is a well-known stereotype most frequently found on shields of the 7th century like Valsgärde 7 and

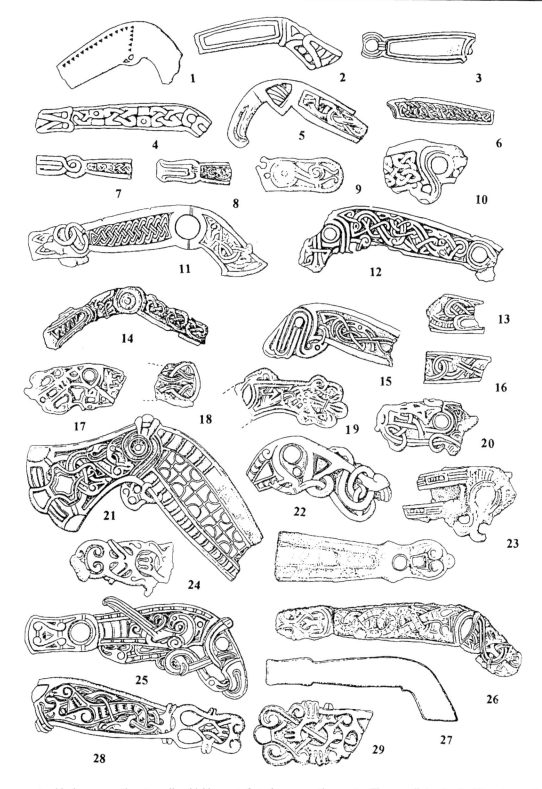

Fig. 8. Dress mounts with close connections to earlier shield mounts featuring an aquatic monster. They are all dated to the 8th century and come with the exception of No. 22 (Småland) from Eastern Middle Sweden.

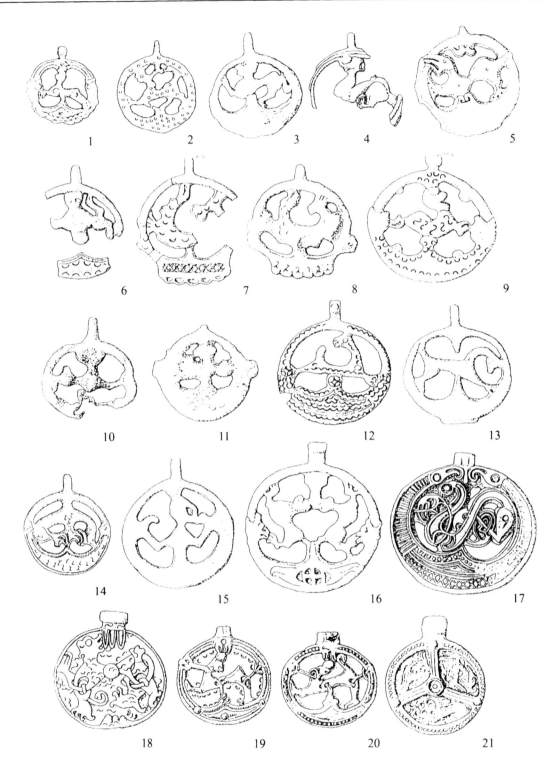

Fig.9. Pelta-shaped pendants with the compact animal motif. They come from Eastern Middle Sweden with the exception of Nos. 17 (Öland), 19-21 (Gotland).

Vendel I (Arwidsson 1977 Abb. 43, 49) and it is obviously not confined to Eastern Middle Sweden. A splendid example comes from the high status Sutton Hoo grave (Bruce Mitford 1978 Fig. 50). The connection with the defensive shield is highly interesting and suggests an apotropheic meaning. The animal itself must derive from a myth (lost to posterity) featuring a benign, resourceful and forceful monster. There is no direct clue to this being a god in animal disguise since the monster character is so strong. Dress mounts of this type were produced from ca. A.D. 700 to 800. The Anglo-Saxon shield mounts have recently been treated by Dickinson (2005) and she classifies them as type iii dragons. When she however arrives at the interpretation of mounts she rightly stresses the aquatic qualities of these and some other mounts. The Anglo-Saxon monuments thus support an interpretation of the animal as a underwater monster. This is most probably not Grendel's mother but the ideas behind it may have been similar.

Other stereotype elements of the long pre-Christian tradition, which we encounter in our phase of interest, are horse figurines and rider figurines. The rider figurines may have roots in the continental ornamental corpus of the 6th century. The horse fibulae may be Scandinavian and of slightly later date (Almgren 1940, Olsén 1945 p. 79 ff.). The strong connection between the horse and fertility cult is well known. There is an important observation to be made at this point. The motifs dealt with here were only as rare exceptions reproduced later than the beginning of the 9th century. The majority of this rich iconography becomes obsolete in the Viking Period proper. A long and strong mytho-religious tradition – certainly an iconographic complex- dies at that time. The Viking Period ornamentation has fundamentally a different character and probably as well another spiritual background. This change must be connected to considerable social transformations but above all to changes in the production and distribution of the ornaments. This is also the end point of some special and significant forms, most notably the most prestigious piece of feminine jewellery, the button-on-bow fibula. It had a great significance as a social signal indicating the dominant female in a social community of the extended family type. This symbol probably indicated considerable power in the lineage and the carriers were the only women who could give birth to a legitimate heir to a major farm or manor. This fibula is not replaced in the Viking Period. Only on Gotland the button-on bow

fibulae were produced until the late Viking Period.

7.2. The quasi-Christian/Pagan Sphere of the Compact Animals, Non-aggressive birds,and Related Symbols

We shall now turn to animal ornamentation, which does not link up closely with earlier traditions and stereotypes. These ornaments are predominantly found on oval fibulae, pelta shaped and circular pendants and some equal armed fibulae. The pelta shape or strike-a-light shape must be considered highly intentional and significant. Although it can be ascertained that the prosaic, real lyre shaped strike-a-light was never so exclusively connected with the masculine sphere that a taboo was in fact in force it can be maintained that the link to the feminine sphere was very weak. The symbolic significance of the making of fire is great in many cultural and religious systems. Very often making fire is a metaphor for reproduction and fertility (cf. Klintberg 1978 pp. 7-12). Since reproduction is where the masculine and the feminine spheres overlap the transfer of the symbol is possible and meaningful. Introduced in the middle of the 8th century pelta shaped rings and pendants of various types were in use as symbols continuously until the end of the pre-Christian religion. It is of great interest that the strike-a-light also had a strong symbolic meaning in the Finno-Ugric world. It remains unclear if this is the result of cultural influence or cultural parallelism.

On pelta shaped pendants there are frequently two animal heads laterally placed. This standard design is found both in an expressive variant and a highly stylised variant (Figs. 9-10, 12-14). This element constitutes a dramatic framework since the heads are frequently depicting the pelta shaped ring. A potential association of this motif is Jormundgandr, the Midgard worm, framing the world for better or worse. The inner apex of the pelta shape is also a very significant location, to which we have reason to come back soon. The opposite location sometimes carries the phi symbol. This symbol is frequently found on the garnet fields of the button-on-bow fibulae and on the Gotlandic late bracteates (from ca. A.D. 700). The inter-relationship between these two locations is the most significant on the pelta shaped pendants.

The central field of decoration of the pendants carries a motif – in almost all known cases- pertaining to five different design groups: 1. the compact animal, 2. the bird/s, 3. the rods, 4. the split pennant and 5. the triple bud.

The compact quadruped to begin with (Fig. 8) is only

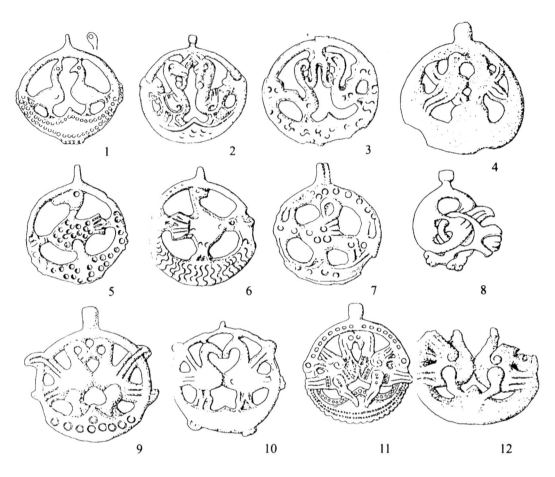

Fig.10. Pelta-shaped pendants with the bird motif from Eastern Middle Sweden except No. 3 (Östergötland).

once depicted doubled. Its oneness and identity is consequently important. The head is with one exception always depicted in profile. The head seldom has a crest. The mouth is marked, but not big. The eyes in most cases are big and globular. The body is powerfully built with a broad chest and muscular loins. The waist is slim. The feet are in a few cases fin like but mostly distinctly clawed. In the material from Eastern Middle Sweden the feet are not gripping. The pose of the animal is suggesting forceful movement forward. These animals have often been interpreted as lions and explained as copies of Carolingian and Anglo-Saxon lions of the Christian tradition (von Blankenburg 1943). It is most likely that the animal shape was transferred from that ornamental milieu but was their Christian meaning also brought over? An ambiguous case sets an animal-shaped brooch featuring a winged compact animal (Atterman 1935).

The second motif, the bird motif (Fig. 9), has a number of traits in common with the compact animal motif. The double projection with affronted birds is however dominating. The model must be sought among the non-aggressive birds. The birds have long necks and small heads with straight or duck like beaks. Also in other respects the birds have characteristics of the Anatidae. The wing feathers and the tail are sometimes long. Three closely design variants depict the birds affronted as if they were engaged in confrontation display. The feet are sometimes finned and in one case definitely clawed. In two cases there is a phi symbol in the upper inside location of the pelta ring. Similar designs are well known from the Byzantine and Langobard art on the continent from the 7th century on (Lother 1929, Reimbold 1983). Zoologically these birds are however not Anatidae but peacocks and thus belong to Christian iconography. We must assume that the peacock was known in the North already in the 8th century according to a striking bird fibula from Lindholm Hoeje

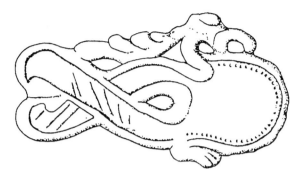

Fig.11. Bird-shaped fibula from Lindholm Höje, North Jutland dating
to the 8th century.

(Northern Jutland) (Fig. 11) (c.f. also the peacock in the
Gokstad ship). The birds on the pendants must, however,
rather bee understood as a mixture of the peacock motif
with the Anatidae. Birds of the latter affiliation begin to
appear already around A.D. 400. They are well known
from fifth and sixth century dress pins, Gotlandic memorial stones (7th century) and there is a bird figure in bone
of this kind in one of the "royal" barrows of Uppsala (ca.
A.D. 600). There are hardly any good arguments for a
derivation from outside Scandinavia. These clearly Anatidae birds are fundamentally different from other birds of
the Germanic Animal ornamentation, where birds of prey
are so usual. The Anatidae birds, as strong symbols, are
well known from the European Late Bronze Age. Strong
evidence for a special mytho-religious importance of the
Anatidae (bird figurines and finned feet) in the Finno-Ugric cultural milieu of North-eastern Europe in the Early
Middle Ages and later is important to consider (Golubeva
1979). There are few early examples from Finland and
Estonia but further east they are much more numerous.
In this predominantly Volga-Finnish milieu they are definitely closely connected with feminine gender and probably fertility, which also is a most likely interpretation of
the Scandinavian Anatide bird motif.

Apart from the figurative motives there are also three
distinct pictogram motives. The first of these I have arbitrarily called the rod motif (Fig. 12). It features a symmetrical duplicate representation of a rod like symbol. The
rod has mostly a certain volume but could in some cases
be reshaped as band form ribbons with or without animal
head terminals. In its typical form the rod is straight with
only the tip curved. The rods are centred on the inner apex
of the pelta shape and on the opposite position. In some

cases animal heads are shown biting rods. The rod motif is frequently used in Eastern Middle Sweden but it is
also known from Gotland where a large rod is sometimes
seen bundled with two shorter rods. The rod motif should
however probably be understood as a more widespread
stereotype symbol of the pre-Christian religion. On some
gold foils (guldgubber) female figures wield a stave or
rod of similar kind (Watt 1992 p. xx). Rods and staves as
attributes indicating power and competence are central.
In this case the interpretation as the seeress' (völva) stave
lies close at hand (Solli 2004). On other gold foils e.g.
from Klepp in Rogaland (Petersen 1955 fig. 101), on the
crest on a horse collar from Mammen in Jutland (Näsman
1991 p. 236) and on a carved stone from Kirk Michael,
Isle of Man we can observe female figurines carrying very
similar attributes with distinct plant character (Allium).
This connection strengthens the link with fertility and reproduction. Among later (9th and 10th century) symbolic
pendants of iron in Eastern Scandinavia the stave is very
common. For a probable link between the rod motif and
Freyja, see below.

Closely linked to the rod motif is the split pennant
symbol (Fig. 13). It is also consistently centred on the inner apex of the pelta shape. The pennants are not seldom
short and bi- or tripartite. In some cases they resemble
feet or impressions of feet of animals. Either the pennants
reach up to the opposite position of the pelta shape or a
rod shaped element joins the apex and the opposite position above. The motif is also known from Finnish chain
spacers (Salo 1997 pp. 349-350). The idea that something
or somebody can only be shown as footmarks or feet is
central.

The third pictogram motif also centred on the inner
apex of the pelta shape is the triple buds motif (Fig. 14).
Relatively small in size but very distinctly worked out
there is an ornament of three rounded elements forming
a triangular shape. In one case the top round element is
drawn out giving the apex a cross like impression. In several cases there is a similar triangular shape in the opposite position of the pelta ring. In one case there is a
rod connecting the two opposite positions. Two pendants
have motives connecting the split pennant design with the
three buds motif. A general connection with the sphere of
fertility seems to be likely.

When we now turn to the further discussion of the
mytho-religious character of these motifs, we should
once more remember what was initially maintained about

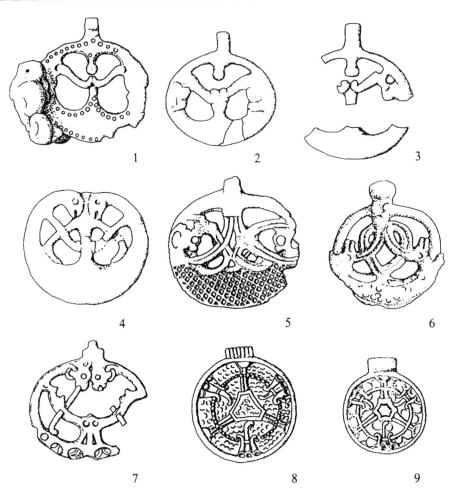

Fig.12. Pelta-shaped pendants with the rod symbol from Eastern Middle Sweden with the exception of Nos. 8 and 9 (Gotland).

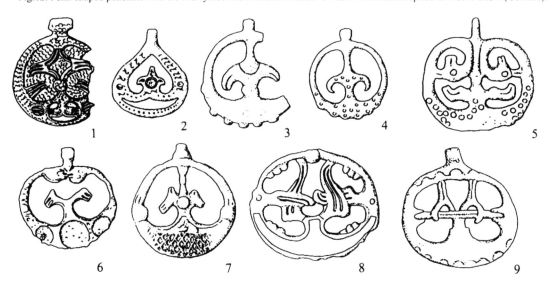

Fig.13. Pelta-shaped pendants with the split pennant symbol from Eastern Sweden with the exception of No. 8 (Gotland).

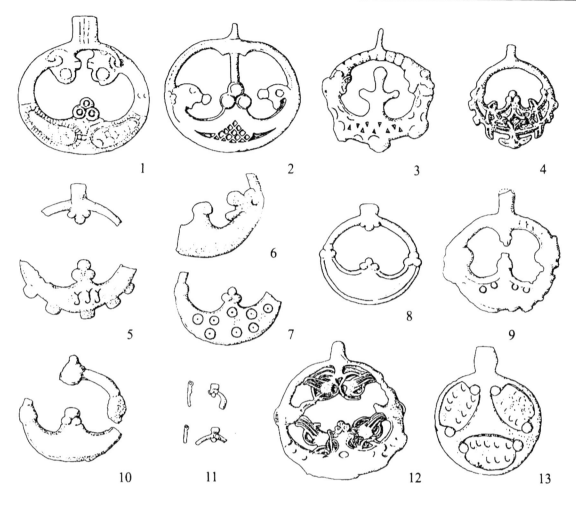

Fig.14. Pelta-shaped pendants with the triple buds symbol from Eastern Sweden.

the feminine gender role in the society of the period. Reproduction and fertility was central in this role. Exclusive feminine competences both in everyday life and in special religious practices and divination were also important. Only with the basis in this role could relative feminine power be constructed and maintained.

Considering the two animal motifs both have close connections with Christian iconography of the time. It is as well likely that this Christian symbolism was ambiguous and could as well be interpreted according to a traditional local religious conception. The three pictogram symbols strongly corroborate this idea. We should also add the phi symbol already commented on in connection with the button-on-bow fibulae and their meaning. The late Hayo Vierck in an exciting interpretation of the Hedeby miniature throne provides an interesting opening to the problem (Vierck 2002). This throne, which in our opinion

must date from ca. A.D. 800, is thus more than a hundred years older than the grave context in which it was found. The considerable age of the object is not surprising per se. The throne is an empty throne like a number of other throne or chair like pendants of the Viking period. The Hedeby throne has a, for us very interesting, decoration with two affronted Anatidae birds closely following the design on the pelta shaped pendants on the back and on the sides quadrupeds sharing all the characteristics of the compact animal (Fig. 15). The East Mediterranean if not Oriental character of the throne should be appreciated. The Hedeby throne is rather modelled on the throne of Salomon. The empty throne motif is also Mediterranean and Oriental and has a central place in Christian iconography (hetoimasia). Vierck interestingly enough does not agree with the somewhat one-eyed interpretation by Hauck of this pendant as the throne of Woden (Drescher&Hauck

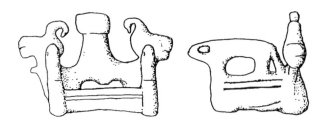

Fig.15. Throne-shaped pendant ca. A.D. 800 from a 10th century inhumation grave at Hedeby, Schleswig-Holstein.

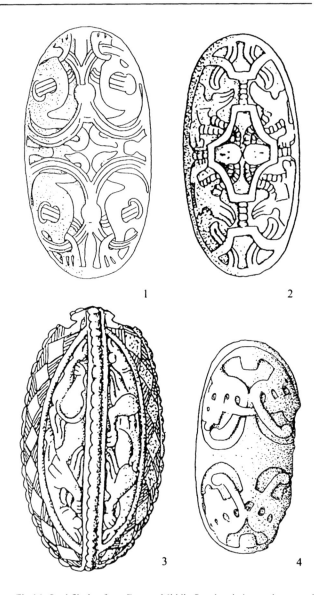

Fig.16. Oval fibulae from Eastern Middle Sweden dating to the second half of the 8th century and ca. A.D. 800.

1982). On the contrary Vierck argues that the empty throne cannot be the throne of Woden and suggests that the throne is the icon of a high seat of a völva. We can follow Vierck in his argumentation for an interpretation of this find in the sphere of feminine religiosity, but the seat of the völva must rather be understood as an ad hoc arrangement and not as an elaborate ceremonial piece of furniture with a fixed iconography. Further the absence of the holder of the throne must be explained. A tenable interpretation must comprise all the attributes discussed here. The Christian connection is more than likely but the meaning is adapted to the local ideology. We find it more reasonable to turn to one of the deities of reproduction and fertility. Whom we should chose of Freyr and Freyja is difficult to say. Three of the four pictograms certainly have a sexual meaning. The phi symbol could of course easily be interpreted as a picture of masculine genitalia and then be connected with the priapic aspect of Freyr. However, we must ask ourselves why a married female person should display a conspicuous pictogram with this particular meaning. A more likely interpretation is that the symbol is connected with the, for fertility, more important union of woman and man. Via the button-on-bow fibulae this symbol shows the feminine godly connection. The meaning of the three buds symbol is most likely similar. The connection with fertility and sexuality of the völva role is also likely at hand. That there was a connection between the völva role and seid and Freyja is known. On one of the Eschwege discs Freyja is probably depicted with a long stave (Sippel 1987). What was most interesting to find out from the seid was how the reproduction of the lineage would be in the future. The split pennant motif, if we agree to an interpretation of the design as the rendering of the feet or imprints of feet, links up neatly with the empty throne motif and the invisible deity.

This has something important to say about how frag-

ments of Christianity were adopted into the pre-Christian religion. In the beginning Christianity was introduced fragmented as stories and tales about strong religious power or magic. Christian symbols like the lion and the peacocks were consequently readily accepted as standard attributes of a major local deity. The empty throne motif, very likely, is another additional symbol transformed from the Christian iconography. A number of more unambiguous Christian motifs and symbols will be treated below.

The preceding discussion has only treated the pelta

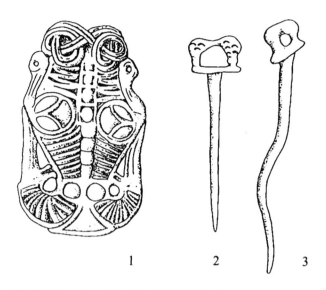

Fig.17. Examples of the beheaded animal motif in Eastern Middle Sweden.

shaped pendants. We shall not have the space necessary for treating other types of jewellery with a related ornamentation in detail but a few comments on oval fibulae, pins and keys will be included. The majority of the oval fibulae (Fig. 16), which we may assume are produced in Eastern Middle Sweden in the second half of the 8th and the very beginning of the ninth century, feature the compact animal and the bird motives. Especially the bird motif follows closely the design on the pendants. The compact animal also generally has great similarity with the animals on the pendants. It is however more usual that the head has a crest and the mouth in some cases is beak like. The lion prototype is corroborated by the occurrence of a realistic tail. The oval fibulae in grave 655 of the Birka cemeteries shows examples of compact animals reshaped according to some style E principles (Jansson 1985 pp.19-20). Among the oval fibulae there is also one example of the rod symbol being used as the main ornament. A number of oval fibulae have the crouching beast design so common in Southern Scandinavia. The majority of these finds should be interpreted as imports to eastern Middle Sweden. As already pointed out, the ovoid shape of the oval fibulae perhaps gives the strongest link to fertility symbolism.

In Eastern Middle Sweden pins with animal ornaments are rare compared to Southern Scandinavia. Whether or not they are imports is impossible to decide. The bird motif is however represented in a form, which

closely follows the design on the pendants (cf. Fig. 10). In Southern and Western Scandinavia bronze keys commonly with animal ornaments very similar to the animals discussed here are used (Almgren 1955). The majority of the designs are however definitely different from the eastern ones. They lack almost completely in Eastern Middle Sweden and the few examples found there (e.g. in the Birka cemeteries) are imports. Consequently we can maintain that the animal ornamentation on the oval fibulae and pins follows the same lines as the pendants and can be interpreted correspondingly.

7.3. The Beheaded Animal

The standard animal ornamentation on oval fibulae in the early and mid 8th century in Southern Scandinavia is the crouching beast. This is almost always a complete animal with four limbs and a head with two eyes and jaws. As just pointed out this animal does not appear to be part of the regional ornamental motives of Eastern Middle Sweden. The oval fibulae made in Eastern Middle Sweden feature other designs and the non-figurative ornamentation of the preceding period is sometimes still applied in the second half of the 8th century. The equal armed fibulae of this region (Nerman 1952) are carriers of animal ornamentation but they never feature complete animals. On the contrary they consequently contain parts of cut up animal bodies (cf. Jennbert 2004 pp. 191-4). Mostly there are limbs and chests. The head is either missing (most frequently) or occurs separately. This observation does not stand isolated. Ornamental animals with missing heads occur also in several other connections (Fig. 17). The motif is also known from Gotland. In some cases the cut throat is deliberately marked. The three buds symbol, discussed in connection with the pelta shaped pendants, is connected with this motif in a number of cases. Here I will only point out that the main theme in this iconographic sphere is the sacrifice. Since the head in the perception also of most Early Medieval traditions, non-Christian and Christian, is the location of identity, power and of wisdom the sacrifice of the head may be the ultimate form of the pagan sacrifice. The important but poorly understood Mimir myth should also be compared. The supreme wisdom of Mimir is inherent in the head and Woden exploits this source of deep knowledge. Since the physical character of Mimir is completely unknown we cannot exclude that this theme is connected to the ornamental motif of the beheaded animal. Since Christian motives were transferred to Eastern

Middle Sweden already in this pre-Viking phase the potential link with the Christian John the Baptist motif must be an open question.

7.4. The Christian Motives and Symbols

Several scholars have discussed the prehistory in Eastern Scandinavia of Christian ideas and motifs if not a complete Christian ideology has been suggested (for Gotland cf. Nerman 1941). The historical sources seem to indicate that the first visit to Western Scandinavia, to Jutland, by Willibrord ca. A.D. 700 was not followed up by the Western Church until the mission of St. Ansgar. There is however little reason to think that the Christianisation process can be followed in the few written sources. Holmquist (1975), Vierck (1984) and Hyenstrand (1996 pp. 107-119) have argued the gradual transfer and acceptance of elements of Christianity and Christian culture. Holmquist argued the presence of a strong Christian influence and a mission mainly from his observations that the crosswise division of ornamental fields becomes a regular feature ca. A.D. 800 (definitely antedating St. Ansgar). From the craftsman's ideas about design there is however a big gap to Christian religion. More convincing is a similar argument by Jansson concerning the oval fibulae in grave Nr 655 at Birka (Jansson 1985 p.20).

Eastern Middle Sweden has a little-known but very interesting source material for a further discussion. The primary Christian symbol, the Holy Cross is represented in several finds (Fig. 18: 1-8, 11-13). The earliest Christian cross comes from a cremation grave not far from Stockholm. It dates to the first half of the 8th century and is most probably an import from Western Europe (Fig. 18:17). More interesting are of course crosses, which we can classify as local products. A small group of more or less equal armed crosses with irregular globular or even cross-shaped ends is found in cremation graves in Uppland and Södermanland (cf. Duczko 1997 p.299) (Fig. 18:4-8). The centre of the cross is covered by a rectangle, the corners of which are marked with a circle or even with a circle on a shaft. This central quadrangle suggests the inclusion of a relic in the prototype cross. The mass import of relics to the West begins in the Carolingian phase. Duczko, who has shortly discussed these rather old finds, thinks that the prototypes are English. It is however very difficult to fix their background more precisely. Both Western and Eastern crosses have definite similarities. The important thing is however that very realistic and dis-

tinct cross pendants were produced in considerable numbers in Eastern Middle Sweden. Duczko dates these cross pendants to the 9th century, which in my opinion is too late. The second half of the 8th century and ca. A.D. 800 is more convincing. In addition to these veritable pendant crosses there is also a number of circular pendants with an inscribed cross (Fig. 18:18:1-3,10-16). Some of these pendants can only conditionally (sensu Holmquist) be considered Christian crosses Cruciform fibulae are known from Birka (Arbman 1940 Taf. 85:8), which could be imports from Southern Scandinavia (there is another find in Hedeby) (Fig. 18:9). These cruciform fibulae were carried as a pair at Birka. The form is closely connected to one of the variants of the equal armed Valsta fibulae from ca. A.D. 800 or slightly later.

A special development of the Christian cross is the Finnish round fibulae with an inscribed cross. Although the majority of the finds are from South-western Finland there are also four finds from the Åland Islands (Salo 1997 p. 341-7). Their connection with West European forms is very likely (cf. Koch 2003)

The quasi-Christian character of the compact animal and bird motives on the pelta-shaped pendants has already been pointed out. Here I would like to point out a purely Christian motive, which obviously became much appreciated by the Scandinavians. With the extraordinary find at Uppåkra of a Continental mount for a reliquary of the 8th century featuring a lion fighting snakes (Helgesson 1999) we have at our disposal an unusual key for the understanding of how a very special variant of this motif became part of the Scandinavian iconography of the second half of the 8th century. Examples are known both from Western and Eastern Scandinavia. However the main theme occurs in a number of variations, which are not closely related to the Uppåkra group. We may note both ornamental dress mounts and an unusual ronde bosse fibula with this motif (Fig. 19). The central ideological content with good versus evil was easily transferred over the cultural border. The snake in this case is malign and deadly. The snake motif in Scandinavia is however highly ambiguous. Especially the coiled snake is a positive symbol connected with the house and with happiness.

We may conclude that especially the 8th century and the time around A.D. 800 is a period with very strong Christian influences in Eastern Middle Sweden as well as in other parts of Northern Europe. This means that St. Ansgar's mission falls in a somewhat later period when

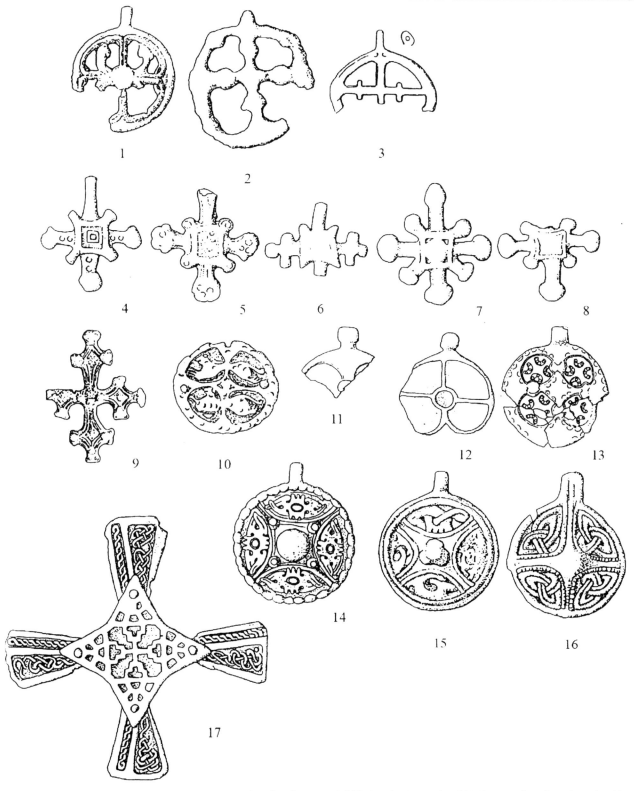

Fig.18. Christian symbols on 8th and early 9th century dress jewellery in Eastern Middle Sweden. Nos. 1-8 and 11-13 are pendants from the region. No. 10 and Nos. 14-16 are related pendants from Östergötland and Öland. No. 9 is a cruciform fibula from Birka and No. 17 is an 8th century cross imported to the region, possibly from the continent.

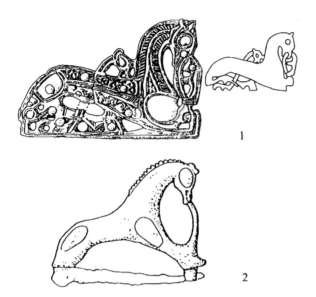

Fig.19. Examples of the beast fighting a snake motif in Eastern Middle Sweden.

we have very little evidence of Christian influences. Only in the 10th century Christian cross pendants become common again. Most scholars have been little aware of these early indications of Christian symbolic language and concentrate on the 10th century (Jesch 1991 pp. 22-24, Gräslund 1997, Staecker 1999).

8. CONCLUSIONS

The iconographic material of Eastern Middle Sweden has a characteristic regional flavour and forms of ornaments, motifs, symbols and style differs from that further south, especially in relation to what we find in Southern and Western Scandinavia. Most of the forms are the same but the motives are different. When there are close connections they are with South-eastern Scandinavia. This means that it is most likely that the ideological background is different from that in other parts of Scandinavia. This is of course of special importance in relationship to the literary sources. There is much to indicate that religious beliefs and customs are in perpetual flux. The iconography also changes with time. We have been able to demonstrate that animal ornamentation plays different roles over time. In some special connections it is not appreciated at all (arm rings and combs). The interesting relationship between animal ornament and gender has been paid little attention to. Between the masculine and feminine spheres

there are great differences and it is most likely that these differences correspond to differences regarding ideology and religion. More or less the masculine gender is drifting away from animal ornamentation already in the 8th century. As already stated this should not be understood as if there existed sexually different systems but rather that gender tend to emphasise different elements and aspects of religion and mythology. There are some bridges between masculine and feminine in the iconographic material but they are not many. In some cases typical men's motifs have been taken over by women like the shield monster and the Ekhammar type figurines. The vast majority of motifs and elements are however exclusive for one gender. The masculine elements were taken over to the feminine side only when they fall into disuse so that the exclusivity is maintained. For a deeper understanding of the differences between feminine and masculine a corresponding study of the male sphere is necessary. However, it is possible to maintain that the masculine gender distanced itself from animal ornamentation already in the 8th century. Especially in the 10th century there is some revival of animal ornamentation in the masculine sphere in Eastern Scandinavia. In the West and the South it remains rather insignificant. The animal ornamentation of the local tradition flows into the early Romanesque art. Of course this has something to say about the meaning of animal ornamentation and its relationship to the pre-Christian religion. Probably this relationship was problematic throughout the Viking Period and possibly even earlier. Our investigation has not been able to show other social differences. The approach of Hauck (e.g. 1983) and later also taken up by Hedeager (2004) to view the Germanic animal ornamentation as a homogenous and coherently structured bloc must be seriously questioned. Also the widespread idea among historians of religion and students of the Icelandic literature, that the pre-Christian religion was coherent and meaningfully structured must be doubted. There were individuals with special knowledge of (and interest in) the pre-Christian religion who brought the tradition on to the next generation but there were no "theologians", no popes and imams. The oral transmission of religious formulae, statements and myths meant that a continuous dynamic change of content must have been characteristic of the pre-Christian religion. What we can glimpse is (like most religions) an incoherent, chaotic and ambiguous pre-Christian religion. This has of course something to say about how we understand traditional religion ourselves. Is it something really built as a standing construction by some "theologians" of old or has it more to do with psycho-therapeutical practice with a disparate and ever changing corpus of beliefs and ideas and even parallel phenomena?

The approach chosen concentrating on iconography means that we are dealing with individuals belonging to the upper social strata. Although differences in social position certainly were relevant for our discussion of differences in religious beliefs and ideology we must try to activate other sources (probably intensive settlement studies could be more rewarding) to penetrate this question.

The iconographic material and the jewellery items themselves indicate that the most important religious element in the feminine sphere is reproduction. The button-on-bow fibulae, the oval fibulae and the pendants are without doubt signalling the ability to produce an heir (second priority a heiress) as well as the competence to play the full feminine role in local society. The iconography, notwithstanding its often clear Christian links (see below), is mainly connected with the reproductive sphere. Symbolic signs used also belong to this sphere. The attribution of these ornaments and symbols to one specific fertility deity is however problematic. Relationships with other religious and mythological beings are likely. Miniature shears as a sign of relationship with the norner are known from nearby Östergötland (Fig. 20) (cf. Lamm 2004). The severed head motif (Mimir?) could indicate similar special relationships. The special competence of the völva is clearly connected with the feminine gender in Eastern Middle Sweden through the use of the stave symbol. Other special domains and competences are difficult to indicate. Keys could be relevant, but are little used in display in Eastern Middle Sweden (cf. Arwill-Nordbladh 1990).

There is ample evidence of strong Christian influence. However it seems mainly to have a secondary character. The cemeteries in Eastern middle Sweden from which almost all the artefacts with iconographic material stem are pre-Christian cremation cemeteries. The number of inhumations is extremely low. Only at Birka, towards the end of our period of interest, we seem to have potentially Christian west-east inhumations in some numbers (Gräslund 1980). It is most likely that the Christian motifs were included in existing mytho-religious ideas and practise but it is also likely that these Christian elements contributed to changes in this sector. It agrees well with

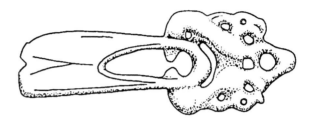

Fig.20. Shears-shaped pendant from Ringstad, Östra Eneby parish, province of Östergötland.

ideas formulated concerning the stronger readiness of the feminine than the masculine side to adopt elements of Christianity. However many Christian elements were included in the pagan fertility sphere. The presence of some Christian symbols like the cross pendants could indicate a missionary activity before St. Ansgar in Eastern Middle Sweden.

The women of eastern Middle Sweden did not produce their own jewellery and it is also most unlikely that their husbands did. We know very little about the production of jewellery during the period of interest (cf. Callmer 2002). Observations from an earlier period (the Helgö workshops and others) and comparative material from other parts of Scandinavia show us that specialists-artisans produced ornamental metalwork. The social position of these artisans is not completely clear in detail but it is unlikely that they were slaves or serfs although there could have been other forms of bondage. Production probably took at some central places although we until now have not been able to locate them. The mould material from Birka, as far as it has been communicated, is later. The artefacts and the ornamentation they created in the second half of the 8th century and in the early 9th century must have been acceptable and understood by those who later carried them. However the cognitive background, after all, remains primarily with the producer. The special social milieu of these artisans and other people engaged in exchange and trade with their frequent contacts to the south and southwest was a platform for the intricate mixture of pre-Christian and Christian ideas, which characterize the period. We can perceive them as examples of local traditional themes and of continental and insular ornamental art influences. It is most likely that we even find the first Christians among them. The broad Christianization of Scandinavia is one and a half century later. The period from the middle of the 8th century to ca. A.D. 800 however stands between two worlds, the old spiritual tradition developed in the Migration Period and the Viking Period proper when so much changes and when the final transformation to Christianity takes place.

REFERENCES

Almgren, B.1940. Runstenen vid Skokloster en bildsten från vendeltiden. Uppländsk bygd. Stockholm.

-1948. Romerska drag i nordisk figurkonst från folkvandringstiden. Tor, 1. Uppsala.

-1955. Bronsnycklar och djurornamentik. Uppsala.

Andersson, G. 2006. Among trees, bones and stones. In A. Andrén et al. (eds) Old Norse religion in long-term perspectives. Origins, changes and interactions. Stockholm.

Arbman, H.1940. Birka I. Die Gräber. Stockholm.

Arwidsson,G. 1942A. Vendelstile, Email und Glas. Uppsala.

-1942B. Valsgärde 6. Uppsala.

-1977. Valsgärde 7. Uppsala.

Arwill-Nordbladh, E.1990. Nyckelsymbolik i järnålderns kvinnogravar. Fornvännen, 85. Stockholm.

-1994. Begriper vi begreppen? Om androcentrismen i några vanliga analytiska begrepp. Meta, 94:1. Lund.

Atterman, I.1935. Nya fynd från Hovgårdsberg i Vendel. Fornvännen, 30. Stockholm.

Bruce-Mitford, R.1978. The Sutton Hoo ship burial, II. Arms, armour and regalia. London.

von Blankenburg, W. 1943. Heilige und dämonische Tiere. Die Symbolsprache der deutschen Ornamentik im frühen Mittelalter. Leipzig.

Callmer,J. 2002. Wayland. An essay on craft production in the Early and High Middle ages in Scandinavia. In L.Larsson&B.Hårdh (eds.) Centrality and regionality. The social structure of Southern Sweden during the Iron Age. (Uppåkra studies, 7.) Lund.

Dickinson, T. 2005. Symbols of protection: the significance of animal-ornamented shields in early Anglo Saxon England. Medieval archaeology, vol. XLIX. London.

Dommasnes, L.H. 1994. Hva önsker vi å få vite om middelalderens samfunn? Kjönsroller, genderverdier og forandringer. Meta, 94:1. Lund.

Drescher, H.&Hauck, K.1982. Götterthrone des heidnischen Nordens. Frühmittelalterliche Studien, 16. Berlin.

Duczko, W. 1997. Byzantine presence in Viking Age Sweden. Archaeological finds and their interpretation. In M.Müller-Wille (Hrsg.) Rom und Byzanz im Norden. Mission und Glaubenswechsel im Ostseeraum während des 8.-14. Jhds. Stuttgart.

Golubeva, L.A.1979. Zoomorfnye ukrasenia finno-ugrov. Svod archeologiceskich istocnikov, vyp. E1-59. Moskva.

Gräslund, A.-S.1980. The burial customs. A study of the graves on Björkö. Birka. Untersuchungen und Studien, 4. Stockholm.

-1997. The Christianization of Central Sweden from a female perspective. In M. Müller-Wille (Hrsg.). Rom und Byzanz im Norden. Mission und Glaubenswechsel im Ostseeraum während des 8.-14. Jhds. Stuttgart.

Hauck, K. 1981. Überregionale Sakralorte und die vorchristliche Ikonographie der Seegermanen (Zur Ikonologie der Goldbrakteaten, XXII). Nachrichten der Akademie der Wissenschaften in Göttingen. Philosofisch-Historische Klasse, Nr 8. Göttingen.

-1983. Text und Bild in einer oralen Kultur. Antworten auf die zeugniskritische Frage nach der Erreichbarkeit mündlicher Überlieferung im frühen Mittelalter. Frühmittelalterliche Studien,17. Berlin.

Hedeager,L.2004. Dyr og andre mennesker - mennesker og andre dyr. Dyreornamentikkens transcendentale realitet. In Andrén,A.&Jennbert,K.&Raudvere,C. Ordning mot kaos-studier av nordisk förkristen religion. Lund.

Helgesson, B.1999. HELGE- ett spår av en tidig kristen mission i Uppåkra? In B.Hårdh (Red.) Fynden i centrum. Keramik, glas och metall från Uppåkra. (Upåkrastudier,2) Lund.

Hjörungdahl,T.1991. Det skjulte kjönn. Patriarkalisk tradition og feministisk visjon i arkeologien belyst med fokus på en jernalderskontekst. Lund.

Holmquist,W. 1975. Was there a Christian mission to Sweden before Ansgar? (Early Medieval studies, 8) Antikvariskt arkiv, 57.

Hyenstrand, Å. 1996. Lejonet, draken och korset. Lund.

Jansson,I. 1985. Ovala spännbucklor. En studie av vikingatidens standardsmycken med utgångspunkt från Björköfynden. Uppsala.

Jennbert, K. 2004. Människor och djur. Kroppsmetaforik och kosmologiska perspektiv. In Andrén, A.& Jennbert, K. & Raudvere,C (eds) . Ordning mot kaos - studier av nordisk förkristen religion. Lund.

Jesch, J.1991. Women in the Viking Age. Woodbridge.

af Klintberg, B. 1978. Harens klagan: studier i gammal och ny folklore. Stockholm.

Koch,R.2003. Eine durchbrochene Scheibenfibel mit Kreuz aus Lund-Uppåkra. In B.Hårdh (ed.) Fler fynd i centrum. Materialstudier i och kring Uppåkra.(Uppåkrastudier, 9.) Lund.

Lamm, J.P. 1973. Fornfynd och fornlämningar på Lovö. Arkeologiska studier kring en uppländsk järnåldersbygd. Stockholm.

-2004. Sächsisches? und fränkisches, einige Neufunde aus Uppåkra und Hammarby in Schweden. Acta Archaeologica Lovaniensia, Monographiae 15. Leuven.

Leroi-Gourhan, A.1965. Préhistoire de l'art occidental. Paris.

Lillehammer, G. (1985) 1996. Död og grav. Gravskikk på Kvassheimfeltet, Hå i Rogaland, SV Norge.Arkeologisk museum i Stavanger. Skrifter, 13. Stavanger.

Lother, H. 1929. Der Pfau in der altchristlichen Kunst. Leipzig.

Magnus, B.1999. Das große Tier im Moor. In U. von Freeden (Hrsg.) Völker an Nord- und Ostsee und die Franken: Akten des 48. Sachsensymposiums in Mannheim von 7. bis 11. September 1979. Bonn.

Nerman,B. 1952. Några likarmade svenska spännen från yngre vendeltid och deras ättlingar. Corolla archaeologica in honorem C.A. Nordman. Helsingfors.

-1941. En kristen mission på Gotland vid tiden omkring år 800 e. Kr.? Fornvännen, 36. Stockholm.

Näsman, U. 1991. Mammen 1871. Ett vikingatida depåfynd med beslag till selbågskrön och annat skrot. In Iversen,M (ed.) Mammen. Grav, kunst og samfund i vikingetid. Århus.

Olsén, P. 1945. Die Saxe von Valsgärde. Uppsala.

Ørsnes, M. 1966. Form og stil i Sydskandinaviens yngre Germanske jernalder. Köbenhavn.

Petersen, J. 1928. Vikingetidens smykker. Stavanger.

-1955. Vikingetidens smykker i Norge. Stavanger.

Reimbold, E.T. 1983. Der Pfau. Mythologie und Symbolik. München.

Ringquist, P.O.1969. Två vikingatida uppländska människofigurer i brons. Fornvännen, 64. Stockholm.

Salo.U.1997.Früher christlicher Einfluss in Finnland. In Müller-Wille, M. (Hrsg.) Rom und Byzanz im Norden. Mission und Glaubenswechsel im Ostseeraum während des 8.-14. Jhds. Stuttgart.

Schjödt, J. P. 1991. Relationen mellem aser og vaner og dens ideologiske implikationer. In Steinsland, G. (red.). Nordisk hedendom. Et symposium. Odense.

Sippel, K. 1987. Ein Merowingisches Kammergrab mit Pferdegeschirr aus Eschwege, Werra-Meissner-Kreis (Hessen). Germania, 65:1. Frankfurt a.M.

Solli, B. 2002. Seid- Myter, sjamanisme og kjönn i vikingenes tid. Oslo.

-2004. Det norröne verdensbildet og ethos.In A.Andrén&K. Jennbert&C.Raudvere. Ordning mot kaos. Studier av nordisk förkristen kosmologi. Lund.

Staecker, J.1999. Rex regum et dominus dominorum. Die wikingerzeitliche Kreuz- und Kruzifixanhänger als Ausdruck der Mission in Altdänemark und Schweden. Lund.

Steinsland, G. 1986. Giants as recipients of cult in the VikingAge? In G. Steinsland (ed.) Words and objects. Towards a dialogue between archaeology and history of religion. Oslo.

Steinsland, G. & Meulengracht Sörensen, P. 1994. Mennesker og makter i vkingenes verden. Oslo.

Stolpe, H. & Arne, T.1912. Graffältet vid Vendel. Stockholm.

Strömbäck, D. 1935. Sejd. (Nordiska texter och undersökningar,5.) Stockholm.

Turville-Petre, G.1964. Myth and religion of the North. London.

Vierck, H. 1984. Mittel- und westeuropäische Einwirkungen auf die Sachkultur von Haithabu/Schleswig. In H.Jankuhn&K.Schietzel&H. Reichstein(Hrsg.) Archäologische und naturwissenschaftliche Untersuchungen an Siedlungen im deutschen Siedlungsgebiet vom 5. Jahrhundert v. Chr. bis zum 11. Jahrhundert n. Chr. 2. Handelsplätze des frühen und hohen Mittelalters. Weinheim.

-2002. Zwei Amulettbilder als Zeugnisse des Ausgehenden Heidentums in Haithabu. Berichte über die Ausgrabungen in Haithabu, 34. Neumünster.

Watt, M. 1992. Die Goldblechfiguren von Sorte Muld. In Hauck, K. (ed.) Der historische Horizont der Götterbilder-Amulette aus der Übergangsepoche von der Spätantike zum Frühmittelalter. Abhandlungen der Göttinger Akademie der Wissenschaften. Philosophisch-Historische Klasse, Nr 200. Göttingen.

Authors address
Tunavägen 21
SE-22363 Lund, Sweden
johancallmer@hotmail.com

Acta Archaeologica vol. 79, 2008, pp 208-215
Printed in Denmark · All rights reserved

SKRIÐUKLAUSTUR MONASTERY
MEDICAL CENTRE OF MEDIEVAL EAST ICELAND?

Steinunn Kristjánsdóttir

Skriðuklaustur monastery was the youngest of nine cloisters operated in Iceland during the Catholic period of the Middle Ages (figure 1). The first one was founded at Þingeyrar in 1133 and the last one three and a half centuries later in 1493 at Skriðuklaustur. The monastic institutions were seven in number, four in the bishopric at Skálholt and three in the bishopric at Hólar. There were two nunneries, one in each bishopric. Icelandic cloisters were all either Augustinian or Benedictine, and Skriðuklaustur monastery is commonly thought to have belonged to the Augustinian order. Other religious orders were not represented in Iceland during the Catholic period. All of Iceland's nine Medieval cloisters were dissolved during the Lutheran Reformation (Gunnar F. Guðmundsson 2000: 212 f).

Despite the fact that the cloisters in Iceland were equally divided between the two bishoprics, Hólar and Skálholt, their geographical distribution within the country was rather unequal. One monastery, Helgafellsklaustur, was located in West Iceland. There were three monasteries and one nunnery in North Iceland: Þingeyraklaustur, Reynistaðaklaustur (nunnery), Möðruvallaklaustur and Munkaþverárklaustur. Two monasteries and one nunnery were located in South Iceland: Viðeyjarklaustur, Þykkvabæjarklaustur and Kirkjubæjarklaustur (nunnery). There was neither a monastery nor a nunnery in the West Fjords. East Iceland was without cloisters as well until the last phase of the Catholic period, when Skriðuklaustur monastery was founded during the reign of Bishop Stefán Jónsson (Björn Þorsteinsson and Guðrún Ása Grímsdóttir 1990: 152-153; Gunnar F. Guðmundsson 2000: 217).

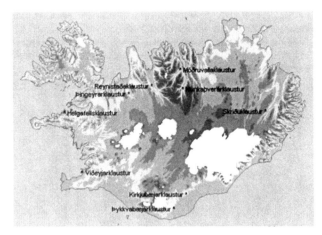

Figure 1. Nine cloisters operated in Iceland during the Catholic period of the Middle Ages. They were all dissolved during the Lutheran Reformation.

ARCHAEOLOGICAL, ORAL AND WRITTEN SOURCES ON SKRIÐUKLAUSTUR MONASTERY

The excavation of the ruins of Skriðuklaustur monastery began in 2002. Before archaeological investigation commenced, it was not known exactly where on the farm Skriða the buildings of the monastery had stood. Though no ruins were visible on the surface, oral sources and various written documents about monastic activities at Skriðuklaustur dispelled all doubt about their existence. Despite its short tenure, the monastery acquired a large amount of land, and its library seems to have been comparable to that of other Icelandic cloisters. It was known that

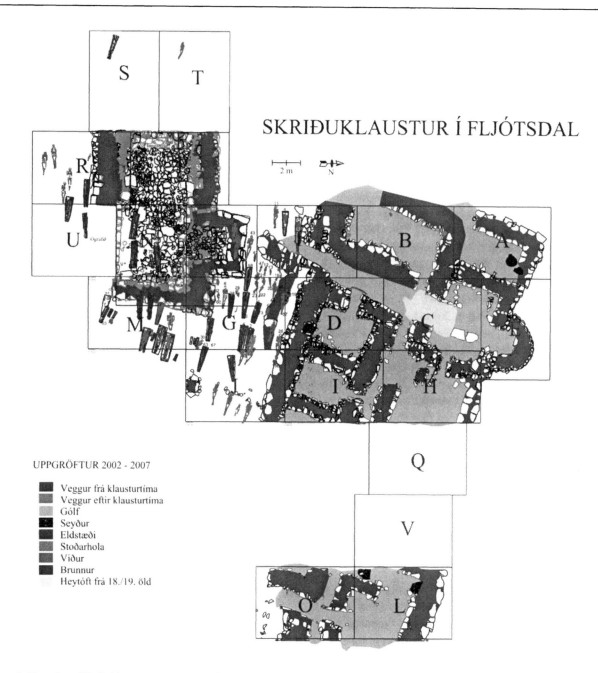

SKRIÐUKLAUSTUR Í FLJÓTSDAL

UPPGRÖFTUR 2002 - 2007

■ Veggur frá klausturtíma
■ Veggur eftir klausturtíma
Gólf
■ Seyður
■ Eldstæði
■ Stoðarhola
■ Viður
■ Brunnur
Heytóft frá 18./19. öld

Figure 2. The ruins of Skriðuklaustur monastery. Despite the excavation's being only half finished, the parts of the monastic buildings that have been uncovered show that it did not resemblance the medieval farmhouses in Iceland, as it consisted of several small cells, a church, and a cloister garden with a well.

a children's school was operated there, as well as an outer school; i.e., schola exterior. Furthermore, it is known that the cloister was dedicated to God the Father, the Virgin Mary, and the holy blood of Jesus Christ, in accordance with a legend about the founding of the Skriðuklaustur monastery in the fifteenth century. Skriðuklaustur is Iceland's only example of a cloister so dedicated (Gunnar F. Guðmundsson 2000: 223, 324).

The ancient sacred legend of the dedication tells of the occurrence of a miracle when a cleric from Valþjófsstaður parish church, located a few kilometres away from the monastic site, went down to the valley to visit a dying parishioner. Along the way, he lost his chalice and paten. A man was sent to look for them and found them on a knoll on the field called Kirkjutún, below the farm at Skriða. The chalice was filled with wine and the paten laid neatly on top, with bread on it. This event was viewed as a miracle and was commemorated with the construction of a chapel whose altar was placed on the knoll where the holy items were found. According to the legend, a cloister dedicated to the Virgin Mary and the blood of Christ was founded on the site (Helgi Hallgrímsson 1999: 34-35).

A cemetery was consecrated at Skriðuklaustur in 1496, and a monastic church in 1512. The church deteriorated after the closing of the monastery but was rebuilt around the year 1670. The church, called Skriðukirkja, was finally discontinued in 1792, nearly three centuries after the founding of the monastery. The cemetery was closed at the same time. During the period from 1554 until its closing, it was used by the farm's post-monastic inhabitants (Heimir Steinsson 1965).

The ruins of this church and a churchyard around it are clearly visible on Kirkjutún, one of Skriða's cultivated fields. Despite this, it was commonly thought that the monastery itself had stood by the farmhouses at Skriða, rather than on Kirkjutún field with the monastic church (Daniel Bruun 1974; Helgi Hallgrímsson 1999; Heimir Steinsson 1965, 1966). The farmhouses at Skriða farm were nonetheless located approximately 150 metres away from Kirkjutún field.

THEORIES ABOUT ICELANDIC CLOISTERS

The hypothesized location of the Skriðuklaustur monastery was based on a commonly held theory about Icelandic cloisters in general: namely, that their buildings were fundamentally different from other contemporary cloisters as regards architecture, purpose, and function. This commonly held view supposes that the Icelandic cloisters were either operated in the farmhouses themselves or that their buildings did not differ considerably from contemporary farm houses in Iceland, although the cloisters are considered to have been more sophisticated than the homes of common farmers (Hörður Ágústsson 1989; Björn Þorsteinsson and Guðrún Ása Grímsdóttir 1990; Guðrún Harðardóttir 1998, 2006).

Though this deeply rooted theory is supported primarily by the supposed isolation of Icelandic society during Medieval times, it is also bolstered by the limited building resources in Iceland. The available building materials – mainly turf, stones and driftwood – are usually not regarded as suitable for the construction of large and complex buildings. In fact, buildings of turf and stones do not last long, and they usually need to be rebuilt frequently. Furthermore, older buildings or structures are commonly used again and again, and in most cases the foundations of older structures are reused for new buildings if possible.

There are several reasons for the wide acceptance of this theory about Icelandic cloisters' similarity to Medieval farmhouses, chief among them the general lack of archaeological investigations of Icelandic monastic sites. In addition, although non-archaeological resources have contributed substantially to this field of research, Medieval written sources contain minimal information about activities other than economic or political ones. These sources may also have contributed to this unverified and stagnant view of the form, purpose, and function of the Icelandic Medieval cloisters. Last but not least, the historical memory of Medieval Iceland as being isolated from foreign influence during the pre-independent times of the 13th -20th centuries may have shaped the image of Icelandic cloisters.

For these reasons, it has generally been believed that Icelandic cloisters functioned primarily as seats of power for Medieval chieftains and that their activities centred on the accumulation of economic wealth, as well as prayer, writing, and the education of clerics. Indeed, Icelandic scholars have maintained that the Catholic Church in Iceland was inactive, if not indifferent, as regards providing social assistance (Helgi Þorláksson 2003). The findings from the excavation at Skriðuklaustur, however, provide compelling evidence to the contrary.

ARCHAEOLOGICAL INVESTIGATIONS OF OTHER ICELANDIC CLOISTERS

Archaeological investigations have been performed at two monastic sites in Iceland apart from Skriðuklaustur. These are the investigation of the ruins of a monastery located on the island of Viðey, outside Reykjavik, and a nunnery at Kirkjubæjarklaustur on the south coast of Iceland. The excavation at Viðey lasted for eight years, from 1987-1995 (Margrét Hallgrímsdóttir 1993; Steinunn Kristjánsdóttir 1995). The excavation of the Kirkjubæ-

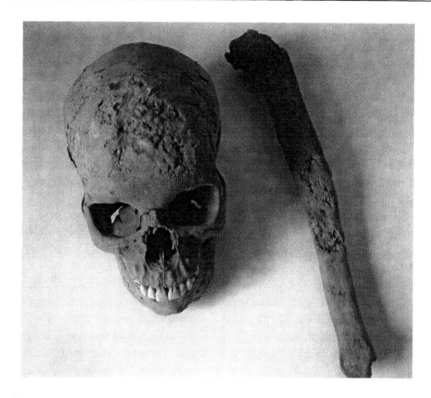

Figure 3. Syphilis has been identified in three cases from the cemetery at Skriðuklaustur monastery.

jarklaustur nunnery began in 2002 and is still underway (Kristján Mímisson and Bjarni F. Einarsson 2005).

Both of these sites are known for a long history of diverse settlements, including monastic activities and farming lasting from the 10th to the 20th century. The monastic ruins at both Viðey and Kirkjubæjarklaustur are therefore intertwined with the ruins of various phases of common farmhouses built both before and after the monastic institutions. As is explained above, because building materials in Iceland consist mainly of turf and stones, the foundations of older buildings were commonly used in the construction of new ones. This has frequently built up of special mounds of buildings at both sites, caused by a long and complicated history of various activities. Moreover, this situation makes the interpretation of each building phase in the mounds very difficult, as the ruin at the top is usually the only one that has lain undisturbed.

Unfortunately, neither of these cloisters has, as yet, been excavated fully enough to produce evidence of architectural plans or inner function. Nevertheless, the excavation at Viðey monastery has been used to support the simplified picture of Icelandic monasteries and nunner-

ies because a large farmhouse, whose different phases of construction have obviously been mixed with monastic buildings through the ages, has been excavated at the site (Margrét Hallgrímsdóttir 1993).

Furthermore, investigations based on written resources describing the form and function of Icelandic cloisters can be criticized for several reasons. Most importantly, contemporary written sources describing Icelandic monastic buildings are limited in number. The vast majority of the written resources used in this context – mainly registers, appraisals and agreements of various kinds –date to the period following the Lutheran Reformation; i.e., the late 16th century or later. Therefore, these documents most likely describe the farmhouses then standing on the sites but not the monastic buildings that had already been abandoned or even demolished.

In short, large farms were situated at monastic sites both before and after the Lutheran Reformation because of the political and economic power the cloisters gained through their activities. To confuse matters further, monastic farmsteads also retained the names of the abandoned monasteries or nunneries after the Reformation.

THE EXCAVATIONS AT SKRIÐUKLAUSTUR

Before the excavation of the Skriðuklaustur ruins commenced in 2002, a pre-excavation was performed on two sites on the land belonging to the farmstead Skriða. The aim was to search for the ruins of the monastic building. The two sites were the immediate vicinity of the farmstead's living quarters, in accordance with the commonly held view presented above, and the area around the old church ruin located on the Kirkjutún field. During the pre-excavation, both sites were surveyed geophysically and several test-pits were dug (Steinunn Kristjánsdóttir 2001).

The pre-excavation indicated a long history of activity, from the 10th century onward, in the area near the farmstead living quarters, and did not rule out the possibility that monastic buildings might have stood there. However, the pre-excavation of Kirkjutún indicated strongly that the monastic building had been attached to the ruin of the old, abandoned church. The test-pits proved that an advanced building had stood on the site during the monastic period, and the geophysical survey indicated that this building had covered an area of at least 1200 m2, which included the ruin of the church. The ruins were very well preserved, and more importantly, no younger structures appeared to have been built on top of the ruins from the monastic period, except for the church because of its longer history of active use (Steinunn Kristjánsdóttir 2001).

This is the first time a monastic building from the Catholic period has been uncovered in Iceland, and after several years of excavation, the layout of the monastic building and the monastery's multi-functional activities during late Medieval times are becoming clearer (Steinunn Kristjánsdóttir 2003, 2004, 2005, 2006, 2007). The excavation at Skriðuklaustur has revealed a monastic building that does not resemble any Medieval farmhouse in Iceland. In fact, the building is laid out in a manner similar to that of most Medieval monastic buildings in Europe. Despite the excavation's being only half finished, the parts of the monastic buildings that have been uncovered show that it consisted of several small cells, a church, and a cloister garden with a well.

The building itself is much larger than anticipated. Steps found in two of the cells indicate that the building was two stories high, or a single story and a cellar. A corridor connects the church and a room that has been interpreted as a chapter house. Midway between them is an entrance to a small cell with a stove and a bookshelf. One of the cells has been interpreted as a refectory and the one beside it as a kitchen. In the latter, two cooking pits were found, but these may have been used partially or exclusively for cooking ink. Artefacts such as sulphur, colouring stones, wax, and pimp-stones have been found inside the ruins, and they indicate that, in addition to writing, parchment- and ink-making may have been a part of the work done in the monastery.

SKRIÐUKLAUSTUR MONASTERY'S INTERFERENCE WITH SOCIAL MATTERS

The skeletons from the site, together with surgical equipment and the cultivation of some healing plants, have also broadened the view of the central function of the monastery at Skriða, as they indicate strongly that the monastery may have functioned as a hospice. The skeletal material indicates that sick, needy and even poor people sought healing or a resting place at the monastery. Some of them may have died of their diseases, while others might have been unable to work because of illness or disability of some kind.

Approximately 90 graves have been identified from the surface inside the cloister garden and the church, and 70 of these have been exhumed. Identification of the human bones shows clearly that the monastic cemetery differs greatly from other contemporary cemeteries in Iceland. Bones of foetuses, neonates, adolescents and, in particular, young females have been discovered in the graves (Elsa Pacciani 2006; Guðný Zoëga 2007). Five graves of males have been unearthed so far, but three of these were located inside the church. This social division according to sex and age differs from what can be found in the cemeteries of other Medieval parish churches. Furthermore, the majority of the youngest children were buried together in the northern corner of the cloister garden. The remains of progressively older individuals take up larger areas towards the east.

Most of the adult skeletons bear clear signs of various chronic diseases, such as syphilis (figure 3), tuberculosis, lung infection, cleft palate, echinococcus granulosus, gum diseases of various kinds, broken bones, and some unidentified infections (Elsa Pacciani 2006; Guðný Zoëga 2007). In addition, several lancets have been excavated from two cells and the church area. In the church's choir an effigy of St. Barbara was found but is known she belonged to a group of fourteen saints that were venerated together in Roman Catholicism, as their intercession was thought to protect against diseases.

Finally, pollen analysis of samples from the site shows that gardening was carried out at the monastery and that both healing plants and vegetables were cultivated there during the monastic period. Ten species of healing plants were discovered, including three that do not belong to the Icelandic fauna: Allium, Urtica major and Plantage major (Hákon Jensson 2005). These findings may be regarded as an indication of intentional gardening in the monastery, similar to that practiced in contemporary monasteries outside Iceland (Samson B. Harðarson 2007). This evidence for the existence of a horticultural garden of healing plants at the site supports the theory that a hospice was operated in the monastery.

STANDARD FORM AND FUNCTION

Although it can be stated that, in general, no two Catholic monasteries and nunneries looked the same architecturally, they were arranged in accordance with a standard plan where the monastic rooms and the church were arranged around a cloister garden, forming a cluster of houses. The garden, which was regarded as the central place in the building, was meant to be free from structures other than a well and was used either as a horticultural garden, or a cemetery, or both (Gilchrist, Roberta and Sloane, Barney 2005).

The outer walls of the monastic buildings formed a visible boundary between the sacred world inside the monastery and the secular world outside it. The religious aims of the Catholic monasteries and nunneries are therefore regarded as having profoundly affected their architectural form. Cloisters were places of introversion and religious intercession, isolated from the secular world in spite of the worldly existence of those who lived in them. As portals to heaven, cloisters were also societies of men and women who sought spiritual shelter by abandoning the secular world in order to save their souls (Gilchrist, Roberta 2000; Gunnar F. Guðmundsson 2000; Gilchrist, Roberta and Sloane, Barney 2005).

Although European monasteries and nunneries have been regarded as powerful cultural and educational institutions whose existence was founded on both on political

and economic strength, one of the fundamental aims of the Catholic Church was to provide social care in a broad sense, beyond spiritual matters. Charity and mercy were well known bywords in the cloisters, where altruistic gestures were visible. Indeed, cloisters met the very real need of Medieval societies for hospitals for sick, needy, poor, and aged people (Vilborg Ísleifsdóttir 1997: 99 f, 2003: 32; Dahlerup Koch, Hanne and Lynnerup, Niels 2003: 11 f; Jón Ólafur Ísberg 2005; Gilchrist, Roberta and Sloane, Barney 2005: 37 f).

FOUNDING OF SKRIÐUKLAUSTUR MONASTERY

Cloisters' ultimate purpose of acting on the basis of charity and mercy has not been regarded as one of the underlying reasons for the late foundation of Skriðuklaustur. Traditionally, Icelandic monasteries have been regarded merely as institutions of education and of political and economic power. It is commonly thought that the reason for the late foundation of the Skriðuklaustur monastery was the lack of such an institution in East Iceland (Heimir Steinsson 1965, 1966). Still, the traditional emphasis on economic and political matters certainly shaped the history of cloisters in Iceland, although it can be stated that many important decisions often had roots other than the merely economic or political.

Perhaps one of the reasons for the founding of Skriðuklaustur monastery can be found, after all, in the history of Cecilía Þorsteinsdóttir, the woman who gave the farm Skriða for the founding of the monastery. Although written documents from the monastery had previously been examined rather thoroughly, this woman was been given any attention at all. Cecilía was a well-born and wealthy woman who married her second cousin, although such marriages were prohibited in Iceland at the time (Agnes Arnórsdóttir 2003). Cecilía gave birth to seven children with her husband, who died while she carried their youngest child. Because of their illegal marriage, their children were treated as a burden to God and to other people. Cecilía then began to fight for their rights, both in life and in death, and repeatedly begged the bishop, Stefán Jónsson, for a special dispensation in her case. She even sought an exemption from the Pope, but without success. Her last attempt in this campaign was to donate the farm at Skriða for the founding of a monastery (Margrét Gestsdóttir 2008). Stefán Jónsson may have been involved in her decision, for it would certainly have increased his political and economic power. Nonetheless, this decision was informed directly by the emotions of a mother who was fighting for her children's rights.

SKRIÐUKLAUSTUR MONASTERY AS AN INTERNATIONAL INSTITUTION

Stefán Jónsson, the bishop who founded the monastery at Skriðuklaustur, was educated in France, and one of his first actions in office was to found the ninth Icelandic monastery at Skriða (Gunnar F. Guðmundsson 2000: 174). He must have been familiar with other Catholic monasteries and their function and distinctive buildings. The lack of a hospice in East Iceland at the time of a series of disasters like the 1477 eruption in Vatnajökull glacier may also have affected his decision to accept Cecilía Þorsteinsdóttir's charitable gift. Furthermore, the fifteenth century is known for a number of serious diseases and natural catastrophes that may have exacerbated the short-age of hospices all over the country. This is supported by the findings from the excavation at Skriðuklaustur monastery, as it demonstrates that the monastery there was built in accordance with the standard plan of monastic buildings. Its purpose as a charitable institution may have been fulfilled through the operation of a hospice, as the skeletal material indicates strongly that sick and needy people may intentionally have sought physical and spiritual comfort there. Furthermore, these findings from the excavation of Skriðuklaustur monastery confirm that the Church interfered with social matters during the Catholic period in Iceland, as it did in neighbouring countries.

Despite the fact that Skriðuklaustur monastery was founded late and was only in operation for roughly half a century, it made a niche for itself in Medieval Icelandic society, as did other cloisters in contemporary societies in Europe. The business of Skriðuklaustur monastery, its mission, and its assignments were obviously shaped by the spirit of the Medieval times in which the Catholic Church played a profoundly important part.

REFERENCES

Agnes Arnórsdóttir. 2003. "Icelandic Marriage Dispensations in the Late Middle Ages." The Roman Curia, the Apostolic Penitentiary and the Partes in the Later Middle Ages Acta Instituti Romani Finlandiae(28):159-169.

Björn Þorsteinsson and Guðrún Ása Grímsdóttir. 1990. "Enska öldin." In Saga Íslands V, ed. Sigurður Líndal. Reykjavik: Hið íslenska bókmenntafélag and Sögufélagið.

Bruun, Daniel. 1974. "Við norðurbrún Vatnajökuls. Rannsóknir á Austurlandi sumarið 1901." Múlaþing 7:163-164.

Gilchrist, Roberta. 2000. "Unsexing the body: the interior sexuality of medieval religious women." In Archaeologies of Sexuality, eds. Robert A. Schmidt and Barbara L. Voss. London/New York: Routledge.

Gilchrist, Roberta and Sloane, Barney. 2005. Requiem. The Medieval Monastic Cemetery in Britain. London: Museum of London Archaeological Service.

Guðný Zoëga. 2007. "Fornmeinafræðileg rannsókn á fimm beinagrindum úr klausturkirkjugarðinum á Skriðu." Sauðárkrókur: Byggðasafn Skagfirðinga.

Guðrún Harðardóttir. 1998. "Nokkrar kynslóðir kirkna og klausturhúsa á Munkaþverá." Árbók Hins íslenska fornleifafélags 1996-97:5-42.

Guðrún Harðardóttir. 2006. "Vangaveltur um íslensk klausturhús - íslenskum erlenda áhrifa." In Sjöunda landsbyggðarráðstefna Sagnfræðingafélags Íslands og Félags þjóðfræðinga á Íslandi Eiðum 3.-5. June 2005., ed. Hrafnkell Lárusson. Egilsstaðir: Héraðsnefnd Múlasýslna og Sagnfræðingafélags Íslands.

Gunnar F. Guðmundsson. 2000. "Íslenskt samfélag og Rómakirkja." In Kristni á Íslandi II, ed. Hjalti Hugason. Reykjavik: Alþingi.

Hákon Jensson. 2005. "Klausturgarðurinn á Skriðu. Niðurstöður frjókornagreininga." In Department of History and Archaeology Reykjavik: Háskóli Íslands.

Heimir Steinsson. 1965. "Munklífi að Skriðu í Fljótsdal." In Guðfræðideild Reykjavik: Háskóli Íslands.

Heimir Steinsson. 1966. "Jarðir Skriðuklausturs og efnahagur." Múlaþing 1:74-103.

Helgi Hallgrimsson. 1999. "Höfuðbólin þrjú í Fljótsdal II. Skriðuklaustur." In Lesbók Morgunblaðsins. Reykjavik.

Helgi Þorláksson. 2003. "Undir einveldi." In Saga Íslands VII, ed. Sigurður Líndal. Reykjavik: Hið íslenska bókmenntafélag.

Hörður Ágústsson. 1989. "Húsagerð á síðmiðöldum." In Saga Íslands IV ed. Sigurður Líndal. Reykjavík: Hið íslenska bókmenntafélag and Sögufélag.

Jón Ólafur Ísberg. 2005. Líf og lækningar. Íslensk heilbrigðissaga. Reykjavík: Hið íslenska bókmenntafélag.

Koch, Hanne Dahlerup and Lynnerup, Niels. 2003. Skælskør karmeliter kloster og dets kirkegård. Copenhagen: Det Konglige Nordiske Oldskriftselskab AB.

Kristján Mímisson and Bjarni F. Einarsson. 2005. "Rannsókn á rústum nunnuklaustursins í Kirkjubæ." In Skýrsla VI. Reykjavík: Kirkjubæjarstofa.

Margrét Gestsdóttir. 2008. "Cecilía Þorsteinsdóttir." In Skriðuklaustur í Fljótsdal, ed. Hrafnkell Lárusson. Egilsstaðir: Gunnarsstofnun.

Margrét Hallgrímsdóttir. 1993. "Húsakostur Viðeyjarklausturs." In Department of History and Archaeology. Reykjavík: University of Iceland.

Pacciani, Elsa. 2006. "Anthropological description of skeletons from graves no. 4, 62, 63, 65, 66, 67 and 68 at Skriðuklaustur monastery." In Skýrslur Skriðuklaustursrannsókna, ed. Steinunn Kristjánsdóttir. Reykjavík: Skriðuklaustursrannsóknir.

Samson B. Harðarson. 2007. "Klausturgarðar til lækningar líkama og sálar." In Þriðja íslenska söguþingið. Reykjavík: Sagnfræðingafélag Íslands.

Steinunn Kristjánsdóttir. 1995. "Klaustureyjan á Sundum." Árbók Hins íslenska fornleifafélags 1994:29-52.

Steinunn Kristjánsdóttir. 2001. "Klaustrið á Skriðu í Fljótsdal. Hvers vegna fornleifarannsókn?" Múlaþing 28:129-139.

Steinunn Kristjánsdóttir. 2003. "Skriðuklaustur - híbýli helgra manna. Áfangaskýrsla fornleifarannsókna 2002." In Skýrslur Skriðuklaustursrannsókna I, ed. Steinunn Kristjánsdóttir. Reykjavik: Skriðuklaustursrannsóknir.

Steinunn Kristjánsdóttir. 2004. "Skriðuklaustur - híbýli helgra manna. Áfangaskýrsla fornleifarannsókna 2003." In Skýrslur Skriðuklaustursrannsókna IV, ed. Steinunn Kristjánsdóttir. Reykjavik: Skriðuklaustursrannsóknir.

Steinunn Kristjánsdóttir. 2005. "Skriðuklaustur - híbýli helgra manna. Áfangaskýrsla fornleifarannsókna 2004." In Skýrslur Skriðuklaustursrannsókna IX. Reykjavik: Skriðuklaustursrannsóknir.

Steinunn Kristjánsdóttir. 2006. "Skriðuklaustur - híbýli helgra manna. Áfangaskýrsla fornleifarannsókna 2005." In Skýrslur Skriðuklaustursrannsókna XI, ed. Steinunn Kristjánsdóttir. Reykjavik: Skriðuklaustursrannsóknir.

Steinunn Kristjánsdóttir. 2007. "Skriðuklaustur - híbýli helgra manna. Áfangaskýrsla fornleifarannsókna 2006." In Skýrslur Skriðuklaustursrannsókna XV, ed. Steinunn Kristjánsdóttir. Reykjavik: Skriðuklaustursrannsóknir.

Vilborg Ísleifsdóttir. 1997. Siðbreytingin á Íslandi 1537-1565. Byltingin að ofan. Reykjavik: Hið íslenska bókmenntafélag.

Vilborg Ísleifsdóttir. 2003. "Öreigar og umrenningar. Um fátækraframfærslu á síðmiðöldum og hrun hennar." Saga XLI(2):91-126.

Author's address
#Archaeology, University of Iceland/National Museum of Iceland, Setberg, IS-101 Reykjavik,
Icelandsjk@hi.is

Acta Archaeologica vol. 79, 2008, pp 216-229
Printed in Denmark • All rights reserved

THE ORIENTATION OF DANISH PASSAGE GRAVES

Claus Clausen, Ole Einicke & Per Kjærgaard

The megalithic monuments found in large numbers throughout most of Western Europe have been the object of extensive archaeo-astronomical investigations over the past decades. In recent years, two main contributions have been the comprehensive works of Clive Ruggles (Ruggles 1999) and Michael Hoskin (Hoskin 2001) dealing in-depth with megalithic monuments in Britain/Ireland and South-Western Europe respectively. Strangely, few investigations of megalithic monuments in Northern Europe have been published. Especially in Denmark and northern Germany, around the western part of the Baltic Sea, the concentration of megalithic graves is very high, probably as high as in Bretagne and the Orkney Islands. In Denmark, about 7,000 megalithic graves have been plotted out of an estimated original total number of 40,000 (Jensen 2001)[1]. The official Danish preservation register lists 2,800 graves. Of these, about 500 are of the special type known in Danish as jættestuer, 'tombs of the giants'. For the sake of brevity, this article will refer to them as passage graves, as in the title. These passage graves will be the subject of the present investigation.

The passage graves seem to be the culmination of a long development from the older simple dolmens with a single small chamber to great dolmens and finally to the passage graves, a type of large, elaborate tomb built by specialists. The passage graves that we consider in this paper are defined by an entrance passage approximately perpendicular to an almost rectangular main chamber. Potsherds found in front of the entrance passages (belonging to the so-called "Klintebakke" type) place the date of construction from around 3200 to 3100 BC (Nielsen 2004). A handful of carbon-14 dates are established from birch bark found in the so-called 'dry wall' between the orthostats (Dehn and Hansen 2005). The dates of eight of the passage graves point to a main construction period reaching from 3350 to 3050 BC[2]

Different forms of these passage graves exist (Hansen 2005). The most common is a single rectangular main chamber with a single narrower entrance passage. The whole construction is usually covered by a circular earthen mound surrounded by kerbstones. The size of both the main chamber and the entrance passage can vary considerably. Another quite common form is a double grave with two separate main chambers in the same earthen mound, each with its own entrance passage (Dehn and Hansen 2000). Twin graves are like double graves, except that the main chambers are adjacent, sharing stones on their short sides. Even triple graves have been found. Sometimes passage graves and dolmens form small groups, typically containing 5-7 graves. An example of the layout of a single passage grave is given in Figure 1, below (Hansen 1993). Figures 2 and 3 show the layout of a twin grave and its earthen mound.

Recently, archaeologists have shown that sight lines

---

1 Other authors evaluate the total number as more likely to be around 25,000. See, for example, Hansen 2005.

2 Seven of the eight dates fall within this interval. A single grave is dated (based on two independent measurements) at 2900 BC.

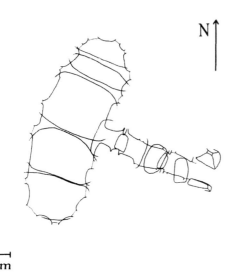

Fig. 1. The ground plan of the typical passage graves - 'Nissehøj'. See Table 1A, unit nr. 3026:58. The contours of the horizontal and vertical stones are shown.

were used when establishing the entrance passage. It seems that the innermost part of the entrance passage was the first part of the passage graves to be built, and that special care was taken in establishing its direction and maintaining this throughout the building process (Hansen 2005, Dehn and Hansen 2002, 2006). From the point of view of construction, such sight lines do not seem to be necessary. This could indicate that the entrance passage relates to some direction in the landscape or to some point on the horizon.

We do not know much about the function of the passage graves. We know that they were used for burials, perhaps in separate, distinct events over a period of time, and that certain rituals were performed which might have included the moving around of bones. Also, a large quantity of pottery of high quality has been found outside the entrances – this pottery seems to have been offered on the occasions of numerous large offering ceremonies.

An earlier study by Hårdh and Roslund (Hårdh and Roslund 1991, H&R in the following), on the orientation of passage graves in Scandia and north-eastern Zealand was made on a sample of 41 graves. They found that most of the entrance passages pointed between east and southeast with a smaller number pointing south south-east. They argued in favour of a relationship between this orientation and the rising of the moon, identifying the south south-eastern direction with the southernmost 'standstill'

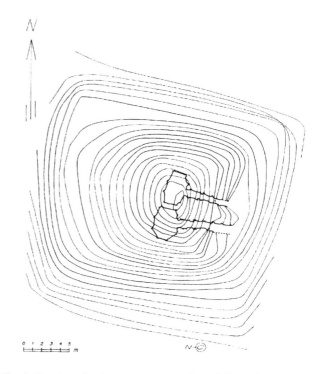

Fig. 2. Drawing of twin passage grave, unit nr. 3127:16 from table 1A, showing contour levels of the earthen mound and the underlying layers. The drawing shows that the passage grave is placed on a kind of platform. If the platform is artificial, it means that the builders have been able to level the terrain during construction. Also note that the two passages seem nearly parallel.

of the moon[3] (see Figure 4, 11 and 12). They concluded that "The distribution pattern of orientations is fully in line with a lunar explanation that the passages point at specific phases of the lunar cycle" (H&R 1991).

Our motivation for the present study was to enlarge the sample of passage graves with accurately determined directions of the entrance passages. Furthermore, we wanted to use this larger sample to see whether H&R's conclusions could be substantiated or if other explanations were possible.

The orientation of the passage graves is in this paper described as the direction of the entrance passage as seen from the main chamber out through the middle of the en-

---

3 Both the moon and sun have 'standstill' points, also known as extreme points. The sun has two extreme points: the northern one corresponds to the point where the sun rises at the winter solstice and the southern one corresponds to the point where it rises at the summer solstice. Likewise, the Moon has similar extreme northern and southern points; however, due to the Moon's 18.61-year cycle, it has two northern and two southern extreme points. (See also the section entitled "The azimuth distributions of the rising sun and moon" and figures 11 and 12.)

Fig. 3. This photo shows the 3127:16 unit from the west side before it was restored in 1991. The mound is clearly placed on a platform or ledge.

trance passage. This direction, measured clockwise from the north, is called the azimuth. Thus, for example, an entrance passage pointing due east has an azimuth of 90° (see figure 5).

The paper is composed as follows: first, we describe our fieldwork and the measurements of the directions of the passages. Then we compare our measurements with the survey by H&R and discuss the significance of specific features in the distribution of the directions. Next, we calculate the distribution of points on the horizon at which the sun and moon rise and we try to interpret the observed distribution in terms of three hypotheses: a) the rising sun; b) the rising (full) moon; and c) the rising full moon before an eclipse of the moon. All tables are placed at the end of this paper, just prior to the references.

OBSERVATIONS – THE FIELDWORK

Measurements were initially made at 56 locations (i.e. registration numbers) on Zealand between the geographical latitude 55.5° N and 56° N. To begin with, measurements were made using a GPS, a magnetic compass and a theodolite.

The GPS was used to measure the altitude above sea level (not tabulated), geographical position and to determine a north–south baseline. The distance between the two reference points on the north–south baseline was from 500 to 600 metres. The theodolite was used to measure the azimuths and the apparent horizon altitude (h) at the azimuth found. The apparent horizon mentioned is the horizon as we see it. In many cases, local topography

(trees, houses, etc.) prevented measures of the horizon altitude, but from the 22 measurements of this type, the landscape was found to be rather flat (see Table 1A), with an average h of about 0.8°. A correction of the azimuths would be of approximately the same order as the horizon altitude according to the true or astronomical horizon, except for the most southern directions. It means that the exclusion of a correction of the azimuth is not critical in relationship to the uncertainty of the measurements (see below). Deduced from 47 measurements, the average altitude was about 42m above sea level, and in some cases there was an extremely good view of the horizon. It has been shown that many passage graves were built in open fields, because underneath the grave itself one sometimes finds traces of agriculture.

The resulting azimuths showed that measurements using the magnetic compass alone were sufficiently accurate; therefore, later measurements of the azimuths were done using only a magnetic compass. Such measurements were done on a supplementary five passage graves on Zealand and for five on of the island of Samsø to the west of Zealand, but still at the same latitude. Thus, the total number of graves measured was 66. The geographical latitude and longitude were measured using the GPS, except for the five graves on Samsø, where the position was found using high resolution maps.

Good measurements were obtained for 51 graves with a total of 63 entrance passages; these measurements are presented in Table 1A. Considering the accuracy in establishing the north–south base line and, correspondingly, the entrance sight line (determined to be the mean line between the two sides), we evaluate the accuracy of the azimuths to be ±2°. This was confirmed by a repeat measurement of four graves, which always agreed to better than ±2°.

The data for the passage graves with uncertain measurements are given in Table 1B, which contains 17 locations (two in common with Table 1A) with a total of 18 estimated entrance passage directions. Reasons that good measurements could not be obtained were that the entrance passage 1) was missing altogether or 2) so damaged that no meaningful measurement could be obtained, or 3) that the local topography made measurements difficult. The uncertainty of measurements given in Table 1B is larger than ±3°. Thus, only the data from Table 1A is taken into further consideration in the present paper.

The distribution of the resulting 63 entrance direc-

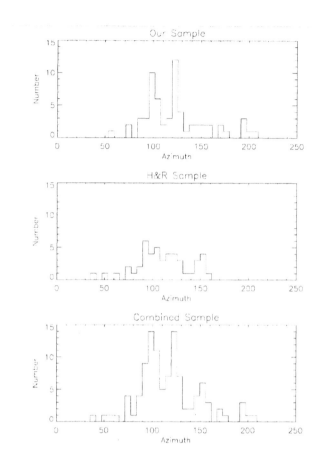

Fig. 4. The distribution of the azimuths of the entrance passages of the passage graves measured by us (upper panel – 51 graves with 63 entrance directions) and by H&R (middle – 41 graves with 47 entrance directions) and the combined sample (88 graves with 105 entrance directions).

tions from Table 1A is given in histogram form in Figure 4 and also, for the combined sample, as a circle azimuth diagram in Fig. 5. Considering the accuracy and number of measurements, we have chosen a bin-size of 6° (and started at 29.5°) for the histograms. At a glance, it is immediately obvious that the distribution is far from random. We find that most azimuths (70%) fall between 80° and 135°, with two peaks around 100° and 120°.

During our investigation, we discovered that large groups of passage graves existed within which most of the passage graves and other megalithic units were related to each other. We call these large groups clusters; they typically contain 15-30 megalithic units and cover an area of around 10-25 km².

Our sample of passage graves includes parts of – probably the central part – of three clusters of passage graves

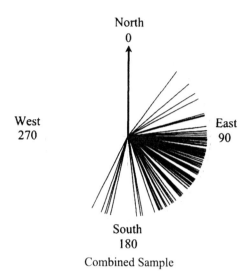

Fig. 5. The azimuth distribution for the combined sample, shown as an azimuth circle diagram. It is easily seen that most of the observations lie in the east to south quadrants.

(Table 1A: Tranebjerg (Samsø cluster), Ubby (Kalundborg cluster), Rye, Kirkehyllinge (Ejby cluster)). Looking for 'astronomical' sight lines, we discovered that about 75% or more of the passage graves in the clusters were pointing towards other passage graves (or dolmens) in the surrounding area, up to five kilometres from the central part. This discovery was so striking that we started a survey of 20 cluster candidates (fig. 6) for which we here present some interesting preliminary results. A more detailed account will be given in Kjærgaard and Clausen 2008.

The Samsø-cluster is shown in Figure 8, and the measurements of this cluster are given in Table 2. The central part of the cluster is shown in Figure 9, in which the reconstructed topography of prehistoric times is also presented. At the moment, this cluster is the one we have investigated most intensively. The cluster consists of 20 units: 14 passage graves, three dolmens, one great dolmen (with a passage) and two unclassified megalith units. The entire cluster covers an area of about 25 km2.

An interesting quantity is what we call the 'alignment azimuth'. The alignment azimuth is defined as the azimuth of the line drawn from one cluster unit (the primary unit) to another cluster unit (the target unit). We use the word 'alignment azimuth' for this new quantity because we know from our investigation that a line can be drawn through at least 4 cluster units, including one or more of the passages. Table 2 shows that for nine primary units of the Samsø-cluster, one can find a corresponding tar-

Fig. 6. The map shows the distribution of identified and potential clusters in Denmark and southern Sweden (Scania). 1) The Samsø cluster, 2) the Kalundborg cluster and 3) the Ejby cluster.

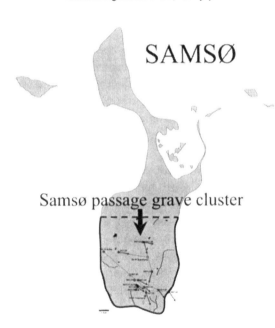

Fig. 7. This map shows the island of Samsø as it appears at the present time and marks the position of the Samsø cluster.

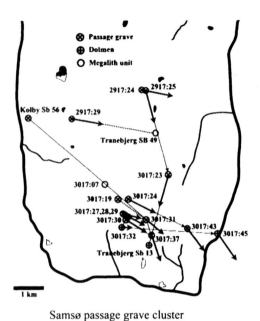

Samsø passage grave cluster

Figure 8. The map shows the southern part of Samsø with small lakes, ponds and creeks at the present time. Eight passage graves are located at the central part of the cluster, which covers about one square km. The distribution of the alignment azimuths in the cluster is quite similar to the main distribution in Table 1A for azimuths greater than 90°. The thin solid lines represent directions for the alignment azimuths tabulated in Table 2. The dotted lines represent an uncertain azimuth alignment direction. The short arrows represent passage directions and the numbers refer to the unit registration number (Table 2).

Figure 9. The reconstructed coastline in prehistoric times and the topography around the central part of the Samsø cluster. Measurements show that nearly all the megalithic units are placed at local high points. The map shows a more complex shoreline, informing us that this part of the island was fragmented into many small islands in the past.

get unit such that the alignment azimuth is the same as the azimuth of the passage of the primary unit (in other words, here the passage points towards the target unit). For 3 other primary units, one can find a target unit such that the alignment azimuth minus 180° is the same as the azimuth of the passage of the primary unit (which means that the opposite direction of the passage azimuth points

Figure 10. Unit 3017:31 seen from the left passage of unit 3017:37 (Table 2). This photo was taken during the restoration of 3017:37 in the late summer of 2007. At that time, it was possible to stand where the passage is connected to the chamber and make a sighting 180□ opposite the direction in which the passage points. Standing in the middle of the passage probably does not give the correct position; one should rather make the sighting along one of the sides of the passage (Hansen 2005). In a few cases, the established sightline has been known to continue at the back of the chamber (Hansen 2005).

towards the target unit). Thus, for the 14 measurable units in the Samsø-cluster, the passage azimuths of nine (64%) point forward, three (22%) point 'backward' and two (14%) have no 'target unit'. All units enter into a source unit–target unit relationship.

One of the two other clusters investigated, the Kalundborg-cluster, with 32 units, shows nearly the same characteristics as the Samsø-cluster. It is also remarkable that the same alignment azimuths are represented in both clusters. This result suggests that the same underlying idea is the basis for the layouts of the two clusters, and certainly that the placement of the individual passage graves and dolmens cannot be random.

Based on the above results, we suggest that lines/directions must have played a very important role in the burial praxis.

COMPARISON WITH THE ORIENTATIONS FOUND BY H&R

As mentioned above, a similar investigation had been done earlier by H&R, who measured typologically similar passage graves in Scandia and North-Zealand. H&R measured 41 graves using a theodolite and a magnetic compass. H&R have an accuracy of ±2° on their measured azimuths. Included in our sample are four graves (with five entrance passages) from H&R's investigation. For these, our measurements are in agreement with those of H&R to less than one degree in the mean (the largest deviation is two degrees). We are therefore confident that H&R's results can be directly compared with ours and that the two samples can be combined. The distribution of the azimuths found by H&R is also shown in Figure 4, together with the distribution of the combined sample. A general agreement can be seen between our sample and that of H&R in the sense that most azimuths are found to be between 80° and 135°. The difference between the two distributions is that our sample clearly displays two peaks; this is not clearly visible in H&R's distribution. However, H&R themselves interpret their broad distribution as having two components, one at around 90° and another at around 125°. We note that the two peaks are clearly visible in the combined sample. Other differences are the small peak at 150°, which is more pronounced in H&R's sample, and the direction due south which is found in our material but not in H&R's. For the combined sample we find the position of the two main peaks to be 100° and 120°.[4]

In order to investigate the observed material a bit further, we have divided the combined sample into three parts according to geographical region: Zealand west of longitude 11° 40' (where the broad fjord "Issefjorden" cuts north Zealand in two); Zealand east of this longitude; and Scania. We have done this in order a) to investigate whether there is a trend in the distributions according to geographical location, and b) to see whether the peaks in the distribution found for the combined sample can be seen in these individual, smaller samples. The result is that all three peaks, at 100°, 120° and 150°, are noticeable in all three distributions. We take this result as a confirmation of the reality of the three peaks in the distribution – they are not due to statistical chance.

THE AZIMUTH DISTRIBUTIONS OF THE RISING SUN AND MOON

From the observed distribution of azimuths (Figures 4 and 5), an interpretation in terms of the rising sun or moon seems natural. Also, the preliminary results from the two clusters of passage graves makes it obvious that not only were the constructors very conscious of the direction of the entrance passage, but also that directions must have played an important role in the burial practice.

The azimuth distribution for the rising (or setting) sun and moon is well known and relatively simple (see, for example, Ruggles 1999, pp. 24-25 and pp. 36-37 or Hoskin 2001, p. 20). The azimuths of the rising sun vary between their extreme values at the solstices. The determining variables are the geographical latitude and the inclination of the ecliptic, ε, which varies slightly with time. For the relevant geographical location, the azimuth of the rising sun would vary between approximately 42° and 135° around the time period where the passage graves were built. The sun would spend most of its time at the extreme points. The azimuth distribution of the rising moon also depends on the inclination of the orbit of the moon and the 18.61-year period of the regression of the line of nodes (the intersection of the line of nodes with the ecliptic). The combined effect causes the lunar extreme points to move along the horizon with the same period as

the lunar cycle (18.61 year). Thus the rising moon has two northern and two southern extreme points (often referred to as the northern/southern major and minor lunar standstills), which are covered in the 18.61-year period. For the sake of the following discussion, we have calculated not only the extreme points but the actual distribution of azimuths for both the sun and the moon.[5] These distributions are given in Figure 10.

From earlier investigations of megalithic monuments, alignment with both the sun (for example, Stonehenge and the passage tombs at Newgrange and Maes Howe) and the moon (for example, the recumbent stone circles in north-eastern Scotland and the short stone rows) have been found (see Ruggles, 1999). In his comprehensive work on the orientation of dolmens in Iberia and France, Hoskin argued in favour of an orientation related to the rising of the sun.

INTERPRETATION IN TERMS OF THE RISING SUN

When we consider the observed distribution of the combined sample from Figures 4 and 5, we notice, in fact, that it very closely resembles some of the distributions found by Hoskin for Iberian and French megalithic tombs. In our case, 78% of the azimuth directions fall within the azimuth range of the rising sun. Thus the same interpretation could be invoked, namely that the entrance direction is related to the direction of the rising sun, and that 17% of the directions could be related to the direction of the sun climbing just above the horizon or close to culmination; in Hoskin's terminology, 95% are sun rising or sun climbing (SR/SC). Hoskin advanced the hypothesis that the tombs were laid out to face sunrise on the day the construction began, when manpower for the enterprise was available after the harvest (see Hoskin 2001, p. 127). So this hypothesis could very well also apply to the Danish passage graves. There are, however, important differences: in general, our distribution of azimuths is skewed

---

4 The calculated mean values for the intervals 75° to 105° (included) and 105° to 130° (included) are 97° and 119° respectively.

5 The computations were done using our set of computer programs. The distribution for the Sun is the same today, with only a small shift in distribution due to today's slightly lower value of the inclination of the ecliptic, ε (the distribution now lies between 44° and 134°). Note that we refer to the apparent rising of the centre of the sun (taking into account the effect of refraction at the horizon). We have calculated the distribution of the rising Moon's azimuth for an 18.61-year period, starting from 3300 BC. The distribution is the same today, with only a small shift in the extreme points of 1-2°.

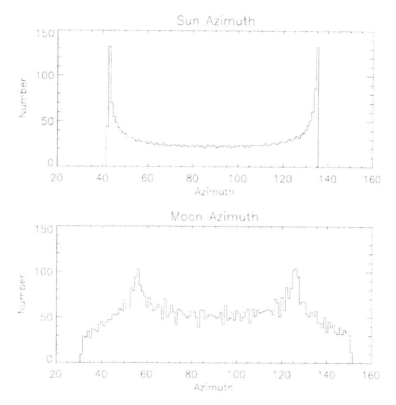

Fig. 11. The azimuth distribution of the number of sunrises for an eight-year period (upper panel) and for the number of moonrises (lower panel) during the moon's 18.6-year cycle for the time around 3300 BC. The bin-size used here is 1 degree.

more towards the South; and in general the passage graves are larger and more elaborate constructions than the simpler dolmens studied by Hoskin. Finally, the climates of the two locations differ. For the Danish passage graves, an azimuth for the rising sun of 120° would correspond to a date close to either the first of November or early February. Since the climate in November and February is cold and wet, with short days and little light, it makes no sense to start building an elaborate passage grave involving the handling of 40-50 large stones, each weighing up to several tons, at this time of the year – even though the actual construction time was probably relatively short; perhaps weeks rather than months. We would consider it highly unlikely that the construction of more than 40% of the passage graves (those with azimuths larger than 119°) would have begun at that time. This argument does not, of course, rule out a solar explanation, but then it requires that the direction of the rising sun be marked for later use. Further, we cannot fit the southern direction into the solar explanation. We then face a more complicated explanation – and, why mark directions around 100° and 120°

preferentially when a whole continuum of directions is available? Besides, the argument for the building process starting after the harvest is really not that strong, since farming at that time was most likely only a supplement to hunting, fishing and herding. Finally, we notice that there is a lack of observed azimuths around the solstices where the sun spends the longest periods of time.

INTERPRETATION IN TERMS OF THE RISING FULL MOON

Some of the features in the observed distribution of azimuths (Figures 4 and 5) could be related to an explanation in terms of the moon. First of all, there is the – admittedly small – clump of azimuths around 150° which corresponds nicely with the southern outer standstill of the moon (which was also the argument that led H&R to suggest a lunar explanation). However, it is also worth mentioning that the two peaks in the observed distribution around 100° and 120° both have a width of around 20° and are separated by this same amount. In the mean, a

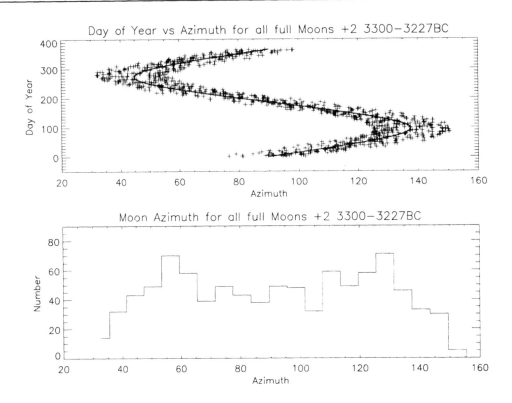

Figure 12. The day of the year versus the azimuth for the rising full moon. The vernal equinox is taken as the start day. The fully drawn line represents the ideal case, in which the moon rises precisely opposite to the setting sun. The azimuth of 90° corresponds in mean to the vernal and autumn equinoxes and the azimuths of approximately 45° and 135° correspond to mid-winter and mid-summer. The diagram is for the geographical latitude 56° and for the time zone +2. The diagram also nicely illustrates the two northern and two southern standstills or extreme points. The lower figure gives the corresponding azimuth distribution.

difference in the rising full moon's azimuth of 20° would roughly correspond to one lunar month (if one is reasonably far from the standstills – see Figure 11).

This leads us to suggest that the important direction is the direction of a certain full moon, for example the first full moon of spring/autumn, the so-called 'megalithic equinox' (Marciano Da Silva 2004) or the first full moon after sowing/harvest. In fact, the azimuth of 100° would roughly correspond to the beginning of April or the middle of September, and the azimuth of 120° would roughly correspond to the beginning of May or the middle of August. The relationship between the azimuth of the rising full moon and the date of the year has been calculated and is given in Figure 11. Due to the moon's 18.61-year period, this relationship is not very sharp, as can be seen from the figure.

The moon hypothesis has the advantage of involving particular directions which eventually could be marked

for later construction. However, it can also be noted that the obvious directions of interest related to spring/autumn and sowing/harvest occur at times of the year when it was practical to start and carry out the construction work. We also find that the special emphasis on the direction revealed by the clusters of passage graves is easier to accommodate in a hypothesis involving the rising of a special full moon. Here we notice that the southern azimuths or lines could refer to the summer full moon, which moves at southern directions just above the horizon.

Most of the above arguments would also apply to the rising of the new moon (or rather, the rising of the moon just before the new moon), the only difference being that the dates upon which this would occur around 100° and 120° would be nearly the same as those for the rising sun.

INTERPRETATION IN TERMS OF ECLIPSES OF THE MOON

An interpretation of the observed azimuth distribution in terms of eclipses of the moon may seem far-fetched. Nevertheless, there are a number of interesting facts which could point in this direction. Here we will consider the distribution of azimuths of the rising full moon prior to an eclipse (later the same night). This distribution should be rather similar to the sun's azimuth distribution, since the moon will be directly opposite the sun at an eclipse. However, due to the moon's different periods, the distribution is not at all smooth. In fact, for limited periods of time and for a limited range of geographical longitudes, one finds a distribution in which peaks occur around the azimuths of 100° and 120° with a trough in between. This is actually the case for the geographical location we consider and for the time period 3300 BC to 3100 BC (but most pronounced for the period 3300 BC to 3200 BC). The two peaks and the trough, which we call the 'fingerprint feature', are not found in the centuries before or after 3300-3100 BC, nor are they found outside a limited range of geographical longitudes.[6] Also when we calculate the moonrise azimuth distribution for the day after the eclipse we do not see the 'fingerprint feature'. Long-term calculations running throughout a period of 8000 years show that the 'fingerprint feature' appears now and then. Roughly speaking, the feature can persist from 100 to approximately 350 years with pauses from 100 to 200 years. We also find that in the time period 3300-3200 BC, there were about 50% more eclipses of the moon than normal for full moonrises in the azimuth interval of 90° to 130°. There is, however, a problem here. We can calculate very accurately when an eclipse will occur in "absolute" time, i.e. in what is called ephemeris time (ET – popularly speaking, the time that enters into Newton's second law). However, due to the accumulated effect of the Earth's faster rotation in earlier times, we do not know the corresponding universal time (UT, i.e. roughly speaking the mean solar time), or equivalently the geographical longi-

tude at which this eclipse will occur. The difference between the ephemeris time and the universal time, known as Delta T, is not known with any great accuracy when considering the time interval relevant here. The best estimate for Delta T for 3300BC is around 23 hours, with an uncertainty of about ±5 hours.[7] We can take this effect into account by simply using our computations at the next following time zone; i.e. for our geographical location, which is the present-day time zone +1, we should use our computations for present day time zone +2. In Figure 13, we show that the fingerprint feature is visible through time zones -5 to +2. Thus our hypothesis is consistent with a Delta T of 23h.

We note that it would have been possible for Neolithic man to a certain degree to 'predict' a lunar eclipse using simple means. Actually, when the sun sets opposite the rising full moon (to within certain natural limits[8]), then about 1 out of 3 full moonrises are followed by an eclipse on the same night.

We do not suggest that the passage graves or the clusters of passage graves and dolmens acted as advanced prehistoric observatories. Rather, we propose the hypothesis that rituals concerning burials and the dead were so important that they necessitated keeping an eye on the rising of the (full) moon, so that these rituals could be performed when an eclipse occurred. In our view, the near-obsession with particular directions indicated by the clusters of passage graves and dolmens points to a special phenomenon,

---

6 Our computer program is based on the lunar theory developed by E. W. Brown, in which analytical expressions for the lunar motion are used and expressions for the Earth's orbit are included – it also gives the Solar ephemeris. The actual version of Brown's theory used is taken from the Nautical Almanac Office's "Improved Lunar Ephemeris" (Jet Propulsion Laboratory,"Long Ephemeris" DE406, see http://ssd.jpl.nasa.gov/horizons.html); however, we used only a limited number of terms. For the classification of the eclipses of the Moon (i.e. whether partial/total/penumbral), we used the recipe given by Jean Meeus (Jean Meeus, *Astronomical Algorithms*, 1991).

7 An account of the problem of the Earth's rotation is given in the review paper by F. Richard Stephenson, "Historical eclipses and the Earth's rotation", *Astronomy & Geophysics*, vol. 44, 2.22, 2003. The difference between the Newtonian time and the universal time (mean solar time) is called delta T. The effect is mainly due to the tidal force of the moon, which slows the Earth's rotation. The value of delta T is relatively well known back in time to about 700BC. When we extrapolate back to the time period considered here, we find a delta T of around 23 hours (for 3300 BC) with a considerable uncertainty, probably around ±5 hours (or ±5 time zones) corresponding to ±75° along the same latitude. The effect of delta T can be taken into account by adjusting the time zone for which the eclipses are computed. A delta T of 23h corresponds to using the time zone +2h for the Danish passage graves. The "fingerprint feature" is visible for time zones from -5h to +2h, and most pronounced for time zones from -4h to 0h.

8 To be precise, the sun and moon should be on a straight line to within ±5° (i.e. the sun and moon are directly opposite to within ±5°) and the full moon should rise between 15 minutes before sunset and 3 minutes after sunset. If this condition is fulfilled, there is a probability that 1 out of 3 full moon rises are followed by an eclipse of the moon within the following 12 hours (this probability is independent of the azimuth). If the moon rises later than 3 minutes after the sunset, one will not be able to determine whether or not the sun and moon are aligned. If the sun is approximately 15 minutes or less from setting, then the rising full moon will appear to be very red, in fact almost as red as the setting sun.

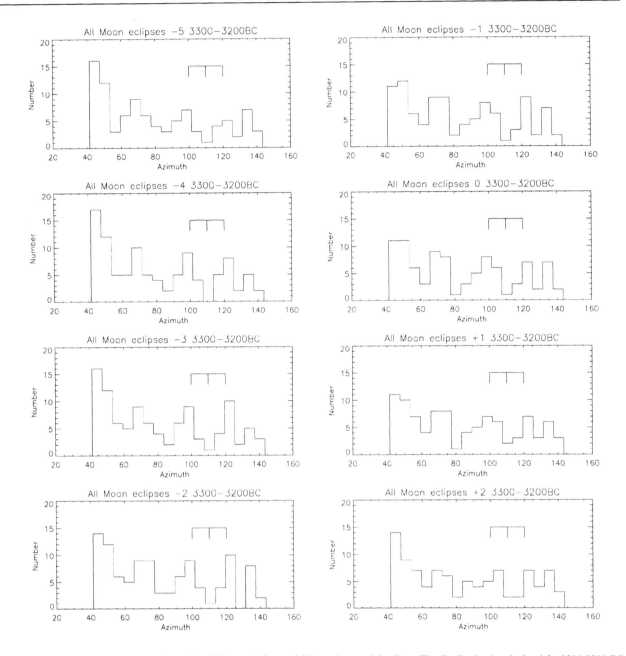

Fig. 13. The distribution of azimuths of the rising full moon before a visible total or partial eclipse. The distribution is calculated for 3300-3200 BC for the geographical latitude 56° and for the time zones from -5h (90° west) to +2 (15° east). The position of the 'fingerprint feature' is indicated by the position of the 'comb' with 3 teeth.

for example, an eclipse. In this case, we suggest that the southern azimuths or lines could be in the direction of the eclipse itself. Many – even most – summer eclipses occur at southern directions low on the horizon.

Actually, one could imagine that some of the full moon risings at the time of spring/autumn and sowing/harvest mentioned before were observed to be followed by an eclipse later the same night, which could have led to a strengthened interest in the two directions of 100° and 120°. Thus the two hypotheses involving the rising of certain full moons and the same followed by an eclipse need not exclude each other.

SUMMARY

We have measured the directions of the entrance passages for 51 passage graves situated mainly on north Zealand. Together with previously published measurements, the combined sample of 105 entrance directions shows a strong preference for the azimuth directions of 100° and 120°. Nearly all directions fall within the azimuths for the rising sun or the (full) moon. From clusters of passage graves, we find a very strong tendency for the entrance passage to point towards another passage grave or dolmen. We discuss our findings in terms of three hypotheses: in terms of the rising sun; the rising full moon; and the rising full moon before an eclipse. Taking all the evidence into consideration, we tend to favour a lunar hypothesis for the entrance directions.

ACKNOWLEDGEMENTS

We would like to thank Svend I. Hansen of the Danish National Museum and Torben Dehn of the Cultural Heritage Foundation (Danish: Kulturarvsstyrelsen) for their valuable help and inspiring conversations. We also thank Svend Hansen for the use of Figures 1 and 10, and The Danish National Museum for the use of Figure 2 (made by N. Chr. Clemmensen), Figure 3, and Figure 9 (made by Jørgen Westphal). Thanks also go to our colleagues, Jens Viggo Clausen and Uffe Gråe Jørgensen of the Niels Bohr Institute, for their careful reading of an early draft of the manuscript and their valuable suggestions, and finally to Elizabeth Bramsen for linguistic corrections.

REFERENCES

Dehn, T. and Hansen, S. I., 2000: "Doubleness in the Construction of Danish Passage Graves", in Neolithic Orkney in its European context, ed. Anna Ritchie, McDonald Institute Monographs, p. 215.

Dehn, T. and Hansen, S. I., 2005: "Birch bark in Danish passage graves", Journal of Danish Archaeology, xiv, pp. 23-42.

Dehn, T. and Hansen S. I., 2006: "Architecture Mégalithique en Scandinavie", in Origine et développement du mégalithisme de l'ouest de l'Europe, Actes du Colloque international du Musée de Bougon 26/30 octobre 2002, p. 39-62.

Hansen, S., 1993: "Jættestuer i Danmark (konstruktion og restaurering)", Miljøministeriet, Skov- og Naturstyrelsen.

Hansen, S. I., 2005: "Der var en gang - danske jættestuers indgangskonstruktioner", preprint.

Hoskin, M., 2001: "Tombs, Temples and Their Orientations", Ocarina Books.

Hårdh, B. and Roslund, C., 1991: "Passage Graves and the Passage of the Moon", in Regions and Reflections, in Honour of Märta Strömberg, eds. K. Jennbert, L. Larsson, R. Petré, and B. Wyszomirska-Werbart, p. 35.

Jensen, J., 2001: "Danmarks Oldtid – Stenalder 13.000 – 2.000 f.Kr"., Gyldendal, p. 347.

Kjærgaard, P. and Clausen, C., 2008: in preparation.

Marciano Da Silva, C., 2004: "The Spring Full Moon", Journal for the History of Astronomy, xxxv, p. 475.

Nielsen, P. O, 2004: "Causewayed camps, palisade enclosures and central settlements of the Middle Neolitic in Denmark", Journal of Nordic Archaeological Science, xiv, pp. 19-33.

Ruggles, C., 1999: "Astronomy in Prehistoric Britain and Ireland", Yale University Press.

Addresses of the authors
C.C. Auto-Transport
Jenagade 19, DK-2300
Copenhagen, Denmark

TABLES

Passage grave		Location		Azimuth	Horizon altitude
Registration number	Name / Place	Lattitude ° ' "	Longitude ° ' "	Az° *Note	h°
3017:24	Ørby / Tranebjerg Sb 36	55 47 24,0	10 35 16,8	116	-
3017:27	Aamarks Høj/ Tranebjerg Sb 33	55 47 13,2	10 35 16,8	105	-
3017:29	Østlige Hyldehøj /Tranebjerg Sb 31	55 47 13,2	10 35 16,8	115	-
3017:30	Sydlige Hyldehøj /Tranebjerg Sb 32	55 47 13,2	10 35 16,8	L 207/R 122 *1	-
3017:31	Ingeborgs hø i/Tranebjerg Sb 38	55 47 13,2	10 35 42,0	128	-
3120:19	Slaaenhøj / Raklev Sb 159	55 42 20,2	11 01 48,7	L 125 *2	-
3120:21	Nyrup / Raklev Sb 158	55 42 19,3	11 02 19,2	171	-
3220:68	Melby / Årby Sb 40	55 38 38,8	11 06 12,4	125	-
3221:38	Ormshø j/ Årby Sb 3	55 38 57,4	11 07 55,5	L121 / R 116	0,2/0,2
3421:08	Rævehøj / Kirke Helsinge Sb 26	55 30 48,0	11 10 09,7	135	-
3221:24	Nordenhøj / Rørby Sb 1	55 39 09,5	11 10 11,8	L 160 / R 140	-
3321:01	Regnarshøj / Svallerup Sb 20	55 34 48,8	11 10 33,8	L 108/103 *2 *3	0,8
3221:10	Ræverøgel/Ubby Sb 24	55 37 41,2	11 10 36,7	101	-
3221:11	Udby / Ubby Sb 29	55 37 49,3	11 10 56,2	199	-
3221:26	Olshøj / Rørby Sb 12	55 39 17,3	11 10 58,3	R 174 *4	0,7
3221:12	Grønhøj / Ubby Sb 26	55 37 47,3	11 10 59,3	123	0,4
3221:06	Værslev / Værslev Sb 10	55 39 12,9	11 11 37,5	L 196/ M 192/ R 195	-
3421:12	Baunehøi / Kirke Helsinge Sb 4	55 30 22,3	11 11 50,7	154	-
3221:03	Værslev / Værslev Sb 4	55 39 43,9	11 11 56,0	156	-
3221:04	Værslev / Værslev Sb 5	55 39 39,0	11 12 13,4	121	-
3221:16	Korshøj / Ubby Sb 3	55 37 18,2	11 12 29,8	L 122/ R 122	1,2
3222:31	Rugtved / Viskinge Sb 20	55 38 46,7	11 16 43,8	94	-
3322:09	Selchausdal / Buerup Sb 19	55 34 55,0	11 19 26,3	L 98 *2	-
3322:10	Frendved / Buerup Sb 43	55 34 47,1	11 20 13,2	103	-
3323:08	Niløse / Niløse Sb 8	55 33 02,6	11 29 52,9	101	-
2823:05	Troldstuerne / Højby Sb 123	55 55 51,2	11 32 28,9	L 123/ R 87	0,4/0,4
3324:11	Bounsdysse / Undløse Sb 5	55 35 24,5	11 36 11,5	L 99 *2	-0,2°
3325:03	Stedstrup / Kirke Eskilstrup Sb 3	55 34 21,7	11 47 25,6	99	-
3125:37	Egby / Rye Sb 94	55 41 57,0	11 50 57,5	98	-
3125:39	Egby / Rye Sb 89	55 41 34,6	11 51 01,2	110	1,2
3325:13	Nørre Hvalsø / Kirke Hvalsø Sb 5	55 35 54,2	11 51 05,0	130	-
3125:34	Møllehøj /Kirke Hylling Sb 6	55 42 12,2	11 51 18,6	L 74/ R 73	-
3125:38	Egby / Rye Sb 93	55 41 45,9	11 51 20,8	85	1,4
3125:44	Præstemarken / Rye Sb 17	55 41 00,4	11 52 17,8	123	1,6
3026:58	Nissehøj / Vellerup Sb 19	55 44 54,3	11 52 49,1	109	0
3326:04	Kvandrup Skovfogedbolig / Kirke Hvalsø Sb 18	55 34 35,2	11 53 22,3	L 169 *5	-
3026:40	Klangdys / Krogstrup Sb 26	55 47 09,8	11 57 48,5	105	0,1
3326:34	Rishøj / Osted Sb 5	55 32 42,6	11 57 55,3	M 100/R 57 *6	M 1,2
2926:10	Slotshegnet / Dråby Sb 155	55 51 39,3	11 59 00,3	154	-
3226:62	Hørhøj / Kornerup Sb 2	55 37 09,7	11 59 02,0	101	2,3
3226:66	Tværhøj / Glim Sb 13	55 35 59,1	11 59 41,6	100	2,2
2926:50	Tørslev Marker/Gerlev Sb 98	55 48 23,9	12 00 41,8	98	0,4
3227:01	Børnehøjen / Himmelev Sb 24	55 39 42,3	12 06 37,9	L 130/ R 138	1,6/1,6
3027:20	Møllehøj / Snostrup Sb 33	55 47 05,9	12 06 42,6	120	-
3027:24	Stuehøj / Ølstykke Sb 53	55 47 52,0	12 06 56,7	123	-
3127:16	Gundsølille / Kirkerup Sb 33	55 41 59,2	12 09 02,4	L 91/ R 95	L 0,7
3027:28	Stenhøj / Stenløse Sb 65	55 45 12,2	12 09 52,8	103	1,1
2728:10	Holmgård / Alsøndrup Sb 3	55 57 46,2	12 12 44,2	126	-
2728:03	Mutter Gribs Hule / Nødebo Sb 5	55 58 48,4	12 17 22,0	85	-
2929:11	Grethes Høj / Farum Sb 10	55 48 12,9	12 20 24,3	104	-
2829:03	Kirkehelte / Karlebo Sb 10	55 54 02,7	12 23 47,3	L 145/ R 144	-

Table 1A

L, M, and R before the azimuth denote the left, middle and right entrance passages (as seen from the outside) for double, twin or triple graves. The Sb number is an old registration number for the location. Notes: *1) the left chamber is elongated in the direction of the entrance passage and resembles a dolmen more; *2) the right entrance passage is missing; *3) the passage makes a bend from 108° to 103° – the latter value is used; *4) the direction of the left entrance passage is uncertain, see Table 1B; *5) only one stone remains of the right entrance; *6) the measurement for the left entrance passage is uncertain, see Table 1B.

Passage grave		Location		Azimuth	
Registration number	Name/Place	Latitude ° ' "	Longitude ° ' "	Az°	*Note
3121:15	Ubberud /Tømmerup Sb 38	55 41 35,30	11 10 24,6	R 195	*1
3221:01	Bøgebjerg / Værslev Sb 14	55 40 18,70	11 10 34,8	?	*2
3221:09	Udby / Ubby Sb 31	55 37 44,80	11 10 41,0	L 116/ R 118	
3221:26	Olshøj / Rørby Sb 12	55 39 17,30	11 10 58,3	L 172	*3
3221:19	Teglværksminde / Ubby Sb 53	55 38 42,20	11 13 51,8	134	
3222:01	Svebøllegavn / Avnsø Sb 5	55 38 45,90	11 16 44,7	90	
3322:24	Sæbygaard / Sæby Sb 6	55 33 05,30	11 18 05,3	46	
3423:03	Skeldebjerg / Skellebjerg Sb 2	55 32 01,90	11 26 36,7	L 197	*4
2824:01	Birkehøj / Højby Sb 95	55 55 48,40	11 36 11,7	164	
3325:08	Stedstrup / Kirke Eskilstrup Sb 8	55 33 04,60	11 48 10,4	115	
2826:04	Hjortegårdene / Dråby Sb 25	55 54 49,50	11 54 45,4	151	
2726:15	Trollerup / Melby Sb 25	55 59 40,20	11 55 10,7	125	
3326:34	Rishøj / Osted Sb 5	55 32 42,60	11 57 55,3	L 190	*5
2926:02	Julianehøj / Dråby Sb 216	55 51 39,30	11 58 03,9	100	
3026:45	Onsved Marker / Krogstrup Sb 43	55 46 47,50	11 59 16,7	121	
3027:32	Elmehøj / Selsø Sb 14	55 44 48,00	12 02 20,0	65	
3027:27	Stenløse By / Stenløse Sb 70	55 45 46,20	12 09 42,6	L 173 ?/ R 103	

Table 1B

L, M, and R before the azimuth denote the left, middle, and right entrance passages for double, twin or triple graves.

*Notes: *1) the left entrance passage is missing; *2) the entrance passage is missing; *3) the right entrance passage is given in Table 1A; *4) the right entrance passage is so disturbed that no meaningful measurement could be made; *5) the middle and right entrance passages are given in Table 1A.

'Primary unit' Registration nr.	Latitude ° '	Longitude ° '	Azimuth +/- 2°	'Alignment azimuth' +/- 1°	'Target unit' Registration nr.
2917:24	55 49,449	10 35,541	100	100	2917:25
2917:25 twin	55 49,446	10 35,596	L 161	163	3017:23
2917:29	55 48,943	10 33,367	100	98	Sb 49 Tranebjerg megalith unit
3017:07 megalith unit	55 47,813	10 34,268	*1		
3017:19			*2	125	3017:31
3017:23	55 47,960	10 36,340	196	196	3017:37
3017:24	55 47,535	10 35,000	116	115	3017:43
3017:27			105	105	3017:31
3017:28			*3		
3017:29	55 47,237	10 35,041	116	115+180	3017:28
3017:30 *4	55 47,175	10 34,965	122	122	3017:37 twin
3017:30 dolmen*4	55 47,175	10 34,965	207	207	3017:32 dolmen
3017:31	55 47,176	10 35,593	128	125+180	3017:19
(3017:31)			128	130+180	3017:07 megalitic unit
(3017:31)			128	130+180	Kolby Sb 56 destroyed
3017:32 dolmen	55 47,052	10 34,846	95	93	3017:45
3017:37 twin	55 46,901	10 35,769	L 160	159+180	3017:31
3017:43	55 47,017	10 36,883	145	none	none
3017:23	55 47,960	10 36,340	196	196	Tranebjerg Sb 13 destroyed dolmen
3017:45 great dolmen	55 46,924	10 37,899	144	none	none
Tranebjerg Sb 49 megalith unit			*1		
Kolby Sb 56 destroyed			*1		
Tranebjerg Sb 13 destroyed dolmen			*1		

Table 2

L, before the azimuth denotes the left entrance passages for twin graves.

The alignment azimuths are deduced from maps and GPS measurements. Notes: *1 Not measurable, *2 Not measured, An old measurement gives the azimuth as south-east for 3017:19, *3 passage missing, *4 Registration number 3017:30 is a hybrid unit with a dolmen and a giant's tomb in the same earthen mound. The 3017:31 and 3017:37 units seem to play a central role in the cluster because of the many line relations. **

Acta Archaeologica vol. 79, 2008, pp 230-245
Printed in Denmark • All rights reserved

Copyright 2008
ACTA ARCHAEOLOGICA
ISSN 0065-101X

STABILITY & CHANGE
IN SCANDINAVIAN ROCK-ART
THE CASE OF BARDAL IN TRØNDELAG, NORWAY

KALLE SOGNNES

ROCK-ART IN CENTRAL NORWAY

In an early issue of Acta Archaeologica Gutorm Gjessing (1935) discussed some aspects of the large Bardal rock-art site in Steinkjer (Nord-Trøndelag) Norway. In this article Gjessing focused on the chronology of the Bronze Age horizon(s), that is, the carvings belonging to the South Scandinavian genre or tradition. However, also carvings belonging to the Stone Age or Arctic tradition are found at this site; these were presented in a later monograph (Gjessing 1936). Bardal holds a unique position within Scandinavian rock-art because both traditions are represented with a substantial number of images and because these images take part in numerous superimposition (Figure 1).

These two rock-art traditions were defined almost a century ago (Brøgger 1906, Hansen 1904). They were found to be separated in space and time as well as in subject matter. Although these dichotomies have been contested (e.g. Ekholm 1916, Hagen 1970, Helskog 1993), there is a strong tendency to deal with each tradition separately. In Norway most emphasis has been put on the Arctic rock-art (Bøe 1932, Gjessing 1932, 1936, Engelstad 1934, Hagen 1970, Hallström 1938, Helskog 1988, Simonsen 1958). Regarding sites and images the Arctic rock-art is outnumbered by the Bronze Age Tradition (here referred to as the BAT) rock-art, which, however, has not been studied as extensively (but see Coll 1902, Fett & Fett 1941, Gjessing 1939, Mandt Larsen 1972, Marstrander 1963, Marstrander and Sognnes 1999, Østmo 1990, Sognnes 2001).

Fifty some Arctic rock-art sites are known from central Norway, most of which contain carvings but paintings

occur too. These sites are found scattered along the coast and at the central and inner parts of the Trondheim Fjord (Sognnes 2002) mostly in areas that were submerged by the sea during the Early Holocene. The subject matter is limited, consisting predominantly of animals, especially elks and whales. Other land mammals are rare but depictions of reindeer, red deer, roe deer, bear and beaver are identified. Seal and fish occur, as do aquatic birds. Anthropomorphs are rare, while boat images are frequent, albeit found at a limited number of panels. Statistically birds and boats follow the whales. A dichotomy between motifs referring to land (elk/reindeer/bear) and sea (whale/boat/bird) may be postulated. In addition to these representational images some geometrical designs are found. Cupmarks are extremely rare in this tradition. Hoof and paw prints apparently are not present.

The BAT panels number around two hundreds, of which the majority is found in Stjørdal (Nord-Trøndelag). Most panels contain representational images but some have cup-marks only. Boats represent the most frequent representational motif. Other motifs are footprints and animals, most likely horses. Hoof prints occur but are extremely rare. Geometrical designs are represented too. Anthropomorphs occur at a few panels. This tradition contains images that are similar to the rock-art of southern Scandinavia. The relative frequencies of the motifs may, however, differ. Footprints, for instance, constitute c. 18 % in Stjørdal (Sognnes 2001: 69) as compared to 2-3 % for most Swedish rock-art regions (Bertilsson 1989: 39). Horses too are more frequent in central Norway, while the frequency of anthropomorphs is much lower than in southern Scandinavia.

Fig. 1. The Bardal I rock-art panels in Steinkjer, Nord-Trøndelag (photo Vitenskapsmuseet).

EPISODIC CONTINUITY
– AND BREAK

The making of rock-art in central Norway arguably lasted a long time, perhaps more than six millennia (Sognnes 2000: 104-108). Dating this rock-art, however, is difficult. For the BAT tradition clues can be found in decorated bronzes. Boats and other symbols represented on rocks were, for instance, engraved also on razors dated to the entire South Scandinavian Bronze Age, c. 1700-500 BC (Kaul 1998). The existence of older carvings has been claimed; cup-and rings in Denmark and Scania (Burenhult 1980) and western Norway (Walderhaug 1994) and boat images in western and central Norway (Fett & Fett 1941: 137, Sognnes 2001: 54). Possible later boat images are especially frequent in central Norway (Sognnes op. cit. 51-52).

Arctic rock-art is more difficult to date but the Holocene land uplift provides some clues. The dating of ancient shorelines indirectly provides maximum dates also for rock-art. In central Norway the earliest maximum dates for some panels are almost 9,000 bp. Most sites cannot, however, be older than from the sixth or seventh millennium bp, that is, from the Late Mesolithic and/or Early Neolithic (Sognnes 2003). Marine deposits covered some panels shortly after the carvings were made (Bakka 1975, 1987). In these cases the land uplift provides minimum dates too. This was the case at the panel Hammer

V (Nord-Trøndelag), which can be fairly well dated to c. 5,400 bp. On the other hand, the maximum date for the Evenhus site (Nord-Trøndelag) is as late as c. 3,700 bp. At this time the first BAT carvings likely were already made in this region, virtually within site from Evenhus.

The Neolithic/Bronze Age transition apparently represented a break in the making of rock-art in central Norway. The subject matter changed and other topographical settings where chosen (Sognnes 1992). Thus, the rock-art-making era in this region seems to consist of two chronologically separate traditions – albeit with some overlap. Superimpositions are rare for both traditions.

Looking into the sites we find that they mostly contain a few images only, which may have been made during one event. In average decades passed between each time new images were made and centuries between the establishing of new sites. A limited subject matter is represented and images at each site often are stylistically similar and executed in the same technique(s). This holds especially true for Arctic rock-art. At a micro scale we get the impression of episodic short-time usage. Yet, when we see all sites together at a macro scale, we get the impression of continuity. Occasionally these episodic events took place at the same panels, the most important of which, is found at Bardal (Nord-Trøndelag).

Fig. 2. The geographical setting of Bardal and neighbour rock-art sites.

BARDAL REVISITED

Prehistoric rock-art has been known from the Bardal farm since the middle of the 1890s (Lossius 1897a), and the Bardal I panel has become one of the best-known rock-art panels in Norway due to it large number and palimpsest of both Arctic and BAT carvings (Gjessing 1936, Hallström 1938). This is not, however, the only panel with rock carvings known from this farm. Already during his first visit the Swedish archaeologist G. Hallström (1907) found some panels eight hundred metres to the northeast. More panels were found also later (Bull 1935). These panels contain BAT images only and were ignored for almost a century. There was one exception from this, however; at a field called Lamtrøa a panel with some small zoomorphic images (Bardal III) was found (Gjessing 1936).

Bardal is located at 64° 3' N and 11° 23' E (Figure 2). From a shallow bay at the northern side of the Beitstad Fjord – the inner larger Trondheim Fjord basin – a narrow valley leads towards the northeast, following the foot of the steep-sided Bardalshalla mountain ridge towards the Følling parish at Lake Snåsavatn. Before c. 4,000 bp this lake formed the innermost part of the Trondheim Fjord.

The present farmstead is located at a raised marine terrace; the site being situated in a "quiet, peaceful inner-fjord landscape with fields and woody ridges", which differs from most other Arctic rock-art sites in northern

Scandinavia (Hallström 1938: 285). The terrace in front of Bardal I (35-45 m above sea level) emerged during the sixth millennium bp. The foot of this terrace, which is thirty metres above sea level, emerged c. 4,500 bp. The distance from the panel to the terrace edge is around seventy metres. It thus remained fairly close to the seashore for almost two millennia. After that topography changed rapidly. A shallow tidal beach emerged, at which five meters uplift represented a horizontal increase in new land of up to four hundred metres. Today the panel lies around one and a half kilometre from the shore.

The foot of the Bardal I panels is levelled to 42 m above sea level (Gjessing 1936: 31). The rock, which is facing southeast, is almost thirty metres long and nine metres high measured along the surface (Hallström 1938: 291). It is divided into two panels by a wide almost vertical crack. The southwestern part (panel a) is around twenty metres, the northeastern part (panel b) ten metres long. The inclination of the rock is c. 35° but more gently sloping in the upper part. Most images are found at panel a, at which also most of the superimpositions are found too.

Panel b contains fewer carvings but here too superimpositions are found. The rock is cut by narrow cracks following at least three major directions. Where three cracks meet pieces of the rock now may be missing. Some of the missing blocks certainly contained carvings. These blocks may still exist, however, during the initial investigation Lossius (1897b: 3-4) removed between one and three metres with soil and dirt in a length of thirteen metres at the left-hand part of panel a. He dug through the original topsoil but found nothing of interest. Whether he looked for missing blocks is unknown.

The fact that Bardal I contain so many images made during a long time span, representing several eras and periods makes this site particularly suitable as a laboratory for developing and testing methods for direct dating of rock carvings. Direct dating of rock art still is in its infancy and is much debated. For rock carving Robert G. Bednarik in particular has attempted to develop a reliable dating method. Bednarik (1992, 1993) focuses on micro erosion, which is contingent upon the presence of crystals or grains that were exposed by the prehistoric makers of the rock-art. In particular the progressive roundedness or wane of the minerals caused by weathering is studied (Bednarik 1992: 281).

Bednarik (op.cit. 282-283) postulates the existence of universal laws of wane formation, which can be applied both macroscopically and microscopically. Weathering processes attack minerals at different rates and the rates of micro-wane may vary through time due to environmental factors. Based on a number of independently dated measurements a calibration curve may be constructed, with which other measurements may be compared. The difficulty is, of course, to provide these independent dates. Bardal I, however, seems to be a suitable panel for testing this method. As stated by Gjessing (1935, 1936) images must have been carved at this site during a long time and a relative sequence based on superimpositions may be established. This sequence, then, may tentatively be calibrated by dates obtained from other, indirect, methods. For the BAT images these tentative datings likely will not differ significantly from the 'real' dates, since the material culture of the Scandinavian Bronze Age show repeatedly patterns of chronologically dependent stylistic variations. Each style was in favour during a short period and based on this the Bronze Age is divided into six periods.

The superimpositions – if it is possible to establish their relative chronological order – may be sorted into a Harris (1989) matrix. This matrix was created for studies of complex soil stratigraphy, but has also been used for sequences of rock paintings (Magar & Davila 2004). For Bardal I the numerous superimpositions in principle may provide a matrix in which several major phases should be identified. For the BAT images it is possible to provide tentative dates, which may serve as fix-points. The Arctic rock-art part of the matrix, however, is without this possibility, since similar images engraved on artefacts are rare and themselves difficult to date. However, the 'undisturbed' rock itself may contribute to a maximum date for the relevant curve (Bednarik 1993: 151). The latest glacial striae at Bardal likely should be dated to 10,400-10,300 bp when the glacier still was active, with an active ice front across the central Beitstad Fjord (Dahl et al. 1997: 121).

A couple of years ago a large rock was uncovered during construction work around fifty metres to the northeast of Bardal I. Marine deposits have covered this rock until today. Thus it is possible to study also a pristine glacially polished rock at which weathering processes have not yet started, a situation that further emphasises the key position Bardal has for Scandinavian rock-art.

GJESSING'S BARDAL

Gutorm Gjessing (1936) and Gustaf Hallström (1938) investigated Bardal I during the early 20th century. Some minor differences exist between these documentations, which are described by Hallström (op. cit. 292-309). I use Gjessing's publications as base for this study. This is because Hallström discussed the Arctic images only. These images were also Gjessing's primary concern but in addition he also made a separate study of the BAT images (Gjessing 1935), which thus makes his work the most complete and hence is used here (Figures 3-4). Gjessing also presented a tracing containing the Arctic images alone, however, he did not treat the BAT images in the same way. Later there has been no systematic documentation or attempts to analyse the panel.

Gjessing catalogued fifty-one Arctic images at Bardal I. The total number of BAT images is around three hundred and sixty, of which one hundred and eighty-five were identified as boats (Gjessing 1935: 126). Most of the Arctic carvings are found at panel a. At the left-hand edge of this panel are several large elks, of which the larger are between three and three and a half metres long. The rock ends abruptly to the left of these images. At the upper edge of the panel is an incomplete six metres long whale. Remnants of cervidae are found almost everywhere on this panel. Near the foot of the panel the images are smaller, some elks being less than two metres long. In this part anthropomorphs are found too, together with aquatic birds and geometric designs. Geometric designs, especially zigzags are found also in the central part of the panel. One little elk only is found at panel b.

Following H. Shetelig (1925) and E. S. Engelstad (1934) Gjessing (1936: 158) argued that the Arctic rock-art in Norway constituted stylistic sequence from large naturalistic to small schematic renderings of animals, sorting the central Norwegian record into three styles:

I.   This stage is characterised by naturalistic images, often in full size or even larger. Bardal I represents this style.
II. The naturalism is less cogent; the images often have some interior line patterns.
III. The images are represented by full schematism, as exemplified by Bardal III (Gjessing 1936: 108).

Gjessing also tried to date these styles. First of all, the strong weathering of the Arctic images suggested that

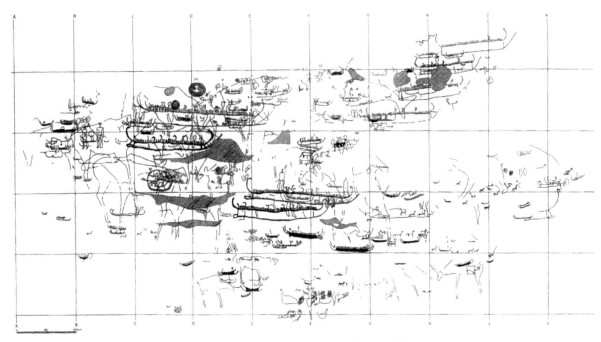

Fig. 3. Tracing of Bardal I panel a (after Gjessing 1936).

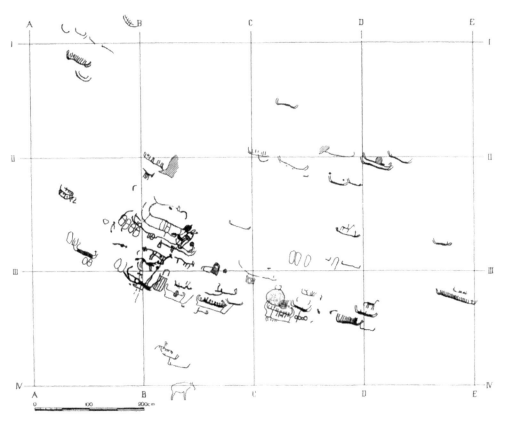

Fig. 4. Tracing of Bardal I panel b (after Gjessing 1936).

these were considerable older than the BAT images. On the other hand, Gjessing believed that the Bardal III images also should be dated to the Bronze Age (Montelius' periods I-II). Based on stylistic arguments he claimed that the Arctic images at Bardal I were much older (Gjessing 1936: 170-171). At that time few data existed regarding the Holocene land uplift in Central Norway, which made it difficult to use this method for dating the rock-art. However, Gjessing dated the Bardal I images tentatively to the Middle Neolithic ('Passage Grave Period'), perhaps earlier for the very first images made (op. cit. 177).

In his study of the BAT horizons Gjessing focused on individual images, for which he tried to construct a chronological sequence. He suggested a priori that the large number of BAT images cover a large time span. The images found could be sorted into a number of major types, which likely mirror the contemporary development in boat building technology – or at least that the images render different kinds of boats (Gjessing 1935: 127). Gjessing started his discussion with some large (more than four metres) boat images with two-lined hulls, two strongly curved lines protruding from keel and gunwhale in one end and one similarly curved line protruding from the gunwhale in the other end (Figure 5). Together with this type of boat images two double spirals he found to be of importance. These spirals strongly resemble decorations found on brooches from the Late Bronze Age. Gjessing believed that the large boats and the spirals were contemporary and therefore dated these boat images to the same time, that is, period IV, the technique used for these images he found to be similar. In his discussion Gjessing (op. cit. 128-131) also referred to the dating of the Brandskog ship from Uppland Sweden, which is equipped with animal head prows typical of this period. This kind of boats is, however, elsewhere in Scandinavia found in earlier contexts and a number of smaller images at Bardal I may also be earlier than these large ones.

In general Gjessing found that where small and large boat images were superimposed, the smaller were the earlier ones (op. cit. 132). Studies of superimpositions further revealed that the boat images could be sorted into three (four) major types (Figure 6):

I. The hull is drawn with one single line, which in both ends curve upwards, indicating prows. They normally have short lines above the hull indicating crewmembers.

IIa. Both gunwhale and keel are indicated. In one end

Fig. 5. Tracing of one of the Larger Bronze Age boat images at Bardal Ia (after Gjessing 1935).

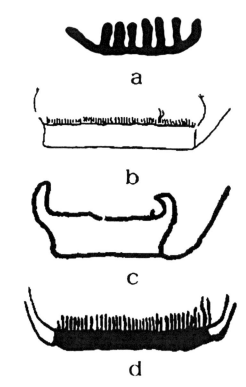

Fig. 6. Gjessing's (1936) sequence of Bronze Age/Pre-Roman Iron Age boat images (compiled after Gjessing 1935).

the keel is strongly elongated. Lines indicating prows are strongly curved.

IIb. Small contoured boat images. The prows are strongly curved and the keel line in the stem end is exceptionally long.

III. Boat images with hammered-out hulls. Gunwhale and keel lines are strongly elongated in both ends.

The claim that the single-line boat images with one-lined hull goes back to a classification system created by Coll's (1902, cf. Ekholm 1916), which was based on an assumed evolutionary sequence from single-lined simple to complex images with distinctly drawn hulls. These im-

Fig. 7. A section of the lower row of rock 'eyes' at Bardal Ia (photo K. Sognnes)

ages I found difficult to fit into the sequence established for Stjørdal (Nord-Trøndelag), which is the most studied record in central Norway. Here the single-line boats tend to occur together with late types (Sognnes 1990: 75-76). Type III Gjessing (op. cit. 135) claimed was later than the Bronze Age, primarily belonging to the beginning of the Iron Age. However, he also found it likely that the types IIb and III were contemporary. An important argument in favour of Iron Age dating of the type III images, Gjessing found at Bjørngård in Stjørdal, where some boats apparently are equipped with side rudder (loc. cit. 135, cf. Sognnes 2002: 176).

TENTATIVE ANALYSIS

At panel a a peculiar natural phenomenon is found. The rock consists mainly of calcite-rich greywacke sandstone. Main minerals are quartz, muscovite and calcite with some chlorite and epidote, the calcite being dissolved from the outermost 5 mm (Prestvik 1981). However, undulating narrow quartz veins occur. In two warped converging belts these veins surround some strongly weathered elongated grooves. These deep and dark grooves together with surrounding white quartz veins give distinct eye-like appearances (Figure 7). During favourable light conditions it is as if the rock has many eyes looking back at the spectators. This may a major reason why this particular rock was selected as a place for rock-art.

Virtually the whole area with Arctic images later was covered with BAT images too. This was, however, done during a long time span, primarily by carving boat images. Based on a thorough study of boat images found on

rocks and engraved on bronze artefacts, particularly razors, from southern Scandinavia F. Kaul (1998) proposed a new chronological sequence for the Bronze Age boat images. In this sequence we do not find Gjessing's type I represented. This emphasizes that this type are difficult to date. Perhaps a detailed study of the Bardal superimpositions will help solving this puzzle. Kaul's sequence starts in Period I of the Scandinavian Bronze Age (1700-500 BC). The boat type depicted on these images, which is identical with Gjessing's type IIa and IIb apparently was depicted during the entire Bronze Age; it was, however, drawn in different styles (Sognnes 1987: 24-25, cf. Kaul 1998). Images like Gjessing's type IIb should be dated to period I, while the type IIB should be dated to period VI (700-500 BC), likely from the very end of the Bronze Age (cf. Bakka 1988: 25).

Some of the early boat images are exceptionally deeply carved and more than four metres long. They are situated at the central and upper left-hand part of the panel. The extreme depth of these carvings may be the result of repeated pecking. This is supported by the two lower fore protrusions on the carving shown as figure 5. Normally the lower protrusion of the earlier examples is short. Here, this is also the case, but a larger protrusion has been added. A number of similar but smaller less deeply carved images are found scattered over large parts of the panel. Details on the end of the prows indicate that these images should be dated to Period III (1300-1000 BC). According to Kaul's sequence the making of BAT engravings must have started earlier than Gjessing suggested, however, Gjessing and Kaul agree that the contoured boats are among the later Bronze Age images.

Kaul's scheme is, however, flawed since several significant types of boat images found at rocks are not represented at the bronzes and therefore not included in the sequence. Å. Fredell (2003: 13) found it necessary to expand Kaul's scheme with types dated to the pre-Roman Period (500-1 BC), which is in accordance to my own study of the record from Stjørdal (Sognnes 1987, cf. 2001), which revealed that even later types of boat images may exist in this region. Gjessing's type III represents the Pre-Roman Iron Age type (500-1 BC), apparently depicting boats like the one excavated at Hjortspring in Denmark (Crumlin-Pedersen & Trakadas 2003), which has curved protrusions from gunwhale and bottom lines in both ends.

This is not the place for a full presentation of the Bardal images. Gjessing's (1936) tracings are, however,

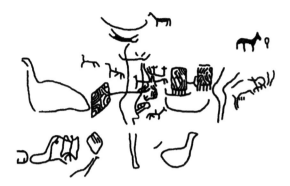

Fig. 8. Superimpositions and juxtapositions in the lower central part of Bardal Ia (after Gjessing 1936).

Fig. 9. Superimpositions in the upper southwestern part of Bardal a (after Gjessing 1936).

presented as figures 3-4. Here I concentrate on some sections in which superimpositions occur. The lower central section of panel a (Figure 8) is dominated by Arctic images, anthropomorphs and birds, but also some geometrical patterns. In addition are found some small animals, likely horses, one of which is superimposed on the larger anthropomorph. This is also the case for two boat images. The Arctic images today are hardly visible, their furrows being strongly weathered. The furrows of the BAT images are deeper and less weathered and frequently each individual peck-mark can be identified.

The upper left-hand section (Figure 9) contains a more complicated stratigraphical/chronological sequence. The focus in this area is four large elk images, one of which is involved in superimpositions with the three others. Their furrows are so strongly weathered that nothing macroscopically can be said about the order in which these images were made. Superimposed on the elks are boat images of Bronze Age and Pre-Roman Iron Age types. This section also includes some oval-shaped images, two of which have interior double spirals. Of special interest are two humans with square bodies.

At panel b no Arctic images are involved in superimpositions. Motifs represented in this section are boats, footprints, animals, anthropomorphs and some geometrical designs (Figure 10). In the upper part two footprints are filling the space between keel and gunwhale of a period III boat images. The lower part is dominated by three contoured boat images from period VI. They are all involved in superimpositions. From a chronological point of view the central one is the most important, being superimposed by a pre-Roman Iron Age boat with seven

crewmembers. This superimposition confirms that this type is later than the Bronze Age types.

These sections demonstrate that boat images are involved in a number of superimpositions representing a long chronological sequence. Compared with the Stjørdal record (Sognnes 1987, 2001) some earlier and later types are not represented.

Elsewhere in central Norway superimpositions are rare but they occur at some panels, apparently for different reasons. At Stykket (Sør-Trøndelag) four large elk images (Figure 11are depicted on a vertical ten metres long panel (Sognnes 1981). These images are carefully placed on the panel; the animals follow each other in a row facing left. One animal has a different posture; the body is oriented towards the right but the head is turned and thus facing the same direction as the others. This row of elks is followed by a smaller image, which I suspect representing a roe deer. On a small panel a few metres to the left a fourth elk is found, facing the others. This seems to be a deliberate composition rendering a herd of real elks. The artist may have used superimposition as a means of creating perspective like for the large elks at Bardal I.

At Holte (Nord-Trøndelag) an almost horizontal rock of similar size is filled with a palimpsest of more than one hundred small cervidae, mostly elks but reindeer and red deer seem to be depicted too (Møllenhus 1968). This panel gives an impression of chaos, not order (Figure 12). The images are similar, yet several styles can be identi-

Fig, 10. Superimpositions on Bardal 1b (after Gjessing 1936).

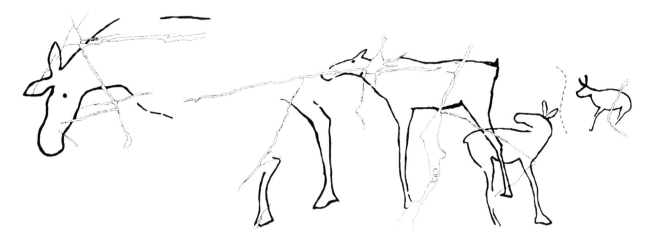

Fig. 11. A herd of elks at Stykket in Rissa, Sør-Trøndelag (after Sognnes 1981).

fied. Most animals have interior body patterns consisting of lines and small cup-marks. Also geometrical patterns are found, especially zigzags and net-like patterns. Considering the recent international debate on entoptics/phosphenes (e.g. Clottes & Lewis-Williams 1996, Dronfield 1995, Lewis-Williams & Dowson 1988, cf. Grønnesby 1998 for central Norway) this panel may represent Shamanic visions. The act of making the carvings was the important issue. Composition apparently played little or no role at all.

Evenhus (Nord-Trøndelag) (Gjessing 1936) represents yet another set of superimpositions (Figure 13). In some way this site resembles Stykket but at the same time look more chaotic. However, the superimpositions found at the Evenhus panels clearly were deliberately made,

representing a kind of 'competition' between land and sea, that is, between elks and whales/boats respectively and thus perhaps between two totemic systems (cf. Hesjedal 1994).

At some sites two temporally separated Arctic rock-art phases seem to be represented. Examples are found at Lånke (Nord-Trøndelag) (Sognnes 1983) and Røsand (Møre og Romsdal) (Sognnes 1996), where some vague strongly weathered remains of large-size animals may be identified (Figure 14). At these sites superimposition seems to represent a re-establishing of the rocks as special spiritual places after a long time with no apparent use.

Re-use of Arctic sites by the makers of BAT rock-art is rare, Evenhus being a well-known example (Gjessing 1936) but also Hammer should be mentioned (Bakka

Fig. 12. At Holte superimpositions are frequent, resulting in a palimpsest of elks, geometrical patterns and lines (photo K. R. Møllenhus).

1987, Gjessing 1936, Rygh 1909). The general picture for central Norway is, however, that reuse of Arctic rock-art panels during Bronze Age/Pre-Roman Iron Age as evidenced by superimpositions, alteration and juxtapositions (where Arctic and BAT rock-art occur together) is most unusual.

THE WHY QUESTIONS

The number and distribution of the Bardal I images raise a number of questions. Here, focus will be on why superimpositions are so frequent at this particular panel. This question is, however, linked to a number of other why questions at several levels. Since they intertwine it is necessary also trying to answer some of these other questions; however, they all go back to one basic question: why do humans make rock-art? I will not try to answer this question but rather: why was rock-art made at Bardal? This lies underneath the question of why the frequent use of superimpositions. The question of why motifs and types are distributed differently also relates to the super-

imposition question. Although focusing on the uniqueness of Bardal I I hope to get closer to understanding this phenomenon also at a more general level.

Most central Norwegian rock-art panels contain a limited number of images but some sites, especially where BAT rock-art is found, may contain hundreds of individual images. These large sites often consist of aggregations of smaller panels and clusters of carvings, frequently focusing on a peculiar motif and/or style. This is especially evident at Leirfall (Nord-Trøndelag) (Marstrander and Sognnes 1999). Looking at Bardal I we find that the situation to a large extent is similar. In content and style panel b, for instance, differs from panel a, the larger animals are clustered, as are anthropomorphs and birds, as well as types of different boat images.

While approaching Bardal I the panels look quite impressing; however, hundreds of other rocks suitable for rock-art exist in the area. Proximity to the sea clearly was of importance but again one should have no problem in finding many suitable rocks also at contemporary shores. The images have been documented several times (Lossius

Fig. 13. Superimpositions at Evenhus (panel V) in Frosta, Nord-Trøndelag (after Gjessing 1936).

Fig. 14. Superimpositions at Rødsand in Averøy, Møre og Romsdal (redrawn after Sognnes 1996).

1897a, Gjessing 1936, Hallström 1938) albeit not based on modern methods. It is a problem, however, that the present documentation is two-dimensional and focused on the images alone and not on the rock as such, which we clearly must do if we want to find out why the carvings were made at this particular panel.

Here I concentrate on panel a where the earlier images are found. This panel is divided by numerous cracks that follow different directions and planes. This is, however, the case also at many other engraved (and non-engraved) rocks. What then comes to mind is the series of eye-like grooves. These grooves were also noted by Gjessing (1936: 31), who described them as looking like man-made steps, being almost regularly distributed across the surface. As Gjessing (loc. cit.) also observed, they actually represent a natural phenomenon and existed when the first carvings were made. Hallström (1938: 285) noticed that these grooves formed a horizontal V-shaped band across the panel.

These grooves form two converging rows warped across the panel. Seen from a distance they form an 'arrow' pointing at the panel's left-hand edge, at which we find the legs of the four large naturalistic elk images. If we accept Gjessing and Hallström's dates the very first images made at Bardal I were made at the spot where the two rows of rock 'eyes' meet (Figure 15). This may have happened when the rock still was close to the shore c. 6,300 bp (Sognnes 2003). Arctic images (mostly animals) later were made virtually everywhere at the panel. Most of these images today are so fragmented that they cannot

Fig. 15. At the focal point of Bardal Ia four large elks are superimposed (redrawn after Gjessing 1936).

be identified, classified or dated, however, a large whale was depicted at the upper central edge of the panel, humans and birds at the lower central edge.

The large elk images represent the first major phase that can be identified at Bardal I. The whale marking the upper edge may be contemporary with these elks. Some smaller animals apparently superimpose this carving. The large elks are the best preserved Arctic images today; likely they also were deeper engraved from the very beginning and thus during the entire Neolithic remained the focal point. Little can be said about the fragmentary images but, according to conventional style dating (Gjessing

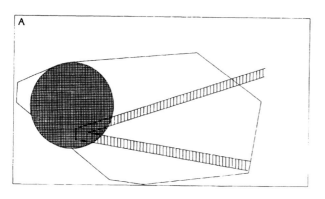

Fig. 16a. Distribution of rock carvings at the Bardal Ia panel from the Late Mesolithic and Neolithic with focus at the left-hand edge of the panel.

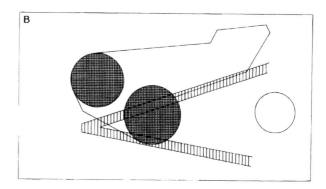

Fig. 16b. Distribution of rock carvings from the Early Bronze Age at the Bardal Ia panel with two foci at the central part of the panel.

1936), the smaller animals at the lower part of the panel were made during this period.

The Bronze Age period I boat images represent a second identifiable major phase, being located in the central and upper left-hand part of the panel. The extraordinary depth of these images may be due repeated remaking during a long time. The size, depth and location of these boats indicate a deliberate defacing of the earlier phase. Their appearance creates two new loci, one in the central part of the panel and one slightly to the right of the large elks' heads. The making of many new images during period III did not change this, although the area with BAT images was expanded towards the right, especially in the upper part of the panel. Most of these images are located above the upper row of rock 'eyes' but some are found between the two rows. A large boat image belonging to this type apparently marks the focal point of panel b. At this panel three period VI boats were added about a half millennium later, near the end of the Bronze Age.

A fourth major phase is represented by the Pre-Roman Period images boats and horses (cf. Sognnes 2001: 68), which dominate panel b. At panel a, these images are found scattered all over the panel, the majority forming a belt at the lower part of the panel and at its left-hand edge. Although these boats and horses are superimposed on some other motifs, they carefully encircle the earlier boats except in the panel's upper part. The larger dominant examples of this type are found immediately below the central Period II images, strengthening the visual importance of this focal point.

Graphically these observations are summed up on figure 16. The larger superimposed elks deliberately were placed at the point of a natural 'arrow' of rock 'eyes'. Lat-

er an unknown number of smaller, now badly preserved animal images were made almost all over this panel. Today it is difficult to decide whether these images were placed in a similar chaotic way as at Holte. However, the cluster of anthropomorphs and birds at the lower part of the panel, below the rock's 'eyes', rather gives the impression of being a deliberate composition.

Bardal I is one of the largest rock-art panels in Norway. As evidenced by the many individual images and frequent superimpositions images were made at these panels for millennia, from the Late Mesolithic through to the Early Iron Age. However, it was used episodically with (at least) four major phases. The images gradually were spread across the surface and not until the latest phase did they cover both panels.

The superimpositions may have a number of causes. The very first making of rock-art at this site likely was due to the special qualities of the panel itself, a point that was stressed already by Brøgger (1925: 91). This start must, however, be seen within the general archaeological context. During the first millennia after the central Norwegian coast was settled, no rock-art seems to have been made. Carvings and paintings found at the coast apparently were made much later than the initial Early Mesolithic Fosna horizon. Although the maximum dates for some locales fall in the 9th millennium bp (early Middle Mesolithic) the majority of the sites cannot be older than from the Late Mesolithic and/or Early Neolithic (Sognnes 2003). This was the time when the hinterland apparently was settled. The making of rock-art may mirror this shift in habitation, representing the symbolic take-over – the domestication – of a new and hitherto alien land (Sognnes 1994: 43).

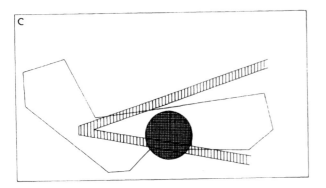

Fig. 16c. Distribution of rock carvings from the Pre-Roman Iron Age at the Bardal Ia panel with focus at the lower central part of the panel.

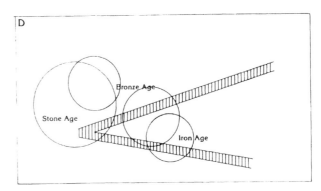

Fig. 16d. Distribution of rock carvings at the Bardal Ia panel, with foci from different periods indicated.

Based on the number of Arctic images panel a was used for a long time. The degree of superimpositions at the earlier stages is difficult to estimate due to strong weathering of the rock. The later Arctic styles (Gjessing 1936, cf. Sognnes 1994) are, however, not represented, neither is the earlier BAT stage (Sognnes 2001). At the Mesolithic/Neolithic transition rock-art making started at Hammer, which is located around six kilometres to the west of Bardal. Here styles missing at Bardal are represented. During the Neolithic Hammer apparently was the centre for rock-art making at the southern shores of the Beitstad Peninsula. However, the supposed final Arctic horizon (Sognnes 1995: 132, cf. Gjessing 1936) is not represented at Hammer but at Bardal III, some hundred metres from Bardal I.

The second major Bardal phase corresponds to the earlier horizon of the BAT rock-art, representing a different visual symbolic system. These images deliberately were superimposed on and defacing the Arctic rock-art. The potency of the rock was still recognised but the former visual system was no longer of interest.

Later during the Early Bronze Age (phase three) some of the larger boat images were remade, which resulted in extraordinary deep carvings. About the same time also new images were made. At the end of the Bronze Age focus was shifted to the lower part of panel B. In this fourth major phase the large boat images were respected but some Early Iron Age images were superimposed also on marginal Early Bronze Age boats. New motifs were introduced, which became especially frequent in this region. To some extent this likely was due to changes in boat building technology. Depictions of old and obsolete boat types no longer gave meaning. During the pre-Ro-

man Period agriculture became common along the Trondheim Fjord (Hafsten 1987: 74) and rock-art making was revitalised. Numerous horses and boat images particular for this period were made at old and new sites and earlier carvings were redesigned.

As above-mentioned superimpositions are rare in central Norwegian rock-art. When a panel was 'full' other panels were chosen for new carvings. The superimpositions at Bardal clearly were results of deliberate decisions. The reasons why this happened likely varied but common for all must be the sanctity and/or potency of this particular rock. For the very first carvings the left-hand edge of the panel, the spot pointed at by the 'arrow' formed by the rock's many 'eyes', was the natural centre in relation to which all later carvings were placed. So important was this centre that one image was not enough, a herd of full-sized elks was necessary to fully express its potency.

CONCLUSIONS

The Bardal I panel today are filled with rock carvings – in total more than four hundred. This, however, has been the situation only since shortly before the beginning of our era. The majority of the images were juxtaposed relatively to other images but a considerable amount was superimposed on previous ones. Today many of the earlier images hardly are visible under normal light conditions but in low afternoon sunlight, or artificial light, the still existing images can be seen. These vague images, of course, were more visible two to three millennia ago and there should be no doubt that the makers of the later carvings were fully aware of the older ones. Except for Bardal I superimpositions are most uncommon in central Norway.

Numerous suitable rock outcrops exist; when superimpositions are found, therefore, there should be little doubt that they are the results of deliberate decisions.

When the first images were made at Bardal, the artist(s) apparently was facing a problem of location. Conflicting interests had to be dealt with: a herd of elks was to be rendered, the animals had to be full size (or even larger) and they had to be carved at one particular spot. The solution to this problem was superimpositioning. In doing so, the artists created a kind of perspective. In the following centuries many smaller images were made. Whether these images were superimposed in a similar way cannot be told today due to their bad state of preservation. However, some geometrical patterns apparently were superimposed on these animals. This is not discussed further here but geometrical patterns are found also at other Arctic rock-art sites in central Norway, sometimes superimposed on full-size cervidae, for instance at Berg (Nord-Trøndelag), a panel that is not yet published.

The later superimpositions also were made at will, apparently as an act of defacing the older ones, replacing them with a new symbolic system. The Bronze Age agriculturalists took the rock in possession, using their own symbols. By doing this, the old symbolic system of the hunter-gatherers became alienated and obsolete. The earlier large boat images were sorted into two clusters separated by the upper row of rock 'eyes'. The lower cluster was kept clear of the large elks, while the upper one to some degree was superimposed on these images. The share size of these boat images combined with the depth of the furrows moved the visual focus towards the centre of the panel.

Boats remained the major symbol within the BAT rock-art but new motifs were added and at the same time the boat building technology apparently changed. This development is mirrored in the choice of motifs and their location on the panels during the later phases. During Bronze Age panel a once again was filled with images but the large elks still were respected and the Period I foci was kept. The very last Bronze Age images were made at panel b, which at that time contained only a few images.

During the Pre-Roman Period new images again were added. They further filled the panels but at the same time generally avoided the Bronze Age images. The larger boat images dating from this period were placed immediately below the central cluster with large Bronze Age boats, further emphasizing the importance of this cluster as the main focus for BAT rock-art. Albeit several other panels were used for rock-art making at Bardal and at the neighbour farm Lagtu during this phase, Bardal I remained the central place for rock-art making in the area. Here we again likely are dealing with re-enactment of ancestral rituals and enhancement of the potency embedded in the rock. The rock itself was constantly observing and watching new generations of people through its omnipresent eyes.

REFERENCES

Bakka, E. 1975. Geologically dated Arctic rock carvings at Hammer near Steinkjer in Nord-Trøndelag. Arkeologiske skrifter 2: 7-48. Bergen, Historisk museum.

Bakka, E. 1987. Helleristningane på Hammer i Beitstad, Steinkjer, Nord-Trøndelag. Rapport arkeologisk serie 1987: 7. Trondheim, Vitskapsmuseet.

Bakka, E. 1988. Bronsealderristningane på Bogge i Romsdal. Gunneria 57. Trondheim, Vitskapsmuseet.

Bednarik, R. G. 1992. A new method to date petroglyphs. Archaeometry 34: 279-291.

Bednarik, R. G. 1993. Developments in rock art dating. Acta Archaeologica 63: 141-155.

Bertilsson, U. 1989. Hällristningar och bygden. In S. Janson, E. B. Lundberg and U. Bertilsson (eds.): Hällristningar och hällmålningar i Sverige, 29-42. Stockholm, Forum.

Brøgger, A. W. 1906. Elg og ren paa helleristninger i det nordlige Norge. Naturen 30: 356-360.

Brøgger, A. W. 1925. Det norske folk i oldtiden. Instituttet for sammenlignende kulturforskning serie A 6a. Oslo, Aschehoug.

Bull, E. 1935. Bardal, Beitstad, Nord-Trøndelag. Kutrøa (Bardalsaune). Report on file at Vitenskapsmuseet, Norwegian University of Science and Technology, Trondheim.

Burenhult, G. 1980. Rock Carvings of Götaland. Theses and Papers in North European Archaeology 10. Stockholm.

Bøe, J. 1932. Felsenzeichnungen im westlichen Norwegen 1: die Zeichnungsgebiete in Vingen und Henøya. Bergens museums skrifter 15. Bergen.

Coll, A. L. 1902. Fra helleristningernes omraade. Foreningen til norske fortidsmindesmærkers bevaring aarsberetning 1901: 33-59. Kristiania [Oslo].

Clottes, J. & D. Lewis-Williams 1996. Les chamanes de la Préhistoire. Paris, Éditions du Seuil.

O. Crumlin-Pedersen & A. Trakadas (eds) 2003. Hjortspring: A

Pre-Roman Iron-Age Warship in Context. Ships and boats of the North 5: 141-186. Roskilde, The Viking Ship Museum.

Dahl, R. H. Sveian & M. K. Thoresen (eds) 1997. Nord-Trøndelag og Fosen: Geologi og landskap. Trondheim, NGU.

Dronfield, J. 1995. Subjective vision and the source of Irish megalithic art. Antiquity 69: 539-549.

Ekholm, G. 1916. De skandinaviska hällristningarna och deras betydelse. Ymer 1916: 275-308

Engelstad, E. S. 1934. Østnorske ristninger og malinger av den arktiske gruppe. Instituttet for sammenlignende kulturforskning serie B 26. Oslo, Aschehoug.

Fett, Eva Nissen and Per Fett 1941. Sydvestnorske helleristninger: Rogaland og Lista. Stavanger, Stavanger museum.

Fredell, Å. 2003. Bildbroar: Figurativ kommunikation av ideologi och kosmologi under sydskandinavisk bronsålder och förromersk järnålder. Gotarc series B 25. Gothenburg.

Gjessing, G. 1932. Arktiske helleristninger i Nord-Norge. Instituttet for sammenlignende kulturforskning serie B 21. Oslo, Aschehoug.

Gjessing, G. 1935. Die Chronologie der Schiffdarstellungen auf den Felsenzeichnungen zu Bardal. Acta Archaeologica 6: 125-139.

Gjessing, G. 1936. Nordenfjelske ristninger og malinger av den arktiske gruppe. Instituttet for sammenlignende kulturforskning serie B 30. Oslo, Aschehoug.

Gjessing, G. 1939. Østfolds jordbruksristninger: Idd, Berg og delvis Skjeberg. Instituttet for sammenlignende kulturforskning serie B 39. Oslo, Aschehoug.

Grønnesby, G. 1998. Skandinaviske helleristninger og rituell bruk av transe. Arkeologiske skrifter 9: 59-82. Bergen, Bergen museum.

Hafsten, U. 1987. Vegetasjon, klima og landskapsutvikling i Trøndelag etter siste istid. Norsk geografisk tidsskrift 37: 63-79.

Hagen, A. 1970. Studier i vestnorsk bergkunst: Ausevik i Flora. Årbok for Universitetet i Bergen humanistisk serie 1969: 3. Bergen, Universitetsforlaget.

Hallström, G. 1907. Hällristningarna vid Trondhjemsfjorden. Det Kongelige Norske Videnskabers Selskabs skrifter 1907: 10. Trondhjem.

Hallström, G. 1938. Monumental Art of Northern Europe from the Stone Age 1: the Norwegian Localities. Stockholm, Thule.

Hansen, A. M. 1904. Landnaam i Norge: En udsigt over bosætningens historie. Kristiania [Oslo], Fabricius.

Harris, E. C. 1989. Principles of Archaeological Stratigraphy (2nd edition). London, Academic Press.

Helskog, K. 1988. Helleristningene i Alta: spor etter ritualer og dagligliv i Finnmarks forhistorie. Alta.

Helskog, K. 1993. Fra tvangstrøyer til 90-åras pluralisme i helleristningsforskning. In Nordic TAG: Report from the Third Nordic TAG Conference 1990, 70-75. Bergen, Historisk museum.

Hesjedal, A. 1994. The hunters' rock art in northern Norway: problems of chronology and interpretation. Norwegian Archaeological Review 27: 1-14.

Kaul, F. 1998. Ships on Bronzes: A Study in Bronze Age Religion and Iconography. Publications from the National Museum, Studies in Archaeology and History 3. Copenhagen.

Lewis-Williams, J. D. & T. A. Dowson 1988. The signs of all times: entoptic phenomena in Upper Palaeolithic art. Current Anthropology 29 (2): 201-217.

Lossius, K. 1897a. Helleristningen paa Bardal i Beitstaden. Foreningen til norske Fortidsmindesmærkers Bevaring Aarsberetning 1896: 145-149. Kristiania [Oslo].

Lossius, K. 1897b. Arkæologiske Undersøgelser i 1897. Det Kongelige Norske Videnskabers Selskabs skrifter 1897: 5. Trondhjem.

Magar, V. & V. Davila 2004. Considerations on the dating of rock art from the Sierra de San Francisco, Baja California, Mexico. Rock Art Research 21: 129-136.

Mandt Larsen, G. 1972. Bergbilder i Hordaland: En undersøkelse av bildenes sammensetning, deres naturmiljø og kulturmiljø. Universitetet i Bergen årbok humanistisk serie 1970: 2. Universitetsforlaget, Bergen.

Marstrander, S. 1963. Østfolds jordbruksristninger: Skjeberg. Instituttet for sammenlignende kulturforskning serie B 53. Oslo, Universitetsforlaget.

Marstrander, S. and K. Sognnes 1999. Trøndelags jordbruksristninger. Vitark 1. Trondheim, Tapir.

Møllenhus, K. R. 1968. Helleristningene på Holtås i Skogn. Det Kongelige Norske Videnskabers Selskabs skrifter 1968: 4. Trondheim

Prestvik, Tore 1981. Rapport vedrørende undersøkelse av bergartsprøver fra ristningsfelt. Report on file at Vitenskapsmuseet, Norwegian University of Science and Technology, Trondheim.

Rygh, K. 1909. En nyfunden helleristning. Det Kongelige Norske Videnskabers Selskabs skrifter 1909: 8. Trondhjem.

Shetelig, H. 1925. Norsk kunst i de ældste tider. Norges kunsthistorie 1: 1-28. Oslo, Aschehoug.

Simonsen, P. 1958. Arktiske helleristninger i Nord-Norge 2. Instituttet for sammenlignende kulturforskning serie B 49. Oslo, Universitetsforlaget.

Sognnes, K. 1981. Helleristningsundersøkelser i Trøndelag 1979 og 1980. Rapport arkeologisk serie 1981: 2. Trondheim, DKNVS museet.

Sognnes, K. 1983. Helleristninger i Stjørdal II: Stjørdal og Lånke sogn. Rapport arkeologisk serie 1983: 6. Trondheim, DKNVS museet.

Sognnes, K. 1987. Bergkunsten i Stjørdal 2: Typologi og kronologi i Nedre Stjørdal. Gunneria 56. Trondheim, Vitenskapsmuseet.

Sognnes, K. 1990. Bergkunsten i Stjørdal 3: Hegraristningane. Gunneria 62. Trondheim, Vitenskapsmuseet.

Sognnes, K. 1992. A spatial approach to the study of rock art in Trøndelag, Norway. In S. Goldsmith, S. Garvie, D. Selin and J. Smith (eds.): Ancient Images, Ancient Thought: The Archaeology of Ideology, 107-120. Calgary, Department of Archaeology.

Sognnes, Kalle 1994. Ritual landscapes: Toward a reinterpretation of Stone Age rock art in Trøndelag, Norway. Norwegian Archaeological Review 27: 29-50.

Sognnes, Kalle 1995. The social context of rock art in central Norway; Rock art at a frontier? In K. Helskog and B. Olsen (eds.): Perceiving Rock Art: Social and Political Perspectives, 130-145. Instituttet for sammenlignende kulturforskning serie B 92. Oslo, Novus.

Sognnes, K. 1996. Helleristningene på Averøya. Nordmøre museum årbok 1996: 74-85. Kristiansund.

Sognnes, K. 2000. Det hellige landskapet: Religiøse og rituelle landskapselementer i et langtidsperspektiv. Viking 63: 87-121.

Sognnes, K. 2001. Prehistoric Imagery and Landscapes: Rock Art in Stjørdal, Trøndelag, Norway. British Archaeological Report International Series 998. Oxford, Archaeopress.

Sognnes, K. 2002. Land of elks – sea of whales: Landscapes of the Stone Age rock-art in central Scandinavia. In G. Nash and C. Chippindale (eds): European Landscapes of Rock-Art, 195-212. London, Routledge.

Sognnes, K. 2003. On shoreline dating of rock-art. Acta Archaeologica 74: 189-208.

Walderhaug, E. M. 1994. "Ansiktet er av stein": Ausevik i Flora –

en analyse av bergkunst og kontekst. Thesis for the cand. philol. degree at the University of Bergen.

Østmo, E. 1990. Helleristninger av sørskandinaviske typer på det indre Østlandet: Fylkene Buskerud, Akershus, Oslo, Oppland og Hedmark. Universitetets oldsaksamlings skrifter ny rekke 12. Oslo.

Author's address
Norwegian University of Science and Technology (NTNU)
Department of Archaeology and Studies of Religion
N 7491 Trondheim, Norway
kalle.sognnes@vm.ntnu.no

Acta Archaeologica vol. 79, 2008, pp 246-249
Printed in Denmark • All rights reserved

Copyright 2008
ACTA ARCHAEOLOGICA
ISSN 0065-101X

PERMANENT LINES
REGISTERED TERRITORIALITY IN THE BRONZE AGE?

KLAVS RANDSBORG

In memory of Mats P. Malmer (1921-2007)

DENMARK

In 2004, a new find appeared - this time from Northern Jylland/Jutland - of the mysterious lines of cooking-pits with burned stones.[1] The lines are broadly dated to the Late Bronze Age, but are devoid of small-finds (Kristensen 2004; generally, Gustafson et al. 2005). The lines are often single, as the one on a new locality at Roskilde, Sjælland/Zealand (Christensen 2000), but may also be double or multiple - even a 16-liner is known - with both parallel and converging lines. Multiple lines may have served to stress or rather repeating a particular phenomenon.

Excavations have followed lines over 300 metres, but probably they are even longer. At single locality, Rønninge on Fyn/Funen, the number of pits is at least 1600 (Thrane 1974; 1989). Sometimes, the lines take their starting point in an Early Bronze Age barrow and are thus part of an already defined cultural landscape, at the same time as they are dividing, thus re-defining a landscape.

Interpretation has been difficult, but the monuments are usually considered "cultic" by Scandinavian archaeologists. One perhaps imagines a ritual in which traces of fire should be viewed both from the night sky and from the underworld. Possibly, the lines might then imitate the journeys of the sun and other celestial bodies both above

and below the disc of the Earth (cf. the model in Kaul 1998, Vol. 2, 262 Fig. 170). Lines, even multiple, of cupmarks are also seen on Bronze Age rock-carvings, resembling rows of cooking-pits.

The idea of common meals for a whole region, prepared in the pits, has put emphasis on the social aspects of the supposed ritual. But fellowship does not necessarily imply identical earth-ovens arranged in long, long lines at short, regularly spaced intervals. Furthermore, would one not expect to find traces of other activities, including broken pots? The "normal" cooking-pits are usually found in or at house structures.

Lines and bordered clusters of regularly spaced iron ovens of the Roman Iron Age have given rise to the idea that the Late Bronze Age cooking-pits were industrial in nature (cf. Voss 1993). But no convincing production has been suggested.

A different - and very fanciful - explanation is to view the lines, in particular the multiple ones, as a sort of defensive position at a prepared battle field. The hot pits might serve as obstacles, at the same time at one may counterattack easily from behind them. One could even think of military sports games.

The latest Danish survey of the data and problems related to the lines of cooking pits is by M.B. Henriksen (Henriksen 1999). Henriksen stresses the potentially multiple functions of the cooking pits and at the same time their indication of the presence of many people at the same location - a settlement, a burial ground, or a sanctuary in the open landscape.

But new finds are constantly appearing.

---

1 This small note is dedicated to the memory of a great archaeologist from Sweden, and Skåne, the late Professor Mats P. Malmer, an admirer of Danish archaeology. Mats P. Malmer worked devotedly to make archaeology a science. The author is particularly greatful to Mats for his scholarly inspiration, and his interest and help when a very young Danish archaeologist visited Swedish collections and institutions for the first time.

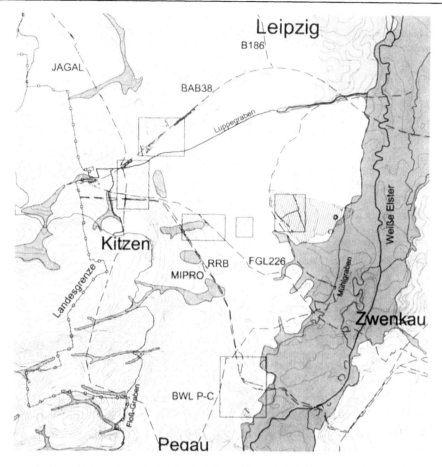

Fig. 1. Cross-country lines of pits to the south of Leipzig, Sachsen (Saxony), including excavated areas (after Stäuble 2002).

GERMANY

In the province of Sachsen-Anhalt and in Sachsen/Saxony in the eastern part of Germany, lines of regularly spaced pits have been found along with other monuments suggesting an explanation not akin to the above ones (cf. Figs 1-2).

These permanent lines are clearly territorial markers: divisions of areas of fields and other plots (Schwartz 2003; cf. Stäuble 2002; Mattheuser & Petzschmann 2003). Likely, the underlying idea is almost "archaeological" in nature, related to the fact that it is impossible to change marks left in the subsoil. Long time before charters, lists of properties, maps, registration books, etc., needs no doubt existed to establish inalienable rights to land. Only, the manifestation of these rights took different forms before writing.

The Saxon finds comprise single lines of usually oval or, in particular, rectangular pits as well as long narrow

ditches which have been followed for at least 500 metres. Lines of pits may merge with ditches, and the lines divide as well as be crossed by other lines. A main difference from the Danish pits is that the Saxon ones do not contain fired stone; they are, in other words, not cooking pits. The lines of pits are always single in the Saxon cases, but may be accompanied by other structures, like multiple rows of posts and palisades.

Nevertheless, the function may well be the same North as South, as emphasized by the fact that the eastern German lines of pits without stones are substituted by the Nordic lines of cooking-pits as one moves beyond Berlin, in fact into the area of the well-known large three-aisled longhouses of the North (Lütjens 1999). The precise date of the Saxon finds is not yet clear, but the monuments certainly belong to a period parallel with the Nordic Late Bronze Age. The North German lines of cooking-pits are of the same age.

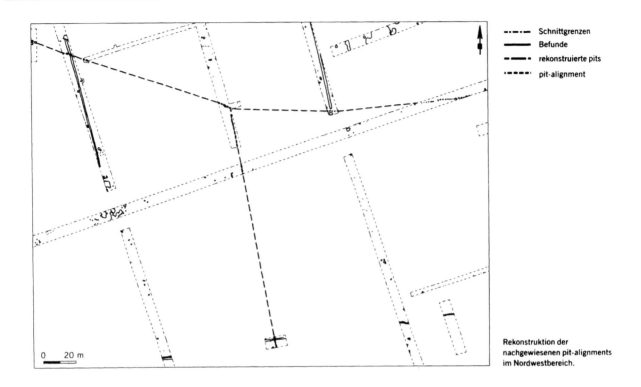

Fig. 2. Line of pits near Halle, Sachsen-Anhalt (Saxony): plan and airphoto (after Mattheusser 2003). Photo seems to be reversed.

On recent air-photos, the said Saxon lines make up large territorial borders and divisions, no doubt pertaining to the issue of bordering whole field-systems belonging to a village. German archaeologists tend towards different and varying interpretations of the phenomenon, from cattle fences, even foundations for tracks, or defensive systems, to the mentioned area divisions.

Incidentally, such lines ("pit alignments") are also known from England, among other countries (Pollard (et al.) 1996). In England, as well as in Germany, it is in particular air-photos which have served to make the alignments known. Most excavations, covering only limited areas, will not catch such massive monuments.

Taking this model to Scandinavia, we would suggest the existence of territorial divisions much, much larger than the small oval fields from the Early Bronze Age at Bjerre in Thy, Jylland (Rasmussen & Adamsen 1993, 142f.), or the larger rectangular fields known from the Pre-Roman Iron Age, which even seems to go back to the Late Bronze Age, perhaps even the earlier part, as Carbon-14 dates might suggest (Nielsen 1984).

PERSPECTIVES

If the suggested territorial interpretation stands the test, it throws a novel light on phenomena like associations and rights of land in later Prehistory, in addition to posing a series of interesting questions concerning the cultural landscape towards the close of the Bronze Age. Danish archaeologists, until this point in time, have mainly investigated cultural landscapes from the point of perspective of burial mounds and the very many settlements and longhouse structures. The question now arises whether a proper culture landscape, characterized not only by points and tracks, but also of field-divisions, existed before the arrival of the lines of cooking-pits. It likely did, but only the cooking-pit lines can so far prove it.

A huge task of documentation in the landscape is waiting. Even the ritual aspects need clarification as indicated by the momentous task of framing areas in fire, thus creating ritually sanctioned and socially accepted "registered charters", which cannot be changed - only challenged -by future generations.

BIBLIOGRAPHY

Christensen, T. 2000. Hvass 2000. 84f.

Gustafson, L., T. Heibreen & J. Martens (eds.). 2005. De gåtefulle kokegroper. Varia 58. (Oslo.)

Henriksen, M.B. 1998. Guden under gulvet - ofringer under fynske huse fra ældre jernalder. Fynske Minder 1998. 191ff.

- . 1999. Bål i lange baner. Fynske Minder 1999. 93ff.

Hvass, S. & B. Storgaard (eds.). 1993. Da klinger i muld ... 25 års arkæologi i Danmark. København & Århus (Det Kgl. Nordiske Oldskriftselskab & Jysk Arkæologisk Selskab) 1993.

Hvass, S. (et al.) (ed.). 2000. Vor skjulte kulturarv. Arkæologien under overfladen. Til Hendes Majestæt Dronnning Margrethe II 16. april 2000. København & Århus (Det Kgl. Nordiske Oldskriftselskab & Jysk Arkæologisk Selskab).

Kaul, F. 1998. Ships on Bronzes. A Study in Bronze Age Religion and Iconography. Publications from the National Museum. Studies in Archaeology & History 3;1-2. Copenhagen.

Kristensen, I.K. 2004. Rad og række. Skalk 2004;2 (April). 11ff.

Lütjens, I. 1999. Langgestreckte Steingruben auf einem jungbronzezeitlichen Siedlungsplatz bei Jürgenshagen, Kreis Güstrow. Offa 56. 21ff.

Mattheusser, E. & U. Petzschmann. 2003. „Die lange Grubenreihen" (two papers). Meller 2003. 83ff.

Meller, H. (ed.). 2003. Ein weites Feld. Ausgrabungen im Gewerbegebiet Halle/Queis. Archäologie in Sachsen-Anhalt. Sonderband 1. Halle (Saale) (Landesamt für Archäologie Sachsen-Anhalt).

Nielsen, V. 1984. Prehistoric Field Boundaries in Eastern Denmark. Journal of Danish Archaeology 3, 1984. 135ff.

Pollard, J. (with V. Fryer, P. Murphy, M. Tylor & P. Wiltshire). 1996. Iron Age Riverside Pit Alignments at St Ives, Cambridgeshire, Proceedings of the Prehistoric Society 62, 1996. 93ff.

Rasmussen, K. & C. Adamsen. 1993. Bebyggelsen. Hvass & Storgaard 1993. 136ff.

Schwarz, R. 2003. Pilotstudien. Zwölf Jahre Luftbildarchäologie in Sachsen-Anhalt. Halle (Saale) (Landesamt für Archäologie Sachsen-Anhalt - Landesmuseum für Vorgeschichte Halle (Saale)). 83ff.

Stäuble, H. 2002. Lineare Gräben und Grubenreihen in Nordwestsachsen. Eine Übersicht. Arbeits- und Forschungsberichte zur Sächsischen Bodendenkmalpflege 44. 9ff.

Thrane, H. 1974. Hundredvis af energikilder fra yngre broncealder. Fynske Minder 1974. 96ff.

- . 1989. De 11 guldskåle fra Mariesminde - vidnesbyrd om en broncealderhelligdom? Fynske Minder 1989. 13ff.

Voss, O. 1993. Snorup. Et jernudvindingsområde i Sydvestjylland. Nationalmuseets Arbejdsmark 1993. 97ff.

Author's address
Saxo-institute, Univesity of Copenhagen, Njalsgade 80,
DK- 2300 Copenhagen, Denmark
randsb@hum.ku.dk
www.worldarchaeology.net

Acta Archaeologica vol. 79, 2008, pp 250-273
Printed in Denmark • All rights reserved

Copyright 2008
ACTA ARCHAEOLOGICA
ISSN 0065-101X

THE GREAT MOUND OF NEWGRANGE

AN IRISH MULTI-PERIOD MOUND SPANNING FROM THE MEGALITHIC TOMB PERIOD TO THE EARLY BRONZE AGE

PALLE ERIKSEN

In June 1999, I travelled to Ireland together with two other Danish archaeologists, Niels H. Andersen and Anders Jæger, in order to see the country's many remarkable passage tombs and dolmens. In the course of eight days we visited Fourknocks, Newgrange, Knowth, Loughcrew, Carrowmore, Knocknarea with Maeve's Cairn, Carrowkeel, Proleek, Brownshill and many other megaliths. It was a truly impressive and fascinating experience to see, in the course of such a short period of time, all these megaliths and the landscape within which they lie.

There was, however, one unpleasant and provocative sight, which we probably were expecting but which still shocked us: Newgrange. This fantastic monument, more than 5000 years old, has been defaced by an exceptionally severe restoration involving a large and conspicuous, high white wall (Fig. 1). It looks very modern and we were left with more than the faintest suspicion that there is something seriously wrong with Newgrange. Or was it us who had a problem because we still lived "in the romantic days of candlelight and cattle"? (M. O'Kelly 1982, 53)

The day after our depressing meeting with Newgrange we were in Loughcrew, which lies only 40 km distant, where there are about 30 more-or-less disturbed cairns with passage tombs. On sight of cairn L and the unrestored cairn T we realised what was wrong with Newgrange: In the Neolithic, Newgrange had resembled these cairns, apart from the fact that it was twice as big. Later in prehistory, every similarity to the two cairns at Loughcrew disappeared when the Newgrange passage-tomb mound was completely encapsulated within a great mound so that the kerbstones and the entrance to the passage tomb became hidden.

This discovery of Newgrange as a multi-period mound was in direct conflict with the traditional view (Eriksen 2004; 2006). During the great investigation and restoration of Newgrange between 1962 and 1975 under the direction of Professor Michael J. O'Kelly it had been demonstrated that Newgrange was a single-period mound (M. O'Kelly 1982). The great quantities of mound fill, which covered the kerbstones and extended far beyond them, had – according to O'Kelly – slid out from the mound when the wall, which held the mound fill in place, had collapsed (M. O'Kelly 1973; 1979; 1982).

O'Kelly was so certain of his collapse theory that he did not even consider that Newgrange could be a multi-period mound. And with his convincing book "Newgrange. Archaeology, Art and Legend" which was published in 1982 – the same year in which he died – he silenced critics and sceptics many years into the future. The book was, as Colin Renfrew wrote in the foreword, "the final and definite report".

The aim of this paper is to present the arguments for Newgrange as a multi-period mound and, especially, to take a closer look at the late Newgrange with its great mound: What did it look like? When was it built – and in which context? The early Newgrange in the Passage-Tomb Period has been discussed previously, but the later phases of Newgrange were only dealt with very briefly (Eriksen 2004).

Fig. 1. Newgrange today. Photo by Pauline Asingh.

RUDE STONE MONUMENTS

Of the many antiquarians who have studied Newgrange since the discovery of its passage tomb in 1699 there is, however, one – James Fergusson – who as early as 1872 was of the opinion that Newgrange was a multi-period mound.

Fergusson had a detailed knowledge of the history of architecture. In 1854, his book "Handbook of Architecture" was published; a revised edition of this, "History of Architecture", appeared in 1864. In both cases, when working with the manuscripts for his books, he had felt the great lack of, and had sought, an overview of "the Rude Stone Monuments then known" (Fergusson 1872, v); an overview which he could use in his research for writing a chapter on these monuments that we today call megaliths. As no antiquarian had yet produced such a book, he wrote it himself! This well-illustrated book "Rude stone monuments in all countries; their ages and uses" was published in 1872 and comprised 559 pages! Fergusson was aware that as a non-specialist he could make mistakes and that many of his suggestions and theories could be untenable: "In one respect I cannot but feel that I may have laid myself open to hostile criticism. On many minor points I have offered suggestions which I do not feel sure that

I could prove if challenged, and which, consequently, a more prudent man would have left alone. I have done this because it often happens that such suggestions turn the attentions of others to points which would otherwise be overlooked, and may lead to discoveries of great importance; while if disproved, they are only so much rubbish swept out of the path of truth, and their detection can do no harm to any one but the author" (Fergusson 1872, ix).

One of Fergusson's many suggestions refers to the disproportionate situation at Newgrange, where the entrance to the passage tomb was located far inside the foot of the mound (Fig. 2). His explanation is almost prophetic and presumably arises from the fact that, with his great knowledge of architecture, he was aware that a building, for example a cathedral, had often been extended and could, therefore, comprise two or more phases:"The position of the entrance so much within the outline of the Tumulus, is a peculiarity at first sight much more difficult to account for. As it now stands, it is situated at a distance of about 50 feet horizontally within what we have every reason to believe was the original outline of the mound. Not only is there no reason to believe that the passage ever extended further, but the ornamented threshold [the kerbstone K1], and the carved stringcourse [the lintel at the roof-box] above, and other indications, seem to point

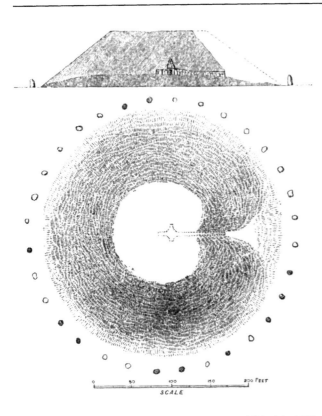

Fig. 2. Section and ground plan of Newgrange, published in 1872 by James Fergusson. In the side of the mound fanning out from the entrance to the passage tomb there is a large notch arising from stone robbing. The flat top and the stone circle are clearly emphasised. At the time, 11 of the circle's orthostats were visible, they are marked in black. The other stones are just a fiction as the original number of orthostats is unknown. Fergusson was of the opinion that Newgrange was built in two stages. After Fergusson 1872.

out that the tumulus had what may be called an architectural facade at this depth. One mode of accounting for this would be to assume that the original mound was only about 200 feet in diameter at the floor level, and that the interior was then accessible, but that after the death of the king who erected it, an envelope 50 feet thick was added by his successors, forming the broad platform at the top, and effectually closing and hiding the entrance to the sepulchre" (Fergusson 1872, 205-6).

Nobody has paid attention to Fergusson's multi-period theory concerning Newgrange. In order to confirm it, it is necessary to take a closer, critical look at the stratigraphy of the mound by studying the sections recorded by O'Kelly.

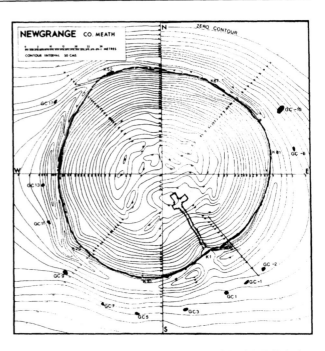

Fig. 3. Ground plan of Newgrange, surveyed by Michael O'Kelly before the alterations of the mound in his 1962-74 campaign. The position of the section, Fig. 4, is indicated. After M. O'Kelly 1982.

LAYERS OF STONES, TURVES AND SNAIL SHELLS

Prior to O'Kelly's restoration of Newgrange the great mound had a diameter of c. 100 m, of which the passage-tomb mound comprised 85 m. It was surrounded by 97 kerbstones (K1-97). As today, the mound was 11 m high and the flat top had, according to O'Kelly, a diameter of 32 m. Just outside the foot of the great mound there are 12 standing stones or orthostats, which can be fitted within a circle with a diameter of c. 105 m (Fig. 3). A 19 m-long passage leads into a cruciform vaulted chamber, 6 m in height. The mound is a cairn, as its fill comprises fist- to hand-sized stones.

O'Kelly cut a trench into the southeastern side of the mound, 10 m to the east of the entrance, in order to study the structure of the mound. The location of a section belonging to this trench is shown in figure 3 and 6. Behind kerbstone K95 the section revealed that the mound consisted of four layers of stones separated by three layers of turf (Fig. 4) (M. O'Kelly 1982, 69). The whole sequence of layers was perceived by O'Kelly as being coeval, as he was of the opinion that the turves in each layer had been placed there by human hand as one great continuous blanketing layer intended to stabilise the stones and prevent

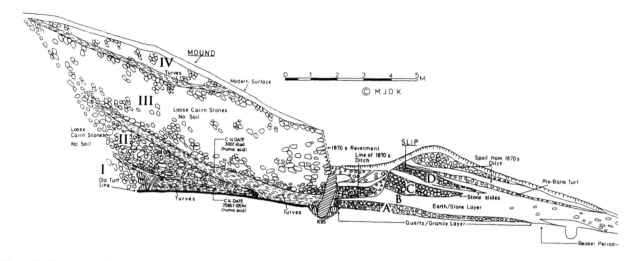

Fig. 4. Section showing the stratigraphic sequence from the Newgrange mound at kerbstone K95. The position of the section is shown at figure 3. The mound's stone fill comprises four layers (I-IV), separated by three turf layers which each represent an old vegetation layer. The stratigraphy shows that the mound has four phases. Outside the kerbstones the quartz/granite layer (A) and the earth/stone layer (B) originated through ceremonial activities in front of the kerbstones in the Passage-Tomb Period and the Late Neolithic. Subsequently, in the Early Bronze Age, they became partially overlain by a great mound with two phases. In the section, these are seen as the two stone slides C and D. This explanation is quite the opposite to that of Michael O'Kelly, who was of the opinion that Newgrange was a single-period mound. The numbers I-IV and the letters A-D have been added in connection with this article. After M. O'Kelly 1982.

them from slipping. The fact that the fill of the mound far exceeded the top of the kerbstones was explained in terms of extensive slippage of the mound fill, because in the Neolithic the mound fill had been held in place by a three-metre high wall, erected on top of the kerbstones. The front of the wall was clad with pieces of white quartz and granite, which were found in front of the kerbstones after the wall had collapsed.

However, this interpretation of the stratigraphy is untenable. Had the turves been placed by human hand they should lie with the vegetation facing downwards, as was normal when turf was used as a building material in prehistoric mounds. But they do not – on the contrary, the vegetation layer is uppermost (M. O'Kelly 1982, 85-6) – and therefore provide evidence for the fact that the turf layers were more probably formed naturally. Each turf layer represents a grass-covered surface at a particular point in time in its developmental history. The three turf layers therefore represent boundaries between the four phases of the mound.

On the diametrically opposed side of the mound, by kerbstone K53, a trench was also cut and a section surveyed (M. O'Kelly 1982, 71). Lowermost, there is a substantial turf layer, the thickness of which increases inwards towards the centre of the mound. This layer probably belongs

to a turf-built mound with a passage tomb, which became encapsulated by the subsequent construction of the great mound (M. O'Kelly 1982, 92; Lynch 1989; 1990). On top of the thick turf layer rests the fill of the great mound in the form of quantities of stones separated by three very thin layers of soil, each containing thousands of snail shells (Spoel 1982, 226; Mason & Evans 1982, 227-8). The three thin soil horizons with snail shells were explained by O'Kelly as follows: "It has already been shown that there are at least three very thin soil horizons in the mound which are not layers of transported turves but represent stadia in the progress of the work, stoppages of perhaps no more than a very few years duration, but long enough for a slight vegetation cover to develop on the stones. We have no way of estimating the duration of the stadia, but if each represents a 5-year interlude we must then add on a maximum of 15 years to the 16 or so already allowed for, making a total of 30 years or more [for the total building of the mound]" (M. O'Kelly 1982, 118).

O'Kelly's interpretation of these thin soil layers containing snail shells as old mound surfaces seems plausible, in contrast to his interpretation of the turf layers in the southern part of the mound, where he – as mentioned – was of the opinion that the corresponding layers were man-made. The time intervals involved are, however,

Fig. 5. Capeshøj during excavation in 1977. The mound, which lies on the island of Tåsinge in Denmark, has two phases: A Neolithic 36 m long and 7 m wide long dolmen with a chamber was covered by a great mound in the Bronze Age. The curved line of the stones along the edge of the excavation area represents the kerbstones of the round Bronze Age mound. At the time of the investigation, the great mound was substantially levelled out due to the effects of cultivation. Photo by Jørgen Holm.

probably much greater than O'Kelly imagined. When O'Kelly proposed that the whole mound could have been constructed in 30 years it relates to his theory that the mound is a single-period structure.

THE STRATIGRAPHY BEHIND THE KERBSTONES

The possible turf-built passage tomb, of which there were traces in the north section and which actually has nothing to do with the large passage-tomb mound we know today, will be assigned to phase 0. If the three turf layers in the south section are perceived as man-made, four phases can be distinguished (I-IV), each corresponding to a single layer (Fig. 4).

Phase 0: Construction of a small turf-built mound with a passage tomb (?) in the area where the later, large passage-tomb mound with the chamber, we know today, was constructed in phases I-II.

Phase I – layer I: A mound containing the present passage-tomb chamber was erected. The foot of the mound was marked by a small stonewall and there were no kerbstones. A parallel to the appearance of the mound in this phase is the passage-tomb mound Fourknocks I (Hartnett 1957; Eriksen 2004, 63).

Phase II – layer II: The mound with the passage tomb was extended and "its toe was again roughly retained by boulders" (M. O'Kelly 1982, 87). The passage was extended in length (Eriksen 2004, 64-5) and the kerbstones were positioned so that there was an open belt just less than 2.5 m wide between them and the foot of the mound. Parallels to the appearance of the mound in this phase are the passage-tomb mounds Loughcrew L (Eogan 1986, 63 and Photo 40; Eriksen 2004, 54), Newgrange site E (C. O'Kelly 1978, 59; Stout 2002, 24 and Fig. 13) and Dowth (O'Kelly & O'Kelly 1983, 148).

Phase III – layer III: A great mound was built and it completely covered the passage-tomb mound, its kerbstones and entrance. The newly added layer was up to 3 m thick and overlay, for example, kerbstone K95 by at least 1.5 m. The upper part of the layer from the kerbstone and 4 m inwards was truncated. I know of no Irish paral-

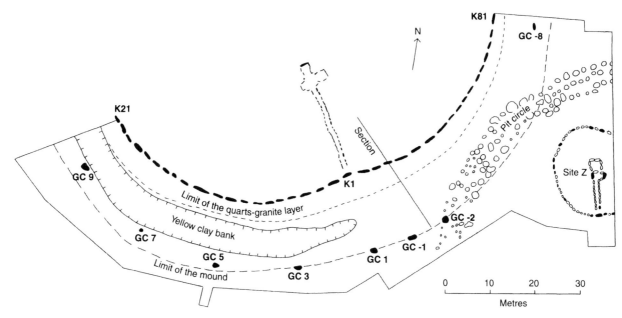

Fig. 6. Simplified plan of the area which Michael O'Kelly investigated at Newgrange. Selected structures in the large excavation area are shown in a very schematic form. Many structures have been omitted. The pit circle was termed by O'Kelly "the multiple arc of pits". Site Z is a demolished passage tomb. The "section" is that shown in Fig. 4. Note that the quartz/granite layer continues beyond the limits of the excavation area and that the foot of the great mound follows the stones belonging to the stone circle. Source: M. O'Kelly 1983 and Mount 1994.

lels for this situation, but there are several examples from Denmark of dolmens and passage tombs which were completely encapsulated within mounds in the Late Neolithic and Early Bronze Age (Fig. 5). For example, the passage tombs of Jordhøj (Kjærum 1970, 13) and Bigum (Dehn et alii 2000, 235-54) as well as the round dolmen Tårup (Holst 2006) and the long dolmen Capeshøj (Eriksen 1980; Skaarup 1985, 315-8).

Phase IV – layer IV: The great mound was extended. This phase – the latest in the section – is represented uppermost by an 8 m long layer, which is truncated at both sides, probably due to stone robbing in recent times.

THE STRATIGRAPHY IN FRONT OF THE KERBSTONES

From the kerbstones and outwards to the orthostats in the large stone circle there was a substantial culture layer which, according to O'Kelly, was deposited by settlement and slippage from the mound (Fig. 4). Here, in front of the mound and with the entrance to the passage of the megalithic tomb as a centre point, O'Kelly (1982, 66-7) investigated a c. 120 m long and 22 m wide area in which

25 sections were surveyed; these radiated out from the kerbstones (Fig. 6). Further to these was the section in the northern side of the mound mentioned above. Of the 26 sections, eight have been published (M. O'Kelly 1982, 69-71, 77; 1983, Figs. 3, 5, 9, 11, 13, 15) and they all show a very uniform stratigraphy: "The profiles showed minor variations from place to place, as was to be expected, but basically they were the same throughout, and a profile which commenced at K95 serves as a good example" (M. O'Kelly 1982, 68).

There are primarily four prehistoric layers (A-D) in the sections (Fig. 4). The formation of these was interpreted by O'Kelly in a very different way to that suggested here:

Phase A – The quartz/granite layer: Lowermost in the section outside the kerbstones lies the quartz/granite layer. This extends all the way up to the kerbstones and stretches 6-7 m outwards and about 50 m to each side of the entrance to the passage tomb. Both to the east and the west the quartz/granite layer continues outside the limits of the excavation area (Fig. 6). The layer is "composed entirely of angular pieces of white quartz and water-or glacially-rolled grey granite boulders, the quartz being very much the predominant material. The layer is wedge-shaped in section, thickest at the kerb and tails off to nothing farther out" (M. O'Kelly 1982, 68).

The quartz/granite layer was – as mentioned previously – perceived by O'Kelly as belonging to the cladding on a collapsed wall that had stood on the kerbstones. There are, however, several factors, which argue against the existence of such a wall:

1) It is unlikely that the wall would at one and the same time collapse along all of its length, like a gate blowing over. But even if this had happened, the layer would not be so thick and dense in by the kerbstones.

2) If such a wall had existed, and it had collapsed, the stone material lying behind it would also come clattering out, overlying the collapsed wall. This is not the case as the quartz/granite layer is overlain by the up to several hundred years younger earth/stone layer (phase B, see below).

3) O'Kelly maintained that an experiment, in which a section of wall clad with quartz stones was erected on top of the kerbstones and subsequently pushed over, confirmed his theory (M. O'Kelly 1982, 73). The experiment, which is only mentioned in general terms, must however have demonstrated the opposite: In the experiment the quartz/granite layer was covered by the stones which slipped out from the mound, i.e. a stratigraphic sequence that was not seen in any one of the 25 sections of which this layer was a part. In these sections the earth/stone layer lay between the quartz/granite layer and the presumed slip of stones.

4) In front of the entrances to the two passage tombs at Knowth, a mound of the same size as Newgrange and less than 2 km distant from it, belts of "exotic stones" have been found, which correspond to the quartz/granite layer at Newgrange. The excavator of Knowth, George Eogan, is most inclined to interpret the stone belts at Knowth as being deposited in connection with ceremonial activities (Eogan 1986, 48, 180).

5) The fact that no quartz was found under the fallen kerbstone K96 "shows that the quartz was not on the ground outside the kerb before it fell over" (M. O'Kelly 1982, 68). This situation is presented several times as proof of the existence of the wall and its collapse at a later point in the history of the mound, when kerbstone K96 had fallen over and decay had set in. The statement in the quote is correct but the explanation must be another, as there was no wall. The quartz/granite layer was

formed through ritual activities in the Neolithic after the kerbstones had fallen over.

The latter two objections also find support in the situation at Danish passage tombs where, instead of quartz, white-burnt flint was used (Dehn et alii 1995, 83-96; Skaarup 1985, 208, 373; Eriksen 2004, 69-70 and note 18).

6) There is a further argument against the wall: No parallels have yet been found at other passage tombs of similar walls erected on top of kerbstones.

All in all, these objections demonstrate that O'Kelly's wall-and-collapse theory must be rejected. The wall did not exist in the Neolithic. Instead, the white quartz stones were intentionally placed on a horizontal surface – a platform – in connection with cultic activities at the passage tomb (Kaul 1995 (in Dehn et alii 1995, 114); Eriksen 2004; Cooney 2006; Scarre 2007, 140).

Phase B – The earth/stone layer: "Above the quartz the profile shows a fairly thick layer of ordinary cairn stones in a matrix of soil, a noteworthy feature of which was the presence in it of innumerable snail shells ... During the excavation this was referred to as the earth/stone layer ... It continued outwards beyond the tail of the quartz/granite and petered out at a distance of up to 14 m from the kerb ... it contained flint artefacts, pottery, animal bones and a number of bone objects denoting the presence of squatters in Late-Neolithic/Beaker times" (M. O'Kelly 1982, 69-70).

The earth/stone layer was considered by O'Kelly to have been created and deposited by an ordinary domestic settlement due to the many postholes, pits, stone-set hearths and artefacts and the great amount of waste (M. O'Kelly 1982, 75; 1983, 52-3). The thickness and extent of the layer, as well as the many structures associated with it, is evidence that it arose from extended occupation or by way of regularly repeated activities. This is also clearly apparent from the many structures on the overview plan of the investigated area (M. O'Kelly 1983, Figs. 4, 8, 10, 12; Mount 1994, Fig. 2). It is very appropriately said of this layer that: "There are a number of phases or episodes of activity" (Mount 1994, 438).

The interpretation of the earth/stone layer as having been deposited by an ordinary settlement was maintained for a long time (Cooney & Grogan 1994, 79-81), until Charles Mount (1994), in his epoch-making article, dealt with this interpretation. Instead, Mount argued convincingly for the layer having been created in connection with cultic ceremonies, primarily on the grounds of its unnaturally large content of pig bones (Van Wijngaarden-Bakker 1974; 1986), which stands in stark contrast to an environment which favours cattle. At a later domestic settlement, such as Haughey's Fort from the Late Bronze Age, cattle dominate, whereas the faunal remains from the Late Bronze Age/Early Iron Age layers at the important ceremonial and religious centre at Navan Fort show dominance of pig (Mount 1994, 436-7).

The many pig bones often found at henges – for exampel at Durrington Walls, three kilometres from Stonehenge – show that pigs were butchered and consumed in great numbers at the religious ceremonies. The preference for pigs "is probably partly in their fecundity, making them an ideal creature for repeated mass slaughter. Compared to cattle and sheep, pigs have larger and more frequent litters. A herd can be killed down and bred up again with little threat to its continued existence" (Pitts 2000/2001, 260, with reference to Richard & Thomas 1984, 206).

The perception that the earth/stone layer at Newgrange accumulated due to ritual activities is also supported by the massive presence at Newgrange of other Late Neolithic/Early Bronze Age cultic monuments mentioned later in this article. Mount's new interpretation is generally accepted today (Bradley 1998, 110; 2007, 147; Cooney 2006, 699, 207; Stout 2002, 33).

Within the earth/stone layer there lies encapsulated a structure termed "the bank of boulder clay" or "the yellow clay bank" (M. O'Kelly 1982, 78; 1983, 26). This is a bank of yellow clay with a width of 5.5 m and a maximum height of 60 cm. It followed the course of the kerbstones at a distance of 4.5-8 m. The bank could be traced over a distance of 70 m from its beginning by the entrance to the passage tomb until it disappeared to the west into the uninvestigated area (Fig. 6).

The bank can be seen in section in four of the published section drawings (M. O'Kelly 1982, 77; 1983, Figs. 9, 11, 13). It has been laid over postholes, hearths, waste etc. belonging to the earth/stone layer, but at an early stage, as the underlying part of the same layer is not particularly thick. With the continued activity on the spot, the deposition of the earth/stone layer progressed up the sides of the bank and also on top of it.

The yellow clay bank is important as it respects the mound by being concentric with the curved course of the kerbstones. It is tempting to imagine that it continues all the way around the mound even though it has not been observed in the cut on the north side of the mound. However, there could have been an opening in the yellow clay bank here, and similarly in the eastern part of O'Kelly's excavation area. Mount (1994, 435) has drawn attention to the fact that the yellow clay bank is similar in construction to henges like Newgrange sites A and P and Monknewton (Sweetman 1976). The yellow clay bank would, perhaps, better be termed the yellow clay bank circle!

Phase C and Phase D – The slide layers: Over the earth/stone layer, and separated from it by a vegetation layer, lie two compact layers of stones, corresponding to the stones which make up the core of the mound. The layers, which are also separated from each other by a vegetation layer, are wedge-shaped and thickest closest to the mound. O'Kelly (1983, Figs. 9, 11, 13) called the lower layer "slide 1" (Fig. 4, layer C) and the upper layer "slide 2" (Fig. 4, layer D) as he took them to be slumping from the mound after his proposed wall had collapsed. They can be seen in all the published sections from the Newgrange mound outside the kerbstones, with the exception of one where they merge into one (M. O'Kelly 1983, Fig. 13). From the sections with kerbstones, K6, K10, K14, K53, K81, K95 and K96, it is apparent that the C-layer terminates on average 5 m from the kerbstones and the D-layer 8 m from them.

It is, however, unlikely that the layers C and D are slides, and why exactly are there two slides in each of the sections? The solution may be that the stones in layers C and D have not slumped out but that they lie in situ. Stones in cairns lock together with each other and do not slide down unless they are disturbed (Eriksen 2006). This can be seen on the exceptionally well-preserved passage-tomb mound Loughcrew T (Conwell 1873, 28-9) and on the best preserved parts of the passage-tomb mound at Dowth (O'Kelly & O'Kelly 1983, Plate IVb). In both cases, the kerbstones lie freely exposed and visible and are not covered by slippage from the stones in their mound, despite the fact that more than 5000 years have elapsed and Dowth (O'Kelly & O'Kelly 1983, 149) is, furthermore, taller and with steeper sides than Newgrange.

The relationship between the two slides and the stratigraphy in the mound behind the kerbstones can, unfortunately, not be seen in the sections as in 1870 and sub-

Fig. 7. The orthostats in the great circle of stone stands just outside the foot of the mound. Originally there probably were around 19 stones spaced at intervals of 14-20 m. Of these, 12 stones survive today. The stones were erected in the Early Bronze Age. Photo by S.P. Ó Ríordáin before the excavation which begun in 1962. After Ó Ríordáin & Daniel 1964.

sequently a deep ditch was dug in front of the kerbstones so that these could be seen more clearly. But the fact that there are two late mound phases (III and IV) in the mound behind the kerbstones, and also two phases (C and D) in the mound in front of the kerbstones, makes it seem reasonable that the two pairs match up, so that layer III and layer C represent the same phase, and these are followed by the phase comprising layer IV and layer D.

THE PIT CIRCLE

In the eastern part of O'Kelly's excavation area a 5-6 m wide curved belt appeared in the form of three concentric rows of pits termed the multiple arc of pits (Fig. 6) (M. O'Kelly 1982, 67, 80; 1983, 16-21). The distance from the outer part of the circle to the closest of the passage-tomb mound's kerbstones was only 7 m.

Subsequently, in 1982-83, it was investigated in more detail by David Sweetman (1985) who followed it further to the south to a point 90 m from O'Kelly's exca-

vation area. It was demonstrated that this actually was a pit circle – a henge – with an outer diameter of 100 m. Sweetman's meticulous investigation showed that the pit circle comprised six concentric rows of pits and postholes within a 7 m wide belt. In the outermost two rows there were substantial postholes. These were followed by two rows with pits and innermost two rows with small postholes. The postholes and the pits in the innermost four rows contained animal bones that had been burnt in connection with the ritual activities.

Within the pit circle there was, in addition to the remains of an earlier passage tomb (site Z), traces of habitation belonging to the cultic activities associated with the pit circle. As the earth/stone layer outside the mound overlies the traces of the pit circle, the pit circle is the oldest known large structure/activity from the Late Neolithic/Early Bronze Age at Newgrange. This dating is also underlined by the circumstance that, in addition to Beaker pottery, there were also sherds of the earlier Grooved Ware (Sweetman 1985, 209-10) together with several radiocarbon dates falling within the first half of the 3rd Millennium BC (Sweetman 1985, 197, 218; Grogan 1991, 130).

THE STONE CIRCLE

Just outside the great mound there are, set within in a great circle 105 m in diameter, 12 standing stones, of which five are intact (Fig. 7). Their GC-numbers are shown at figure 3. GC means Great Circle. The largest orthostats protrude 2-2.5 m up above the grassy turf. Ten of the orthostats lie within one half of the circle. The two remaining orthostats GC -8 and GC -10, which stand side by side approximately in the middle of the other half of the circle, make it seem probable that some stones are missing and that, accordingly – just like the course of other stone circles – the orthostats stood at regular intervals all the way around the mound. As stones have not been removed from the circle since Newgrange was first described 300 years ago, the removal of the missing stones must have taken place previous to this. They were probably cleared away when the area was cultivated after the Cistercian monks from Mellifont Abbey had taken it over in 1348 (O'Kelly et alii 1978, 344; Sweetman 1985, 204; Stout 2002, 82).

A frequently recurring discussion regarding the stone circle concerns the number of orthostats it originally comprised. Just outside the entrance to the passage tomb there are three orthostats standing 7-9 m apart. If all the stones stood so closely all the way round there must have been about 38 stones. But if the middle (GC -1) of the three orthostats is excluded and perceived as an abnormality, the distance between the orthostats was 14-20 m and in that case there were originally 19 orthostats (C. O'Kelly 1978, 96-7; Eriksen 2004, 67). In favour of the 19 orthostats and the large interval is the fact that, in O'Kelly's investigation comprising 2/5 of the stone circle's perimeter, no certain stone traces or sockets from orthostats were found which had stood at the lesser interval. The regularity with which the six orthostats stand, from stone GC 1, outside the entrance to the passage tomb, to stone GC 13, west of the mound (Fig. 3), also supports this assumption and that there were originally c. 19 orthostats around the mound.

In the southeastern part of the stone circle, one of its stones (GC -2) stands in the area of the pit circle (Fig. 6). This must mean that the stone circle is later than the pit circle. Had the pit circle been the later of the two, it would be expected that the stone would have been removed when

constructing the pit circle (Sweetman 1985, 216). This is consistent with the traditional perception that the stone circles, at one and the same time, replaced pit and timber circles (Sweetman 1985, 216; Cooney 2006, 705). But there are also examples that stones and posts could have stood at the same time, side by side in the same henge (Pitts 2000/2001, 255-6; Bradley 2007, 124). Sweetman's investigations of the stratigraphy, and the position of the GC -2 stone in the large stone circle, also indicate that the stone circle is the latest, even though there is no unequivocal proof of this (Sweetman 1985, 208).

The perimeter of the stone circle is concentric and, indeed, almost coincidental with that of the great mound. As a consequence, it is not concentric with the perimeter of the passage-tomb mound. This fact has, often with wonderment, been pointed out time and again. Now, with the newly-acquired realisation that Newgrange is a multiperiod monument, this can be explained by the builders of the great mound having hidden the old passage-tomb mound and its kerbstones and being solely interested in the new mound – their mound.

But how does the stone circle relate to the great mound? Is it contemporary with it or is it later? The most informative and detailed investigation of one of the stone circle's orthostats – GC -10 – was carried out in 1954 by Seán Ó Ríordáin and Marcus Ó hEochaide (Fig. 8). The stone had fallen over completely and lay directly on the old ground surface permitting the conclusion that "It is certain that the stone was erected clear of the edge of the cairn and that it fell before any collapse took place because none of the cairn material lay beneath it" (Ó Ríordáin & Ó hEochaide 1956, 56).

The stratigraphy and the description of the layers (Fig. 8) are interesting and contain important information: "The stratification consisted of following layers: (a) a light sod cover, (b) cairn collapse, (c) ... the old ground surface and (d) the natural sub-soil" (Ó Ríordáin & Ó hEochaide 1956, 55).

Today – about 50 years later – and in the light of our knowledge concerning the existence of the great mound, the lowest archaeological layer, b3, which in addition to animal bones also contained numerous fragments of quartz, could correspond to the quartz/granite layer (phase A) in O'Kelly's investigation and the layer b2 to his "slide 2" and, accordingly, the outermost part of the great mound in phase D. The uppermost layer, b1, extended right up to the stone and overlay its socket. The

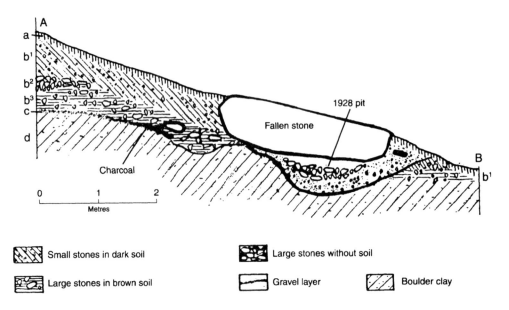

Fig. 8. Section with the fallen orthostat GC -10 in the stone circle. The mound lies to the left, and just to the left of the fallen stone its socket can be seen. "1928 pit" refers to an investigation carried out in 1928. When the section was surveyed in 1954, the b-layers were interpreted as cairn collapse: b1 consisted of small stones embedded in dark soil, b2 was of large stones free from soil, b3 had large stones similar to those in b2 but they were embedded in brown soil. Today, they can be interpreted quite differently: b3 is the quartz/granite layer (Fig. 4: A-layer), b2 is slide 2 (Fig. 4: D-layer) and b1 was formed partially after the stone fell over. As the b1-layer, which continues on the other side of the stone, contained animal bones, its formation could be due to ritual activity. After Ó Ríordáin & Ó hEocadhe 1956.

formation of the layer therefore also took place after the orthostat had fallen over, possibly because of cairn collapse but more probably due to ritual activities as it also contained animal bones. This latter observation is important as it demonstrates that cultic activities continued to take place at this point in Newgrange's history.

If we also include the observations made during O'Kelly's campaign concerning the relationship between the stone circle and the mound, we must conclude that the stones could be coeval with the mound, but they could also have been erected later.

STANDING STONES

In the southernmost of his cuts, no. 1, just less than 90 m to the south of the kerbstones of the Newgrange passage-tomb mound, Sweetman (1985, 203-4) found the sockets of two standing stones. One of the stones, of which a remnant was preserved, was estimated to have been 2.9 m high. Removal of the stones possibly took place as early as the Middle Ages with the monks' cultivation of their newly-acquired land at Newgrange.

It was not possible to date the erection of the two stones. Similarly, it could not be established in which context they belonged, but they were placed just outside the pit circle. Could these stones have belonged to a completely demolished stone circle or did they stand alone?

Single, undated stones also occur elsewhere in the Newgrange area. 800 m ESE of Newgrange there is a 3.5 m-high standing stone (site C) and 85 m from this there is another standing stone (site D) (C. O'Kelly 1978, 52, 59; M. O'Kelly 1982, 49).

THE STONE ON THE TOP

When Edward Lhwyd, as the first, described Newgrange following his visit in 1699, he wrote in a letter: "... a stately mound ... having a number of huge stones pitch'd on end round about it, and a single one on the top". And in another letter written three months later, in March 1700, he tells that the stone on the top is smaller than those that stand around the mound (Ó Ríordáin & Daniel 1964, 31-3).

The first known drawing of Newgrange may originate from Lhwyd's visit in 1699 (Fig. 9). The drawing, which

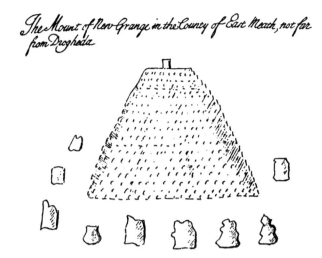

The Mount of New-Grange in the County of East Meath, not far from Drogheda

Fig. 9. The earliest known drawing of the Newgrange mound was probably produced by Edward Lhwyd in 1699. Note the stone on the top. The mound could have been more-or-less intact until this point in time, but subsequently many cartloads of stones were removed from it and ten years later the stone on the top was gone. After Ó Ríordáin & Daniel 1964.

was "most probably done by Edward Lhwyd" (Daniel 1967, Fig. 4.), clearly shows a stone standing on the flat top of the mound.

When Samuel Molyneux (Herity 1967, 135) visited Newgrange ten years later, the stone on the top had been removed in the comprehensive stone robbing which took place in the first half of the 18th century and which is dealt with in more detail below.

This stone on the top, which probably stood 1.5 m tall, must necessarily be coeval with or later than the last phase of the great mound. It could have been erected in the same operation as the stones in the great stone circle.

NEWGRANGE'S PHASES
After dealing with, in the above, the stratigraphy of the mound on both sides of the kerbstones and considering the pit circle, the stone circle and the stone on the top of the mound, we will now position the phases inside and outside the kerbstones and the aforementioned structures relative to each other (Figs. 10-11).

Phase 0: Small turf-built mound with passage tomb (?).

Phase 1: Phase I. The first large passage-tomb mound with its present chamber. The foot of the mound termi-

nates 6.5 m from the kerbstones erected in phase 2.

Phase 2: Phase II and phase A. The mound is enlarged, the passage is extended and the kerbstones are put in position so there is a 2.5 m wide stone-free belt between them and the foot of the mound. After a while, the quartz/granite layer is formed by accumulation as a consequence of several ritual activities in front of the kerbstones.

Phase 3: The pit circle and phase B. The pit circle appears to be earliest, after which the earth/stone layer is successively deposited from the kerbstones and outwards. Finally, the yellow clay bank circle is constructed. However, this later becomes encapsulated in a further culture layer belonging to the earth/stone layer. This dense settlement-like layer must be perceived as having been deposited by way of several cultic/ceremonial activities.

Phase 4: Phase III and phase C. The passage-tomb mound is included within, and hidden by, a great mound.

Phase 5: Phase IV and phase D. Further extension of the great mound. The structures assigned to phase 6 may possibly have been erected in phase 5.

Phase 6: The orthostats in the large stone circle are erected and a stone is positioned on the top of the mound. The stone circle could, however, as mentioned above, have been established already in phase 5 and the stone on the top could have been erected much later. Ritual activity continued even after some of the orthostats had toppled over.

DATING
With regard to dating the individual phases and their cultural associations, phases 1-3 are well-documented by virtue of the datable artefacts, analogous structures and calibrated radiocarbon dates.

Phases 1-2, with construction of the passage tomb and its mound together with its enlargement and use, took place in the Passage-Tomb Period, which in the Bend of Boyne is radiocarbon dated to 3350-2900 BC (Grogan 1991, 128-9). The Newgrange passage tomb and similar Irish passage tombs are dated to 3400-3200 BC in the Middle Neolithic (3600-3100 BC) (Cooney 2000, 11).

Phase 3 comprises both the Late Neolithic (3100-2500 BC) and the Early Bronze Age, the beginning of which in Ireland, 2500 BC, coincides with the appearance of the Beaker culture (Cooney 2000, 18). The radiocarbon dates suggest that the Beaker horizon does not continue after 2300 BC (Grogan 1991, 131). The oldest structure

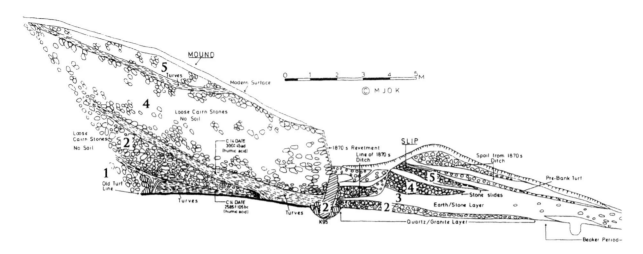

Fig. 10. The whole section at kerbstone K95 with the layers corresponding to Newgrange phases 1-5. The layers are separated by vegetation layers. Phase 1: Mound with passage tomb without kerbstones. Phase 2: The passage-tomb mound is enlarged and kerbstones are erected at a distance from its foot; the quartz/granite layer accumulates. Phase 3: By continued ceremonial activity in the Late Neolithic/Beaker period a dense layer is deposited in front of the passage-tomb mound. Phase 4: In the Early Bronze Age a great mound is constructed, which also covers the kerbstones of the passage-tomb mound. Phase 5: Enlargement of the phase 4 great mound.

in phase 3 – the pit circle – is dated to 2800 BC, corresponding to the Grooved Ware culture (2900-2700 BC) (Cooney 2000, 17). According to the radiocarbon dates, the end of phase 3 lies around 2300 BC (Grogan 1991, 131).

There is a great deal of uncertainty and disagreement concerning the dating of the individual periods and the degree to which the Beaker horizon should be placed at the end of the Neolithic or in the beginning of the Bronze Age. It is easy to envy the researchers who previously used broad period terms such as "the Late Neolithic/ Beaker period settlement" concerning the earth/stone layer (C. O'Kelly (ed.) 1983) or "a Late Neolithic/Early Bronze Age pit circle" concerning the pit circle (Sweetman 1985). Both are correct, as phase 3 comprises both the Late Neolithic, the Beaker period and the Early Bronze Age.

The subsequent phases, 4-6, are not dated in detail. This is due to the fact that they have only recently been recognised and that there is, with a single exception, no radiocarbon dates. The exception is an erroneous date of 300 ad (uncalibrated) for the turf layer on which the earliest great mound (phase 4) rests (Fig. 4) (M. O'Kelly 1982, 230-1). So until new radiocarbon dates become available we must make do with very broad dates. On the whole, the three latest phases appear to lie in the Early Bronze Age from about 2300 BC until the time when the large

stone circle was erected. These three phases together may well cover a period of only 100-300 years, so the beginning of phase 6 should be dated to before 2000 BC.

The artificial division into six phases could give the impression of a step-wise development with "dead" intervals in between – just like the steps of a staircase without people and therefore without movement. This was not the case; Newgrange is more than a monument: Newgrange is also a process.

QUARRYING

In order to form a picture of how the great mound may have looked, it is first necessary to examine the extent of the changes to which it has been subjected since its destruction began 300 years ago. The great mound was visible until O'Kelly's activities in the 1960s and 1970s changed its appearance in a major way. On early aerial photos one can clearly see an uneven flat surface on the top and a disturbed, pitted mound side towards the southeast (Fig. 12). The other parts of the mound appear – with exception of the ditch by the kerbstones – undisturbed. The destruction of the top and the southeast side, together with the digging of the ditch, were caused by stone robbing and a wish to expose the fronts of the kerbstones.

Whereas it is common knowledge that large quantities of stone were removed from the two other large Neolithic

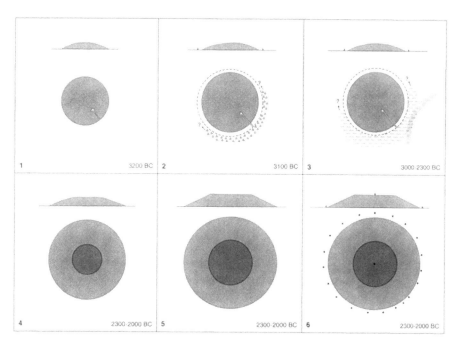

Fig. 11. Newgrange's six phases. 1: Passage-tomb mound without kerbstones. 2: The passage-tomb mound is enlarged and kerbstones are erected a little outside the mound foot. The quartz/granite layer (small triangles) accumulates. 3: A new culture layer, the earth/stone layer (small waves), accumulates over the quartz-granite layer and beyond. The rounded narrow belt with the many dots indicates the pit circle. 4: The passage-tomb mound and its kerbstones are covered by a great mound. 5: The great mound is enlarged and given a flat top. 6: The mound is encircled with large stones and a stone is possibly erected on the flat top. Phases 5 and 6 could be one phase.

Fig. 12. Newgrange seen from the air during Michael O'Kelly's campaign. Previous stone robbing has altered the surface of the flat top and caused a large indentation in the southeastern part, over the chamber and the passage to the passage tomb. The ditch and the associated bank, created in 1870 in front of the kerbstones, are clearly visible outside the investigation area. The arc of holes uppermost belongs to the pit circle. Photo by D.L. Swan, after M. O'Kelly 1983.

View of a New Grange

Fig. 13. In 1776 Charles Vallancey made this drawing of the Newgrange mound. The concave top of the mound is due to extensive stone robbing, begun in 1699. The two horns – one at each side – on the mound top are the bank along the edge of the original mound which is accentuated on Fig. 14. The bank could have arisen from the stone robbers not taking stones all the way out to the edge of the mound summit. After Brennan 1983.

mounds nearby, Dowth (O'Kelly & O'Kelly 1983, 126) and Knowth (Stout 2002, 69), it is today generally accepted that this was not the case at Newgrange. At least O'Kelly (1982, 33) rejected the idea that "wholesale removal of cairn material had taken place".

When the Cistercian monks took over the area in the 14th century, as mentioned a couple of times previously, in order to facilitate cultivation they could have destroyed and removed some of the stones in the large stone circle.

But it is first with Edward Lhwyd's two letters from 1699-1700, written just after the passage tomb was discovered, that more tangible testimony is provided. In August 1699, the lands of Newgrange were leased for ninety years to Charles Campbell (Stout 2002, 128). Charles Campbell was an exceptionally enterprising gentleman who transformed the Newgrange area into a viable estate. He also saw the economic and practical potential of the many stones in the great mound as he had, according to Lhwyd, "employed his servants to carry off a considerable parcel of them" (Ó Ríordáin & Daniel 1964, 32), for buildings and the improvement of roads. The reason that the passage tomb was discovered in 1699 was very probably that a considerable parcel of stones was removed from the mound and it is likely that this continued in the following years when the large stone on top of the mound also disappeared. The explanation for stones being removed just here was that the road leading from the farm Newgrange met the mound at this point. Had the farm lain on the opposite side of the mound, perhaps the entrance to the passage tomb would never have been discovered so early.

Robbing of the cairn for stone appears to have proceeded apace in the following years, for when Thomas Pownall described Newgrange as he saw it in 1769, he stressed its continued use as a quarry: "... but a ruin of what is was. It has long served as a stone quarry to the country round about it. All the roads in the neighbourhood are paved with its stones; immense quantities having been taken away" (Pownall 1773, 253). Pownall was of the opinion that a large triangular segment, measuring 40 feet at ground level and 70 feet far up the sloping mound side, was removed from in front of the entrance. This great cut into the mound at the entrance can be very clearly seen on the "Section of the Tumulus" which land-surveyor Samuel Bouie drew for Pownall (1773, pl. XX). One hundred years later, the drawing was "improved" by James Fergusson (Fig. 2). Pownall has probably over-dramatised the extent of the stone robbing because he thought the top of the mound had originally been pointed like a pyramid, in which case a very considerable amount of stone was missing.

In his long description of Newgrange, Pownall does not mention the famous kerbstone (K1) in front of the entrance, almost certainly because it was covered by a great heap of stones, as shown on Gabriel Beranger's drawing a few years later, in 1775 (Stout 2002, 41). Already the following year – 1776 – another drawing by Charles Vallancey became available in which it can be seen that the top of the mound had been hollowed out as a consequence of the stone robbing (Fig. 13). On both sides, a raised area can be seen – a bank – which is shown here in 1776 for the first time and which existed right up until the time of O'Kelly's campaign.

In 1844 there were alarming plans "that the removal of a portion, if not the whole, of the mound of Newgrange was contemplated to be broken up for the repair of the roads" (M. O'Kelly 1982, 33). Fortunately, Newgrange avoided this fate and stone robbing appears to have ceased completely by 1849 when William Wilde (1849/1949, 165-6) briefly described the destruction: "Various excavations made into its sides, and upon its summit, at different times ... have assisted to lessen its original height, and also to destroy the beauty of its outline; but this defect has been obviated in part by a plantation chiefly of hazel, which has grown over its surface." The same "peaceful" state is also conjured up by Fergusson's description of Newgrange in 1872, where an accompanying drawing shows that the mound had become somewhat overgrown with trees and bushes (Fergusson 1872, 201).

Under the provisions of the Ancient Monuments Protections Act 1882, Newgrange was taken into State care, and the Board of Public Works became the authority responsible for it. With this, a definite end was brought to the use of the mound as a source of stone.

THE SHAPE AND SIZE OF THE MOUND

Edward Lhwyd does not mention the shape of the mound, but he was probably responsible for the first known drawing of the mound (Fig. 9). Even though the drawing is very naive it gives a good impression: The mound has very steep sides and a flat top on which there stands a stone. Nine large stones belonging to the large stone circle can be seen around the mound.

When Samuel Molyneux visited Newgrange around 1710, he made a sketch from which it is apparent that the mound had a flat top with a diameter of 105 feet, corresponding to 32 m (Herity 1967, 132). Since then, this has been the generally accepted value for the diameter of the mound's top surface (O'Kelly 1982, 21).

The mound's original shape has prompted very divergent opinions. For example, Thomas Pownall (1773) thought that the mound had had a pointed top like a pyramid, and R.A.S. Macalister (1929) believed in a shapely hemispherical mound. Both explained the missing peak either by extensive stone robbing or erosion. It was generally very common – prior to O'Kelly's campaign – to presume that Newgrange had once been much higher. As late as 1964, Glyn Daniel stated that "the mound was probably considerably higher than at present" (Ó Ríordáin & Daniel 1964, 49), and that the present lower mound was the result of its extensive use as a quarry. There were,

however, antiquarians, like James Fergusson (1872, 206) and George Coffey (1912/1977, 16), who were of the opinion that the flat top was an original feature.

O'Kelly argued vehemently that the stone robbing had been limited and had not changed the mound significantly. The flat top was also an original feature in O'Kelly's eyes. He went radically against previous perceptions when he – mistakenly – thought the mound's original perimeter was identical with the line of the kerbstones, over which there had been a 3 m high wall responsible for retaining the mound fill lying between the circle of kerbstones and the large circle of orthostats.

As revealed by the new analyses of O'Kelly's numerous sections through the mound, the great mound in its final form – phase 5 – had a diameter of 100 m. It extended almost all the way out to the stone circle, which is possibly a little later, being erected in phase 6.

If we presume that stone robbing was limited in extent, then the best method of revealing the original appearance of the mound is to study the very detailed contour map O'Kelly had produced. If we lay a section through the middle of the mound onto this map and include two of the stones in the stone circle – GC 11 in the west and GC -10 in the east – we gain a good impression of the flat top (Fig. 14). At each side it is delimited by a 1 m high and 4-6 m wide bank. The top has here its maximum extent which, including the top of the bank, comprises 40 m. The highest point on the bank corresponds to the 16 m contour on the contour map. The outer side of the bank corresponds to the 15 m contour. If we then mark the two contours on the map, we can evaluate the appearance and size of the flat top. It is far from circular in outline; it is almost kidney shaped with a large notch in the southeastern part running from the kerbstones and all the way up to the top. This great notch corresponds to that which Pownall saw on his visit in 1769.

It is likely that the top surface was originally roughly circular in outline, because the mound has a circular ground-plan – normally the case with mounds – and the contours at the top are also concentric and circular where the surface of the mound is undisturbed. If we also assume that the original top surface was approximately horizontal at a level corresponding to the top of the bank, we can calculate the size of the top surface by reconstructing the original 16 m contour on the contour map. This reveals that the top surface measured 35-40 m in diameter and had an area of 1100 m2.

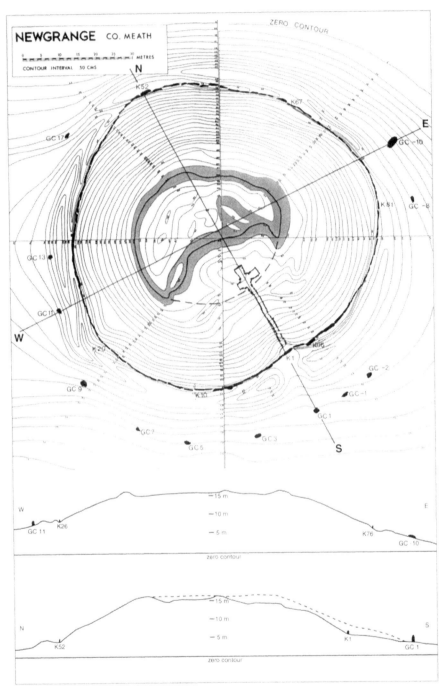

Fig. 14. This contour map, which was surveyed by Michael O'Kelly prior to his restoration of Newgrange, gives a good impression of the surface and form of the mound in 1962. The distance between the contour lines is 0.5 m. The highest area lies along the edge of the mound top at the 16 m contour, which is accentuated. The original course of the 16 m contour in the damaged area is shown with a broken line. The marking of the area 16-15.5 m gives a good impression of the bank along the edge of the mound top. The location of the two sections below is shown.

On the W-E section, the bank can be clearly seen along the edge of the mound top. The top of the bank probably marks the surface of the original top before the stone robbing. In front of both kerbstones there is a ditch and a bank, which arose from the digging free of the kerbstones in 1870 and subsequently.

On the N-S section, the broken line shows the presumed surface of the great mound. The reconstructed mound side has been drawn on the basis of a presumed even course of the contour lines. Stone robbing has led to the removal of parts of the top of the mound and the mound side to the south.

Fig. 15. With its size, flat top and dating to the second half of the 3rd Millennium BC, Silbury Hill is the most obvious parallel to the great mound of Newgrange. Photo by Palle Eriksen.

With the sections through the mound we can now calculate its height very accurately. As the mound lies on an east-west oriented ridge, we will use the section that runs in approximately the same direction. If we join the ground surface at the two diametrically opposed stones in the large stone circle with a line and measure from the middle of this line up to the 16 m contour, we obtain a height of 11 m.

The great mound has, accordingly, had the form of a truncated cone with a basal diameter of c. 100 m, and a top diameter, on average, of 37.5 m and a height of 11 m. Its volume was therefore 43,646 m3 or c. 43,500 m3. If we estimate the density of stone to be 2.75, the whole of the stone fill of the mound weighs 119,625 tons, i.e. about 120,000 tons, which is a lot less than the 180,000-200,000 tons previously suggested (Wilde 1849/1949, 165; M. O'Kelly 1982, 117).

THE BIG "BEAKER BUILDING-BOOM"

If one searches for parallels to Newgrange's great mound in Ireland and Britain in the form of flat-topped mounds with a diameter of 100 m or more, constructed in the latter half of the 3rd Millennium BC, the choice available is very limited. There is only one contender, i.e. Silbury Hill in Southern England (Fig. 15).

Silbury Hill, with a diameter of 162 m and a height of 37 m, is Europe's largest prehistoric man-made mound. The ground-plan of the mound is completely circular. The flat top has a diameter of 30 m and an area of 700 m2 (Whittle 1997).

The mound has prompted several archaeological investigations, the earliest being in 1776 and the most recent Richard Atkinson's investigations in 1968-70. Further to this are investigations in 2000 and 2007 prompted by damage to the top of the mound. The investigations carried out so far reveal that Silbury Hill has three related construction phases (Malone 1989, 95-9; Whittle 1997, 1). The earliest mound, which had a diameter of less than 40 m, has been radiocarbon dated to 2871-2486 BC. The latest mound, with the present diameter, has been radiocarbon dated to 2398-2202 BC and 2270-2042 BC (Whittle 1997, 1).Chronologically, there is coincidence between Silbury Hill and Newgrange's great mound; the latter can probably be dated to 2300-2000 BC. Linking these two mounds with both reference to form and age is nothing new; James Fergusson (1872, 202) did it!

Fig. 16. The Newgrange mound and its immediate surroundings have many traces of structures and activities from the Late Neolithic and Early Bronze Age, though no. 7 could be even earlier and contemporary with the construction of the passage tomb. This figure shows those we know today. 1: The great mound. 2: The earth/stone layer. 3: The stone circle. 4: The pit circle. 5: A smaller pit circle. 6: Two standing stones. 7: The cursus. Photo by Con Brogan, Photographic Unit, Department of Environment Heritage and Local Government, Ireland.

Perhaps the stone Lhwyd saw on the top of New-grange just over 300 years ago was erected on the newly constructed great mound, in which case there could also be a parallel here to Silbury Hill. A small fragment of a bluestone, possibly part of a larger stone, has been found on top of the latter. The bluestone fragment was found during Atkinson's investigations and was described by Atkinson, who was also the excavator of Stonehenge and was familiar with bluestones, as being "apparently identical with one of the varieties of Stonehenge bluestone (volcanic ash)" (Atkinson 1970, 314). Atkinson therefore made the suggestion that at least some of the bluestones of Stonehenge were already at Silbury Hill some centuries before their first use at Stonehenge itself. Subsequently, Flemming Kaul (1999, 33) has proposed the theory that Stonehenge's bluestones – or some of them – had previously stood on Silbury Hill during the period when, according to Atkinson (1956) they were not standing at Stonehenge. However, the phase without bluestones at Stonehenge is far from certain (Cleal 1995, 210).

Despite the fact that several excavations have been carried out at Silbury Hill no trace has been found of a buried king or chieftain worthy of a mound of these dimensions. This is hardly surprising as Silbury Hill – just like Newgrange's great mound – is unlikely to have been a burial mound in the traditional sense associated with burials but rather a large scale cultic monument (Fergusson 1872, 79; Malone 1989, 99-100; Whittle 1997, 142-51; Bradley 2007, 131).

Only slightly more than 1 km to the north of Silbury Hill lies Avebury, another of the Late Neolithic/Early Bronze Age's great monuments which, like Silbury Hill, is one of the largest and most labour-demanding monuments from the European Late Neolithic and Early Bronze Age. A circular ditch, originally 21 m wide at the top and 11 m deep, with an associated external bank, encloses an area of 115,000 m2. The diameter of this henge, which is one of the largest examples, is 420 m! A circle of stones has stood along the inner edge of the ditch, corresponding to the stone circle at Newgrange but with its diameter of 335 m it is undeniably somewhat larger and also the largest of its kind. Within the large circle there were two lesser circles, although these were of the same size as that at Newgrange. Further to these are two stone-set avenues, which led from outside up to two of the four openings in this great henge. Avebury comprises several phases, probably all lying within the period 2800-2400 BC (Burl 1979; Malone 1989).

35 km further south lies the best known of all Late Neolithic/Early Bronze Age monuments: Stonehenge (Cleal et alii 1995). This world-famous and unique monument has a long construction history with three phases and several sub-phases extending over the period 2950-1600 BC, i.e. contemporary with the construction of Newgrange's great mound. Stonehenge phase 3ii with the rising of the trilithons and the sarsen circle has just been re-dated to 2600-2400 BC (Pearson et alii).

In addition to the obvious similarities between Newgrange and Silbury Hill, mention is made of this site, together with the two other famous English monuments – Avebury and Stonehenge, in order to demonstrate that in the second half of the 3rd Millennium BC it was typical to build big in Ireland and Britain. It was truly a "Hengeworld " (Pitts 2000/2001), with innumerable henges and circles of various kinds and sizes, ranging from pit and/or timber circles, ditch and/or bank enclosures to stone circles. These monuments are something completely unique to Ireland and Britain as they are virtually absent from the Continent.

Further to these there is in Hengeworld the occurrence of round mounds of exceptional local size associated with henges: The Hatfield mound and the Marden henge and the Conquer barrow and the Mount Pleasant henge, both in Wessex. The great barrow at Knowlton in Dorset, the great mound at Duggleby Howe in Yorkshire and Maes Howe with the famous passage tomb in the Orkneys all lie within henges. Despite their being just over 1 km apart, there was probably also an association between Silbury Hill and Avebury. And at Newgrange there is again the same combination: great mound and henges, where the henges are represented by the pit circle and perhaps also the yellow clay bank circle, later superseded by the large stone circle around the mound after the enlargement of the latter in the Early Bronze Age.

Seen in the light of this big "Beaker building-boom" it is not difficult to understand that the large passage-tomb mound at Newgrange was also "modernised". The contemporary monument builders in the Late Neolithic/Early Bronze Age often took over earlier monuments, created several hundreds years previously, and altered them so they fitted with their own cultic requirements. This applies, for example, to Stonehenge and now also to Newgrange.

Many of the henges in Britain and Ireland, including the pit circle at Newgrange, were large open structures where many people could follow and take part in the ceremonies (Bradley 1998, 109). Silbury Hill and the late Newgrange mound are, of course, not henges but are, perhaps, related to them in that cultic activities could have taken place on their elevated flat tops which could accommodate several hundred people. The great mound of Newgrange has a furthr link to the henges with standing stones: The mound was surrounded by a circle of stones, of which 12 survive.

THE LATE NEOLITHIC AND EARLY BRONZE AGE AT NEWGRANGE

Newgrange's great mound with its stone circle is, as is apparent from the above, far from the only cultic monument at Newgrange dating from the Late Neolithic and the Early Bronze Age (Fig. 16). First, the earth/stone layer, rich in finds and structures including the yellow clay bank, was discovered by O'Kelly (1983) in the 1960s. The pit circle, with a diameter of 100 m, was also found during O'Kelly's campaign, but this henge was first comprehensively investigated and understood following the excavations in 1982-83 by David Sweetman (1985). When Sweetman investigated the pit circle he also found traces of two standing stones, 90 m south of the Newgrange mound. In 1985 Sweetman (1987) excavated part of another pit circle with a diameter of only 20 m situated 50 m west of the Newgrange mound. It is also Sweetman's credit to have dated Newgrange's large stone circle to the Late Neolithic/Early Bronze Age (Sweetman 1985).

Earlier, in 1971, Sweetman (1976) had investigated a henge at Monknewton, about 3 km to the north of Newgrange. This henge, which had a diameter of 100 m, is the smallest in a group of 13 prehistoric enclosures in County Meath. These enclosures are unique to Ireland by having an earth bank but no ditch and are, therefore, termed "embanked enclosures" (Stout 1991). The material for the banks in these henges has been scraped from the inner surface. Three of these enclosures lie in the Bend of the Boyne, of which there are two – Newgrange A and Newgrange P (C. O'Kelly 1978, 49-52; Stout 1991, 268-71) each with an outer diameter of 175 m – within 1 km of Newgrange.

Further to these henges, Tom Condit (1997a) and later Gabriel Cooney (2000, 165-7) and Geraldine Stout (2002, 33-8) have also drawn attention to other of the Late Neolithic/Early Bronze Age's monuments near Newgrange

Fig. 17. Newgrange as it appeared prior to 1962. Photo by M. O'Kelly, after M. O'Kelly 1982.

and the mutual relationships existing between them. These include a couple of single standing stones – not the two found by Sweetman – and a cursus, perceived as a ceremonial avenue where ritual processions took place through the landscape.

The Newgrange Cursus located 100 m east of the Newgrange mound on a north-south axis, consists of two parallel banks 20 m apart, the southern end closed off by a convex terminal. It can be followed over a distance of 100 m but was even longer in prehistory (Condit 1997a). No investigations have been carried out into this cursus and there are no finds to date it. Even so, it is thought to be functionally, and thereby also chronologically, associated with the other Late Neolithic monuments from the 3rd Millennium BC in the area around Newgrange (Condit 1997a; Cooney 2000, 214; Stout 2002, 33; Loveday 2006, 195). This late date for the cursus in the Late Neolithic is problematic as the earliest cursus extend back to the early 4th Millennium BC, i.e. the Early Neolithic

(Gibson 1994, fig. 28) and the monument type generally is well-dated to the Middle Neolithic (Loveday 2006, 10, 105, 144). Late radiocarbon dates such as, for example, for the Stonehenge Cursus have also been doubted and are not thought to give the time of their construction (Cleal & Allen 1995, 477).

In addition to these many monuments from the Late Neolithic and Early Bronze Age it is to be expected that, in the area around Newgrange, there lie many undiscovered structures from the same period. Perhaps future investigations will also be able to determine whether a pair of deliberately created ponds in the area near Newgrange were included in the religious activities of that time (Condit 1997b; Cooney 2000, 166).

The cultic activities of the Late Neolithic/Early Bronze Age thus clearly made their mark on the landscape at Newgrange and the Bend of the Boyne by adapting earlier monuments and constructing many new. The overall plan was to shape a ceremonial and sacred landscape in which the great mound with the flat top was a striking participant, perhaps even a centre for the cult.

The discovery of Newgrange's great mound opens up, accordingly, new and fascinating perspectives of far-reaching significance for the understanding and communication of the cultural development in the area.

THE MOUND AND THE PRESENT

The old antiquarians Molyneux, Wilde, Fergusson, Coffey and many others were of the opinion that the foot of the Newgrange's mound lay at the stone circle. This was the general perception, also in the first half of the 20th century (Fig. 17). So when O'Kelly, at the beginning of the 1960s, was selected to carry out the restoration of Newgrange, he was also given the instruction that "The original sloping face of the mound to be restored" (M. O'Kelly 1982, 72).

However, as is now well known, things worked out quite differently when the subsequent archaeological investigations of the 1960s apparently confirmed that Newgrange was a single-period mound and that the great stone masses of the mound sill had been retained by a high white-clad wall rising from the top of the kerbstones. As a consequence of this, O'Kelly reconstructed Newgrange as he thought it had appeared in the Neolithic. This is the appearance that Newgrange has now had for just less than 40 years. Criticism from some quarters has been severe (e.g. Michell 1982, 149; Giot 1983; Kaul 1998, 61; Cope 2004, 238), but has primarily been directed at the appearance or the modern concrete construction technique without pointing out actual errors in the reconstruction, i.e. that in the Neolithic there never was a wall, and not even a sloping mound side clad in white quartz (Eriksen 2004).

Recently, restored megalithic monuments have been assigned to one of three classes where Newgrange is used as the type example of the worst: radical reconstruction (Scarre 2006, 28-30).

With the newly-acquired realisation that there was no white wall in the Neolithic, the scientific basis for the modern wall has crumbled. At the same time, the demonstration of the existence of the great mound has introduced new perspectives of crucial importance for a possible future "re-restoration" of Newgrange. The great mound ought to be recreated more-or-less as it appeared prior to the beginning of the archaeological investigations in 1962.

But since O'Kelly created Newgrange's white wall, it has become incorporated into people's consciousness and has become an (Irish) icon (Cooney 2000, 1; 2006, 706). Nevertheless, the wall is a fake and, with the discovery of the great mound, half of the real Newgrange story is not now being communicated to the monument's annual 200,000 visitors. Furthermore, Brú na Bóinne with Newgrange was, in 1993, designated a UNESCO World Heritage Site which led, among other things, to the establishing of a fine visitor centre. But with such fame and designation comes responsibility and this ought to lead to the demolition of the contentious white wall. This should not be a source of regret or complaint, the wall is – excuse me – hideous, and the story of Newgrange has now become even better and more colourful. Instead of one monument – the passage-tomb mound from the Neolithic – there are now, with the discovery of the great mound from the Early Bronze Age, two monuments. Furthermore, there is the dramatic story of a white wall which, for just less than half a century (?), has characterised Newgrange.

ACKNOWLEDGEMENTS

I am most grateful to Dronning Margrethe II's Arkæologiske Fond for a grant enabling me to visit Ireland in 1999, to Niels H. Andersen and Torben Dehn for comments of the text, to Geraldine Stout for discussions, to Con Brogan for the photo figure 16, to Thames and Hudson for permission to use Figs. 3, 4 and 17 in Newgrange. Archaeology, Art and Legend by Michael O'Kelly, to Torben Egeberg and Louise Hilmar for technical assistance with the figures, to David Earle Robinson and Anne Bloch Jørgensen who translated this article into English and last but not least to Jesper Laursen.

BIBLIOGRAPHY

Atkinson, R.J.C. 1956. Stonehenge. London.
- 1970. Silbury Hill, 1969-70. Antiquity 44, 313-4.
Bradley, R. 1998. The significance of monuments. London: Routledge.
- 2007. The Prehistory of Britain and Ireland. Cambridge: Cambridge University Press.
Brennan, M. 1983: The Stars and the Stones. Ancient art and astronomy in Ireland. London: Thames and Hudson.
Burl, A. 1979. Prehistoric Avebury. New Haven and London: Yale University Press.
Cleal, R.M.J. 1995. The stone settings, phase 3. In Cleal, R.M.J., Walker, K.E. & Montague, R. (eds) 1995, 168-331.
Cleal, R.M.J. & Allen, M. 1995. Stonehenge in its landscape. In Cleal, R.M.J., Walker, K.E. & Montague, R. (eds) 1995, 464-91.
Cleal, R.M.J., Walker, K.E. & Montague, R. (eds) 1995. Stonehenge and its landscape. Twentieth-century excavations. London: English Heritage Archaeological Report 10.
Coffey, G. 1912/1977. New Grange and other incised tumuli in Ireland. Dublin: Hodges Figgis/Poole: Dolphin Press.
Condit, T. 1997a. The Newgrange cursus and the theatre of ritual. In
Condit, T. & Cooney, G. (eds), Brú na Bóinne, 26-7. Dublin: Archaeology Ireland.
- 1997b. Monknewtown ritual pond. In Condit, T. &
Cooney, G. (eds), Brú na Bóinne, 23. Dublin: Archaeology Ireland.
Conwell, E. 1873. Discovery of the Tomb of Ollamh Fodhla. Dublin: McGlashan and Gill.
Cooney, G. 2000. Landscapes of Neolithic Ireland. London: Routledge.
- 2006. Newgrange – a view from the platform. Antiquity 80, 697-708.
Cooney, G. & Grogan, E. 1994. Irish prehistory: a social perspective. Dublin: Wordwell.
Cope, J. 2004. The Megalithic European. London: Element.
Daniel, G. 1967. The Origins and Growth of Archaeology. New York: Galahad Books.
Dehn, T., Hansen, S. & Kaul, F. 1995. Kong Svends Høj. Restaureringer og undersøgelser på Lolland 1991. København: Nationalmuseet, Skov- og Naturstyrelsen.
- 2000. Klekkendehøj og Jordehøj. Restaureringer og undersøgelser 1985-90. København: Nationalmuseet, Skov- og Naturstyrelsen.
Eogan, G. 1986. Knowth and the passage-tombs of Ireland. London: Thames and Hudson.
Eriksen, P. 1980. Capeshøj på Tåsinge. En langdysse dækket af en bronzealderhøj. Antikvariske studier 4, 31-48.
- 2004. Newgrange og den hvide mur. Kuml 2004, 45-77.
- 2006. The rolling stones of Newgrange. Antiquity 80, 709-10.
Fergusson, J. 1872. Rude Stone Monuments in all Countries; their Age and Uses. London: John Murray.
Gibson, A. 1994. Excavations at the Sarn-y-bryn-caled cursus complex, Welshpool, Powys, and the timber circles of Great Britain and Ireland. Proceedings of the Prehistoric Society 60, 143-223.
Giot, P.-R. 1983. Review of M.J. O'Kelly 1982: Newgrange. Archaeology, Art and Legend. Antiquity 57, 149-50.
Grogan, E. 1991. Radiocarbon dates from Brugh na Bóinne. Proceedings of the Royal Irish Academy 91 C, 126-32.

Hartnett, P.J. 1957. Excavation of a Passage Grave at Fourknocks, Co. Meath. Proceedings of the Royal Irish Academy 58 C, 197-277.
Herity, M. 1967. From Lhuyd to Coffey: New Information from Unpublished Descriptions of the Boyne Valley Tombs. Studia Hibernica 7, 127-44.
Holst, M.K. 2006. Tårup, a round dolmen and its secondary burials. Journal of Danish Archaeology 14, 7-21.
Kaul, F. 1998. Europas dysser og jættestuer. København.
- 1999. Stonehenge var et vanvittigt byggeri. Illustreret Videnskab 1999-2, 30-3.
Kjærum, P. 1970. Jættestuen Jordhøj. KUML 1969, 9-66.
Loveday, R. 2006. Inscribed across the Landscape. The Cursus Enigma. Briscombe Port: Tempus.
Lynch, A. 1989. Newgrange Passage Tomb. In Bennett, I. (ed.), Excavations 1988: 33. Dublin: Wordwell.
- 1990. Newgrange Passage Tomb. In Bennett, I. (ed.), Excavations 1989: 42-3. Dublin: Wordwell.
Macalister, R.H.S. 1929. Newgrange Co. Meath. Dublin: Baile Atha Cliath.
Malone, C. 1989. Avebury. London: Batsford/English Heritage.
Mason, C. & Evans, J.G. 1982. Land molluscs (2). In M.J. O'Kelly 1982, 227-8.
Michell, J. 1982. Megalithomania. Artists, antiquarians and archaeologists at the old stone monuments. London: Thames and Hudson.
Mount, C. 1994. Aspects of Ritual Deposition in the Late Neolithic and Beaker Periods of Newgrange, Co. Meath. Proceedings of the Prehistoric Society 60, 433-43.
O'Kelly, C. 1978. Illustrated Guide to Newgrange and the other Boyne Monuments. Cork: C. O'Kelly.
O'Kelly, C. (ed.) 1983. Newgrange, Co. Meath, Ireland. The Late Neolithic/Beaker Period Settlement. Oxford: British Archaeological Reports 190.
O'Kelly, M.J. 1973. Current Excavations at Newgrange, Ireland, in Daniel, G. & Kjærum, P. (eds), Megalithic Graves and Rituals. Papers presented at the III Atlantic Colloquium, Moesgård 1969, 137-46. Århus: Jutland Archaeological Society Publications 11.
- 1979. The restoration of Newgrange. Antiquity 53, 205-10.
- 1982. Newgrange. Archaeology, Art and Legend. London: Thames and Hudson.
- 1983. The excavation. In C. O'Kelly (ed.) 1983, 1-57.
O'Kelly, M.J., Lynch, F.M. & O'Kelly, C. 1978. Three passage-tombs at Newgrange, Co. Meath. Proceedings of the Royal Irish Academy 78 C, 249-352.
O'Kelly, M.J. & O'Kelly, C. 1983. The tumulus of Dowth, County Meath. Proceedings of the Royal Irish Academy 83 C, 5-190.
Ó Ríordáin, S.P. & Daniel, G. 1964. New Grange. London: Thames and Hudson.
Ó Ríordáin, S.P. & Ó hEochaidhe, M. 1956. Trial excavation at Newgrange. The Journal of the Royal Society of Antiquaries of Ireland 86, 52-61.
Pearson, M.P., Cleal, R., Marshall, P., Needham, S., Pollard, J., Richards C., Ruggles, C., Sheridan, A., Thomas, J., Tilley, C., Welham, K., Chamberlain, A., Chenery, C., Evans, J., Knüsel, C., Linford, N., Martin, L., Montgomery, J., Payne, A. & Richards, M. 2007. The age of Stonehenge. Antiquity 81.
Pitts, M. 2000/2001. Hengeworld. London: Century/Arrow Books

Pownall, T. 1773. A Description of the Sepulchral Monument at New Grange, near Drogheda, in the County of Meath, in Ireland. Archaeologia 2, 236-75.

Richards, C. & Thomas, J. 1984. Ritual activity and structured deposition in Later Neolithic Wessex. In Bradley, R. & Gardiner, J. (eds), Neolithic Studies. A Review of Some Current Research. Oxford: British Archaeological Report 133, 189-218.

Scarre, C. 2006. Consolidation, reconstruction and the interpretation of megalithic monuments. In Cruz, R. & Oosterbeek, L. (eds), ARKEOS – perspectivas em diálogo 16, 13-43.

– 2007. The Megalithic Monuments of Britain and Ireland. London: Thames and Hudson.

Skaarup, J. 1985. Yngre stenalder på øerne syd for Fyn. Rudkøbing: Langelands Museum.

Spoel, S. van der, 1982. Land molluscs (1). In O'Kelly, M.J. 1982, 226.

Stout, G. 1991. Embanked enclosures of the Boyne region. Proceedings of the Royal Irish Academy 91 C, 245-84.

– 2002: Newgrange and the Bend of Boyne. Dublin: Cork University Press.

Sweetman, P.D. 1976. An earthen enclosure at Monknewton, Slane, Co. Meath. Proceedings of the Royal Irish Academy 76 C, 25-72.

– 1985. A Late Neolithic/Early Bronze Age pit circle at Newgrange, Co. Meath. Proceedings of the Royal Irish Academy 85 C, 195-221.

– 1987. Excavation of a Late Neolithic/Early Bronze Age site at Newgrange, Co. Meath. Proceedings of the Royal Irish Academy 87 C, 283-98.

Van Wijngaarden-Bakker, L.H. 1974. The animal remains from the Beaker settlement at Newgrange, Co. Meath: first report. Proceedings of the Royal Irish Academy 74 C, 313-83.

– 1986. The animal remains from the Beaker settlement at Newgrange, Co. Meath: final report. Proceedings of the Royal Irish Academy 86 C, 17-112.

Whittle, A. 1997. Sacred Mound, Holy Rings. Silbury Hill and the West Kennet palisade enclosures: a Later Neolithic complex in north Wiltshire. Oxford: Oxbow Monograph 74.

Wilde, W.R. 1849/1949. The beauties of the Boyne and its Tributary the Blackwater. Dublin.

Author's address:
Ringkøbing-Skjern Museum
Herningvej 4
6950 Ringkøbing
Denmark
pe@riskmus.dk

Acta Archaeologica vol. 79, 2008, pp 274-281
Printed in Denmark • All rights reserved

AISTULF AND THE ADRIATIC SEA

RICHARD HODGES

> *... the Adriatic Sea is a miniature Mediterranean; the Adriatic has, since the early Middle Ages, brought the inhabitants of Italy face-to-face with Slavs, Albanians, and other Balkan peoples... The Adriatic was a special theatre of operations for Venice...*
>
> (Abalafia 2005:67)

On 7 July 751 the Lombard king Aistulf issued an official act at 'Ravenna in palatio'.[1] Hardly momentous in itself, this act confirmed that the old Byzantine capital had fallen to the Lombards and with it, almost certainly, other centres as well. In Constantinople the imperial court could only lament and prepare for comparable assaults on its remaining territories in Venice, Apulia, Calabria and Sicily (Herrin 1987:370). Aistulf's audacity almost certainly paved the way for great changes not just in Lombardy but throughout the length and breadth of the Adriatic Sea.

Since early prehistoric times the Adriatic Sea connected the far points of the Mediterranean to the Danube and Rhine valleys. Controlled from what was to become the Venetian archipelago, the passage of Neolithic, Bronze and Iron Age traders and travellers presaged its huge importance as a thoroughfare in Roman times. In many ways, resembling the North Sea, with the Baltic Sea being the Mediterranean, the Adriatic connected many disparate communities from Friuli to the Peloponnese. Along its seaboard lay the Dalmatian archipelago, the mountains of Montenegro and Albania as well as Arcadia, the plains of the Apulian Tavoliere, the Abruzzi Mountains and the sprawling Po estuary. Yet, strangely, except when Ravenna served as a Byzantine capital, its real authority has always been implicit in the promise of what lay beyond – across the Alps and to the east of the Cyclades on the Bosphorus. Ravenna, therefore, was an aberration. It was a capital rather than an entropôt. As the architecture of the Emperor Justinian's capital as well as the new excavations in its port at Classe show, it was a late antique destination aimed at eclipsing the imperial and commercial authority of Rome (and Ostia Antica) (Augenti et al 2007). The new excavations at Classe emphasize the colossal growth of the port in the late 5th and 6th centuries, and then as the power of Byzantium wained, the demise of trade by the mid to later 7th century (Augenti et al 2007). Classe, like Constantinople itself, was reduced to the tiniest fraction of its former self by AD700, as the full impact of the so-called Dark Ages overwhelmed the Mediterranean reducing its ports and trade to mere shadows of even their shape in prehistory. When Aistulf seized Ravenna he was seeking to conquer the old capital's symbolic prowess rather than its coffers.

New excavations, however, are beginning to shed light on the changing 8th and 9th century fortunes of the Adriatic Sea. As recently as a decade ago it seemed to be a seaway that enjoyed revival only at the very end of the millennium. The origins of Venice itself were speculative, while the Lombard emporium of Comacchio at the mouth of the river Po was no more than an intriguing enigma. Further south the coastal ports of Albania and Apulia

1 Acknowledgements. Thanks to the Butrint Foundation in partnership with the Packard Humanities Institute for supporting the excavations at Butrint. Special thanks to Sauro Gelichi for introducing me to Comacchio. In writing this paper I am grateful to Paul Arthur, Kim Bowes, Andy Crowson, Florin Curta, Simon Greenslade, Solinda Kamani, Sarah Leppard, Matthew Logue, Michael McCormick, John Moreland, John Mitchell, Nevila Molla, Pagona Papadopolou, Paul Reynolds, Sandro Sebastiani, Joanita Vroom and Chris Wickham.

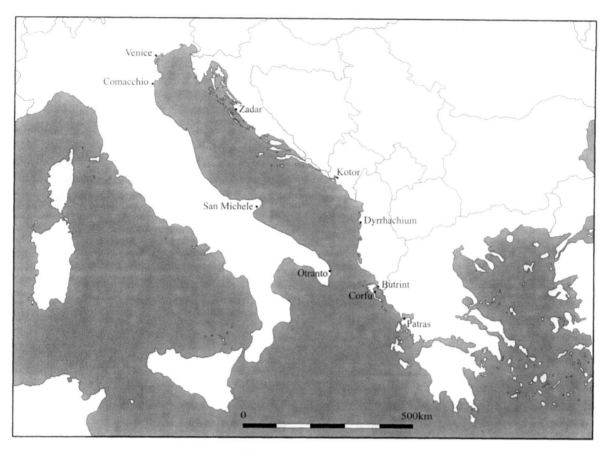

Fig. 1. Adriatic Sea sites mentioned in the text.

– with the exception of Otranto – were also unknown. New surveys of Venice (Gelichi 2004), the discovery of Comacchio (Gelichi 2007a; 2007b) and the large-scale excavations of Butrint in southern Albania on the Straits of Corfu chart the beginnings of a new era for Adriatic Sea history (Hodges 2006) (Fig. 1).

With the acquisition of the relics of St. Mark in AD 827, Venice appeared to be establishing itself as a powerful centre. Its strategic significance was very evident to Charlemagne who repeatedly despatched Frankish armies in order to conquer it and the adjacent regions. After a negotiated peace in AD 812, it was to become an important Carolingian mint, yet remained a coalition of islands managed by a doge. New surveys by Albert Ammerman (2003) of the physical and man-made topography of the archipelago in this era, and by Sauro Gelichi of the archaeology (2004) show beyond doubt that with a nucleus gathered around Rialto it emerged as a major emporium covering as many as 50 hectares around 800 (cf. McCormick 2007). The eclipse of Ravenna was indubitably its

making but perhaps, no less significantly, the Venetians were able to win support against their great competitors, the traders of Comacchio.

Comacchio with its canals is a miniature Venice today. Occupying one of the web of branches of the Po close to the Adriatic, it was a surprisingly important port in Etruscan times. Lombard sources show that this role was renewed in the later 7th and 8th centuries and evidently prospered as Ravenna became an increasingly isolated outpost of Byzantium. The Comaclenses are best known from a capitulary or pact issued between 715-30 by the Lombard King Liutprand (Balzaretti 1996:219-20; Wickham 2005:733). This extraordinary document provides instructions to the leaders of the port on harbour and other fees in Po valley towns like Bergamo, Brescia, Cremona, Mantua, Parma and Piacenza. Salt from the estuary pans seems to have the principal cargo to these Lombard riverine wharfs. The pact, of course, has attracted much interest among historians. The present interpretation is that Comacchio was the outcome of a treaty made between the Lombards and their neighbours, the Byzantines resident in the Exarchy of Ravenna. But differences exist on whether it was an independent centre located between the two territories or a Byzantine stronghold. It was evidently in Lombard hands in 756 when the Frankish King Pepin marched into Italy to support the beleagured Pope Stephen. Pepin compelled King Aistulf to sue for peace and appropriated Comacchio for the papacy (Herrin 1987:377-79).

The scale of the emporium, like Venice, has until now been a matter of speculation. Again, a new survey by Sauro Gelichi accompanied by excavations in the centre of the modern town up against the cathedral have shown beyond doubt that the emporium was full of post-built dwellings covering as many as thirty to forty hectares (2004). More to the point, its ample deposits of amphorae and other objects confirm the volume of its trade between the Po valley and the upper Adriatic, with some containers coming from as far away as the Black Sea. When this sprawling town is compared to the tiny aristocratic nuclei in Lombard urban centres such as Brescia and indeed to contemporary villages, there is little doubt about its importance. In common with the better-known 8th-century emporia around the North Sea, this was undoubtedly the motor of the regional political economy. No wonder, then, that hard on the heels of the truce with the Carolingians, successive Doges of Venice set out to crush their neighbour. By the 10th century, as the new investigations show, like many North Sea emporia of its generation, Comacchio was effectively eclipsed, soon to be a backwater.

No excavation along the 1000 km length of the Adriatic coastline of Italy has produced anything as remotely as revealing as Comacchio. On the contrary, it is the near absence of evidence until now which has been most striking. Odd sherds of east Alpine soapstone jars turn up from time to time, minor illustrations of an Adriatic Sea traffic that the 9th-century written sources certainly considered substantial. The sherds apart, the settlement evidence is sparse. A dig in the centre of Rimini located a small later 7th -or 8th-century nucleus of indifferent character (Negrelli 2007). In Pescara (ancient Aternum), for example, numerous salvage excavations in the 1990s brought to light a line of undistinguished 9th-century post-built houses along the shore-front (Staffa 1991). Siponto, for example, the port below the celebrated 9th-century sanctuary of San Michele on the Gargano peninsula, remains essentially unexplored. The great Beneventan sanctuary

above it, that drew pilgrims from as far afield as England and Francia, is no less enigmatic (Castelfranchi and Mancini 1994). Only the graffiti left by these travellers record the importance of the traffic, mostly destined for the Holy Land. What form the late antique shrine itself took is a matter of speculation (Trotta and Renzulli 2003). Otranto, on the other hand, the Byzantine naval stronghold at the heel of Italy has become noteworthy in medieval archaeology thanks to its pottery kilns, several of which have now been excavated. Otranto's potters produced prodigious numbers of globular carriage wares containing Apulian oils and wines (cf. Arthur et al 1992). None, it seems, found their way to Comacchio. At Otranto, too, systematic excavations have produced the distinctive Byzantine bronze folles – low denomination coins – of the later 9th and 10th centuries (Michaelides 1991).

The archaeology of the Balkan coastline is hardly any better known until Butrint on the Straits of Corfu. Its principal ports, of course, are mentioned in the sources, such as the travelogue of Amalarius of Metz, who acting as a Carolingian diplomat to the Byzantine court in AD 813 sailed by way of Zadar (in Croatia) Dyrrachium (in Albania) and around the Peloponnese to Constantinople (McCormick 2001:138-43; map 5.3). The archaeology and architecture of Zadar and neighbouring Nin show that they were within a Lombard sphere on influence. This much is readily evident at the cathedral of St. Donatus occupying the north end of the old Zadar's Roman forum as well as the stone furnishing from neighbouring churches such as Holy Cross at Nin (cf. Curta 2006:142). Close by, excavations at Nin have brought to light a Croat cemetery with rich grave goods, including Lombard sword blades. South of Split such north Adriatic associations disappear. In Lezha (ancient Lissus) in north Albania, like Dyrrachium, Amalarius would have noted the scarse but evident use of Byzantine folles (Serjina 2005). By the 860s, these towns, judging from the inventory of the Albanian coin cabinet, were being lost in profligate numbers. Amalarius sailed southwards rather than taking the Via Egnatia, perhaps because he learnt that many of the ancient bridges – repaired in late antiquity, to judge from a recent survey – were once again un-passable (Amore et al 2005; cf. the historical debate - Curta 2003:288; McCormick 2003:318-9). In Saranda, ancient Onchesmos, evidence of a small seafront nucleus was found in rescue excavations in 2007 (Gilkes, Kondo and Vroom forthcoming), while the massive late antique shrine to the Forty Saints

Fig. 2. The location of the towers in the western defences at Butrint.

directly above the city, was completely rebuilt at this time albeit on a less ambitious scale (Mitchell 2004; Hodges 2007). An extraordinary painting in one of its many crypts also belongs to the revival of the cult. In bright, ochrous colours it depicts Christ tugging firmly on the beard of an unfortunate saint (Hodges 2007:47).

The Forty Saints was a seamark stationed at the north end of the Straits of Corfu. Halfway along its eastern length lies Butrint, ancient Buthrotum. Here, perhaps the most extensive campaign of modern excavations, has charted what happened to an Adriatic port of classical origins in the early Middle Ages (Hodges 2006).

Like most ancient cities, Butrint in the 7th century was reduced to little more than a castle. But instead of occupying the acropolis with its prominent late antique basilica, the nucleus of the first Mid Byzantine community appears to have been located in two towers in the lower city's seaward defences (cf. Andrews, Bowden, Gilkes and Martin 2004). Vivid remains of the ground and upper floors of both towers were found, thanks to a cataclysmic fire - per-

Fig. 3. A view of the late 8th-century amphorae found in tower 1.

haps a sack of some kind (cf. Curta 2004) - which around 800 engulfed them at the same time (Fig. 2). In each case, the upper floors collapsed downwards, crushing the stored contents just inside the ground-floor door. In the first tower these included a crate of glass comprising 61 goblets and cullet – a consignment destined for a glass-maker somewhere. Next to this was a line of smashed amphorae from Otranto and other parts of Apulia (Fig. 3), as well as the Aegean, perhaps Crete, and the Crimea. There were White Ware table wares from Constantinople and the strangest local pots, so-called Avaro-Slavic types, as well as two portable ovens which may have been the cause of the conflagration.

This rich assemblage emphasizes a chapter in Butrint's history when it could once more seek traded goods from as far afield as the Crimea as well as Italy. This assemblage is very different from that discovered on the Vrina Plain outside Butrint (see below), or indeed, from anything known from north-west Greece, Albania or south-east Italy to date. Being in the lower city rather than on the acropolis, we can only assume the commander who occupied the tower(s) wished to have direct control over traffic plying the straits as Frankish pilgrims and travellers such as Amalarius sailed southwards.

South of Butrint, excavations in its Roman suburb on the Vrina Plain, brought to light the successor to the commander's tower-house (Fig. 4). Here, in the ruins of the 5th-century monastery that in turn occupied the remains of the Roman colonial settlement, the manor-house or oikos of the commander was discovered. Post-holes found within the paved narthex of the 5th-century basilica show that its upper floor was reinforced to take a new residence. Fire-blasted through the paving stones, the primitive architecture of the house cannot be understated. No less fascinating are the contemporary conditions. Its ground floor, like the areas around the church were covered in a thick deposit of black earth in which 48 bronze *folles* spanning c.840-950 were found as well as 5 Byzantine lead seals belonging to the same period (Greenslade et al 2006). The black earth deposit also extended into

Fig. 4. Reconstructed late 8th-century south Italian, principally Otranto, wares from tower 1.

the south aisle of the earlier church, while the north aisle, judging from hearths discovered here, was deployed as a workshop. A small side chapel of 5th-century date off the north aisle now housed at pottery kiln. The nave of the 5th-century basilica was made into a cemetery from the mid 9th century, graves rudely puncturing the earlier mosaic. A grave with a fine copper-alloy openwork ornamental buckle accompanied one adult, perhaps the aristocrat himself. A secondary cemetery lay beyond the apse of the church included a disturbed adult associated with whom was a silver-plated horse bit. One adult appeared to have been interred with a Byzantine folles in his pocket. The ceramics, like the prolific coins, appear to distinguish the culture of this household from that found in the tower at Butrint. Amphorae of a distinctive Otranto type make up about fifty per cent of the pottery, while, local kitchen wares made here amount to most of the rest.

The first-floor dwelling with the associated high-status burials, occupying the monastic church, dates to the mid 9th to mid 10th centuries. The material culture shows a steady revival of trade with the heel of Italy while the ornamental metal fittings and jewellery points to far-flung Balkan connections. The coins and seals confirm the administrative role of this household. Certainly, the material culture and art distinguishes the household from anything yet found in the large excavations in Butrint, including the tower described above. Was this, then, the residence of the archon of Vagenetia, the region opposite Corfu, whose seal has been discovered in excavations in Bulgaria (Curta 2006: 103)? Indeed, was this the household at Butrint (polis epineios) in which according to the Vita Eliae iunioris St. Elias the Younger and his companion, Daniel, were held prisoner at Butrint in 881-2, on suspicion of being Arab spies, on returning from the Peloponnese (Rossi Taibbi 1962: XVI, 116 (c73), 182; cf. McCormick 2001:957, no.686)?

Little more is known about Butrint as a town at this time. Arsenios of Corfu (876-953) who apparently visited Epirus to plead with Slav pirates to desist their raids, recorded that Butrint was rich in fish and oysters, with a fertile hinterland (Soustal 2004:22). Were these simple local products, like the salt Comacchio distributed throughout the Po valley, the bases of Butrint's revival as an Adriatic sea port?

Fig. 5. An annotated aerial view of the 9th- to 10th-century Vrina Plain settlement.

The archaeology is of course still very fragmentary. Yet with these new excavations there is beginning to be some definition of size and shape to the maritime world of the Adriatic Sea in the 8th and 9th centuries. Rather like the North Sea at this time, separated by the influence of competing traders emanating from the rivers Rhine and Seine, so the Adriatic after antiquity appears to have been reduced to two very different spheres of commerce. Dominated first by Comacchio then Venice, the head of the Adriatic reaching down to the Abruzzi and opposite to southern Croatia fell within their orbit. Byzantine domination appears to have stretched to northern Albania and perhaps, intermittently, to northern Apulia. Ravenna after 754 plainly lay beyond the reach of Constantinople. The western Veneto's axis with Istria was clearly behind Charlemagne's eager pursuit of Venice. Frankish armaments and Lombard church furniture in Croatia were probably exchanged for slaves needed to make the levees and timber sub-structures for the town at Rialto as well as the investment in new manorial estate farming (cf. McCormick 2007). The other axis joined the heel of Italy, and

Otranto in particular, to ports like Butrint. Fish for wine, it seems, brought new vigour to these otherwise exposed western provinces of the Byzantine Empire. New vigour, too, was injected by the increasing numbers of pilgrims, many (unlike the diplomat Amalarius) setting out from Beneventan and Byzantine ports to head southwards.

Until now, with many archaeological excavations around the Bay of Naples, great emphasis has been given to the commercial drive of the Beneventans and Neapolitans in the revival of Mediterranean trade (cf. Arthur 2002). Their sights were on the new markets of Aghlabid North Africa, commerce which with time drew pirates and invaders as well as merchants to 9th-century Italy. Aided by the exceptional status of Rome, the Tyrrhennian sea has always appeared more active than the Adriatic. Now, with the discoveries made at Comacchio, Venice and far to the south at Butrint, it is evident that spurred on by Aistulf's bold seizure of Ravenna in 754, the Adriatic sea slowly re-established itself as the paramount thoroughfare in the western world before Columbus found the New World.

BIBLIOGRAPHY

Abulafia, D. (2005) Mediterraneans, in Harris, W. V. (ed.), Rethinking the Mediterranean, Oxford, Oxford University Press: 64-93.

Ammerman, A.J. (2003) Venice before the Grand Canal, Memoirs of the American Academy of Rome 48: 141-58.

Amore, M.G., Bejko, L., Cerova, Y. and Gjipali, I. (2005) Via Egnatia (Albania) project: results of fieldwork 2002, Journal of Roman Archaeology 18: 336-60.

Andrews, R. Bowden, W., Gilkes, O. and Martin, S. (2004) 'The late antique and medieval fortifications of Butrint', in Hodges, Bowden and Lako (eds.), 126-50.

Arthur, P. (2002) Naples, from Roman town to city state: an archaeological perspective, London, British School at Rome.

Arthur, P., Caggia, M.P., Ciongoli, G.P., Melissano, V., Patterson, H., and Roberts, P. (1992) Fornaci altomedievali ad Otranto. Nota preliminare, Archeologia Medievale19: 91-122.

Augenti, A., Cirelli, E., Nannetti, M.C. Sabetta, T., Savini, E., Zantedeschi, E. (2007) Nuovi dati archeologichi dallo scavo di Classe, in S.Gelichi and C.Negrelli (eds.) La circolazione delle ceramiche nell'Adriatico tra tarda antichitá e altomedievale: 257-95. Mantova, SAP.

Balzaretti, R. (1996) Cities, emporia and monasteries: local economies in the Po. Valley, c.AD 700-875, in N. Christie and S.T. Loseby (eds.) Towns in Transition. Urban evolution in late antiquity and the early MiddleAges: 213-34. Aldershot, Scolar Press.

Castelfranchi, M. F. and Mancini, R. (1994) Il culto di San Michele in Abruzzo e Molise dalle origini all'altomedioevo (secoli V-XI). In C. Carletti and G. Otranto (eds.), Culto e Insediamenti Micaelici nell'Italia Medridionale fra Tarda Antichità e Medioevo. Atti del Convegno Internazionale di Monte Sant'Angelo 18-21 November 1992: 507-51. Bari, EdiPuglia.

Curta, F. (2003) East central Europe, Early Medieval Europe 12: 283-91.

- . (2004) Barbarians in Dark-Age Greece: Slavs or Avars, in Stepanov, T. and Vachkova, V. (eds.), Civitas Divino-Humana. In Honorem Annorem LX Georgii Bakalov, Sofia, 513-50.

- . (2006) Southeastern Europe in the Middle Ages 500-1250, Cambridge, Cambridge University Press.

Greenslade, S., Hodges, R., Leppard, S., and Mitchell, J. (2006) Preliminary report on the Early Christian basilica on the Vrina Plain, Albania, Archeologia Medievale, 33: 397-408.

Gelichi, S. (2004) Venezia tra archeologia e storia: la costruzione di un identitá urbana, in A. Augenti (ed.) Le citta italiana tra la tarda antichita e l'alto medievo. 151-83. Florence, Insegna del Giglio.

- . (2007a) Tra Comacchio e Venezia. Economia, societá e insediamenti nell' arco nord adriatico durante l'Alto Medievo, in Genti nel Delta da Spina a Comacchio. 365-86. Ferrara, Corbo editore.

- . (2007b) Flourishing places in north-eastern Italy: towns and emporia between late antiquity and the Carolingian age, in J. Henning (ed.) Post-Roman towns, trade and settlement in Europe and Byzantium. Vol. 1.The heirs of the Roman West: 77-104. Berlin, Walter de Gruyter.

Gilkes, O. Kondo, K and Vroom, J. (forthcoming) New light on early-medieval Saranda, ancient Onchesmos: excavations at the Bashkia of Saranda.

Herrin, J. (1987) The Formation of Christendom, Princeton, Princeton University Press.

Hodges, R. (2006) Eternal Butrint: a Unesco World Heritage Site in Albania, London, General Penne Publishing.

- . (2007) Saranda, ancient Onchesmos. A short history and guide, Tirana, Migjeni

Hodges, R., Bowden, W. and Lako, K. (eds.) (2004) Byzantine Butrint. Excavations and Survey 1994-1999, Oxford, Oxbow Books.

McCormick, M. (2001) Origins of the European Economy, Communications and Commerce AD 300–900, Cambridge, Cambridge University Press.

- . (2003) Complexity, chronology and context in the early medieval economy, Early Medieval Europe 12: 307-23.

- . (2007) Where do trading towns come from? Early medieval Venice and the northern emporia, in J. Henning (ed.) Post-Roman towns, trade and settlement in Europe and Byzantium. Vol. 1. The heirs of the Roman West: 41-68. Berlin, Walter de Gruyter.

Michaelides, D. (1991) Excavations at Otranto, Lecce, Congedo Editore.

Mitchell, J. (2004) The archaeology of pilgrimage in late antique Albania: the Basilica of the Forty Martyrs. In W. Bowden, L. Lavan and C. Machado (eds.), Recent Research on the Late Antique Countryside: 145-186. Leiden, Brill.

Negrelli, C. (2007) Vasellame e contenitore da trasporto tra tarda antichitá ed altomedioevo: L'Emilia Romagna e l'area medio-Adriatica, in S.Gelichi and C.Negrelli (eds.) La circolazione delle ceramiche nell'Adriatico tra tarda antichitá e altomedievale: 297-330. Mantova, SAP.

Rossi Taibbi, G. (ed. and trans.) (1962) Vita di Sant'Elia il Giovane, Palermo, Istituto Siciliano di Studi Bizantini e Neoellenici.

Serjani, E. (2005) La città tra tarda anticha ed Alto Medevo in Albania, Unpublished Ma dissertation, University of Siena.

Soustal, P. (2004) The historical sources for Butrint in the Middle Ages, in Hodges, Bowden and Lako (eds.), 20-26.

Staffa, A 1991) Scavi nel centro storico di Pescara. 1: primi elementi per una riconstruzione dell'assetto antico ed altomedievale dell'abitato di 'Ostia Aterna-Aternum', Archeologia Medievale 17: 201-57

Trotta, M. and Renzulli, A. (2003) La caverna di S. Michele al Gargano: funzione d'uso e funzione monumentale delle fabbriche antistanti all'imboccatura, in R.Fiorillo and P.Peduto (eds.) III Congresso Nazionale di Archeologia Medievale: 736-40. Florence, Insegna del Giglio.

Wickham, C. (2005) Framing the Middle Ages, Oxford, Oxford University Press.

Author's address
Penn Museum, 3260 South Street
Philadelphia, PA 19104, USA
r.hodges@uea.ac.uk

Acta Archaeologica vol. 79, 2008, pp 282-295
Printed in Denmark • All rights reserved

Copyright 2008
ACTA ARCHAEOLOGICA
ISSN 0065-101X

THE *LONGPHORT* IN VIKING AGE IRELAND

JOHN SHEEHAN

INTRODUCTION

There are several bodies of archaeological evidence that may be used, alongside historical, literary and other sources, to elucidate and interpret the nature of the Scandinavian and Hiberno-Scandinavian impact and settlement in Ireland during the ninth and tenth centuries.[1] These comprise, first and foremost, the results of the excavations of the Hiberno-Scandinavian towns, most notably those at Dublin and Waterford,[2] as well as the evidence of associated rural settlements in the hinterlands of these and other towns.[3] The large number of silver hoards on record represents the second body of evidence,[4] and this is of primary importance in understanding both the nature of Scandinavian activity in Ireland and the economic and social relationships that existed between the Irish and the Scandinavians. The information that can be inferred from the grave-finds, on the other hand, though limited due to the fact that most of them were unearthed during the nineteenth century, has been enhanced by current work on the antiquarian sources relevant to them[5] as well as by several recent discoveries of burials.[6] Much the same limitation applies to the single-finds of weapons and other objects of Scandinavian workmanship.[7] The only focus of research to have taken place on a major 'new' aspect of the archaeology of the Scandinavians in Ireland over recent years, apart from various artefact and related studies, is that on the *longphuirt* (sing. *longphort*). The aim of this paper is to summarise and evaluate this work particularly in the context of the relationship between the *longphort* phenomenon and silver in Viking-age Ireland.

LONGPHUIRT

The initial phase of seasonal Scandinavian raiding in Ireland, commencing according to the annals in 795, gave way to the establishment of the first winter-camps in Ire-

land during the 830s, and of the historically documented *longphuirt* of the 840s and their successors. The annalistic sources record the establishment of such permanent bases at two locations in 841, at Duiblinn (Dublin) and Linn Dúachaill (Louth) – the latter location generally being identified as Annagassen, on the south side of Dundalk Bay. Their foundation, and the recording of other bases at Lough Neagh, Lough Ree, Cork, Limerick, and elsewhere, during the 840s, is associated with the 'second phase' of Scandinavian activity in Ireland, as identified by Byrne and Doherty.[8] This phase, dating to between 837 and 876 and recently referred to as '*The Time of the Longphort*' by Mytum,[9] was initiated by the arrival of large Viking fleets at the mouths of the Liffey and Boyne and was characterised by heavy raiding and over-wintering in the *longphuirt*. Duiblinn and Linn Dúachaill became permanent and enduring bases. The construction and use of *longphuirt* should not be confined to this phase, however, as a second series of foundations is recorded in the 920s and 930s.[10]

The term *longphort*, according to Doherty, was a new compound based upon two Latin loanwords that were borrowed into Irish at an earlier period, *long* from L. (*navis*) *longa* 'ship' and *port* from L. *portus* 'port', 'landing place', 'shore', and he suggested that the term was originally coined by the annalists to describe a new and specific phenomenon, that is 'an earthen bank thrown up on the landward side to protect ships that had been drawn up on a beach or river-bank'.[11] The word *dúnad* is also used in the annalistic sources to refer to Viking (and Irish) bases of the ninth century and later, though it may well be synonymous with *longphort*. Doherty has proposed that the two words, *longphort* and *dúnad*, may distinguish, respectively, between 'coastal and riverine encampments enclosing ships' and 'encampments made while the army was on the march in the interior', and suggested that from the contemporary Irish perspective there may have been little apparent difference in these phenomena.[12] By the late tenth century *longphort* had become a broader term, usually used to describe a military encampment, Irish or Scandinavian, and need not necessarily have had any association with ships; later its meaning was broadened further and it came to signify other things, such as 'dwelling'.

The longevity and varied uses of the term *longphort* has led to interpretative and contextual difficulties amongst scholars in recent decades. In this paper, however, the term is used, along with those sites sometimes referred to as *dúnad*, to refer only to Scandinavian or Hiberno-Scandinavian bases located in coastal, lacustrine or riverine contexts from the period encompassing the mid-ninth to the mid-tenth centuries; these were initially established for offensive or raiding purposes, though some developed trading and other economic functions.

From an archaeological perspective, it is difficult to assess the precise physical nature of these sites. Part of the problem is that many of them are referred to only once in the historical sources, usually in reference either to their establishment or destruction, and consequently it is difficult to ascertain how enduring individual examples actually were. A short-lived *longphort*, perhaps established simply as a winter base, is likely to be different in form to one that endured and developed over decades, such as the Duiblinn and Linn Dúachaill examples. Another difficulty lies in actually identifying these sites in the field, as the historical sources that refer to them often do not assign them anything more than a broad location; for instance, the "encampment [*dúnad*] of the foreigners" in Lough Ree in 844-45, from where the Viking leader Turgesius plundered "Connacht and Mide, and burned Cluain Moccu Nóis with its oratories, and Cluain Ferta Brénainn, and Tír dá Glas and Lothra and other monasteries",[13] is not given even a general location along the shoreline or islands of this very large Shannon lake. The likelihood that some *longphuirt* were not referred to at all in the historical sources should also be borne in mind.

Another problem concerns whether *longphuirt* were generally purpose-built monuments, or whether pre-existing monuments or even islands were used. Ó Floinn has suggested that "an existing complex of buildings, surrounded by an earthen bank on a riverside location such as that afforded by an early monastic site, would have

been perfect as a base",[14] and proposed that such was the case at the documented bases at Linn Dúachaill, Clúain Andobair, Co. Kildare, and Clondalkin, Co. Dublin.[15] This is a plausible theory, bolstered by the fact that Scandinavian bases in England were sometimes located at or near monasteries, as at Thanet and Sheppey, both in Kent, in the 850s, and at Repton, Derbyshire, in 873-74. Both Thanet and Sheppey, furthermore, were on islands, and it is interesting to note Clarke's suggestion that while the original Duiblinn *longphort* was located around the tidal pool of the River Poddle, it was shortly afterwards relocated to the nearby river crossing of Áth Cliath, possibly on the island subsequently called Usher's Island.[16]

The characteristics of the *longphort* that are inherent in the term itself suggest that they took the form of ship-bases situated in coastal, lacustrine or riverine locations. There are no associated descriptions of landward defences in the annalistic sources, but it is evident from some references concerning the use of these sites that they were designed to be raiding bases, whether permanent or semi-permanent; therefore, these examples, at least, must have had both defensive and settlement elements to them. The concept of the *longphort* as a settlement, with associated agricultural interests, is supported by an annalistic entry that records how, in 866, Áed Finnliath, king of the Northern Uí Néill, 'plundered all the strongholds of the foreigners [*longportu Gall*] ... both in Cenél Eógain and Dál Araidi, and took away their heads, their flocks, and their herds from camp [*longport*] by battle...'.[17] The defences of a *longphort* could have been, as Ó Floinn suggests, pre-existing, or, in the case of islands, natural, and he warns against the notion of the *longphort* acquiring "the status of a monument in some minds".[18] Nevertheless, a not inconsiderable body of evidence has now accumulated to suggest that several *longphuirt* did, in fact, conform to a novel and fairly standardised site-type. Kelly and Maas, who have identified and discussed several possible examples, such as the enclosure on the River Barrow at Dunrally, Co. Laois, have pioneered this proposal.[19]

The Dunrally site is a large D-shaped enclosure, 360m long and 150m in maximum width, defined by a bank and external ditch, within which is a sub-circular enclosure, 52m x 41m in diameter, also defined by a bank and ditch (Fig. 1). It is not known if this latter enclosure is contemporary with the larger D-shaped one. The site is situated at the confluence of a minor stream and a bend of the River

1: Site location of the D-shaped enclosure, identified as the *Longphort Rothlaibh* of the annals, at Dunrally (townland: Vicarstown), Co. Laois (based on 1908 Ordnance Survey mapping).

Barrow, at which point there was formerly a pool, and has a marshy area on its landward side. Kelly and Maas proposed that it be identified as the Scandinavian *longphort* specifically named as *Longphort Rothlaibh* in the annals, the destruction of which is recorded by the combined forces of the kings of Loígis and Osraige in 862. One of the relevant annalistic entries for this event records the defeat of Rodolb's fleet, "which had come from Lochlann shortly before that"[20], confirming the association of ships with the base. The essential components of this site, a D-shaped enclosure, open to the water, located at the confluence of a river and tributary, adjacent to a pool, close to a fording point, and protected on the landward side by marshy ground, along with other factors, sometimes including place-name evidence, has led to the identification of several potential *longphuirt* elsewhere in Ireland.

These include the D-shaped, cliff-edge enclosure, measuring 73m by 34m, known as Lisnarann, at Annagassan, which, along with an adjacent river island, has been suggested as the location of the Linn Dúachaill *longphort*,[21] as well as an apparently historically undocumented D-shaped enclosure, measuring 75m by 30m, located on a bend of the River Shannon at Fairyhill, Co.

Clare, near Athlunkard (*Áth Longphuirt* – the Ford of the *Longphort*), and protected on its landward side by marshy ground and flanked on one side by a stream.[22] Neither of these sites has been excavated, but it may be significant that Scandinavian-type objects, comprising two conical silver weights, have been found in the immediate vicinity of the Athlunkard site.[23] Viking-age weights in silver are practically unique, and it is interesting to note that the only other example on record from Ireland, an unusual example of ninth-century Scandinavian type, also derives from a *longphort*, that at Woodstown, Co. Waterford (see below). The interior of the Athlunkard site also produced a rare example of a long-tanged coulter, a type that Brady has associated with the large plough-shares known from tenth-century Hiberno-Scandinavian Dublin,[24] as well as a spear-butt, spearhead and a hooped iron band which were found in close proximity and may well have belonged to the same spear; the spear-butt is of a type that is also represented amongst the finds from the Scandinavian cemetery at Kilmainham/Islandbridge, in Dublin. The evidence clearly indicates that the most likely cultural context for these Athlunkard objects is a Scandinavian one.[25]

A potential *longphort* site, first identified as such by the late Thomas Fanning in the 1970s, is located at Ballaghkeeran Little, Co. Westmeath, on the southern side of Killinure Lough, a large inlet on the eastern shore of Lough Ree, on the River Shannon (Fig. 2). It consists of a triangular promontory of land, *c*.200m by *c*.100m, bounded on its southern side by the Breensford River, and defined on its landward side by two banks and an intervening ditch, beyond which lies a low-lying, marshy area; a gap in the banks and ditch may represent an original entrance. On the southern side of the enclosure, alongside the small river, is a large, embanked, hollow feature that Fanning interpreted as a possible Scandinavian-type *naust*, while the remains of an apparently ancient oak-plank jetty projected into the lake on its north-western side.[26] Considering that the site was possibly a *longphort* associated with the historically attested Scandinavian occupation of Lough Ree in 845 and/or the 920s and 930s,[27] he conducted minor trial excavations there in 1981.[28] Cuttings within the enclosure revealed two shallow parallel trenches, but no evidence of occupation, while a cutting through one of the landward banks showed this to have been substantial. A cutting within the *naust*-like feature produced iron slag and fragments of fired clay. Fanning

2: Aerial view of the possible *longphort* at Ballaghkeeran Little, Lough Ree, Co. Westmeath (Photo: Thomas Fanning: inset, bottom left, depicts site location on the River Shannon; inset, top right, depicts site location based on 1913 Ordnance Survey mapping).

obtained two radiocarbon dates from the site, and these yielded 4th/5th century AD determinations; both, however, were from wood charcoal that was apparently derived from the old ground surface beneath the enclosing bank and consequently merely provide *terminus post quem* dates for the construction of the enclosure. It is apparent, nonetheless, that the orientation of the site was towards the lake rather than the land, and the occurrence of the possible *naust* and jetty appear to confirm its association with ships. Fanning's hypothesis that it is a *longphort* may well be supported by the fact that significant finds of Viking-age silver and gold are provenanced to within its immediate environs (see below).

Connolly and Coyne have recently tentatively identified another potential *longphort*, at Rathmore, near Castlemaine, Co. Kerry (Fig. 3).[29] It is located on the southern bank of the River Maine, upstream from Dingle Bay, at the point where it changes from being tidal. It consists of a large D-shaped enclosure, *c.* 250m by *c.*170m, open to the river and defined on its landward side by two massive banks and an intervening ditch. This may well be the Scandinavian site that is referred to as 'Dún Mainne'

in *Cogadh Gaedhel re Gallaibh*, where its destruction around the year 867 is recorded. Another account of this event, as identified by Ó Corráin,[30] is recorded in the *Fragmentary Annals*, where it is noted: 'At this time the Ciarraige besieged the followers of that Tomrar ... Old Congal, king of the Ciarraige, took the victory in this conflict. A few of the Norwegians [*Lochlannaibh*] escaped, naked and wounded; great quantities of gold and silver and beautiful women were left behind'. Evidently Dún Mainne was considered a major threat to the area, as the force that destroyed it comprised the kings of Ciarraige Luachra, Eóganacht Locha Léin and Uí Fidgeinte, the leading kings of west Munster. This is in keeping with the identification of the Rathmore enclosure as this *dún*, given its size and the strength of its defences. The record of the taking of women prisoners and the capture of precious booty, including gold and silver, implies that Dún Mainne was probably a strong, enduring, defended settlement rather than simply a short-term fortified raiding base.

In overall terms, therefore, there is evidence to suggest that both the location and morphology of several potential *longphuirt* do, in fact, conform in a rather strik-

3: Aerial view of the potential longphort, possibly to be identified with the historically attested site of *Dún Mainne*, at Rathmore, Co. Kerry (Photo: Ordnance Survey Ireland)

ing manner to one another, and it is not, consequently, unreasonable to describe the *longphort* as a monument-type. Ó Floinn has objected to such a conclusion on the grounds that it implies "some form of pre-existing model of a defended settlement, for which there is no real evidence either in Ireland or elsewhere in the Viking world in the ninth century".[31] It could be argued, however, that the D-shaped or semi-circular enclosures, open to the water, that characterise the early settlements at Birka and Hedeby are of relevance in this regard, and it should also be noted that later Scandinavians did, in fact, develop highly-standardized fortifications for which there were no obvious pre-existing models, the Trelleborg-type forts of tenth-century Denmark being conspicuous cases in point. Given, however, the recorded degree of Irish hostility to the Scandinavian attacks from the 830s onwards, which had not been matched elsewhere in the west by this time, it would not be entirely surprising if the Scandinavians were forced to devise a novel form of fortification to provide both security for their fleets and a land base for themselves. In other words, it is possible that Ireland in the 840s was the first place and time that fortifications

which met both of these needs were actually required by the Scandinavians. This is not to say that all *longphuirt* were of this form, or that islands, monasteries or various forms of pre-existing fortifications could not have been used as *longphuirt*, but it does appear that there was a formal *longphort* concept in existence which was developed and regularly adhered to by the Scandinavians in Ireland, and was somewhat later transferred to Britain.

A final point that links together the potential *longphuirt* sites noted above, and others, concerns the fact that they tend to be located on Early Medieval political boundaries: Linn Dúachaill, for instance, was located on the borders of Conaille and Cíannachta;[32] Dunrally was positioned at the point of convergence of three kingdoms, those of Loígis, Uí Failge and Uí Muiredaig;[33] Ballaghkeeran Little, being located on the Shannon, was at the boundary of Clann Cholmain of Mide and Connachta, and close to their boundaries with Tethba; Rathmore, is located on the River Maine which formed the boundary between Ciarraige Luachra and Eóganacht Locha Léin; Duiblinn lay between Brega and Laigin; while Woodstown was positioned on the border of the Déisi Muman and Osraige. This trend is hardly coincidental and suggests that the Scandinavians, as Kelly and Maas have proposed, may have had a considered strategy of taking advantage of the rivalries that existed between bordering territories.[34] This is certainly what seems to be suggested, for instance, by a mid-ninth-century entry in the Annals of the Four Masters which recounts how Maelseachlainn, King of Ireland, marched into Munster and, upon arrival at Indeoin na nDéisi, enforced hostages and submission from them 'for they had given him opposition at the instigation of the foreigners'.[35] It is also entirely likely that the establishment of *longphuirt* in such boundary zones may occasionally have had the support of local rulers, who hoped to benefit from trading opportunities as well as the local availability of mercenaries.

WOODSTOWN, CO. WATERFORD

The Woodstown site, discovered and subjected to limited archaeological investigations in advance of a planned road-building scheme in 2003-04,[36] features most of the diagnostic *longphort* characteristics outlined by Kelly and Maas who, incidentally, had earlier suggested the existence of a Scandinavian base in the Waterford harbour area on the evidence of ninth-century annalistic references to fleets operating from there.[37] Located on the southern bank of the River Suir, near a bend and about five kilometers upstream from the location of later Viking-age and Medieval Waterford, the Woodstown site appears to have comprised a large, shallow D-shaped area, *c.*450m long by up to 160m wide, enclosed by a bank and a external ditch, now ploughed out; it was open to the water, located at the confluence of the river and a small tributary, and protected along portion of its landward side by a wetland area (Fig. 4). The excavated portion of the enclosing bank was topped with a palisade. Within the enclosure testing resulted in the discovery of a large number of features, including post-holes, hearths and cobbled surfaces, which may represent structures and houses of both rectangular and oval/circular plan.[38] A Viking burial, complete with sword, shield-boss, spearhead, axe-head, and other items, was excavated just outside the enclosure.[39]

An extensive number of artifacts, numbering over 5000, were recovered from the investigations, most of which, however, were not excavated archaeologically. Many of those finds that are culturally diagnostic are indubitably of Scandinavian or Hiberno-Scandinavian character, including hack-silver, lead pan-weights, a fragment of a Kufic coin, ringed pins, ships' roves, sword fittings, rotary whet-stones and some hones.[40] Among the remainder of the culturally affiliated material is a small collection of Irish ecclesiastical metalwork items,[41] of the type that also forms part of the find assemblages from the ninth-century Scandinavian cemeteries in Dublin and from Viking burials of similar date in Norway.

The evidence, as it currently stands, indicates that the cultural context of the Woodstown site is Scandinavian or Hiberno-Scandinavian. In terms of its locational and physical characteristics it is in keeping with the essentials of the other proposed *longphort* sites, as noted above. Apart from the aforementioned grave-finds, the artefacts from the site include weaponry,[42] which conforms to what one would expect from a *longphort* given that it is evident from the historical sources that they functioned as raiding bases. The linguistic evidence implies that these sites also had an inherent association with ships, and it is instructive to note in this regard that the Woodstown find assemblage includes over two hundred roves and clench nails of the type used in the construction of boats' hulls. In fact, when staples, spikes and other forms of nails are taken into account, the total number of examples of this category of material from Woodstown exceeds 1500. [43]

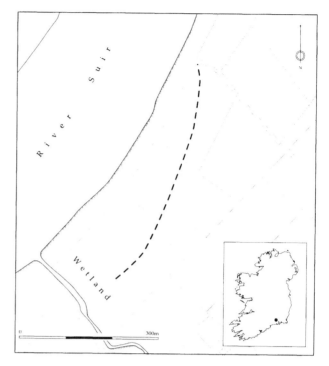

4: Site location of the *longphort* at Woodstown, Co. Waterford, showing the approximate extent of the defences as revealed by geophysical survey and excavation (after O'Brien and Russell 2005, Fig. , based on 1907 Ordnance Survey mapping)..

It has, however, been argued by O'Brien, Quinney and Russell, each of whom was involved in the investigations at the site, that the Woodstown enclosure was built in the fifth century, possibly as a 'monastic settlement', otherwise unevidenced in the historical and archaeological sources, and was later, from the ninth century onwards, reoccupied by Scandinavians[44]. If this interpretation could be sustained it would clearly qualify the notion of the development of the *longphort* as a distinct type-site, given that Woodstown is the only potential *longphort* - apart from the small-scale work carried out at Ballaghkeeran - to have been subjected to any archaeological investigation. On the basis of the published evidence, however, it is difficult to support the arguments of O'Brien *et al* concerning the date of origin of the site. Firstly, there is a complete absence of the sort of features and artefacts that one would expect to find in an early ecclesiastical site of this date in Munster, such as imported Mediterranean and continental pottery, cross-inscribed stones, etc. More importantly, however, it is evident that the early dating of the site is based solely on three radiocarbon determinations, all of which derive from the fills of its enclosing ditch.[45] These dates, when calibrated at 2-sigma level, fall within the fifth to seventh centuries AD, but in each case they derive from oak charcoal; clearly, this charcoal could be derived from old wood, as oak is a long-lived species. That this was almost certainly the case is inferred when the artefacts from this ditch are considered, for these include amber and ivory as well as a silver ingot. These are materials that one would not normally expect to find in Ireland during the fifth to seventh centuries, though they are familiar from Scandinavian and Hiberno-Scandinavian contexts of the Viking Age. Indeed, the ingot is an example of somewhat unusual form that is closely paralleled in the Viking-age hoard from the Scottish island of Tiree, the deposition of which is coin-dated to the later tenth century.[46]

Given that the seven other radiocarbon dates from elsewhere within the site, when calibrated, yield date-ranges that either fall within, or overlap with, the period of the Viking Age, it seems that there is little evidence to support the claim that Woodstown "does not represent a Viking-only settlement".[47] It appears that the ethnic and cultural monomorphic aspects of the post-processual revisionist paradigm have overly influenced O'Brien *et al*,[48] but the problem is that their consequent theorising is inconsistent with the archaeological evidence from the site itself. An alternative model, that deserves testing, is simply that the enclosure at Woodstown was built as a Scandinavian *longphort*.

In this regard it is interesting to note Ó Cíobháin's proposed identification of the placename *Cammus Hua Fathaid Tire* - which is recorded as a base with a fleet of 120 Viking ships in 821 in *Cogadh Gaedhel re Gallaibh* - with the bend of the River Suir just upstream from Woodstown.[49] It is also possible that the Woodstown site dates to the 860s, during which Downham notes a "radical increase" in the recording of Scandinavian attacks that emanate from Waterford Harbour[50] - and that it may have endured to become a Hiberno-Scandinavian settlement, probably with broader functions, into the tenth and possibly even the early eleventh centuries. Whether it was the focus of unbroken settlement is debatable on present evidence. It may appear curious that such a large and strategically located site is not directly referred to in the historical sources. In this regard, however, Etchingham's point about 'demonstrable geographical bias' in the reporting of the annals, and the fact that the south-east of Ireland lay outside the areas of bias, should be borne in mind.[51]

It is, of course, also possible that the Woodstown enclosure dates to the second decade of the tenth century, during which the annals record, for 914, 'A great new fleet of foreigners came to Loch dá Chaech, and placed a stronghold [*longphort*] there',[52] and, for the following year, 'A great and frequent increase in the number of heathens arriving at Loch dá Chaech, and the laity and clergy of Mumu were plundered by them'.[53] The name Loch dá Chaech refers generally to the Waterford Harbour area, though Downham has recently drawn attention to the fact that from 914 to 918 it is exclusively used in the annalistic sources to refer to a Scandinavian settlement at Waterford; both before and after this period the name Port Láirge is used.[54] The final entry for the Loch dá Chaech base, 'The foreigners of Loch dá Chaech, i.e. Ragnall, king of the Dubgaill [Dark Foreigners], and the two jarls, Oitir and Gragabai, forsook Ireland',[55] implies its abandonment. The name-change from Port Láirge to Loch dá Chaech might indicate, as Downham has suggested, that a new Scandinavian base was established in the area in 914. Is Loch dá Chaech to be identified with the Woodstown site? It seems possible that this is the case, and this question should become a focus of further research. Some of the information contained in the annalistic references to Loch dá Chaech, such as the mentions of 'a great new fleet',[56] the arrivals of 'great and frequent reinforcements of foreigners'[57] and the 'plundering of Munster and Leinster' from it,[58] as well as the use of the term *longphort* to describe it,[59] serve to create the impression that it was a very large defended base with, of course, access to water, and this is entirely consistent with the broad picture that has emerged from the archaeology of the Woodstown site to date.

DUIBLINN/ÁTH CLIATH

The most important historically attested *longphort* in Ireland was established at Duiblinn (Dublin) in 841, though Clarke has proposed that shortly afterwards it may have been relocated upstream to the nearby river crossing of Áth Cliath, by which name it is referred to after 845.[60] According to the historical sources it was occupied until 902, when it was apparently destroyed and abandoned following an attack by the combined forces of Brega and Laigin.[61] During this period there are many references to its use as a raiding base, and it seems to have become strong enough to establish other bases further inland at Clúain

Andobair and Clondalkin.[62] Slave raiding from the base is recorded,[63] with the most significant reference to its role in slaving occurring in the Annals of Ulster under the year 871, where it is recorded: 'Amlaíb and Ímar returned to Áth Cliath from Alba with two hundred ships, bringing away with them in captivity to Ireland a great prey of Angles and Britons and Picts'.[64] This international aspect of raiding from Áth Cliath may also be attested by the hoard from Coughlanstown West (Mullaghboden), Co. Kildare, deposited *c*.847, possibly in a Viking grave,[65] for this was composed of Carolingian coins that, according to Dolley, probably represent loot from the documented Viking raids on Aquitaine in the mid-840s.[66]

There is considerable archaeological evidence, however, that the Áth Cliath *longphort* developed beyond being a mere raiding base to become an important trading and market settlement during the second half of the ninth century. Clarke has noted that this stage of economic activity paralleled that in Norway, where Kaupang came to function as an international emporium, and suggested "in Ireland Áth Cliath became its equivalent".[67] Ó Floinn has observed that evidence for the paraphernalia of trade, such as balance scales, weights and purse mounts, is well represented among the grave-finds of the Dublin cemeteries, and suggested that these finds were "those of a military elite engaged in commerce".[68] It is also evident that considerable amounts of silver, the common currency of the Scandinavians, had already been amassed in Ireland before the establishment of the Hiberno-Scandinavian towns during the opening decades of the tenth century, and this can only have come about through the involvement of the *longphuirt*, particularly Áth Cliath.[69] Downham has recently made the suggestion that some of the Scandinavian raids on ecclesiastical sites may "also have served as strikes against rival trading-centres, as Vikings sought to develop their bases as permanent trading-sites".[70]

The location of the Duiblinn/Áth Cliath *longphort* has been debated at length over recent decades,[71] while the current state of knowledge arising from several important recent excavations in ninth-century Dublin has been discussed by Simpson.[72] She notes that early Scandinavian occupation has been unearthed along both the northern and southern sides of the Black Pool (*Duiblinn*) that gave the *longphort* its original name. This pool is on the Poddle, a tributary of the River Liffey, close to their point of confluence, a location that reflects the topographical trends noted above in relation to other potential *longphort*

sites. It should be noted, however, that there was probably an early ecclesiastical settlement located close to the pool, and its enclosure may have been adapted for use as a *longphort* by the Scandinavians, as has been suggested for this and other sites by Ó Floinn.[73] Along the southern side of the pool early settlement evidence, represented by post-holes, refuse pits, hearths and large quantities of butchered animal bone, was revealed. The pool itself produced a collection of ship-rivets, suggesting that boats were docked there, and along its southern rim five furnished graves were excavated. Osteological examination revealed that these burials were all of young men, each radiocarbon dated to between the late seventh and the late ninth century; their grave-goods included shield-bosses and weapons. On the northern side of the pool the ninth-century settlement, which was apparently established somewhat later than the one on its southern shore, included examples of Wallace's Type 1 houses, flood banks, property boundaries, animal pens and a stone roadway. In Temple Bar West, a part of the site on which portion of the tenth-century town was later superimposed, no evidence was found to suggest a break in occupancy following 902 when, according to the documentary sources, the *longphort* was abandoned. In the light of the currently available evidence, Simpson has proposed that the *longphort* may have been located on the eastern side of the Poddle, within an area subsumed by later settlement.[74]

The date-range of the burials from the southern side of the Black Pool, several of which have pre-841 intercept dates, prompted Simpson to suggest that there may have been a Scandinavian encampment in this area before the 841 establishment of the annalistically recorded *longphort*.[75] This may well have been the case, even though there are no direct records of such, and it should not be assumed that all Scandinavian activity in Ireland was recorded in the historical sources. Indeed, Downham has recently suggested that a 'short-term Viking base' may have been set-up in the Dublin area in the late 790s, partly on the basis that the Annals of Ulster record that 'the heathens ... took the cattle-tribute of the territories' following their raid on Inis Pátraic (perhaps Holmpatrick, north county Dublin) in 798.[76] As she points out, cattle-tribute was not a practical way of transferring wealth overseas, and the implication is that it represented supplies for a Scandinavian base in the locality.

To date, the excavated mid- to late ninth-century levels of Scandinavian Dublin conform to what might be predicted of an important *longphort*, particularly the focus around the confluence of a river and its tributary, the presence of a pool that offers protection for boats, and the occurrence of settlement evidence and 'warrior' burials. There is as yet, however, no clear evidence for the presence of an early defensive bank in an appropriate location. The existence of an apparently undefended settlement on the north side of the Black Pool implies that the *longphort* and its associated settlements had a large population that manifestly did not perceive itself as being under constant danger. It may well be that there was a considerable amount of associated settlement strung out along both sides of the Liffey estuary, as may be indicated by the distribution of early cemeteries and single burials along a two kilometre long stretch, [77] and that the *longphort* came to function as the military and administrative nucleus of this early Scandinavian settlement zone. Indeed, this zone, protected by the outlying bases at Clúain Andobair and Clondalkin, probably formed the original core of the broader settlement's agricultural hinterlands, which were later to be called *Fine Gall/Crích Gall* and *Dyflinarskiri* in native Irish and Icelandic sources respectively.

LONGPHUIRT AND WEALTH

The annalistic reference, quoted above, which recorded that 'great quantities of gold and silver' fell into Irish hands following the defeat of the Scandinavians at Dún Mainne, *c*.867, serves as a reminder that the predominantly tenth-century range of deposition dates of Ireland's Viking-age coin hoards does not actually reflect the period during which the Scandinavians first introduced silver into Ireland. Analysis of the hoards containing non-numismatic material, and the recognition of the Hiberno-Scandinavian and Irish silver-working traditions, indicate that the period during which by far the greatest amounts of silver was imported lies between *c*.850 and *c*.950. [78] This is of particular interest for a number of reasons, but in the present context the most important one is that considerable silver resources had clearly been amassed in Ireland well before the establishment of the formal Hiberno-Scandinavian towns during the opening decades of the tenth century. The fact that silver was in circulation in large quantities in the later ninth century serves to focus attention back on the nature of Scandinavian activity and settlement in Ireland at this time and, in particular,

it raises questions concerning the role and functions of the *longphuirt*, suggesting that some of these, especially Duiblinn/Áth Cliath, should be viewed primarily as important trading and market settlements rather than simply as fortified raiding bases.

That ninth-century Dublin was a prosperous and wealthy settlement has been elegantly demonstrated by Graham-Campbell in his preliminary analysis of the massive silver hoard from Cuerdale, Lancashire, the greatest known Viking-age treasure from both Scandinavia and the West. [79] Weighing over forty kilograms, it comprised over a thousand individual pieces of bullion and over seven thousand coins, the latter enabling its deposition to be dated to *c*.905. The major part of the bullion is demonstrably of Hiberno-Scandinavian origin, as characterised by its large quantity of broad-band arm-rings, and it has been proposed that it comprised the capital of some of the exiled leaders of Dublin following their expulsion in 902. Other hoards, on both sides of the Irish Sea, may relate to the same event and also testify to the wealth of the Dublin *longphort*. Chief amongst these is the hoard found at Drogheda, Co. Louth, in 1846, also deposited *c*.905, [80] that reportedly contained almost 'two gallons' of coins of both Kufic and Viking York type. [81] Downham has suggested that this hoard may represent booty gathered from Dublin by Mael Finnia, king of North Brega, who played a prominent role in the dramatic events of 902. [82] Equally important is the Dysart Island (no.4) hoard, from Lough Ennell, Co. Westmeath, deposited *c*.907, which, in addition to coins and ingots, contained a large quantity of hack-silver derived from Hiberno-Scandinavian, Irish, Norwegian and Baltic material. Both in terms of its date and the wide variety of its components it is closely comparable to the Cuerdale hoard, and Ryan and Ó Floinn have suggested that it derives, at least in part, from the 902 sack of Dublin. [83]

The later ninth-century hoards are indicative of a flourishing bullion economy, with Scandinavian, Baltic and Islamic connections, and this economy was confident enough to develop its own distinctive ornament forms. Many of their components occur in hack-silver form, often displaying nicking, indicating that they formed part of a pool of silver that circulated through economic transactions. It is evident that the economic outcomes of the original activities associated with *longphuirt*, raiding, ransoming and slaving, were sufficient to set up trading undertakings, and thus trading became as much a part as raiding in the economics of the Dublin *longphort*. What is surprising, particularly in the light of the recent discovery of significant amounts of hack-silver at Woodstown, is that virtually no material of this kind has been found in the excavation of Dublin's ninth-century levels. It may well be, however, that the excavated areas around the Black Pool may be associated settlements, rather than the nucleus, of the *longphort*. However, as Simpson has recently pointed out, the tenth-century Hiberno-Scandinavians of the 're-founded' Dublin continued raiding activities, yet little evidence of torn up metalwork or hack-silver has emerged in its excavated levels. She notes that this should serve as a warning 'against dismissing any potential *longphort* site in Dublin merely because it did not produce this kind of material'.[84]

Reference was made above to the fact that significant finds of Viking-age silver and gold are on record from the vicinity of the potential *longphort* site at Ballaghkeeran Little, Co. Westmeath. These finds may relate to the occupation of this site and, if so, may testify to its importance as a base with commercial functions. The two best known of these finds comprise a pair of lost hoards, one gold and one silver, which were discovered only a few metres apart in the early nineteenth century on Hare Island,[85] otherwise known as *Inis Ainghin*, a monastic centre with Clonmacnoise connections. The silver find comprised an unknown number of ingots and arm-rings, while the gold hoard comprised ten massive arm-rings with a combined weight of about five kilos, making it by far the largest gold hoard on record from the Viking world (Fig. 5). Indeed, it is possible that the Lough Ree *longphort* was located on Hare Island itself, within the enclosure of *Inis Ainghin*, though the evidence supporting the Ballaghkeeran Little enclosure as the site of the *longphort* is difficult to dismiss. In fact, Hare Island is located close to the entrance of Killinure Lough, within which Ballaghkeeran Little is located. An important discovery of a hack-silver hoard, consisting of fragments of arm-rings and ingots, together with one complete ingot, was made in the 1980s on a small natural island in Killinure Lough, at Creaghduff, close to the Ballaghkeeran Little site.[86] This could well be contemporary with the Hare Island hoards, but it is clearly different in character, relating more directly to the type of silver that presumably circulated in the *longphuirt* at Dublin and, as has recently emerged, at Woodstown.

To date, thirty-eight items of Viking-age silver derive from the Woodstown site. These comprise complete in-

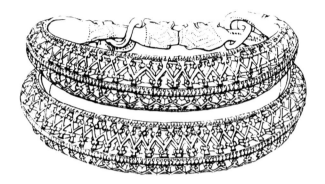

5: Gold arm-ring from the Hare Island hoard, Co. Westmeath (Source:*Vetusta Monumenta* (1835))

gots, ingot and arm-ring fragments, a weight, a wire fragment and pieces of casting waste. Unfortunately, with only one exception, all of these finds were retrieved from topsoil contexts. In numerical terms the collection represents more non-numismatic silver than had been found in over forty years of excavation in Viking-age Dublin. On the basis of the dating evidence for its various components, it is clear that as an assemblage it contains elements from as early as the later ninth century to, potentially, as late as the mid-eleventh century. The bulk of the material, however, as represented by ingots and ingot-derived hack-silver, most likely dates to the period encompassing the later ninth and tenth centuries. The collection also includes some casting waste and this should probably be regarded as evidence for silver-working on the site, along with the excavated evidence for a smithing hearth.[87] Given the nature of the overall assemblage it is likely that the main product of such silver-working would have been ingots.

Amongst the silver material from Woodstown is a small silver scale-weight of polyhedral form (Fig. 6). Weights of this form and size are of particularly common occurrence in Scandinavia, especially in its Baltic region, where they are usually made in copper alloys. The Woodstown example weighs 2.51 gm, and it is interesting to note that this was one of the target weights identified by Kyhlberg in his analysis of a series of such weights from Birka.[88] Weights of polygonal type are absent from the large assemblage of Viking-age weights from Dublin,[89] though a small number are on record from England. For example, three copper-alloy polyhedral weights, with ornamentation, were amongst the finds from the Viking winter camp at Torskey, Lincolnshire, associated with the

6. Scale-weight of polyhedral form, in silver, from Woodstown (Photo: Archaeological Consultancy Services Ltd)

872-873 campaign by the Danish 'Great Army' during the period 865 to 877. The Woodstown weight is the only diagnostically Scandinavian silver object from the site, and most probably dates to the late ninth century.

Hack-silver deposits are relatively rare in Ireland, where few such finds may be classified as 'true' hack-silver hoards in the sense in which this phenomenon is understood in Scandinavia. Hårdh, for instance, has defined hack-silver hoards as finds 'where half or more of the objects are fragments, and where most of the objects weigh less than five grams'.[90] The Woodstown collection, however, is exceptional in that it does satisfy these criteria, and this adds to its importance. 'True' hack-silver hoards from Ireland date to the tenth century, though it is clear that they must also have been a feature of the late ninth century. The importance of the Woodstown assemblage is that, for the first time in Ireland, a large collection of hack-silver has been found in a demonstrably Scandinavian or Hiberno-Scandinavian cultural context. It exceeds the amount of such material from ninth-century Dublin, and is best paralleled by the hack-silver material from Kaupang. The presence of this material at Woodstown, alongside a large number of Viking scale-weights, clearly indicates that this *longphort* site had important and developed economic functions. It may well be, as has been suggested in the case of the Kilmacomma hoard,[91]

that other finds of Viking-age silver from Munster derive from this and other *longphuirt*.

Finally, it should be noted that the occurrence of Viking-age silver and hoards in the vicinity of *longphuirt* need not necessarily imply that these were buried by Scandinavian hands. An interesting case in point concerns four hoards from the Inishowen region of Co. Donegal, those provenanced to 'north-west Inishowen', Carrowmore/Glentogher, Roosky, and 'near Raphoe'.[92] This is a striking concentration of finds, especially given the rarity of silver hoards from elsewhere in the north-west of Ireland, and their general contemporanity is suggested by the fact that all feature broad-band arm-rings in their composition. Graham-Campbell has interpreted them as relating to the historically attested presence of a Scandinavian fleet, led by one Acolb, in the Inishowen region during the early 920s, and has suggested that they were deposited during this period.[93] The annalistic records of Acolb's presence in the region notes that he commanded a fleet of thirty-two ship in Lough Foyle and that he occupied a place named 'Cennrig'.[94] Although neither '*longphort*' nor any other specific term was used in connection with this place in the annalistic sources, it may be assumed that even a short-lived land settlement associated with a fleet of this size was likely to have been a defended one. One of the annalistic entries recounts that 'it was quickly(?) and completely abandoned by them, except for a few who remained behind in it through sloth' and that a local king 'killed the crew of one of their ships and wrecked the ship and took its booty'.[95] The equation of the Inishowen hoards with Acolb and his ill-fated expedition is supported by Ó Floinn, who presents additional literary evidence relating to it, and suggests that the finds are representative of silver bullion that was acquired as loot by local rulers during the campaign against Acolb.[96] The fact that at least two of the four hoards in question were buried in ringforts, the dominant Irish settlement type of the Early Medieval period, supports the idea that the hoards were in Irish ownership. The implication of this case study is that some of the silver wealth known from the vicinities of *longphuirt* elsewhere may represent Irish loot, or Scandinavian tribute, rather than just the proceeds of trade.

CONCLUSION

On the basis of the evidence to date it may be concluded that the *longphort* existed both as a specific concept and as a monument type in Ireland during the Viking Age, particularly during the mid- to late ninth and the opening decades of the tenth century. This does not exclude the likelihood of pre-existing and naturally defended sites also being used by the Scandinavians for the same purposes, but there is no reason why these would not also be referred to as *longphuirt* in the contemporary historical sources. Though it is certain that very few *longphuirt*, if any, endured and developed to become permanent multifunctional settlements like Duiblinn/Áth Cliath, it seems probable that most examples functioned solely or predominantly as raiding bases and thus may have been relatively short-lived. In most cases historical records refer to a *longphort* only once, and consequently it is impossible on the basis of this evidence to gauge whether the use of an individual site extended over months, years or decades, or whether its occupation was continuous or periodic. Archaeological excavation in the future, however, should be able to throw light on these questions. At present the archaeological evidence from Woodstown indicates that

it was a strongly defended site with settlement and raiding functions, while the nature of its silver assemblage suggests that it also participated in a broader economic framework. The evidence of Cuerdale, and other hoards, has already established a link between silver and *longphuirt* in the case of Duiblinn/Áth Cliath. The suggested association of silver, and sometimes of gold, with other potential *longphuirt*, such as Athlunkard, Ballaghkeeran and Rathmore, indicates that this link may have been a common one. It may, perhaps, have been mainly due to the role these types of sites played in the slave trade though, given the historical evidence for the establishment of political and military alliances between the Scandinavians and the Irish from the mid-ninth century onwards, it is also likely that some of them may have developed local trading and market functions. The evidence of Ireland's hoards demonstrates that considerable silver resources had already been amassed there before the establishment of the formal Hiberno-Scandinavian towns, and the *longphuirt* must have played a key role in this.

ACKNOWLEDGEMENTS

The author is grateful to Professor Donnchadh Ó Corráin, Department of Medieval History, University College Cork, and E.P. Kelly, Keeper of Antiquities, National Museum of Ireland, for the benefit of their discussions on this paper. He is also grateful to Nick Hogan, Department of Archaeology, University College Cork, for preparing figs. 1, 2 and 4, Michael Connolly, Kerry County Archaeologist, for supplying fig. 3, and Archaeological Consultancy Services Ltd for permission to refer to the silver finds from Woodstown.

ENDNOTES

1   In this paper the terms 'Scandinavian' and 'Hiberno-Scandinavian' are used in accordance with the definitions that are proposed in Sheehan *et al* 2001:93-4.

2   Wallace 1992; Simpson 2000; Hurley et al 1997.

3   Bradley 1988.

4   Sheehan 1998.

5   Harrison and Ó Floinn, *forthcoming*.

6   Simpson 2005: 37-48; Connolly & Coyne 2005: 49-78; O'Brien & Russell 2005: 121-22, fig.7,8; O'Donovan 2005.

7   Ó Floinn 1998: 148-53.

8   In Moody et al 1982:20-21.

9   Mytum 2003: 118-22.

10   See Downham 2004: 75, fn. 7, for a listing of the annalistic references to these foundations. Downham 2007, figs 4 and 8, conveniently lists the ninth- and tenth-century chronicle references to 'viking-camps' in Ireland.

11   Doherty 1998: 324.

12   Ibid.: 326.

13   Annals of Ulster: s.a. 844, 845.

14   Ó Floinn 1998:164.

15   Ibid.: 162-64.

16   Clarke 1998:348. Simpson   reports that a limited area of

this island was subjected to archaeological testing in 1995 and that no apparent Viking-age material was found (2000:21).

17   Annals of Ulster: s.a. 866.

18   Ó Floinn 1998: 161.

19   Kelly and Maas 1995; Kelly and Maas 1999: 132-43.

20   Fragmentary Annals: s.a. 862.

21   Kelly and Maas 1999:141.

22   Kelly and O'Donovan 1998.

23   Ibid.: illustrated on p.14.

24   Brady 1993, 40. The object is illustrated in Kelly and O'Donovan 1998. I am grateful to Michael A. Monk for discussing this object with me and for drawing my attention to the Brady reference.

25   The author is grateful to E.P. Kelly, Keeper of Antiquities, National Museum of Ireland, for information on the Athlunkard material.

26   This was noted and recorded by Victor Buckley, then of the Archaeological Survey of Ireland.

27   Annals of Ulster: s.a. 845; Annals of the Four Masters: s.a. 922, 927, 929, Annals of Inisfallen: s.a. 922. It should be noted that John O'Donovan, the nineteenth-century scholar, proposed that the location of the Lough Ree *longphort* may have been on the promontory of Rindoon, on the Co. Roscommon side of the lake. See *Journal of the Old Athlone Society* 1.4 (1974-75), 288. I am grateful to E.P. Kelly, National Museum

of Ireland, for drawing my attention to this reference.

28 Fanning 1983: 221. The two radiocarbon dates obtained from the site are recorded in the topographical file for the site in the National Museum of Ireland.

29 Connolly and Coyne 2005: 172-73, pl.42.

30 Ó Corráin 1996, 273. Ó Corráin suggested that the site of the Scandinavian dún was near Castlemaine, where there later was a medieval castle, but this was prior to the discovery of the Rathmore enclosure.

31 Ó Floinn 1988:164.

32 Ibid.: 162.

33 Kelly and Maas 1999: 140.

34 Ibid.:140.

35 Annals of the Four Masters: s.a. 852.

36 O'Brien and Russell 2005; O'Brien, Quinney and Russell 2005; McNamara 2005.

37 Kelly and Maas 1999:133.

38 O'Brien, Quinney and Russell 2005:33.

39 Ibid.: 35, fig.14.

40 Preliminary accounts of the finds are included in ibid.: 58-73 and McNamara 2005. The rotary whetstones from Woodstown belong to the pan-Scandinavian type, datable from the ninth to the early thirteenth century, recently published by Stummann Hansen and Sheehan (2001).

41 O'Brien, Quinney and Russell 2005:69.

42 Ibid.: 71.

43 Ibid.: 68-69, pl.23.

44 Ibid.: 74-78, 82; O'Brien and Russell 2005: 115, 119, 124

45 O'Brien, Quinney and Russell 2005: 43-45, figs.12, 15-16. The relevant ditch is numbered F2174.

46 Graham-Campbell 1995: 97-98, pl.3a.

47 O'Brien, Quinney and Russell 2005: 82.

48 See, for instance, ibid.: 57, fn.15.

49 See Ó Cíobháin, B., 'Camas Ó bnFathaidh Tíre: a note on its location and significance', http://www.vikingwaterford.com/images_documents/woodstown_camas.pdf (January 2005).

50 Downham 2004: 77-82.

51 Etchingham 1996: 21-2, map 3.

52 Annals of the Four Masters: s.a. 912.

53 Annals of Ulster: s.a. 915.

54 Downham 2004: 82-84.

55 Annals of Ulster: s.a. 918.

56 Ibid.: s.a. 914, Annals of the Four Masters: s.a. 912.

57 Annals of Ulster: s.a. 915, Annals of the Four Masters: s.a. 913.

58 Annals of Ulster: s.a. 916, Annals of the Four Masters: s.a. 914.

59 Annals of the Four Masters: s.a. 912.

60 See note 14.

61 Annals of Ulster: s.a. 902.

62 Ibid.: s.a. 845, 867.

63 Holm 1986: 318-26.

64 This event is also recorded in Annales Xantenses: s.a. 871.

65 Shearman 1872, 13, records that the hoard was associated with a group of burials from which was also recovered 'a small bronze pin, with a ring at the top'. This appears to have been a ringed pin.

66 Dolley 1961:60-62.

67 Clarke 1998: 352.

68 Ó Floinn 1998: 143.

69 Sheehan 1998: 171-73.

70 Downham 2004: 88.

71 See Wallace 1981: 138-39, O'Brien 1998: 217-19, Clarke 1998: 346-51, Simpson 2000: 20-24.

72 Simpson 2005.

73 Ó Floinn 1998, 163-64.

74 Ibid., 56-59.

75 Simpson 2005, 53-54.

76 Downham 2004: 75.

77 Clarke 1998, 315; Ó Floinn 1998, 137.

78 Sheehan 1998: 167-83.

79 Graham-Campbell 1992, 113-14.

80 Dolley 1966: 49, no.57.

81 Crofton Croker 1848. See, however, Dolley's comments regarding the size of this hoard (1966: 26-27).

82 Downham 2003, 251.

83 In Ryan et al 1984: 361.

84 Simpson 2005: 23-24.

85 Graham-Campbell 1974.

86 Sheehan 1992: 51-52; 1998: 201, fig. 6.1.

87 O'Brien, Quinney and Russell 2005: 45, pl.5.

88 Kyhlberg 1980: 281.

89 Wallace 1987: 212.

90 Hårdh 1996: 33.

91 Sheehan, *forthcoming*.

92 Details of these finds, and published references for them, are included in Graham-Campbell 1988.

93 Ibid., 109-10; the two annalistic references are the Annals of Ulster, s.a. 921 and the Annals of the Four Masters, s.a. 919.

94 Ó Floinn (1995, 103) suggests that this 'Cenrig' may be equated with the site of Dunree fort in north-west Inishowen.

95 Annals of Ulster, s.a. 921.

96 Ó Floinn 1995, 101-03.

BIBLIOGRAPHY

Bradley, J, 1988. The interpretation of Scandinavian settlement in Ireland, in Bradley, J (ed.), *Settlement and Society in Medieval Ireland*, Kilkenny, 49-78.

Brady, N. 1993. Reconstructing a medieval Irish plough, *Primeras Jornadas Internacionales Sobre Tecnologia Agraria Tradicional*, Madrid, 31-44.

Clarke, H.B., 1998. Proto-towns and towns in Ireland and Britain in the ninth and tenth centuries', in Clarke, H.B. et al (eds.), *Scandinavia and Ireland in the Early Viking Age*, Dublin, 331-80.

Connolly, M. and F. Coyne, 2005. *Underworld: Death and Burial in Cloghermore Cave, Co. Kerry*, Bray.

Crofton Croker, T., 1848. Report of hoard from Drogheda, *Journal of the British Archaeological Association* 3, 334.

Doherty, C., 1998. The Vikings in Ireland: a review, in Clarke, H.B. et al (eds.), *Scandinavia and Ireland in the Early Viking Age*, Dublin, 288-330.

Dolley, R.H.M., 1961. The 1871 Viking-age find of silver coins from Mullaghboden as a reflection of Westfalding intervention in

Ireland, *Årbok Universitetets Oldsaksamling* 1960/61, 49-62.

Dolley, R.H.M., 1966. *The Hiberno-Norse Coins in the British Museum*, London.

Downham, C., 2003. The Vikings in Southern Uí Néill to 1014, *Peritia* 17-18 (2002-04), 233-55.

Downham, C., 2004. The historical importance of Viking-age Waterford, *Journal of Celtic Studies* 4, 71-96.

Downham, C., 2007. *Viking Kings of Britain and Ireland: The Dynasty of Ívarr to A.D. 1014*, Edinburgh.

Etchingham, C., 1996. *Viking Raids on Irish Church Settlements in the Ninth Century*, Maynooth.

Fanning, T., 1983. Ballaghkeeran Little, Athlone, Co. Westmeath, *Medieval Archaeology* 27, 221.

Graham-Campbell, J.A., 1974. A Viking age gold hoard from Ireland, *Antiquaries Journal* 54, 269-72.

Graham-Campbell, J.A., 1988. A Viking-age silver hoard from near Raphoe, Co. Donegal, pp.102-11 in Wallace, P.F. and G. Mac Niocaill (eds), *Keimelia: Studies in Medieval Archaeology and History in Memory of Tom Delaney*. Galway.

Graham-Campbell, J.A., 1992. The Cuerdale hoard: comparisons and context, in Graham-Campbell, J.A. (ed.), *Viking Treasure from the North West: the Cuerdale hoard in its context*, Liverpool, 107-115.

Graham-Campbell, J.A., 1995. *The Viking-Age Gold and Silver of Scotland (AD 850-1100)*, Edinburgh.

Harrison, S. and Ó Floinn, R., *forthcoming. A Catalogue of Irish Viking Graves and Grave-Goods*, Dublin.

Holm, P., 1986. The slave trade of Dublin, ninth to twelfth centuries, *Peritia* 5, 317-45.

Hurley, M.F., Scully, O.M.B and McCutcheon, S.W.J., 1997. *Late Viking Age and Medieval Waterford: Excavations 1986-1992*, Waterford.

Hårdh, B.,1996. *Silver in the Viking Age: A Regional-Economic Study*. Acta Archaeologica Lundensia, Series in 8°, 25. Stockholm.

Kelly, E.P. and Maas, J., 1995. Vikings on the Barrow, *Archaeology Ireland* 9.3, 30-32.

Kelly, E.P. and Mass, J., 1999. The Vikings and the kingdom of Laois, in Lane, P.G. and Nolan, W. (eds.), *Laois History and Society: interdisciplinary essays on the history of an Irish county*, Dublin, 123-160.

Kelly, E.P. and O'Donovan, E., 1998. A Viking *longphort* near Athlunkard, Co. Clare, *Archaeology Ireland* 12.4, 13-16.

Kyhlberg, O. 1980. *Vikt och värde*. Stockholm Studies in Archaeology. Stockholm.

McNamara, S., 2005. Woodstown 6: the finds, in O'Sullivan, J. and M. Stanley (eds), *Recent Archaeological Discoveries on National Road Schemes 2004*, Dublin, 125-130.

Moody, T.W., Martin, F.X. and Byrne, F.J. (eds.), 1982. *A New History of Ireland, 8, A Chronology of Irish History to 1976*, Oxford.

Mytum, H., 2003. The Vikings and Ireland: ethnicity, identity, and culture change, in Barrett, J.H. (ed.), *Contact, Continuity, and Collapse: The Norse Colonization of the North Atlantic*, York, 113-37.

O'Brien, R. and Russell, I., 2005. The Hiberno-Scandinavian site of Woodstown 6, County Waterford, in O'Sullivan, J. and M. Stanley (eds), *Recent Archaeological Discoveries on National Road Schemes 2004*, Dublin, 111-124.

O'Brien, R., Quinney, P. and Russell, I., 2005. Preliminary report on the archaeological excavation and finds retrieval strategy of the Hiberno-Scandinavian site of Woodstown 6, County Waterford, *Decies: Journal of the Waterford Archaeological and Historical Society* 61, 13-122.

Ó Cíobháin, B., n.d. *Camas Ó bhFathaidh Tire*: a note on its location and significance, http://www.vikingwaterford.com/svwag_event_lecture.htm

Ó Corráin, D., 1996. Vikings III: Dún Mainne, *Peritia* 10, 273.

O'Donovan, E., 2005. There is an antiquarian in us all, *Archaeology Ireland* 19.3, 16-17.

Ó Floinn, R. (1995). Sandhills, silver and shrines – fine metalwork of the medieval period from Donegal, pp.85-148 in Nolan, W., Ronayne, L. and Dunlevy, M. (eds), *Donegal History and Society: interdisciplinary essays on the history of an Irish county*, Dublin.

Ó Floinn, R., 1998. The archaeology of the Early Viking Age in Ireland, in Clarke, H.B. et al (eds.), *Scandinavia and Ireland in the Early Viking Age*, Dublin, 131-65.

Ryan, M. *et al.*, 1984. Six silver finds of the Viking period from the vicinity of Lough Ennell, Co. Westmeath, *Peritia* 3, 334-81.

Shearman, J.F., 1872. 'Discovery of Carolingian coins at Mullaboden, Ballymore Eustace', *Journal of the Kilkenny Archaeological Society* 2, 13-16.

Sheehan, J., 1992. Coiled armrings: an Hiberno-Viking silver armring type, *Journal of Irish Archaeology* 6, 41-53.

Sheehan, J., 1998. Early Viking-age silver hoards from Ireland and their Scandinavian elements, in H. Clarke *et al.* (eds), *Scandinavia and Ireland in the Early Viking Age*. Dublin, 166-202.

Sheehan, J., *forthcoming*. The Viking-age silver hoard from Kilmacomma, Co. Waterford: a Woodstown connection ?, *Peritia: Journal of the Medieval Academy of Ireland*, 2008.

Sheehan, J., Stummann Hansen, S. and Ó Corráin, D., 2001. A Viking-age maritime haven: a reassessment of the island settlement at Beginish, Co. Kerry, *Journal of Irish Archaeology* 10, 93-119.

Simpson, L., 2000. Forty years a-digging: a preliminary synthesis of archaeological investigations in medieval Dublin, in S. Duffy (ed.), *Medieval Dublin I*, Dublin, 11-68.

Simpson, L., 2005. Viking warrior burials in Dublin: is this the *longphort?*, in Duffy, S. (ed.), *Medieval Dublin*, 6, Dublin, 11-62.

Stummann Hansen, S. and Sheehan, J., 2001. Roterende slibesten: et upåagtet nordbofund fra osterbygde, *Tidsskriftet Grønland* 8, 289-292

Wallace, P.F., 1981. The origins of Dublin, in Scott, B.G. (ed.), *Studies on Early Ireland*, Belfast, 129-43.

Wallace, P.F., 1987. The economy and commerce of Viking-age Dublin, in Düwel, K. *et al.* (eds.), *Untersuchungen zu Handel und Verkehr der vor- und frügeschichtlichen Zeit in Mittel- und Nordeuropa, 4, Der Handel der Karolinger - und Wikingerzeit*, Göttingen, 200-45.

Wallace, P.F., 1992. *The Viking Age Buildings of Dublin*, Dublin.

Author's address
#Arhaeology, University College Cork
Cork
Irland
jsheehan@archaeology.ucc.ie

Acta Archaeologica vol. 79, 2008, pp 296-304
Printed in Denmark • All rights reserved

DETAILED BRONZE AGE CHRONOLOGY AT 1850

KLAVS RANDSBORG

In memory of Jørgen Jensen (1936-2008)

FAMED MUSEUM DISPLAYS

Surveys of the development of prehistoric archaeology are rightly giving credits to the great C.J. Thomsen (1788-1865), a Dane, for having defined the Bronze Age as one of the major stages in the archaeological history of the Old World.[1] Thomsen served as the secretary of the Royal Commission for the preservation of Antiquities (established 1807) during the very difficult years from 1817 onwards (cf. Jensen 1992; Jakobsen 2007).

Denmark was assaulted by Great Britain in 1801, and again in 1807-14: Copenhagen was bombarded and the great navy - the largest on the Continent after Trafalgar - was carried away, the country went bankrupt in 1813, and at the Vienna Conference in 1815 (after the Napoleonic Wars) Norway finally was lost to the crown. Obviously, a symbolic offensive was needed after the setbacks for the once great nation, which in the late 18th century had the second largest merchant fleet in the World.

Already in 1817+, soon after his nomination, the young Thomsen demonstrated the properties and workings of the famous chronological so-called Three Age System for Antiquity - "Stone · Bronze · Iron" - in the novel Royal Museum of Nordic Antiquities, which was founded on the Commission's collection of Danish artefacts (cf. Jakobsen 2007, 136f. & 139ff.). However,

a publication proper of the system, which gave "eyes" to Prehistory, did not appear until nearly 20 years later (Thomsen 1836), even though in 1831, a small pamphlet on the collection was published by Thomsen ([Thomsen] 1831; cf. Jakobsen 2007, 150). The late publication has given rise to various speculations that Thomsen was not the inventor of the Three Age System, speculations which can be clearly rejected on the bases of correspondence, minutes and letters (Jakobsen 2007, 140, 153f.).

In essence, the Three Age System of 1817+ was but an evolutionary chronological postulate based on the supposed temporal sequence of same-function artefacts in different materials. In reality, the system was generated on the basis of a series of stratigraphic observations in the field during several centuries, as well as many other studies (Randsborg 1992; 1994). Thomsen may not have been the first scholar to think along these lines, but he certainly through his museum was the one systematizing and making archaeologically operational a directional, even evolutionary, technological and chronological system (Schnapp 1993). The classical Palaeolithic classification is much later, introduced by de Mortillet in 1869 and later (e.g., de Mortillet 1872).

Thomsen's first museum was housed in the University Library, in the huge loft above Trinitatis (Trinity) Church, Copenhagen. The acquisition of new artefacts went fast indeed, especially from the 1830s onwards, where the annual acquisition rose to far more than 400 (Jakobsen 2007, Fig. 103). In the very first period it was about 100, but Thomsen quickly drove it towards the 200 mark. Even the Danish overseas possessions responded to Thomsen's call for artefacts for the museum (Randsborg 2001).

The museum premises were in a sad state upon Thomsen's nomination in 1817, but quickly improved with the new exhibition soon after (Jakobsen 2007, 122ff.). Never-

---

1 This paper is dedicated to the memory of the late Dr. Jørgen Jensen, author of Danmarks Oldtid I-IV and a lover of archaeology, at home as abroad. The author is particularly grateful for Jørgen's help and interest in supporting young archaeologists joining the university institute of archaeology in Copenhagen (then housed at the National Museum). Later on, Jørgen devoted his life to the National Museum, its exhibitions and long history.

I am also grateful to Conservators T.B. Jakobsen, H. Brinch Madsen & J. Holme Andersen for discussions over the years on the present topic, as well as to Professor Bo Gräslund, Uppsala for information.

theless, the many acquisitions necessitated new cabinets and constant rearrangements, and in 1832+ the museum moved to a suite of rooms at the Christiansborg Castle, where it stayed for 20 years till 1852+, when it was relocated to its present location in the nearby "Palace of the Prince" (Prinsens Palais) complex (today, the "National Museum"), likely another promotion of this important national collection in the aftermath of the First Slesvig War (1848-50) and the full introduction of democracy (1848+). Thomsen's publication of the Three Age system thus belongs to an earlier period when the Royal Museum of Nordic Antiquities had recently been transferred to Christiansborg Castle (Thomsen 1836).

The constant changes no doubt left an impact on the character of the display, though hardly on its essence, but little is known about the details before the catalogues of the 1840s by Thomsen's assistant J.B. Sorterup (1815-49) (Sorterup 1845; 1846). Incidentally, Sorterup is most likely seen standing right behind Thomsen in J. Magnus Petersen's (1827-1917) famous and slightly humoristic drawing of 1846, where the master is demonstrating artefacts to a clearly awed public in the museum at its new premises in the very royal castle (Jakobsen 2007, Cover; cf. same 2007, Fig. 17c).

CHRONOLOGICAL ACCOMPLISH-MENTS & PUBLICATIONS

J.J.A. Worsaae (1821-85), an assistant and collaborator of C.J. Thomsen, is acknowledged for an argued division of the Stone Age of Thomsen into an "Early" (in the North, Mesolithic) and a "Late" (or, Neolithic) phase (Worsaae 1860 [1859]; cf. Gräslund 1974, 115, note 10). This observation dates to 1857, or, incidentally, to a period when the Royal Museum of Nordic Antiquities had been transferred to its lasting premises at the "Palace of the Prince".

Worsaae is also credited for a division of the Nordic Bronze Age into an early and a late phase, mainly on the basis of different burial customs: the Early Bronze Age having inhumations, the Late Bronze Age cremations (Worsaae 1860). Worsaae's quoted publication is of 1860, but already in a publication of 1854 [in fact of 1853, the date of the preface] he notes that inhumations belong to an early part of the Bronze Age, cremations to a late one (Worsaae 1854). In 1854, in a fine paper in the annual of the Royal Commission for the preservation of Antiqui-

ties, Swedish N.G. Bruzelius stated that cremations were later than inhumations in the Bronze Age (Bruzelius 1854, 357). Gräslund gives Bruzelius the credit of a "first", but is seemingly overlooking Worsaae's remarks of a year earlier (cf. Gräslund 1974, 119f.).

On the basis of proper excavations, scholars already of the 18th century noted that graves with inhumations and stone artefacts in Denmark were earlier than cremations with bronzes (Randsborg 1992, 218f.; cf. 1994, 144f.). Such observations were no doubt basic to the establishment of Thomsen's Three Age system. Even in the Renaissance, other excavations in burial mounds (no doubt of the Bronze Age) established that cremations were later than inhumations (cf. Randsborg 1994, 144f.). There were other opinions as well, sustained by referring to statements from the historical tradition of Snorri in the Islandic Sagas, where it was claimed that cremations were earlier than inhumations, which they no doubt were as far as the Iron Age and Viking Age are concerned.

Credits for the full detailed artefact chronology of the Scandinavian Bronze Age should be given to a great Swedish archaeologist, Oscar Montelius (1843-1921), who ultimately established the six-period system still very much in professional use in his seminal work "Om tidsbestämning" of 1885 (Montelius 1885). The six-period system was one of earliest relative chronological systems in archaeology as based classifications of metal artefacts, in particular from closed finds (Montelius Period I-VI) (Montelius 1885) (cf. Gräslund 1974, 174ff.). Some years earlier, Montelius had established a distinction between artefacts from the Early versus from the Late Bronze Age, even though the outline, and even details, of this system must have been common knowledge among Danish and other archaeologists of the age, as we shall see below (Montelius 1869; 1872-73; etc.; cf. Gräslund 1975, 168). But like Thomsen, much earlier in the 19th century, Montelius was the one who made the observations operational and integrated them into a single archaeological system.

Montelius, in particular late in life, became an ardent advocate of the position that artefacts, when organized in series according to their typological features, would "by themselves" reveal their relative chronological position (Montelius 1899). Already in 1884, the Dane S. Müller, criticized Montelius for having put this principle to the fore, stressing instead the need to study the artefacts as found together, and in closed contexts (Müller 1885). The

Danish-Swedish rivalry in early archaeology was in fact a very fruitful way of collaborating.

EVIDENCE OF ILLUSTRATIONS

Studying the early Danish publications with illustrations of bronzes, a modification of the uniqueness of Montelius' work should be presented, since, seemingly, elements of his full system must have been recognized in Copenhagen - with the richest collection on the Nordic Bronze Age - already around 1850, if not earlier.

In Thomsen's work from 1836 - which was meant to be a popular one - there are only few illustrations, including a few surprisingly professional drawings of flint artefacts (rendered in Jakobsen 2007, Fig. 143). On the whole, Thomsen was an organizer and administrator and did not write very much. Also, he had to tend to a number of other collections, as well as his own business. However, the work of 1836 was freely mailed to all priests in the country, spreading the message of archaeology very widely and no doubt helping to augment the Copenhagen collection, as did free entry and free guided tours, re Magnus Petersen's drawing of Thomsen himself heading a guided tour in 1846 (Jakobsen 2007, Cover). Incidentally, illustrations were very costly to reproduce in the 19th century.

In 1843, also Worsaae (only born in 1821) published a popular volume on the prehistory of Denmark, again with relatively few and rather simple illustrations, even though this volume may be regarded as the first reflective treatise on prehistoric archaeology in the World, outlining a number of basic principles. This volume is published earlier than Worsaae's division of the Bronze Age in an early and a late phase (Worsaae 1860; cf. 1854).

A decade later still, upon the transfer of the Royal Museum of Nordic Antiquities to its present premises at the "Palace of the Prince" in 1852+, Worsaae published the comprehensive and well illustrated volume on "Nordic Artefacts" already mentioned above (Worsaae 1854 [1853]; 2nd ed. 1859). In this work, the main chronological ordering of the artefacts is that of the Three Age system (plus the Medieval period, early and late, equivalent to the Romanesque and the Gothic periods respectively, the latter extending to the Protestant Reformation in 1536). The artefacts are arranged on the plates according basically to main functional type, certain aesthetical considerations, and the provision of space.

Surprisingly, clear elements of a typologically correct sorting or ordering of the Bronze Age artefacts along the chronological division by Montelius' by 1869+ into an early and a late phase are already evident in Worsaae's work of 1854 [1853], as are elements, however few, of Montelius' full periodical system of 1885 (Worsaae 1854; Montelius 1869; 1872-73; 1885).

On Plate 25 in Worsaae's work, apart from one untypical sword from the very Early Bronze Age, are four Late Bronze Age specimens. On Plate 26, to the left, are four Late Bronze Age swords (all with "antennas"); to the right are two specimens from of the Early Bronze Age, both of Montelius' Period III; below are three miniature swords from the Late Bronze Age. On Plate 27, all eight swords are from the Early Bronze Age. Other elements of a correct typological-chronological ordering can be detected on the other plates and bear witness to the discussions which were taking taken place among Danish archaeologists and others at least by 1850.

Even more surprising in the present context is the very large and still impressive "Atlas for Nordic Antiquities displaying Samples from the Bronze Age and the Iron Age", in fact metal artefacts from the Bronze Age and golden ones from the Iron Age (cf. below). "Atlas" was obviously meant to leave an impact on learned international readers, and published in both Danish and French by C.C. Rafn (1795-1864), including very fine illustrations by J. Magnus Petersen (Rafn 1856; "Atlas" 1857). Likely, the "Atlas" was also meant as a prestigious gift. Rafn was the founder of the Royal Society for Nordic Antiquities, in 1825, a highly international society - indeed, a Danish centre of world archaeology - in its early days and still an important organization, with its home at the Danish National Museum. In 1830, Rafn became a member of the above-mentioned Royal Commission for the preservation of Antiquities headed by C.J. Thomsen, the base of the Royal Museum of Nordic Antiquities.

In Rafn's "Atlas", Bronze Age artefacts, in particular the series of fine swords are arranged "correctly" in quite a number of cases, even when taking the finer chronological periods of Montelius' system of 1885 into consideration (Montelius 1885) (cf. Figs. 1-2). Thus, while elements of a correct distribution of artefacts from respectively the Early and the Late Bronze Age is noted in Worsaae's work of 1854 [1853], Rafn's volume is displaying clear approaches to the scientific stage represented in Montelius' classical chronological treatise of 1885, "Om tidsbestämning", outlining the full six-period system for the Bronze Age still very much in use (Montelius 1885).

The typological-chronological arrangements transpiring from the "Atlas" are presented and discussed in detail in Fig. 1 here (cf. the illustrations rendered in Jakobsen 2007, 145f., with Figs. 135f., including interesting printer's drafts by the draftsman, and Fig. 2 here). Incidentally, some of the artefacts in "Atlas" are also included in Worsaae's work from 1854, but the illustrations in "Atlas", all of a superb quality, were new. Clearly, a new interest in artefact details was dawning - accurate rendering being a must in artefact typology and chronology, as in other sub-branches of archaeology at 1850.

MUSEUM DISPLAYS OF 1807 · 1817 · 1824 · 1832

In summary, the chronological order of the Bronze Age artefacts C.C. Rafn's "Atlas" is hardly accidental and must, at the very minimum, be recognized as artefact sorting according to at least two basic principles: (A) Specimen similarity - or typology - at a level beyond functional identity, approaching chronologically correct interpretation, and, (B) Adaptation to spatial and aesthetical demands of the plates in the process of production.

It is quite plausible that plates of Rafn's "Atlas", and the typological-chronological ordering they are putting at display, are reflections of contemporary exhibition arrangements. Support for this view may be found in Sorterup's catalogue of 1846, which describes the Bronze Age exhibition in the Christianborg Castle period of the Royal Museum of Nordic Antiquities in much the same terms as the plates in Worsaae's volume of 1854 (cf. below and Sorterup 1846; Jakobsen 2007, 136ff.).

The organization of the museum exhibition after its transfer to the "Palace of the Prince" in 1852+ was structurally largely identical with the one at Christiansborg Castle, but the number of artefacts on display was higher, including "ca. 140 Bronze swords" (Jensen 1992, 367f.) (cf. Fig. 3). On the basis of such exhibition, a "typological mind", such as Montelius', would relatively easily have drawn chronological conclusions, studying also the artefacts accompanying the swords in graves and other finds (Montelius 1885). Montelius was in Copenhagen at least in connection with the archaeological congress of 1869 (cf. Montelius 1875). It is known that the important Swedish archaeologist Hans O. Hildebrand (1842-1913)

- also of the typological "school" - visited Copenhagen 1858, as a teenager, as well as three years later in 1861. At that time the full new exhibition at "The Palace of the Prince" was open to the general public, which happened in 1855 (cf. below).

Certainly, all kinds of observations were much easier to make as time went by and the collection grew drastically in number of artefacts and closed finds, from 1844+ even including fine specimens from the ancient King's Art Chamber (cf. Jakobsen 2007, Fig. 103, with an annual peak after 1850; Sorterup 1846). It is quite possible that the observed order had even older roots, going back - at least in a rudimentary form - to the period of the museum at the loft of the University Library above Trinitatis Church: (A) 1807-17, the Pre-Thomsen period; (B) 1817/1818 to 1832, the Thomsen period, including a re-arrangement of 1824-25 (Jakobsen 2007, 150).

As to the Pre-Thomsen exhibition of 1807+, next to nothing is known about the Bronze Age artefacts, a Late Bronze Age lur trumpet was suspended in a window, though (cf. Jakobsen 2007, 136f.).

As to the early Thomsen period from 1817+ more is known about the Bronze Age artefacts, including their place in a display arranged according to the three "ages", plus the Middle Ages, the latter in two sections - a mundane one and one related to the "Catholic cult" (cf. Jakobsen 2007, 139f.). Sub-groups were weapons from the Bronze Age and pertaining artefacts, e.g. lurs (supposed to be for battle) and shields, and jewellery. The weapons etc. from the Bronze and Iron Ages (only a few from the latter due to poor preservation) were displayed according to their similarities in a special showcase. In a note from 1824, Thomsen mentions that this particular display of swords enabled the viewer to detect their "development" (Jakobsen 2007, 149f.; cf. [Thomsen] 1831). The slim publication by Thomsen (even though his name does not figure) from 1831 describes the exhibition as it stood during the period from 1824 until the time of the removal of the museum to Christiansborg Castle in 1832+.

At Christiansborg Castle, each main prehistoric period had its own room (cf. Jakobsen 157f.). The first room held stone artefacts, the second one, ceramics, etc. The third and larger room held the Bronze and Iron Age items, arranged separately. Sorterup's catalogue is listing the various showcases etc. with bronzes and other artefacts in detail (Sorterup 1846). From this period we also have Magnus Petersen's drawing from 1846 of Thom-

Pl. I. Spearheads and axes, etc. - No particular chronologically motivated order is noticed from the artefacts on this plate.

Pl. II. Swords, etc. - The swords are mainly of the Late Bronze Age (Montelius Periods IV-VI), both Nordic and imported. However, two specimens and a dagger from the last phase of the Early Bronze Age (Montelius Period III) are included, seemingly where they fit the best. No other chronological arrangement is noted.

Pl. III. Swords, almost all from the Early Bronze Age, both Nordic and imported. - At the top, from left to right, the following sequence is seen Montelius Periods III, II (with traits similar to Period III swords), III, III, V (!), II, II, II (all octagonal-hilted swords), and I. At the bottom, again from left to right, are specimens of Montelius Periods II, II, II (the latter two octagonal-hilted), II, II, and III. Between the latter two is a Late Bronze Age miniature, or symbolic, sword.

Pl. IV. Swords (and sword pommels), both Nordic and imported. - At the top, from left to right, specimens of Montelius Periods II, II, II, II, II, IV, V, V, and V. At the bottom, from left to right, specimens of Montelius Periods II, II, II, IV, IV, and V. (cf. Fig. 2.)

Pl. V. "Helmet" and two shields. - The "helmet" is from Montelius Period II, the two shields (imported) from the Late Bronze Age. No particular order is seen.

Pl. VI. Shield, tutuli, and belt-plates. - At the top is a shield (imported) likely of Montelius Period IV. Next row displays tutuli of Montelius Periods II, and II. The third row from the top carries tutuli and a belt-plate (centre) of Montelius Periods II, III, and III. At the bottom are belt-plates (in the middle a tututus) from Montelius Periods II, II, and II.

Pl. VII. Lur trumpets. - Lurs of Montelius Period V; below is a fragment of a specimen of Period IV, with pieces of carrying chains.

Fig. 1. Descriptions of the contents of plates with Bronze Age artefacts: from C.C. Rafn's "Atlas" (Rafn 1856; cf. Atlas 1857).

sen demonstrating artefacts to the public in the museum (Jakobsen 2007, Cover). In the drawing, showcases and even parts of their contents are clearly seen. Thomsen is standing in the Iron Age section, with a Migration period golden necklace in his hand, ready to slip it over the neck of a visitor, as the story goes.

Thus, the series of typological museum displays, in part of the same artefacts - in the stages outlined above - may well have lead to chronological speculations about divisions of the Bronze Age, among other things, relatively soon after the establishment of the Three Age system in the exhibition of the Royal Museum of Nordic Antiquities in Copenhagen, possibly in connection with the re-arrangement of 1824, likely by the transfer of the collection to the Christiansborg Castle in 1832+.

AT THE "PALACE OF THE PRINCE"

The transfer of the steadily, even rapidly growing collection to the "Palace of the Prince" of 1852+ and the arrangement of a new exhibition was not completed as far as the Bronze Age is concerned until very late in 1854 (Jensen 1992, 368ff.) (Fig. 3). Thus, Rafn's "Atlas" of 1857 (1856) may well refer directly to the new exhibition at the "Palace of the Prince", while it is less likely that

Worsaae's work of 1854 (1853) does (Atlas; Rafn 1856; Worsaae 1854). Certainly, the novel and even richer display would have enabled any visiting archaeologist to perceive chronological dimensions in the artefact data far more detailed than the Three Age system. The new exhibition was opened to the public in the Summer of 1855.

Not too long after that followed the Second Slesvig War 1863-64 and the loss of Slesvig-Holstein. H.C.C. Engelhardt (1825-81) bravely evacuated and hid the archaeological finds from Danish Slesvig in face of the German offensive, including famous weapons deposits of the Migration Period. But the artefacts ended up as a clause in the peace treaty. A great loss to the Copenhagen museum and to archaeology was C.J. Thomsen's death in 1865. Denmark's hope after the wars was a strong France (and England, even Russia) to counterbalance German Continental might. On the cultural front, to enhance Denmark's status, an international archaeological congress was planned for 1869.

An illustrated guide to the new exhibition in the "Palace of the Prince" was published by Engelhardt in 1868 in connection with, and preparation of, the international archaeological congress of 1869 (Engelhardt 1868). The booklet gives a showcase by showcase description of the displays, from which it transpires that closed finds of the

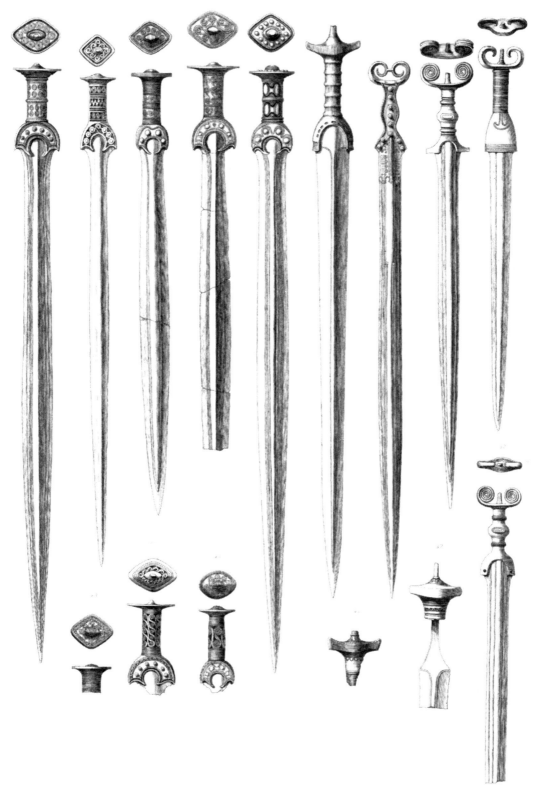

Fig. 2. Plate (No. IV) from C.C. Rafn's "Atlas" (Rafn 1856; cf. Atlas 1857).

Fig. 3. The oldest photo of the sixteen metre long Bronze Age room at the "Palace of the Prince" as it stood during the last quarter of the 19th century. The exhibition is still much like it was arranged by C.J. Thomsen after 1852+, with some re-arrangement by J.J.A. Worsaae during the 1860s. The oak-coffin graves (chokingly open) are later. After Jensen 1992.

Bronze Age were kept separate and that a division in an early and a late phase on the basis of types of graves (in-humation-cremation) was prevalent, even supported by artefacts. It is expressively noted that a series of swords and daggers below in ten showcases (also displaying other artefacts) is arranged "according to their presumed age" (cf. the photo in Fig. 3): Indeed, a perfect typological display for keen visitors to observe and discuss, even to take notes of, copy, and publish, as we know Hildebrand and Montelius must have done.

Nevertheless, it took a couple of generations before O. Montelius (only born in 1843) perceived the full and comprehensively documented chronological system of Nordic Bronze Age artefacts in 1885 (Montelius 1885). More than one hundred years later still, further ramifications of this system are still being studied, in part by natural scientific methods, in part by the same typological, as well as contextual, ones that Thomsen and Montelius employed (cf. Randsborg & Christensen 2006).

IRON AGE TYPOLOGY

Interestingly, the "Atlas" by Rafn of 1857 (1856) is also displaying typological observations of the same order as the Bronze Age artefacts (with chronological ramifications) in the plates referring to the Iron Age, in particular the golden bracteates of largely the fifth century AD (cf. Fig. 3, all so-called D-bracteates, for an example).

In fact, numismatics and related topics were a particular interest of C.J. Thomsen, who in 1855 had presented the earliest scientific classification of bracteates (a small work of 1824 was merely a prelude), even with reference to Rafn's (coming) "Atlas" (Thomsen 1855; with Rafn 1856, and 1857). Thomsen's classification is the basis of all later typological-chronological systems regarding the bracteates (cf. Malmer 1963, 76ff.). Also here, in his late and mature work (he died in 1865) Thomsen produced a true and lasting "first", pertaining to the requirement of details of the archaeology at 1850. Still, Thomsen was hardly a typical academic. His engagements with the written word were limited; rather, he was a man of action and material display, but great nonetheless.

Fig. 4. Plate (No. IX) from C.C. Rafn's "Atlas" displaying so-called D-bracteates (Rafn 1856; cf. Atlas 1857).

BIBLIOGRAPHY

Atlas = 1857. Atlas for nordisk Oldkyndighed fremstilende Pröver fra Bronzealderen og fra Jernalderen/Atlas de l'archéologie du nord représentant des échantillons de l'age de bronze et de l'age de fer. Kjöbenhavn (Thiele). [See Rafn.]

Bruzelius, N.G. 1854. Beskrifning om åtskilliga i Skåne och Södra Halland belägna fornlemningar, hvilke under åren 1853 och 1854 bifvit undersökte. Annaler for Annaler for nordisk Oldkyndighed og Historie. 339ff.

Engelhardt, C. 1868. Guide illustré du Musée des Antiquités du Nord à Copenhague. Copenhague (Thiele).

Gräslund. 1974. Relativ datering. Om kronologisk metod i nordisk arkeologi. Tor 1974. Uppsala (Almqvist & Wiksell).

Jakobsen, T.B. (et al.). 2007. Birth of a World Museum. Acta Archaeologica Supplementa VIII = Acta Archaeologica 78:1.

Jensen, J. 1992. Thomsens Museum. Historien om Nationalmuseet. København (Gyldendal).

Malmer, M.P. 1963. Metodproblem inom järnålderns konsthistoria. Acta Archaeologica Lundensia. Series in 8o. No. 3.

Montelius, O. 1872-73. Bronsåldern i norra och mellersta Sverige. Antiqvvarisk Tidskrift för Sverige 3:2-4. 173ff.

- . 1875. L'âge du bronze en Suède. Congrès international d'anthropologie & d'archéologie préhistoriques. Compte rendu de la 4e session, Copenhague, 1869. Copenhague. 249ff.

- . 1885. Om tidsbestämning inom bronsåldern med särskild hänsyn till Skandinavien. Kongl. Vitterhets Historie och Antiqvitets Akademiens Handlingar 30. Ny följd 10. Stockholm.

- . 1899. Typologien eller utvecklingslären tillämpad på det menskliga arbetet. Svenska Fornminnesföreningens Tidskrift.10:3. 237ff.

de Mortillet, G. 1872. Classification des diverses périodes de l'âge de la pierre. Revue d'anthropologie 1872. 432ff.

Müller, S. 1884. Mindre Bidrag til den forhistoriske Archaeologis methode. Aarbøger for nordisk Oldkyndighed og Historie 1884. 161ff.

Oversigt = Oversigt over det Kongelige danske Videnskabernes Selskabs Forhandlinger og dets Medlemmers Arbeider i Aaret 1859. Kjöbenhavn. [See Worsaae 1860.]

Rafn, C.C. 1856. Om Vaaben fra Nordens Bronzealder. Forudskikket Underretning om ATLAS FOR NORDISK OLDKYNDIGHED. Annaler for nordisk Oldkyndighed og Historie. 331ff.

Randsborg, K. 1992. Antiquity and Archaeology in "Bourgeois" Scandinavia 1750-1800. Acta Archaeologica 63. 209ff.

- . 1994. Ole Worm. An Essay on the Modernization of Antiquity. Acta Archaeologica 65. 135ff.

- . 2001. Archaeological Globalization. The First Practitioners. Acta Archaeologica 72:2. 1ff.

- . 2006. Opening the Oak-coffins. New Dates - New Perspectives. Randsborg & Christensen 2006. 1ff.

Randsborg, K. & K. Christensen 2006. Bronze Age Oak-coffin Graves. Archaeology & Dendro-dating. Acta Archaeologica Supplementa VII = Acta Archaeologica 77.

Schnapp, A. 1993. La Conquête du passé: aux origines de l'archéologie. Paris (Carré).

Sorterup, J.B. 1845. Kort Veiledning gjennem Museet for nordiske Oldsager. (For Deltagere i det nordiske Studentermöde 1845). Kjöbenhavn.

- . 1846. Kort Udsigt over Museet for nordiske Oldsager. Til Veiledning for de Besögende. Kjöbenhavn (Schultz).

[Thomsen, C.J.] 1831. Om Nordiske Oldsager og deres Opbevaring. [Kjöbenhavn.]

Thomsen, C.J. 1824. Guldbracteater. [Kiöbenhavn.]

Thomsen, C.J. 1836. Ledetraad til Nordisk Oldkyndighed udgiven af det kongelige Nordiske Oldskrift-Selskab. Kjøbenhavn (Det kgl. nordiske Oldskriftselskab).

- . 1855. Om Guldbracteaterne og Bracteaternes tidligste brug som Mynt. Annaler for Nordisk Oldkyndighed og Historie. 265ff.

Worsaae, J.J.A. 1843. Danmarks Oldtid oplyst ved Oldsager og Gravhøie. Kjøbenhavn (Selskabet for Trykkefrihedens rette Brug/Louis Klein).

- . 1854 [1853]. Nordiske Oldsager i det Kongelige Museum i Kjöbenhavn. Ordnede og forklarede. Kjøbenhavn (Kittendorf & Aagaard).

- . 1859. Nordiske Oldsager i det Kongelige Museum i Kjöbenhavn. Ordnede og forklarede. Forøget udgave af "Afbildninger fra det Kgl. Museum for nord. Oldsager i Kjöbenhavn. 1854." Kjöbenhavn (Kittendorff & Aagaard).

- . 1860. Om en ny Deling af Steen- og Bronzealderen. Og om Et mærkeligt Fund fra den ældre Stenalder ved Engestofte på Laaland. Særskilt aftrykt af Oversigt 1859.

Author's address
University of Copenhagen, SAXO-institute, Archaeology division, Centre of World Archaeology/CWA, Acta Archaeologica, Njalsgade 80, DK-2300 Copenhagen S., DENMARK
randsb@hum.ku.dk www.worldarchaeology.net

Lightning Source UK Ltd.
Milton Keynes UK
14 March 2010

151361UK00001B/4/P